Conflict and Continuity

A History of Ideas
on Social Equality
and Human Development

Edited by
JOHN R. SNAREY
TERRIE EPSTEIN
CAROL SIENKIEWICZ
PHILIP ZODHIATES

REPRINT SERIES NO. 15

HARVARD EDUCATIONAL REVIEW

Library of Congress Number 80-83476. ISBN 0-916690-17-2.
Printed by Capital City Press, Montpelier, Vermont 05602. Cover design by Cyndy Brady.

Harvard Educational Review
Longfellow Hall, 13 Appian Way
Cambridge, Massachusetts 02138

This volume is dedicated to
Margaret K. O'Hara
for her guidance and service
over the past twenty-two years to the
Harvard Educational Review
and for her steadfast commitment
to excellence in publishing.

Conflict and Continuity

A History of Ideas
on Social Equality
and Human Development

WITHDRAWN

PART II   Education and Social Equality

Preface

The history of educational thought has been marked by uncertainty and conflict about the aims of education and its ability to foster either human development or social equality. The *Harvard Educational Review* in celebrating its first half-century brings together here in one volume articles from its own pages which reflect the search for the purposes of education and for the strategies to achieve them. We hope this volume will contribute to the inquiry by reminding us that the salient issues of the past and those of today remain essentially the same. Looking back over a half-century of educational thought also shows us which questions have changed and why, and which have remained constant.

The articles were selected by the four editors, though our choices were sometimes directed by suggestions from former and present Board members, requests for reprints, and citations in other journals. Whatever the limitations of our choice, we hope it serves as a representative sample of *HER*'s best contributions to education over the past fifty years. Since the majority of articles in *HER* fall into the category either of the psychology of human development or of the sociology of education, we have decided to organize the volume around those two themes.

Education and Human Development

The *Harvard Educational Review's* publications on human development are an integral part of the history of psychology in general. In its first year the journal published an essay by John Dewey that reflected psychology's origins in philosophy. In "Appreciation and Cultivation," he explores the psychology of emotions and discovers in it a tool for teaching. Dewey conceived of mental functions as the organization of sensations that were psychologically significant only when they were used in making adaptations to the environment. Dewey's philosophy of education was founded on the principle of the reconstruction of experience. At his famous laboratory elementary school at the University of Chicago, he applied many innovations, such as new methods of instruction, reduction in student conformity, students' evaluation of their own work, and the elimination of grading.

The connection between psychology and philosophy is also evident in an article by philosopher Israel Scheffler (1965). Drawing on the works of Plato, St. Augustine, John Locke, and Immanuel Kant, Scheffler analyzes three models that attempt to describe the nature of the mind and the process of teaching. Each theory on its own is incomplete, but together they serve as a useful explanation of teaching and learning processes.

In the 1940s and 1950s *HER* published articles from the major competing schools of psychology—learning theory and psychoanalysis—though the former is more solidly represented. Edward L. Thorndike, the leading figure in educational psychology until his death in 1949, formulated one of the earliest empirically based theories of learning, "the law of effect," also called "instrumental conditioning." It states that any act that produces a successful effect becomes learned, while an act that produces an unpleasant effect is not "stamped in." In an alternative theory, classical conditioning, Ivan Pavlov argued that association or the conditioned response is the fundamental unit of learning. While other learning theorists tried to account for all learning in terms of either the law of effect or conditioned responses, O. Hobert Mowrer (1948) formulated a two-factor theory that integrates these competing learning models. According to Mowrer's article, learning has two processes, the conditioning of emotional responses and the learning of particular problem-solving behaviors.

The foremost contemporary exponent of education in this learning theory tradition is B. F. Skinner, who contributed "operant conditioning" — learning in which the subject actively responds to, or performs operations on, his or her environment which in turn produces positive or negative reinforcements. Skinner insists that terms must be operationally defined and further links the Pavlovian and Thorndikian types of learning. Operant conditioning, he argues, is functional both in acquiring concrete skills or communicating simple information and in teaching abstract concepts of problem-solving. When students begin to learn concepts, they need to master stimulus-response associations; only then do they generalize to a principle or law which guides abstract thought. Problem solving is simply applying principles to arrive at a tentative solution to a problem. In "The Science of Learning and the Art of Teaching" (1954), Skinner extends the principles of operant conditioning to the classroom through the teaching machine. That article has been credited by some with starting the programmed-learning movement in education.

Among the few psychoanalytic pieces is Anna Freud's article, "The Role of the Teacher" (1956), which is strikingly similar to her famous lectures to *Hort* (i.e., daycare) teachers in Vienna. According to Anna Freud, the educator should consider education as a part of the broader context of human development that begins on the first day of life, not just when the child enters school. She suggests that teachers adopt a developmental viewpoint and an interest in the entire process of development to avoid becoming too attached to individual children.

Humanistic psychology evolved out of a humanist attack on psychoanalysis and behaviorism; this "third force" became the perspective that psychology, and *HER*, would emphasize in the 1960s. Carl Rogers's "The Interpersonal Relationship: The Core of Guidance," is typical of that perspective. Rogers introduces new procedures in psychotherapy that distinguish it both from prevailing psychoanalytic techniques and from behavioral therapy. Rogers's client-centered, or nondirective, therapy attempts to help clients select and initiate their own actions and assume responsibility for them. In the classroom, Rogers suggests, students learn when they capitalize on their natural drive to manipulate their environment. Learning, then, is the process of "becoming" a person, the humanist's view of the purpose of education.

Abraham H. Maslow, in "Some Educational Implications of the Humanistic Psychologies," also offers a humanistic alternative to contemporary classroom practices. Maslow emphasizes the whole person rather than subsystems or parts of the individual, and places responsibility for learning on the learner and not on the teacher. The intrapersonal, not the interpersonal, forms the basis of Maslow's psychology.

A seminal article by Heinz Werner (1937) anticipated *HER*'s current psychological perspective. Challenging behaviorist psychology, Werner argued for a comparative developmental approach to mental processes that function in qualitatively different ways at different periods in the life cycle. Such a developmental psychology, Werner concluded, requires cooperation between psychological theory and educational practice. Werner's work, like that of Piaget, was ignored in the United States and in *HER* for many years, but it foreshadowed and has been partially assimilated by the current structural-developmental perspective that some now consider the theoretical alternative to psychoanalysis and behaviorism. Structural-developmental theory emerged in *HER* during the 1960s and became dominant in the 1970s; four of the eighteen articles that share this perspective are included in this volume.

Jerome S. Bruner's "The Act of Discovery," published thirty years after Dewey and twenty-three years after Werner, argues for the participation of the learner in the construction and appreciation of knowledge. Bruner, like Dewey, believes that the motivation to understand the world lies within the learner and does not depend on external rewards; like Werner and Piaget, he believes that instruction must be adjusted to the student's stage of development. Bruner organized the 1959 Woods Hole Conference, the first such meeting aimed at utilizing Piagetian theory to improve educational practice. He also contributed to the rediscovery of Piaget in the United States by providing popularized accounts of structural-developmental theory for lay readers.

Roger Brown and Ursula Bellugi apply a developmental perspective to children's language in "The Child's Acquisition of Syntax" (1969), which contrasts sharply with the Skinnerian view of language learning. This pathbreaking study of language acquisition identified parent-child speech interaction patterns through which children grasp the latent structures of their language. This suggests an innate ability to infer the syntactic rules underlying language.

Lawrence Kohlberg and Rochelle Mayer drew from both Dewey's progressive philosophy and Piaget's developmental psychology in "Development as the Aim of Education" (1972). This influential article analyzes such competing conceptions of education as maturation, cultural transmission, and cognitive development. Kohlberg and Mayer argue that only a progressive educational philosophy and a structural-developmental psychology can provide an adequate basis for educational reform. *HER* has published several criticisms of developmental psychology. Carol Gilligan's "In a Different Voice: Women's Conceptions of the Self and of Morality," criticizes Kohlberg and other developmentalists for ignoring male-female differences and argues for an integration of the feminine voice into an expanded conception of human development.

Education and Social Equality

At the center of U. S. liberal thought is the idea of a society in which anyone with talent and ambition can succeed. Since World War II educational policy and research in the United States have largely been shaped by the conviction that an accelerating economy would be derailed by a shortage of highly skilled workers, and by the continuing attempt to achieve equality of opportunity. Federal legislative action and business support encouraged the expansion in enrollments and in research in education. Not surprisingly, educational researchers began to respond to pressures from outside the school and to pay attention to the relationship between research and policy-making. The new emphasis of sociology differed from the old in its concern with applied research, but the questions remained the same: How do schools inculcate attitudes, values, and behavior in individual students? How do schools impart technical and intellectual skills to students? How much influence do schools, as opposed to parents and peers, exert on children? How do various methods of teaching affect students from different social classes?

James Bryant Conant and the poet Stephen Spender raised some of the fundamental questions about the function of education in modern society. In a 1948 article, "Selection and Guidance in the Secondary School," Conant reaffirmed the traditional view that the nation's hope for a democratic future lay in the training and selection of its youth. He, along with other policymakers of the time, wanted to ensure that every student among the top quarter or third of high school graduates could attend college, regardless of background. Education, Conant argued, was a social investment, and the educator's first responsibility was to society, to sort and fit students into jobs that best matched their talents.

Conant's argument that working-class students were underrepresented in higher education suggests that he was aware of the role social class played, but it remained a subsidiary and undeveloped concern. For Spender, on the other hand, class divisions stood at the very center of his account of the English adolescent (1948). The principal social experience for any English child was belonging to a particular social class. Spender found the socializing function of the English school, along with the family, to be to teach middle-class adolescents civic responsibility, while in the process stunting their emotional and sexual development. In contrast, he claimed, working-class students grew up into emotionally healthy adults, but lacking the civic virtues associated with the middle class.

Joseph A. Kahl (1953) shares Conant's concern with social mobility and Spender's sensitivity toward the effects of class. Yet, like other people who shared the structural-functionalist view that dominated the 1950s, Kahl was interested in social integration based on shared values and in the factors that determine individual aspirations. Working-class parents accept as legitimate the evaluation and selection process that goes on in school. His article provides a glimpse into working-class life in the 1950s and argues persuasively that the belief in getting ahead through hard work is really a middle-class belief which only a fraction of the working class shares. It serves to justify middle-class success as being the result of effort rather than of luck or social status. In typical U.S. fashion the psychological problem of motivation submerged the thornier political problem of structural barriers to social and economic equality.

Talcott Parsons (1959) supported Kahl's finding that student aspirations differ widely depending on socioeconomic background. In his classic formulation of the sociology of education, Parsons found that academic success was partly the result of characteristics such as the family's socioeconomic status and partly of factors such as individual ability. Differentiation occurs early in elementary school when cognitive tasks are still relatively easy and the difficult challenge is in mastering social skills; achievement at that level consists of living up to the teacher's expectations. His analysis of the function of the peer group and the teacher in a child's socialization is new; his treatment of the educated woman in the family harks back to the nineteenth-century concept of woman as wife and mother. Like others in the 1950s, Parsons describes the elementary-school classroom as the embodiment of the fundamental American belief in equality of opportunity that places value both on initial equality and on differential achievement.

The definition of equality of opportunity has always been at the core of political debate in the United States. In the 1960s the tenor of that discussion radically changed as blacks, youth, and later women challenged established power, and schools became the battleground for the struggle over equality. James S. Coleman (1968) reflects on the various guises the notion of equality of educational opportunity has assumed and shows how its meaning is affected by the times. At the beginning of the common-school movement it meant a common curriculum for all; by the turn of the century it meant a differentiated curriculum to train people for jobs to fit the needs of an industrializing economy. Recently it has become synonymous with equal educational resources. Since the *Brown* decision in 1954, the emphasis has shifted to educational outcomes while incorporating the ideal of racial integration.

Charles Hamilton's article, published in the same year as Coleman's essay, is a radical challenge to mainstream, liberal notions of equality. Unlike most academic advocates of desegregation, who suggested that acquisition of verbal and math skills should be the criteria for equal opportunity, he argues that equality depends on the degree of control that black parents have over their schools. Hamilton speaks for those in the black community who question the legitimacy of schools run by white administrators and white policymakers. He calls for new relations of power: a curriculum that incorporates Afro-American history and culture, schools controlled by black teachers and parents, and more black principals. Implicit in Hamilton's view is a lingering faith in the power of the schools to affect an individual's chances, though he adds to that the argument that black students will take school seriously only if they view it as a legitimate institution. The failure of blacks and, by extension, of some other minorities, is for him a political rather than an academic problem.

The themes of emancipation, power, and self-determination are also found in Paulo Freire (1970), who, like Hamilton, sees an inextricable connection between educational and political issues. Freire argues that knowledge is not something one "digests" as if it were food. Literacy must engage students by enabling them to reflect upon their lives. The teacher's task is not simply to teach people how to read but to enable students to find their political voice, to raise their consciousness.

Optimism in the power of schools to distribute opportunity more fairly dissolved into the belief that schools alone cannot eradicate inequality. Radicals used social class to analyze their failure, while liberals struggled to redefine what educational opportunity might involve. Disappointment with liberal reform even brought back hereditarian theories of intelligence, like Arthur Jensen's 1969 article.

Ray Rist's ethnographic study of a ghetto school (1970), like Parsons's article more than ten years earlier, showed how a teacher's attitudes toward students beginning in kindergarten plays a decisive role in determining who will succeed and who will fail.

Rist observed that teachers have an image in their minds of what the ideal student ought to be and that this image is determined by middle-class attitudes. Like Parsons, Rist showed how adult expectations and definitions of success affect the behavior of students. But while Parsons remains neutral in defining achievement in terms of the child's fulfillment of adult expectations, Rist sees the criteria for achievement as clearly class bound. According to him, the class-based distinctions that teachers and administrators perpetuate are part of a larger system of class domination.

Jerome Karabel (1972) looks at the effects of the community college movement on students and society. Contrary to popular belief, community colleges are not the vehicle for an open, egalitarian society, but merely another instance of class-based tracking and educational inflation. The major function of the community college is to adjust students' unrealistic aspirations downward, to make students blame themselves for their failure, and to legitimize the process of sorting—"to cool out" working-class students who dream of upward mobility.

Marxist theory, on which Karabel bases his analysis of the growth of community colleges, has served as a powerful explanatory tool for studying history, but it is only one of a number of plausible models. David Tyack (1976) argues that social scientists ought to entertain alternative theories so as to guard against the danger of selecting evidence to fit a particular thesis. He examines the phenomenon of compulsory universal education in the United States and suggests that there are at least five different plausible explanations for it: as an effort to produce a loyal citizenry out of a heterogeneous population; as an outcome of ethnic and religious conflict; as part of the organizational transformation of U.S. society toward greater central control and management by experts; as the result of individual economic calculation that schooling produces higher earning; and, finally, as the result of class conflict. Each theory, Tyack suggests, captures some important facet of compulsory education.

Social policy is usually regarded as a response to political demands for a greater degree of equality, but David Cohen (1976) detects another theme that is less frequently recognized, a concern with the decline of the family, the community, and tradition. Cohen examined the idea of loss as it has influenced school policy and discovered that, beginning in the nineteenth century, the fear that familiar community forms would pass away often came into conflict with the goal of equality. Social critics in the United States, less fatalistic than the Europeans, believed that they could repair the damage caused by urbanization and industrialization through social institutions such as the schools. Having invested the school from the start with too many conflicting social ideals, society continues to be ambivalent about its purpose.

* * * *

We wish to thank Michael Schudson, historian, sociologist, and former member of the Editorial Board, for his introductory essay on the history of *HER*, and all former editors whose efforts over the last fifty years have made this volume possible. The editors owe a particular debt of gratitude to Francis Keppel, O. Hobart Mowrer, and the late Robert Ulich for establishing *HER* as a student-run journal, and to Deans Theodore R. Sizer and Paul N. Ylvisaker for their continued support. We would also like to express our deep gratitude to former and present staff members, Kathleen Gallagher, the late R. Christine Gill, Dorothy A. Johnson, Valerie Lester, Pam Matz, Ethel Mc-Cready, Margaret O'Hara, Elizabeth Reilly, Anne H. Smith, and Mary Sullivan for their dedication to the *Harvard Educational Review*.

JOHN R. SNAREY
TERRIE EPSTEIN
CAROL SIENKIEWICZ
PHILIP PHAEDON ZODHIATES
Editors

A History of the
Harvard Educational Review

MICHAEL SCHUDSON

The fiftieth birthday of the *Harvard Educational Review* seems an appropriate enough occasion for writing its history, and as former editor, contributor, and reader, I was particularly pleased to take on that assignment. For, while *HER* is now widely regarded as the most influential journal in the field of education, it was not always so.[1] One reward of looking backward lies in finding out how a relatively obscure publication grew up to be the major forum for educational thought that it has now become. *HER* has also in itself been an educational experiment. Since 1950 it has been the editorial responsibility of graduate students in education and related disciplines. In the words of former Dean Francis Keppel, it has served as "the best seminar in education offered at Harvard." Where possible, I will discuss editorial procedures at *HER*, as well as the resulting product. Finally, *HER* is one important index of changing educational thought, and so its history provides some notes on the intellectual history of U.S. education in general.

The *Harvard Educational Review* was first published in 1931 as the *Harvard Teachers Record*, an outgrowth of the alumni bulletin published in the 1920s at the Harvard Graduate School of Education. The avowed purpose of the *Record* was to

[1] An independent study of the *Social Science Citation Index* for 1975 shows that, after controlling for frequency of publication, *HER* is cited more often than any other of the 136 journals in education and related disciplines. See Charles F. Turner and Sara B. Kiesler, *"The Use and Support of Basic Research Relevant to Education"* (Washington, D.C.: National Research Council, 1978). A 1975 survey of only members of the American Educational Research Association (AERA) regarding the prestige of educational journals found that *HER* was the leading non-AERA journal. See Terrence S. Luce and Dale M. Johnson, "Rating of Educational and Psychological Journals," *Educational Researcher*, 7 (1978), 8–10.

I want to thank Harold S. Wechsler for some initial suggestions on what to look for in writing *HER*'s history. Wechsler wrote the history of the University of Chicago's *School Review*, now the *American Journal of Education*, which appeared in its November 1979 and February 1980 issues. I am indebted to the editors of this volume and to the staff at *HER* for supplying me with archival materials and many suggestions. I also want to thank the former editors and friends of the *Review* whom I interviewed, talked to by phone, or corresponded with: John Butler, Patti Cox, Paul DiMaggio, Hendrik Gideonse, George W. Goethals, William Greenbaum, Thomas J. Marx, Donald Moore, O. Hobart Mowrer, Frederick Mulhauser, Arthur G. Powell, Barbara Powell, David Riesman, Bella Rosenberg, Israel Scheffler, Theodore R. Sizer, Lydia A. Smith, Ellen Solomon, Julian C. Stanley, Gregg Thomson, and David Tiedeman.

keep "the alumni and friends of the School in touch with its ideas and activities," and not to "enter into competition with established journals of education." By the second issue, however, it abandoned this stance and called for articles, popular or technical, "from anyone with a vital message."

Despite this open invitation, the *Record* remained a house organ. It devoted more than half its pages to editorials, faculty notes, and reports of Harvard Teachers' Association summer conferences and annual meetings. While it occasionally published authors from other places, the Harvard voice was dominant. A. Lawrence Lowell, president of Harvard between 1909 and 1933, wrote articles in 1931, 1932, 1933, and again in 1934, after James Conant had succeeded him. Conant himself contributed in 1937, 1938, 1947, and 1948. No Harvard president has appeared since. Henry Holmes, dean of the School of Education and advisory editor of the journal, contributed editorials and articles every year between 1932 and 1938, after which his contributions appeared less frequently. Deans since Holmes have rarely written for the journal. Francis T. Spaulding, perhaps preoccupied with directing educational programs in the Army's Special Services branch during the war, wrote only one article, in 1942, on "Education in the Army." Phillip J. Rulon, acting dean from 1944 to 1948, contributed several, but in his capacity as specialist in educational measurement rather than in his administrative position. Francis Keppel's contributions were rare and brief. When the *Record* published his dean's report in 1955, the editors felt they had to explain that the report was published because it provided "unusual insight into the working philosophy of a school of education," even though it did not result from a "research effort."

The first editor of the *Harvard Teachers Record* was Charles Swain Thomas (1868–1943), a native of Indiana, who had received his bachelor's degree from Harvard, and then returned to Indiana to teach English, to become a principal, and then superintendent of schools. Eventually he returned to Massachusetts as head of the English department in the Newton public schools. In 1920 he became an editor at the *Atlantic Monthly* and a part-time lecturer in the School of Education. In 1930, at the age of sixty-two, he was made a full-time faculty member in the School of Education, though the English Department regarded his teaching as "fit only for ordinary minds" and kept him away from Harvard College.[2]

Thomas retired in 1936, but until his death in 1943 he continued to contribute a column, "The Saunterer," a rambling essay, interspersed with jokes and stories, that frequently dealt with words and word usage. He quoted poetry he found instructive or inspiring and talked about holidays and the seasons. In one column of "whimsical cerebrations," he reported a casual conversation with a cartoonist, and mused about how cartoonists can create new pictures every day. In another, he wrote of the Reverend Mr. Beebe, an E. M. Forster character whose chief pleasure was "to provide people with happy memories," an objective Thomas found admirable. "The Saunterer" was by no means a central feature of the journal, but its informality and its distance from political and social issues, which it alluded to rarely and then in very general terms, typify the journal in its early years.

[2] Arthur G. Powell, *The Uncertain Profession: Harvard and the Search for Educational Authority* (Cambridge, Mass.: Harvard Univ. Press, 1980), p. 192.

This is not to say that the journal was without a political stance. It favored increasing the authority and autonomy of professional educators. Commenting on a strike by high school students in Watertown, Massachusetts, in an editorial in the first issue, the journal argued that neither students nor their parents should control the schools: "We believe the nature of an education should be determined by the educated and decision as to how that education shall be given made by the professionally trained." In 1936 Dean Holmes, chairing a summer school conference on equality of educational opportunity, declared that the schools should accommodate the needs of both students and society, and that the task should be entrusted to "the only group that is at all qualified to assume the responsibilities of modifying schools and guiding pupils . . . the teaching profession itself." The only problem was that the teacher "does not always have the broad professional training needed for the job," but that was where the School of Education came in.

The journal, then, spoke not only to, but on behalf of, teachers. It defended the educational profession against its enemies and detractors, and so did its part in defending the School of Education itself. The journal had begun to appear just a year after Abraham Flexner, in a widely noted study, praised American schools of education for enlivening elementary and secondary education, but damned them for their intellectual malnutrition and cited Harvard in this regard.[3] Schools of education were not highly esteemed in academic circles: Arthur G. Powell's recent history of the Harvard School of Education is aptly titled *The Uncertain Profession*. One sign of professional uneasiness was the School's attitude toward women. Education was the only school at Harvard where women were admitted during this period. (Women were admitted to the Medical School in 1945, Law 1950, Divinity 1955, Business 1963.) But, as Powell says, Dean Holmes recognized that "the School's reputation and success within Harvard was directly proportional to its dominance by males," and he would not consider women for regular faculty positions. When women reached 54 percent of the student body in 1928–29, he proposed, unsuccessfully, that they be barred from Harvard degrees.[4]

Boosting professional educators in academic circles was only indirectly of interest to the journal. Rarely in its first decade did it deal with substantive developments in academic disciplines, with the exception of psychological testing and measurement. Defending educators against their critics beyond the university, on the other hand, was a major concern. In "Teaching as Prophecy" (1936), for instance, Dean Holmes noted ominous political interference in the schools and attacked those who "wish teachers to be bound by oaths to routines, to mechanical saluting of flags, to perfunctory teaching of the Constitution, to the teaching of an unscientific biology." He defended the autonomy of professional educators against the intrusion of "politics and dogmatism."

In 1940, the National Association of Manufacturers (NAM) commissioned a study of social studies textbooks, and the faculty at the School of Education saw in this an attack on texts and teachers who did not agree with NAM's views on "free enterprise." Dean Francis T. Spaulding and thirteen other members of the faculty wrote a long

---

[3] Abraham Flexner, *Universities: American, English, German* (New York: Oxford Univ. Press, 1930).
[4] Powell, pp. 154, 169.

letter to NAM which the *Record* printed, along with NAM's conciliatory response. An issue later, associate editor Evan R. Collins suggested that the completed study lived up to the worst fears expressed in the original letter.

Academic freedom was again at issue in January 1942 and was discussed in an article entitled "Should Communists and Fascists Teach in the Schools?" by V. T. Thayer, director of New York City's Ethical Culture Schools, who wrote: "This is a period of genuine soul-searching for all conscientious liberals," defining the audience the editors believed they addressed.

Conscientious liberalism responded to attacks on the schools from the right with considerable vigor; its attitude toward the progressive education movement, which shaded off somewhere to the journal's left, was more detached. Leaders of progressive education rarely wrote for the journal. Harold Rugg never published in the *Record*, although a Harvard faculty member, Richard Ballou, reviewed Rugg's *American Life and the School Curriculum*. He referred to Rugg as an "apologist" for progressivism and criticized his work as "vague." Ballou argued that "to consider the school as the sole agency laden with responsibility for enhancing the life of society is to lose a proper perspective on the school's place in society." John Dewey received more respectful but no more copious treatment. James Harvey Robinson wrote a tribute to him, and in 1931 the journal published Dewey's own brief essay, "Appreciation and Cultivation." The *Record* printed William H. Kilpatrick's debate with Harvard's Truman L. Kelley at the New York Society for the Experimental Study of Education, but otherwise ignored him. Two years later, Dean Holmes reflected on George Counts's manifesto, *Dare the School Build a New Social Order?*, which had attacked progressive education for becoming the captive of the upper middle class. He urged that it become politically progressive as well, and he called on educators to worry less about "indoctrination." Holmes praised Counts for demanding that the schools deal with "the present, vital issues of our common life," but he applauded only what he could reduce to platitudes. He rejected Counts's plea that teachers adopt socialist convictions. For Counts, the social issue teachers needed to face was capitalism. For Holmes, the social question was a medley of social problems—"prohibition, public ownership of power, the tariff, money, birth control, trade-unionism, and unemployment insurance."

The dean and the journal both remained skeptical of progressivism throughout the thirties. The journal published Michael Demiashkevich, one of its strongest critics. His articles appeared in 1933 and 1935, an editorial in 1938, and *An Introduction to the Philosophy of Education* was sympathetically reviewed by Holmes and Thomas Harris, who warned against "partisan condemnation of so genuine and valuable a book." Demiashkevich headed the Essentialist Committee for the Advancement of American Education founded in 1938. The Essentialists, like the recent back-to-basics advocates, objected to the "electivism, options, and choice" in progressivism and advocated a tougher pedagogy. In his 1933 article, "Some Doubts about the Activity Movement," Demiashkevich claimed that progressive education invariably resulted "except for miracles in a sketchy, spotty education." Historian Edward Krug suggests that educators regarded the Essentialists as "inappropriate, possibly in bad taste."[5] Remarked

---

[5] Edward A. Krug, *The Shaping of the American High School*, II (Madison: Univ. of Wisconsin Press, 1972), pp. 291–297. See also Gurney Chambers, "Michael John Demiashkevich and the Essentialist Committee for the Advancement of American Education," *History of Educational Quarterly*, 9 (1969), 46–56.

Charles Swain Thomas in 1938, "The only time I'm tempted to become a Progressive is when I listen to the excited talk of these self-styled Essentialists."

In 1937 the *Harvard Teachers Record* became the *Harvard Educational Review* with Howard Wilson as its new editor. Emphasis on teaching and curriculum remained much the same, and its support of professional educators continued steadfast. For instance, Wilson's second editorial, "The Neglected Teacher," observed, "It is strange that, with all this concern over making the school a fit place for pupils to grow in, we have done so little about providing a fit life for teachers."

In the war years, *HER* concentrated on politics as much as it did on education. It was full of essays about democracy. Sixteen articles have "democracy" or "democratic" in the title between 1937 and 1945, as compared with six articles in the following thirty-five years. There were articles on what a Nazi victory would bring, on education and national defense, on psychological warfare, on American world leadership, on Nazi education, on democracy and world order, on sane patriotism, on German prisoners of war. All educational problems were seen in terms of the world struggle. The journal contributed articles to the war effort just as the School of Education was contributing its dean, faculty, and students—a far cry from the situation in the fifties and sixties when neither the Korean War nor the Vietnam War received any attention in its pages, aside from the editorial board's endorsement of the demands of the national student strike in the May 1970 issue.

Wilson left the School of Education in 1945 to work for the Carnegie Endowment for International Peace. His place was taken by a faculty editor, O. Hobart Mowrer, and a student editorial board. Professors Henry W. Holmes and Robert Ulich continued as associate editors. Eight students were appointed to serve on the editorial board for the academic year 1945-46. The new management stated their editorial policy in the following terms:

> The *Harvard Educational Review* will continue, as in the past, to be devoted to the publication of articles which are concerned with the clarification of, and the discovery of solutions to, the *problems of education*.
>
> It will be the policy of the Editorial Board to interpret the term "education" to mean the process whereby those ways of thinking, feeling, and doing things which are generally useful—i.e., the *culture* of a society—is transmitted from generation to generation. As the problems of a society change, the culture of that society also tends to change. Therefore, the specific *content* of education may vary widely from time to time, but the *function* of education is highly stable: it is to pass on to each succeeding generation those discoveries, acquired from preceding generations, which the present generation has found useful, along with those discoveries which the present generation has made as a result of its own experience.
>
> While by no means minimizing the importance of that segment of the educational process that goes on in classrooms, this definition of education gives equal scope and emphasis to the culture-transmission that goes on—less formally but inexorably—in the home, the church, the office and factory, through newspapers, movies, and the radio, and in ordinary social interaction. By this definition of education, we mean substantially the same as modern social scientists mean by the term *socialization*. As Dean Rulon has said in his 1943-44 report to the President of the University, the total task of education consists of "the rearing of the younger generation and the induction of that generation into adult society when they come of age."

By the 'problems' of education, we mean whatever difficulties or obstacles are encountered, whether in the school, the home, or elsewhere, in attempting to transmit the culture and thereby socialize the members of the oncoming generation.

The journal would, in other words, continue to deal with education broadly conceived, and not confine its attention to the schools, but it now stated that intention in the new language of social science—"culture" and "socialization" are used precisely as social scientists of the time used them. The original draft of the editorial statement was even more laden with the language of social science than the published version, from which terms like "adaptive" and "adjustive" were eventually dropped. Despite the language, however, the statement is as notable for the social science it omits as it is for the social science it uses. In calling for contributions from social science, the editors mention in particular cultural anthropology, social psychology, personality and learning theory, genetics, statistics, and semantics. Neither sociology nor political science has a place. Politics is not relevant when one defines training as "the ways of feeling and acting which are deemed necessary for the survival of society." After *Brown v. Board of Education*, and certainly from the mid-1960s on, the question would be: deemed necessary by whom? The statement assumes a single, homeostatic system. There is no sense that there might be conflict, for instance, between "the school, the home, and other educational agencies"—instead, there is the simple assurance that these agencies "divide responsibility" among themselves for the unified training of the young. Similarly, when "therapy" is discussed, the journal observes that education includes reeducation, remedial teaching, and counseling, any and all efforts devoted to coping with delinquency or neurosis. The statement does not envision any educational problem that cannot be defined as a failure in socialization.

The first meeting that included a student board was called to order September 26, 1945 by Professor Mowrer. Professor Holmes, the former dean, traced the history of *HER* and suggested that it should be made of interest to intelligent laypersons as well as to school and college faculty. "It is in no sense a 'house organ,'" as were the preceding journals," he said, referring to the alumni bulletin and *HTR*. Acting Dean Rulon explained the powers of the editorial board, which was constituted essentially as a committee of the faculty, subject to its authority. Mowrer added that five articles for the October issue were already in galley proof but could be rejected if board members objected to them. Articles were assigned to one or two members of the board who reported back to the whole, which would vote to accept or reject on the basis of what the one or two readers said.

Holmes's claim that *HER* was in no sense a house organ was partly contradicted at the next meeting, when Professor Mowrer reported that the faculty and dean felt *HER* should be "a credit to the School as a scientific publication," but that it should also serve "to some extent as an official house organ." And it was still a house organ, at least to the extent that the faculty, and particularly the faculty editor, Mowrer, and associate editors Rulon and Ulich were well represented in it. While student editors had some autonomy they were understood to be representative of particular fields, and even of the particular faculty members who nominated them to the board. As Mowrer pointed out, "Dean Rulon suggested that the Board members should feel free to utilize the judgments of the various members of the faculty *whom they represent*" (my italics). At the same meeting, Mowrer justified a particular procedure for reading manuscripts on the grounds that Dean Rulon believed board membership should be a "learning experience." From that time on, the *Review* became an educational process as well as an editorial product.

There was a debate between Mowrer and Professor Simpson, who was a visitor at that meeting (the board voted to invite a faculty member to every meeting, but this was not carried through), on the direction the *Review* should take. Mowrer wanted to accept articles on cultural anthropology, learning theory, social-class theory, and psychoanalytic theory. Simpson held that it should be "a general magazine" and not "a social science journal."

That *HER* should remain a house organ in one form or another seemed inevitable. The problem was that the house was divided, and composed increasingly of people more loyal to individual social science disciplines than to the field of education. This was notably true of Mowrer himself. He had received his formative academic experiences as a Sterling Fellow at Yale in 1934–36 and as a member of Yale's Institute for Human Relations in 1936–40. At Harvard from 1940, he felt he was never really "plugged in" to the School of Education. He found it "a rather dull place" and recalled later that he "was never very challenged or stimulated by it." His ties were not to the faculty in education but to a group that formed around Henry A. Murray's psychology clinic. His orientation was heavily toward the social sciences. "In more ways than one," he wrote in 1974 in an autobiographical sketch, "I always had a sense of 'marginality' at Harvard, which was in marked contrast to the deep sense of identification and involvement I had enjoyed at Yale."[6]

Mowrer was indeed "marginal" at the School of Education. Rulon, although or perhaps because he was a psychometrician himself, "continued to have little sympathy for the social sciences," and sought instead to strengthen the faculty in curriculum.[7] There were signs of change. Morris Opler, an anthropologist, came to the school in 1945 (and published twice in *HER* in 1947). But the School's ambivalence was indicated in its stipulation that Opler teach in the schools to acquire experience and research ideas. Still, a shift toward social science was under way. Provost Paul Buck, acting in President Conant's name, promoted the social science orientation and sought a social scientist for the new deanship. Having failed to attract anthropologist Robert Redfield, Carl Hovland, or Charles Dollard, Buck recommended his own thirty-one-year-old assistant, Francis Keppel. Keppel was equipped with only a B.A. and had no experience in education, but he had greatly impressed the social scientists at Harvard as an administrator. His appointment in 1948 signaled a School of Education which would emphasize "research on a high university level . . . closely related to the Social Sciences in the Faculty of Arts and Sciences."[8] This was too late, however, to make Mowrer feel at home. He took a professorship at the University of Illinois in 1948, leaving behind a faculty plan for a more autonomous student board for the *Review*, which

---

[6] O. Hobart Mowrer, "O. Hobart Mowrer," in *A History of Psychology in Autobiography*, VI, ed. Gardner Lindzey (Englewood Cliffs, N.J.: Prentice-Hall, 1974), pp. 338–340.

[7] Powell, p. 233.

[8] Paul H. Buck, quoted in Powell, p. 235. Powell credits Conant with promoting the social sciences, but in a personal communication, 28 Aug. 1980, David Riesman holds that Buck was the key figure.

included an increase in student responsibilities and a faculty chairman of the board rather than a faculty editor.

Just who suggested the idea of a student-run board is not clear, but the *Harvard Law Review* was the model used. Julian C. Stanley, Jr., a faculty member who served as board chairman for the year 1948–49, wrote to the *Review*'s printer that he was to turn it into a student-managed journal over the next three years, "along the lines of the *Harvard Law Review*."[9] As it turned out, one year proved sufficient. Writing to Dean Keppel some months later, Stanley urged that board membership be treated as an honor and asset comparable to *Law Review* membership and expressed "virtually unlimited faith in the possibilities for complete student control of the *Review*, subject only to control by the faculty *as a whole*."[10]

The *Law Review* precedent was a distinguished one. David Riesman has described the *Law Review* as "an island of teamwork in a sea of ruthless rivalry." The articles contributed to the *Law Review* by teachers and practicing lawyers "are markedly inferior to the student work both in learning and in style and, in fact, often have to be rewritten by the brashly serious-minded student editors."[11] The *Harvard Educational Review* quickly fit that mold. Some of social science's most opaque writers have published lucid articles in *HER* in the past thirty years, thanks to student editing. Others have been exasperated by the editorial board. Some members over the years assumed proprietary attitudes over the articles they edited. Several former *HER* editors have recalled the "arrogance" of the editorial board. David Tiedeman recalls the student board's first years: "Student editors in the beginning took to their task with a will and unflaggingly exhibited the reformational zeal which became characteristic of the *Review*."[12]

Whether or not *HER* should be a house organ for the School of Education remained at issue. When Dean Keppel urged that more Harvard dissertation abstracts be published, the board did not react enthusiastically. Although it never took a definite stand on the question, *HER* continued to reflect the interests of the School of Education faculty and at the same time to maintain its editorial autonomy.

By 1950 the student-run journal was still small and relatively unknown. Circulation had decreased from 850–900 in 1937 to 630 in 1943, rose to 800–850 in 1946, and was holding its own at about 800 in 1950. More than half the subscribers were members of the Harvard Teacher's Association, another quarter were libraries. One serious problem the journal faced was a lack of good manuscripts from which to choose. Few manuscripts were submitted, and even fewer were published: between 1945 and 1950, 50–70 percent were rejected. The editors complained that few people knew about the journal. Even inside the school, few students understood that the *Review* was a student endeavor. To try to solve these problems, the 1949–50 board set about learning how other publications were run, looking mainly to the *Harvard Law Review* and the *Har-*

[9] Julian C. Stanley, Jr., Letter to Neil Heffernan, 25 Aug. 1948, *HER* files.

[10] Julian C. Stanley, Jr., Letter to Francis Keppel, 9 Feb. 1949, *HER* files. In a telephone interview, Aug. 1980, O. Hobart Mowrer says the idea for a student-run journal may have been his, but he is not sure, and thinks it likely that the idea was conceived at the same time by a number of faculty members.

[11] David Riesman, "Toward an Anthropological Science of Law and the Legal Profession," in his *Individualism Reconsidered* (New York: Free Press, 1954), p. 452.

[12] Personal communication with David Tiedeman, 29 July 1980.

vard Business Review as models. Both journals, they discovered, actively solicited articles; *HER* did not. That policy began to change when, in April 1950, Howard Wilson, former *Review* editor, suggested that all the papers presented at a recent UNESCO conference on education be published in one issue. In May, chairperson Alvin Schmidt met with Wilson. The board's interest in the papers lay partly in the likelihood that the issue would bring publicity to the *Review* in new quarters and sell extra copies. The board committed itself to publication before seeing a single manuscript. Eventually 1500 copies, 500 more than usual, were printed. Extensive publicity sold them all and added 117 new subscriptions.

This issue was more financially than editorially auspicious but the idea of the "special issue" began to take form. (See Table 1.) The next special issue, on teachers' salaries, was also unusual in that the board contacted a whole group of authors, many of whom had worked together on the subject. In the fall of 1952 the board began making plans for a special issue on social class. Shildrick Kendrick, a former student board member, came to a meeting and, according to the minutes, helped persuade the board to take on the project on the grounds that it would be a "mature test" of the special-

TABLE 1
HER Special Issues and Symposiums

1945	Intercultural Education
1950	UNESCO Conference on Education
1952	Teachers' Salaries
1953	Social Class Structure and American Education, Parts I and II
1954	Comparative Education
1956	The Philosophy of Education
1958	A Symposium: What Can Philosophy Contribute to Educational Theory?
1959	A Symposium: Can the Laws of Learning be Applied to the Classroom?
	A Symposium: The Physical Science Study Committee Theory and Research in Sociology and Education
1960	Negro Education in the United States
1961	Education and American History
	A Symposium: The Computer and Educational Research
1962	Guidance: An Examination
1964	Language and Learning
1966	American Intellectuals and the Schools
1968	Equal Educational Opportunity
	Political Socialization
1969	Architecture and Education
1970	Illiteracy in America
1972	Alternative Schools
1973	Perspectives on Inequality
	The Rights of Children, Part I
1974	The Rights of Children, Part II
1975	Education and Development
1976	Education and History
1977	Reading, Language, and Learning
1979	Women and Education, Part I
1980	Women and Education, Part II

issue policy, since this time the board would have to start from scratch. Kendrick and David Tiedeman, a faculty member who had once served on the board, concluded that the topic was so complex that two issues might be required and urged the board not to set too rigid a schedule.

The board planned the issue to include an article about "the values and characteristics of the six major classes," a description which indicates that the definition of "social class" they were using was that developed by W. Lloyd Warner. Social class was treated by the editors as a new and technical social scientific concept and not as a basic element of social criticism.

The board developed an outline for the issue and drew up lists of academic luminaries to write the articles. The board was clearly too sanguine. On March 31, 1953, chairman John J. O'Neill admitted that they were still without contributors to the historical and governmental sections. The minutes of April 10 report that they would have to be satisfied with one article in the Measurement section, and would substitute an article on British education by G. Z. F. Bereday.

The special issues, when they finally did appear, showed a new level of seriousness, sophistication, and self-consciousness. Indeed, the editors took these articles so seriously that they asked Neal Gross, a sociologist new to the faculty, to criticize their contents in an article. He concluded that the two issues showed some evidence that the behavioral sciences could aid the study of education, but also that "the liaison between the behavioral sciences and education may not in all instances yield significant developments."

This intellectual solemnity is a far cry from the intimacy and amateurism of *HER*'s early years. Absent in these issues was the kind of "general" essay on education that had once been so ubiquitous. Authors like Ordway Tead, who had published five articles in the *Review* from 1941 to 1950, and one last time—a commencement address at Briarcliff Junior College—in 1955, disappeared from the pages of *HER*. His 1950 discussion, "Has Higher Education Any Unifying Principles?" sounds rather quaint in 1980:

> All of our courses of study bearing as they do directly or indirectly upon the nature of man and the science of nature are now seen to illuminate some aspect of our understanding of a human destiny which is at once mundane and transcendent. The educational mandate is toward a salvation which is of this earth but a salvation which also has divine resonance and overtones.
>
> Man's education is helping him to struggle to know himself and to be himself as a creative partner in divine purposes which he can progressively both learn and share.
>
> Integration in education is the collaborative search for meaning, natural law, directions for fulfillment,—all as the basis for being most fully human and as a condition for realizing our divine nature and stature.

The decline of piety did not necessarily herald its immediate replacement by the social sciences. In the 1950s and early 1960s *HER* was close to the humanities, particularly the philosophy of education. These contributions were not discursive essays by university deans and presidents, as in the 1930s and 1940s, but sophisticated analyses of educational ideas by philosophers. From 1950 through 1965, *HER* published forty articles on philosophy; from 1966 on, it published only five.

The emphasis on the humanities was also reflected in the board's minutes; in deliberations, for example, on a proposal submitted in 1957 by Reginald Archambault to reorganize *HER* "with a heavy orientation toward the Philosophy and History of Education." The board was aware that it needed a more coherent editorial policy, but nevertheless rejected Archambault's proposal for fear it would destroy "the essential quality of the *Review*—a journal devoted to the promotion of communications among the several areas of Education."

The *Review* in the 1950s mirrored Dean Keppel's School of Education as a whole: it supported scholars trained in the various disciplines who demonstrated an interest in education rather than those trained in education who had a special attachment to one of the disciplines. The topic that aroused perhaps the greatest passion in the *Review* during that period was behaviorism, both its proposals for curriculum and its models of the person. B. F. Skinner opened the debate in 1954 with "The Science of Learning and the Art of Teaching," and returned to it with his advocacy in 1961 of programmed instruction, "Why We Need Teaching Machines." Teaching machines allowed students to learn at their own rate, and they assured that instruction would follow a coherent sequence. Thus they promoted individual instruction and "learning by doing" at the same time. Students working with teaching machines regularly "engaged in behavior." Skinner presented his position as revolutionary, though it was not a revolution toward anything in particular but a revolution away from all traditions:

> When the nature of the human organism is better understood, we may begin to consider not only what man has already shown himself to be, but what he may become under carefully designed conditions. The goal of education should be nothing short of the fullest possible development of the human organism. An experimental analysis of behavior, carried out under the advantageous conditions of the laboratory, will contribute to progress toward the goal.

Teaching machines and programmed instruction received further support in 1963 from Lauren Resnick's "Programmed Instruction and the Teaching of Complex Intellectual Skills: Problems and Prospects." But there was also a spirited rebuttal. Israel Scheffler, philosopher at the Harvard School of Education, responded to Skinner as follows:

> At any rate, Mr. Skinner does not appear troubled by the fact that "the fullest possible development of the human organism" is not merely a vague but a virtually *empty* prescription for education, because there is no *single* fullest possible development of the human organism: *Conflicting* possibilities exist with qualitatively different characteristics; education theory *starts* from this fact. Unless we indicate what *purposes* are projected, what *direction* we shall follow in developing human possibilities, we shall be in danger of rushing headlong in all directions, or finding ourselves on a path we never properly evaluated. Without such indication of purpose, the ideal of the *new man* is no ideal at all, but only a morally dangerous facsimile.

Later, behaviorism would be more often ignored than attacked. Jean Piaget was in the meantime developing a "genetic" or "developmental" view of the child's learning which American education, dominated by the behaviorist debate, at first paid little attention to, but which it later embraced. Jerome Bruner's 1961 article in *HER* was a harbinger. Bruner stressed that people are motivated to learn for reasons they establish for themselves rather than for extrinsic rewards. David Elkind discussed Piaget's work in articles in 1967 and 1969. Lawrence Kohlberg worked out his theory of moral development which maintained Piaget's notion of a balance between inner and outer forces, biological maturation, and environmental response. By the 1970s, Piagetian structural models of human development in general were the dominant psychological voice of *HER*.

In the meantime, whatever the prevailing controversy, the editorial board continued to worry about the *Review*'s finances. Better office management and secretarial help were needed. Each new board of editors hoped to increase circulation and to erase the deficit which year after year the School of Education underwrote. The School was much less alarmed about deficits than the student editors. The *Review* was not only the best seminar at Harvard but also "the cheapest," Dean Keppel observed.[13] But in 1959 *HER* finally acquired its first permanent office staff in the person of Margaret O'Hara, who had already begun to work there half-time. Dorothy Johnson, who had for years overseen the business management of *HER* while serving as financial officer to the School, gave up her duties, and Margaret O'Hara became the *Review*'s first full-time office manager. In 1964 board chairperson Fred Newmann wrote to Dean Theodore Sizer requesting a promotion for Mrs. O'Hara, noting that circulation had grown from 1300 to 4500, thanks to the promotional mailings she had supervised, and that she had become "the major element of continuity in the organization."[14] In 1965 she was made general manager, a position she still holds. Ethel McCready, circulation manager, came in 1964 and is also still with *HER*, Anne Smith, editorial assistant and frequent counsel to board members, came in 1965 and retired in 1980. Kathleen Gallagher, in charge of accounts and billing, has been at the *Review* since 1968. Elizabeth Reilly, assistant in sales, has worked for *HER* since 1969.

Money problems, however, were also growing. In 1958-59 *HER*'s expenses were $11,000; in 1964-65 they were $53,000. Today the *Review* has close to a $300,000 budget. In 1961-62 Dean Keppel approved a grant of $2,000 for a Business School student to study *HER*'s circulation and how it might be increased, and the board asked for $30,000 from the dean over the next few years to pay for a circulation drive. The dean's job was to seek an "angel." In the meantime board chairman Hendrik Gideonse recommended redesigning the *Review* to appeal to "the great mass of responsible influential people in the field of education. . . . I am not being cynical, I think, when I stress the importance of packaging. If we want to be catholic in our concerns and nationwide in our interest then we ought to look the part. We have the role now. I think we ought to assume an appropriate costume." The result was a cleaner, brighter design. It still featured the name "Harvard" on the cover but dropped the university's seal.

The dean never found the angel, and the *Review* received no special subsidy, but promotion through direct mail became a regular part of the board's activities. For some years the board designated one of its members "promotions editor," but Margaret O'Hara continued to be the key figure in circulation growth, "the architect of the

[13] Telephone interview with Francis Keppel, Sept. 1980.
[14] Fred Newmann, Letter to Theodore Sizer, 13 April 1964, *HER* files.

FIGURE 1
HER *Subscription Figures: 1934-1980*

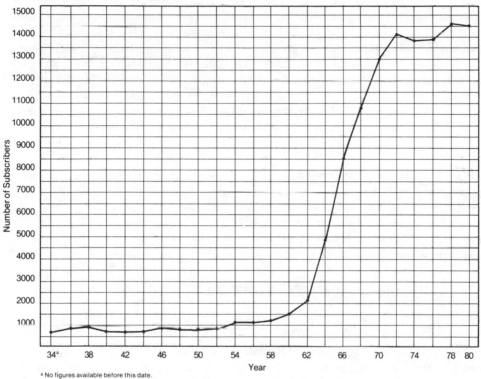

^a No figures available before this date.

national spread of *HER*," as former Dean Sizer put it.[15] In 1957 when *HER*'s circulation was 1,300, Dean Keppel suggested that it try for a circulation of 5,000 by 1970. Actually, it reached 5,000 in 1965, and by 1970 stood at 12,800. (See Figure 1.)

By the late sixties, *HER* was certainly among the most prominent journals in U.S. education. It received some 300 unsolicited manuscripts a year, and its circulation in 1968 stood at 11,700. It faced controversial issues and was rewarded with publicity. This was notably the case in 1967 when Christopher Jencks and David Riesman published the chapter on black colleges that would appear the following year in their book, *The Academic Revolution*. The article caused an uproar, particularly from leaders of the black colleges it evaluated so critically.

At the same time, the School of Education was undergoing changes of its own. Theodore Sizer, himself a member of the *HER* board from 1959 to 1960, became dean of the School of Education when Francis Keppel went on to become United States Commissioner of Education in 1962. Larsen Hall was added, and the faculty expanded from ten senior faculty members in 1962 to twenty-six by 1967. While some faculty thought the school was galloping off in too many directions at once, others were ex-

[15] Personal communication with Theodore Sizer, 18 July 1980.

cited by the new responses to the social and political problems of education, and the generally high spirits.

In 1966–67 a faculty seminar, underwritten by the Carnegie Corporation and the U.S. Office of Education, reanalyzed data from the 1966 Coleman report, and in 1968 *HER* published a special issue on the reanalysis and the politics of social research. This special issue was significant for financial as well as editorial reasons. *HER* printed 18,000 copies, well in excess of the subscription list, and engaged in an extensive promotional campaign. It also arranged with Harvard University Press to publish the volume as a hard-cover edition. *HER*'s own reprint series was initiated the following year with *Socialization and the Schools*. The reprints, of which this is the fifteenth volume, have altogether sold more than 125,000 copies and have proved to be *HER*'s only profit-making venture. Thanks to them the journal has shown a surplus in the past decade. (See Table 2.)

Few statements on U.S. education produced such an immediate and serious response both in the community and among educators as the Coleman report, which suggested that social background affected student academic performance far more than the quality of a school, and that financial investment in schooling made little difference in student achievement scores. Since its appearance, educators and researchers have wrestled with Coleman's findings. As a British observer notes, the Coleman report "has dominated the debate on educational inequality."[16]

In its special issue, *HER* sought a wide variety of comment, notably including radical as well as mainstream opinions. One contributor, Samuel Bowles, was a radical economist. Another, William Ayres, then running a free school in Ann Arbor, later joined the antiwar resistance and was underground until 1980. Nor were these radical voices isolated. The preceding issue of *HER* included an essay by Charles Hamilton, coauthor with Stokely Carmichael of *Black Power*. Hamilton argued that, for black people, the issue about schools was not their effectiveness but their legitimacy. To have taken this position to its logical conclusion would have preempted the Coleman discussion, which focused almost entirely on effectiveness. It was a fitting prelude, however, to the work of radical educator Paulo Freire, to be published in *HER* in 1970. Freire held that educational effectiveness depends on the political legitimacy and relevance of the schooling to the students involved.

The same issue that included Hamilton's essay featured David Kirp's article, "The Poor, the Schools, and Equal Protection." Kirp held that Supreme Court interpretations of the 14th Amendment in cases of criminal process and suffrage should be extended to education, so that, in education, the state would be "constitutionally obliged, not merely to open its doors to all comers, but to provide *effective* equality to all." This was the first of several articles Kirp would contribute (others appeared in 1974, 1976, and 1977), and signaled increased attention in the *Review* to legal issues in education. From 1950 to 1959, three articles appeared on law and education, eight between 1960 and 1969, and thirteen from 1970 to 1979 plus two special issues on legal topics.

The *Review* of 1968 showed two developments: first, that educational thought was increasingly shaped by social science research; and, second, that the growing political

[16] J. R. Pole, *The Pursuit of Equality in American History* (Berkeley: Univ. of California Press, 1978), p. 344.

TABLE 2
HER Monographs and Reprints

1969	*Community and the Schools*
	Environment, Heredity, and Intelligence
	Socialization and Schools
1970	*Cultural Action for Freedom,* by Paulo Freire, Monograph No. 1
	Science, Heritability & IQ
1971	*Challenging the Myths: The Schools, the Blacks and the Poor*
	Education and the Legal Structure
1973	*Perspectives on Inequality*
1974	*Education and Black Struggle: Notes from the Colonized World,*
	edited by the IBW, Monograph No. 2
	The Rights of Children
1976	*Education, Participation, and Power: Essays in Theory and Practice*
	School Desegregation: The Continuing Challenge
1977	*Education and Life Chances*
1978	*Stage Theories of Cognitive and Moral Development: Criticisms and Applications*
	Thought & Language/Language & Reading

movements of the 1960s and the ideological crisis of liberalism had opened the pages of the *Review* to radical opinion. In the context of the Coleman report, in the winter of 1969, *HER* published an article which began, "Compensatory education has been tried and it has apparently failed." The author, a coeditor of the 1968 volume, *Race, Social Class, and Psychological Development*, dedicated to the memory of Martin Luther King, Jr., was Berkeley psychologist Arthur Jensen, who had done well-regarded work on language learning in children. He had become convinced that the environmentalist side of the nature/nurture question had been overstated and that social scientists were deliberately neglecting the genetic component in assessing intellectual abilities. He believed that compensatory education failed to raise IQ scores in large measure because IQ is to a great extent genetically determined. Jensen had published his views in a number of academic periodicals, but they had thus far remained without significant notice outside academic circles. This silence ended when the *HER* article came out, partly because Jensen stated his position more provocatively than he had before:

> There is an increasing realization among students of the psychology of the disadvantaged that the discrepancy in their (Negroes') average performance cannot be completely or directly attributed to discrimination or inequalities in education. It seems not unreasonable, in view of the fact that intelligence variation has a large genetic component, to hypothesize that genetic factors may play a part in this picture. But such an hypothesis is anathema to many social scientists. The idea that the lower average intelligence and scholastic performance of Negroes could involve, not only environmental, but also genetic, factors has indeed been strongly denounced (e.g. Pettigrew, 1964). But it has been neither contradicted nor discredited by evidence.

The article was given great prominence in *HER*; it was far and away the longest article the *Review* had ever published (123 pages). That it appeared in a journal attached to the Harvard name also contributed to its prominence.

The press, rather than *HER*, first announced the article to the public at large. According to Jensen's own account, a reporter from *U.S. News and World Report* came to see him (and other Berkeley professors) to write a story on campus unrest. In the course of their discussion, Jensen mentioned his forthcoming work. The result was an article published in *U.S. News* on March 10, 1969, entitled "Can Negroes Learn the Way Whites Do?" The implicit answer was "no." The article listed as "findings" what were, at best, hypotheses, and stated them in ways that suited the perspective of *U.S. News*. "Unfortunately, big programs of 'compensatory' education, now costing taxpayers hundreds of millions of dollars a year, are doomed to failure as long as they pursue old approaches stressing 'cognitive' learning."[17]

The *Review* was entirely unprepared for the furor that followed. The office was deluged with requests for copies of the Jensen article, some ten days before the board received its copies from the printer. The board had not originally intended that the Jensen article appear by itself. It had asked for a short article, which was to be followed by commentary from psychologists and geneticists, but, according to the board chairpersons' report (Jensen's account does not mention it), Jensen's article "arrived four months later and five times longer than we had anticipated," so the responses could not be published in the same issue, as had been planned. The *Review* found itself less an intellectual forum than a political battlefield.

Why did the board not hold Jensen to the original agreement and insist that he cut two hundred manuscript pages to forty or fifty? One board member claims that failure to do this was the board's biggest mistake. If the manuscript had been unsolicited, it would surely have been cut, if printed at all. But the board had solicited the article and negotiated with the author over a year's time. The obligations and expectations this imposed precluded the board's considering the alternative of cutting the article or delaying its publication. In any case, newspapers and magazines all over the country picked up the story.[18] Students at Berkeley demanded that Jensen be fired. A year later, during the student strike that followed the invasion of Cambodia, the Strike Committee at the Harvard Graduate School of Education demanded that *HER* contribute any profits from the sales of Jensen reprints—and there were profits—to the Black Panther Defense Fund. The editorial board turned them down but endorsed the strike. For a time, *HER* refused even to sell the Winter issue, stating that it would not be sold until the responses were also available in the Spring issue. At one point the board even denied Jensen reprints of his own article until the rejoinders were available. One editor recalls late-night phone calls with a Harvard faculty member who advised that Jensen could sue if he chose, and would win. The policy was reversed.

[17] Arthur C. Jensen, Jr., *Genetics and Education* (New York: Harper & Row, 1972).

[18] Jensen's account does not square with *HER*'s on some matters and a full history of the Jensen article is still to be written. While Jensen praises the *U.S. News* story for its accuracy, the Board believed it to be unusually misleading and so released the Jensen article and the responses to other news media. The 1968-69 chairpersons' report says, "We learned a few things about how to deal with political cross-pressures and manipulatory newsmen." According to Jensen, the *Boston Globe* was the first publication to report on the article. According to *HER*, Jensen released his story to *U.S News* before any other publication knew of the matter. *U.S. News* published March 10. The *Globe* published a story March 16 and an editorial March 17, beaten to the punch by an editorial in the *Christian Science Monitor* March 13 and a syndicated column by Joseph Alsop the same day. The wider public clearly learned of Jensen from *U.S. News* and from the Alsop column. However, local news media did have word earlier. The *Harvard Crimson* published a story February 28 and an editorial March 6. Several small New England papers picked up an Associated Press story February 28. See *HER* clipping file.

The aftermath of the Jensen case for the board itself can be traced in the chairpersons' reports:

> *HER* articles have been "noticed" occasionally in the past; this time it was different, as members awoke all too late to the realization that what may appear to us to be academic debates have wider ramifications, and some more unscrupulous partisans, than we realized. The politics of education suddenly became very real, as the article became "evidence" for some alarming policy recommendations—which neither the author nor the Board had the foresight to predict. This may be excusable, but when the subject was race, it is unhappy to report that even at this late date, the Board was utterly insensitive.

The editors advised that "future boards will need to be more aware of their board responsibilities—responsibilities that go far beyond our readership and beyond our parochial view of the need to present academic debates." Three years later, the 1972–73 chairpersons' report was still referring to the article as *HER*'s "most widely known publication and most clinging albatross."

Editorial boards in the early 1970s actively sought articles on race and education. The *Review*'s emphasis on articles about desegregation and busing in the late seventies can also be understood as in part a consequence of the Jensen controversy. In the early seventies, the *Review* also undertook some additional activities—advising inner-city high school students in Boston about publishing a journal in 1971–72 and helping to secure funding for *The Rican*, a journal by and about Puerto Ricans edited by a former School of Education student, in 1972–73.

The Jensen controversy led to changes in *HER* election practices. The School of Education Strike Committee in 1969 recommended that the board find ways to represent not only different research specialties in its membership but different racial and ethnic backgrounds as well. The editorial board, independently seeking the same end after Jensen, revised its procedures. The 1970–71 board became the first to be selected without relying exclusively on nominations by faculty members, board members, and former board members. Of candidates for the 1970–71 board, 33 were nominated by faculty and 16 by students; 9 were self-nominated. For the 1971–72 board, only 11 of 41 applicants were faculty nominations. For the 1973–74 board, almost all of the 46 applicants nominated themselves.

Despite the board's best intentions, the 1972–73 editorial board was again all white, when its sole minority member resigned early in the year. The annual report noted:

> We had felt, at various times in the course of the year, intellectually handicapped and politically endangered by the absence of minority group members. These considerations led some board members, as individuals, to actively recruit new board members, and led the board as a whole to assign two board members to contact personally every organization at the school to inform students about *HER*.

Larry Browning, a new member of the 1971–72 board, made special efforts to solicit black authors for the *Review*, writing to scholars around the country, assuring them that Blacks like himself were represented on the board and that the board was sympathetic to the work of black scholars. The 1972–73 chairpersons' report notes one of the results:

IBW (Institute of the Black World), an independent institute of radical black scholars in Atlanta, replied that they had no intention of submitting manuscripts to a predominantly white board but that they would be willing to produce an issue of the journal for us. Larry took this reply seriously and discussed the matter with the board. This resulted in representatives of IBW coming to Boston on January 11 and 12, 1972, to meet with the *HER* board as a whole. On January 18, 1972 the board voted to collaborate with IBW and have IBW guest-edit the November 1972 issue of the *Review*. What had been the most critical issue in the negotiations—the nature of the editorial control—was resolved much as IBW had wished; IBW would have complete decision-making power over the contents of the issue with *HER* serving in an active advisory capacity. *HER* retained the right ultimately to decide to publish or not publish the whole issue.

The question of editorial control raised serious legal as well as intellectual problems, since no one knew whether a publication of Harvard University with university copyright could legally assign editorial control to another institution. Nevertheless, an agreement between IBW and *HER* was negotiated and signed in May 1972, specifying that IBW would supply the contents for the February 1973 issue, and including a schedule for IBW's submission of copy. As it turned out, IBW missed the October printer's deadline. The board then voted to offer IBW a monograph rather than an issue, and the IBW edition appeared as the second in the *HER* monograph series.

It seemed to board members in the years following the Jensen publication that everyone writing on IQ sent the results to *HER*. Some were publishable, and one in particular raised troubling issues for the board in 1972–73. It was a serious effort to explain by environmental variables the same kinds of racial differences in IQ that Jensen sought to explain largely by heredity. The board found the article (since published elsewhere) substantial, but narrowly decided against publication. The scholarly merits of the article were clear, but its political consequences were hard to estimate. Some board members contended that it was a vindication of environmentalist and social-reform positions and should be published in the journal identified with Jensen. Others argued that it would be better for educational research, and ultimately for education, to let the Jensen controversy fade away. The article in question was no more definitive than the Jensen article had been, and it was difficult even to imagine a decisive end to the battle. Better, then, some argued, not to encourage research which contributed very little to improving the quality of, or our understanding of, education. Several board members raised another concern: would publishing more articles on Jensen, pro or con, turn the *Harvard Educational Review* into the *Harvard Review of IQ Studies*?

Jensen made the board self-conscious. Educational research, the editors noted, like schools themselves, exists in a social context. It became board dogma, and even a source of pride, that the social consequences, as well as the intellectual merits, of articles be anticipated and considered in making judgments about publication. Discussion of the social and political consequences of publication came to have an accepted place in board deliberations. The self-consciousness of the board is reflected in the demand for self-consciousness in the articles *HER* publishes. David Quattrone, 1971–72 co-chairperson, defined the distinguishing characteristic of *HER* articles as "self-consciousness," an awareness of the nature and limits of the scholar's eye-view of the world. This has been, at least, a goal of the editorial board.

The Jensen article is the most famous, or notorious, article *HER* has ever published, but it only "briefly readmitted" the question of race, genes, and intelligence to polite conversation.[19] The Coleman report, in contrast, lives on. Where Jensen argued that compensatory education might fail because, on the average, Blacks may be genetically different in some respects from whites, Coleman had argued that schools fail to make a difference in student achievement because social factors, especially family background, overpower school effects. The Jensen article fit into the mood that the Coleman report had established: disenchantment with school reform as a vehicle for social change.

Schools do not work to change the social order: this seemed to be the message of the Coleman report. From quite a different quarter, this conclusion was reinforced by radical or "revisionist" educational history. In his book, *The Irony of Early School Reform*, Michael Katz opened the revisionist attack. Writing about nineteenth-century school reforms, Katz argued that schools do not change society *because they never intended to*.[20] School reforms ostensibly designed to widen educational opportunity benefit only the middle and professional classes who promote the reform in the first place. *HER*'s reviewer, Neil Harris, admired the Katz volume, but argued, "Irony is not what one ends up with in history; it is what one begins with," and he accused Katz of replacing the traditional view of inevitable progress with his own view of irresistible failure.

From then on, *HER* became a forum for debating the question raised by Coleman: do schools make a difference? and the question raised by the revisionist historians: did they ever mean to? Revisionist history, and sociology with a similar view of educational reform, appeared in articles by Michael Katz (1971), Jerome Karabel (1972), Norton Grubb and Marvin Lazerson (1975), and several contributors to the 1976 special issue on Education and History. By that time, revisionism was, if not the new orthodoxy, at least the most coherent perspective in the field, and its adherents the most prolific.

As for the Coleman question—do schools make a difference?—the *Review* closely followed the debate, especially in printing a set of reviews on Christopher Jencks's *Inequality*,[21] and articles on the Follow-Through evaluations, both of which undermined the liberal belief in school reform. The evidence continued to support Coleman.

Several objections were possible, however, and *HER* sought them out. Introducing the series of essays on Jencks in 1973, the editors noted once more that schooling had not reduced inequality. Additional school resources had neither increased achievement scores nor reduced differences in achievement between rich and poor, Black and white. But the editors refused to concede that this meant the schools had little effect:

> The editors of *HER* share with many of our readers the predisposition to believe that the schools routinely *do* have powerful effects on the children attending them. We would like to ask the question, what are these effects? This will involve developing ways of talking about schooling which are not now in existence in the research community.

[19] Henry Aaron, *Politics and the Professors: The Great Society in Perspective* (Washington, D.C.: Brookings Institution, 1978), p. 44.

[20] *The Irony of Early School Reform* (Cambridge, Mass.: Harvard Univ. Press, 1968).

[21] Christopher Jencks, Marshall Smith, Henry Ackland, Mary Jo Bane, David Cohen, Herbert Gintis, Barbara Heyns, and Stephan Michelson, *Inequality: A Reassessment of the Effect of Family and Schooling in America* (New York: Basic Books, 1972).

Without new questions, we fear that the current tendency to find that nothing relates to anything will continue, and that it will be misunderstood by the American public to mean that the schools are doing nothing.

Perhaps there were errors in Coleman's and Jencks's research methods—not in application but in the procedures themselves. In August 1975 Luecke and McGinn were critical of Coleman and Jencks on these grounds. They created a model which included among its assumptions that various features of schooling—for example, teacher quality and per pupil expenditures—did influence achievement. They ran hypothetical students through this hypothetical system and then collected data on the students at a single point in time just as the Coleman report had done. The results again systematically understated the role of schooling and overstated the importance of students' family background. The implication was that Coleman's methods preordained his results.

Perhaps one needed to examine the schools directly, not through the refractions of survey research. Wesley Becker reported in 1977 on one very successful field experiment from the University of Oregon and concluded: "The Direct Instruction Model has demonstrated that children from low-income homes can be taught at a rate sufficient to bring them up on most achievement measures to national norms by the end of third grade." In 1978 Pederson et al. described the effects of one teacher on achievement, and Hugh Mehan argued that there are classroom effects. In 1978 Jonathan Kozol, reporting on the Cuban literacy campaign, argued that schooling can greatly affect student achievement. But contrary to Becker, Kozol argues that academic achievement is connected not to a technology of instruction but to a politics of pedagogy. Genuine prospects for a better life, not particular instructional methods, make the difference.

By 1978, however, Kozol's hopeful missionary spirit was further removed from the center of editorial board sentiment than Freire's optimism had been eight years before. In their introduction to a critique of the Follow-Through evaluations, the editors remarked: "Today education is rarely esteemed as a potent social force," in contrast to the late 1960s, "a now poorly remembered era of optimism." But then, despite the editors' short memory, they spoke in a rhetoric of optimism about "how we can best serve our children."

Although the word "children" ought, one would think, to be common in educational literature, "child," "childhood," or "children" in fact appear only once in the titles of *HER* articles between 1931 and 1940, not at all between 1941 and 1950, three times between 1951 and 1960, six times between 1961 and 1970, and fifteen times since 1971, five of them in the special issues on "children's rights" published in 1973 and 1974. Perhaps, as educators have grown disheartened with the power of schools to affect students or change society, they have turned to a faith in the natural abilities of children to achieve for themselves. This emphasis is most evident in research on the child's capacity for learning language.

Language became a central concern of *HER* in the 1970s. Its beginnings lay in Mowrer's admission, in his 1947 essay on models of learning, that traditional learning theory had contributed very little to understanding the complexities of how language is acquired. Despite B. F. Skinner's own contributions to that field, its main thrust has been sharply antibehaviorist. The model of the language learner has not been the pigeon in a box, studied for a brief period, but the child in the family, maturing over years. Biology, not mechanism, has provided the leading metaphor of the psychology of language. The motif is explicit in Roger Brown and Ursula Bellugi's 1964 article: "The very intricate simultaneous differentiation and integration that constitute the evolution of the noun phrase is more reminiscent of the biological development of an embryo than it is of the acquisition of a conditional reflex."

The emphasis on the child's native abilities in both Jean Piaget's biological orientation and Noam Chomsky's Cartesian leanings comes through again and again in these articles on language. Carol Chomsky's essay on the stages of language development (1972) concludes that every child "enters the classroom equipped to learn language and able to do so by methods of his own." That the study of language touched on universal themes, revealed common human elements, and illuminated the biological nature of learners and, perhaps, their divine spark as well, was symbolized in Brown and Bellugi's decision to provide the two children they studied with the names Adam and Eve.

The study of language reached beyond psychology and linguistics to sociology. In 1970 *HER* published two essays that joined language to politics. Paulo Freire, writing of his work in adult literacy campaigns in Latin America, promoted the idea that since reading was a source of power, learning to read was less a psychological stage than a level of political awareness or "conscientisation." Joan and Stephen Baratz attacked various educational interventions from a radical perspective. Rejecting the "social pathology" model, they argued that Blacks were not "deficient," as both supporters and opponents of compensatory education had assumed, but "different," and they based that assumption on the conviction that the urban Black has a consistent, though different, linguistic system. An understanding of language, then, seemed to offer a way through social policy debacles and intellectual despair. A focus on language and the ability of the preschool child to show the most remarkable capacity for rule-governed behavior and the learning of exquisitely complex grammatical systems — regardless of genes, family background, or the quality of schooling — offered hope for the liberal position that the educational community had long tried to sustain. There was almost a new theology of education arising out of the study of language.

At the same time that language became the central focus of educational research, research itself was reconceived as a linguistic process. In a series of articles, David Cohen and colleagues discussed, not the Coleman problem of school effects, but the language in which that problem was debated. Cohen and Michael Garet, in "Reforming Educational Policy with Applied Research" (1975), observed that a decade of debate over the Coleman report had paradoxically produced "knowledge which is better by any scientific standard, no more authoritative by any political standard and often more mystifying by any reasonable public standard." Here, and in his other writings, Cohen wrote about language — how educational practice is based on "stories" we tell ourselves or "central metaphors." And so, likewise, in educational research. Cohen and Garet write:

> The function of policy research is at least as much to describe and discuss the premises and objectives of policy as it is to predict policy effects. In this sense, applied research

resembles a discourse about social reality—a debate about social problems and their solutions (pp. 113–137).

In a sense, Cohen's position seems the ultimate collaboration with what Joseph Featherstone called the "prevailing defeatist intellectual fashion in education." But Cohen's disenchantment was not with schooling but with social research; not with the capacities of the schools to teach but with the academic community's ability to learn with certainty about what schools do. Social research is seen not as answering questions but as expressing intellectual moods.

The implications of this position are not easily assimilated into a research community that has been wedded to the assumptions of conventional social science for more than a generation or into a journal which for fifteen years has had such a pronounced social science orientation. If social research is supposed to interpret texts rather than explain findings, then presumably a plurality of positions is not only possible but likely and desirable. This *is* disconcerting. Here the rediscovery of language, a product of academic inquiry, threatens to suck in the old academic enterprise and make it over. Just how this might be done is not clear, but it is apparent that the epistemological chasm opened by the politics of the 1960s has been widened by the intellectual advances of the 1970s.[22]

Review editors of the late seventies claim that there had been a decline in political awareness of the editorial board in the mid-1970s and link it to a growing loss of interest in social policy in the School of Education and to the shift of intellectual enthusiasm for programs in human development. They are right in linking trends at the *Review* to developments in the School of Education curriculum. At the same time, the concern with human development clearly did not preclude a concern for politics. The 1979 volume included articles on the *Bakke* decision, on open admissions at City University, a number of feminist essays, in addition to the special issue on women and education (most notably Carol Gilligan's criticism of Kohlberg, psychology, and moral philosophy from the perspective of the woman's life cycle), and others. What may be more significant than whether or not there has been a decline in the political content of the *Review* is the fact that former editors worry that there might have been. The attitude that *HER* has a responsibility for the world beyond the ivory tower is a legacy editors are largely unaware of when they come to the *Review*, learn to cherish while working on it, and pass on anxiously to new editors when they leave it.

The effort of editorial boards to be "at the cutting edge" of educational thought, and the excitement and intense seriousness that accompany it, are hard to recapture in this brief account. But some editors may speak for themselves about their experience with *HER*. The co-chairpersons for 1972–73 wrote in the annual report:

> We should say that *HER* meetings have more fun and sparkle and learning than any others we have experienced. There is shared concern about issues, there *is* listening, and there is argument that makes people see something in what they read they had not

[22] Cohen's call for interpretation of texts rather than explanation of causes and effects is very much like the program for anthropology outlined by Clifford Geertz, although Cohen does not cite Geertz. See Clifford Geertz, *The Interpretation of Cultures* (New York: Basic Books, 1973). It is worth noting here that of the various social sciences, anthropology has been notably underrepresented in the pages of the *Review*. The same may be said for economics.

seen on their own. Minds change in the course of board discussions — and votes. Indeed, this happens so often that the board has chosen not to count the vote of a member absent from the meeting, even if he or she has written a memo or otherwise made an initial reaction to the manuscript known.

And Theodore Sizer recalls of his own time on the board in 1959-60:

> It was (sad to say) the one arena where each of us graduate students was forced to make decisions on matters outside of our technical fields. . . . The real genius of the exercise was the fact that we came out in print: there was clear and unmistakable accountability. As they say, it focused the mind. Because the journal was the product of a committee of graduate students, it showed all the attendant weaknesses of such an arrangement. We were often sloppy; as soon as we became sophisticated in the ways of the publishing world we got our degrees and moved along, leaving another naive crop in our wake; we sometimes confused slickly written articles with deep articles, and accordingly published some rather harmless nonsense; in our lack of experience we often missed important scholarly matters which were shortly to break upon us and concentrated rather on what was in fact conventional. However, when one balances the strengths and the weaknesses, I clearly think the strengths win out.[23]

That judgment is modest enough, and affectionate enough, to serve as a graceful preamble to *HER*'s next fifty years.

[23] Personal communication with Theodore Sizer, 18 July 1980.

PART I

Education and Human Development

Appreciation and Cultivation

JOHN DEWEY

John Dewey examines the role of emotion in the processes of teaching and learning and its relation to subject matter. The author observes that while subjects such as literature and the fine arts easily arouse appreciation—personally experienced value—this experience is not restricted to particular school subjects. Dewey argues that the development of appreciation can be maximized only if all curriculum subject matter actively contributes to the stirring of emotion and the cultivation of the learner's powers of imagination.

A great deal has been said of late of the importance of appreciation in education and of its neglect. Much of the discussion turns about the growing significance of leisure in American life and the need that education should prepare for proper use of leisure, as well as for vocations. The revolt against domination by the "business mind," whether in life or in the schools, is all to the good. But I think I see signs that appreciation is taken too narrowly—that its universal scope as a function of all normal experience is not sufficiently perceived.

The narrow tendency to which I just referred concerns the limitation of appreciation to a few subjects, studies like literature and the fine arts. Now I do not wish to inflict anything upon you about the old topic of interest. Without attempting an accurate definition of appreciation, we can at least say that it is a sense, a personal realization, of value. One conclusion seems inevitable. If there is value in any subject, a value which is actual to students and teachers and not merely nominal and external, then the place and the role of appreciation cannot be restricted to any particular list of studies.

If there is not appreciation in geography, history, yes, in arithmetic and algebra, we are forced to the conclusion that although there may be value somehow in those subjects, the students do not personally come into possession of it. What then is appreciation? What is its nature that it may extend to all subjects and themes? Literature and the fine arts may give us the key to the answer. For while not having a monopoly of power to arouse appreciation, they exemplify it in a conspicuous way.

I suppose that all would agree without labored argument that capacity to arouse emotion and imagination is a distinctive feature of poetry, novels, the drama, music, painting, and other arts. If this be admitted, then we have the clue to two marked traits of appreciation. It involves a stirring of emotion and an immediate development of imagination. If certain school subjects do not offer material which is appreciated, it

Harvard Teachers Record   Vol. 1   No. 2   April 1931, 73-76

must then be because of lack of emotional and imaginative power as these subjects are taught and learned.

The psychology of emotion is a somewhat obscure matter. But some characteristics of it are evident to ordinary inspection. It involves at least personal participation. The things that leave us cold are things indifferent to us. They may be so and so, but they make no difference to *us*.

> Be she fairer than the day
> Or the flowery meads in May,
> If she be not so to me,
> What care I how fair she be?

To be emotionally stirred is to care, to be concerned. It is to be *in* a scene or subject, not outside of it. A slight and passing emotional stir occurs when something at least touches us. A deep emotion is more than tangency; it is secancy. The more anything, whether an object, scene, idea, fact, or study, cuts into and across our experience, the more it stirs and arouses. An emotion is the register of the extent and way in which we are personally implicated, involved, in anything, no matter how external it is to us physically.

Some emotions are gross. They manifest themselves in direct unmistakable, observable, changes of the face, the hand, and the postures of the body. Rage, extreme grief and elation, fear when it reaches the point of terror, are examples. In such cases, there is no manner of doubt as to the degree in which some physically external event comes home to one. The event so enters into us, is so experienced as a part of our own very selfhood, that we are lifted up, cast down, attracted so that we want to make it more fully our own, or repelled so that we want to cast it out and destroy it. But emotions exist on the most extensive scale from the coarse to the refined and subtle. We are elated by a victory of *our* side in a football game, a political election; by an access of sudden fortune, by the recovery of a critically ill friend. But we also may be elated, set up, by a sunset, a picture, by a new idea that has dawned on us, by the perception of a relevancy of a fact to some problem that has been occupying us. Then we relish the object; we are drawn to appropriate, possess, and linger with affection. In short, we appreciate.

Transformation of the coarser, instinctively organic emotions into subtler and more delicate forms, of the glaring hues of black and white, red and green, into variegated tints and shades, is a large part of the process of refinement of personality. Aristotle said that anybody could get angry, but to get angry at the right time, place, object and in the right degree is the mark of a moralized human being. The principle of the saying applies to all the emotions; as they are nicely and justly adapted to conditions, they are shaded and refined. While refinement and cultivation are not wholly synonymous in all respects, they are identical in some of their phases. No amount of possession of facts and ideas, no matter how accurate the facts in themselves and no matter what the sweep of the ideas — no one of these in itself secures culture. They have to take effect in modifying emotional susceptibility and response before they constitute cultivation.

I am not concerned to make a too explicit and literal application to the matter of instruction and learning. But it should be clear that while certain subjects, like the fine arts, may be more easily employed than some others to secure emotional appropriation of material and thereby effect a transformation of native crude emotions, it is fatal to confine appreciation to them. Unless pupils, for example, acquire a certain fastidiousness of taste in the use of words in all classes, a sensitiveness to shades of meaning, the lack cannot be made up by set subjects of composition and literature. Unless a fact or piece of information in geography, history or botany is emotionally responded to, and in a way which makes emotional disposition more graded and delicate, we cannot safely depend upon music and poetry to perform the task.

I think one could go through the defects and mistakes of teaching and learning generally and find that they are associated with failure to secure emotional participation. Take two of the universally deplored features. Mere receptive passivity on the part of a pupil and mere pouring in by textbook and teacher are themselves proof of absence of that personal participation which we call emotion. The schooling that puts chief stress upon mere memorizing, upon committing to heart, is an instance of the same failure. The trouble is that material is not committed to *heart*; it is only entrusted to some portion of the cerebrum. In consequence, personal cultivation is not attained.

Unless there is emotional sensitiveness to facts and ideas, to problems and solutions, wherever they present themselves, there is great likelihood that the attempt to secure genuine appreciation through the means of specially selected subjects will fail and go wrong. It is one thing for a child, youth, or adult to *feel* a sunset, and another thing for him to learn that certain rhapsodic utterances are conventionally expected of him. There is a like danger in the educational use of music, poetry, and the drama. Unless the pupil comes to these subjects with a background of experience in which prior perceptions of meanings and relationships of form are configured, his emotional response is bound to be one in which the cruder emotions are dominant, or else one that is factitious because irrelevant to actual subject matter. Limitation of appreciation makes some subjects dull and dead while it renders others the occasion of temporary excitation, amusement, and escape into the realm of reverie.

With respect to imagination I should approach its definition, educationally, through the spontaneous carrying power which information and ideas sometimes possess. There is a kind of study and learning in which what is acquired falls with a dead weight. It stops short with itself. It has no propulsive charge. Such knowledge, if we dignify it by that name, points, by contrast, to the nature of imagination. The connection of emotion and imagination is not accidental. Emotion provides the carrying impetus. Imagination denotes that to which we are carried when the emotion is not so coarsely organic as to lead to direct overt action. A man in a rage may smash and tear about. If his emotion is refined and controlled by thought of objects, it leads to consequences in imagination. The resentful man may fancy his foe placed in all sorts of predicaments in which he suffers dire distress, or he may project himself, taking sweet revenge in some public humiliation of the object of his wrath. A more refined indignation may set to work to explore imaginatively the source of a public wrong and to construct measures of remedy. Or a Dickens may be led to an imagination which discloses the situation to others through the medium of a novel.

Such instances should not obscure the educational bearings of the power of emotion to awaken and direct imagination in all sorts of situations. A fact of natural science or a principle in mathematics, if it does not drop dead with a thud into the mind, will suggest other facts and ideas; it will propel the mind forward. Suggestion is a simple case of imagination; apt and vivid metaphors are the work of that carrying power named imagination. An obverse example is the irrelevant play of fancy so common among pupils. Attention can be held only as it is carried forward. Absence of power to stir in subject-matter presented has its counterpart in mind-wandering; the mind lets itself go into all kinds of scenes and situations which do afford congenial imaginative exercise.

None of these illustrations is very fundamental compared with that absorption in a subject, problem, or undertaking which of itself carries one forward to all sorts of relations and consequences which have the tang of novelty and surprise. Imagination is nought but a free play of mind, a play which, if it is really of the mind, does a work which no reluctant and enforced toil can accomplish. The caricature of interest and attention which disfigures the schoolroom is due to acting as if a closed object or situation had interest and intellectual possibilities. Degradation of interest into amusement results when it is forgotten that only expanding movement, intrinsic development of subject-matter can sustain interest; nothing is more boring or exhausting than momentary excitation; and that is all any situation or activity that is closed, that ends with itself, can provide. The statements do not signify that interest or imagination should be conscious or be consciously appealed to. They mean that wherever there are freely moving ideas, wherever information is fruitful in suggesting other meanings than those contained in what is immediately at hand, there is of necessity imagination and intellectual interest.

Appreciation, in short, is more than immediate and transient emotional stir and turmoil. It shapes things that come home to us, that we deeply realize have possibilities, entail consequences. To appreciate is to trace mentally these outleadings, to place the possibilities before the mind so that they have felt significance and value. There is no fact and no idea or principle that is not pregnant, that does not lead out into other things. The greatest and the commonest defect in teaching lies in presenting material in such fashion that it does not arouse a sense of these leadings and a desire to follow them. There is then no appreciation, no personally experienced value, because what is presented is presented as if it had its meaning complete in itself, as if it were closed and shut. Think over the teachers that you would call inspiring and you will find that they were the teachers who made you aware of possibilities in the things which they taught and who bred in you desire to realize those possibilities for yourself. I can give no better exemplification of the true nature of appreciation nor of its capacity to attend all subjects of instruction.

Process and Achievement:
A Basic Problem of Education and
Developmental Psychology

HEINZ WERNER

Heinz Werner challenges the behaviorist focus on quantitative levels of achievement and end-products from the perspective of genetic (developmental) psychology. In this seminal article, he urges a developmental analysis of qualitatively different levels of underlying mental processes that are directed toward the same achievement. Werner concludes by discussing the need for intense cooperation between such a genetic psychology and pedagogy.

The question of the relation between accomplishment and the underlying mental processes is one of the most significant problems of genetic psychology, as well as of the theory and the practice of education. It is doubtless of great value to analyze the genesis of human mentality in terms of a gradual increase of accomplishment. Measuring development by means of achievements has proved to be a successful approach, and has provided valuable insight into the laws of mental growth. Nevertheless, this method of understanding must be supplemented by an analysis of the mental processes which underlie the achievements themselves.

A fundamental issue is involved. Does the genesis of "learning," "abstraction," "reasoning," or whatever term one chooses to use, mean the development of a unitary function? Or does it mean the history of an accomplishment achieved by process-patterns which are quite different at different levels? It is correct, if development is interpreted according to the first assumption, to take the degree of accomplishment as the objective measure of the genetic stage of the unitary function in question. If it is admitted, following a growing tendency among psychologists, that the latter assumption is more tenable, the conclusion must be drawn that mental development, or training, does not consist so much of a quantitative increase in accomplishment, one based on a unitary function, as of a reorganization of processes conditioned either by the introduction of a new

Harvard Educational Review Vol. 7 No. 3 May 1937, 353–368

function, or by a change of dominance of function in a given process-pattern. From this latter stand-point, processes at different levels are involved in any improvement within a special field of mental activity, no matter whether this improvement is due to training or to a natural ripening of the mentality. The analysis of these levels of process then becomes a task of considerable importance for child psychology and pedagogy as well.

Analogous Mental Functions

In order to attack this problem of process-levels, it might be expedient to make use of a familiar concept of biology and anatomy, the concept of "analogous function." In comparative anatomy, the term "analogous function" refers to a type of function which may be accomplished by organs distinctly different in structure. The respiration of vertebrates, for example, is carried on by gills in fishes and by lungs in mammals. Analogous mental functions, which we may define here as functions on different genetic levels directed toward the same achievement, can be easily demonstrated to be present in almost any field of mental activity.[1]

A good illustration is furnished by the ability to apprehend objects according to their constant properties. The brightness of objects, for instance, may appear approximately the same to us throughout different intensities of illumination. Chalk appears to have about the same degree of whiteness, and coal of blackness, even though the physical intensity of the light reflected from the surfaces of the objects may vary considerably because of a change of illumination.[2] There is an effective mechanism which tends to keep the color properties of objects approximately constant. It is as if the eye were making the proper allowances for a change in the frame of reference, that is, the illumination.

This tendency of the organism to stabilize the properties of objects is evident in processes on three different levels. The most primitive level of this adaptation to varying illuminations is the physiological light and dark adaptation of the retina. Again, there is the previously mentioned tendency to perceive the brightness of the objects as being more or less constant despite varying illumination. This is a higher level of function, a level of perceptual interpretation on which the illumination is perceptually related to the object. Physiological adaptation is probably fully developed in early childhood, while perceptual constancy in color and brightness develops more slowly, and reaches its final peak at about 15 years

---

[1] See my *Einführung in die Entwicklungs-psychologie*, 2nd ed., (Leipsic: J. A. Barth, 1933).
[2] See David Katz, *The World of Color* (London: Paul, Trench, Trubner and Co., 1935).

of age. The perceptual interpretation of brightness and color is in turn super-seded by a mental activity on a higher level. This activity is a process by means of which the properties of things are determined conceptually; it is "known" that chalk is white and coal black. It can readily be seen that these three different processes achieve their goal with increasing efficiency. The least effective is, of course, the retinal adaptation, and the most effective, the conceptually under-stood relation between things and their characteristic color properties.

Analogous processes can again be seen in the interpretation of other proper-ties of objects — for instance, their size and shape. The size and shape of an ob-ject may, within certain limits, remain approximately constant even though there has been a definite change in the retinal image because of a variation in the distance of the object, or in the visual angle. Furthermore, approximate con-stancy of size and shape on the perceptual level is superseded by a constancy re-sulting from conceptual operations — logical inferences, measurements, etc.[3]

As Figure I shows, the curve for perceptual shape-constancy arrives at its peak at the age of 14 years. The decline of the curves for perceptual constancy of brightness, color, shape, and size is very likely due to the growth of the concep-tual operation, which will now replace, partially at least, the function on the lower level. Numerous other examples of analogous, genetically related pro-cesses could be cited. E. Jaensch sees such a relationship between after images, eidetic images, normal images. Brunswik, Goldscheider, and Pilek,[4] by their studies on memory, demonstrate analogous processes at the following genetic levels: memory for unorganized meaningless material (with the peak of accom-plishment at 11-13 years of age); memory for perceptually organized material (peak at 15-18 years); memory for conceptually organized material (peak after 20).

Levels of Abstract Mental Functions

The discussion of the general problem may be directed toward such mental ac-tivities as abstraction and conceptual thinking, problems with which education is specifically concerned. Textbooks of psychology tell us that abstraction is a mental function by means of which parts of a unit are separated from the whole, and detached qualities — color, form, etc. — are understood in isolation. Such a definition usually implies that abstraction is a unitary function which comes into

---

[3] S. Klimpfinger, "Entwicklung der Gestaltkonstanz," *Arch. f. d. ges. Psychol.* (88, 1933).
[4] "Untersuchungen zur Entwicklung des Gedächtnisses," Beiheft 64, *Zeitschr. f. angew. Psychol.* (1932).

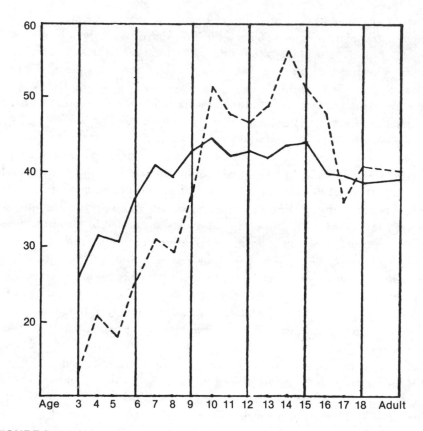

FIGURE I

Graph representing development of brightness-constancy (solid line) and shape-constancy (dotted line). Ordinate represents relative percentage of ideal constancy (100 per cent). Abscissa represents age (3–18)—also the adult level. (Redrawn from Brunswik, Bericht XI, *Kongress f. Psychol.* 1930, p. 53).

being at a certain stage of mental development, and increases gradually with age. But if one holds that the term "abstraction" does not mean a unitary function, but rather denotes an accomplishment effected by processes on quite different levels, any such question as determining the age at which the faculty of abstraction first appears becomes meaningless.

To further the analysis of the development of abstraction, we may turn to some results from the numerous experiments dealing with this subject. An experiment frequently made is the grouping test. Children are presented with geometrical figures of diverse shapes and colors, which they are told to order in groups.

It has been found by various experimenters that, up to about 4 years of age, the grouping is done usually according to only one category. This category may be either color or shape, but never both. Moreover, there is little or no freedom of choice in the grouping. It appears that the conspicuous properties of objects themselves—color or form—quasi-automatically force similar things into groups: blue objects "come together," and the same is true of red ones or green ones. In consequence of this apparent coercion, the young child is unable to change his grasp of the situation in order to arrange the objects into sub-groups. The blue objects, once having been brought together, cannot be subdivided further according to the different shapes.

FIGURE II

In analyzing this primitive type of a rigid, one-sided abstraction, which seems to be occasioned by the objects themselves instead of being directed by the will of the child, it will be found that such abstraction is based on a primary law of organization, a law effective in the simplest of perceptions. Gestalt psychology calls this the "law of equality." If, for example, one closely observes Figure II, it will be seen that the number "2" is based on the phenomenon that certain elements of the optical field with equal qualities tend to attract each other.

This quasi-automatic attraction of equal elements seems to be effective also in the so-called "primitive abstraction." Things having equal qualities tend to come to the fore, organizing themselves into a unit. It may even be—as experiments with both children and adults have shown—that if objects of the same color are scattered over a surface, these objects may be seen as a different group before the color common to all of them has been clearly discerned. It is therefore justifiable to conclude that there is a primitive abstraction which is quite close to primary sensory organization.

What are the next steps in the development of abstraction? Intentionality may be taken as a discriminating factor in describing the genetic levels revealed in the grouping process. By intentionality is meant the ability to shift spontaneously from one point of view to another, from one category to another. In this respect it is interesting to note an experiment made by Usnadze.[5] The child is presented with a number of figures of different sizes, shapes, and colors which he is told to bring into a logical grouping. The younger child, that is, one working on a lower level, although capable of grouping according to one category, must learn to follow the example set by the teacher in order to be able to divide into sub-groups. An older child, usually one who has reached the age of 7, after he has exhausted the possibilities of grouping according to color, will continue without aid to make sub-groups on the basis of shape. When he has done this, he will continue still further, and group according to size. In the highest type of performance characteristic of the average adult there is a preliminary conception of the task, so that it becomes possible to take into account all three categories at once in the ordering process.

This development does not simply indicate a gradual growth of a unitary, intellectual function called "abstraction." It involves, to my way of thinking, specific changes in the process of abstraction itself. He who is able to shift his point of view during a deliberate grouping is no longer passively subject to the forces of sensory stimulation. Such a person consciously perceives that the objects have different signs according to which order is possible. In other words, this development indicates an immensely important change from abstraction which works close to sensory organization, to abstraction which is guided by purposively conceived categories, such as color, shape, number, size, etc. The behavior involved in this higher form of abstraction has been called "categorical behavior." Not one child in Usnadze's experiments between the ages of 3 and 8 was able to reach the level of categorical abstraction in the strict sense of the adult performance. According to the experiments conducted with the same type of material in the Hamburg Psychological Laboratory, it was found that children usually reached the level of categorical abstraction at the age of 11–12.[6]

[5] "Begriffsbildung im vorschulpflichtigen Alter," *Zeitschr. f. angew. Psychol.* (34, 1929).
[6] It must, however, be kept in mind that all results gained from any experiments are, to a large ex-

A deeper insight into the genesis of abstraction as revealed in the experiments with children can be obtained if one considers the facts resulting from the analysis of individuals who, in consequence of a deterioration of the brain, have more or less lost the higher forms of abstraction. A most instructive case of a "regression" towards a more primitive stage of abstraction is described by Gelb and Goldstein.[7] In the experiment the patient was asked to name the colors of objects. This he was unable to do. He was then asked to select the correct colors from a pile of differently colored woolen threads. He failed in this as well. Superficially this inability either to name or to point to the desired colors would appear to be a peculiar language defect. But Gelb and Goldstein, after a thorough experimental analysis, concluded that the deficiency is not primarily one of language, but of categorical behavior. The patient has lost his capacity for using names as symbols for categories ("green," "red," "blue," etc.). At the same time, his ability to name "concrete" colors, that is, colors associated with objects in his experience ("strawberry-like," etc.), is not disturbed. His behavior in the grouping experiment is highly significant. If the patient is asked to bring differently colored woolen threads into order, he shows a marked loss in the power to group things according to a principle which normal persons follow. He is not guided by a conceptual scheme according to which things are divided into groups, but rather by the "concrete coherence" of the sensory qualities of the objects. The patient therefore shows a loss of spontaneity of intentionality comparable to that of the younger children of the previously mentioned experiments. Depending on a change in the coherence of the sensory stimuli, the patient sometimes groups colors which are perfectly equal in their qualities; another time it may be brightness, or certain aesthetic-emotional qualities, which guides the ordering process.

Such evidence from pathology again leads us to the conclusion that there are different levels of abstraction—that primitive abstraction, close to the level of perceptual organization, is, during development, superseded by higher processes of abstraction which operate on the level of conceptual, categorical thinking.

The genesis of abstraction is one of the numerous phenomena which suggest that learning, development, should be conceived as a transformation of one pat-

---

tent, dependent on the particular experimental situation. So far as the relative age is concerned, the steps in the growth of abstraction may therefore more or less vary with the conditions of the experiment. The sequence, as pointed out here, and as we have other strong evidence to believe, will follow the general scheme outlined above.

[7] "Ueber Farbennamen-Amnesie," *Psychol. Forsch.* (6, 1924). See also K. Goldstein, "The Problem of the Meaning of the Words, Based upon Observation of Aphasic Patients," *Journal of Psychology*, II (1936).

tern of processes into another. Such a conception of development raises a great many problems of concern to both theoretical child psychology and educational practice. One of these problems with the relation between the higher and lower processes which we have termed "analogous." Is the lower type of process, we may ask, a stage that must be reached before advancing to a higher form? And again, is this lower level completely lost if one continues on to higher functional types of achievement? These two questions are intimately linked. Unfortunately, there is really not enough experimental evidence to justify a complete answer to these problems. Nevertheless, certain observations point to the following conclusions: First, there are analogous processes of a lower order which must take place before the higher process occurs. Second, the lower level, in many instances, is not lost, but becomes an integral part of an organization in which the higher process dominates the lower. Great educators have at all times implicitly recognized the principle underlying these two conclusions embodying the law of "organic development."[8]

Very little has been done, however, to subject this principle to scientific tests. Two groups of facts may be cited which shed some light on the relation between the higher and lower processes in an integrated activity. The first group of facts is concerned with the adult manner of carrying out tasks involving abstraction. It has been found in many of these experimental analyses—regardless of whether it is a question simply of abstracting equal elements out of a multitude of different items, or one of putting into effect a highly abstract conceptual formation— that primitive abstraction on a perceptual level is more or less involved in all these performances.

If a subject is presented with a number of figures of the following type (Figure III), and is asked to tell how many systematic groupings can be made with these figures, it seems to be the natural procedure for the subject to gaze at the field and allow the primitive forces of organization inherent in the field to have their effect. In the course of this subject's experimentation with the material, he will find that the figures cohere in three distinctly different ways: according to size, thickness, and shape. Such a perceptual grouping is the basis for a rather abstract, and verbally expressed judgment. This procedure is typical of many other instances where abstraction on the perceptual level is put at the service of the higher conceptual process of abstraction.

Suppose that a child, because of external or internal circumstance, lacks the opportunity of sufficient practice in primitive abstraction. What will this mean

[8] John Dewey, *Democracy and Education* (New York: The Macmillan Co., 1919). Pp. 130 ff.

FIGURE III

for him? There are many facts—some of which will be mentioned later in discussing the genesis of number—indicating that this situation means a violation of the principle of organic development when higher forms of abstraction operating in judgments of comparison, construction of concepts, have to be carried out. Here again strong evidence for this conclusion can be derived from pathological facts. At this point we may refer to the case of a patient who, because of a brain injury, suffered from a general inability to configurate in the sensory field ("Gestalt-blindness").[9] Primitive abstraction, based on perceptual organization, was therefore lacking. In consequence of this, the patient was unable to make any judgment of a higher order of abstraction—for example, unable to judge which of two lines was longer or which of two tones was higher.

The patient lost the ability to carry out higher processes of abstraction not because he was lacking in potential intelligence of a higher order, but because, lacking perceptual organization, he could not actualize this intelligence. His ac-

[9] Benary, "Intelligenz bei einem Fall von Seelenblindheit," *Psychol. Forsch.* (2, 1922).

tive intelligence was disturbed "from below," and not from the higher centers. A further analysis of this case proves the correctness of such an interpretation. The patient learned to act intelligently in dealing with the problems of abstraction by substituting movements for the missing optical configurations. He could, for instance, recognize printed letters, providing that he was permitted to follow the outlines of the letters with movements of his head. If he were allowed to use such organizations as a substitute, he would be able to peform all judgments of comparison concerning length of line, tone-pitches, etc., simply because he would now be able, through movements, to select and configurate the necessary properties out of the given material.[10]

This intelligence defect "from below" again became apparent when the patient's ability to abstract on the purely verbal, conceptual level was tested. He could find no meaning in the analogy of "head—hat: foot—shoe." But as soon as it occurred to him to relate the objects designated in the analogy by means of movements, substituting this device for what, with the normal person, would perhaps be an optical-schematic image, he was able to conceive the relationship.[11]

If development is conceived as being not an increasing efficiency in accomplishment, but as the transformation of mental processes from lower to higher forms, a further consequence arises. It is of equal importance to the child psychologist and the educator to bear in mind that the degree of accomplishment in a certain test does not always indicate the stage of development that has been reached by the child in this particular field. The teacher in the classroom and the diagnosing psychologist very often neglect the fact that the child who is accomplishing a task by employing functions of a lower level may ultimately be more successful than another who attempts to employ functions of a higher order. In the previously mentioned grouping experiments, for example, a 10-year-old child does not experience any particular difficulty. He orders first by color, then by shape, proceeding smoothly in separate successive steps. On the other hand, we have often observed that a child of the same age who is conscious from the start that the objects should be ordered according to several categories may not succeed nearly so well. This child, although more advanced so far as the mental processes are concerned, will work more slowly, encounter more difficul-

---

[10] If, for example, two tones were given, he could indicate the lower pitch by a downward movement of the head. Or, if the tones were of different duration, he could indicate the longer tone by a more protracted movement.

[11] The behavior of a patient whose intelligence is disturbed because of a lack of perceptual organization is quite different from that of a person who is deficient on the level of higher abstraction itself. The latter will always fail in an analogy test; his is a deficiency which cannot be overcome.

ties, than the other more näive child whose abstractive processes are nearer to the purely perceptual organization. It is well known that there is usually a decrease in accomplishment during the transition from the use of a primitive mental tool to the use of one that is more refined.

Genesis of the Idea of Number

The genesis of abstraction is repeated in specialized forms in all fields of activity in the learning process. The development of any such mental activity, occasioned and guided by appropriate school instruction, follows in principle the same rules which can be detected in the child's reaction to carefully prepared experimental situations. In order to illustrate this point, let us turn to a brief discussion of the genesis of number-ideas.

In the genesis of the number-idea there is a metamorphosis of processes similar to that observed in the experiments on abstraction. One of the first steps, counting, is pretty close to the configuration of objects on the plane of rhythmic, motor activity.[12] Another important step is represented by the understanding of numbers as perceptually organized units — as "number-groups," for example, :·: representing 5. The great progress here lies in the fact that the double aspect of a number which is a single unit and a plurality at the same time is inherent in any properly conceived number-form. In order to reach a still higher level of abstract number, a new metamorphosis of the process-pattern occurs. The number-forms or concrete number-groups are stripped of their picture-like properties; they develop into schemata representative of a number-concept. Such a transition implies two characteristics of development which have been previously discussed. First, analogous processes appear at genetically different levels — especially the level of concrete number-group and of number-concept. Second, the lower level of perceptual organization will still persist, at least for a long time, within the higher activity, although it is subordinated to the conceptual thinking.

In a careful study on "The Development of Children's Number Ideas in the Primary Grades,"[13] William A. Brownell comes to conclusions much like our

---

[12] W. Oehl, *Zeitschr. f. angew. Psychol.*, XLIX (1935), 300, stresses the fact that mentally backward children of school age are usually unable to count objects without motor accompaniment. One of the boys observed by Oehl, a child of 8 years, could count objects only when allowed to touch them one after the other. We are here reminded of counting methods found among some of the primitive tribes, e.g., the Bakairi, of whom K. von d. Steinen reports that they cannot count unless the hands are free to touch the objects.

[13] *Supplementary Educational Monographs*, No. 35 (Chicago: University of Chicago Press, 1928).

own. He points out the intrinsic developmental relationship between the two (analogous) functions of conceiving number as concrete groups and as concepts that are abstract. He substantiates quite convincingly the assumption that "those pupils who have developed mature methods of dealing with concrete numbers have little difficulty in making the transition to abstract numbers, and in learning the additive combinations" (p. 146). He specifically distinguishes between two types of pupils who have difficulty in handling abstract numbers. The pupils of the first type have never developed mature methods in dealing with concrete numbers. (For example, they will count off point by point the elements of a point-group, instead of perceiving the elements of the group simultaneously as a single unit.) They carry over the immature methods and apply them, as best they can, to abstract numbers. The pupils of the second type fail to relate the new work in abstract numbers to their former experience with concrete numbers. Usually they attempt blindly to memorize the new material (p. 158). This latter type of deficiency shows clearly that, even in higher forms of conceptual thinking, the processes of the lower developmental level ought not to be lost, but should play an integral part in the total performance.

This relationship is illustrated rather strikingly by those pathological cases which are characterized by a deficiency, or a complete loss, of perceptual organization. I refer again to the case analyzed by Benary.[14] This analysis proved that complete "Gestalt-blindness" will lead to an inability to construct sensory schemata which again will affect the processes of conceptual mathematical operations. The patient could perform mathematical operations only by substituting a primitive motor scheme (counting with the hands) for the lost optical scheme. If, for example, he was asked to add 4 and 3, he first counted 4 fingers on the left hand and then 3 fingers on the right hand. Having done this, he brought both his hands together and counted off the total represented by his outstretched fingers. Moreover, having lost the ability to think of a definite plurality as a unit, he was unable to tell immediately which of the two members, 7 or 3, was the greater. Only by counting on his fingers did he conclude that 7 came after 3 and therefore must be the bigger number. He could solve the problem of $5 + 4 - 4 = ?$ only by means of his motor counting scheme. In doing this he had first to count 4 forwards and then 4 over again backwards. He had no inkling that the same result could be obtained by a single operation. This and similar cases suggest that some sort of schematization, however remote it may be from the original con-

[14] See note 9.

crete organization, plays an actual role on the conceptual level of number operations.

The problem of analogous function in the field of number formation leads back to the problem of the relationship between accomplishment and the processes involved. With reference to this problem, Brownell has reached some enlightening conclusions which seem to be of general importance for educational psychology. It was found that there is no strict relation between greater achievement and more mature processes. Individual analysis shows that one pupil may do better than another so far as accuracy is concerned, although he may use more immature methods. Actually he ranks decidedly lower in development, although on the basis of results he should rank higher. Group tests which score accomplishment only, have to be supplemented by individual analysis. Group tests reveal the *product* of thinking, not the *processes* responsible for the product. Any notion of development expressed merely in terms of accuracy or speed in achievement seems inadequate. The true measure of development is not the degree of accuracy, but the manner in which the pupil thinks of numbers. "Effective instruction in arithmetic is contingent upon an understanding of the mental processes of the pupils. The teacher who secures all her information from such inadequate data as the correctness of their responses and the speed with which these responses are made is neglecting the essential element in the situation, namely, the processes which underlie this correctness and this speed" (Brownell, p. 117).

Genetic Psychology and Education

If, then, developmental psychology and pedagogy are both interested in the analysis of mental processes appearing at different genetic levels, processes tending toward the same cultural goal, one should in this regard expect a very intense cooperation between the two sciences. One of the most important tasks of genetic psychology which should prove of utmost significance to pedagogy is an exhaustive experimental analysis of the mental tools which culture offers to the growing child. Unfortunately, experimental genetic psychology has concerned itself, up to the present, but very little with the problem. To inquire into the special and general laws of development of mental instruments, specific types of experimental situations will have to be introduced. Among the very few examples of this kind of work I may cite the pioneer experiments made by Russian psychologists (Vigotski, Leontiev, Luria). In all their various experiments the child is offered some mental instrument. The experimental situation is so constructed that the experimenter is able to observe the manner in which the child makes use of the instrument, the way the tool changes the process involved, and the way the tool itself may change at different stages of mental growth.

In one type of experiment, for instance, the child is tested in his ability to use artificial (mnemo-technical) means presented to him by the experimenter.[15] The child is faced with the task of remembering a number of words. If the task is easy, that is, if there are only a few words to be remembered, he will master it by the relatively primitive method of creating associative connections between the words. This simple method, however, appears quite inefficient if a great many words are to be memorized. The experimenter then puts a group of objects before the child, objects quite unrelated to the words to be memorized — a series of pictures, for instance, arranged in some definite sequence. While the younger children cannot make any use at all of this mental instrument, children between 7 and 8, of normal intelligence, will begin to use the pictures as mnemo-technical means of remembering words. For every given word the child chooses one of the pictures, the one which, for him, is most closely associated with the given word. At first he tries to use very natural associations which might exist between picture and word, a method which may prove to be fairly successful. A child of greater mental development will pass on to more remote and abstract intellectual connections which will prove to be even more efficient. A higher step in using such an instrument is reached when the child replaces the external picture-diagram with an internal scheme. In such a case he does not refer to the actual picture, but associates the word material with the titles of the pictures which he has learned to keep in mind in a strict order.

This development suggests a general principle governing the genesis of mental tools, which may be thought of as the law of the metamorphosis of an external mental instrument into one that is internal. It was found to be evident in the fulfillment of all tasks given to the children. The development of the concrete number-group until it becomes a rather remote and abstract inner scheme of number might, perhaps, be considered as a special case of this general rule. Such types of experiments, however imperfect they may at first appear, at least suggest the possibility of constructing experimental situations by which the worker in the field of child psychology might attack those problems which concern education in its essence.

In this paper an attempt has been made to show that the analysis of mental process in the course of development is a task vital to both genetic psychology

[15] L. S. Vigotski, "The Problem of the Cultural Development of the Child," *Pedagogical Seminary*, XXXVI (1929).

and education. The fruitful cooperation of workers in both fields, however, will depend on the basic assumption that education itself is conceived in terms, not of static accomplishment, but of dynamic processes.

On the Dual Nature of Learning:
A Reinterpretation of "Conditioning" and
"Problem-Solving"

O. HOBART MOWRER

In this often-cited article O. Hobart Mowrer describes three major traditions in the psychology of learning: hedonism, associationism, and rationalism. Many writers have attempted to base their understanding of learning exclusively upon one or another of these traditions, whereas others have unsystematically drawn from all three. Mowrer takes the position that there are only two basic learning processes: associationism's "conditioning," or learning based in the person's autonomic nervous system, and hedonism's "problem-solving," or learning based in the central nervous system. Rationalism is simply a complex derivative of these other two. Mowrer uses this formulation to resolve a number of theoretical paradoxes and to open the way for applying learning theory to the two types of education, which he also distinguishes: "teaching" for problem solving and "training" for conditioned responses.

One of the distinguishing features of science is that it strives for maximal simplicity, parsimony, and consistency in its basic assumptions, whereas comon sense is content with complexity, multiplicity, and inconsistency. Folk explanations often take the form of proverbs, which are notorious for their variety, unrelatedness, and mutual contradiction. Scientific explanations, by contrast, tend to be interrelated, rigorous, and systematic. Whereas common sense has an "explanation" for everything—once it has happened—but lacks general principles with high predictive power, the ways of science often bring its practitioners up short in the face of paradoxes and set problems which those who rely upon a ubiquitous eclecticism do not encounter.

The history of scientific learning theory, though brief, reflects some of the best traditions in scientific method. In America, William James was the first great writer in this field, and for him *repetition* was "the great law of habit." His student, E. L.

A portion of this paper was presented by invitation at the meeting of the Society for the Study of Psychosomatic Medicine in Boston, October 1946, and the paper as a whole was presented as a lecture to the Psychological Colloquium of Brown Unversity, in November 1946. In February 1947, the paper was discussed with the Psychology Seminar of Western Reserve University. The writer is indebted for many useful criticisms and suggestions received on these occasions, and from his students and colleagues.

Harvard Educational Review   Vol. 17   No. 2   Spring 1947, 102-148

Thorndike, found it impossible to make the law of repetition (or "use") account for all his experimental findings and posited the *law of effect* in addition. John B. Watson accepted the law of repetition (or "frequency") but rejected *effect* in favor of *recency*. At a somewhat later stage he came under the sway of Pavlovian thought and concluded that the *conditoned response* was the "fundamental unit of habit."

That those pioneer investigators have been in disagreement concerning their basic hypotheses has sometimes been allowed to overshadow the more important fact that they were all following the behest of science, that one's basic assumptions be explicit, simple, and, if possible, few in number. The wealth of experimental fact which has been accumulated during the past half-century as a result of the systematic formulations and logical deductions of these writers abundantly testifies to the value of this method.

During this period still other hypotheses concerning the learning process have been put forward, explicitly by Gestalt psychology, for example, and by psychoanalysis implicitly; but these hypotheses have not readily lent themselves either to precise experimentation nor to rigorous logical analysis and may therefore be dismissed from further consideration at this time.[1]

Within the past two decades there have been no major innovations in basic learning theory, but many investigators have vigorously pursued the implications and possible relatedness of the various fundamental concepts which were formulated during the first and second decades of the century. The last and in many respects most ambitious attempt to base a psychology of learning exclusively upon the principle of conditioning was made by E. B. Holt (1931). While it is uniformly conceded that there is something real and important about the conditioning concept, it is now generally acknowledged that it does not provide a comprehensive learning theory. In the hands of E. R. Guthrie (1935), the principle of recency has received its most vigorous and able exploitation, but O'Connor (1946) has pointed out what would seem to be a fatal defect in this type of theory. The principle of repetition (use, exercise, frequency) has come in for a bombardment of criticism from many sides, and is today perhaps the least important of the historically notable concepts in the field. By contrast, the law of effect, which was for a long time "an unpopular doctrine" (Thorndike, 1931, p. 33), has stood up exceedingly well and is today probably more influential than any other single conception of the learning process.

For a number of years the present writer and a small group of colleagues and students have attempted to push the law of effect as hard and as far as possible in an effort to determine the full extent of its potentialities—and its limitations, if any. For a time it looked as if this law were indeed *the* basic law of learning, from which all seemingly divergent types of learning could be derived. This view was tentatively suggested by the writer in 1938 and has been more confidently proposed in a series of later papers. McGeoch (1942), in *The Psychology of Human Learning*, has taken a similar position; and numerous other writers have subscribed to this view in varying degree.

---

[1] The writer has recently discussed some of the implications of Gestalt psychology for scientific learning theory in an article entitled, "The law of effect and ego psychology" (Mowrer, 1946). For a discussion of psychoanalysis in this connection, see "Time as a determinant in integrative learning" (Mowrer & Ullman, 1945).

But it remained for Hull (1943), in his *Principles of Behavior*, to make the first thoroughgoing attempt to make effect theory serve all purposes.[2]

The purpose of the present paper is to adduce evidence for believing that the law of effect is not valid as a *universal* principle of learning and that it has to be ranged alongside a second, and independent, type of learning.

*   *   *   *

Association and Effect

Since science strives for parsimony in its basic assumptions, it is understandable that attempts should have been made to account for all learning solely in terms of the law of effect. While acknowledging the molar differences between "habits," and so-called conditioned responses, a number of writers have attempted to account for both as instances of the same fundamental learning process.

In 1938 the present writer made such an attempt, as follows: "Just as incidental . . . stimuli which are temporally contiguous with those responses which are made at the time of escape from hunger, for example, become integrated with the hunger stimulus into a total stimulus pattern which, with repetition, becomes more and more specifically connected with these responses, so would it appear that stimuli which are temporally contiguous with those responses which occur at the time of escape from an anticipatory tension [e.g., fear] likewise become integrated with the anticipatory tension into a total stimulus pattern which, with repetition, becomes likewise more and more specifically connected with these responses. Eventually such incidental stimuli may acquire sufficient excitatory value as to be capable alone of eliciting the responses with which they have been temporarily associated, without the accompanying presence of the original motivating stimuli" (Mowrer, 1938, pp. 73–74).

Mowrer and Lamoreaux (1942) attempted to make this hypothesis more explicit by distinguishing between "parasitic" reinforcement and "intrinsic" reinforcement. "Parasitic" reinforcement is here used to designate the strengthening of the tone-running (conditioned) sequence through the action of the basic rewarding situation provided by the shock-termination. The strengthening of the shock-running (trial-and-error) sequence may, in contradistinction, be termed "intrinsic" reinforcement (pp. 3–4). It was here again assumed that there was only one basic reinforcing process, namely, that which occurs when a drive is reduced, a problem solved.

The concept of "redintegration," which is very likely to be suggested to the reader by the foregoing quotations, is, of course, an old one. However, in these quotations the attempt is made to make redintegrative, or associative, learning dependent upon the law of effect, rather than to explain it in terms of a separate principle, as has been the common practice.

In Hull's (1943) book, *Principles of Behavior*, there appears a section entitled "The

[2] It is debatable whether Thorndike can be said ever to have adopted this monistic conception of the learning process. In 1931, he wrote: "Repetition of a connection in the sense of the mere sequence of the two things in time has then very, very little power, perhaps none, as a cause of learning" (pp. 28–29). This might seem to constitute a repudiation of the law of exercise and an endorsement of the law of effect, as the sole principle of learning. But in the next sentence he adds, "Belonging is necessary." Moreover, in later publications Thorndike (1943, 1946) has continued to speak as if exercise and effect were both valid principles; see also later discussion of Thorndike on exercise and effect.

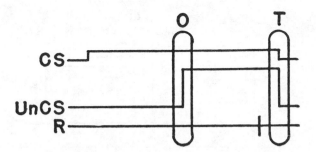

FIGURE 1

Diagram illustrating two theories of conditioning. According to Pavlov, reaction R becomes connected with the conditioned stimulus, CS, because of what happens at O. According to Hull, reaction R becomes connected with the CS because of what happens at T. For Pavlov it is the contiguity of the CS and the *onset* of the UnCS that is crucial, whereas for Hull it is the contiguity of the CS and the *termination* of the UnCS that is all important. In this illustration, the UnCS may be thought of as any noxious stimulus, such as an electric shock, and the CS as any innocuous stimuli, such as a tone or a light.

conditioned reflex as a special case of ordinary learning reinforcement," in which the author develops the same monistic conception of learning.[3] He says:

> Because of the current differences of opinion concerning the relationship between selective learning and conditioned-reflex learning, an explicit and somewhat detailed comparison of them as types will be made. . . . [Illustrative examples] suggest that the differences between the two forms of learning are superficial in nature; i.e., that they do not involve differences in the conditions under which the principle operates. . . . On one critical point both cases are identical—the reinforcing state of affairs in each consists in the abolition of the shock-injury or need, together with the associated decrement in the drive and drive receptor impulse, at once after the temporal conjunction of the afferent receptor discharge and the reaction. This is, of course, all in exact conformity with the law of primary reinforcement formulated above.
>
> Pavlov differs from the law of reinforcement by regarding as the critical element of the reinforcing state of affairs the occurence of S_u, in this case the *onset* of the shock. On the other hand, the critical element in the reinforcing state of affairs by our own hypothesis is the reduction in the drive receptor impulse which accompanies the reduction of the need, i.e., reduction of the physiological injury of the feet, caused by the termination of the shock.
>
> It is an easy matter to show the inadequacy of Pavlov's formulation as a general theory of learning. . . . It is not difficult to understand how Pavlov could have made such an error. His mistaken induction was presumably due in part to the exceedingly limited type of experiment which he employed. (pp. 76–79)

Figure 1 presents these two theories of reinforcement diagramatically. Each of these theories accounts well enough for those instances in which the response elicited by the conditioned stimulus [CS] is an exact replica of the response [R] elicited by the unconditioned stimulus [UnCS]; but a theory of conditioning must also be able to explain those instances in which the so-called conditioned response differs radically from the unconditioned response, as, for example, in the experiment by Mowrer and Lamo-

---

[3] See also a series of papers by Youtz (1938a, 1938b, 1939) in which a number of seeming parallels between "Pavlovian" and "Thorndikian" learning are adduced; also an earlier paper by Symonds (1927).

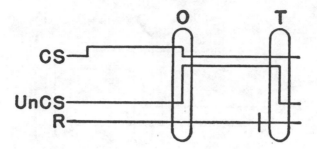

FIGURE 2

The important feature of this diagram is that it shows an experimental procedure in which the CS is turned off at O instead of being kept on until T, as in Fig. 1. If the reinforcement of the connection between CS and R were dependent on what happens at T, this connection would be expected to develop less readily with this procedure than with the one depicted in Fig. 1. The fact that the CS-R connection seems to develop just as readily when the CS terminates at O as when it extends to T suggests that for this kind of learning the reinforcement is provided by what happens at O, not at T. However, this analysis presupposes the division of labor posited in the text between reactions which are mediated by the autonomic nervous system and those mediated by the central nervous system. No attempt is made either in Fig. 1 or in Fig. 2 to indicate this relatively complex relationship.

reaux (1946) previously described. Such results can be made intelligible only if fear is posited as an intervening variable (cf. Tolman, 1932), and neither Pavlov's nor Hull's type of analysis has any place in it for such an intermediate factor. What clearly happens when a CS is paired with a noxious UnCS is that the CS becomes a danger signal and arouses fear, and it is the fear which then serves to motivate the externally observed defensive behavior. The latter seems to be largely determined by effect learning and may be like or quite unlike the overt behavior aroused by the original noxious drive.

Having established this much, the question which now arises is: How is fear learned? Is it acquired on the basis of what happens at O or at T (Figure 1)? If Pavlov had ever interested himself in the phenomenon of fear, he would presumably have said that it becomes attached to the CS by virtue of the mere conjunction of the CS and the UnCS. Hull's theory, on the other hand, would lead us to expect that the fear would become attached to the CS because of the satisfying state of affairs experienced when the UnCS is terminated. The latter expectation is contrary to intuitive common sense and to biological considerations. Why, one asks, should living organisms be so constructed that they can learn to fear traumatic stimulation only when that stimulation is "all over"? Would it not seem preferable for them to be constructed in such a way that fear-learning is produced by the coincidence of a danger signal and the impact of the trauma?

In an experiment which will shortly be reported by Suter, Horton, and Traum, evidence has been obtained which shows that fear-learning is indeed dependent, not upon situation T, but upon situation O (Figure 1). The logic of this experiment is as follows. If the capacity of the CS to become a danger signal is dependent upon its coincidence with the termination of the UnCS, then the CS should become more ominous to the subject if it overlaps and terminates with the UnCS than if the CS does not overlap with the UnCS, as shown in Figure 2. It is not possible here to give all the details of this experiment; but the important fact for the present purposes is that the above prediction is not confirmed: there even appears to be a slight tendency for the CS to become more ominous to the subject if the CS and the UnCS do *not* overlap.

No one will gainsay the importance and legitimacy of the attempt to derive a single, monistic principle of learning. For the teacher of learning theory no less than for the investigator, it would be very convenient if learning were a simple, unitary process. But the fact seems to be that learning is a more complicated procedure, and it is unrealistic to try to adduce a theory which does not appropriately acknowledge this complexity. We know that in certain instances of learning what happens when a drive is terminated and satisfaction is experienced is crucially important; but it now appears equally clear that certain other instances of learning depend upon the onset, rather than upon the termination, of a drive. Some other principle which is quite different from either the law of effect or the principle of association may ultimately make possible a unified theory of the reinforcement process; but for the present it seems necessary to assume that there are *two basic learning processes:* the process whereby the solutions to problem, i.e., ordinary "habits," are acquired; and the process whereby emotional learning, or "conditioning," takes place.[4]

This distinction, because it employs the term "conditioning" in a much more restricted and rigorous sense than has been common practice, immediately requires a word of explanation. As we have seen in the preceding section, the broader and more usual usage applies the term "conditioning" to the acquisition of any response which occurs to a signal, or CS, of any kind. This usage has broken down on both logical and pragmatic grounds and should be discontinued. As we have seen, many *so-called* conditioned responses are simply solutions to secondary-drive problems and are learned in the same way as are problem-solutions in general, i.e., through trial-and-error and the law of effect.[5] But it is also apparent that the law of effect is not adequate to account

[4] This conclusion has been forced upon the writer, not only by the experimental findings which are reviewed in this and the preceding section, but also by some particularly cogent and forceful criticisms which Professors P. B. Rice (1946) and G. W. Allport (1946) have recently directed against the author's earlier view that "living organisms learn when and only when they solve a problem in the sense of reducing a tension, relieving a discomfort, deriving a satisfaction" (Mowrer & Lamoreaux, 1946, p. 326).

Although convinced of the validity and importance of the law of effect, Rice prefers "to leave it an open question whether the Law of Effect can be taken as the sole principle of learning, or whether a Law of Exercise is also needed, perhaps together with still other principles." "It is hard to see how mere exercise or repetition, without satisfaction or need-reduction, could fail to have some effect on the associative neural tracts, even though this effect may be slighter than the 'retroflex' action of reward" (p. 309).

And Allport, while accepting effect as a secondary principle of learning, maintains that "effect cannot possibly be the *only* law of learning" (p. 338) and remarks that it is easy "to demonstrate that learning takes place when no drives have been reduced. Suppose while using a cleaning fluid I am careless with a match. . . . Suppose I mispronounce a word in a public speech . . . and suffer mounting shame and discomfort. Tension has been *created*, not reduced; *dissatisfaction* and not satisfaction has resulted; but in this sequence of events I shall surely learn . . ." (p. 342). These critcisms are well taken, and it is hoped that the point of view presented in the present paper will meet them, but will, at the same time, avoid the manifest difficulties which multiple-principle learning theories have previously encountered (see the later discussion of Thorndike's principles of effect and exercise).

[5] In earlier publications the author has stressed the usefulness of the distinction which Hilgard and Marquis (1940) have drawn between the "classical" conditioning procedure (invariable pairing of CS and UnCS) and the "instrumental" conditioning procedure (pairing of CS and UnCS only when the CS does not elicit the expected response). An "instrumental conditioned response" now appears to be a contradiction in terms. Only *skeletal* responses are instrumental in the sense of performing "work," producing "results," changing the external world; and if the term conditioning is to be restricted, as now seems desirable, to the process whereby responses of the smooth muscles and glands are acquired, it is clearly inappropriate to speak of a conditioned response as instrumental. This point will be returned to on a later page.

for the process whereby these secondary drives are themselves acquired; and it is for this latter process, exclusively, that the term "conditioning" should be reserved.

Such a procedure has a number of advantages which will be reviewed in a later section; first, however, it will be useful to note certain other justifications for using the term "conditioning" in this, and only this, sense and for making the conditioning process separate and distinct from the learning process denoted by the law of effect.

Collateral Support for a Two-Factor Theory of Learning

There are reasons other than that of conceptual convenience for supposing that there are two distinctive learning processes. In stressing the "unity of the individual," or the "organism as a whole," we are likely to gloss over the fact that in all mammals and in many other phyla the individual organism is divided into two great response systems, that of the *skeletal muscles* and that of the *smooth muscle* and *glands*. The responses mediated by the latter are appropriately termed *physiological*, whereas those mediated by the former are *behavioral* in the usual sense of that term. Just as an army must have both its "supply" units and its "action" units, so must the individual organism have organs of supply and organs of action.

The fundamental quality of this dichotomy is further emphasized by the fact that mammals and other complex living organisms have, not "a nervous system," but two distinct *nervous systems*. Responses of the skeletal muscles are mediated by the *central nervous system*, whereas responses of the visceral and vascular parts of the organism are mediated by the *autonomic nervous system*. In terms of structure and organization, as well as mode of functioning, these two nervous systems are radically different; and it is by no means unreasonable to suppose that the responses which they mediate are subject to very different learning processes.[6]

As a further parallel to this basic dichotomy we may note the familiar differentiation between *voluntary* and *involuntary* responses. Without exception, the visceral and vascular responses are beyond direct voluntary control, whereas all of the skeletal responses (with the unimportant exception of a few "reflexes") are or may be brought under voluntary control. Under ordinary circumstances, the visceral and vascular responses occur in a smoothly automatic fashion, and serve what Cannon (1932) has called the "homeostatic," or physiological, equilibrium-restoring function. These same responses may, however, be made to occur, not only in response to actual physiological needs, but also in response to conditioned stimuli, or signals, of various kinds. And when the visceral and vascular responses occur on the latter basis, as *anticipatory states*, they *produce*, rather than eliminate, physiological disequilibrium and are con-

---

[6] If one assumes that effect learning is a basic and that conditioning is dependent upon it, then one might expect to find that, phylogenetically and ontogenetically, the central nervous system is laid down first and the autonomic later. Kempf (1918) believes that the autonomic is the primitive nervous system and far older than the central nervous system. Although the central nervous system is now "dominant" in higher organisms, this was presumably not the case at an early stage in organic evolution. And Hewer (1927) has shown that in the human embryo the unstriped musculature develops first, to be followed later by the striped musculature. There is thus converging evidence that the autonomic-physiological system is more primitive than the central-behavioral system. From this it may seem to follow that conditioning is the basic form of learning and effect learning a "secondary form" (as Allport has proposed, Footnote 4). Whether such an inference is justifiable, on the basis of present knowledge, is uncertain.

sciously experienced as *emotion*. As such, they play enormously important motivational roles, roles so important to the survival of the organism that it is easily understood why the learning of these responses should be automatic, involuntary, distinct from the type of learning whereby ordinary habits are acquired. Biologically, it is clearly necessary that living organisms be equipped with a nervous system which will cause to be fixated those skeletal responses which reduce drives and give pleasure. But it is equally evident that living organisms must also be equipped with another nervous system which will cause emotional responses to be learned, not because they solve problems or give pleasure in any immediate sense, but because without such responses the organism would have slight chance of survival. There are grounds for believing that all emotions (including fear, anger, and the appetites) are basically painful (i.e., all have drive quality); and it is hard to see how they could be acquired by the same mechanism which fixes those responses (of the skeletal musculature) which are problem-solving, drive-reducing, pleasure-giving. The latter are learned when a problem is resolved, ended; whereas it is often necessary that emotional responses become conditioned to signals which are associated with the *onset*, not the termination, of a problem.[7]

Another way of making the same point is to note (as one of the author's students, Mr. C. G. Chmielenski, has recently done) that trial-and-error learning is parallel to what Freud (1911) has called the *pleasure-principle*, whereas conditioning is more closely related to the *reality-principle*. In other words, living organisms acquire conditioned responses, or emotions, not because it is pleasant to do so, but because it is *realistic*. It is certainly not pleasant to be afraid, for example, but it is often very helpful, from the standpoint of personal survival (cf. Mowrer & Kluckhohn [1944], on the distinction between "adjustment" and "adaptation"). At the same time, it is biologically useful for living organisms to be able to learn those responses which reduce their drives, regardless of whether these drives be primary (as in the case of hunger) or secondary (as in the case of fear); but it is apparently quite necessary that the neural mechanism which mediates this kind of learning be different from the mechanism whereby emotional, or "attitudinal," learning comes about.

Nor does the usefulness of differentiating between conditioning and effect learning end here. Anthropologists are tending more and more to define *culture* as accumulated and transmitted problem-solutions (Ford, 1939; Kluckhohn & Kelly, 1945; Linton, 1936). However, unless a distinction is immediately made, this definition leads to a serious dilemma; i.e., some items of culture, far from solving problems for the individual in any immediate sense, actually *make* problems for him. This dilemma is quickly resolved if we note that certain items of culture are problem-solving primarily, or perhaps exclusively, in the sense of being *individually* useful; whereas certain other items of culture are problem-solving primarily, or perhaps exclusively, in the sense of being *socially* necessary. By and large, the solutions to individual problems involve the

---

[7] This discussion raises a particularly important, but difficult question: How are appetites learned? Superficially they appear to represent an anticipation of drive-reduction, or satisfaction. Thus, for example, salivation (as a physical concomitant of food appetite) may be said to represent an anticipation of hunger-reduction. But whether an appetite is learned in the same way as are responses of the skeletal musculature which produce drive-reduction, or by the mere pairing of a signal and food (as Pavlov apparently believed) is at present impossible to say. Even less is known about the conditions of anger-learning.

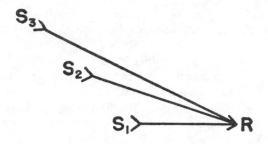

FIGURE 3

Diagramatic representation of conditioning, or stimulus-substitution. Originally only S_1 is capable of producing R; but as a result of the contiguous occurrence of S_2 and S_1, S_2 becomes able to elicit R. This change represents "first-order" conditioning. And if R becomes attached to S_3 through the pairing of S_3 and S_2, this change is referred to as "second-order" conditioning. In this type of learning, R is a response mediated by the autonomic nervous system.

central nervous system and the skeletal musculature, whereas the solutions to social problems involve the autonomic nervous system and the organs which mediate emotional responses. Intrinsically, it is hardly helpful to the individual to be told, "thou shalt not do thus and so," but it may be socially very necessary, and, in the long run but not in any immediately discernible psychological sense, also advantageous to the individual.[8]

Similarly, in the field of education it is useful to differentiate between *teaching* and *training*. Teaching may be defined as the process whereby one individual helps another learn to solve a problem more quickly or effectively than would be likely on the basis of that individual's own unaided, trial-and-error efforts. Here we are dealing with "items of culture" which are individually helpful. Training, by contrast, may be thought of as involving learning whose primary objective is social rather than individual. In this connection one naturally thinks of "items of culture" which are associated with such words as "morality," "character," "social responsibility," etc. Such a distinction as the one here proposed between teaching and training is helpful in deciding the oft-debated question as to whether "indoctrination" is a legitimate function of education. It is also relevant to some of the issues which have arisen between Progressive Education and more traditional educational philosophies.[9]

Although current laboratory practice is not completely differentiated in this connection, it may nevertheless be worth noting that the method of plotting "learning curves" tends to be different when trial-and-error learning is involved from what it is when conditioning is involved. What is probably the commonest procedure, in the former instance, is to note and graph the *time required* by the subject to make the "correct" response after the "problem" is presented. Learning is thus seen graphically as a descending curve. In the case of conditioning, on the other hand, the usual practice is to note whether a specified response does or does not occur (and possibly to what

[8] See also Mowrer and Ullman (1945) on the distinction between "adjustment" and "integration." See also the concluding paragraphs of the present paper on the "problem of conscience."
[9] See Kilpatrick's (1925) discussion of "concomitant" learnings, i.e., the unintentional emotional conditioning which often accompanies supposedly pure "teaching."

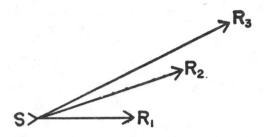

FIGURE 4

Diagrammatic representation of problem-solving, or response-substitution. Originally S produces R_1; but if R_1 does not lead to a satisfactory outcome, it is inhibited and R_2 occurs. If R_2 likewise fails to prove rewarding, R_3 occurs. If this latter response "solves the problem," i.e., eliminates S, the connection between S and R_3 is reinforced, and R_3 tends to replace both R_1 and R_2. In this type of learning R_1, R_2, and R_3 are mediated by the central nervous system.

extent) in response to the so-called "conditioned stimulus." This type of learning is therefore represented graphically as an ascending curve.

An even more explicit difference arises from the fact that conditioning involves what may be termed stimulus-substitution, whereas problem-solving learning involves response-substitution. This contrast is presented diagramatically in Figure 3. Thus, if S_1 is a stimulus which can be relied upon to elicit the emotional response R, and if S_2 is presented along with S_1, then S_2 quickly becomes a substitute for S_1. This is commonly known as "first-order" conditioning. But if, after S_2 has become capable of producing the same response as S_1, S_3 is paired with S_2, then S_3 may become capable of eliciting the response in question. This is known as "second-order" conditioning. Pavlov (1927) has shown that salivary conditioning in dogs can be carried to the "third order." How far "higher-order" conditioning, involving different subjects and different responses, can be carried has not been fully determined. (To the reader who is not accustomed to think in terms of this type of learning, the analogy of the teaching of a foreign language by the "direct" and "indirect" methods may be useful. The first method corresponds roughly to first-order conditioning and the indirect method to second-order conditioning, i.e., in the first case the "word" is associated directly with the "thing," whereas in the second case the "word" is expected to acquire the proper meaning by virtue of association with another "word," rather than with the "thing.")

The diagram shown in Figure 4 represents learning of the problem-solving, or response-substitution, type. If S is a drive, or a "problem-situation," the subject's first response, R_1, may not be effective. It is followed by R_2, which may likewise not be effective. R_2 is followed in turn by R_3, which, let us suppose, is effective. On subsequent occasions, when S recurs, R_3 will tend to be the dominant response. It may be said to have become a substitute for R_1.

This distinction between conditioning and problem-solving has recently been expressed by Scott (1947) somewhat differently but very explicitly, as follows:

> The behavior of an animal can be divided into two categories: modifiable and non-
> modifiable behavior. In the first class falls most of the external behavior. If an animal's
> first reaction does not produce satisfactory adjustment to stimulation, he can alter it
> and produce a more satisfactory one. In the second class is most of the internal behav-

ior of an animal, including the secretion of glands and the contractions of smooth mus-cles. Such activities follow a standard pattern, and while they can be associated with certain stimuli, and thus be affected by learning, the nature of the reaction never var-ies except in its strength. In this same class of behavior also belong certain types of ex-ternal behavior which have been usually termed reflexes. It is, of course, this non-mod-ifiable behavior which has the closest association with the term emotion (quoted from MS).[10]

That there is a fundamental difference between the two forms of learning which are here designated as conditioning and as problem-solving is made clear in yet another way. There have been many experiments and discussions on "the gradient of reinforce-ment," but if there are two basically different types of reinforcement, one would ex-pect to find *two* gradients of reinforcement. This expectation is well founded. In the gradient of reinforcement of the problem-solving type, the variable that is important is the interval of time between the occurrence of the correct response and the occurrence of the ensuing rewarding state of affairs. If this interval is short, the reinforcement is great; if the interval is long, then the reinforcement is slight. On the other hand, in the gradient of reinforcement of the conditioning type, the variable that is important is the interval of time between the occurrence of the CS and the occurrence of the UnCS. If the CS precedes the UnCS only slightly or actually coincides with it, then the rein-forcement is great; but if the interval between the CS and the UnCS is greater, then the reinforcement is proportionately lessened. We thus arrive at what is one of the most clear-cut distinctions between the two types of learning which are here under dis-cussion.

In summary, then, we see that there are many and highly diverse sources of evidence for the two-factor theory of learning which is here under consideration. Such a theory presupposes a delimitation of the term "conditioning" as it is usually employed and an extension of the traditional concept of "effect" learning. The term "conditioning" has commonly been used, erroneously as it now seems, to denote the process whereby a liv-ing organism comes to make any response, skeletal or visceral, immediate or delayed, to a stimulus which has "signal value." As we saw in the preceding section, this usage is too broad for precise scientific purposes. It now seems preferable to apply the term "conditioning" to that and only that type of learning whereby *emotional* (visceral and vascular) responses are acquired. By contrast, effect learning has been previously con-ceived as applying mainly in those situations in which the motive, or "problem," is an unlearned biological drive, such as hunger, thirst, pain, etc. It is now clear that effect learning must be expanded to include those situations in which the motive, or "prob-lem," is a *learned* drive, i.e., an emotion such as fear or an appetite (Mowrer, 1939, 1940; Mowrer & Lamoreaux, 1942). Many responses involving the skeletal muscula-ture, which have previously been termed "conditioned responses," are, in the present conceptual scheme, not conditioned responses at all. Only those responses which in-

[10] This way of dichotomizing the responses of living organisms has the interesting incidental effect of re-solving the quesion: Why do conditioned responses, so-called, sometimes differ from their unconditioned prototypes? The answer is that if the term, "conditioned response," is restricted to visceral-vascular re-sponses, the problem disappears, since such responses are always much the same, whether elicited by a CS or an UnCS. (This is not to say, however, that their subjective counterparts are necessarily the same. See the earlier discussion of emotions as physiological preparations.)

volve visceral and vascular tissue and which are experienced subjectively as emotion are assumed to be conditioned responses. If an emotion, or secondary drive, causes the skeletal musculature to be activated and if such activity results in secondary drive-reduction, then the overt response thus acquired is here conceived as an instance of effect learning, not conditioning.

One other matter remains to be considered, although the limitations of both space and precise knowledge are such that it can be considered only in the most general terms. In the foregoing pages we have repeatedly spoken of *two* nervous systems, the central and the autonomic. We must now briefly examine their interrelationship and, in one important respect, the dependence of one upon the other.

Of the two, the central nervous system is the more complete, composed as it is of sensory nerves, internuncial nerves, and motor nerves, by means of which it is possible, at least in principle, for an impulse from any sense organ to be relayed to any part of the skeletal musculature. On the other hand, the autonomic nervous system, strictly speaking, is an exclusively motor, or efferent, system. As Fulton (1943) remarks, "The sympathetic chain and vagus obviously carry many afferent fibres, some sensory in nature, giving rise to visceral pain, and others involved in viscero-visceral and viscero-somatic reflexes that never reach consciousness. There is some question, however, whether such fibres should be classified as 'autonomic,' the term adopted by Lashley for a purely efferent out-flow, and it is perhaps better to use the standard morphological term 'visceral afferent' " (p. 194). It is obvious, therefore, that communication, if communication there be, between the so-called autonomic nervous system and the sensorium of the individual must be supplied by the sensory pathways of the central nervous system. And the fact that both external and internal stimuli of various kinds may activate the autonomic leaves no doubt that such communication does exist. The question is how and where it is that ordinary sensory impulses, traveling inward on the central nervous system, get shunted onto fibres communicating with the autonomic system.

For an answer we may again turn to Fulton (1943). He says:

> Autonomic nerves . . . are in no way independent of somatic. The two are interdependent. . . . We find somatic and autonomic functions regulated from common levels in the cord, brain, stem, hypothalamus and cortex. (p. 191)
>
> In the cortex there is extensive overlapping between autonomic and somatic motor representation, making possible unified correlation between the reactions of the two systems. In general, the topographical relation between the cortical areas influencing specific autonomic functions is close to the cortical area influencing the corresponding functions. Thus lacrimation is observed on stimulating the eye fields, salivation, on stimulation of the motor representation of the face and tongue. (p. 444)

In other words, it is now established that there are numerous "representations" of the autonomic nerves in the most complex parts of the central nervous system, and that from the standpoint of neuroanatomy there is no difficulty in getting an impulse which enters the central nervous system from any sensory organ to discharge through the autonomic system. The structural basis is thus laid for the occurrence of that form of learning which is involved in conditioning; but how this is achieved, functionally, is still a mystery. What is important to note for present purposes is merely that, anatomically, there is just as much basis for assuming that conditioning occurs in the cerebral cortex as for supposing that problem-solving learning occurs there. There is, in other words, no neuroanatomical evidence which argues against the two-factor theory of learning, and there is some such evidence which is at least implicitly supportive of this theory.

*   *   *   *

Clarifying Consequences

In the present section we shall review some of the paradoxes which are resolved by adopting the two-factor theory of learning presented in the preceding sections. In the final section, we shall consider, by contrast, some of the problems which remain unsolved or are specifically created by this theory.

Failures to Obtain "Conditioning"

Nowhere is it more apparent how confused the concept of conditioning has been than in the numerous apparent failures to obtain this type of learning. Let us consider first an example of such a "failure" with animal subjects and then one involving human subjects.

Warner (1932) published a paper entitled, "An experimental search for the 'conditioned response,' " in which he reported a would-be conditioning experiment in which "no rat, even after 1000 trials, responded to the sound or light by hopping [i.e., making a CR]. The secondary stimuli did come to affect the animals' behavior but not in this way. The most frequent responses given by them were change in respiratory rate and lowering of the head" (p. 112). Using a different experimental set-up, Warner found it possible to produce successful avoidance reactions, but these reactions were very different from the so-called unconditioned responses of his subjects (cf. Mowrer and Lamoreaux [1946]. "The four rats which quite consistently scrambled under the fence [which divided two compartments] in response to the shock did learn to get to the other side of the fence in response to the sound — *but by leaping over it"* (p. 113).

In conclusion, Warner says:

> Even though a rat be placed in a situation wherein all stimulation is relatively uniform with the exception of two potent stimuli, and even though these stimuli be often repeated in a close temporal juxtaposition, it does not necessarily follow that the response to one of these stimuli can ultimately be aroused by the presentation of the other. (p. 113)
>
> The conditioned response hypothesis has been just as susceptible to over-application and misapplication as have, for example, the Freudian principles. One should not conclude that the hypothesis is faulty but rather that it should be employed far more critically, and that it should be made the subject of less speculation and more experimentation. (p. 113–114)

It will be neither possible nor necessary to go into all of the probable reasons why Warner failed to get the kind of response-modification which he felt one should expect on the basis of traditional conditioning doctrine. Only two points are here essential. It will be noted, first of all, that by changing the definition of a "conditioned response" from a vague, conventional one to the more limited and precise one suggested above, an experiment which ostensibly failed to produce "conditioning" in the conventional sense changes to one in which "conditioning," in the restricted sense, was obviously obtained: "the secondary stimuli did come to affect the animals' behavior but not in this way. The most frequent responses given to them were change in the respiration rate. . . ." From this phrase it is apparent that the subjects did condition in the sense that they acquired an emotional response.

The other point to be noted is that at least part of Warner's failure to obtain avoidance reactions involving the skeletal musculature was due to a failure to appreciate that such responses develop and persist only if they are *problem-solving* with respect to the underlying emotion, in this case *fear*. As the various experiments reported in Section III indicate, it is possible to get rats to begin making such responses after six to ten trials and, after 60 to 80 trials, to make these responses nearly 100% of the time.

"Failures" to obtain conditioning have been reported particularly often when human beings have been used as subjects, but nowhere does one find a more illuminating example of this than in the article, already cited, which was published by Watson in 1916. Watson says:

> In the best cases we begin to get a conditioned reflex [flexion of the great toe] after fourteen to thirty combined stimulations. We have found several refractory subjects: subjects in which even the primary reflex will not appear in the toe when the current is strong enough to induce perspiration. Whether this is due to atrophy of the toe reflex through the wearing of shoes, or to some other cause, we have never been able to determine. (pp. 96-97)

We may now safely surmise that Watson's "refractory subjects" were simply individuals whose conception of themselves and of what was expected of them in the experimental situation was such that they "voluntarily" refrained from solving either the problem of shock, or the problem of fear of shock, by lifting their toe from the metal grill against which it rested between trials. That they conditioned, however—in the sense of reacting emotionally to the conditioned stimulus—can hardly be doubted: ". . . strong enough to induce perspiration."

A number of studies, which the reader will find reviewed by Hilgard and Marquis (1940), have shown that instructions are enormously important in determining what skeletal responses human beings will or will not allow themselves to make to the fear which is aroused by a danger signal. However, comparatively little control over the fear reaction itself is possible. Investigators who have looked for physiological, rather than skeletal, indices of "conditioning," whether in human or animal subjects, have rarely, if ever, failed to find it.

Pavlovian Conditioning Reconsidered

The present writer and others have criticized the Pavlovian paradigm of conditioning on the grounds that it is really reward learning, i.e., that the subject learns to respond to a signal by salivating, not because the food (of which the signal is premonitory) produces salivation (on a reflex basis), but because the food reduces hunger (Hull, 1943; Mowrer & Lamoreaux, 1946). According to the bifurcated conception of learning which is here under consideration, the Pavlovian paradigm, based as it is on a response (salivation) which involves glands and which is mediated by the autonomic nervous system, would qualify as a conditioned response and would be expected to involve, not effect learning, but association.

Whether salivary conditioning occurs because of the appearance of food in the mouth (and reflex stimulation of salivation) or because of the disappearance of hunger (due to distension of the stomach and associated effects) has apparently not been fully determined. Two experimental possibilities come to mind. (A) If a "sham-feeding" preparation were arranged, so that food taken into the mouth and swallowed by a dog would not reach the stomach and so that food could be placed in the stomach without being first in the mouth, differential predictions concerning salivary conditioning would be made on the basis of the two factors mentioned above, i.e., the appearance of food in the mouth vs. the disappearance of hunger. (B) If hunger-reduction, or reward, is the important element in salivary conditioning, it should be possible to make the salivary response instrumental in the following way. Suppose a dog had been trained to secrete a few drops of saliva in the response to a signal that food is about to be presented. Then suppose that conditions were made such that food would materialize *only* if the subject secreted a certain minimum quantity. By successively raising the "production standard," it should be possible, if the reward theory of salivary conditioning is correct, to convert the subject into a veritable "saliva factory."

If the preliminary observations reported by Skinner (1938) and by Mowrer (1938) are valid, it would seem highly improbable that the salivary response could be made to function in any such instrumental manner. But even though salivary conditioning be true conditioning and not problem-solving, as these terms are here defined, Pavlov seems completely to have overlooked what is perhaps the most important function of the conditioned salivary response. Pavlov thought of it exclusively as a physiological preparation for eating; the present analysis would see it as an indicator, perhaps a veritable part of the mechanism, of the secondary motivation known as "appetite." While a good deal is known concerning the role of fear as a motive, we are only beginning to explore the systematic behavioral implications of the appetitive drives.[11]

Hull's "Dilemma"

In 1929 Hull formulated what he termed "The dilemma of the conditioned defense reaction," as follows:

> For a defense reaction to be wholly successful, it should take place so early that the organism will completely escape injury, i.e., the impact of the nocuous (unconditioned) stimulus. But in case the unconditioned stimulus fails to impinge upon the organism, there will be no reinforcement of the conditioned tendency, which means one would expect that experimental extinction will set in at once. This will rapidly render the conditioned reflex impotent which, in turn, will expose the organism to the original injury. This will initiate a second cycle substantially like the first which will be followed by another and another indefinitely, a series of successful escapes [i.e., *avoidances*] always alternating with a series of injuries. From a biological point of view, the picture emerging from the above theoretical considerations is decidedly not an attractive one.

[11] See Tuttle's remark that "Pavlov died without recognizing the most significant implications of his researches" (1946, p. 270).

There is thus presented a kind of biological dilemma apparently not at all the product of misplaced ingenuity on the part of the theorist. If experimental extinction operates fully the organism seems doomed to suffer the injury of the nocuous stimulus periodically in order to renew the strength of its conditioned defense reactions. If, on the other hand, experimental extinction does not operate, the organism seems doomed to dissipate much of its energy reacting defensively to irrelevant stimuli. . . . The problem presents a fascinating field for experimental investigation. (pp. 510-511)

At this stage Hull was apparently thinking of "reinforcement" entirely in terms of association, or paired presentation of stimuli. As we have already seen, he later came to the position that all reinforcement is ultimately reducible to drive-reduction, problem-solving, satisfaction. The dilemma outlined above seems to arise, at least in part, from a neglect of the possibility that there are *two* reinforcement processes, one whereby emotions are conditioned and another whereby habits are acquired which reduce emotions (or, in other instances, primary drives). Because the type of reinforcement that is involved in emotional learning fails to occur, i.e., because the CS fails to be followed by the UnCS, is no reason for saying "there will be no reinforcement of the conditioned tendency," if by the latter one means, as Hull evidently did, not the emotion of fear, but "the conditioned defense reaction." Defense reactions involving the skeletal musculature are "reinforced" if they reduce the emotion of fear which produces them; they are not dependent for their strengthening, in any direct sense, upon the coincidence of CS and UnCS.

In this situation, as in all situations involving the extinction of a so-called "conditioned defense reaction," we must differentiate between (a) the tendency for a danger signal to elicit the emotion of fear and (b) the tendency for the fear reaction to produce a skeletal adjustment which has been acquired because it is fear-reducing. Clarity on this score does not entirely resolve Hull's dilemma, but it seems to bring us a step nearer a resolution. A little thought will show that this dilemma is closely related to some of the basic problems in the field of "personality and culture," for example, that of "survivals," or "lag," in culture, and of "fixations" in individuals. These problems have been considered more fully elsewhere (Mowrer, 1948).

A "Vicious Circle" Explained

Another puzzling phenomenon which was brought to the writer's attention a few years ago (by Dr. Judson S. Brown) is the following. If a rat is put at one end of a straight alley about four feet long and if, after a period of ten seconds, the floor of alley (consisting of a metal grill) is electrified, the rat will soon scamper to the opposite end of the alley and, if a small non-electrified compartment is available, escape into it. After a few repetitions of this procedure, the subject, as might be expected, will run to the opposite end as soon as placed in the alley, without receiving the shock. What obviously happens is that the rat's fear becomes conditioned to the "danger situation" and since the running response carries the rat out of that situation, with an attendant reduction in fear, this response is quickly fixated.

Once this response is well established, it will persist for many trials; but the rat will tend to become more and more leisurely in making the run and will eventually delay beyond the ten-second period. If shock is not applied under these circumstances, the tendency on the part of the rat to flee from the end of the maze where it is introduced deteriorates still further; and ultimately the flight response will disappear completely.

This behavior is, of course, in no way surprising, since it conforms perfectly to what is well known concerning the extinction of avoidance reactions. What is surprising, however, is this: If, after a "conditioned" response of the kind just described is well established, a small section of the floor-grill, at the far end of the alley, is permanently electrified so that in the process of getting from the starting point to the safety compartment, the rat must always receive at least a momentary shock, the running response does not extinguish! Even though shock is never again experienced in the part of the alley where the animal is introduced, flight from this area continues to occur indefinitely.

When subjected to the first procedure described above, rats behave in a perfectly "normal" and understandable manner. But in the case of the second procedure, their behavior is very surprising, strange, "abnormal"—for they seem to be manifesting a "masochistic trend," a "need for punishment," "pleasure in pain." They continue to cross the electrified segment of the floor-grill and get shocked, whereas if they merely "sat tight" in the first part of the alley, nothing would happen to them. Under these circumstances, the running response obviously gets "punished," and yet, instead of being inhibited by this punishment, it is apparently strengthened by it.[12]

How can this paradox be resolved? The answer seems to be relatively simple on the basis of a two-factor theory of reinforcement. Each time the rat is placed in the experimental apparatus and gets a brief shock on the way to the safety compartment, the part of the alley where the rat is introduced gets "reinforced" as a danger situation (or "conditioned stimulus"), since it continues to be temporally associated with pain. This means that the fear continues to be aroused each time the animal is placed in the alley and this fear is most effectively reduced by the running response, which carries the animal to the safety compartment. The running response, as skeletal behavior, is thereby reinforced (through effect learning); but this behavior is of such a nature that it also provides the kind of reinforcement whereby the fear, or motivation for running, is kept alive.

It is always hazardous to interpret clinical phenomena on the human level in terms of animal experiments, yet there seems to be more than a superficial resemblance between the behavior just described and the "compulsive," "self-defeating," "masochistic" behavior which Horney (1937) and others (Mowrer & Ullman, 1945) have discussed under the concept of the "vicious circle." Perhaps the two-factor theory of learning will turn out to have important clinical significance.

By thus sharply differentiating between two types of learning process, or "reinforcement," one is able to resolve the paradox involved in the experiment just described (and possibly also in at least certain types of "vicious circles" found at the human level). Yet a question remains as to what happens to the inhibitory tendency which is undoubtedly created by the fact that the response of running is consistently punished,

---

[12] Although the experiment just described is not strictly comparable to the situations employed by Muenzinger and Wood (1935) and others in studying the facilitation of learning by means of punishing "right" responses, there is at least an oblique similarity. Perhaps the latter studies can be usefully re-examined with the assumptions underlying the present analysis in mind.

i.e., regularly followed by electric shock. As a tentative hypothesis, one may assume that this tendency is present but that it is overridden by the reinforcement processes just described.[13]

Thorndike on "Punishment"

In his early statements of the law of effect Thorndike posited punishment as the antithesis of reward. Rewarding or satisfying consequences of an act were assumed to "stamp in" the connection between this act and the drive which produced it. Punishing or annoying consequences of an act, on the other hand, were asssumed to "stamp out" the connection between this act and the drive which produced it. Learning was thus conceived as a reversible process, which was carried in one direction by reward and in the opposite direction by punishment. Whatever it was that learning, under the impact of reward did, unlearning, under the impact of punishment, supposedly undid.

In later studies, however, Thorndike (1931) has taken a different position, based largely on the results of an experiment which was designed to answer this question:

> Other things being equal, does one right response to a certain situation rewarded by the announcement of "Right" strengthen the connection in question more than one wrong response to the situation punished by the announcement of "Wrong" weakens that connection? (p. 38)

From the results thus obtained, Thorndike drew the following conclusions:

> An announcement of "Right" strengthens its corresponding connection much more than an announcement of "Wrong" weakens its connection.
>
> Indeed the announcement of "Wrong" in our experiments does not weaken the connection at all, so far as we can see. Rather there is more gain in strength from the occurrence of the response than there is weakening by the attachment of "Wrong" to it. (p. 45)

By way of providing further support for these statements, Thorndike continues:

> I have studied in the same way the records of the rats, crows, monkeys, and pigs who learned by reward and punishment in the experiments of Yerkes, Kuo, and others. In the case of Kuo's thirteen rats the learning is largely, and perhaps entirely, explainable by the strengthening of the rewarded responses. In the other experiments the relative influence of the rewards and the punishments is not easily measurable, but the former are apparently more potent. I have also supplemented the experiments reported above by additional ones with other subjects and kinds of learning, and have found them fully corroborated. (pp. 45–46)

From these findings and Thorndike's remarks concerning them, the inference has sometimes been drawn that there is no such thing as "punishment," psychologically speaking, and that the only kind of learning is reward learning. Thorndike's own, rather guarded, statement on this score follows:

[13] Since the above was written, experimental results obtained by U. E. Whiteis indicate that this hypothesis is well founded. Once the shock on the right side of the grill is removed, the running response quickly deteriorates, reflecting a conflict on the part of the subject between a fear of not running and a fear of running.

These experiments do not, of course, mean that punishment is always futile. The contrary is demonstrable from general observation and from such experiments with animals as those of Warden and Aylesworth. They need not necessarily predispose us to any change of attitude toward punishment save with such learning and for such learners as I have described. . . . Since in these experiments with these subjects, the wrong connections were simply displaced or nullified by the right ones, not intrinsically weakened, we may properly expect that something similar may happen in many sorts of learning, and we may increase our confidence in positive rather than negative learning and teaching. (p. 46)

That there is something amiss with the older conception of punishment, as the antithesis of reward, is clearly apparent; but it does not seem that Thorndike's work has quite brought us to a satisfactory new understanding of this phenomenon. Let us therefore see if the two-factor conception of learning will handle the problem any more effectively.

According to this conception of learning, the first thing to be noted is that "punishment," i.e., a relatively sudden and painful increase of stimulation following the performance of some act, provides the necessary conditions for the establishment of a conditioned fear reaction. The performance of any given act normally produces kinesthetic (and often visual, auditory, and tactile) stimuli which are perceptible to the performer of the act. If these stimuli are followed a few times by a noxious ("unconditioned") stimulus, they will soon acquire the capacity to produce the emotion of fear. When, therefore, on subsequent occasions the subject starts to perform the previously punished act, the resulting self-stimulation will arouse fear; and the most effective way of eliminating this fear is for the subject to stop the activity which is producing the fear-producing stimuli. The cessation, or inhibition, of activity thus becomes the solution to the fear problem and may be expected to be fixated as are other habits.[14]

This analysis agrees with Thorndike's newer view that punishment does not simply cancel out, or "dissolve," the effects of learning which are produced by past rewards; and it also agrees that the inhibition of punished responses comes about because of the learning, through reward, of new responses (such as doing nothing or something else) which are incompatible with the old (punished) ones. What Thorndike's analysis seems to lack is a sufficiently explicit recognition of the role of fear-learning and fear-reduction. It is apparently fear which constitutes the new problem that instigates responses which, if they prove capable of reducing the fear, become fixated and which, if more powerful, tend to inhibit the older, original responses.

Thorndike's remarks on this score are less explicit but not necessarily incompatible. He says:

Annoyers do not act on learning in general by weakening whatever connection they follow. If they do anything to learning they do it indirectly by informing the learner that such and such a response in such and such a situation brings distress, or by making the learner feel fear of a certain object, or by making him jump back from a certain place,

---

[14] The only qualification which this statement requires is that "other habits" do not necessarily result in conflict, whereas an "inhibitory habit," which is acquired because it reduces fear, causes some other problem to go unsolved, or at least prevents that problem from being solved in the way that has previously been customary, and thus leads to at least temporary conflict. For a closely similar treatment of the problem of punishment, see Miller and Dollard (1941).

or by some other definite and specific change which they produce in him. Satisfiers seem to act more directly and generally and uniformly and subtly, but just what they do should be studied with much more care than anybody has yet devoted to it. (p. 46)

Punishment and Conditioning

It is instructive to note that if one uses a noxious or painful stimulus in a conditioning experiment, one does not speak of it as a "punishment," even though one would so characterize it in other circumstances. If it is applied as a result of something which the *subject* has done, then it is a punishment, but if it is applied because of something the *experimenter* has done, i.e., because he has presented a "conditioned stimulus," then it is called an "unconditioned stimulus." One wonders if this somewhat arbitrary terminological distinction is followed by very different consequences in the subject and, if so, what they are. In both cases the fear reaction is conditioned, but in the one case it becomes attached to an *external* stimulus which, on one or more occasions, has preceded the noxious event; while in the other case the fear becomes attached to the *internal*, viz., kinesthetic, stimulation which, on one or more occasions, has preceded the noxious event. In the one case the resulting fear may be resolved by *making* a skeletal response and in the other case by *inhibiting* a skeletal response. In both cases the "conditioned response" is fear, but there is a difference in the resulting "problem-solving" behavior.

Perhaps this is one of the striking differences between clinicians and experimentalists: the former are interested in fears that are "cued off" by internal as well as external events, whereas the latter are usually interested only in fears which are elicited by external events. It now appears that each group has much to learn from the other. Clinicians can sharpen their thinking if they familiarize themselves with the work of experimentalists. Experimentalists, on the other hand, have been peculiarly slow to appreciate some of the mechanisms which clinicians understand very well. It is, for example, remarkable that anyone should not have anticipated the conflict which arises if, after an external stimulus becomes capable of arousing a fear reaction and the subject begins to make a skeletal response to it, the experimenter continues pairing the CS and UnCS. What obviously happens in such cases is that the kinesthetic stimulation resulting from the subject's response begins to elicit fear, and the subject is then motivated both to make and not to make the skeletal response which produces this type of stimulation. Small wonder that Liddell (1944) has characterized such a procedure as "pathogenic" and that it sometimes makes experimental subjects "neurotic"!

Thorndike originally spoke of reward "stamping in" responses and of punishment as stamping them out. It now appears that both reward and punishment "stamp in" response, but different kinds of responses: reward fixates skeletal responses, and punishment establishes the emotion of fear. That punishment serves to inhibit responses which have been established through reward learning is apparently due, not to a direct and antithetical action, but to an indirect process of the kind described.

This line of thought may be extended one step further. There has been much discussion and research on the question of whether pleasant "memories" are more or less durable than unpleasant ones. The results, as is well known, are highly equivocal. Perhaps this is because "memories" are of two kinds—those laid down by effect learning and those laid down by conditioning. An action which is followed by pleasant consequences will be better preserved as one type of "memory," whereas an action that is followed by unpleasant consequences will be better preserved as the other type. This problem needs to be more fully considered with the two-factor theory of learning in mind.

James on the Nature of Emotion

The present analysis, with its recurrent emphasis upon emotion, both as a consequence of learning (conditioning) and as an occasion for learning (problem-solving), naturally calls for a clear and explicit statement of assumptions concerning the nature of emotion. In any comprehensive sense, such a statement is not possible in the present paper. However, it is illuminating to consider the present view of the learning process and the significance of the emotions against the background of the James-Lange theory of emotion.

In his *Principles of Psychology* James (1890) introduces this theory in the following words:

> The merely descriptive literature of the emotions is one of the most tedious parts of psychology . . . [The usual descriptive statements] give one nowhere a central point of view, or a deductive or generative principle . . . [The difficulty is that 'emotions' have been too often] set down as so many eternal and sacred psychic entities. . . . Now the general causes of the emotions are indubitably physiological. Prof. C. Lange, of Copenhagen, in the pamphlet from which I have already quoted, published in 1885 a physiological theory of their constitution and conditioning, which I had already broached the previous year in an article in *Mind*. None of the criticisms which I have heard of it have made me doubt its essential truth. (pp. 448–449)

James then proceeds, under the heading, "Emotion follows upon the bodily expression in the coarser emotions at least," to state his theory in this way:

> Our natural way of thinking about these coarser emotions is that the mental perception of some fact excites the mental affection called the emotion, and that this latter state of mind gives rise to the bodily expression. My theory, on the contrary, is that *the bodily changes follow directly the perception of the exciting fact, and that our feeling of the same changes as they occur IS the emotion.* (p. 449)

This formal statement of the theory coincides perfectly with the conception of emotion upon which the present discussion is based. However, in attempting to explicate the theory, James provided the grounds for a serious ambiguity. In a now famous passage James intimated that it is not that we run because we see a bear and are afraid; it is rather that we "see the bear, and judge it best to run," and then, because we run, we feel afraid. This interpretation is clearly at variance with the present conception of emotion, as a cause of skeletal behavior, but not as a consequence thereof. Paraphrased in the light of this conception, James' illustration would go: We see a bear, we become *physiologically prepared to run*, are afraid, and then may run (or do whatever the fear forces us to do).

That this may, in fact, have been what James meant to imply is suggested by a number of passages, of which the following is typical:

> We may catch the trick with the voluntary muscles, but fail with the skin, glands, heart, and other viscera. Just as an artificially imitated sneeze lacks something of the

reality, so the attempt to imitate an emotion in the absence of its normal instigating cause is apt to be rather "hollow." (p. 450)

Although the James-Lange theory has been criticized vigorously and often (Cannon, 1927; Dunbar, 1938), it has shown a remarkable vitality and may only now, more than half a century after its formulation, be coming fully into its own. With the minor reformulation just suggested, it is completely consonant with the present conception of emotion as a conditioned viscero-vascular response which then produces a state of affairs which may motivate any of an infinitely wide variety of skeletal response and whose reduction may powerfully fixate whatever response brings the reduction about. And equally important is the extent to which it agrees with current formulations concerning the "psychosomatic" disorders. It is now well established that excessively powerful or protracted emotional states may not only produce functional disturbances of an organic nature but may also lead to actual structural pathology, as in the case of stomach ulcers and other comparable conditions.

The whole problem of emotion needs to be rethought from the standpoint of contemporary learning theory, with special reference to the problem of "neurosis" and personality disturbances generally.

The Problem of Response Variability

Perhaps the most important single difficulty which is encountered in attempting to base the psychology of learning wholly upon the law of effect arises from the phenomena of response variability, or response equivalence. In an earlier study the writer (Mowrer & Jones, 1943) has attempted, and failed, to deal satisfactorily with this phenomenon within the framework of effect theory.

The difficulty, specifically, is this. If for example, there are several equally good routes whereby a hungry rat or other animal can go from a starting compartment to a food compartment, one might expect, on the basis of the law of effect, that the habit of choice (to speak loosely) which is strongest in the beginning would be progressively strengthened, to the point where, ultimately, that choice would cause the subject to be completely fixated upon one particular route to the goal. What is actually observed is that there continues to be a great deal of vacillation between the various routes. In the case of some subjects a clearcut "preference" eventually may be established, but in other cases variability continues indefinitely. [15]

The dual learning theory which is here under consideration suggests that in a situation in which two or more equally "effective" responses are possible, the observable alternation of response may be explainable, not on the basis of effect learning, but on the basis of conditioning. As a means of quickly communicating an otherwise rather complex thought the following illustration may be useful. The writer used to eat lunch rather regularly at a particular restaurant. His hunger was seemingly well satisfied by the food he obtained there, and one might have predicted, on the basis of the law of effect alone, that, barring untoward incidents, the writer would continue indefinitely to eat lunch at this restaurant. One day, however, as he started to enter the restaurant

---

[15] It may be expected that the current researches of Professor J. G. Beebe-Center on taste preferences in rats, in which learning factors are being given special attention, may soon throw new and important light on this problem. See also recent unpublished researches by Dr. R. C. Solomon.

in question (and without any identifiable unpleasant experience associated therewith), he experienced an emotion of aversion which was strong enough to cause him to turn about and go to another restaurant, and he has never since returned to the first restaurant.

It would be premature at this point to assume that concomitant emotional learnings, at times perhaps very subtle ones, provide the sole explanation of response variability of the kind under consideration; but such a possibility warrants careful scrutiny. It is, in fact, conceivable that emotional conditioning, of appetites and aversion, provides, respectively, the positive and negative "vectors" which Lewin (1935) and others have posited as essential parts of "field theory." "Change in cognitive structure," may, in many instances be merely a matter of subtle, or perhaps not-so-subtle, conditioning.

"Field" theorists have made a great deal of "latent" learning and have sometimes cited it as "disproof" of the law of effect.[16] That a hungry rat may learn his way about in a maze without benefit of food does not demonstrate that reward is not involved in such learning. Secondary drives are almost certainly active under such circumstances, and it is therefore possible that their periodic reduction may provide rewards which are no less potent than those provided, for example, by hunger-reduction. However, a two-factor theory of learning leaves open another possibility, namely, that some, perhaps most, of the learning that occurs under these circumstances is based on conditioning. Tolman (1935) has offered "sign-gestalt expectations" as an explanation of latent learning. Such "expectations" seem clearly relatable to the results of conditioning, although the details of this relationship have not as yet been worked out. In a recent article, entitled "Expectation," Thorndike (1946) has made some interesting suggestions in this connection, among them this, "that what S-R psychology has to learn from Tolman's work is the need for a satisfactory account of primitive forms of knowledge, and of how they operate" (p. 281).

"Knowledge" has often been regarded as something "mental" and behavior as something physical. Perhaps the feeling of "knowing" is merely the subjective counterpart of what we objectively perceive as the results of learning. A two-factor theory of learning would then suggest that there might be two basic forms of knowledge. And such a dichotomy is indeed implied by the two idioms, "to know *how*" to do this or that and "to know *that*" this or that is so. An epistemological investigation which was grounded in this type of learning theory might lead to interesting outcomes.

* * * *

References*

Allport, G. W. Effect: A secondary principle of learning. *Psychological Review*, 1946, **53**, 335–347.

Brogden, W. J., Lipman, E. A., & Culler, E. The role of incentive in conditioning and extinction. *American Journal of Psychology*, 1938, **51**, 109–118.

---

[16] For a penetrating experimental analysis of latent learning, see Karn and Porter (1946).

* Although this article has been abridged, the references are in their original complete form — ED.

Cannon, W. B. The James-Lange theory of emotions: A critical examination and an alternative theory. *American Journal of Psychology*, 1927, **39**, 106–124.

Cannon, W. B. The wisdom of the body. New York: Norton, 1932.

Dunbar, H. F. *Emotions and bodily changes: A survey of literature on psychosomatic interrelationships, 1910–1933*. New York: Columbia University Press, 1938.

Ford, C. S. Society, culture, and the human organism. *Journal of General Psychology*, 1939, **20**, 135–179.

Freud, S. Formulations regarding the two principles in mental functioning (1911). *Collected papers* (Vol. 4). London: Hogarth Press, 1934.

Fulton, J. F. *Physiology of the nervous system* (2nd ed.). New York: Oxford Press, 1943.

Guthrie, E. R. *The psychology of learning*. New York: Harper, 1935.

Hewer, E. E. The development of muscle in the human foetus. *Journal of Anatomy*, 1927, **62**, 72–78.

Hilgard, E. R. The relationship between the conditioned response and conventional learning experiments. *Psychological Bulletin*, 1937, **34**, 61–102.

Hilgard, E. R., & Marquis, D. G. *Conditioning and learning*. New York: Appleton-Century, 1940.

Holt, E. B. *Animal drive and the learning process*. New York: Holt, 1931.

Horney, K. *The neurotic personality of our time*. New York: Norton, 1937

Hull, C. L. A functional interpretation of the conditioned reflex. *Psychological Review*, 1929, **36**, 498–511.

Hull, C. L. *Principles of behavior*. New York: Appleton-Century, 1943.

Hunter, W. S. Conditioning and extinction in the rat. *British Journal of Psychology*, 1935, **26**, 135–148.

James, W. *The principles of psychology*. New York: Holt, 1890.

Karn, H. W., & Porter, J. M. The effects of certain pre-training procedures upon maze performance and their significance for the concept of latent learning. *Journal of Experimental Psychology*, 1946, **36**, 461–469.

Kempf, E. J. The autonomic functions and the personality. *Nervous and Mental Disease Monograph No. 28*, 1918.

Kilpatrick, W. H. *Foundations of method*. New York: Macmillan, 1925.

Kluckhohn, C., & Kelly, W. H. The concept of culture. In R. Linton (Ed.), *The science of man in world crisis*. New York: Columbia University Press, 1945.

Konorski, J., & Miller, S. On two types of conditioned reflex. *Journal of General Psychology*, 1937, **16**, 264–272.

Lamoreaux, R. R., & Mowrer, O. H. Avoidance conditioning as discrimination. Unpublished paper, n.d.

Lashley, K. S. The human salivary reflex and its use in psychology. *Psychological Review*, 1916, **23**, 446–464.

Lewin, K. *Principles of topological psychology*. New York: McGraw-Hill, 1935.

Liddell, H. S. Conditioned reflex method and experimental neurosis. In J. McV. Hunt (Ed.), *Personality and the behavior disorders* (Vol. 1). New York: Ronald Press, 1944.

Linton, R. *The study of man*. New York: Appleton-Century, 1936.

Maier, N. R. F., & Schneirla, R. D. Mechanisms in conditioning. *Psychological Review*, 1942, **49**, 117–134.

McGeoch, J. A. *The psychology of human learning*. New York: Longmans, Green, 1942.

Miller, N. E., & Dollard, J. *Social learning and imitation*. New Haven: Yale University Press, 1941.

Morris, C. *Signs, language, and behavior*. New York: Prentice-Hall, 1946.

Mowrer, O. H. Preparatory set (expectancy) — A determinant in motivation and learning. *Psychological Review*, 1938, **45**, 62–91.

Mowrer, O. H. A stimulus-response analysis of anxiety and its role as a reinforcing agent. *Psychological Review*, 1939, **46**, 553–565.

Mowrer, O. H. Anxiety-reduction and learning. *Journal of Experimental Psychology*, 1940, **27**, 497–516.

Mowrer, O. H. Motivation and learning in relation to the national emergency. *Psychological Bulletin*, 1941, **38**, 421–431.

Mowrer, O. H. The law of effect and ego psychology. *Psychological Review*, 1946, **53**, 321–334.

Mowrer, O. H. What is normal behavior? In L. A. Pennington & I. A. Berg (Eds.), *An Introduction to Clinical Psychology*. New York: Ronald Press, 1948.

Mowrer, O. H., & Jones, H. Extinction and behavior variability as functions of effort-fulness of task. *Journal of Experimental Psychology*, 1943, **33**, 369–386.

Mowrer, O. H., & Kluckhohn, C. Dynamic theory of personality. In J. McV. Hunt (Ed.), *Personality and the behavior disorders*. New York: Ronald Press, 1944.

Mowrer, O. H., & Lamoreaux, R. R. Avoidance conditioning and signal duration: A study of secondary motivation and reward. *Psychological Monographs*, 1942, **54** (No. 5).

Mowrer, O. H., & Lamoreaux, R. R. Fear as an intervening variable in avoidance conditioning. *Journal of Comparative Psychology*, 1946, **39**, 29–50.

Mowrer, O. H., & Miller, N. E. A multi-purpose learning-demonstration apparatus. *Journal of Experimental Psychology*, 1942, **30**, 163–170.

Mowrer, O. H., & Ullman, A. D. Time as a determinant in integrative learning. *Psychological Review*, 1945, **52**, 61–90.

Muenzinger, K. F., & Wood, A. Motivation in learning. IV. The function of punishment as determined by its temporal relation to the act of choice in the visual discrimination habit. *Journal of Comparative Psychology*, 1935, **20**, 95–106.

O'Connor, V. J. Recency or effect?: A critical analysis of Guthrie's theory of learning. *Harvard Educational Review*, 1946, **16**, 194–206.

Ogden, C. K., & Richards, I. A. *The meaning of meaning*. New York: Harcourt, Brace, 1938.

Pavlov, I. P. [*Conditioned reflexes*] (G. V. Anrep, trans.). London: Oxford University Press, 1927.

Pavlov, I. P. *Lectures on conditioned reflexes*. New York: International Publishers, 1928.

Rice, P. B. The ego and the law of effect. *Psychological Review*, 1946, **53**, 307–420.

Richards, I. A. *Interpretation in teaching*. New York: Harcourt, Brace, 1938.

Richards, I. A. *How to read a page*. New York: Norton, 1942.

Russell, B. *Philosophy*. New York: Norton, 1927.

Schlosberg, H. Conditioned responses in the white rat. *Journal of Genetic Psychology*, 1934, **45**, 303–335.

Schlosberg, H. Conditioned responses in the white rat: II. Conditioned responses based on shock to the foreleg. *Journal of Genetic Psychology*, 1936, **49**, 107–138.

Schlosberg, H. The relationship between success and the laws of conditioning. *Psychological Review*, 1937, **44**, 379–394.

Scott, J. P. "Emotional" behavior in fighting mice. *Journal of Comparative and Physiological Psychology*, 1947, **40**, 275–282.

Sherrington, C. S. *The integrative action of the nervous system*. New Haven: Yale University Press, 1906.

Skinner, B. F. Two types of conditioned reflex and a pseudo type. *Journal of General Psychology*, 1935, **12**, 66–77.

Skinner, B. F. Two types of conditioned reflex: A reply to Konorski and Miller. *Journal of General Psychology*, 1937, **16**, 272–279.

Skinner, B. F. *The behavior of organisms*. New York: Appleton-Century, 1938.

Stevens, J. M. Expectancy vs. effect: Substitution as a general principle of reinforcement. *Psychological Review*, 1942, **49**, 102–116.

Symonds, P. M. Laws of learning. *Journal of Educational Psychology*, 1927, **18**, 405–413.

Thorndike, E. L. *Human learning*. New York: Century, 1931.

Thorndike, E. L. *The psychology of wants, interests and attitudes*. New York: Appleton-Century, 1935.

Thorndike, E. L. *Man and his works*. Cambridge: Harvard University Press, 1943.

Thorndike, E. L. Expectation. *Psychological Review*, 1946, **53**, 277–281.

Tolman, E. C. *Purposive behavior in animals and men*. New York: Appleton-Century, 1932.

Tolman, E. C. Sign-gestalt or conditioned reflex? *Psychological Review*, 1935, **40**, 246-255.

Tuttle, H. S. Two kinds of learning. *Journal of Psychology*, 1946, **22**, 267-277.

Warner, L. H. An experimental search for the "conditioned response." *Journal of Genetic Psychology*, 1932, **41**, 91-115.

Watson, J. B. The place of the conditioned-reflex in psychology. *Psychological Review*, 1916, **23**, 89-116.

Whatmore, G. B., Morgan, E. A., & Kleitman, N. The influence of avoidance conditioning on the course of non-avoidance conditioning in dogs. *American Journal of Physiology*, 1945-1946, **145**, 432-435.

Whatmore, G. B., & Kleitman, N. The role of sensory and motor cortical projections in escape and avoidance conditioning in dogs. *American Journal of Physiology*, 1946, **146**, 282-292.

Whiting, J. W. M., & Mowrer, O. H. Habit progression and regression: A laboratory study of some factors relevant to human socialization. *Journal of Comparative Psychology*, 1943, **36**, 229-253.

Wolf, S., & Wolff, H. G. Evidence on the genesis of peptic ulcer in man. *Journal of American Medical Association*, 1942, **120**, 670-675.

Youtz, R.E.P. Reinforcement, extinction, and spontaneous recovery in a non-Pavlovian reaction. *Journal of Experimental Psychology*, 1938, **22**, 305-318. (a)

Youtz, R.E.P. The change with time of a Thorndikian response in the rat. *Journal of Experimental Psychology*, 1938, **23**, 128-140. (b)

Youtz, R.E.P. The weakening of one Thorndikian response following the extinction of another. *Journal of Experimental Psychology*, 1939, **24**, 294-304.

The Role of the Teacher

ANNA FREUD

The school is expected to perform many functions formerly thought to belong exclusively to the home. The teacher's role has expanded to include assisting the child's emotional and social development as well as his or her intellectual growth. Along with this expanding role came the belief that the teacher of young children should serve as a mother-substitute. Psychoanalyst Anna Freud points out that teachers cannot and should not be maternal substitutes if they are to perform effectively. She suggests that a general focus on the whole process of development will allow teachers to avoid this pitfall. The article is based on a lecture that Freud delivered to students at the Harvard Graduate School of Education, and concludes with her responses to their questions.

It is not a good practice for teachers to be confined to one age group because this encourages them to disregard the fact that any given age is merely a transitional stage within the whole process of childhood. It is important for the school teacher to have knowledge of children of all ages. The good teacher and child psychologist see every phase of childhood in terms of what has gone before and what will come afterwards. Teachers of children of every age should keep this outlook and not confine their interest to their own age group. It is a disadvantage for teachers of elementary school children that they do not see the earlier stages of infancy which have led up to the picture of the child as it is seen in the classroom.

What an enormous difference there is in the evaluation of the child's personality by the school teacher and by the parents. For example, when I used to work with one- and two-year-olds in the day nursery, I saw the children act within their community as full and independent personalities. These children asserted their wishes and influenced the conduct of the nursery school. For example, I would walk in and ask the nursery worker why the children had not yet gone out on the terrace. The teacher would say that Johnny was involved in work and had said they should wait, or Billy had said the weather wasn't fine enough. One day no one was eating lunch. It was because Jimmy had said the food wasn't good today, and the other children had followed his lead. Then one would meet these same "important" children on the street with their parents — they would be pushed in prams, and appear in relation to the adults as small, insignificant infants.

Three Dangers of Teaching School

First, working too closely with children fosters a loss of perspective between the child's world and the adult world. The teacher who works with young children only sees them

Harvard Educational Review   Vol. 22   No. 4   Fall 1952, 229-234

out of proportion. She gets caught up in the children's lives, loses her adult values, and begins to live in a children's world where everything comes down to the child's size.

Second, the teacher may come to look at childhood stages as valued within themselves, and not as a preparation for the future. One way to avoid this danger is for the worker with young children to develop an interest in later phases of development.

The third danger for the teacher is to attach herself to the individual child so much as to think of him as her own. Every teacher of young children is in a difficult emotional situation. It is only natural for her to develop strong positive feelings for the children on whom she spends so much of her care; she can hardly avoid valuing, and over-valuing, them in the manner of a mother. At the same time she has to accept the necessity that her children leave her after comparatively short periods and she has to avoid rivalry with the mothers of her children. Teachers who are too possessive in their attitude to the children will suffer from the repeated separations and harden their personalities in defence against this experience; and they will get involved in battles with the mothers who are the legitimate owners of the child. There is one way for the teacher who wishes to escape this danger. Her interest in the individual child has to develop further until it becomes a more general and less personal interest in the whole process of childhood with all its implications.

Questions and Answers

If we adopt this point of view, don't we become impersonal in our relations with the children?

I don't think so. This way each child becomes a figure of real interest for the teacher. We ask how far he has gone in his development, how we can help him, which direction he is taking. It gives the possibility of looking at the child and wondering what is happening in him.

If the teacher sees in a child something that reminds her of her own childhood, she wants to help that child and save him from what she experienced. She will give him infinite patience and care. But what of the child who reminds her either of a brother with whom she fought constantly or of something in her own development which she cannot face? For every child who benefits because he means something in her life, another child suffers. This is the danger of the personal approach. It is too selective to want to work only with groups who need special help, such as deprived or retarded children. This is not a good basis for professional work because it means that in a subtle way the teacher identifies with the children she has chosen and is trying to help herself rather than the child. Since teaching is a profession, she ought to have an over-all relationship with childhood. A teacher cannot be completely objective, but once she becomes interested in the processes of childhood, all children become interesting in a more objective way.

Would you discuss the problem of the child who comes from a home in which he is emotionally deprived?

To answer the question with a few historical facts: there was a time when teachers were interested only in the child's learning capacity; other sides of the child's life were added gradually. In Europe, about 1914 to 1918, teachers began to realize that the child's physical state had something to do with his learning capacity. Children were not getting sufficient food due to deprivations caused by the war, and it was noticed that the hungry child does not learn as well as the adequately fed. The first school meals were begun at this time. Then it was observed that the child without sufficient sleep could not learn well either. People realized that you can't deal with a child's intellect without taking care of his bodily needs first. The latter observation resulted in rest periods for younger children. The next step was the realization that affectional deprivation also influenced school behaviour. This came as a surprise because of the lack of knowledge concerning the connection between the emotions and learning. Equally, the influence of social conditions of the home upon the intellect became recognized. Thus teachers in time acquired knowledge concerning the child's bodily needs, his social environment, his emotional atmosphere, and his need for affection.

To satisfy a deprived child's need for affection the teacher may want to play the part of the mother. She had better know that in this case the child will cease to accept her in the teacher's role. The teacher's role is not that of a mother-substitute. If, as teachers, we play the part of a mother we get from the child the reactions which are appropriate for the mother-child relationship — the demand for exclusive attention and affection, the wish to get rid of all the other children in the classroom. This makes it more difficult to deal with the child. Although it fills a need of the child, it is not the teacher's role.

There is a difference in a child's attitudes toward his mother and toward his teacher. He wants to be loved by his mother and doesn't want to be taught by her. His attitude toward his mother is a demanding one based on his instinctive wishes; his attitude toward his teacher is farther removed from drive-activity, it is one of willingness to give and take in. To illustrate: In the war-time nursery, the nurses who acted as mother-substitutes for the children separated from their families, could not function as teachers. Only when taken to another building and put with other nursery workers did the children behave as if in school.

It is inevitable that in the classroom the children will act out the attitudes which they transfer from home. But, normally, when the teacher stays within her role, the home situation does not develop fully in school. It is the privilege of the teacher to introduce the child to a new experience, to life within a social community, not merely to duplicate his experiences within the family.

Should the teacher try to help the problem child?
It may depend on the child's age. Helping the child with personal problems by understanding them is within the teacher's role. But if this presupposes as close a relationship between the child and the teacher as between a child and a therapist, then it transgresses the limits within which the teacher can work. She can help the child by varying her demands on him and her behaviour toward him. But it should be remembered that the teacher is neither a mother, nor a therapist.

Should the teacher show affection to the children?
The teacher with an objective attitude can respond warmly enough to satisfy the child

without getting herself involved. In that way emotional involvements cannot develop to a dangerous extent.

On the whole, bodily contact should be left to the mother. This is true for children of all ages. The normal child will not make these demands for bodily contact in the classroom since they are satisfied at home. The child who doesn't have these contacts needs a mother-substitute, a function which — as said before — the teacher should not perform. The communication between teacher and child should take a form different from that of physical contact.

What will be the teacher's interest in the child if her emotional approach has to be under such strict control?

The teacher who has a firm grounding in psychoanalytic child psychology will look at the individual child in terms of his personality structure, i.e., not as a unified being but as a being consisting of several parts who, during his development, has to struggle to create an inner equilibrium, a state of harmony within himself. There are three agencies within the personality: (1) the drives, which clamour for satisfaction; (2) the ego, which regulates drive satisfaction and establishes connections with the environment; (3) the super-ego, derived from identifications, which embodies the individual's demands on himself, his ideals, his morality. The teacher has to recognize in the child the working of these three agencies as well as their interactions.

So far as the detailed observation of children is concerned, the elementary school teacher is in a difficult position. By the time the child has reached school-age, much of the activity of his drives is under control, unconscious, and not visible on the surface; he would not be fit for school if his ego were not built up and functioning. The elementary school teacher therefore lacks the advantages of the nursery school teacher who sees the child during his early conflicts and struggles. Therefore it is of great advantage for the teachers of school children to observe infants in day-nurseries and even babies in their cribs. On the one hand they will realize how early the personality traits of the school child reveal themselves in the infant; on the other hand they will be impressed by the enormous changes which every individual undergoes in the first five years of his life, i.e., the long and strenuous way from the newborn with his primitive animal-like attitudes to the almost civilized and socialized human being which the child presents himself as at the beginning of his school career. Such observations will enable the teacher to understand the interactions between innate and environmental forces in the individual child.

A deeper understanding of personality structure will help teachers to avoid a common mistake: namely to approach children of varying ages in the same manner. At nursery age the teacher deals more or less directly with the child's instinctive wishes; she offers opportunities for satisfying wishes or restricts and deflects drive-activity by means of play-material. At school age the teacher only draws indirectly on drive-energy (as for instance in the sublimations); on the whole she deals with the ego and its intellectual interests. In moral matters the child with a fully developed super-ego has to be approached quite differently from one where this step in development has not taken place yet. Instead of receiving permission or being thwarted in his wish-fulfillments by the teacher he should be given scope to solve moral conflicts within himself, i.e., he should be approached indirectly through his ideals and values.

How far are the child's drives still visible in the elementary school period?

The degree to which drives are still visible at school age varies from child to child, and according to his upbringing. After six years, the most common surface remnants of past instinctive wishes are greediness, mouth play such as thumb-sucking, interest in lavatory matters, day-dreaming, masturbation, aggressiveness, and showing-off. Some children fail to outgrow the need for immediate drive satisfaction; they do not settle down to school occupations, but are always searching for immediate gratifications. They cannot wait or work for their pleasures. In this, they still have the attitudes of infants.

If the teacher observes behavior remnants of early development, their occurrence can give clues to the inner life of the child as well as to his present stage of drive-development. Thumb-sucking, rocking, and dirty language do not indicate abnormality, but a stage of development over which the child has not yet achieved control. The teacher cannot do much to correct such behaviour unless she knows more about the relevant facts.

Curiosity is one of the early drives which can be used to the full by the elementary school teacher. The child's intellectual activity is a function of his mental apparatus activated by energy from the drives. The child's early curiosity concerning sex matters can be displaced most profitably to the school subjects, if these are selected carefully to come close enough to the child's original interests. But the progressive school has to accomplish more than provide the child with welcome outlets for his drive energy. Such "sublimation" of sexual curiosity will only be of real benefit if simultaneously the child is guided towards exchanging play for work, i.e., if he becomes able to pursue occupations which do not yield immediate and unrestricted fulfillment of his primitive wishes but lead to pleasurable experiences by more difficult circuitous routes.

The Science of Learning and
the Art of Teaching[1]

B. F. SKINNER

B. F. Skinner's experimental work has been concerned with the effects of reinforcement in learning and the designing of techniques by which reinforcement can be manipulated. He criticizes current classroom practice for the relative infrequency of positive reinforcement and suggests how the results of certain scientific research in the field of learning can be applied to practical problems in education. In order to take advantage of these advances, the teacher must have the help of mechanical devices. In presenting the advantages to be gained from the use of teaching machines, Skinner also addresses objections to his position.

SOME promising advances have recently been made in the field of learning. Special techniques have been designed to arrange what are called "contingencies of reinforcement"—the relations which prevail between behavior on the one hand and the consequences of that behavior on the other—with the result that a much more effective control of behavior has been achieved. It has long been argued that an organism learns mainly by producing changes in its environment, but it is only recently that these changes have been carefully manipulated. In traditional devices for the study of learning—in the serial maze, for example, or in the T-maze, the problem box, or the familiar discrimination apparatus—the effects produced by the organism's behavior are left to many fluctuating circumstances. There is many a slip between the turn-to-the-right and the food-cup at the end of the alley. It is not surprising that techniques of this sort have yielded only very rough data from which the uniformities demanded by an experimental science can be extracted only by averaging many cases. In none of this work has the behavior of the individual organism been predicted in more than a statistical sense. The learning processes which are the presumed object of such research are

[1] Paper presented at a conference on Current Trends in Psychology and the Behavioral Sciences at the University of Pittsburgh, March 12, 1954.

Harvard Educational Review Vol. 24 No. 2 Spring 1954, 86-97

reached only through a series of inferences. Current preoccupation with deductive systems reflects this state of the science.

Recent improvements in the conditions which control behavior in the field of learning are of two principal sorts. The Law of Effect has been taken seriously; we have made sure that effects *do* occur and that they occur under conditions which are optimal for producing the changes called learning. Once we have arranged the particular type of consequence called a reinforcement, our techniques permit us to shape up the behavior of an organism almost at will. It has become a routine exercise to demonstrate this in classes in elementary psychology by conditioning such an organism as a pigeon. Simply by presenting food to a hungry pigeon at the right time, it is possible to shape up three or four well-defined responses in a single demonstration period—such responses as turning around, pacing the floor in the pattern of a figure-8, standing still in a corner of the demonstration apparatus, stretching the neck, or stamping the foot. Extremely complex performances may be reached through successive stages in the shaping process, the contingencies of reinforcement being changed progressively in the direction of the required behavior. The results are often quite dramatic. In such a demonstration one can *see* learning take place. A significant change in behavior is often obvious as the result of a single reinforcement.

A second important advance in technique permits us to maintain behavior in given states of strength for long periods of time. Reinforcements continue to be important, of course, long after an organism has learned *how* to do something, long after it has acquired behavior. They are necessary to maintain the behavior in strength. Of special interest is the effect of various schedules of intermittent reinforcement. Charles B. Ferster and the author are currently preparing an extensive report of a five-year research program, sponsored by the Office of Naval Research, in which most of the important types of schedules have been investigated and in which the effects of schedules in general have been reduced to a few principles. On the theoretical side we now have a fairly good idea of why a given schedule produces its appropriate performance. On the practical side we have learned how to maintain any given level of activity for daily periods limited only by the physical exhaustion of the organism and from day to day without substantial change throughout its life. Many of these effects would be traditionally assigned to the field of motivation, although the principal operation is simply the arrangement of contingencies of reinforcement.[2]

These new methods of shaping behavior and of maintaining it in strength are a great improvement over the traditional practices of professional animal trainers, and it is not surprising that our laboratory

[2] The reader may wish to review Dr. Skinner's article, "Some Contributions of an Experimental Analysis of Behavior to Psychology as a Whole," *The American Psychologist*, 1953, 8, 69-78. Ed.

results are already being applied to the production of performing animals for commercial purposes. In a more academic environment they have been used for demonstration purposes which extend far beyond an interest in learning as such. For example, it is not too difficult to arrange the complex contingencies which produce many types of social behavior. Competition is exemplified by two pigeons playing a modified game of ping-pong. The pigeons drive the ball back and forth across a small table by pecking at it. When the ball gets by one pigeon, the other is reinforced. The task of constructing such a "social relation" is probably completely out of reach of the traditional animal trainer. It requires a carefully designed program of gradually changing contingencies and the skillful use of schedules to maintain the behavior in strength. Each pigeon is separately prepared for its part in the total performance, and the "social relation" is then arbitrarily constructed. The sequence of events leading up to this stable state is excellent material for the study of the factors important in nonsynthetic social behavior. It is instructive to consider how a similar series of contingencies could arise in the case of the human organism through the evolution of cultural patterns.

Cooperation can also be set up, perhaps more easily than competition. We have trained two pigeons to coordinate their behavior in a cooperative endeavor with a precision which equals that of the most skillful human dancers. In a more serious vein these techniques have permitted us to explore the complexities of the individual organism and to analyze some of the serial or coordinate behaviors involved in attention, problem solving, various types of self-control, and the subsidiary systems of responses within a single organism called "personalities." Some of these are exemplified in what we call multiple schedules of reinforcement. In general a given schedule has an effect upon the rate at which a response is emitted. Changes in the rate from moment to moment show a pattern typical of the schedule. The pattern may be as simple as a constant rate of responding at a given value, it may be a gradually accelerating rate between certain extremes, it may be an abrupt change from not responding at all to a given stable high rate, and so on. It has been shown that the performance characteristic of a given schedule can be brought under the control of a particular stimulus and that different performances can be brought under the control of different stimuli in the same organism. At a recent meeting of the American Psychological Association, Dr. Ferster and the author demonstrated a pigeon whose behavior showed the pattern typical of "fixed-interval" reinforcement in the presence of one stimulus and, alternately, the pattern typical of the very different schedule called "fixed ratio" in the presence of a second stimulus. In the laboratory we have been able to obtain performances appropriate to *nine* different schedules in the presence of appropriate stimuli in random alternation. When Stimulus 1 is present, the pigeon executes the performance appropriate to Schedule 1. When

Stimulus 2 is present, the pigeon executes the performance appropriate to Schedule 2. And so on. This result is important because it makes the extrapolation of our laboratory results to daily life much more plausible. We are all constantly shifting from schedule to schedule as our immediate environment changes, but the dynamics of the control exercised by reinforcement remain essentially unchanged.

It is also possible to construct very complex *sequences* of schedules. It is not easy to describe these in a few words, but two or three examples may be mentioned. In one experiment the pigeon generates a performance appropriate to Schedule A where the reinforcement is simply the production of the stimulus characteristic of Schedule B, to which the pigeon then responds appropriately. Under a third stimulus, the bird yields a performance appropriate to Schedule C where the reinforcement in this case is simply the production of the stimulus characteristic of Schedule D, to which the bird then responds appropriately. In a special case, first investigated by L. B. Wyckoff, Jr., the organism responds to one stimulus where the reinforcement consists of the *clarification* of the stimulus controlling another response. The first response becomes, so to speak, an objective form of "paying attention" to the second stimulus. In one important version of this experiment, as yet unpublished, we could say that the pigeon is telling us whether it is "paying attention" to the *shape* of a spot of light or to its *color*.

One of the most dramatic applications of these techniques has recently been made in the Harvard Psychological Laboratories by Floyd Ratliff and Donald S. Blough, who have skillfully used multiple and serial schedules of reinforcement to study complex perceptual processes in the infrahuman organism. They have achieved a sort of psycho-physics without verbal instruction. In a recent experiment by Blough, for example, a pigeon draws a detailed dark-adaptation curve showing the characteristic breaks of rod and cone vision. The curve is recorded continuously in a single experimental period and is quite comparable· with the curves of human subjects. The pigeon behaves in a way which, in the human case, we would not hesitate to describe by saying that it adjusts a very faint patch of light until it can just be seen.

In all this work, the species of the organism has made surprisingly little difference. It is true that the organisms studied have all been vertebrates, but they still cover a wide range. Comparable results have been obtained with pigeons, rats, dogs, monkeys, human children, and most recently, by the author in collaboration with Ogden R. Lindsley, human psychotic subjects. In spite of great phylogenetic differences, all these organisms show amazingly similar properties of the learning process. It should be emphasized that this has been achieved by analyzing the effects of reinforcement and by designing techniques which manipulate reinforcement with considerable precision. Only in this way can the behavior of the individual organism be brought under such precise control. It is also important to note that through a gradual advance to complex interrelations among responses, the same degree of rigor is being extended to behavior which would usually be assigned to such fields as perception, thinking, and personality dynamics.

From this exciting prospect of an advancing science of learning, it is a great shock to turn to that branch of technology which is most directly concerned with the learning process—education. Let us consider, for example, the teaching of arithmetic in the lower grades. The school is concerned with imparting to the child a large number of responses of a special sort. The responses are all verbal. They consist of speaking and writing certain words, figures, and signs which, to put it roughly, refer to numbers and to arithmetic operations. The first task is to shape up these responses—to get the child to pronounce and to write responses correctly, but the principal task is to bring this behavior under many sorts of stimulus control. This is what happens when the child learns to count, to recite tables, to count while ticking off the items in an assemblage of objects, to respond to spoken or written numbers by saying "odd," "even," "prime," and so on. Over and above this elaborate repertoire of numerical behavior, most of which is often dismissed as the product of rote learning, the teaching of arithmetic looks forward to those complex serial arrangements of responses involved in original mathematical thinking. The child must acquire responses of transposing, clearing fractions, and so on, which modify the order or pattern of the original material so that the response called a solution is eventually made possible.

Now, how is this extremely complicated verbal repertoire set up? In the first place, what reinforcements are used? Fifty years ago the answer would have been clear. At that time educational control was still frankly aversive. The child read numbers, copied numbers, memorized tables, and performed operations upon numbers to escape the threat of the birch rod or cane. Some positive reinforcements were perhaps eventually derived from the increased efficiency of the child in the field of arithmetic and in rare cases some automatic reinforcement may have resulted from the sheer manipulation of the medium—from the solution of problems or the discovery of the intricacies of the number system. But for the immediate purposes of education the child acted to avoid or escape punishment. It was part of the reform movement known as progressive education to make the positive consequences more immediately effective, but any one who visits the lower grades of the average school today will observe that a change has been made, not from aversive to positive control, but from one form of aversive stimulation to another. The child at his desk, filling in his workbook, is behaving primarily to escape from the threat of a series of minor aversive events—the teacher's displeasure, the criticism or ridicule of his classmates, an ignominious showing in a competition, low marks, a trip to the office "to be talked to" by the principal, or a word to the parent who may still resort to the birch rod. In this welter of aversive consequences, getting the right answer is in itself an insignificant event, any effect of which is lost amid the anxieties, the boredom, and the aggressions which are the inevitable by-products of aversive control.[3]

Secondly, we have to ask how the contingencies of reinforcement are arranged. When is a numerical operation reinforced as "right"? Eventually, of course, the pupil may be able to check his own answers and achieve some sort of automatic reinforcement, but in the early stages the reinforcement of being right is usually accorded by the teacher. The contingencies she provides are far from optimal. It can easily be demonstrated that, unless explicit mediating behavior has been set up, the lapse of only a few seconds between response and reinforcement destroys most of the effect. In a typical classroom, nevertheless, long periods of time customarily elapse. The teacher may walk up and down the aisle, for example, while the class is working on a sheet of problems, pausing here and there to say right or wrong. Many seconds or minutes intervene between the child's response and the teacher's reinforcement. In many cases—for example, when papers are taken home to be corrected —as much as 24 hours may intervene. It is surprising that this system has any effect whatsoever.

A third notable shortcoming is the lack of a skillful program which moves forward through a series of progressive approximations to the final complex behavior desired. A long series of contingencies is necessary to bring the organism into the possession of mathematical behavior most efficiently. But the teacher is seldom able to reinforce at each step in such a series because she cannot deal with the pupil's responses one at a time. It is usually necessary to reinforce the behavior in blocks of responses—as in correcting a work sheet or page from a workbook. The responses within such a block must not be interrelated. The answer to one problem must not depend upon the answer to another. The number of stages through which one may progressively approach a complex pattern of behavior is therefore small, and the task so much the more difficult. Even the most modern workbook in beginning arithmetic is far from exemplifying an efficient program for shaping up mathematical behavior.

Perhaps the most serious criticism of the current classroom is the relative infrequency of reinforcement. Since the pupil is usually dependent upon the teacher for being right, and since many pupils are usually dependent upon the same teacher, the total number of contingencies which may be arranged during, say, the first four years, is of the order of only a few thousand. But a very rough estimate suggests that efficient mathematical behavior at this level requires something of

[3] B. F. Skinner, *Science and Human Behavior*. New York: Macmillan, 1953.

the order of 25,000 contingencies. We may suppose that even in the brighter student a given contingency must be arranged several times to place the behavior well in hand. The responses to be set up are not simply the various items in tables of addition, subtraction, multiplication, and division; we have also to consider the alternative forms in which each item may be stated. To the learning of such material we should add hundreds of responses concerned with factoring, identifying primes, memorizing series, using short-cut techniques of calculation, constructing and using geometric representations or number forms, and so on. Over and above all this, the whole mathematical repertoire must be brought under the control of concrete problems of considerable variety. Perhaps 50,000 contingencies is a more conservative estimate. In this frame of reference the daily assignment in arithmetic seems pitifully meagre.

The result of all this is, of course, well known. Even our best schools are under criticism for their inefficiency in the teaching of drill subjects such as arithmetic. The condition in the average school is a matter of **widespread national concern. Modern children simply do not learn** arithmetic quickly or well. Nor is the result simply incompetence. The very subjects in which modern techniques are weakest are those in which failure is most conspicuous, and in the wake of an ever-growing incompetence come the anxieties, uncertainties, and aggressions which in their turn present other problems to the school. Most pupils soon claim the asylum of not being "ready" for arithmetic at a given level or, eventually, of not having a mathematical mind. Such explanations are readily seized upon by defensive teachers and parents. Few pupils ever reach the stage at which automatic reinforcements follow as the natural consequences of mathematical behavior. On the contrary, the figures and symbols of mathematics have become standard emotional stimuli. The glimpse of a column of figures, not to say an algebraic symbol or an integral sign, is likely to set off—not mathematical behavior—but a reaction of anxiety, guilt, or fear.

The teacher is usually no happier about this than the pupil. Denied the opportunity to control via the birch rod, quite at sea as to the mode of operation of the few techniques at her disposal, she spends as little time as possible on drill subjects and eagerly subscribes to philosophies of education which emphasize material of greater inherent interest. A confession of weakness is her extraordinary concern lest the child be taught something unnecessary. The repertoire to be imparted is carefully reduced to an essential minimum. In the field of spelling, for example, a great deal of time and energy has gone into discovering just those words which the young child is going to use, as if it were a crime to waste one's educational power in teaching an unnecessary word. Eventually, weakness of technique emerges in the disguise of a reformulation of the aims of education. Skills are minimized in favor of vague achievements —educating for democracy, educating the whole child, educating for life, and so on. And there the matter ends; for, unfortunately, these philosophies do not in turn suggest improvements in techniques. They offer little or no help in the design of better classroom practices.

There would be no point in urging these objections if improvement were impossible. But the advances which have recently been made in our control of the learning process suggest a thorough revision of classroom practices and, fortunately, they tell us how the revision can be brought about. This is not, of course, the first time that the results of an experimental science have been brought to bear upon the practical problems of education. The modern classroom does not, however, offer much evidence that research in the field of learning has been respected or used. This condition is no doubt partly due to the limitations of earlier research. But it has been encouraged by a too hasty conclusion that the laboratory study of learning is inherently limited because it cannot take into account the realities of the classroom. In the light of our increasing knowledge of the learning process we should, instead, insist upon dealing with those realities and forcing a substantial change in them. Education is perhaps the most important branch of scientific technology. It deeply affects the lives of all of us. We can no longer allow the exigencies of a practical situation to suppress the tremendous improvements which are within reach. The practical situation must be changed.

There are certain questions which have to be answered in turning to the study of any new organism. What behavior is to be set up? What reinforcers are at hand? What responses are available in embarking upon a program of progressive approximation which will lead to the final form of the behavior? How can reinforcements be most efficiently scheduled to maintain the behavior in strength? These questions are all relevant in considering the problem of the child in the lower grades.

In the first place, what reinforcements are available? What does the school have in its possession which will reinforce a child? We may look first to the material to be learned, for it is possible that this will provide considerable automatic reinforcement. Children play for hours with mechanical toys, paints, scissors and paper, noise-makers, puzzles—in short, with almost anything which feeds back significant changes in the environment and is reasonably free of aversive properties. The sheer control of nature is itself reinforcing. This effect is not evident in the modern school because it is masked by the emotional responses generated by aversive control. It is true that automatic reinforcement from the manipulation of the environment is probably only a mild reinforcer and may need to be carefully husbanded, but one of the most striking principles to emerge from recent research is that the *net* amount of reinforcement is of little significance. A very slight reinforcement may be tremendously effective in controlling behavior if it is wisely used.

If the natural reinforcement inherent in the subject matter is not enough, other reinforcers must be employed. Even in school the child is occasionally permitted to do "what he wants to do," and access to reinforcements of many sorts may be made contingent upon the more immediate consequences of the behavior to be established. Those who advocate competition as a useful social motive may wish to use the reinforcements which follow from excelling others, although there is the difficulty that in this case the reinforcement of one child is necessarily aversive to another. Next in order we might place the good will and affection of the teacher, and only when that has failed need we turn to the use of aversive stimulation.

In the second place, how are these reinforcements to be made contingent upon the desired behavior? There are two considerations here—the gradual elaboration of extremely complex patterns of behavior and the maintenance of the behavior in strength at each stage. The whole process of becoming competent in any field must be divided into a very large number of very small steps, and reinforcement must be contingent upon the accomplishment of each step. This solution to the problem of creating a complex repertoire of behavior also solves the problem of maintaining the behavior in strength. We could, of course, resort to the techniques of scheduling already developed in the study of other organisms but in the present state of our knowledge of educational practices, scheduling appears to be most effectively arranged through the design of the material to be learned. By making each successive step as small as possible, the frequency of reinforcement can be raised to a maximum, while the possibly aversive consequences of being wrong are reduced to a minimum. Other ways of designing material would yield other programs of reinforcement. Any supplementary reinforcement would probably have to be scheduled in the more traditional way.

These requirements are not excessive, but they are probably incompatible with the current realities of the classroom. In the experimental study of learning it has been found that the contingencies of reinforcement which are most efficient in controlling the organism cannot be arranged through the personal mediation of the experimenter. An organism is affected by subtle details of contingencies which are beyond the capacity of the human organism to arrange. Mechanical and electrical devices must be used. Mechanical help is also demanded by the sheer number of contingencies which may be used efficiently in a single experimental session. We have recorded many millions of responses from a single organism during thousands of experimental hours. Personal arrangement of the contingencies and personal observation of the results are quite unthinkable. Now, the human organism is, if anything, more sensitive to precise contingencies than the other organisms we have studied. We have every reason to expect, therefore, that the most effective control of human learning will require instrumental aid. The simple fact is that, as a mere reinforcing mechanism, the teacher is out of date. This would be true even if a single teacher devoted all her time to a single child, but her inadequacy is multiplied many-fold when she must serve as a reinforcing device to many children at once. If the teacher is to take advantage of recent advances in the study of learning, she must have the help of mechanical devices.

The technical problem of providing the necessary instrumental aid is not particularly difficult. There are many ways in which the necessary contingencies may be arranged, either mechanically or electrically. An inexpensive device which solves most of the principal problems has already been constructed. It is still in the experimental stage, but a description will suggest the kind of instrument which seems to be required. The device consists of a small box about the size of a small record player. On the top surface is a window through which a question or problem printed on a paper tape may be seen. The child answers the question by moving one or more sliders upon which the digits 0 through 9 are printed. The answer appears in square holes punched in the paper upon which the question is printed. When the answer has been set, the child turns a knob. The operation is as simple as adjusting a television set. If the answer is right, the knob turns freely and can be made to ring a bell or provide some other conditioned reinforcement. If the answer is wrong, the knob will not turn. A counter may be added to tally wrong answers. The knob must then be reversed slightly and a second attempt at a right answer made. (Unlike the flash-card, the device reports a wrong answer without giving the right answer.) When the answer is right, a further turn of the knob engages a clutch which moves the next problem into place in the window. This movement cannot be completed, however, until the sliders have been returned to zero.

The important features of the device are these: Reinforcement for the right answer is immediate. The mere manipulation of the device will probably be reinforcing enough to keep the average pupil at work for a suitable period each day, provided traces of earlier aversive control can be wiped out. A teacher may supervise an entire class at work on such devices at the same time, yet each child may progress at his own rate, completing as many problems as possible within the class period. If forced to be away from school, he may return to pick up where he left off. The gifted child will advance rapidly, but can be kept from getting too far ahead either by being excused from arithmetic for a time or by being given special sets of problems which take him into some of the interesting bypaths of mathematics.

The device makes it possible to present carefully designed material in which one problem can depend upon the answer to the preceding and where, therefore, the most efficient progress to an eventually complex repertoire can be made. Provision has been made for recording the commonest mistakes so that the tapes can be modified as experience dictates. Additional steps can be inserted where pupils tend to have trouble, and ultimately the material will reach a point at which the answers of the average child will almost always be right.

If the material itself proves not to be sufficiently reinforcing, other reinforcers in the possession of the teacher or school may be made contingent upon the operation of the device or upon progress through a series of problems. Supplemental reinforcement would not sacrifice the advantages gained from immediate reinforcement and from the possibility of constructing an optimal series of steps which approach the complex repertoire of mathematical behavior most efficiently.

A similar device in which the sliders carry the letters of the alphabet has been designed to teach spelling. In addition to the advantages which can be gained from precise reinforcement and careful programming, the device will teach reading at the same time. It can also be used to establish the large and important repertoire of verbal relationships encountered in logic and science. In short, it can teach verbal thinking. As to content instruction, the device can be operated as a multiple-choice self-rater.

Some objections to the use of such devices in the classroom can easily be foreseen. The cry will be raised that the child is being treated as a mere animal and that an essentially human intellectual achievement is being analyzed in unduly mechanistic terms. Mathematical behavior is usually regarded, not as a repertoire of responses involving numbers and numerical operations, but as evidences of mathematical ability or the exercise of the power of reason. It is true that the techniques which are emerging from the experimental study of learning are not designed to "develop the mind" or to further some vague "understanding" of mathematical relationships. They are designed, on the contrary, to establish the very behaviors which are taken to be the evidences of such mental states or processes. This is only a special case of the general change which is under way in the interpretation of human affairs. An advancing science continues to offer more and more convincing alternatives to traditional formulations. The behavior in terms of which human thinking must eventually be defined is worth treating in its own right as the substantial goal of education.

Of course the teacher has a more important function than to say right or wrong. The changes proposed would free her for the effective exercise of that function. Marking a set of papers in arithmetic—"Yes, nine and six *are* fifteen; no, nine and seven *are not* eighteen"—is beneath the dignity of any intelligent individual. There is more important work to be done—in which the teacher's relations to the pupil cannot be duplicated by a mechanical device. Instrumental help would merely improve these relations. One might say that the main trouble with education in the lower grades today is that the child is obviously not competent and *knows it* and that the teacher is unable to do anything about it and *knows that too*. If the advances which have recently been made in our control of behavior can give the child a genuine competence in reading, writing, spelling, and arithmetic, then the teacher may begin to function, not in lieu of a cheap machine, but through intellectual, cultural, and emotional contacts of that distinctive sort which testify to her status as a human being.

Another possible objection is that mechanized instruction will mean technological unemployment. We need not worry about this until there are enough teachers to go around and until the hours and energy demanded of the teacher are comparable to those in other fields of employment. Mechanical devices will eliminate the more tiresome labors of the teacher but they will not necessarily shorten the time during which she remains in contact with the pupil.

A more practical objection: Can we afford to mechanize our schools? The answer is clearly yes. The device I have just described could be produced as cheaply as a small radio or phonograph. There would need to be far fewer devices than pupils, for they could be used in rotation. But even if we suppose that the instrument eventually found to be most effective would cost several hundred dollars and that large numbers of them would be required, our economy should be able to stand the strain. Once we have accepted the possibility and the necessity of mechanical help in the classroom, the economic problem can easily be surmounted. There is no reason why the school room should be any less mechanized than, for example, the kitchen. A country which annually produces millions of refrigerators, dish-washers, automatic washing-machines, automatic clothes-driers, and automatic garbage disposers can certainly afford the equipment necessary to educate its citizens to high standards of competence in the most effective way.

There is a simple job to be done. The task can be stated in concrete terms. The necessary techniques are known. The equipment needed can easily be provided. Nothing stands in the way but cultural inertia. But what is more characteristic of America than an unwillingness to accept the traditional as inevitable? We are on the threshold of an exciting and revolutionary period, in which the scientific study of man will be put to work in man's best interests. Education must play its part. It must accept the fact that a sweeping revision of educational practices is possible and inevitable. When it has done this, we may look forward with confidence to a school system which is aware of the nature of its tasks, secure in its methods, and generously supported by the informed and effective citizens whom education itself will create.

The Act of Discovery

JEROME S. BRUNER

In this article Jerome Bruner outlines a method of learning through discovery or "finding-out-for-oneself" within the school setting. Teaching practices that use a hypothesis-generating mode of inquiry result in greater positive effects, Bruner contends, since the students are motivated to achieve their self-established goals and actively participate in the "figuring-out" process. Bruner argues that the aim of education is to make children autonomous learners, and that the process of education should thus be learner-centered.

MAIMONIDES, in his *Guide for the Perplexed*[1], speaks of four forms of perfection that men might seek. The first and lowest form is perfection in the acquisition of worldly goods. The great philosopher dismisses such perfection on the ground that the possessions one acquires bear no meaningful relation to the possessor: "A great king may one morning find that there is no difference between him and the lowest person." A second perfection is of the body, its conformation and skills. Its failing is that is does not reflect on what is uniquely human about man: "he could [in any case] not be as strong as a mule." Moral perfection is the third, "the highest degree of excellency in man's character." Of this perfection Maimonides says: "Imagine a person being alone, and having no connection whatever with any other person; all his good moral principles are at rest, they are not required and give man no perfection whatever. These principles are only necessary and useful when man comes in contact with others." "The fourth kind of perfection is the true perfection of man; the possession of the highest intellectual faculties. . . ." In justification of his assertion, this extraordinary Spanish-Judaic philosopher urges: "Examine the first three kinds of perfection; you will find that if you possess them, they are not your property, but the property of others. . . . But the last kind of perfection is exclusively yours; no one else owns any part of it."

It is a conjecture much like that of Maimonides that leads me to examine the act of discovery in man's intellectual life. For if man's intellectual excel-

[1] Maimonides, *Guide for the Perplexed* (New York: Dover Publications, 1956).

Harvard Educational Review Vol. 31 No. 1 Winter 1961, 21-32

lence is the most his own among his perfections, it is also the case that the most uniquely personal of all that he knows is that which he has discovered for himself. What difference does it make, then, that we encourage discovery in the learning of the young? Does it, as Maimonides would say, create a special and unique relation between knowledge possessed and the possessor? And what may such a unique relation do for a man—or for a child, if you will, for our concern is with the education of the young?

The immediate occasion for my concern with discovery—and I do not restrict discovery to the act of finding out something that before was unknown to mankind, but rather include all forms of obtaining knowledge for oneself by the use of one's own mind—the immediate occasion is the work of the various new curriculum projects that have grown up in America during the last six or seven years. For whether one speaks to mathematicians or physicists or historians, one encounters repeatedly an expression of faith in the powerful effects that come from permitting the student to put things together for himself, to be his own discoverer.

First, let it be clear what the act of discovery entails. It is rarely, on the frontier of knowledge or elsewhere, that new facts are "discovered" in the sense of being encountered as Newton suggested in the form of islands of truth in an uncharted sea of ignorance. Or if they appear to be discovered in this way, it is almost always thanks to some happy hypotheses about where to navigate. Discovery, like surprise, favors the well prepared mind. In playing bridge, one is surprised by a hand with no honors in it at all and also by hands that are all in one suit. Yet all hands in bridge are equiprobable: one must know to be surprised. So too in discovery. The history of science is studded with examples of men "finding out" something and not knowing it. I shall operate on the assumption that discovery, whether by a schoolboy going it on his own or by a scientist cultivating the growing edge of his field, is in its essence a matter of rearranging or transforming evidence in such a way that one is enabled to go beyond the evidence so reassembled to additional new insights. It may well be that an additional fact or shred of evidence makes this larger transformation of evidence possible. But it is often not even dependent on new information.

It goes without saying that, left to himself, the child will go about discovering things for himself within limits. It also goes without saying that there are certain forms of child rearing, certain home atmospheres that lead some children to be their own discoverers more than other children. These are both topics of great interest, but I shall not be discussing them. Rather, I should like to confine myself to the consideration of discovery and "finding-out-for-oneself" within an educational setting—specifically the school. Our aim as teachers is to give our student as firm a grasp of a subject as we can, and to make him as autonomous and self-propelled a thinker as we can—one who will go along on his own after formal schooling has ended. I shall return in the end to the question of the kind of classroom and the style of teaching that encourages an attitude of wanting to discover. For purposes of orienting the discussion, however, I would like to make an overly simplified distinction between teaching that takes place in the *expository mode* and teaching that utilizes the *hypothetical mode*. In the former, the decisions concerning the mode and pace and style of exposition are principally determined by the teacher as expositor; the student is the listener. If I can put the matter in terms of structural linguistics, the speaker has a quite different set of decisions to make than the listener: the former has a wide choice of alternatives for structuring; he is anticipating paragraph content while the listener is still intent on the words; he is manipulating the content of the material by various transformations, while the listener is quite unaware of these internal manipulations. In the hypothetical mode, the teacher and the student are in a more cooperative position with respect to what in linguistics would be called "speaker's decisions." The student is not a bench-bound listener, but is taking a part in the formulation and at times may play the principal role in it. He will be aware of alternatives and may even have an "as if" attitude toward these and, as he receives information he may evaluate it as it comes. One cannot describe the process in either mode with great precision as to detail, but I think the foregoing may serve to illustrate what is meant.

Consider now what benefit might be derived from the experience of learning through discoveries that one makes for oneself. I should like to discuss these under four headings: (1) The increase in intellectual potency, (2) the shift from extrinsic to intrinsic rewards, (3) learning the heuristics of discovering, and (4) the aid to memory processing.

1. *Intellectual potency.* If you will permit me, I would like to consider the difference between subjects in a highly constrained psychological experiment involving a two-choice apparatus. In order to win chips, they must depress a key either on the right or the left side of the machine. A pattern of payoff is designed such that, say, they will be paid off on the right side 70 per cent of the time, on the left 30 per cent, although this detail is not important. What is important is that the payoff sequence is arranged at random, and there is no pattern. I should like to contrast the behavior of subjects who think that there *is* some pattern to be found in the sequence—who think that regularities are discoverable—in contrast to subjects who think that things are happening quite by *chance*. The former group adopts what is called an "event-matching" strategy in which the number of responses given to each side is roughly equal to the proportion of times it pays off: in the present case R70 : L30. The group that believes there is no pattern very soon reverts to a much more primitive strategy wherein *all* responses are allocated to the side that has the greater payoff. A little arithmetic will show you that the lazy all-and-none strategy pays off more if indeed the environment is random:

namely, they win seventy per cent of the time. The event-matching subjects win about 70% on the 70% payoff side (or 49% of the time there) and 30% of the time on the side that pays off 30% of the time (another 9% for a total take-home wage of 58% in return for their labors of decision). But the world is not always or not even frequently random, and if one analyzes carefully what the event-matchers are doing, it turns out that they are trying out hypotheses one after the other, all of them containing a term such that they distribute bets on the two sides with a frequency to match the actual occurrence of events. If it should turn out that there is a pattern to be discovered, their payoff would become 100%. The other group would go on at the middling rate of 70%.

What has this to do with the subject at hand? For the person to search out and find regularities and relationships in his environment, he must be armed with an expectancy that there will be something to find and, once aroused by expectancy, he must devise ways of searching and finding. One of the chief enemies of such expectancy is the assumption that there is nothing one can find in the environment by way of regularity or relationship. In the experiment just cited, subjects often fall into a habitual attitude that there is either nothing to be found or that they can find a pattern by looking. There is an important sequel in behavior to the two attitudes, and to this I should like to turn now.

We have been conducting a series of experimental studies on a group of some seventy school children over the last four years. The studies have led us to distinguish an interesting dimension of cognitive activity that can be described as ranging from *episodic empiricism* at one end to *cumulative constructionism* at the other. The two attitudes in the choice experiments just cited are illustrative of the extremes of the dimension. I might mention some other illustrations. One of the experiments employs the game of Twenty Questions. A child—in this case he is between 10 and 12—is told that a car has gone off the road and hit a tree. He is to ask questions that can be answered by "yes" or "no" to discover the cause of the accident. After completing the problem, the same task is given him again, though he is told that the accident had a different cause this time. In all, the procedure is repeated four times. Children enjoy playing the game. They also differ quite markedly in the approach or strategy they bring to the task. There are various elements in the strategies employed. In the first place, one may distinguish clearly between two types of questions asked: the one is designed for locating constraints in the problem, constraints that will eventually give shape to an hypothesis; the other is the hypothesis as question. It is the difference between, "Was there anything wrong with the driver?" and "Was the driver rushing to the doctor's office for an appointment and the car got out of control?" There are children who precede hypotheses with efforts to locate constraint and there are those who, to use our local slang, are "pot-shotters," who string out hypotheses non-cumulatively one after the other. A second element of strategy is its connectivity of information gathering: the extent to which questions asked utilize or ignore or violate information previously obtained. The questions asked by children tend to be organized in cycles, each cycle of questions usually being given over to the pursuit of some particular notion. Both within cycles and between cycles one can discern a marked difference in the connectivity of the child's performance. Needless to say, children who employ constraint location as a technique preliminary to the formulation of hypotheses tend to be far more connected in their harvesting of information. Persistence is another feature of strategy, a characteristic compounded of what appear to be two components: a sheer doggedness component, and a persistence that stems from the sequential organization that a child brings to the task. Doggedness is probably just animal spirits or the need for achievement —what has come to be called *n-ach*. Organized persistence is a maneuver for protecting our fragile cognitive apparatus from overload. The child who has flooded himself with disorganized information from unconnected hypotheses will become discouraged and confused sooner than the child who has shown a certain cunning in his strategy of getting information—a cunning whose principal component is the recognition that the value of information is not simply in getting it but in being able to carry it. The persistence of the organized child stems from his knowledge of how to organize questions in cycles, how to summarize things to himself, and the like.

Episodic empiricism is illustrated by information gathering that is unbound by prior constraints, that lacks connectivity, and that is deficient in organizational persistence. The opposite extreme is illustrated by an approach that is characterized by constraint sensitivity, by connective maneuvers, and by organized persistence. Brute persistence seems to be one of those gifts from the gods that make people more exaggeratedly what they are.[2]

Before returning to the issue of discovery and its role in the development of thinking, let me say a word more about the ways in which information may get transformed when the problem solver has actively processed it. There is first of all a pragmatic question: what does it take to get information processed into a form best designed to fit some future use? Take an experiment by Zajonc[3] as a case in point. He gives groups of subjects information of a controlled kind, some groups being told that their task is to transmit the information to others, others that it is merely to be kept in mind. In general, he finds

[2] I should also remark in passing that the two extremes also characterize concept attainment strategies as reported in *A Study of Thinking* by J. S. Bruner *et al.* (New York: J. Wiley, 1956). Successive scanning illustrates well what is meant here by episodic empiricism; conservative focussing is an example of cumulative constructionism.

[3] R. B. Zajonc (Personal communication, 1957).

more differentiation and organization of the information received with the intention of being transmitted than there is for information received passively. An active set leads to a transformation related to a task to be performed. The risk, to be sure, is in possible overspecialization of information processing that may lead to such a high degree of specific organization that information is lost for general use.

I would urge now in the spirit of an hypothesis that emphasis upon discovery in learning has precisely the effect upon the learner of leading him to be a constructionist, to organize what he is encountering in a manner not only designed to discover regularity and relatedness, but also to avoid the kind of information drift that fails to keep account of the uses to which information might have to be put. It is, if you will, a necessary condition for learning the variety of techniques of problem solving, of transforming information for better use, indeed for learning how to go about the very task of learning. Practice in discovering for oneself teaches one to acquire information in a way that makes that information more readily viable in problem solving. So goes the hypothesis. It is still in need of testing. But it is an hypothesis of such important human implications that we cannot afford not to test it—and testing will have to be in the schools.

2. *Intrinsic and extrinsic motives.* Much of the problem in leading a child to effective cognitive activity is to free him from the immediate control of environmental rewards and punishments. That is to say, learning that starts in response to the rewards of parental or teacher approval or the avoidance of failure can too readily develop a pattern in which the child is seeking cues as to how to conform to what is expected of him. We know from studies of children who tend to be early over-achievers in school that they are likely to be seekers after the "right way to do it" and that their capacity for transforming their learning into viable thought structures tends to be lower than children merely achieving at levels predicted by intelligence tests. Our tests on such children show them to be lower in analytic ability than those who are not conspicuous in overachievement.[4] As we shall see later, they develop rote abilities and depend upon being able to "give back" what is expected rather than to make it into something that relates to the rest of their cognitive life. As Maimonides would say, their learning is not their own.

The hypothesis that I would propose here is that to the degree that one is able to approach learning as a task of discovering something rather than "learning about" it, to that degree will there be a tendency for the child to carry out his learning activities with the autonomy of self-reward or, more properly, by reward that is discovery itself.

[4] J. S. Bruner and A. J. Caron, "Cognition, Anxiety, and Achievement in the Preadolescent." Unpublished manuscript, 1961.

To those of you familiar with the battles of the last half-century in the field of motivation, the above hypothesis will be recognized as controversial. For the classic view of motivation in learning has been, until very recently, couched in terms of a theory of drives and reinforcement: that learning occurred by virtue of the fact that a response produced by a stimulus was followed by the reduction in a primary drive state. The doctrine is greatly extended by the idea of secondary reinforcement: any state associated even remotely with the reduction of a primary drive could also have the effect of producing learning. There has recently appeared a most searching and important criticism of this position, written by Professor Robert White,[5] reviewing the evidence of recently published animal studies, of work in the field of psychoanalysis, and of research on the development of cognitive processes in children. Professor White comes to the conclusion, quite rightly I think, that the drive-reduction model of learning runs counter to too many important phenomena of learning and development to be either regarded as general in its applicability or even correct in its general approach. Let me summarize some of his principal conclusions and explore their applicability to the hypothesis stated above.

> I now propose that we gather the various kinds of behavior just mentioned, all of which have to do with effective interaction with the environment, under the general heading of competence. According to Webster, competence means fitness or ability, and the suggested synonyms include capability, capacity, efficiency, proficiency, and skill. It is therefore a suitable word to describe such things as grasping and exploring, crawling and walking, attention and perception, language and thinking, manipulating and changing the surroundings, all of which promote an effective—a competent—interaction with the environment. It is true of course, that maturation plays a part in all these developments, but this part is heavily overshadowed by learning in all the more complex accomplishments like speech or skilled manipulation. I shall argue that it is necessary to make competence a motivational concept; there is *competence motivation* as well as competence in its more familiar sense of achieved capacity. The behavior that leads to the building up of effective grasping, handling, and letting go of objects, to take one example, is not random behavior that is produced by an overflow of energy. It is directed, selective, and persistent, and it continues not because it serves primary drives, which indeed it cannot serve until it is almost perfected, but because it satisfies an intrinsic need to deal with the environment.[6]

I am suggesting that there are forms of activity that serve to enlist and develop the competence motive, that serve to make it the driving force behind behavior.

[5] R. W. White, "Motivation Reconsidered: The Concept of Competence," *Psychological Review,* LXVI (1959), 297-333.
[6] *Ibid.,* pp. 317-18.

I should like to add to White's general premise that the *exercise* of competence motives has the effect of strengthening the degree to which they gain control over behavior and thereby reduce the effects of extrinsic rewards or drive gratification.

The brilliant Russian psychologist Vigotsky[7] characterizes the growth of thought processes as starting with a dialogue of speech and gesture between child and parent; autonomous thinking begins at the stage when the child is first able to internalize these conversations and "run them off" himself. This is a typical sequence in the development of competence. So too in instruction. The narrative of teaching is of the order of the conversation. The next move in the development of competence is the internalization of the narrative and its "rules of generation" so that the child is now capable of running off the narrative on his own. The hypothetical mode in teaching by encouraging the child to participate in "speaker's decisions" speeds this process along. Once internalization has occurred, the child is in a vastly improved position from several obvious points of view—notably that he is able to go beyond the information he has been given to generate additional ideas that can either be checked immediately from experience or can, at least, be used as a basis for formulating reasonable hypotheses. But over and beyond that, the child is now in a position to experience success and failure not as reward and punishment, but as information. For when the task is his own rather than a matter of matching environmental demands, he becomes his own paymaster in a certain measure. Seeking to gain control over his environment, he can now treat success as indicating that he is on the right track, failure as indicating he is on the wrong one.

In the end, this development has the effect of freeing learning from immediate stimulus control. When learning in the short run leads only to pellets of this or that rather than to mastery in the long run, then behavior can be readily "shaped" by extrinsic rewards. When behavior becomes more long-range and competence-oriented, it comes under the control of more complex cognitive structures, plans and the like, and operates more from the inside out. It is interesting that even Pavlov, whose early account of the learning process was based entirely on a notion of stimulus control of behavior through the conditioning mechanism in which, through contiguity a new conditioned stimulus was substituted for an old unconditioned stimulus by the mechanism of stimulus substitution, that even Pavlov recognized his account as insufficient to deal with higher forms of learning. To supplement the account, he introduced the idea of the "second signalling system," with central importance placed on symbolic systems such as language in mediating and giving shape to

[7] L. S. Vigotsky, *Thinking and Speech* (Moscow, 1934).

mental life. Or as Luria[8] has put it, "the first signal system [is] concerned with directly perceived stimuli, the second with systems of verbal elaboration." Luria, commenting on the importance of the transition from first to second signal system, says: "It would be mistaken to suppose that verbal intercourse with adults merely changes the contents of the child's conscious activity without changing its form. . . . The word has a basic function not only because it indicates a corresponding object in the external world, but also because it abstracts, isolates the necessary signal, generalizes perceived signals and relates them to certain categories; it is this systematization of direct experience that makes the role of the word in the formation of mental processes so exceptionally important."[9, 10]

It is interesting that the final rejection of the universality of the doctrine of reinforcement in direct conditioning came from some of Pavlov's own students. Ivanov-Smolensky[11] and Krasnogorsky[12] published papers showing the manner in which symbolized linguistic messages could take over the place of the unconditioned stimulus and of the unconditioned response (gratification of hunger) in children. In all instances, they speak of these as *replacements* of lower, first-system mental or neural processes by higher-order or second-system controls. A strange irony, then, that Russian psychology that gave us the notion of the conditioned response and the assumption that higher-order activities are built up out of colligations or structurings of such primitive units, rejected this notion while much of American learning psychology has stayed until quite recently within the early Pavlovian fold (see, for example, a recent article by Spence[13] in the *Harvard Educational Review* or Skinner's treatment of language[14] and the attacks that have been made upon it by linguists such as Chomsky[15] who have become concerned with the relation of language and cognitive activity). What is the more interesting is that Russian pedagogical theory has become deeply influenced by this new trend and is now placing much stress upon the importance of building up a more active symbolical approach to problem solving among children.

[8] A. L. Luria, "The Directive Function of Speech in Development and Dissolution," *Word*, XV (1959), 341-464.

[9] *Ibid.*, p. 12.

[10] For an elaboration of the view expressed by Luria, the reader is referred to the forthcoming translation of L. S. Vigotsky's 1934 book being published by John Wiley and Sons and the Technology Press.

[11] A. G. Ivanov-Smolensky, "Concerning the Study of the Joint Activity of the First and Second Signal Systems," *Journal of Higher Nervous Activity*, I (1951), 1.

[12] N. D. Krasnogorsky, *Studies of Higher Nervous Activity in Animals and in Man*, Vol. I (Moscow, 1954).

[13] K. W. Spence, "The Relation of Learning Theory to the Technique of Education," *Harvard Educational Review*, XXIX (1959), 84-95.

[14] B. F. Skinner, *Verbal Behavior* (New York: Appleton-Century-Crofts, 1957).

[15] N. Chomsky, *Syntactic Structure* (The Hague, The Netherlands: Mouton & Co., 1957).

To sum up the matter of the control of learning, then, I am proposing that the degree to which competence or mastery motives come to control behavior, to that degree the role of reinforcement or "extrinsic pleasure" wanes in shaping behavior. The child comes to manipulate his environment more actively and achieves his gratification from coping with problems. Symbolic modes of representing and transforming the environment arise and the importance of stimulus-response-reward sequences declines. To use the metaphor that David Riesman developed in a quite different context, mental life moves from a state of outer-directedness in which the fortuity of stimuli and reinforcement are crucial to a state of inner-directedness in which the growth and maintenance of mastery become central and dominant.

3. *Learning the heuristics of discovery.* Lincoln Steffens,[16] reflecting in his *Autobiography* on his undergraduate education at Berkeley, comments that his schooling was overly specialized on learning about the known and that too little attention was given to the task of finding out about what was not known. But how does one train a student in the techniques of discovery? Again I would like to offer some hypotheses. There are many ways of coming to the arts of inquiry. One of them is by careful study of its formalization in logic, statistics, mathematics, and the like. If a person is going to pursue inquiry as a way of life, particularly in the sciences, certainly such study is essential. Yet, whoever has taught kindergarten and the early primary grades or has had graduate students working with him on their theses—I choose the two extremes for they are both periods of intense inquiry—knows that an understanding of the formal aspect of inquiry is not sufficient. There appear to be, rather, a series of activities and attitudes, some directly related to a particular subject and some of them fairly generalized, that go with inquiry and research. These have to do with the *process* of trying to find out something and while they provide no guarantee that the *product* will be any *great* discovery, their absence is likely to lead to awkwardness or aridity or confusion. How difficult it is to describe these matters—the heuristics of inquiry. There is one set of attitudes or ways of doing that has to do with sensing the relevance of variables—how to avoid getting stuck with edge effects and getting instead to the big sources of variance. Partly this gift comes from intuitive familiarity with a range of phenomena, sheer "knowing the stuff." But it also comes out of a sense of what things among an ensemble of things "smell right" in the sense of being of the right order of magnitude or scope or severity.

The English philosopher Weldon describes problem solving in an interesting and picturesque way. He distinguishes between difficulties, puzzles, and problems. We solve a problem or make a discovery when we impose a puzzle form on to a difficulty that converts it into a problem that can be solved in such a

[16] L. Steffens. *Autobiography of Lincoln Steffens* (New York: Harcourt, Brace, 1931).

way that it gets us where we want to be. That is to say, we recast the difficulty into a form that we know how to work with, then work it. Much of what we speak of as discovery consists of knowing how to impose what kind of form on various kinds of difficulties. A small part but a crucial part of discovery of the highest order is to invent and develop models or "puzzle forms" that can be imposed on difficulties with good effect. It is in this area that the truly powerful mind shines. But it is interesting to what degree perfectly ordinary people can, given the benefit of instruction, construct quite interesting and what, a century ago, would have been considered greatly original models.

Now to the hypothesis. It is my hunch that it is only through the exercise of problem solving and the effort of discovery that one learns the working heuristic of discovery, and the more one has practice, the more likely is one to generalize what one has learned into a style of problem solving or inquiry that serves for any kind of task one may encounter—or almost any kind of task. I think the matter is self-evident, but what is unclear is what kinds of training and teaching produce the best effects. How do we teach a child to, say, cut his losses but at the same time be persistent in trying out an idea; to risk forming an early hunch without at the same time formulating one *so* early and with so little evidence as to be stuck with it, waiting for appropriate evidence to materialize; to pose good testable guesses that are neither too brittle nor too sinuously incorrigible; etc., etc. Practice in inquiry, in trying to figure out things for oneself, is indeed what is needed, but in what form? Of only one thing I am convinced. I have never seen anybody improve in the art and technique of inquiry by any means other than engaging in inquiry.

4. *Conservation of memory.* I should like to take what some psychologists might consider a rather drastic view of the memory process. It is a view that in large measure derives from the work of my colleague, Professor George Miller.[17] Its first premise is that the principal problem of human memory is not storage, but retrieval. In spite of the biological unlikeliness of it, we seem to be able to store a huge quantity of information—perhaps not a full tape recording, though at times it seems we even do that, but a great sufficiency of impressions. We may infer this from the fact that recognition (i.e., recall with the aid of maximum prompts) is so extraordinarily good in human beings—particularly in comparison with spontaneous recall where, so to speak, we must get out stored information without external aids or prompts. The key to retrieval is organization or, in even simpler terms, knowing where to find information and how to get there.

Let me illustrate the point with a simple experiment. We present pairs of words to twelve-year-old children. One group is simply told to remember the

---

[17] G. A. Miller, "The Magical Number Seven, Plus or Minus Two," *Psychological Review,* LXIII (1956), 81-97.

pairs, that they will be asked to repeat them later. Another is told to remember them by producing a word or idea that will tie the pair together in a way that will make sense to them. A third group is given the mediators used by the second group when presented with the pairs to aid them in tying the pairs into working units. The word-pairs include such juxtapositions as "chair-forest," "sidewalk-square," and the like. One can distinguish three styles of mediators and children can be scaled in terms of their relative preference for each: *generic mediation* in which a pair is tied together by a superordinate idea: "chair and forest are both made of wood"; *thematic mediation* in which the two terms are imbedded in a theme or little story: "the lost child sat on a chair in the middle of the forest"; and *part-whole mediation* where "chairs are made from trees in the forest" is typical. Now, the chief result, as you would all predict, is that children who provide their own mediators do best—indeed, one time through a set of thirty pairs, they recover up to 95% of the second words when presented with the first ones of the pairs, whereas the uninstructed children reach a maximum of less than 50% recovered. Interestingly enough, children do best in recovering materials tied together by the form of mediator they most often use.

One can cite a myriad of findings to indicate that any organization of information that reduces the aggregate complexity of material by imbedding it into a cognitive structure a person has constructed will make that material more accessible for retrieval. In short, we may say that the process of memory, looked at from the retrieval side, is also a process of problem solving: how can material be "placed" in memory so that it can be got on demand?

We can take as a point of departure the example of the children who developed their own technique for relating the members of each word pair. You will recall that they did better than the children who were given by exposition the mediators they had developed. Let me suggest that in general, material that is organized in terms of a person's own interests and cognitive structures is material that has the best chance of being accessible in memory. That is to say, it is more likely to be placed along routes that are connected to one's own ways of intellectual travel.

In sum, the very attitudes and activities that characterize "figuring out" or "discovering" things for oneself also seems to have the effect of making material more readily accessible in memory.

The Interpersonal Relationship:
The Core of Guidance

CARL R. ROGERS

Carl Rogers presents some hypotheses about the conditions that contribute to a growth-promoting relationship between client and counselor. He argues that the quality of the interpersonal encounter is the most critical element in successfully sponsoring the development of another person. In particular, effective guidance counseling requires the empathic understanding of the client's private world and a positive regard for the client, coupled with the client's perception of the genuineness of the counselor.

I WOULD LIKE TO SHARE with you in this paper a conclusion, a conviction, which has grown out of years of experience in dealing with individuals, a conclusion which finds some confirmation in a steadily growing body of empirical evidence. It is simply that in a wide variety of professional work involving relationships with people—whether as a psychotherapist, teacher, religious worker, guidance counselor, social worker, clinical psychologist—it is the *quality* of the interpersonal encounter with the client which is the most significant element in determining effectiveness.

Let me spell out a little more fully the basis of this statement in my personal experience. I have been primarily a counselor and psychotherapist. In the course of my professional life I have worked with troubled college students, with adults in difficulty, with "normal" individuals such as business executives, and more recently with hospitalized psychotic persons. I have endeavored to make use of the learnings from my therapeutic experience in my interactions with classes and seminars, in the training of teachers, in the administration of staff groups, in the clinical supervision of psychologists, psychiatrists, and guidance workers as they work with their clients or patients. Some of these relationships are long-continued and intensive, as in individual psychotherapy. Some are brief, as in experiences with workshop participants or in contacts with students who come for practical advice. They cover a wide range of depth. Gradually I have come to the conclusion that one learning

Harvard Educational Review   Vol. 32   No. 4   Fall 1962, 416–429

which applies to all of these experiences is that it is the quality of the personal relationship which matters most. With some of these individuals I am in touch only briefly, with others I have the opportunity of knowing them intimately, but in either case the quality of the personal encounter is probably, in the long run, the element which determines the extent to which this is an experience which releases or promotes development and growth. I believe the quality of my encounter is more important in the long run than is my scholarly knowledge, my professional training, my counseling orientation, the techniques I use in the interview. In keeping with this line of thought, I suspect that for a guidance worker also the relationship he forms with each student—brief or continuing—is more important than his knowledge of tests and measurements, the adequacy of his record keeping, the theories he holds, the accuracy with which he is able to predict academic success, or the school in which he received his training.

In recent years I have thought a great deal about this issue. I have tried to observe counselors and therapists whose orientations are very different from mine, in order to understand the basis of their effectiveness as well as my own. I have listened to recorded interviews from many different sources. Gradually I have developed some theoretical formulations (4, 5), some hypotheses as to the basis of effectiveness in relationships. As I have asked myself how individuals sharply different in personality, orientation and procedure can all be effective in a helping relationship, can each be successful in facilitating constructive change or development, I have concluded that it is because they bring to the helping relationship certain attitudinal ingredients. It is these that I hypothesize as making for effectiveness, whether we are speaking of a guidance counselor, a clinical psychologist, or a psychiatrist.

What are these attitudinal or experiential elements in the counselor which make a relationship a growth-promoting climate? I would like to describe them as carefully and accurately as I can, though I am well aware that words rarely capture or communicate the qualities of a personal encounter.

CONGRUENCE

In the first place, I hypothesize that personal growth is facilitated when the counselor is what he *is*, when in the relationship with his client he is genuine and without "front" or facade, openly being the feelings and attitudes which at that moment are flowing in him. We have used the term "congruence" to try to describe this condition. By this we mean that the feelings the counselor is experiencing are available to him, available to his awareness, that he is able to live these feelings, be them in the relationship, and able to communicate them if appropriate. It means that he comes into a direct personal encounter with his client, meeting him on a person-to-person basis. It means that he is *being* himself, not denying himself. No one fully achieves this condition, yet the more the therapist is able to listen acceptantly to what is going on within himself, and the more he is able to *be* the complexity of his feelings without fear, the higher the degree of his congruence.

I think that we readily sense this quality in our everyday life. We could each of us name persons whom we know who always seem to be operating from behind a front, who are playing a role, who tend to say things they do not feel. They are exhibiting incongruence. We do not reveal ourselves too deeply to such people. On the other hand each of us knows individuals whom we somehow trust, because we sense that they are being what they *are*, that we are dealing with the person himself, and not with a polite or professional facade. This is the quality of which we are speaking, and it is hypothesized that the more genuine and congruent the therapist in the relationship, the more probability there is that change in personality in the client will occur.

I have received much clinical confirmation for this hypothesis in recent years in our work with randomly selected hospitalized schizophrenic patients. The individual therapists in our research program who seem to be most successful in dealing with these unmotivated, poorly educated, resistant, chronically hospitalized individuals, are those who are first of all real, who react in a genuine, human way as persons, and who exhibit their genuineness in the relationship.

But is it always helpful to be genuine? What about negative feelings? What about the times when the counselor's real feeling toward his client is one of annoyance, or boredom, or dislike? My tentative answer is that even with such feelings as these, which we all have from time to time, it is preferable for the counselor to be real than to put up a facade of interest and concern and liking which he does not feel.

But it is not a simple thing to achieve such reality. I am not saying that it is helpful to blurt out impulsively every passing feeling and accusation under the comfortable impression that one is being genuine. Being real involves the difficult task of being acquainted with the flow of experiencing going on within oneself, a flow marked especially by complexity and continuous change. So if I sense that I am feeling bored by my contacts with this student, and this feeling persists, I think I owe it to him and to our relationship to share this feeling with him. But here again I will want to be constantly in touch with what is going on in me. If I am, I will recognize that it is *my* feeling of being bored which I am expressing, and not some supposed fact about him as a boring person. If I voice it as my *own* reaction, it has the potentiality of leading to a deeper relationship. But this feeling exists in the context of a complex and changing flow, and this needs to be communicated too. I would like to share with him my distress at feeling bored, and the discomfort I feel in expressing this aspect of me. As I share these attitudes I find that my feeling of boredom arises from my sense of remoteness from him, and that I would like to be more in touch with him. And even as I try to express these feelings, they change. I am certainly not bored as I try to communicate myself to him in this way, and I am far from bored as I wait with eagerness and perhaps a bit of apprehension for his response. I also feel a new sensitivity to him, now that I have shared this feeling which has been a barrier between us. So I am very much more able to hear the surprise or perhaps the hurt in his voice as he now finds *him*self speaking more genuinely because I have dared to be real with him. I have let myself be a person—real, imperfect—in my relationship with him.

I have tried to describe this first element at some length because I regard it as highly important, perhaps the most crucial of the conditions I will describe, and because it is neither easy to grasp nor to achieve. Gendlin (2) has done an excellent job of explaining the significance of the concept of experiencing and its relationship to counseling and therapy, and his presentation may supplement what I have tried to say.

I hope it is clear that I am talking about a realness in the counselor which is deep and true, not superficial. I have sometimes thought that the word transparency helps to describe this element of personal congruence. If everything going on in me which is relevant to the relationship can be seen by my client, if he can see "clear through me," and if I am *willing* for this realness to show through in the relationship, then I can be almost certain that this will be a meaningful encounter in which we both learn and develop.

I have sometimes wondered if this is the only quality which matters in a counseling relationship. The evidence seems to show that other qualities also make a profound difference and are perhaps easier to achieve. So I am going to describe these others. But I would stress that if, in a given moment of relationship, they are not genuinely a part of the experience of the counselor, then it is, I believe, better to be genuinely what one is, than to pretend to be feeling these other qualities.

EMPATHY

The second essential condition in the relationship, as I see it, is that the counselor is experiencing an accurate empathic understanding of his client's private world, and is able to communicate some of the significant fragments of that understanding. To sense the client's inner world of private personal meanings as if it were your own, but without ever losing the "as if" quality, this is empathy, and this seems essential to a growth-promoting relationship. To sense his confusion or his timidity or his anger or his feeling of being treated unfairly as if it were your own, yet without one's own uncertainty or fear or anger or suspicion getting bound up in it, this is the condition I am endeavoring to describe. When the client's world is clear to the counselor and he can move about in it freely, then he can both communicate his understanding of what is vaguely known to the client, and he can also voice meanings in the client's experience of which the client is scarcely aware. It is this kind of highly sensitive empathy which seems important in making it possible for a person to get close to himself and to learn, to change and develop.

I suspect that each of us has discovered that this kind of understanding is extremely rare. We neither receive it nor offer it with any great frequency. Instead we offer another type of understanding which is very different, such as "I understand what is wrong with you" or "I understand what makes you act that way." These are the types of understanding which we usually offer and receive—an evaluative understanding from the outside. It is not surprising that we shy away from true understanding. If I am truly open to the way life is experienced by another person—if I can take his world into mine—then I run the risk of seeing life in his way, of being changed myself, and we all resist change. So we tend to view this other person's world only in our terms, not in his. We analyze and evaluate it. We do not understand it. But when someone understands how it feels and seems to be me, without wanting to analyze me or judge me, then I can blossom and grow in that climate. I am sure I am not alone in that feeling. I believe that when the counselor can grasp the moment-to-moment experiencing occurring in the inner world of the client, as the client sees it and feels it, without losing the separateness of his own identity in this empathic process, then change is likely to occur.

Though the accuracy of such understanding is highly important, the communication of intent to understand is also helpful. Even in dealing with the confused or inarticulate or bizarre individual, if he perceives that I am *trying* to understand his meanings, this is helpful. It communicates the value I place on him as an individual. It gets across the fact that I perceive his feelings and meanings as being *worth* understanding.

None of us steadily achieves such a complete empathy as I have been trying to describe, any more than we achieve complete congruence, but there is no doubt that individuals can develop along this line. Suitable training experiences have been utilized in the training of counselors, and also in the "sensitivity training" of industrial management personnel. Such experiences enable the person to listen more sensitively, to receive more of the subtle meanings the other person is expressing in words, gesture, and posture, to resonate more deeply and freely within himself to the significance of those expressions.[1]

---

[1] I hope the above account of an empathic attitude will make it abundantly clear that I am not advocating a wooden technique of pseudo-understanding in which the counselor "reflects back what the client has just said." I have been more than a little horrified at the interpretation of my approach which has sometimes crept into the teaching and training of counselors.

Now the third condition. I hypothesize that growth and change are more likely to occur the more that the counselor is experiencing a warm, positive, acceptant attitude toward what *is* in the client. It means that he prizes his client, as a person, with somewhat the same quality of feeling that a parent feels for his child, prizing him as a person regardless of his particular behavior at the moment. It means that he cares for his client in a non-possessive way, as a person with potentialities. It involves an open willingness for the client to be whatever feelings are real in him at the moment—hostility or tenderness, rebellion or submissiveness, assurance or self-depreciation. It means a kind of love for the client as he is, providing we understand the word love as equivalent to the theologian's term "agape," and not in its usual romantic and possessive meanings. What I am describing is a feeling which is not paternalistic, nor sentimental, nor superficially social and agreeable. It respects the other person as a separate individual, and does not possess him. It is a kind of liking which has strength, and which is not demanding. We have termed it positive regard.

UNCONDITIONALITY OF REGARD

There is one aspect of this attitude of which I am somewhat less sure. I advance tentatively the hypothesis that the relationship will be more effective the more the positive regard is unconditional. By this I mean that the counselor prizes the client in a total, rather than a conditional way. He does not accept certain feelings in the client and disapprove others. He feels an *unconditional* positive regard for this person. This is an outgoing, positive feeling without reservations and without evaluations. It means *not* making judgments. I believe that when this nonevaluative prizing is present in the encounter between the counselor and his client, constructive change and development in the client is more likely to occur.

Certainly one does not need to be a professional to experience this attitude. The best of parents show this in abundance, while others do not. A friend of mine, a therapist in private practice on the east coast, illustrates this very well in a letter in which he tells me what he is learning about parents. He says:

> I am beginning to feel that the key to the human being is the attitudes with which the parents have regarded him. If the child was lucky enough to have parents who have felt proud of him, wanted him, wanted him just as he was, exactly as he was, this child grows into adulthood with self-confidence, self-esteem; he goes forth in life feeling sure of himself, strong, able to lick what confronts him. Franklin Delano Roosevelt is an example . . . "my friends . . . ." He couldn't imagine anyone thinking otherwise. He had two adoring

parents. He was like the pampered dog who runs up at you, frisking his tail, eager to love you, for this dog has never known rejection or harshness. Even if you should kick him, he'll come right back to you, his tail friskier than ever, thinking you're playing a game with him and wanting more. This animal cannot imagine anyone disapproving or disliking him. Just as unconditional regard and love was poured into him, he has it now to give out. If a child is lucky enough to grow up in this unconditionally accepting atmosphere, he emerges as strong and sure and he can approach life and its vicissitudes with courage and confidence, with zest and joy of expectation.

But the parents who like their children—if. They would like them if they were changed, altered, different; if they were smarter or if they were better, or if, if, if. The offspring of these parents have trouble because they never had the feeling of acceptance. These parents don't really like these children; they would like them if they were like someone else. When you come down to the basic fundamental, the parent feels: "I don't like *this* child, this child before me." They don't say that. I am beginning to believe that it would be better for all concerned if parents did. It wouldn't leave such horrible ravages on these unaccepted children. It's never done that crudely. "If you were a nice boy and did this, that and the other thing, then we would all love you."

I am coming to believe that children brought up by parents who would like them "if" are never quite right. They grow up assuming that their parents are right and that they are wrong; that somehow or other they are at fault; and even worse, very frequently they feel they are stupid, inadequate, inferior.

This is an excellent contrast between an unconditional positive regard and a conditional regard. I believe it holds as true for counselors as for parents.

The Client's Perception

Thus far all my hypotheses regarding the possibility of constructive growth have rested upon the experiencing of these elements by the counselor. There is, however, one condition which must exist in the client. Unless the attitudes I have been describing have been to some degree communicated to the client, and perceived by him, they do not exist in his perceptual world and thus cannot be effective. Consequently it is necessary to add one more condition to the equation which I have been building up regarding personal growth through counseling. It is that when the client perceives, to a minimal degree, the genuineness of the counselor and the acceptance and empathy which the counselor experiences for him, then development in personality and change in behavior are predicted.

This has implications for me as a counselor. I need to be sensitive not only to what is going on in me, and sensitive to the flow of feelings in my client. I must also be sensitive to the way he is receiving my communications. I have learned, especially in working with more disturbed persons, that empathy can be perceived as lack of involvement; that an unconditional regard on my part can be perceived as indifference; that warmth can be perceived as a threatening closeness, that real feelings of mine can be perceived as false. I would like to behave in ways, and communicate in ways which have clarity for this specific person, so that what I am experiencing in relationship to him would be perceived unambiguously by him. Like the other conditions I have proposed, the principle is easy to grasp; the achievement of it is difficult and complex.

THE ESSENTIAL HYPOTHESIS

Let me restate very briefly the essentially simple but somewhat radical hypothesis I have set forth. I have said that constructive personality growth and change comes about only when the client perceives and experiences a certain psychological climate in the relationship. The conditions which constitute this climate do not consist of knowledge, intellectual training, orientation in some school of thought, or techniques. They are feelings or attitudes which must be experienced by the counselor and perceived by the client if they are to be effective. Those I have singled out as being essential are: a realness, genuineness, or congruence in the therapist; a sensitive, empathic understanding of the client's feelings and personal meanings; a warm, acceptant prizing of the client; and an unconditionality in this positive regard.

SOME LIMITATIONS

I would like to stress that these are hypotheses. In a later section I will comment on the way these hypotheses are faring when put to empirical test. But they are beginning hypotheses, not the final word.

I regard it as entirely possible that there are other conditions which I have not described, which are also essential. Recently I had occasion to listen to some recorded interviews by a young counselor of elementary school children. She was very warm and positive in her attitude toward her clients, yet she was definitely ineffective. She seemed to be responding warmly only to the superficial aspects of each child and so the contacts were chatty, social and friendly, but it was clear she was not reaching the real person of the child. Yet in a number of ways she rated reasonably high on each of the conditions I have described. So perhaps there are still elements missing which I have not captured in my formulation.

I am also aware of the possibility that different kinds of helping relationships may be effective with different kinds of people. Some of our therapists working with schizophrenics are effective when they appear to be highly conditional, when they do *not* accept some of the bizarre behavior of the psychotic. This can be interpreted in two ways. Perhaps a conditional set is more helpful with these individuals. Or perhaps—and this seems to me to fit the facts better—these psychotic individuals perceive a conditional attitude as meaning that the therapist *really* cares, where an unconditional attitude may be interpreted as apathetic noncaring. In any event, I do want to make it clear that what I have given are beginning formulations which surely will be modified and corrected from further learnings.

THE PHILOSOPHY WHICH IS IMPLICIT

It is evident that the kind of attitudes I have described are not likely to be experienced by a counselor unless he holds a philosophy regarding people in which such attitudes are congenial. The attitudes pictured make no sense except in a context of great respect for the person and his potentialities. Unless the primary element in the counselor's value system is the worth of the individual, he is not apt to find himself experiencing a real caring, or a desire to understand, and perhaps he will not respect himself enough to be real. Certainly the professional person who holds the view that individuals are essentially objects to be manipulated for the welfare of the state, or the good of the educational institution, or "for their own good," or to satisfy his own need for power and control, would not experience the attitudinal elements I have described as constituting growth-promoting relationships. So these conditions are congenial and natural in certain philosophical contexts but not in others.

EMPIRICAL STUDIES

This raises some questions which I have asked myself, and which you too must be asking. Are these characteristics which I have described as essential to a helping relationship simply my personal opinion, preference, and bias? Or do they represent simply a bias growing out of a generally democratic philosophy? Or do they in *fact* promote constructive change and development?

Five years ago I could not have answered these questions. Now there are at least a dozen well-designed research investigations which, approaching the matter in a variety of ways, throw light on the issues (1, 3, 6a through 6j). To report each of these studies would be confusing rather than helpful. Let me try to describe their methods in general terms and then report on the findings.

The studies deal with two rather different classes of clients: students and community members who voluntarily come to counselors for help; and on the other hand, schizophrenic individuals in a state hospital who have been there for periods ranging from a few months to many years. The first group is above the socio-educational average, the second below. The first group is motivated to gain help, the second is not only unmotivated but resistant. The over-all range in adjustment is from well-functioning individuals through varying degrees of maladjustment and disturbance, to those who are completely unable to cope with life, and who are out of contact with reality.

In the different studies there have been three ways of measuring the attitudinal elements I have described. The first method is based on brief segments, usually four minutes in length, taken in a randomized way from the tape-recorded interviews. Raters, listening to these segments, judge the degree to which the counselor is, for example, being accurately empathic, and make a rating on a carefully defined scale. The raters have no knowledge of whether the segment is from an early or late interview, or whether it is a more or less successful case. In most of the studies several raters have made ratings on each of the qualities involved.

A second method of measurement is through the use of the Relationship Inventory (1), filled out by the client at different points in time. The inventory contains statements regarding the degree to which the counselor is acceptant, empathic, and congruent, and the client responds by evaluating the statement on a six point scale from "strongly true" to "definitely untrue." Examples concerning empathy are: "He generally senses or realizes how I am feeling"; "He understands my words but does not realize how I feel." In relationship to congruence some items are: "He behaves just the way that he is in our relationship"; "He pretends that he likes me or understands me more than he really does." The Inventory is scored for each of the four attitudinal elements, and there is also a total score .

The third method is also based on the Relationship Inventory, but this time filled out by the therapist or counselor. The items are identical except for a suitable change in pronouns.

In the various studies different criteria are used for assessing the degree of constructive personality change which has taken place over the course of the interviews. In all cases the criteria of change are independent of the measurement of attitudinal conditions in the relationship. Some of the measures of change are: changes in various Minnesota Multiphasic Personality Inventory scales and indices; changes in projective tests as analyzed "blind" by clinicians having no knowledge of the research; changes in Q-sort adjustment score; changes on a measure of anxiety; therapist's ratings of change in personality and in adjustment.

THE FINDINGS

Let me now give some of the general findings from these studies:

The counselor is the most significant factor in setting the level of conditions in the relationship, though the client, too, has some influence on the quality of the relationship.

Clients who will later show more change perceive more of these attitudinal conditions early in the relationship with their counselor or therapist.

The more disturbed the client the less he is likely to (or able to?) perceive these attitudes in the counselor.

Counselors or therapists tend to be quite consistent in the level of the attitudinal conditions which they offer to each client.

The major finding from all of the studies is that those clients in relationships marked by a high level of counselor congruence, empathy and unconditional positive regard, show constructive personality change and development. These high levels of conditions are associated with: positive change on MMPI scales and indices, including ego-strength; positive change from the pre- to post-test battery as rated by clinicians working "blind"; decrease in anxiety scores and in a self-consciousness score; a higher level on Process Scales designed to measure process in therapy; and positive change in counselor's ratings.

Clients in relationships characterized by a low level of these attitudinal conditions show significantly less positive change on these same indices.

In studies of clinic clients the correlation between the client's perception of the conditions offered early in the relationship and the degree of change at the conclusion of the interviews is somewhat higher than that between the counselor's perception of the conditions offered and the degree of change. The client's perception is, in other words, the better predictor of change.

This finding does not hold for the schizophrenic client, whose inner disturbance makes it difficult for him accurately to perceive the conditions offered by the therapist. With our schizophrenics, the rating of the conditions made by unbiased raters is the best predictor of change.

An unexpected finding with the schizophrenic clients is that low conditions in the relationship are associated with *negative* change in several respects. The clients not only fail to show constructive change but become worse in the judgment of clinicians rating their pre- and post-test batteries; show an increase in anxiety; are worse off than their matched no-therapy controls. Whether this finding holds for clinic clients who come for help has not yet been determined.

A finding which seems to lend validity to the studies is that, as might be expected, more experienced counselors, when compared with inexperienced counselors, offer a higher level of these conditions, and are more successful in communicating these to their clients. Thus they are perceived as offering higher conditions, and their clients show more change over the course of the interviews.

IMPLICATIONS

What are some of the implications of these hypotheses and of these findings for the field of counseling psychology and guidance? I would like to mention four which occur to me.

In the first place, these studies indicate that perhaps it is possible to study cause and effect in counseling and psychotherapy. They are actually, so far as I know, the first studies to endeavor to isolate and measure the primary change-producing influences in counseling. Whether they are still further confirmed by later research, or whether they are contradicted or modified by future studies, they represent pioneering investigations of the question, "What really makes the difference in counseling and psychotherapy?" And the answer they give is that it is the attitudes provided by the counselor, the psychological climate largely created by him, which *really* makes the difference, which really induces change.

There is another highly practical significance to these studies. They indicate quite clearly that, by assessing a relationship early in its existence, we can to some degree predict the probability of its being a relationship which makes for growth. It seems to be quite within the range of possibility that in the not too distant future we will acquire an increasingly accurate knowledge of the elements which make for constructive psychological development, just as we have in the realm of nutrition acquired an increasingly accurate knowledge of the elements which promote physical growth. As this knowledge accumulates, and as our instruments grow sharper, then there is the exciting possibility that we may be able, relatively early in the game, to predict whether a given relationship will actually promote or inhibit individual psychological growth and development, just as we can assess the diet of a child and predict the extent to which this diet will promote or inhibit physical growth.

In this connection the disturbing finding that an inadequate interpersonal relationship can have a negative effect on personal development, at least in the case of highly disturbed individuals, makes such early assessment of a relationship an even more challenging possibility and responsibility.

Another significant meaning for the counseling field is that we now have the beginnings of a theory, and some empirical facts supporting the theory, as to the specific elements in an interpersonal relationship which facilitate positive change. Thus we can now say with some assurance and factual backing that a relationship characterized by a high degree of congruence or genuineness in the counselor, by sensitive and accurate empathy on the part of the counselor, by a high degree of regard, respect and liking for the client by the counselor, and by an absence of conditionality in this regard, will have a high probability of being an effective, growth-promoting relationship. This statement holds, whether we are speaking of maladjusted individuals who come of their own initiative seeking help, or whether we are speaking of chronically schizophrenic persons, with no conscious desire for help. This statement also holds whether these attitudinal elements are rated by impartial observers who listen to samples of the recorded interviews, or whether they are measured in terms of the counselor's perception of the qualities he has offered in the relationship, or whether they are measured by the client's perception of the relationship, at least in the case of the nonhospitalized client. To me it seems to be quite a forward stride to be able to make statements such as these in an area as complex and subtle as the field of helping relationships.

Finally, these studies would, if confirmed by further work, have significant implications for the training of counselors and therapists. To the extent that the counselor is seen as being involved in interpersonal relationships, and to the extent that the goal of those relationships is to promote healthy development, then certain conclusions would seem to follow. It would mean that we would endeavor to select individuals for such training who already possess, in their ordinary relationships with other people, a high degree of the qualities I have described. We would want people who were warm, spontaneous, real, understanding, and non-judgmental. We would also endeavor so to plan the educational program for these individuals that they would come increasingly to *experience* empathy and liking for others, and that they would find it increasingly easier to be themselves, to be real. By feeling understood and accepted in their training experiences, by being in contact with genuineness and absence of facade in their instructors, they would grow into more and more competent counselors. There would be as much focus in such training on the interpersonal experience as on the intellectual learning. It would be recognized that no amount of knowledge of tests and measures, or of counseling theories, or of diagnostic procedures could make the trainee more effective in his personal encounter with his clients. There would be a heavy stress upon the actual experience of working with clients, and the thoughtful and self-critical assessment of the relationships formed.

When I ask myself whether the training programs I know, in guidance, in clinical psychology, in psychiatry, approach this goal, I come up with a strong negative. It seems to me that most of our professional training programs make it *more* difficult for the individual to be himself, and more likely that he will play a professional role. Often he becomes so burdened with theoretical and diagnostic baggage that he becomes *less* able to understand the inner world of another person as it seems to that person. Also, as his professional training continues, it all too often occurs that his initial warm liking for other persons is submerged in a sea of diagnostic and psycho-dynamic evaluation.

Thus to take the findings of these studies seriously would mean some sharp changes in the very nature of professional training, as well as in its curriculum.

Conclusion

Let me conclude with a series of statements which for me follow logically one upon the other.

The purpose of most of the helping professions, including guidance counseling, is to enhance the personal development, the psychological growth toward a socialized maturity, of its clients.

The effectiveness of any member of the profession is most adequately measured in terms of the degree to which, in his work with his clients, he achieves this goal.

Our knowledge of the elements which bring about constructive change in personal growth is in its infant stages.

Such factual knowledge as we currently possess indicates that a primary change-producing influence is the degree to which the client experiences certain qualities in his relationship with his counselor.

In a variety of clients—normal, maladjusted, and psychotic—with many different counselors and therapists, and studying the relationship from the vantage point of the client, the therapist, or the uninvolved observer, certain qualities in the relationship are quite uniformly found to be associated with personal growth and change.

These elements are not constituted of technical knowledge or ideological sophistication. They are personal human qualities—something the counselor *experiences*, not something he *knows*. Constructive personal growth is associated with the counselor's realness, with his genuine and unconditional liking for his client, with his sensitive understanding of his client's private world, and with his ability to communicate these qualities in himself to his client.

These findings have some far-reaching implications for the theory and practice of guidance counseling and psychotherapy, and for the training of workers in these fields.

References

1. Barrett-Lennard, G. T. Dimensions of therapist response as causal factors in therapeutic change. *Psychol. Monogr*, 1963, 76. (Ms. No. 43)

2. Gendlin, E. T. Experiencing: A variable in the process of therapeutic change. *Am. Jour. Psychother.* 15, 1961, 233-245.
3. Halkides, G. An experimental study of four conditions necessary for therapeutic change. Unpublished doctoral dissertation, University of Chicago, 1958.
4. Rogers, C. R. The necessary and sufficient conditions of therapeutic personality change. *Jour. Cons. Psych., 21*, 1957, 95-103.
5. ——. A theory of therapy, personality, and interpersonal relationships as developed in the client-centered framework. In S. Koch (ed.) *Psychology: A Study of a Science, Vol. III.* New York: McGraw-Hill, 1959, 184-256.
6. Wisconsin Psychiatric Institute: Research Reports (unpublished)
    a. Spotts, J. E. The perception of positive regard by relatively successful and relatively unsuccessful clients.
    b. Truax, C. B. Comparison between high conditions therapy, low conditions therapy, and control conditions in the outcome measure of change in anxiety levels.
    c. ——. Constructive personality change in schizophrenic patients receiving high-conditions therapy, low-conditions therapy, and no-therapy.
    d. ——. Effects of therapists and effects of patients upon the amount of accurate empathy occurring in the psychotherapeutic interaction.
    e. ——. Effects of therapists and effects of patients upon the level of problem expression and experiencing occurring in the therapeutic interaction.
    f. ——. The relationship between the patient's perception of the level of therapeutic conditions offered in psychotherapy and constructive personality change.
    g. ——, Liccione, J., and Rosenberg, M. Psychological test evaluations of personality change in high conditions therapy, low conditions therapy, and control patients.
    h. van der Veen, F. The effects of the therapist and the patient on each other's therapeutic behavior early in therapy: A study of the beginning interviews of three patients with each of five therapists.
    i. ——. Perceived therapist conditions and degree of disturbance: A comparison of conditions perceived by hospitalized schizophrenic patients and counseling center clients.
    j. Wargo, D. G. The Barron Ego Strength and LH4 Scales as predictors and indicators of change in psychotherapy.

Three Processes in the Child's Acquisition of Syntax

ROGER BROWN
URSULA BELLUGI

In this pathbreaking study, Roger Brown and Ursula Bellugi identify three processes underlying children's acquisition of syntax. The authors observe that children acquiring language frequently imitate and then reduce parents' speech into telegraphic utterances, preserving both sentence order and major content words; while parents often expand these utterances to adhere more closely to the grammatical regularities of adult speech. Noting the complementary and cyclic nature of these strategies, Brown and Bellugi suggest that the pattern of imitation, reduction, and expansion may lead children to induce the latent structure of their language. As one alternative to this hypothesis, the authors also suggest that children's innate ability to formulate hypotheses about the rules underlying language may overshadow the importance of environmental or parental interactions.

Some time in the second six months of life most children say a first intelligible word. A few months later most children are saying many words and some children go about the house all day long naming things (*table, doggie, ball,* etc.) and actions (*play, see, drop,* etc.) and an occasional quality (*blue, broke, bad,* etc.). At about eighteen months children are likely to begin constructing two-word utterances; such a one, for instance, as *Push car.*

A construction such as *Push car* is not just two single-word utterances spoken in a certain order. As single word utterances (they are sometimes called holophrases) both *push* and *car* would have primary stresses and terminal intonation contours. When they are two words programmed as a single utterance the primary stress would fall on *car* and so would the highest level of pitch. *Push* would be subordinated to *car* by a lesser stress and a lower pitch;

This investigation was supported in whole by Public Health Service Research Grant MH7088 from the National Institute of Mental Health.

Harvard Educational Review Vol. 34 No. 2 Spring 1964, 133–151 the unity of the whole would appear in the absence of a terminal contour between words and the presence of such a contour at the end of the full sequence.

By the age of thirty-six months some children are so advanced in the construction process as to produce all of the major varieties of English simple sentences up to a length of ten or eleven words. For several years we have been studying the development of English syntax, of the sentence-constructing process, in children between eighteen and thirty-six months of age. Most recently we have made a longitudinal study of a boy and girl whom we shall call Adam and Eve. We began work with Adam and Eve in October of 1962 when Adam was twenty-seven months old and Eve eighteen months old. The two children were selected from some thirty whom we considered. They were selected primarily because their speech was exceptionally intelligible and because they talked a lot. We wanted to make it as easy as possible to transcribe accurately large quantities of child speech. Adam and Eve are the children of highly-educated parents; the fathers were graduate students at Harvard and the mothers are both college graduates. Both Adam and Eve were single children when we began the study. These facts must be remembered in generalizing the outcomes of the research.

While Adam is nine months older than Eve, his speech was only a little more advanced in October of 1962. The best single index of the level of speech development is the average length of utterance and in October, 1962, Adam's average was 1.84 morphemes and Eve's was 1.40 morphemes. The two children stayed fairly close together in the year that followed; in the records for the thirty-eighth week Adam's average was 3.55 and Eve's, 3.27. The processes we shall describe appeared in both children.

Every second week we visited each child for at least two hours and made a tape recording of everything said by the child as well as of everything said to the child. The mother was always present and most of the speech to the child is hers. Both mother and child became very accustomed to our presence and learned to continue their usual routine with us as the observers.

One of us always made a written transcription, on the scene, of the speech of mother and child with notes about important actions and objects of attention. From this transcription and the tape a final transcription was made and these transcriptions constitute the primary data of the study. For many purposes we require a "distributional analysis" of the speech of the child. To this end the child's utterances in a given transcription were cross-classified and relisted under such headings as: "*A* + noun"; "Noun + verb"; "Verbs in the past"; "Utterances containing the pronoun *it*," etc. The categorized utterances expose the syntactic regularities of the child's speech.

Each week we met as a research seminar, with students of the psychology of language,[1] to discuss the state of the construction process in one of the two children as of that date. In these discussions small experiments were often suggested, experiments that had to be done within a few days if they were to be informative. At one time, for instance, we were uncertain whether Adam understood the semantic difference between putting a noun in subject position and putting it in object position. Consequently one of us paid an extra visit to Adam equipped with some toys. "Adam," we said, "show us the duck pushing the boat." And, when he had done so: "Now show us the boat pushing the duck."

Another week we noticed that Adam would sometimes pluralize nouns when they should have been pluralized and sometimes would not. We wondered if he could make grammatical judgments about the plural, if he could distinguish a correct form from an incorrect form. "Adam," we asked, "which is right, 'two shoes' or 'two shoe'?" His answer on that occasion, produced with explosive enthusiasm, was "Pop goes the weasel!" The two-year-old child does not make a perfectly docile experimental subject.

The dialogue between mother and child does not read like a transcribed dialogue between two adults. Table 1 offers a sample section from an early

TABLE 1

A Section from Adam's First Record

Adam	Mother
See truck, Mommy.	
See truck.	
	Did you see the truck?
No I see truck.	
	No, you didn't see it?
	There goes one.
There go one.	
	Yes, there goes one.
See a truck.	
See truck, Mommy.	
See truck.	
Truck.	
Put truck, Mommy.	
	Put the truck where?
Put truck window.	
	I think that one's too large to go in the window.

[1] We are grateful for intellectual stimulation and lighthearted companionship to Dr. Jean Berko Gleason, Mr. Samuel Anderson, Mr. Colin Fraser, Dr. David McNeill, and Dr. Daniel Slobin.

transcribed record. It has some interesting properties. The conversation is, in the first place, very much in the here and now. From the child there is no speech of the sort that Bloomfield called "displaced," speech about other times and other places. Adam's utterances in the early months were largely a coding of contemporaneous events and impulses. The mother's speech differs from the speech that adults use to one another in many ways. Her sentences are short and simple; for the most part they are the kinds of sentences that Adam will produce a year later.

Perhaps because they are short, the sentences of the mother are perfectly grammatical. The sentences adults use to one another, perhaps because they are longer and more complex, are very often not grammatical, not well formed. Here for instance is a rather representative example produced at a conference of psychologists and linguists: "As far as I know, no one yet has done the in a way obvious now and interesting problem of doing a in a sense a structural frequency study of the alternative syntactical in a given language, say, like English, the alternative possible structures, and how what their hierarchical probability of occurrence structure is."[2] It seems unlikely that a child could learn the patterns of English syntax from such speech. His introduction to English ordinarily comes in the form of a simplified, repetitive, and idealized dialect. It may be that such an introduction is necessary for the acquisition of syntax to be possible but we do not know that.

In the course of the brief interchange of Table 1 Adam imitates his mother in saying: "There go one" immediately after she says "There goes one." The imitation is not perfect; Adam omits the inflection on the verb. His imitation is a reduction in that it omits something from the original. This kind of imitation with reduction is extremely common in the records of Adam and Eve and it is the first process we shall discuss.

IMITATION AND REDUCTION

Table 2 presents some model sentences spoken by the mothers and the imitations produced by Adam and Eve. These were selected from hundreds in the records in order to illustrate some general propositions. The first thing to notice is that the imitations preserve the word order of the model sentences. To be sure, words in the model are often missing from the imitation but the words preserved are in the order of the original. This is a fact that is so familiar and somehow reasonable that we did not at once recognize it as an empirical outcome rather than as a natural necessity. But of course it is not a necessity, the outcome could have been otherwise. For example, words could

---

[2] H. Maclay and C. E. Osgood, "Hesitation phenomena in spontaneous English speech," *Word*, XV (1959), 19-44.

TABLE 2

Some Imitations Produced by Adam and Eve

Model Utterance	Child's Imitation
Tank car	*Tank car*
Wait a minute	*Wait a minute*
Daddy's brief case	*Daddy brief case*
Fraser will be unhappy	*Fraser unhappy*
He's going out	*He go out*
That's an old time train	*Old time train*
It's not the same dog as Pepper	*Dog Pepper*
No, you can't write on Mr. Cromer's shoe	*Write Cromer shoe*

have been said back in the reverse of their original order, the most recent first. The preservation of order suggests that the model sentence is processed by the child as a total construction rather than as a list of words.

In English the order of words in a sentence is an important grammatical signal. Order is used to distinguish among subject, direct object, and indirect object and it is one of the marks of imperative and interrogative constructions. The fact that the child's first sentences preserve the word order of their models partially accounts for the ability of an adult to "understand" these sentences and so to feel that he is in communication with the child. It is conceivable that the child "intends" the meanings coded by his word orders and that, when he preserves the order of an adult sentence, he does so because he wants to say what the order says. It is also possible that he preserves word order just because his brain works that way and that he has no comprehension of the semantic contrasts involved. In some languages word order is not an important grammatical signal. In Latin, for instance, "Agricola amat puellam" has the same meaning as "Puellam amat agricola" and subject-object relations are signalled by case endings. We would be interested to know whether children who are exposed to languages that do not utilize word order as a major syntactic signal, preserve order as reliably as do children exposed to English.

The second thing to notice in Table 2 is the fact that when the models increase in length there is not a corresponding increase in the imitation. The imitations stay in the range of two to four morphemes which was the range characteristic of the children at this time. The children were operating under some constraint of length or span. This is not a limitation of vocabulary; the children knew hundreds of words. Neither is it a constraint of immediate memory. We infer this from the fact that the average length of utterances produced spontaneously, where immediate memory is not involved, is about the same as the average length of utterances produced as immediate imitations. The constraint is a limitation on the length of utterance the children are able to program or plan.[3] This kind of narrow span limitation in children is characteristic of most or all of their intellectual operations. The limitation grows less restrictive with age as a consequence, probably, of both neurological growth and of practice, but of course it is never lifted altogether.

A constraint on length compels the imitating child to omit some words or morphemes from the mother's longer sentences. Which forms are retained and which omitted? The selection is not random but highly systematic. Forms retained in the examples of Table 2 include: *Daddy, Fraser, Pepper,* and *Cromer; tank car, minute, briefcase, train, dog,* and *shoe; wait, go,* and *write; unhappy* and *old time.* For the most part they are nouns, verbs, and adjectives, though there are exceptions, as witness the initial pronoun *He* and the preposition *out* and the indefinite article *a.* Forms omitted in the samples of Table 2 include: the possessive inflection *-s,* the modal auxiliary *will,* the contraction of the auxiliary verb *is,* the progressive inflection *-ing,* the preposition *on,* the articles *the* and *an,* and the modal auxiliary *can.* It is possible to make a general characterization of the forms likely to be retained that distinguishes them as a total class from the forms likely to be omitted.

Forms likely to be retained are nouns and verbs and, less often, adjectives, and these are the three large and "open" parts-of-speech in English. The number of forms in any one of these parts-of-speech is extremely large and always growing. Words belonging to these classes are sometimes called "contentives" because they have semantic content. Forms likely to be omitted are inflections, auxiliary verbs, articles, prepositions, and conjunctions. These forms belong to syntactic classes that are small and closed. Any one class has few members and new members are not readily added. The omitted forms are the ones that linguists sometimes call "functors," their grammatical *functions* being more obvious than their semantic content.

Why should young children omit functors and retain contentives? There is more than one plausible answer. Nouns, verbs, and adjectives are words that make reference. One can conceive of teaching the meanings of these words by speaking them, one at a time, and pointing at things or actions or qualities. And of course parents do exactly that. These are the kinds of words that children have been encouraged to practice speaking one at a time. The child arrives at the age of sentence construction with a stock of well-practiced nouns, verbs, and adjectives. Is it not likely then that this prior practice causes him to retain the contentives from model sentences too long to be reproduced in full, that the child imitates those forms in the speech he hears which are

[3] Additional evidence of the constraint on sentence length may be found in R. Brown and C. Fraser. "The acquisition of syntax," C. N. Cofer and Barbara Musgrave, eds., *Verbal Behavior and Learning* (New York: McGraw Hill, 1963).

already well developed in him as individual habits? There is probably some truth in this explanation but it is not the only determinant since children will often select for retention contentives that are relatively unfamiliar to them.

We adults sometimes operate under a constraint on length and the curious fact is that the English we produce in these circumstances bears a formal resemblance to the English produced by two-year-old children. When words cost money there is a premium on brevity or to put it otherwise, a constraint on length. The result is "telegraphic" English and telegraphic English is an English of nouns, verbs, and adjectives. One does not send a cable reading: "My car has broken down and I have lost my wallet; send money to me at the American Express in Paris" but rather "Car broken down; wallet lost; send money American Express Paris." The telegram omits: *my, has, and, I, have, my, to, me, at, the, in*. All of these are functors. We make the same kind of telegraphic reduction when time or fatigue constrains us to be brief, as witness any set of notes taken at a fast-moving lecture.

A telegraphic transformation of English generally communicates very well. It does so because it retains the high-information words and drops the low-information words. We are here using "information" in the sense of the mathematical theory of communication. The information carried by a word is inversely related to the chances of guessing it from context. From a given string of content words, missing functors can often be guessed but the message "my has and I have my to me at the in" will not serve to get money to Paris. Perhaps children are able to make a communication analysis of adult speech and so adapt in an optimal way to their limitation of span. There is, however, another way in which the adaptive outcome might be achieved.

If you say aloud the model sentences of Table 2 you will find that you place the heavier stresses, the primary and secondary stresses in the sentences, on contentives rather than on functors. In fact the heavier stresses fall, for the most part, on the words the child retains. We first realized that this was the case when we found that in transcribing tapes, the words of the mother that we could hear most clearly were usually the words that the child reproduced. We had trouble hearing the weakly stressed functors and, of course, the child usually failed to reproduce them. Differential stress may then be the cause of the child's differential retention. The outcome is a maximally informative reduction but the cause of this outcome need not be the making of an information analysis. The outcome may be an incidental consequence of the fact that English is a well-designed language that places its heavier stresses where they are needed, on contentives that cannot easily be guessed from context.

We are fairly sure that differential stress is one of the determinants of the child's telegraphic productions. For one thing, stress will also account for the way in which children reproduce polysyllabic words when the total is too much for them. Adam, for instance, gave us *'pression* for *expression* and Eve gave us *'raff* for *giraffe*; the more heavily-stressed syllables were the ones retained. In addition we have tried the effect of placing heavy stresses on functors which do not ordinarily receive such stresses. To Adam we said: "You say what I say" and then, speaking in a normal way at first: "The doggie will bite." Adam gave back: "Doggie bite." Then we stressed the auxiliary: "The doggie *will* bite" and, after a few trials, Adam made attempts at reproducing that auxiliary. A science fiction experiment comes to mind. If there were parents who stressed functors rather than contentives would they have children whose speech was a kind of "reciprocal telegraphic" made up of articles, prepositions, conjunctions, auxiliaries, and the like? Such children would be out of touch with the community as real children are not.

It may be that all the factors we have mentioned play some part in determining the child's selective imitations; the reference-making function of contentives, the fact that they are practiced as single words, the fact that they cannot be guessed from context, and the heavy stresses they receive. There are also other possible factors: for example, the left-to-right, earlier-to-later position of words in a sentence, but these make too long a story to tell here.[4] Whatever the causes, the first utterances produced as imitations of adult sentences are highly systematic reductions of their models. Furthermore, the telegraphic properties of these imitations appear also in the child's spontaneously produced utterances. When his speech is not modeled on an immediately prior adult sentence, it observes the same limitation on length and the same predilection for contentives as when it is modeled on an immediately prior sentence.

IMITATION WITH EXPANSION

In the course of the brief conversation set down in Table 1, Adam's mother at one point imitates Adam. The boy says: "There go one" and mother responds: "Yes, there goes one." She does not exactly reproduce the model sentence of the child but instead adds something to it or expands it. What she adds is a functor, the inflection for third-person on the verb, the very form that Adam had omitted when he imitated his mother.

One of the first things we noticed when we began to study child speech several years ago was the frequency with which adults imitated children. Indeed they seemed to imitate more often than did the children themselves. We later came to realize that adult imitations are seldom exact reproductions; they are usually expansions. The mothers of Adam and Eve responded to the

[4] Brown and Fraser, *ibid.*

123

speech of their children with expansions about thirty per cent of the time. We did it ourselves when we talked with the children. Indeed we found it very difficult to withhold expansions. A reduced or incomplete English sentence seems to constrain the English-speaking adult to expand it into the nearest properly formed complete sentence. Table 3 lists a few sample expansions from the hundreds in the records.

The first thing worthy of attention in the expansions of Table 3 is the fact that the words spoken by the mother preserve the order of the words in the child's sentences. To be sure, words and inflections are added but they are fitted in—before, and after and between the words the child used; they are not generally permitted to disturb the order of the child's words. It is as if these latter were taken as constants by the mother, constants to which some sentence had to be fitted. She acts as if she were assuming that the child means everything he says, all the words and also their order, but as if he might also mean more than he says. From the mother's point of view an expansion is a kind of communication check; it says in effect: "Is this what you mean?"

The second thing to notice about Table 3 is the character of the forms added to the child's utterances. They include the auxiliaries *is* and *will;* the prepositions *in, on, to,* and *up;* the verb forms *is, have, had,* and *having;* the articles *a* and *the;* the pronouns *her, he,* and *it.* For the most part, the words added are functors, and functors are of course the words that the child omits in his reductions.

The interaction between mother and child is, much of the time, a cycle of reductions and expansions. There are two transformations involved. The reduction transformation has an almost completely specifiable and so mechanical character. One could program a machine to do it with the following instructions: "Retain contentives (or stressed forms) in the order given up to some limit of length." The expansion accomplished by Adam's mother when she added the third-person inflection to the verb and said "There goes one"

TABLE 3

Expansions of Child Speech Produced by Mothers

Child	Mother
Baby highchair	*Baby is in the highchair*
Mommy eggnog	*Mommy had her eggnog*
Eve lunch	*Eve is having lunch*
Mommy sandwich	*Mommy'll have a sandwich*
Sat wall	*He sat on the wall*
Throw Daddy	*Throw it to Daddy*
Pick glove	*Pick the glove up*

is also a completely specifiable transformation. The instructions would read: "Retain the forms given in the order given and supply obligatory grammatical forms." To be sure, this mother-machine would have to be supplied with the obligatory rules of English grammar but that could be done. However, the sentence "There goes one" is atypical in that it only adds a compulsory and redundant inflection. The expansions of Table 3 all add forms that are not grammatically compulsory or redundant and these expansions cannot be mechanically generated by grammatical rules alone.

In Table 3 the topmost four utterances produced by the child are all of the same grammatical type; all four consist of a proper noun followed by a common noun. However, the four are expanded in quite different ways. In particular the form of the verb changes: it is in the first case in the simple present tense; in the second case the simple past; in the third case the present progressive; in the last case the simple future. All of these are perfectly grammatical but they are different. The second set of child utterances is formally uniform in that each one consists of a verb followed by a noun. The expansions are again all grammatical but quite unlike, especially with regard to the preposition supplied. In general, then, there are radical changes in the mother's expansions when there are no changes in the formal character of the utterances expanded. It follows that the expansions cannot be produced simply by making grammatically compulsory additions to the child's utterances.

How does a mother decide on the correct expansion of one of her child's utterances? Consider the utterance "Eve lunch." So far as grammar is concerned this utterance could be appropriately expanded in any of a number of ways: "Eve is having lunch"; "Eve had lunch"; "Eve will have lunch"; Eve's lunch," etc. On the occasion when Eve produced the utterance, however, one expansion seemed more appropriate than any other. It was then the noon hour, Eve was sitting at the table with a plate of food before her, and her spoon and fingers were busy. In these circumstances "Eve lunch" had to mean "Eve is having lunch." A little later when the plate had been stacked in the sink and Eve was getting down from her chair the utterance "Eve lunch" would have suggested the expansion "Eve has had her lunch." Most expansions are not only responsive to the child's words but also to the circumstances attending their utterance.

What kind of instructions will generate the mother's expansions? The following are approximately correct: "Retain the words given in the order given and add those functors that will result in a well-formed simple sentence that is appropriate to the circumstances." These are not instructions that any machine could follow. A machine could act on the instructions only if it were provided with detailed specifications for judging appropriateness and no such specifications can, at present, be written. They exist, however, in implicit form in the brains of mothers and in the brains of all English-speaking adults and so judgments of appropriateness can be made by such adults.

The expansion encodes aspects of reality that are not coded by the child's telegraphic utterance. Functors have meaning but it is meaning that accrues to them in context rather than in isolation. The meanings that are added by functors seem to be nothing less than the basic terms in which we construe reality: the time of an action, whether it is ongoing or completed, whether it is presently relevant or not; the concept of possession and such relational concepts as are coded by *in, on, up, down,* and the like; the difference between a particular instance of a class ("Has anybody seen *the* paper?") and any instance of a class ("Has anybody seen *a* paper?") ; the difference between extended substances given shape and size by an "accidental" container (*sand, water, syrup,* etc.) and countable "things" having a characteristic fixed shape and size (*a cup, a man, a tree,* etc.) . It seems to us that a mother in expanding speech may be teaching more than grammar; she may be teaching something like a world-view.

As yet it has not been demonstrated that expansions are *necessary* for learning either grammar or a construction of reality. It has not even been demonstrated that expansions contribute to such learning. All we know is that some parents do expand and their children do learn. It is perfectly possible, however, that children can and do learn simply from hearing their parents or others make well-formed sentences in connection with various nonverbal circumstances. It may not be necessary or even helpful for these sentences to be expansions of utterances of the child. Only experiments contrasting expansion training with simple exposure to English will settle the matter. We hope to do such experiments.

There are, of course, reasons for expecting the expansion transformation to be an effective tutorial technique. By adding something to the words the child has just produced one confirms his response insofar as it is appropriate. In addition one takes him somewhat beyond that response but not greatly beyond it. One encodes additional meanings at a moment when he is most likely to be attending to the cues that can teach that meaning.

INDUCTION OF THE LATENT STRUCTURE

Adam, in the course of the conversation with his mother set down in Table 1, produced one utterance for which no adult is likely ever to have provided an exact model: "No I see truck." His mother elects to expand it as "No, you didn't see it" and this expansion suggests that the child might have created the utterance by reducing an adult model containing the form *didn't*. However, the mother's expansion in this case does some violence to Adam's original version. He did not say *no* as his mother said it, with primary stress and final contour; Adam's *no* had secondary stress and no final contour. It is not easy to imagine an adult model for this utterance. It seems more likely that the utterance was created by Adam as part of a continuing effort to discover the general rules for constructing English negatives.

In Table 4 we have listed some utterances produced by Adam or Eve for which it is difficult to imagine any adult model. It is unlikely that any adult said any of these to Adam or Eve since they are very simple utterances and yet definitely ungrammatical. In addition it is difficult, by adding functors alone, to build any of them up to simple grammatical sentences. Consequently it does not seem likely that these utterances are reductions of adult originals. It is more likely that they are mistakes which externalize the child's search for the regularities of English syntax.

We have long realized that the occurrence of certain kinds of errors on the level of morphology (or word construction) reveals the child's effort to induce regularities from speech. So long as a child speaks correctly, or at any rate so long as he speaks as correctly as the adults he hears, there is no way to tell whether he is simply repeating what he has heard or whether he is actually constructing. However, when he says something like "I digged a hole" we can often be sure that he is constructing. We can be sure because it is unlikely that he would have heard *digged* from anyone and because we can see how, in processing words he has heard, he might have come by *digged*. It looks like an overgeneralization of the regular past inflection. The inductive operations of the child's mind are externalized in such a creation. Overgeneralizations on the level of syntax (or sentence construction) are more difficult to identify because there are so many ways of adding functors so as to build up conceivable models. But this is difficult to do for the examples of Table 4 and for several hundred other utterances in our records.

The processes of imitation and expansion are not sufficient to account for the degree of linguistic competence that children regularly acquire. These processes alone cannot teach more than the sum total of sentences that speak-

TABLE 4

Utterances Not Likely to be Imitations

My Cromer suitcase	You naughty are
Two foot	Why it can't turn off?
A bags	Put on it
A scissor	Cowboy did fighting me
A this truck	Put a gas in

ers of English have either modeled for a child to imitate or built up from a child's reductions. However, a child's linguistic competence extends far beyond this sum total of sentences. All children are able to understand and construct sentences they have never heard but which are nevertheless well-formed, well-formed in terms of general rules that are implicit in the sentences the child has heard. Somehow, then, every child processes the speech to which he is exposed so as to induce from it a latent structure. This latent rule structure is so general that a child can spin out its implications all his life long. It is both semantic and syntactic. The discovery of latent structure is the greatest of the processes involved in language acquisition and the most difficult to understand. We will provide an example of how the analysis can proceed by discussing the evolution in child speech of noun phrases.

A noun phrase in adult English includes a noun but also more than a noun. One variety consists of a noun with assorted modifiers: *The girl*; *The pretty girl*; *That pretty girl*; *My girl*, etc. All of these are constructions which have the same syntactic privileges as do nouns alone. One can use a noun phrase in isolation to name or request something; one can use it in sentences, in subject position or in object position or in predicate nominative position. All of these are slots that nouns alone can also fill. A larger construction having the same syntactic privileges as its "head" word is called in linguistics an "endocentric" construction, and noun phrases are endocentric constructions.

For both Adam and Eve, in the early records, noun phrases usually occur as total independent utterances rather than as components of sentences. Table 5 presents an assortment of such utterances at Time 1. They consist in each

TABLE 5

Noun Phrases in Isolation
and Rule for Generating Noun Phrases at Time 1

A coat	More coffee
A celery*	More nut*
A Becky*	Two sock*
A hands*	Two shoes
The top	two tinker-toy*
My Mommy	Big boot
That Adam	Poor man
My stool	Little top
That knee	Dirty knee

$$NP \rightarrow M + N$$

M $\rightarrow$ *a, big, dirty, little, more, my, poor, that, the, two.*
N $\rightarrow$ *Adam, Becky, boot, coat, coffee, knee, man, Mommy, nut, sock, stool, tinker-toy, top,* and very many others.

* Ungrammatical for an adult.

case of some sort of modifier, just one, preceding a noun. The modifiers, or as they are sometimes called the "pivot" words, are a much smaller class than the noun class. Three students of child speech have independently discovered that this kind of construction is extremely common when children first begin to combine words. [5, 6, 7]

It is possible to generalize the cases of Table 5 into a simple implicit rule. The rule symbolized in Table 5 reads: "In order to form a noun phrase of this type, select first one word from the small class of modifiers and select, second, one word from the large class of nouns." This is a "generative" rule by which we mean it is a program that would actually serve to build constructions of the type in question. It is offered as a model of the mental mechanism by which Adam and Eve generated such utterances. Furthermore, judging from our work with other children and from the reports of Braine and of Miller and Ervin, the model describes a mechanism present in many children when their average utterance is approximately two morphemes long.

We have found that even in our earliest records the M + N construction is sometimes used as a component of larger constructions. For instance, Eve said: "Fix a Lassie" and "Turn the page" and "A horsie stuck" and Adam even said: "Adam wear a shirt." There are, at first, only a handful of these larger constructions but there are very many constructions in which single nouns occur in subject or in object position.

Let us look again at the utterances of Table 5 and the rule generalizing them. The class M does not correspond with any syntactic class of adult English. In the class M are articles, a possessive pronoun, a cardinal number, a demonstrative adjective or pronoun, a quantifier, and some descriptive adjectives—a mixed bag indeed. For adult English these words cannot belong to the same syntactic class because they have very different privileges of occurrence in sentences. For the children the words do seem to function as one class having the common privilege of occurrence before nouns.

If the initial words of the utterances in Table 5 are treated as one class M then many utterances are generated which an adult speaker would judge to be ungrammatical. Consider the indefinite article *a*. Adults use it only to modify common count nouns in the singular such as *coat, dog, cup,* etc. We would not say *a celery*, or *a cereal*, or *a dirt; celery, cereal,* and *dirt* are mass nouns. We would not say *a Becky* or *a Jimmy; Becky* and *Jimmy* are proper nouns. We would not say *a hands* or *a shoes; hands* and *shoes* are plural nouns. Adam and Eve, at first, did form ungrammatical combinations such as these.

[5] M. D. S. Braine, "The ontogeny of English phrase structure: the first phrase," *Language,* XXXIX (1963), 1-13.
[6] W. Miller and Susan Ervin, "The development of grammar in child language," Ursula Bellugi and R. Brown, eds., *The Acquisition of Language, Child Developm. Monogr.* (1964).
[7] Brown and Fraser, "The acquisition of syntax."

The numeral *two* we use only with count nouns in the plural. We would not say *two sock* since *sock* is singular, nor *two water* since *water* is a mass noun. The word *more* we use before count nouns in the plural (*more nuts*) or mass nouns in the singular (*more coffee*). Adam and Eve made a number of combinations involving *two* or *more* that we would not make.

Given the initial very undiscriminating use of words in the class M it follows that one dimension of development must be a progressive differentiation of privileges, which means the division of M into smaller classes. There must also be subdivision of the noun class (N) for the reason that the privileges of occurrence of various kinds of modifiers must be described in terms of such sub-varieties of N as the common noun and proper noun, the count noun and mass noun. There must eventually emerge a distinction between nouns singular and nouns plural since this distinction figures in the privileges of occurrence of the several sorts of modifiers.

Sixteen weeks after our first records from Adam and Eve (Time 2), the differentiation process had begun. By this time there were distributional reasons for separating out articles (*a, the*) from demonstrative pronouns (*this, that*) and both of these from the residual class of modifiers. Some of the evidence for this conclusion appears in Table 6. In general one syntactic class is distinguished from another when the members of one class have combinational privileges not enjoyed by the members of the other. Consider, for example, the reasons for distinguishing articles (Art) from modifiers in general (M). Both articles and modifiers appeared in front of nouns in two-word utterances. However, in three-word utterances that were made up from the total pool of words and that had a noun in final position, the privileges of *a* and *the* were

TABLE 6

Subdivision of the Modifier Class

A) PRIVILEGES PECULIAR TO ARTICLES

Obtained	Not Obtained
A blue flower	*Blue a flower*
A nice nap	*Nice a nap*
A your car	*Your a car*
A my pencil	*My a pencil*

B) PRIVILEGES PECULIAR TO DEMONSTRATIVE PRONOUNS

Obtained	Not Obtained
That my cup	*My that cup*
That a horse	*A that horse*
That a blue flower	*A that blue flower*
	Blue a that flower

---

different from the privileges of all other modifiers. The articles occurred in initial position followed by a member of class M other than an article. No other modifier occurred in this first position; notice the "Not obtained" examples of Table 6A. If the children had produced utterances like those (for example, *blue a flower, your a car*) there would have been no difference in the privileges of occurrence of articles and modifiers and therefore no reason to separate out articles.

The record of Adam is especially instructive. He created such notably ungrammatical combinations as "a your car" and "a my pencil." It is very unlikely that adults provided models for these. They argue strongly that Adam regarded all the words in the residual M class as syntactic equivalents and so generated these very odd utterances in which possessive pronouns appear where descriptive adjectives would be more acceptable.

Table 6 also presents some of the evidence for distinguishing demonstrative pronouns (Dem) from articles and modifiers. (Table 6B). The pronouns occurred first and ahead of articles in three-and-four-word utterances—a position that neither articles nor modifiers ever filled. The sentences with demonstrative pronouns are recognizable as reductions which omit the copular verb *is*. Such sentences are not noun phrases in adult English and ultimately they will not function as noun phrases in the speech of the children, but for the present they are not distinguishable distributionally from noun phrases.

Recall now the generative formula of Table 5 which constructs noun phrases by simply placing a modifier (M) before a noun (N). The differentiation of privileges illustrated in Table 6, and the syntactic classes this evidence motivates us to create, complicate the formula for generating noun phrases. In Table 7 we have written a single general formula for producing all noun phrases at Time 2 [NP $\rightarrow$ (Dem) + (Art) + (M) + N] and also the numerous more specific rules which are summarized by the general formula.

By the time of the thirteenth transcription, twenty-six weeks after we began our study, privileges of occurrence were much more finely differentiated

TABLE 7

Rules for Generating Noun Phrases at Time 2

$NP_1 \rightarrow Dem + Art + M + N$	$NP \rightarrow (Dem) + (Art) + (M) + N$
$NP_2 \rightarrow Art + M + N$	
$NP_3 \rightarrow Dem + M + N$	
$NP_4 \rightarrow Art + N$	( ) means class within
$NP_5 \rightarrow M + N$	parentheses is optional
$NP_6 \rightarrow Dem + N$	
$NP_7 \rightarrow Dem + Art + N$	

and syntactic classes were consequently more numerous. From the distributional evidence we judged that Adam had made five classes of his original class M: articles, descriptive adjectives, possessive pronouns, demonstrative pronouns, and a residual class of modifiers. The generative rules of Table 7 had become inadequate; there were no longer, for instance, any combinations like "A your car." Eve had the same set except that she used two residual classes of modifiers. In addition nouns had begun to subdivide for both children. The usage of proper nouns had become clearly distinct from the usage of count nouns. For Eve the evidence justified separating count nouns from mass nouns, but for Adam it still did not. Both children by this time were frequently pluralizing nouns but as yet their syntactic control of the singular-plural distinction was imperfect.

In summary, one major aspect of the development of general structure in child speech is a progressive differentiation in the usage of words and therefore a progressive differentiation of syntactic classes. At the same time, however, there is an integrative process at work. From the first, an occasional noun phrase occurred as a component of some larger construction. At first these noun phrases were just two words long and the range of positions in which they could occur was small. With time the noun phrases grew longer, were more frequently used, and were used in a greater range of positions. The noun phrase structure as a whole, in all the permissible combinations of modifiers and nouns, was assuming the combinational privileges enjoyed by nouns in isolation.

In Table 8 we have set down some of the sentence positions in which both nouns and noun phrases occurred in the speech of Adam and Eve. It is the close match between the positions of nouns alone and of nouns with modifiers in the speech of Adam and Eve that justifies us in calling the longer constructions noun phrases. These longer constructions are, as they should be, endocentric; the head word alone has the same syntactic privileges as the head word with its modifiers. The continuing failure to find in noun phrase positions whole constructions of the type "That a blue flower" signals the fact

TABLE 8

Some Privileges of the Noun Phrase

Noun Positions	Noun Phrase Positions
That (flower)	*That (a blue flower)*
Where (ball) go?	*Where (the puzzle) go?*
Adam write (penguin)	*Doggie eat (the breakfast)*
(Horsie) stop	*(A horsie) crying*
Put (hat) on	*Put (the red hat) on*

that these constructions are telegraphic versions of predicate nominative sentences omitting the verb form *is*. Examples of the kind of construction not obtained are: "That (that a blue flower)"; "Where (that a blue flower)?"

For adults the noun phrase is a subwhole of the sentence, what linguists call an "immediate constituent." The noun phrase has a kind of psychological unity. There are signs that the noun phrase was also an immediate constituent for Adam and Eve. Consider the sentence using the separable verb *put on*. The noun phrase in "Put the red hat on" is, as a whole, fitted in between the verb and the particle even as is the noun alone in "Put hat on." What is more, however, the location of pauses in the longer sentence, on several occasions, suggested the psychological organization: "Put . . . the red hat . . . on" rather than "Put the red . . . hat on" or "Put the . . . red hat on." In addition to this evidence the use of pronouns suggests that the noun phrase is a psychological unit.

The unity of noun phrases in adult English is evidenced, in the first place, by the syntactic equivalence between such phrases and nouns alone. It is evidenced, in the second place, by the fact that pronouns are able to substitute for total noun phrases. In our immediately preceding sentence the pronoun "It" stands for the rather involved construction from the first sentence of this paragraph: "The unity of noun phrases in adult English." The words called "pronouns" in English would more aptly be called "pro-noun-phrases" since it is the phrase rather than the noun which they usually replace. One does not replace "unity" with "it" and say "The *it* of noun phrases in adult English." In the speech of Adam and Eve, too, the pronoun came to function as a replacement for the noun phrase. Some of the clearer cases appear in Table 9.

Adam characteristically externalizes more of his learning than does Eve

TABLE 9

Pronouns Replacing Nouns or Noun Phrases and Pronouns Produced Together with Nouns or Noun Phrases

Noun Phrases Replaced by Pronouns	Pronouns and Noun Phrases in Same Utterances
Hit ball	*Mommy get it ladder*
Get it	*Mommy get it my ladder*
Ball go?	*Saw it ball*
Go get it	*Miss it garage*
Made it	*I miss it cowboy boot*
Made a ship	*I Adam drive that*
Fix a tricycle	*I Adam drive*
Fix it	*I Adam don't*

and his record is especially instructive in connection with the learning of pronouns. In his first eight records, the first sixteen weeks of the study, Adam quite often produced sentences containing both the pronoun and the noun or noun phrase that the pronoun should have replaced. One can here see the equivalence in the process of establishment. First the substitute is produced and then, as if in explication, the form or forms that will eventually be replaced by the substitute. Adam spoke out his pronoun antecedents as chronological consequents. This is additional evidence of the unity of the noun phrase since the noun phrases *my ladder* and *cowboy boot* are linked with *it* in Adam's speech in just the same way as the nouns *ladder* and *ball*.

We have described three processes involved in the child's acquisition of syntax. It is clear that the last of these, the induction of latent structure, is by far the most complex. It looks as if this last process will put a serious strain on any learning theory thus far conceived by psychology. The very intricate simultaneous differentiation and integration that constitutes the evolution of the noun phrase is more reminiscent of the biological development of an embryo than it is of the acquisition of a conditional reflex.

Philosophical Models of Teaching

ISRAEL SCHEFFLER

Israel Scheffler offers three philosophical models of teaching and suggests new criteria for assessing the purposes of education. Each model contributes an important but incomplete insight into the activity of teaching; together, they form a complementary whole. The input or impression model, associated with John Locke, views learning as the receiving and processing of information. The insight model, found in the writings of Plato and St. Augustine, holds that the teacher's words prompt the student to acquire new knowledge, to understand external reality in his or her own terms. Finally, the rule model, associated with Immanuel Kant, suggests that learning involves deliberation and judgment, and emphasizes the role of principles as well as cognition in guiding action.

INTRODUCTION

Teaching may be characterized as an activity aimed at the achievement of learning, and practiced in such manner as to respect the student's intellectual integrity and capacity for independent judgment. Such a characterization is important for at least two reasons: First, it brings out the intentional nature of teaching, the fact that teaching is a distinctive goal-oriented activity, rather than a distinctively patterned sequence of behavioral steps executed by the teacher. Secondly, it differentiates the activity of teaching from such other activities as propaganda, conditioning, suggestion, and indoctrination, which are aimed at modifying the person but strive at all costs to avoid a genuine engagement of his judgment on underlying issues.

This characterization of teaching, which I believe to be correct, fails, nevertheless, to answer certain critical questions of the teacher: What sort of learning shall I aim to achieve? In what does such learning consist? How shall I strive to achieve it? Such questions are, respectively, normative, epistemological, and empirical in import, and the answers that are provided for them give point and substance to the educational enterprise. Rather than trying to separate these questions, however, and deal with each abstractly and explicitly,

This paper was presented at Brown University as the Marshall Woods lecture on Education for 1964. Variant versions were delivered to the Harvard-Lexington Summer Program for 1964, and to the Boston University Philosophy Club.

Harvard Educational Review Vol. 35 No. 2 Spring 1965, 131-143

I should like, on the present occasion, to approach them indirectly and as a group, through a consideration of three influential models of teaching, which provide, or at any rate suggest, certain relevant answers. These models do not so much aim to *describe* teaching as to *orient* it, by weaving a coherent picture out of epistemological, psychological, and normative elements. Like all models, they simplify, but such simplification is a legitimate way of highlighting what are thought to be important features of the subject. The primary issue, in each case, is whether these features are indeed critically important, whether we should allow our educational thinking to be guided by a model which fastens upon them, or whether we should rather reject or revise the model in question. Although I shall mention some historical affiliations of each model, I make no pretense to historical accuracy. My main purpose is, rather, systematic or dialectical, that is, to outline and examine the three models and to see what, if anything, each has to offer us in our own quest for a satisfactory conception of teaching. I turn, then, first to what may be called the "impression model."

The Impression Model

The impression model is perhaps the simplest and most widespread of the three, picturing the mind essentially as sifting and storing the external impressions to which it is receptive. The desired end result of teaching is an accumulation in the learner of basic elements fed in from without, organized and processed in standard ways, but, in any event, not generated by the learner himself. In the empiricist variant of this model generally associated with John Locke, learning involves the input by experience of simple ideas of sensation and reflection, which are clustered, related, generalized, and retained by the mind. Blank at birth, the mind is thus formed by its particular experiences, which it keeps available for its future use. In Locke's words, (Bk. II, Ch. I, Sec. 2 of the *Essay Concerning Human Understanding*):

Let us then suppose the mind to be, as we say, white paper, void of all characters, without any ideas; how comes it to be furnished? Whence comes it by that vast store, which the busy and boundless fancy of man has painted on it with an almost endless variety? Whence has it all the materials of reason and knowledge? To this I answer, in one word, From experience; in that all our knowledge is founded, and from that it ultimately derives itself. Our observation, employed either about external sensible objects, or about the internal operations of our minds, perceived and reflected on by ourselves, is that which supplies our understandings with all the materials of thinking. These two are the fountains of knowledge, from whence all the ideas we have, or can naturally have, do spring.

Teaching, by implication, should concern itself with exercising the mental powers engaged in receiving and processing incoming ideas, more particularly powers of perception, discrimination, retention, combination, abstraction, and representation. But, more important, teaching needs to strive for the optimum selection and organization of this experiential input. For potentially, the teacher has enormous power; by controlling the input of sensory units, he can, to a large degree, shape the mind. As Dewey remarked,[1]

Locke's statements ... seemed to do justice to both mind and matter.... One of the two supplied the matter of knowledge and the object upon which the mind should work. The other supplied definite mental powers, which were few in number and which might be trained by specific exercises.

The process of learning in the child was taken as paralleling the growth of knowledge generally, for all knowledge is constructed out of elementary units of experience, which are grouped, related, and generalized. The teacher's object should thus be to provide data not only useful in themselves, but collectively rich enough to support the progressive growth of adult knowledge in the learner's mind.

The impression model, as I have sketched it, has certain obvious strong points. It sets forth the appeal to experience as a general tool of criticism to be employed in the examination of all claims and doctrines, and it demands that they square with it. Surely such a demand is legitimate, for knowledge does rest upon experience in some way or other. Further, the mind is, in a clear sense, as the impression model suggests, a function of its particular experiences, and it is capable of increased growth with experience. The richness and variety of the child's experiences are thus important considerations in the process of educational planning.

The impression model nevertheless suffers from fatal difficulties. The notions of absolutely simple ideas and of abstract mental powers improvable through exercise have been often and rightly criticized as mythological:[2] Simplicity is a relative, not an absolute, concept and reflects a particular way of analyzing experience; it is, in short, not given but made. And mental powers or faculties invariant with subject matter have, as everyone knows, been expunged from psychology on empirical as well as theoretical grounds. A more fundamental criticism, perhaps, is that the implicit conception of the growth of knowledge is false. Knowledge is not achieved through any standard set of operations for the processing of sensory particulars, however conceived. Knowledge is, first and foremost, embodied in language, and involves a conceptual apparatus not derivable from the sensory data but imposed upon

---

[1] John Dewey, *Democracy and Education*. New York: The Macmillan Company, 1916, p. 62.

[2] Dewey, *Ibid.*, "the supposed original faculties of observation, recollection, willing, thinking, etc., are purely mythological. There are no such ready-made powers waiting to be exercised and thereby trained."

them. Nor is such apparatus built into the human mind; it is, at least in good part a product of guesswork and invention, borne along by culture and by custom. Knowledge further involves *theory*, and theory is surely not simply a matter of generalizing the data, even assuming such data organized by a given conceptual apparatus. Theory is a creative and individualistic enterprise that goes beyond the data in distinctive ways, involving not only generalization, but postulation of entities, deployment of analogies, evaluation of relative simplicity, and, indeed, invention of new languages. Experience is relevant to knowledge through providing tests of our theories; it does not automatically generate these theories, even when processed by the human mind. That we have the theories we do is, therefore, a fact, not simply about the human mind, but about our history and our intellectual heritage.

In the process of learning, the child gets not only sense experiences but the language and theory of his heritage in complicated linkages with discriminable contexts. He is heir to the complex culture of belief built up out of innumerable creative acts of intellect of the past, and comprising a patterned view of the world. To give the child even the richest selection of sense data or particular facts alone would in no way guarantee his building up anything resembling what we think of as knowledge, much less his developing the ability to retrieve and apply such knowledge in new circumstances.

A *verbal* variant of the impression model of teaching naturally suggests itself, then, as having certain advantages over the *sensory* version we have just considered: What is to be impressed on the mind is not only sense experience but language and, moreover, accepted theory. We need to feed in not only sense data but the correlated verbal patterning of such data, that is, the *statements* about such data which we ourselves accept. The student's knowledge consists in his stored accumulation of these statements, which have application to new cases in the future. He is no longer, as before, assumed capable of generating our conceptual heritage by operating in certain standard ways on his sense data, for part of what *we* are required to feed into his mind is this very heritage itself.

This verbal variant, which has close affinities to contemporary behaviorism, does have certain advantages over its predecessor, but retains grave inadequacies still, as a model of teaching. To *store* all accepted theories is not the same as being able to *use* them properly in context. Nor, even if some practical correlation with sense data is achieved, does it imply an understanding of what is thus stored, nor an appreciation of the theoretical motivation and experimental evidence upon which it rests.

All versions of the impression model, finally, have this defect: They fail to make adequate room for radical *innovation* by the learner. We do not, after all, feed into the learner's mind all that we hope he will have as an end result of our teaching. Nor can we construe the critical surplus as generated in standard ways out of materials we do supply. We do not, indeed cannot, so construe insight, understanding, new applications of our theories, new theories, new achievements in scholarship, history, poetry, philosophy. There is a fundamental gap which teaching cannot bridge simply by expansion or reorganization of the curriculum input. This gap sets *theoretical* limits to the power and control of the teacher; moreover, it is where his control ends that his fondest hopes for education begin.

The Insight Model

The next model I shall consider, the "insight model," represents a radically different approach. Where the impression model supposes the teacher to be conveying ideas or bits of knowledge into the student's mental treasury, the insight model denies the very possibility of such conveyance. Knowledge, it insists, is a matter of vision, and vision cannot be dissected into elementary sensory or verbal units that can be conveyed from one person to another. It can, at most, be stimulated or prompted by what the teacher does, and if it indeed occurs, it goes beyond what is thus done. Vision defines and organizes particular experiences, and points up their significance. It is vision, or insight into meaning, which makes the crucial difference between simply storing and reproducing learned sentences, on the one hand, and understanding their basis and application, on the other.

The insight model is due to Plato, but I shall here consider the version of St. Augustine, in his dialogue, "The Teacher,"[3] for it bears precisely on the points we have dealt with. Augustine argues roughly as follows: The teacher is commonly thought to convey knowledge by his use of language. But knowledge, or rather *new* knowledge, is not conveyed simply by words sounding in the ear. Words are mere noises unless they signify realities present in some way to the mind. Hence a paradox: If the student already knows the realities to which the teacher's words refer, the teacher teaches him nothing new. Whereas, if the student does not know these realities, the teacher's words can have no meaning for him, and must be mere noises. Augustine concludes that language must have a function wholly distinct from that of the signification of realities; it is used to *prompt* people in certain ways. The teacher's words, in particular, prompt the student to search for realities not already known by him. Finding these realities, which are illuminated for him by internal

[3] *Ancient Christian Writers*, No. 9, St. Augustine, "The Teacher," edited by J. Quasten and J. C. Plumpe, translated and annotated by J. M. Colleran, Newman Press, Westminster, Md: 1950; relevant passages may also be found in Kingsley Price, *Education and Philosophical Thought*, Boston: Allyn and Bacon, Inc., 1962, pp. 145-159.

vision, he acquires new knowledge for himself, though indirectly as a result of the teacher's prompting activity. To *believe* something simply on the basis of authority or hearsay is indeed possible, on Augustine's view; to *know* it is not. Mere beliefs may, in his opinion, of course, be useful; they are not therefore knowledge. For knowledge, in short, requires the individual himself to have a grasp of the realities lying behind the words.

The insight model is strong where the impression model is weakest. While the latter, in its concern with the conservation of knowledge, fails to do justice to innovation, the former addresses itself from the start to the problem of *new* knowledge resulting from teaching. Where the latter stresses atomic manipulable bits at the expense of understanding, the former stresses primarily the acquisition of insight. Where the latter gives inordinate place to the feeding in of materials from the outside, the former stresses the importance of firsthand inspection of realities by the student, the necessity for the student to earn his knowledge by his own efforts.

I should argue, nevertheless, that the case offered by Augustine for the prompting theory is not, as it stands, satisfactory. If the student does not know the realities behind the teacher's words, these words are, presumably, mere noises and can serve only to prompt the student to inquire for himself. Yet if they *are* mere noises, how can they even serve to prompt? If they are not understood in any way by the student, how can they lead him to search for the appropriate realities which underlie them? Augustine, furthermore, allows that a person may believe, though not know, what he accepts on mere authority, without having confronted the relevant realities. Such a person might, presumably, pass from the state of belief to that of knowledge, as a result of prompting, under certain conditions. But what, we may ask, could have been the content of his initial belief if the formulation of it had been literally unintelligible to him? The prompting theory, it seems, will not do as a way of escaping Augustine's original paradox.

There is, however, an easier escape. For the paradox itself rests on a confusion of the meaning of *words* with that of *sentences*. Let me explain. Augustine holds that words acquire intelligibility only through acquaintance with reality. Now it may perhaps be initially objected that understanding a word does not always require acquaintance with its signified reality, for words may also acquire intelligibility through definition, lacking such direct acquaintance. But let us waive this objection and grant, for the sake of argument, that understanding a word *always* does require such acquaintance; it still does not follow that understanding a true sentence similarly requires acquaintance with the state of affairs which it represents. We understand new sentences all the time, on the basis of an understanding of their constituent words and of the grammar by which they are concatenated. Thus, given a sentence signifying some fact, it is simply not true that, unless the student already knows this fact, the sentence must be mere noise to him. For he can understand its meaning indirectly, by a synthesis of its parts, and be led thereafter to inquire whether it is, in reality, true or false.

If my argument is correct, then Augustine's paradox of teaching can be simply rejected, on the ground that we *can* understand statements before becoming acquainted with their signified realities. It follows that the teacher can indeed *inform* the student of new facts by means of language. And it further seems to follow that the basis for Augustine's prompting theory of teaching wholly collapses. We are back to the impression model, with the teacher using language not to prompt the student to inner vision, but simply to inform him of new facts.

The latter conclusion seems to me, however, mistaken. For it does *not* follow that the student will *know* these new facts simply because he has been *informed;* on this point Augustine seems to me perfectly right. It is knowing, after all, that Augustine is interested in, and knowing requires something more than the receipt and acceptance of true information. It requires that the student earn the right to his assurance of the truth of the information in question. New *information,* in short, can be intelligibly conveyed by statements; new *knowledge* cannot. Augustine, I suggest, confuses the two cases, arguing in effect for the impossibility of conveying new knowledge by words, on the basis of an alleged similar impossibility for information. I have been urging the falsity of the latter premise. But if Augustine's premise is indeed false, his conclusion as regards knowledge seems to me perfectly true: To *know* the proposition expressed by a sentence is more than just to have been told it, to have grasped its meaning, and to have accepted it. It is to have earned the right, through one's own effort or position, to an assurance of its truth.

Augustine puts the matter in terms of an insightful searching of reality, an inquiry carried out by oneself, and resting in no way on authority. Indeed, he is perhaps too austerely individualistic in this regard, rejecting even legitimate arguments from authority as a basis for knowledge. But his main thesis seems to me correct: One cannot convey new knowledge by words alone. For knowledge is not simply a storage of information by the learner.

The teacher does, of course, employ *language,* according to the insight model, but its primary function is not to impress his statements on the student's mind for later reproduction. The teacher's statements are, rather, instrumental to the student's own search of reality and vision thereof; teaching is consummated in the student's own insight. The reference to such insight seems to explain, at least partially, how the student can be expected to apply his learning to new situations in the future. For, having acquired this learning not merely by external suggestion but through a personal engagement with reality, the student can appreciate the particular fit which his theories have with real circumstances, and, hence, the proper occasions for them to be brought into play.

There is, furthermore, no reason to construe adoption of the insight model as eliminating the impression model altogether. For the impression model, it may be admitted, does reflect something genuine and important, but mislocates it. It reflects the increase of the culture's written lore, the growth of knowledge as a public and recorded possession. Furthermore, it reflects the primary importance of conserving such knowledge, as a collective heritage. But knowledge in this public sense has nothing to do with the process of learning and the activity of teaching, that is, with the growth of knowledge in the individual learner. The public treasury of knowledge constitutes a basic source of materials for the teacher, but he cannot hope to transfer it bit by bit in growing accumulation within the student's mind. In conducting his teaching, he must rather give up the hope of such simple transfer, and strive instead to encourage individual insight into the meaning and use of public knowledge.

Despite the important emphases of the insight model which we have been considering, there are, however, two respects in which it falls short. One concerns the simplicity of its constituent notion of insight, or vision, as a condition of knowing; the other relates to its specifically cognitive bias, which it shares with the impression model earlier considered. First, the notion that what is crucial in knowledge is a vision of underlying realities, a consulting of what is found within the mind, is far too simple. Certainly, as we have seen, the knower must satisfy *some* condition beyond simply being informed, in order to have the right to his assurance on the matter in question. But to construe this condition in terms of an intellectual inspection of reality is not at all satisfactory. It is plausible only if we restrict ourselves to very simple cases of truths accessible to observation or introspection. As soon as we attempt to characterize the knowing of propositions normally encountered in practical affairs, in the sciences, in politics, history, or the law, we realize that the concept of a *vision of reality* is impossibly simple. Vision is just the wrong metaphor. What seems indubitably more appropriate in all these cases of knowing is an emphasis on the processes of deliberation, argument, judgment, appraisal of reasons *pro* and *con*, weighing of evidence, appeal to principles, and decision-making, none of which fits at all well with the insight model. This model, in short, does not make adequate room for principled deliberation in the characterization of knowing. It is in terms of such principled deliberation, or the potentiality for it, rather than in terms of simple vision, that the distinctiveness of knowing is primarily to be understood.

Secondly, the insight model is specifically cognitive in emphasis, and cannot readily be stretched so as to cover important aspects of teaching. We noted above, for example, that the application of truths to new situations is somewhat better off in the insight than in the impression model, since the appropriateness of a truth for new situations is better judged with awareness of underlying realities than without. But a judgment of appropriateness is not all there is to application; habits of proper execution are also required, and insight itself does not necessitate such habits. Insight also fails to cover the concept of character and the related notions of attitude and disposition. Character, it is clear, goes beyond insight as well as beyond the impression of information. For it involves general principles of conduct logically independent of both insight and the accumulation of information. Moreover, what has been said of character can be applied also to the various institutions of civilization, including those which channel cognition itself. Science, for example, is not just a collection of true insights; it is embodied in a living tradition composed of demanding principles of judgment and conduct. Beyond the cognitive insight, lies the fundamental commitment to principles by which insights are to be criticized and assessed, in the light of publicly available evidence or reasons. In sum, then, the shortcoming of the insight model may be said to lie in the fact that it provides no role for the concept of *principles,* and the associated concept of *reasons.* This omission is very serious indeed, for the concept of principles and the concept of reasons together underlie not only the notions of rational deliberation and critical judgment, but also the notions of rational and moral conduct.

THE RULE MODEL

The shortcoming of the insight model just discussed is remedied in the "rule model," which I associate with Kant. For Kant, the primary philosophical emphasis is on reason, and reason is always a matter of abiding by general rules or principles. Reason stands always in contrast with inconsistency and with expediency, in the judgment of particular issues. In the cognitive realm, reason is a kind of justice to the evidence, a fair treatment of the merits of the case, in the interests of truth. In the moral realm, reason is action on principle, action which therefore does not bend with the wind, nor lean to the side of advantage or power out of weakness or self-interest. Whether in the cognitive or the moral realm, reason is always a matter of treating equal reasons equally, and of judging the issues in the light of general principles to which one has bound oneself.

In thus binding myself to a set of principles, I act freely; this is my dignity as a being with the power of choice. But my own free commitment obligates me to obey the principles I have adopted, when they rule against me. This is what fairness or consistency in conduct means: if I could judge reasons differently when they bear on my interests, or disregard my principles when they conflict with my own advantage, I should have no principles at all. The concepts of *principles, reasons,* and *consistency* thus go together and they apply both in the cognitive judgment of beliefs and the moral assessment of conduct. In fact, they define a general concept of rationality. A rational man is one who is consistent in thought and in action, abiding by impartial and generalizable principles freely chosen as binding upon himself. Rationality is an essential aspect of human dignity and the rational goal of humanity is to construct a society in which such dignity shall flower, a society so ordered as to adjudicate rationally the affairs of free rational agents, an international and democratic republic. The job of education is to develop character in the broadest sense, that is, principled thought and action, in which the dignity of man is manifest.

In contrast to the insight model, the rule model clearly emphasizes the role of principles in the exercise of cognitive judgment. The strong point of the insight model can thus be preserved: The knower must indeed satisfy a further condition beyond the mere receiving and storing of a bit of information. But this condition need not, as in the insight model, be taken to involve simply the vision of an underlying reality; rather, it generally involves the capacity for a principled assessment of reasons bearing on justification of the belief in question. The knower, in short, must typically earn the right to confidence in his belief by acquiring the capacity to make a reasonable case for the belief in question. Nor is it sufficient for this case to have been explicitly taught. What is generally expected of the knower is that his autonomy be evidenced in the ability to construct and evaluate fresh and alternative arguments, the power to innovate, rather than just the capacity to reproduce stale arguments earlier stored. The emphasis on innovation, which we found to be an advantage of the insight model, is thus capable of being preserved by the rule model as well.

Nor does the rule model in any way deny the psychological phenomenon of insight. It merely stresses that insight itself, wherever it is relevant to decision or judgment, is filtered through a network of background principles. It brings out thereby that insight is not an isolated, momentary, or personal matter, that the growth of knowledge is not to be construed as a personal interaction between teacher and student, but rather as mediated by general principles definitive of rationality.

Furthermore, while the previous models, as we have seen, are peculiarly and narrowly *cognitive* in relevance, the rule model embraces *conduct* as well as cognition, itself broadly conceived as including processes of judgment and deliberation. Teaching, it suggests, should be geared not simply to the transfer of information nor even to the development of insight, but to the inculcation of principled judgment and conduct, the building of autonomous and rational character which underlies the enterprises of science, morality and culture. Such inculcation should not, of course, be construed mechanically. Rational character and critical judgment grow only through increased participation in adult experience and criticism, through treatment which respects the dignity of learner as well as teacher. We have here, again, a radical gap which cannot be closed by the teacher's efforts alone. He must rely on the spirit of rational dialogue and critical reflection for the development of character, acknowledging that this implies the freedom to reject as well as to accept what is taught. Kant himself holds, however, that rational principles are somehow embedded in the structure of the human mind, so that education builds on a solid foundation. In any event, the stakes are high, for on such building by education depends the prospect of humanity as an ideal quality of life.

There is much of value in the rule model, as I have sketched it. Certainly, rationality is a fundamental cognitive and moral virtue and as such should, I believe, form a basic objective of teaching. Nor should the many historical connotations of the term "rationality" here mislead us. There is no intent to suggest a faculty of reason, nor to oppose reason to experience or to the emotions. Nor is rationality being construed as the process of making logical deductions. What is in point here is simply the autonomy of the student's judgment, his right to seek reasons in support of claims upon his credibilities and loyalties, and his correlative obligation to deal with such reasons in a principled manner.

Moreover, adoption of the rule model does not necessarily exclude what is important in the other two models; in fact, it can be construed quite plausibly as supplementing their legitimate emphasis. For, intermediate between the public treasury of accumulated lore mirrored by the impression model, and the personal and intuitive grasp of the student mirrored by the insight model, it places general principles of rational judgment capable of linking them.

Yet, there is something too formal and abstract in the rule model, as I have thus far presented it. For the operative principles of rational judgment at any given time are, after all, much more detailed and specific than a mere requirement of formal consistency. Such consistency is certainly fundamental, but the way its demands are concretely interpreted, elaborated, and supplemented in any field of inquiry or practice, varies with the field, the state of knowledge, and the advance of relevant methodological sophistication. The concrete rules governing inference and procedure in the special sciences, for example, are surely not all embedded in the human mind, even if the demands of formal consistency, as such, *are* universally compelling. These concrete rules and standards, techniques and methodological criteria evolve and grow with the advance of knowledge itself; they form a live tradition of rationality in the realm of science.

Indeed, the notion of tradition is a better guide here, it seems to me, than appeal to the innate structure of the human mind. Rationality in natural inquiry is embodied in the relatively young tradition of science, which defines and redefines those principles by means of which evidence is to be interpreted and meshed with theory. Rational judgment in the realm of science is, consequently, judgment which accords with such principles, as crystallized at the time in question. To teach rationality in science is to interiorize these principles in the student, but furthermore, to introduce him to the live and evolving *tradition* of natural science, which forms their significant context of development and purpose.

Scholarship in history is subject to an analogous interpretation, for beyond the formal demands of reason, in the sense of consistency, there is a concrete tradition of technique and methodology defining the historian's procedure and his assessment of reasons for or against particular historical accounts. To teach rationality in history is, in effect, here also to introduce the student to a live tradition of historical scholarship. Similar remarks might be made also with respect to other areas, e.g. law, philosophy and the politics of democratic society. The fundamental point is that rationality cannot be taken simply as an abstract and general ideal. It is embodied in *multiple evolving traditions,* in which the basic condition holds that issues are resolved by reference to *reasons,* themselves defined by *principles* purporting to be impartial and universal. These traditions should, I believe, provide an important focus for teaching.

V. Conclusion

I have intimated that I find something important in each of the models we have considered. The impression model reflects, as I have said, the cumulative growth of knowledge in its *public* sense. Our aim in teaching should surely be to preserve and extend this growth. But we cannot do this by storing it piecemeal within the learner. We preserve it, as the insight model stresses, only if we succeed in transmitting the live spark that keeps it growing, the insight which is a product of each learner's efforts to make sense of public knowledge in his own terms, and to confront it with reality. Finally, as the rule model suggests, such confrontation involves deliberation and judgment, and hence presupposes general and impartial principles governing the assessment of reasons bearing on the issues. Without such guiding principles, the very conception of rational deliberation collapses, and the concepts of rational and moral conduct, moreover, lose their meaning. Our teaching needs thus to introduce students to those principles we ourselves acknowledge as fundamental, general, and impartial, in the various departments of thought and action.

We need not pretend that these principles of ours are immutable or innate. It is enough that they are what we ourselves acknowledge, that they are the best we know, and that we are prepared to improve them should the need and occasion arise. Such improvement is possible, however, only if we succeed in passing on, too, the multiple live traditions in which they are embodied, and in which a sense of their history, spirit, and direction may be discerned. Teaching, from this point of view, is clearly not, as the behaviorists would have it, a matter of the teacher's shaping the student's behavior or of controlling his mind. It is a matter of passing on those traditions of principled thought and action which define the rational life for teacher as well as student.

As Professor Richard Peters has recently written,[4]

The critical procedures by means of which established content is assessed, revised, and adapted to new discoveries have public criteria written into them that stand as impersonal standards to which both teacher and learner must give their allegiance. . . . To liken education to therapy, to conceive of it as imposing a pattern on another person or as fixing the environment so that he 'grows', fails to do justice to the shared impersonality both of the content that is handed on and of the criteria by reference to which it is criticized and revised. The teacher is not a detached operator who is bringing about some kind of result in another person which is external to him. His task is to try to get others on the inside of a public form of life that he shares and considers to be worthwhile.

In teaching, we do not impose our wills on the student, but introduce him to the many mansions of the heritage in which we ourselves strive to live, and to the improvement of which we are ourselves dedicated.

[4] *Education as Initiation,* an inaugural lecture delivered at the University of London Institute of Education, 9 December 1963; published for The University of London Institute of Education by Evans Brothers, Ltd., London.

Some Educational Implications of The Humanistic Psychologies

ABRAHAM H. MASLOW

Maslow's theoretical and empirical work made him a leading spokesman for the "third force," or humanistic movement in psychology, that challenged both learning theory and psychoanalysis. In this essay, Maslow examines the relevance of humanistic psychology for education. His discussion includes the reinforcing role of "peak-experiences" and the general educational imperatives to be derived from his theory of the "self-actualization" process.

The upshot of the past decade or two of turmoil and change within the field of psychology can be viewed as a local manifestation of a great change taking place in all fields of knowledge. We are witnessing a great revolution in thought, in the Zeitgeist itself: the creation of a new image of man and society and of religion and science (1, 16). It is the kind of change that happens, as Whitehead said, once or twice in a century. This is not an *improvement* of something; it is a real change in direction altogether. It is as if we had been going north and are now going south instead.

Recent developments in psychological theory and research are closely related to the changes in the new image of man which lie at the center of the larger revolution. There are, to oversimplify the situation, two comprehensive theories of human nature which dominate psychology today. The first is the behavioristic, associationistic, experimental, mechanomorphic psychology; the psychology which can be called "classical" because it is in a direct line with the classical conception of science which comes out of astronomy, mechanics, physics, chemistry, and geology; the psychology which can be called "academic" because it has tended to emanate from and flourish in the undergraduate and graduate departments of psychology in our universities. Since its first detailed and testable formulation by Watson (24), Hull (5), and Skinner (21), "classical," "aca-

Based on a talk given to Superintendents of member schools in the New England School Development Council, July 12, 1967. I would like to acknowledge the assistance of David Napior, Barbara Powell, and Gail Zivin of the *Harvard Educational Review* in preparing this article.

Harvard Educational Review   Vol. 38   No. 4   Fall 1968, 685–696

demic" psychological theory has been widely applied beyond its original limited focus in such diverse areas as acquisition of motor skills, behavior disorders and therapy, and social psychology. It has answers of a kind to any questions that you may have about human nature. In that sense, it is a philosophy, a philosophy of psychology.

The second philosophy of psychology, the one which dominates the whole field of clinical psychology and social work, emerged essentially from the work of Freud and his disciples and antagonists. In light of its emphasis upon the interplay between unconscious emotional forces and the conscious organization of behavior, I refer to this school of thought as "psychodynamic" or "depth" psychology. It, too, tries to be a comprehensive philosophy of man. It has generated a theory of art, of religion, of society, of education, of almost every major human endeavor.

What is developing today is a third, more inclusive, image of man, which is now already in the process of generating great changes in all intellectual fields and in all social and human institutions (2, 6, 8, 20, 25). Let me try to summarize this development very briefly and succinctly because I want to turn as soon as I can to its meaning for learning and education.

Third Force psychology, as some are calling it, is in large part a reaction to the gross inadequacies of behavioristic and Freudian psychologies in their treatment of the higher nature of man. Classical academic psychology has no systematic place for higher-order elements of the personality such as altruism and dignity, or the search for truth and beauty. You simply do not ask questions about ultimate human values if you are working in an animal lab.

Of course, it is true that the Freudian psychology has confronted these problems of the higher nature of man. But until very recently these have been handled by being very cynical about them, that is to say, by analyzing them away in a pessimistic, reductive manner. Generosity is interpreted as a reaction formation against a stinginess, which is deep down and unconscious, and therefore somehow more real. Kindliness tends to be seen as a defense mechanism against violence, rage, and the tendency to murder. It is as if we cannot take at face value any of the decencies that we value in ourselves, certainly what I value in myself, what I try to be. It is perfectly true that we do have anger and hate, and yet there are other impulses that we are beginning to learn about which might be called the higher needs of man: "needs" for the intrinsic and ultimate values of goodness and truth and beauty and perfection and justice and order. They are there, they exist, and any attempt to explain them *away* seems to me to be very foolish. I once searched through the Freudian literature on the feeling of love, of wanting love, but especially of giving love. Freud has been called the philosopher of love, yet the Freudian literature contains nothing but the pathology of love, and also a kind of derogatory explaining-away of the finding that people do love each other, as if it could be only an illusion.

Something similar is true of mystical or oceanic experiences: Freud analyzes them *away*.

This belief in the reality of higher human needs, motives and capacities, that is, the belief that human nature has been sold short by the dominant psychological theories, is the primary force binding together a dozen or so "splinter groups" into this comprehensive Third Force psychology.* All of these groups reject entirely the whole conception of science as being value-free. Sometimes they do this consciously and explicitly, sometimes by implication only. This is a real revolution because traditionally science has been defined in terms of objectivity, detachment, and procedures which never tell you how to find human ends. The discovery of ends and values is turned over to non-scientific, non-empirical sources. The Third Force psychology totally rejects this view of science as merely instrumental and unable to help mankind to discover its ultimate ends and values (11, 18).

Among the many educational consequences generated by this philosophy, to come closer to our topic now, is a different conception of the self. This is a very complex conception, difficult to describe briefly, because it talks for the first time in centuries of an *essence,* of an *intrinsic* nature, of specieshood, of a kind of animal nature (9, 14). This is in sharp contrast to the European existentialists, most especially with Sartre, for whom man is *entirely* his own project, *entirely* and merely a product of his own arbitrary, unaided will. For Sartre and all those whom he has influenced, one's self becomes an arbitrary choice, a willing by fiat to be something or do something without any guidelines about which is better, which is worse, what's good and what's bad. In essentially denying the existence of biology, Sartre has given up altogether any absolute or at least any species-wide conception of values. This comes very close to making a life-philosophy of the obsessive-compulsive neurosis in which one finds what I have called "experiential emptiness," the absence of impulse-voices from within (12, 14).

The American humanistic psychologists and existential psychiatrists are mostly closer to the psychodynamicists than they are to Sartre. Their clinical experiences have led them to conceive of the human being as having an essence, a biological nature, membership in a species. It is very easy to interpret the "uncovering" therapies as helping the person to *discover* his Identity, his Real Self, in a word, his own subjective biology, which he can *then* proceed to actualize, to "make himself," to "choose." The Freudian conception of instincts has been generally discarded by the humanistic psychologists in favor of the conception of "basic needs," or in some cases, in favor of the conception of a single overarching need for actualization or growth (19). In any case, it is implied, if not made explicit, by most of these writers that the organism, in the strictest sense,

* See (16), Appendix, for list.

150

has *needs* which must be gratified in order to become fully human, to grow well, and to avoid sicknesses (9, 14). This doctrine of a Real Self to be uncovered and actualized is also a total rejection of the *tabula rasa* notions of the behaviorists and associationists who often talk as if *anything* can be learned, *anything* can be taught, as if the human being is a sort of a passive clay to be shaped, controlled, reinforced, modified in any way that somebody arbitrarily decides.

We speak then of a self, a kind of intrinsic nature which is very subtle, which is not necessarily conscious, which has to be sought for, and which has to be uncovered and then built upon, actualized, taught, educated (13). The notion is that something is there but it's hidden, swamped, distorted, twisted, overlaid The job of the psychotherapist (or the teacher) is to help a person find out what's already in him rather than to reinforce him or shape or teach him into a prearranged form, which someone else has decided upon in advance, *a priori*.

Let me explore what I call "introspective biology" and its relation to new ideas for education. If we accept the notion of the human essence or the core-self, i.e., the constitutional, temperamental, biological, chemical, endocrinological, given raw material, if we do accept the fact that babies come into the world very different from each other (anyone of you who has more than one child knows that), then the job of any helper, and furthermore the first job of each of us for ourselves, is to uncover and discover what we ourselves are. A good example for pedagogical purposes is our maleness and femaleness, which is the most obvious biological, constitutional given, and one which involves all the problems of conflicts, of self-discovery, and of actualization. Practically every youngster, not to mention a good proportion of the older population also, is mixed up about what it means to be a female and what it means to be a male. A lot of time has to be spent on the questions: How do I get to be a good female, or how do I get to be a good male? This involves self-discovery, self-acceptance, and self-making; discoveries about both one's commonness and one's uniqueness, rather than a Sartre-type decision on whether to be a male or a female.

One constitutional difference that I have discovered is that there are differences in triggers to peak-experiences between the sexes. The mystical and peak-experiences, the ultimate, esthetic, poetic experiences of the male, can come from a football game, for example. One subject reported that once when he broke free of the line and got into the open and then ran—that this was a true moment of ecstasy. But Dr. Deborah Tanzer has found women who use the same kinds of words, the same kind of poetry, to describe their feelings during natural childbirth. Under the right circumstances these women have ecstasies which sound just the same as the St. Theresa or Meister Eckhardt kind of ecstasy. I call them peak-experiences to secularize them and to naturalize them, to make them more empirical and researchable.

Individual constitutional differences, then, are an important variable. It continually impresses me that the same peak-experiences come from different kinds of activities for different kinds of people.* Mothers will report peak-experiences not only from natural childbirth but also from putting the baby to the breast. (Of course this doesn't happen all the time. These peak-experiences are rare rather than common.) But I've never heard of any man getting a peak-experience from putting his baby to *his* breast. It just doesn't happen. He wasn't constructed right for this purpose. We are confronting the fact that people are biologically different, but have species-wide emotional experiences. Thus I think we should examine individual differences in all of our given biochemical, endocrine, neurological, anatomical systems to see to just what extent they carry along with them psychological and spiritual differences and to what extent there remains a common substratum (14).

The trouble is that the human species is the only species which finds it hard to be a species. For a cat there seems to be no problem about being a cat. It's easy; cats seem to have no complexes or ambivalences or conflicts, and show no signs of yearning to be dogs instead. Their instincts are very clear. But we have no such unequivocal animal instincts. Our biological essence, our instinct-remnants, are weak and subtle, and they are hard to get at. Learnings of the extrinsic sort *are more powerful than our deepest impulses.* These deepest impulses in the human species, at the points where the instincts have been lost almost entirely, where they are extremely weak, extremely subtle and delicate, where you have to dig to find them, *this* is where I speak of introspective biology, of biological phenomenology, implying that one of the necessary methods in the search for identity, the search for self, the search for spontaneity and for naturalness is a matter of closing your eyes, cutting down the noise, turning off the thoughts, putting away all busyness, just relaxing in a kind of Taoistic and receptive fashion (in much the same way that you do on the psychoanalyst's couch). The technique here is to just wait to see what happens, what comes to mind. This is what Freud called free association, free-floating attention rather than task-orientation, and if you are successful in this effort and learn how to do it, you can forget about the outside world and its noises and begin to hear these small, delicate impulse-voices from within, the hints from your animal nature, not only from your common species-nature, but also from your own uniqueness.

There's a very interesting paradox here, however. On the one hand I've talked about uncovering or discovering your idiosyncrasy, the way in which you are different from everybody else in the whole world. Then on the other hand I've spoken about discovering your specieshood, your humanness. As Carl Rogers has phrased it: "How does it happen that the deeper we go into ourselves as particular

* For some ways in which educators can use peak-experiences, see (15).

152

and unique, seeking for our own individual identity, the more we find the whole human species?" Doesn't that remind you of Ralph Waldo Emerson and the New England Transcendentalists? Discovering your specieshood, at a deep enough level, merges with discovering your selfhood (13, 14). Becoming (learning how to be) fully human means *both* enterprises carried on simultaneously. You are learning (subjectively experiencing) what you peculiarly are, how you are you, what your potentialities are, what your style is, what your pace is, what your tastes are, what your values are, what direction your body is going, where your personal biology is taking you, i.e., how you are *different* from others. And at the same time it means learning what it means to be a human animal like other human animals, i.e., how you are *similar* to others.

It is such considerations as these that convince me that we are now being confronted with a choice between two extremely different, almost mutually exclusive conceptions of learning. What we have in practically all the elementary and advanced textbooks of psychology, and in most of the brands of "learning theory" which all graduate students are required to learn, is what I want to call for the sake of contrast and confrontation, *extrinsic learning*, i.e., learning of the outside, learning of the impersonal, of arbitrary associations, of arbitrary conditioning, that is, of arbitrary (or at best, culturally-determined) meanings and responses. In this kind of learning, most often it is not the person himself who decides, but rather a teacher or an experimenter who says, "I will use a buzzer," "I will use a bell," "I will use a red light," and most important, "I will reinforce this but not that." In this sense the learning is extrinsic to the learner, extrinsic to the personality, and is extrinsic also in the sense of *collecting* associations, conditionings, habits, or modes of action. It is as if these were *possessions* which the learner accumulates in the same way that he accumulates keys or coins and puts them in his pocket. They have little or nothing to do with the actualization or growth of the peculiar, idiosyncratic kind of person he is.

I believe this is the model of education which we all have tucked away in the back of our heads and which we don't often make explicit. In this model the teacher is the active one who teaches a passive person who gets shaped and taught and who is *given* something which he then accumulates and which he may then lose or retain, depending upon the efficiency of the initial indoctrination process, and of his own accumulation-of-fact process. I would maintain that a good 90% of "learning theory" deals with learnings that have nothing to do with the intrinsic self that I've been talking about, nothing to do with its specieshood and biological idiosyncrasy. This kind of learning too easily reflects the goals of the teacher and ignores the values and ends of the learner himself (22). It is also fair, therefore, to call such learning amoral.

Now I'd like to contrast this with another kind of learning, which is actually going on, but is usually unconscious and unfortunately happens more outside the classroom than inside. It often comes in the great personal learning experiences of our lives.

For instance, if I were to list the most important learning experiences in my life, there come to mind getting married, discovering my life work, having children, getting psychoanalyzed, the death of my best friend, confronting death myself, and the like. I think I would say that these were more important learning experiences for me than my Ph.D. or any 15 or 150 credits or courses that I've ever had. I certainly learned more about *myself* from such experiences. I learned, if I may put it so, to throw aside many of my "learnings," that is, to push aside the habits and traditions and reinforced associations which had been imposed upon me. Sometimes this was at a very trivial, and yet meaningful, level. I particularly remember when I learned that I really hated lettuce. My father was a "nature boy," and I had lettuce two meals a day for the whole of my early life. But one day in analysis, after I had learned that I carried my father inside me, it dawned on me that it was my father, through *my* larynx, who was ordering salad with every meal. I can remember sitting there, realizing that *I* hated lettuce and then saying, "My God, take the damn stuff away!" I was emancipated, becoming in this small way me, rather than my father. I didn't eat any more lettuce for months, until it finally settled back to what my body calls for. I have lettuce two or three times each week, which I now enjoy. But *not* twice a day.

Now observe, this experience which I mentioned occurred just once and I could give many other similar examples. It seems to me that we must call into question the generality of repetition, of learning by drilling (4). The experiences in which we uncover our intrinsic selves are apt to be unique moments, not slow accumulations of reinforced bits. (How do you repeat the death of your father?) These are the experiences in which we discover identity (16). These are the experiences in which we learn who we are, what we love, what we hate, what we value, what we are committed to, what makes us feel anxious, what makes us feel depressed, what makes us feel happy, what makes us feel great joy.

It must be obvious by now that you can generate consequences of this second picture of learning by the hundred. (And again I would stress that these hypotheses can be stated in testable, disconfirmable, confirmable form.) One such implication of the point of view is a change in the whole picture of the teacher. If you are willing to accept this conception of two kinds of learning, with the learning-to-be-a-person being more central and more basic than the impersonal learning of skills or the acquisition of habits; and if you are willing to concede that even the more extrinsic learnings are far more useful, and far more effective if based upon a sound identity, that is, if done by a person who knows what he wants, knows what he is, and where he's going and what his ends are; then you *must* have a different picture of the good teacher and of his functions.

In the first place, unlike the current model of teacher as lecturer, conditioner, reinforcer, and boss, the Taoist helper or teacher is receptive rather than intrusive. I was told once that in the world of boxers, a youngster who feels himself to be good and who wants to be a boxer will go to a gym, look up one of the managers and say, "I'd like to be a pro, and I'd like to be in your stable. I'd like you to manage me." In this world, what is then done characteristically is to try him out. The good manager will select one of his professionals and say, "Take him on in the ring. Stretch him. Strain him. Let's see what he can do. Just let him show his very best. Draw him out." If it turns out that the boxer has promise, if he's a "natural," then what the good manager does is to take that boy and train him to be, if this is Joe Dokes, a *better Joe Dokes.* That is, he takes his style as given and builds upon that. He does not start all over again, and say, "Forget all you've learned, and do it this new way," which is like saying, "Forget what kind of body you have," or "Forget what you are good for." He takes him and builds upon his *own* talents and builds him up into the very best Joe Dokes-type boxer that he possibly can.

It is my strong impression that this is the way in which much of the world of education could function. If we want to be helpers, counselors, teachers, guiders, or psychotherapists, what we must do is to accept the person and help him learn what kind of person he is already. What is his style, what are his aptitudes, what is he good for, not good for, what can we build upon, what are his good raw materials, his good potentialities? We would be non-threatening and would supply an atmosphere of acceptance of the child's nature which reduces fear, anxiety and defense to the minimum possible. Above all, we would care for the child, that is enjoy him and his growth and self-actualization (17). So far this sounds much like the Rogerian therapist, his "unconditional positive regard," his congruence, his openness and his caring. And indeed there is evidence by now that this "brings the child out," permits him to express and to act, to experiment, and even to make mistakes; to let himself be seen. Suitable feedback at this point, as in T-groups or basic encounter groups, or nondirective counseling, then helps the child to discover what and who he is.

In closing, I would like to discuss briefly the role that peak-experiences can play in the education of the child. We have no systematic data on peak-experiences in children but we certainly have enough anecdotes and introspections and memories to be quite confident that young children have them, perhaps more frequently than adults do. However, they seem at least in the beginning to come more from sensory experiences, color, rhythm, or sounds, and perhaps are better characterized by the words wonder, awe, fascination, absorption, and the like.

In any case, I have discussed the role of these experiences in education in (15), and would refer the reader to that paper for more detail. Using peak-experiences or fascination or wonder experiences as an intrinsic reward or goal at *many* points in education is a very real possibility, and is congruent with the whole philosophy of the humanistic educator. At the very least, this new knowledge can help wean teachers away from their frequent uneasiness with and even disapproval and persecution of these experiences. If they learn to value them as great moments in the learning process, moments in which both cognitive and personal growth take place simultaneously, then this valuing can be transmitted to the child. He in turn is then taught to value rather than to suppress his greatest moments of illumination, moments which can validate and make worthwhile the more usual trudging and slogging and "working through" of education.

There is a very useful parallel here with the newer humanistic paradigm for science (11, 18) in which the more everyday cautious and patient work of checking, validating and replicating is seen, not as *all* there is to science but rather as follow-up work, *subsequent* to the great intuitions, intimations, and illuminations of the creative and daring, innovative, breakthrough scientist. Caution is then seen to *follow* upon boldness and proving comes *after* intuition. The creative scientist then looks more like a gambler than a banker, one who is willing to work hard for seven years because of a dazzling hunch, one who feels certain in the *absence* of evidence, *before* the evidence, and only *then* proceeds to the hard work of proving or disproving his precious revelation. First comes the emotion, the fascination, the falling in love with a possibility, and *then* comes the hard work, the chores, the stubborn persistence in the face of disappointment and failure.

As a supplement to this conception in which a noetic illumination plays such an important role, we can add the harsh patience of the psychotherapist who has learned from many bitter disappointments that the breakthrough insight doesn't do the therapeutic job all by itself, as Freud originally thought. It needs consolidation, repetition, rediscovery, application to one situation after another. It needs patience, time and hard work—what the psychoanalysts call "working through." Not only for science but also for psychotherapy may we say that the process *begins* with an emotional-cognitive flash but *does not end there!* It is this model of science and therapy that I believe we may now fairly consider for the process of education, if not as an exclusive model, at least as an additional one.

We must learn to treasure the "jags" of the child in school, his fascination, absorptions, his persistent wide-eyed wonderings, his Dionysian enthusiasms. At the very least, we can value his more diluted raptures, his "interests" and hobbies, etc. They can lead to much. Especially can they lead to hard work, persistent, absorbed, fruitful, educative.

And conversely I think it is possible to think of the peak-experience, the experience of awe, mystery, wonder, or of perfect completion, as the goal and reward of learning as well, its end as well as its beginning (7). If this is true for the *great* historians, mathematicians, scientists, musicians, philosophers and all the rest, why should we not try to maximize these studies as sources of peak-experiences for the child as well?

I must say that whatever little knowledge and experience I have to support these suggestions comes from intelligent and creative children rather than from retarded or underprivileged or sick ones. However, I must also say that my experience with such unpromising adults in Synanon, in T-groups (23), in Theory Y industry (10), in Esalen-type educative centers (3), in Grof-type work with psychedelic chemicals, not to mention Laing-type work with psychotics and other such experiences, has taught me never to write *anybody* off in advance.

References

1. Braden, W. *The private sea: LSD and the search for God.* Chicago: Quadrangle, 1967.
2. Bugental, J. (ed.) *Challenges of humanistic psychology.* New York: McGraw-Hill, 1967.
3. Esalen Institute. *Residential program brochure.* Big Sur, California, 1966 and subsequent years.
4. Holt, J. *How children fail.* New York: Pitman, 1964.
5. Hull, C. L. *Principles of behavior.* New York: Appleton Century-Crofts, 1943.
6. *Journal of Humanistic Psychology.* (Periodical.) American Association of Humanistic Psychology, Palo Alto, California.
7. Leonard, G. *Education and ecstasy.* New York: Delacorte Press, 1968.
8. *Manas.* (Periodical.) Cunningham Press, South Pasadena, California.
9. Maslow, A. Criteria for judging needs to be instinctoid. In M. R. Jones (ed.), *Human motivation: A symposium.* Lincoln, Neb.: University of Nebraska Press, 1965.
10. Maslow, A. *Eupsychian management: A journal.* New York: Irwin-Dorsey, 1965.
11. Maslow, A. *The psychology of science: A reconaissance.* New York: Harper and Row, 1966.
12. Maslow, A. Neurosis as a failure of personal growth. *Humanitas,* III (1967), 153-169.
13. Maslow, A. Self-actualization and beyond. In J. Bugental (ed.), *Challenges of humanistic psychology.* New York: McGraw-Hill, 1967.
14. Maslow, A. A theory of metamotivation: The biological rooting of the value-life. *Journal of Humanistic Psychology,* I (1967), 93-127.
15. Maslow, A. Music education and peak-experiences. *Music Educators Journal,* LIV (1968), 72-75, 163-171.
16. Maslow, A. *Toward a psychology of being.* (Revised edition) Princeton, N.J.: D. Van Nostrand, 1968.
17. Moustakas, C. *The authentic teacher.* Cambridge, Mass.: Howard A. Doyle Publishing Co., 1966.
18. Polanyi, M. *Personal knowledge.* Chicago: University of Chicago Press, 1958.

19. Rogers, C. *On becoming a person*. Boston: Houghton Mifflin, 1961.
20. Severin, F. (ed.) *Humanistic viewpoints in psychology*. New York: McGraw-Hill, 1965.
21. Skinner, B. F. *Science and human behavior*. New York: Macmillan, 1938.
22. Skinner, B. F. *Walden two*. New York: Macmillan, 1948.
23. Sohl, J. *The lemon eaters*. New York: Simon and Schuster, 1967.
24. Watson, J. B. *Behaviorism*. New York: Norton, 1924 (rev. ed., 1930). Also *Psychology from the standpoint of a behaviorist*. Philadelphia: Lippincott, 1924.
25. Wilson, C. *Introduction to the new existentialism*. Boston: Houghton Mifflin, 1967.

Development as the Aim of Education

LAWRENCE KOHLBERG
ROCHELLE MAYER

The authors offer an explanation of the psychological and philosophical positions underlying aspects of educational progressivism. They contrast tenets of progressivism, most clearly identified with the work of John Dewey, with two other educational ideologies, the romantic and the cultural transmission conceptions, which historically have competed in the minds of educators as rationales for the choice of educational goals and practices. Kohlberg and Mayer maintain that only progressivism, with its cognitive-developmental psychology, its interactionist epistemology, and its philosophically examined ethics, provides an adequate basis for our understanding of the process of education.

The most important issue confronting educators and educational theorists is the choice of ends for the educational process. Without clear and rational educational goals, it becomes impossible to decide which educational programs achieve objectives of general import and which teach incidental facts and attitudes of dubious worth. While there has been a vast amount of research comparing the effects of various educational methods and programs on various outcome measures, there has been very little empirical research designed to clarify the worth of these outcome measures themselves. After a deluge of studies in the sixties examining the effects of programs on I.Q. and achievement tests, and drawing policy conclusions, researchers finally began to ask the question, "What is the justification for using I.Q. tests or achievement tests to evaluate programs in the first place?"

The present paper examines such fundamental issues and considers the strategies by which research facts can help generate and substantiate educational objectives and measures of educational outcomes. Three prevalent strategies for defining objectives and relating them to research facts are considered: the desirable trait or "bag of virtues" strategy; the prediction of success or

The position presented in this paper was elaborated in a different form in *Proceedings of the Conference on Psychology and the Process of Schooling in the Next Decade: Alternative conceptions.* Washington, D.C.: U. S. Office of Education, 1971.

Harvard Educational Review   Vol. 42   No. 4   November 1972, 449-496

"industrial psychology" strategy; and the "developmental-philosophic" strategy. It will be our claim in this paper that the first two strategies: 1) lack a clear theoretical rationale for defining objectives which can withstand logical and philosophic criticism; and 2) that as currently applied they rest upon assumptions which conflict with research findings. In contrast, we claim that the developmental-philosophic strategy for defining educational objectives, which emerges from the work of Dewey and Piaget, is a theoretical rationale which withstands logical criticism and is consistent with, if not "proved" by, current research findings.

This presentation begins by making explicit how a cognitive-developmental *psychological* theory can be translated into a rational and viable progressive *educational ideology*, i.e., a set of concepts defining desirable aims, content, and methods of education. We contrast the progressive ideology with the "romantic" and the "cultural transmission" schools of thought, with respect to underlying psychological, epistemological, and ethical assumptions. In doing so we focus on two related problems of value theory. The first is the issue of *value-relativity*, the problem of defining some general ends of education whose validity is not relative to the values and needs of each individual child or to the values of each subculture or society. The second is the problem of relating psychological statements about the actual characteristics of children and their development to philosophic statements about desirable characteristics, the problem of relating the natural *is* to the ethical *ought*. We claim that the cognitive-developmental or progressive approach can satisfactorily handle these issues because it combines a psychological theory of development with a rational ethical philosophy of development. In contrast, we claim that other educational ideologies do not stem from psychological theories which can be translated into educational aims free of the philosophic charge that they are arbitrary and relative to the values of the particular educator or school.

Subsequently, we look at the ways in which these ideologies form the basis for contemporary educational policy. We evaluate longitudinal evidence relevant to the "bag of virtues" definition of education objectives favored in maturationist models of education, and the academic achievement definition of objectives favored in environmental learning models. We conclude that the available research lends little support for either of these alternative educational strategies. More specifically:

1. The current prevalent definition of the aims of education, in terms of academic achievement supplemented by a concern for mental health, cannot be justified empirically or logically.
2. The overwhelming emphasis of educational psychology on methods of instruction and tests and measurements which presuppose a "value-neutral" psychology is misplaced.

3. An alternative notion that the aim of the schools should be the stimulation of human development is a scientifically, ethically, and practically viable conception which provides the framework for a new kind of educational psychology.

Three Streams of Educational Ideology

There have been three broad streams in the development of Western educational ideology. While their detailed statements vary from generation to generation, each stream exhibits a continuity based upon particular assumptions of psychological development.

Romanticism

The first stream of thought, the "romantic," commences with Rousseau and is currently represented by Freud's and Gesell's followers. A. S. Neill's Summerhill represents an example of a school based on these principles. Romantics hold that what comes from within the child is the most important aspect of development; therefore the pedagogical environment should be permissive enough to allow the inner "good" (abilities and social virtues) to unfold and the inner "bad" to come under control. Thus teaching the child the ideas and attitudes of others through rote or drill would result in meaningless learning and the suppression of inner spontaneous tendencies of positive value.

Romantics stress the biological metaphors of "health" and "growth" in equating optimal physical development with bodily health and optimal mental development with mental health. Accordingly, early education should allow the child to work through aspects of emotional development not allowed expression at home, such as the formation of social relations with peers and adults other than his parents. It should also allow the expression of intellectual questioning and curiosity. To label this ideology "romantic" is not to accuse it of being unscientific; rather it is to recognize that the nineteenth-century discovery of the natural development of the child was part of a larger romantic philosophy, an ethic and epistemology involving a discovery of the natural and the inner self.

With regard to childhood, this philosophy involved not only an awareness that the child possessed an inner self but also a valuing of childhood, to which the origins of the self could be traced. The adult, through taking the child's point of view, could experience otherwise inaccessible elements of truth, goodness, and reality.

As stated by G. H. Mead (1936):

The romantic comes back to the existence of the self as the primary fact. That is what gives the standard to values. What the Romantic period revealed was not simply a past but a past as the point of view from which to come back at the self. . . . It is this self-conscious setting-up of the past again that constitutes the origin of romanticism. (p. 61)

The work of G. Stanley Hall, the founder of American child psychology, contains the core ideas of modern romantic educational thought, including "deschooling."

The guardians of the young should strive first to keep out of nature's way and to prevent harm and should merit the proud title of the defenders of the happiness and rights of children. They should feel profoundly that childhood, as it comes from the hand of God, is not corrupt but illustrates the survival of the most consummate thing in the world; they should be convinced that there is nothing else so worthy of love, reverence and service as the body and soul of the growing child.

Before we let the pedagog loose upon childhood, we must overcome the fetishes of the alphabet, of the multiplication tables, and must reflect that but a few generations ago the ancestors of all of us were illiterate. There are many who ought not to be educated and who would be better in mind, body and morals if they knew no school. What shall it profit a child to gain the world of knowledge and lose his own health? (1901, p. 24)

Cultural Transmission

The origins of the cultural transmission ideology are rooted in the classical academic tradition of Western education. Traditional educators believe that their primary task is the transmission to the present generation of bodies of information and of rules or values collected in the past; they believe that the educator's job is the direct instruction of such information and rules. The important emphasis, however, is not on the sanctity of the past, but on the view that educating consists of transmitting knowledge, skills, and social and moral rules of the culture. Knowledge and rules of the culture may be rapidly changing or they may be static. In either case, however, it is assumed that education is the transmission of the culturally given.

More modern or innovative variations of the cultural transmission view are represented by educational technology and behavior modification.[1] Like traditional education, these approaches assume that knowledge and values—first located in the culture—are afterwards internalized by children through the imitation of adult behavior models, or through explicit instruction and reward and punishment. Accordingly, the educational technologist evaluates the individual's success in terms of his ability to incorporate the responses he has been taught and to respond favorably to the demands of the system. Although the technologist stresses the child as an individual learner, learning at his own pace, he, like the traditionalist, assumes that what is learned and what is valued in education is a culturally given body of knowledge and rules.

[1] The romantic-maturationist position also has "conservative" and "radical" wings. Emphasizing "adaptation to reality," psychoanalytic educators like A. Freud (1937) and Bettelheim (1970) stress mental health as ego-control, while radicals stress spontaneity, creativity, etc.

There are, of course, a number of contrasts between the traditional academic and the educational technology variations of the cultural-transmission ideology. The traditional academic school has been humanistic in the sense that it has emphasized the transmission of knowledge considered central to the culture of Western man. The educational technology school, in contrast, has emphasized the transmission of skills and habits deemed necessary for adjustment to a technological society. With regard to early education, however, the two variations of the cultural transmission school find an easy rapprochement in stressing such goals as literacy and mathematical skills. The traditionalist sees literacy as the central avenue to the culture of Western man, the technologist sees it as a means to vocational adaptation to a society depending on impersonal information codes. Both approaches, however, emphasize definition of educational goals in terms of fixed knowledge or skills assessed by standards of cultural correctness. Both also stress internalization of basic moral rules of the culture. The clearest and most thoughtful contemporary elaboration of this view in relation to preschool education is to be found in the writing of Bereiter and Engelmann (1966).

In contrast to the child-centered romantic school, the cultural transmission school is society-centered. It defines educational ends as the internalization of the values and knowledge of the culture. The cultural transmission school focuses on the child's need to learn the discipline of the social order, while the romantic stresses the child's freedom. The cultural transmission view emphasizes the common and the established, the romantic view stresses the unique, the novel, and the personal.

Progressivism

The third stream of educational ideology which is still best termed "progressive," following Dewey (1938), developed as part of the pragmatic functional-genetic philosophies of the late nineteenth and early twentieth centuries. As an educational ideology, progressivism holds that education should nourish the child's natural interaction with a developing society or environment. Unlike the romantics, the progressives do not assume that development is the unfolding of an innate pattern or that the primary aim of education is to create an unconflicted environment able to foster healthy development. Instead, they define development as a progression through invariant ordered sequential stages. The educational goal is the eventual attainment of a higher level or stage of development in adulthood, not merely the healthy functioning of the child at a present level. In 1895, Dewey and McLellan suggested the following notion of education for attainment of a higher stage:

Only knowledge of the order and connection of the stages in the development of the psychical functions can insure the full maturing of the psychical powers. Education is the work of supplying the conditions which will enable the psychical functions, as they

163

successively arise, to mature and pass into higher functions in the freest and fullest manner. (p. 207)

In the progressive view, this aim requires an educational environment that actively stimulates development through the presentation of resolvable but genuine problems or conflicts. For progressives, the organizing and developing force in the child's experience is the child's active thinking, and thinking is stimulated by the problematic, by cognitive conflict. Educative experience makes the child think—think in ways which organize both cognition and emotion. Although both the cultural transmission and the progressive views emphasize "knowledge," only the latter sees the acquisition of "knowledge" as *an active change in patterns of thinking* brought about by experiential problem-solving situations. Similarly, both views emphasize "morality," but the progressive sees the acquisition of morality as an active change in patterns of response to problematic social situations rather than the learning of culturally accepted rules.

. The progressive educator stresses the essential links between cognitive and moral development; he assumes that moral development is not purely affective, and that cognitive development is a necessary though not sufficient condition for moral development. The development of logical and critical thought, central to cognitive education, finds its larger meaning in a broad set of moral values. The progressive also points out that moral development arises from social interaction in situations of social conflict. Morality is neither the internalization of established cultural values nor the unfolding of spontaneous impulses and emotions; it is justice, the reciprocity between the individual and others in his social environment.

Psychological Theories Underlying Educational Ideologies

We have described three schools of thought describing the general ends and means of education. Central to each of these educational ideologies is a distinctive educational psychology, a distinctive psychological theory of development (Kohlberg, 1968). Underlying the romantic ideology is a maturationist theory of development; underlying the cultural transmission ideology is an association-istic-learning or environmental-contingency theory of development; and underlying the progressive ideology is a cognitive-developmental or interactionist theory of development.

The three psychological theories described represent three basic metaphors of development (Langer, 1969). The romantic model views the development of the mind through the metaphor of organic growth, the physical growth of a plant or animal. In this metaphor, the environment affects development by providing necessary nourishment for the naturally growing organism. Maturationist psychologists elaborating the romantic metaphor conceive of cognitive development as unfolding through prepatterned stages. They have usually assumed not only that cognitive development unfolds but that individual variations in rate of cognitive development are largely inborn. Emotional development is also believed to unfold through hereditary stages, such as the Freudian psychosexual stages, but is thought to be vulnerable to fixation and frustration by the environment. For the maturationist, although both cognitive and social-emotional development unfold, they are two different things. Since social-emotional development is an unfolding of something biologically given and is not based on knowledge of the social world, it does not depend upon cognitive growth.

The cultural transmission model views the development of the mind through the metaphor of the machine. The machine may be the wax on which the environment transcribes its markings, it may be the telephone switchboard through which environmental stimulus-energies are transmitted, or it may be the computer in which bits of information from the environment are stored, retrieved, and recombined. In any case, the environment is seen as "input," as information or energy more or less directly transmitted to, and accumulated in, the organism. The organism in turn emits "output" behavior. Underlying the mechanistic metaphor is the associationistic, stimulus-response or environmentalist psychological theory, which can be traced from John Locke to Thorndike to B. F. Skinner. This psychology views both specific concepts and general cognitive structures as reflections of structures that exist outside the child in the physical and social world. The structure of the child's concepts or of his behavior is viewed as the result of the association of discrete stimuli with one another, with the child's responses, and with his experiences of pleasure and pain. Cognitive development is the result of guided learning and teaching. Consequently, cognitive education requires a careful statement of desirable behavior patterns described in terms of specific responses. Implied here is the idea that the child's behavior can be shaped by immediate repetition and elaboration of the correct response, and by association with feedback or reward.

The cognitive-developmental metaphor is not material, it is dialectical; it is a model of the progression of ideas in discourse and conversation. The dialectical metaphor was first elaborated by Plato, given new meaning by Hegel, and finally stripped of its metaphysical claims by John Dewey and Jean Piaget, to form a psychological method. In the dialectical metaphor, a core of universal ideas is redefined and reorganized as their implications are played out in experience and as they are confronted by their opposites in argument and discourse. These reorganizations define qualitative levels of thought, levels of increased epistemic adequacy. The child is not a plant or a machine; he is a philosopher or a scientist-poet. The dialectical metaphor of progressive education is supported by a cognitive-developmental or interactional psychological theory. Discarding the dichotomy between maturation and environmentally determined learning, Piaget and Dewey claim that mature thought emerges through a process of development that is neither direct biological maturation nor direct learning, but rather a reorganization of psychological structures resulting from organism-environment interactions. Basic mental structure is the product of the patterning of interaction between the organism and the environment, rather than a direct reflection of either innate neurological patterns or external environmental patterns.

To understand this Piaget-Dewey concept of the development of mental pattern, we must first understand its conception of cognition. Cognitions are assumed to be structures, internally organized wholes or systems of internal relations. These structures are *rules* for the processing of information or the connecting of events. Events in the child's experience are organized actively through these cognitive connecting processes, not passively through external association and repetition. Cognitive development, which is defined as change in cognitive structures, is assumed to depend on experience. But the effects of experience are not regarded as learning in the ordinary sense (training, instruction, modeling, or specific response practices). If two events which follow one another in time are cognitively connected in the child's mind, this implies that he relates them by means of a category such as causality; he perceives his operant behavior as causing the reinforcer to occur. A program of reinforcement, then, cannot directly change the child's causal structures since it is assimilated by the child in terms of his present mode of thinking. When a program of reinforcement cannot be assimilated to the child's causal structure, however, the child's structure may be reorganized to obtain a better fit between the two. Cognitive development is a dialogue between the child's cognitive structures and the structures of the environment. Further, the theory emphasizes that the core of development is not the unfolding of instincts, emotions, or sensorimotor patterns, but instead is cognitive change in distinctively human, general patterns of thinking about the self and the world. The child's relation to his social environment is cognitive; it involves thought and symbolic interaction.

Because of its emphasis on ways of perceiving and responding to experience, cognitive-developmental theory discards the traditional dichotomy of social *versus* intellectual development. Rather, cognitive and affective development are parallel aspects of the structural transformations which take place in development. At the core of this interactional or cognitive-developmental theory is the doctrine of cognitive stages. Stages have the following general characteristics:

1. Stages imply distinct or qualitative differences in children's modes of thinking or of solving the same problem.
2. These different modes of thought form an invariant sequence, order, or succession in individual development. While cultural factors may speed up, slow down, or stop development, they do not change its sequence.

3. Each of these different and sequential modes of thought forms a "structural whole." A given stage-response on a task does not just represent a specific response determined by knowledge and familiarity with that task or tasks similar to it; rather, it represents an underlying thought-organization.

4. Cognitive stages are hierarchical integrations. Stages form an order of increasingly differentiated and integrated *structures* to fulfill a common function. (Piaget, 1960, pp. 13-15)

In other words, a series of stages form an invariant developmental sequence; the sequence is invariant because each stage stems from the previous one and prepares the way for the subsequent stage. Of course, children may move through these stages at varying speeds and they may be found to be half in and half out of a particular stage. Individuals may stop at any given stage and at any age, but if they continue to progress they must move in accord with these steps.

The cognitive-developmental conception of stage has a number of features in common with maturational-theory conceptions of stage. The maturational conception of stage, however, is "embryological," while the interactional conception is "structural-hierarchical." For maturational theory, a stage represents the total state of the organism at a given period of time; for example, Gesell's embryological concept of stage equates it with the typical behavior pattern of an age period, e.g., there is a stage of "five-year-olders." While in the theories of Freud and Erikson stages are less directly equated with ages, psychoanalytic stages are still embryological in the sense that age leads to a new stage regardless of experience and regardless of reorganizations at previous stages. As a result, education and experience become valuable not for movement to a new stage but for healthy or successful integration of the concerns of the present stage. Onset of the next stage occurs regardless of experience; only healthy integration of a stage is contingent on experience.

By contrast, in cognitive-developmental theory a stage is a delimited structure of thought, fixed in a sequence of structures but theoretically independent of time and total organismic state (Kohlberg, 1969b; Loevinger *et al.*, 1970). Such stages are hierarchical reorganizations; attainment of a higher stage presupposes attainment of the prior stage and represents a reorganization or transformation of it. Accordingly, attainment of the next stage is a valid aim of educational experience.

For the interactionist, experience is essential to stage progression, and more or richer stimulation leads to faster advance through the series of stages. On the other hand, the maturational theory assumes that extreme deprivation will retard or fixate development, but that enrichment will not necessarily accelerate it. To understand the effects of experience in stimulating stage-development, cognitive-developmental theory holds that one must analyze the relation of the structure of a child's specific experience to behavior structures. The analysis focuses upon discrepancies between the child's action system or expectancies and the events experienced. The hypothesis is that some moderate or optimal degree of conflict or discrepancy constitutes the most effective experience for structural change.

As applied to educational intervention, the theory holds that facilitating the child's movement to the next step of development involves exposure to the next higher level of thought and conflict requiring the active application of the current level of thought to problematic situations. This implies: (1) attention to the child's mode or styles of thought, i.e., stage; (2) match of stimulation to that stage, e.g., exposure to modes of reasoning one stage above the child's own; (3) arousal, among children, of genuine cognitive and social conflict and disagreement about problematic situations (in contrast to traditional education which has stressed adult "right answers" and has reinforced "behaving well"); and (4) exposure to stimuli toward which the child can be active, in which assimilatory response to the stimulus-situation is associated with "natural" feedback.

In summary, the maturationist theory assumes that basic mental structure results from an innate patterning; the environmentalist learning theory assumes that basic mental structure results from the patterning or association of events in the outside world; the cognitive-developmental theory assumes that basic mental structure results from an interaction between organismic structuring tendencies and the structure of the outside world, not reflecting either one directly. This interaction leads to cognitive stages that represent the transformations of early cognitive structures as they are applied to the external world and as they accommodate to it.

Epistemological Components of Educational Ideologies

We have considered the various psychological theories as parts of educational ideologies. Associated with these theories are differing epistemologies or philosophies of science, specifying what is knowledge, i.e. what are observable facts and how can these facts be interpreted. Differences in epistemology, just as differences in actual theory, generate different strategies for defining objectives.

Romantic educational ideology springs not only from a maturational psychology, but from an existentialist or phenomenological epistemology, defining knowledge and reality as referring to the immediate inner experience of the self. Knowledge or truth in the romantic epistemology is self-awareness or self-insight, a form of truth with emotional as well as intellectual components. As this form of truth extends beyond the self, it is through sympathetic understanding of humans and natural beings as other "selves."

In contrast, cultural transmission ideologies of education tend to involve epistemologies which stress knowledge as that which is repetitive and "objective," that which can be pointed to in sense-experience and measurement and which can be culturally shared and tested.

The progressive ideology, in turn, derives from a functional or pragmatic epistemology which equates knowledge with neither inner experience nor outer sense-reality, but with an equilibrated or resolved relationship between an inquiring human actor and a problematic situation. For the progressive epistemology, the immediate or introspective experience of the child does not have ultimate truth or reality. The meaning and truth of the child's experience depends upon its relationship to the situations in which he is acting. At the same time, the progressive epistemology does not attempt to reduce psychological experience to observable responses in reaction to observable stimuli or situations. Rather, it attempts to functionally coordinate the external meaning of the child's experiences as *behavior* with its internal meaning as it appears to the observer.

With regard to educational objectives, these differences in epistemology generate differences with respect to three issues. The first issue concerns whether to focus objectives on internal states or external behavior. In this respect, cultural transmission and romantic ideologies represent opposite poles. The cultural transmission view evaluates educational change from children's performances, not from their feelings or thoughts. Social growth is defined by the conformity of behavior to particular cultural standards such as honesty and industriousness. These skill and trait terms are found in both common-sense evaluations of school grades and report cards, and in "objective" educational psychological measurement. Behaviorist ideologies systematize this focus by rigorously eliminating references to internal or subjective experience as "nonscientific." Skinner (1971) says:

We can follow the path taken by physics and biology by turning directly to the relation between behavior and the environment and neglecting . . . states of mind. . . . We do not need to try to discover what personalities, states of mind, feelings, . . . intentions—or other prerequisites of autonomous man really are in order to get on with a scientific analysis of behavior. (p. 15)

In contrast, the romantic view emphasizes inner feelings and states. Supported by the field of psychotherapy, romantics maintain that skills, achievements, and performances are not satisfying in themselves, but are only a means to inner awareness, happiness, or mental health. They hold that an educator or therapist who ignores the child's inner states in the name of science does so at his peril, since it is these which are most real to the child.

The progressive or cognitive-developmental view attempts to integrate both behavior and internal states in a functional epistemology of mind. It takes inner experience seriously by attempting to observe thought process rather than language behavior and by observing valuing processes rather than reinforced behavior. In doing so, however, it combines interviews, behavioral tests, and naturalistic observation methods in mental assessment. The cognitive-developmental approach stresses the need to examine mental competence or mental structure as opposed to examining only performance, but it employs a functional rather than an introspective approach to the observation of mental structure. An example is Piaget's systematic and reproducible observations of the preverbal infant's thought-structure of space, time, and causality. In short, the cognitive-developmental approach does not select a focus on inner experience or on outer behavior objectives by epistemological fiat, but uses a functional methodology to coordinate the two through empirical study.

A second issue in the definition of educational objectives involves whether to emphasize immediate experience and behavior or long-term consequences in the child's development. The progressive ideology centers on education as it relates to the child's experience, but attempts to observe or assess experience in functional terms rather than by immediate self-projection into the child's place. As a result the progressive distinguishes between *humanitarian* criteria of the quality of the child's experience and *educative* criteria of quality of experience, in terms of long-term developmental consequences. According to Dewey (1938):

Some experiences are miseducative. Any experience is miseducative that has the effect of arresting or distorting the growth of further experience. . . . An experience may be immediately enjoyable and yet promote the formation of a slack and careless attitude . . . (which) operates to modify the quality of subsequent experiences so as to prevent a person from getting out of them what they have to give. . . . Just as no man lives or dies to himself, so no experience lives or dies to itself. Wholly independent of desire or intent, every experience lives on in further experiences. Hence the central problem of an education based on experience is to select the kind of present experiences that live fruitfully and creatively in subsequent experience. (pp. 25-28)

Dewey maintains that an educational experience which stimulates development is one which arouses interest, enjoyment, and challenge in the immediate experience of the student. The reverse is not necessarily the case; immediate interest and enjoyment does not always indicate that an educational experience stimulates long-range development. Interest and involvement is a necessary but not sufficient condition for education as development. For romantics, especially of the "humanistic psychology" variety, having a novel, intense, and complex experience is *self-development* or self-actualization. For progressives, a more objective test of the effects of the experience on later behavior is required before deciding that the experience is developmental. The progressive views the child's enjoyment and interest as a basic and legitimate criterion of education, but views it as a humanitarian rather than an educational criterion. The progressive holds that education must meet humanitarian criteria, but argues that a concern for the enjoyment and liberty of the child is not in itself equivalent to a concern for his development.

Psychologically, the distinction between humanitarian and developmental criteria is the distinction between the short-term value of the child's immediate experience and the long-term value of that experience as it relates to development. According to the progressive view, this question of the relation of the immediate to the long-term is an empirical rather than a philosophic question. As an example, a characteristic behaviorist strategy is to demonstrate the reversibility of learning by performing an experiment in which a preschooler is reinforced for interacting with other children rather than withdrawing in a corner. This is followed by a reversal of the experiment, demonstrating that when the reinforcement is removed the child again becomes withdrawn. From the progressive or cognitive-developmental perspective, if behavior changes are of this reversible character they cannot define genuine educational objectives. The progressive approach maintains that the worth of an educational effect is decided by its effects upon later behavior and development. Thus, in the progressive view, the basic problems of choosing and validating educational ends can only be solved by longitudinal studies of the effects of educational experience.

The third basic issue is whether the aims of education should be universal as opposed to unique or individual. This issue has an epistemological aspect because romantics have often defined educational goals in terms of the expression or development of a unique self or identity; "objectivist" epistemologies deny that such concepts are accessible to clear observation and definition. In contrast, cultural transmission approaches characteristically focus on measures of individual differences in general dimensions of achievement, or social behavior dimensions on which any individual can be ranked. The progressive, like the romantic, questions the significance of defining behavior relative to some population norm external to the individual. Searching for the "objective" in human experience, the progressive seeks universal qualitative states or sequences in development. Movement from one stage to the next is significant because it is a sequence in the individual's own development, not just a population average or norm. At the same time, insofar as the sequence is a universally observed development it is not unique to the individual in question.

In summary, the cognitive-developmental approach derives from a functional or pragmatic epistemology which attempts to integrate the dichotomies of the inner versus the outer, the immediate versus the remote in time, the unique versus the general. The cognitive-developmental approach focuses on an empirical search for continuities between inner states and outer behavior and between immediate reaction and remote outcome. While focusing on the child's experience, the progressive ideology defines such experience in terms of universal and empirically observable sequences of development.

Ethical Value Positions Underlying Educational Ideologies

When psychologists like Dewey, Skinner, Neill and Montessori actually engage in innovative education, they develop a theory which is not a mere statement of psychological principle, it is an ideology. This is not because of the dogmatic, non-scientific attitude they have as psychologists, but because prescription of educational practice cannot be derived from psychological theory or science alone. In addition to theoretical assumptions about how children learn or develop (the psychological theory component), educational ideologies include value assumptions about what is educationally good or worthwhile. To call a pattern of educational thought an ideology is to indicate it is a fairly systematic combination of a theory about psychological and social fact with a set of value principles.

The Fallacy of Value Neutrality

A "value-neutral" position, based only on facts about child development or about methods of education, cannot in itself directly contribute to educational practice. Factual statements about what the processes of learning and development *are* cannot be directly translated into statements about what children's learning and development *ought to be* without introduction of some value-principles.

In "value-neutral" research, learning does not necessarily imply movement to a stage of greater cognitive or ethical adequacy. As an example, acquisition of a cognitively arbitrary or erroneous concept (e.g., it is best to put a marble in the hole) is considered learning in the same general sense as is acquisition of a capacity for logical inference. Such studies do not relate learning to some justifiable notion of knowledge, truth, or cognitive adequacy. Values are defined relative to a particular culture. Thus, morality is equivalent to conformity to, or internalization of, the particular standards of the child's group or culture. As an example, Berkowitz (1964) writes: "Moral values are evaluations of actions generally believed by the members of a given society to be either 'right' or 'wrong' " (p. 44).

Such "value-free" research cannot be translated into prescriptions for practice without importing a set of value-assumptions having no relation to psychology itself. The effort to remain "value-free" or "non-ideological" and yet prescribe educational goals usually has followed the basic model of counselling or consulting. In the *value-free consulting model,* the client (whether student or school) defines educational ends, and the psychologist can then advise about means of education without losing his value-neutrality or imposing his values. Outside education, the value-free consulting model not only provides the basic model for counselling and psychotherapy, where the client is an individual, but also for industrial psychology, where the client is a social system. In both therapy and industrial psychology the consultant is paid by the client and the financial contract defines whose values are to be chosen. The educator or educational psychologist, however, has more than one client. What the child wants, what parents want, and what the larger community wants are often at odds with one another.

An even more fundamental problem for the "value-free" consulting model is the logical impossibility of making a dichotomy between value-free means and value-loaded ends. Skinner (1971, p. 17) claims that "a behavior technology is ethically neutral. Both the villain and the saint can use it. There is nothing in a methodology that determines the values governing its use." But consider the use of torture on the rack as a behavior technology for learning which could be used by saint and villain alike. On technological grounds Skinner advises against punishment, but this does not solve the ethical issue.

Dewey's logical analysis and our present historical awareness of the value consequences of adopting new technologies have made us realize that choices of means, in the last analysis, also imply choices of ends. Advice about means and methods involves value considerations and cannot be made purely on a basis of "facts." Concrete, positive reinforcement is not an ethically neutral means. To advise the use of concrete reinforcement is to advise that a certain kind of character, motivated by concrete reinforcement, is the end of education. Not only can advice about means not be separated from choice of ends, but there is no way for an educational consultant to avoid harboring his own criteria for choosing ends. The "value-neutral" consulting model equates value-neutrality with acceptance of value-relativity, i.e., acceptance of whatever the values of the client are. But the educator or educational psychologist cannot be neutral in this sense either.

Values and the Cultural Transmission Ideology

In an effort to cope with the dilemmas inherent in value-neutral prescription, many psychologists tend to move to a cultural transmission ideology, based on the value premise of *social relativity*. Social relativity assumes some consistent set of values characteristic of the culture, nation, or system as a whole. While these values may be arbitrary and may vary from one social system to another, there is at least some consensus about them. This approach says, "Since values are relative and arbitrary, we might as well take the given values of the society as our starting point and advocate 'adjustment' to the culture or achievement in it as the educational end." The social relativist basis of the Bereiter-Engelmann system, for example, is stated as follows:

In order to use the term cultural deprivation, it is necessary to assume some point of reference. . . The standards of the American public schools represent one such point of reference. . . . There are standards of knowledge and ability which are consistently held to be valuable in the schools, and any child in the schools who falls short of these standards by reason of his particular cultural background may be said to be culturally deprived. (1966, p. 24)

The Bereiter-Engelmann preschool model takes as its standard of value "the standard of the American public schools." It recognizes that this standard is arbitrary and that the kinds of learning prized by the American public schools may not be the most worthy; but it accepts this arbitrariness because it assumes that "all values are relative," that there is no ultimate standard of worth for learning and development.

Unlike Bereiter and Engelmann, many social relativist educators do not simply accept the standards of the school and culture and attempt to maximize conformity to them. Rather, they are likely to elaborate or create standards for a school or society based on value premises derived from what we shall call "the psychologist's fallacy." According to many philosophical analysts, the effort to derive statements of *ought* (or value) directly from statements of *is* (or fact) is a logical fallacy termed the "naturalistic fallacy" (Kohlberg, 1971). The psychologist's fallacy is a form of the naturalistic fallacy. As practiced by psychologists, the naturalistic fallacy is the direct derivation of statements about what human nature, human values, and human desires ought to be from psychological statements about what they are. Typically, this derivation slides over the distinction between what is desired and what is desirable.

The following statement from B. F. Skinner (1971) offers a good example of the psychologist's fallacy:

Good things are positive reinforcers. Physics and biology study things without reference to their values, but the reinforcing effects of things are the province of behavioral science, which, to the extent that it concerns itself with operant reinforcement, is a science of values. Things are good (positively reinforcing) presumably because of the contingencies of survival under which the species evolved. It is part of the genetic endowment called 'human nature' to be reinforced in particular ways by particular things. . . . The effective reinforcers are matters of observation and no one can dispute them. (p. 104)

In this statement, Skinner equates or derives a value word (good) from a fact word (positive reinforcement). This equation is questionable; we wonder whether obtaining positive reinforcement really is good. The psychologist's fallacy or the naturalistic fallacy is a fallacy because we can always ask the further question, "Why is that good?" or "By what standard is that good?" Skinner does not attempt to deal with this further question, called the "open question" by philosophers. He also defines good as "cultural survival." The postulation of cultural survival as an ultimate value raises the open question too. We may ask, "Why should the Nazi culture (or the American culture) survive?" The reason Skinner is not concerned with answering the open question about survival is because he is a cultural relativist, believing that any non-factual reasoning about what is good or about the validity of moral principles is meaningless. He says:

What a given group of people calls good is a fact, it is what members of the group find reinforcing as a result of their genetic endowment and the natural and social contingencies to which they have been exposed. Each culture has its own set of goods, and what is good in one culture may not be good in another. (p. 128)

The Fallacy of Value-Relativism

Behind Skinner's value-relativism, then, lie the related notions that: 1) all valid inferences or principles are factual or scientific; 2) valid statements about values must be statements about facts of valuing; and 3) what people actually value differs. The fact that people do value different things only becomes an argument for the notion that values are relative if one accepts the first two assumptions listed. Both assumptions are believed by many philosophers to be mistaken because they represent forms of the fact-value confusion already described as the naturalistic fallacy. Confusing discourse about fact with discourse about values, the relativist believes that when ethical judgment is not empirical science, it is not rational. This equation of science with rationality arises because the relativist does not correctly understand philosophical modes of inquiry. In modern conceptions, philosophy is the clarification of concepts for the purpose of critical evaluation of beliefs and standards. The kinds of beliefs which primarily concern philosophy are normative beliefs or standards, beliefs about what ought to be rather than about what is. These include standards of the right or good (ethics), of the true (epistemology), and of the beautiful (esthetics). In science, the critical evaluation of factual beliefs is limited to criteria of causal explanation and prediction; a "scientific" critical evaluation of normative beliefs is limited to treating them as a class of facts. Philosophy, by contrast, seeks rational justification and criticism of normative beliefs, based on considerations additional to their predictive or causal explanatory power. There is fairly widespread agreement among philosophers that criteria for the validity of ethical judgments can be established independent of "scientific" or predictive criteria. Since patterns for the rational statement and justification of normative beliefs, or "oughts," are not identical with patterns of scientific statement and justification, philosophers can reject both Skinner's notion of a strictly "scientific" ethics and Skinner's notion that whatever is not "scientific" is relative. The open question, "Why is reinforcement or cultural survival good?," is meaningful because there are patterns of ethical justification which are ignored by Skinner's relativistic science.

Distinguishing criteria of moral judgment from criteria of scientific judgment, most philosophers accept the "methodological non-relativism" of moral judgment just as they accept the methodological non-relativism of scientific judgment (Brandt, 1956). This ethical non-relativism is based on appeal to principles for making moral judgments, just as scientific non-relativism is based on appeal to principles of scientific method or of scientific judgment.

In summary, cultural transmission ideologies rest on the value premise of social relativism—the doctrine that values are relative to, and based upon, the standards of the particular culture and cannot be questioned or further justified. Cultural transmission ideologies of the "scientific" variety, like Skinner's, do not recognize moral principles since they equate what is desirable with what is observable by science, or with what is desired. Philosophers are not in agreement on the exact formulation of valid moral principles though they agree that such formulations center around notions like "the greatest welfare" or "justice as equity." They also do not agree on choice of priorities between principles such as "justice" and "the greatest welfare." Most philosophers do agree, however, that moral evaluations must be rooted in, or justified by, reference to such a realm of principles. Most also maintain that certain values or principles ought to be universal and that these principles are distinct from the rules of any given culture. A principle is a universalizeable, impartial mode of deciding or judging, not a concrete cultural rule. "Thou shalt not commit adultery" is a rule for specific behavior in specific situations in a monogamous society. By contrast, Kant's Categorical Imperative—act only as you would be willing that everyone should act in the same situation—is a principle. It is a guide for choosing among behaviors, not a prescription for behavior. As such it is free from culturally-defined content; it both transcends and subsumes particular social laws. Hence it has universal applicability.

In regard to values, Skinner's cultural transmission ideology is little different from other, older ideologies based on social relativism and on subjective forms of hedonism, e.g., social Darwinism and Benthamite utilitarianism. As an educational ideology, however, Skinner's relativistic behavior technology has one feature which distinguishes it from older forms of social utilitarianism. This is its denial that rational concern for social utility is itself a matter of moral character or moral principle to be transmitted to the young. In Skinner's view, moral character concepts which go beyond responsiveness to social reinforcement and control rely on "prescientific" concepts of free will. Stated in different terms, the concept of moral education is irrelevant to Skinner; he is not concerned with teaching to the children of his society the value-principles which he himself adopts. The culture designer is a *psychologist-king*, a value relativist, who somehow makes a free, rational decision to devote himself to controlling individual behavior more effectively in the service of cultural survival. In Skinner's scheme there is no plan to make the controlled controllers, or to educate psychologist-kings.

Values and the Romantic Ideology

At first sight the value premises of the romantic ideology appear to be the polar opposites of Skinner's cultural transmission ideology. Opposed to social control and survival is individual freedom, freedom for the child to be himself. For example, A. S. Neill (1960) says:

How can happiness be bestowed? My own answer is: Abolish authority. Let the child be himself. Don't push him around. Don't teach him. Don't lecture him. Don't elevate him. Don't force him to do anything. (p. 297)

As we have pointed out, the romantic ideology rests on a psychology which conceives of the child as having a spontaneously growing mind. In addition, however, it rests on the ethical postulate that "the guardians of the young should merit the proud title of the defenders of the happiness and rights of children" (G. S. Hall, 1901, p. 24). The current popularity of the romantic ideology in "free school," "de-school," and "open school" movements is related to increased adult respect for the rights of children. Bereiter (1972) carries this orientation to an extreme conclusion:

Teachers are looking for a way to get out of playing God. . . . The same humanistic ethos that tells them what qualities the next generation should have also tells them that they have no right to manipulate other people or impose their goals upon them. The fact is that there are no morally safe goals for teachers any more. Only processes are safe. When it comes to goals, everything is in doubt. . . . A common expression, often thrown at me, when I have argued for what I believed children should be taught, is 'Who are we to say what this child should learn.' The basic moral problem . . . is inherent in education itself. If you are engaged in education, you are engaged in an effort to influence the course of the child's development . . . it is to determine what kinds of people they turn out to be. It is to create human beings, it is, therefore, to play God. (pp. 26-27)

This line of thought leads Bereiter to conclude:

The Godlike role of teachers in setting goals for the development of children is no longer morally tenable. A shift to informal modes of education does not remove the difficulty. This paper, then, questions the assumption that education, itself, is a good undertaking and considers the possibilities of a world in which values other than educational ones, come to the fore. (p. 25)

According to Bereiter, then, a humanistic ethical concern for the child's rights must go beyond romantic free schools, beyond de-schooling, to the abandonment of an explicit concern for education. Bereiter contrasts the modern "humanistic ethic," and its concern for the child's rights, with the earlier "liberal" concern for human rights which held education and the common school as the foundation of a free society. This earlier concern Bereiter sees expressed most cogently in Dewey's progressivism.

The historical shift in the conception of children's rights and human rights leading Bereiter to reject Dewey's position is essentially a shift from the liberal grounding of children's rights in ethical principles to the modern humanistic grounding of children's rights in the doctrine of ethical relativity.

Bereiter is led to question the moral legitimacy of education because he equates a regard for the child's liberty with a belief in ethical relativity, rather than recognizing that liberty and justice are universal ethical principles. "The teacher may try to play it safe by sticking to the middle of the road and only aiming to teach what is generally approved, but there are not enough universally endorsed values (if, indeed, there are any) to form the basis of an education" (Bereiter, 1972, p. 27). Here, he confuses an ethical position of tolerance or respect for the child's freedom with a belief in ethical relativity, not recognizing that respect for the child's liberty derives from a principle of justice rather than from a belief that all moral values are arbitrary. Respect for the child's liberty means awarding him the maximum liberty compatible with the liberty of others (and of himself when older), not refusal to deal with his values and behavior. The assumption of individual relativity of values underlying modern romantic statements of the child's liberty is also reflected in the following quote from Neill (1960):

Well, we set out to make a school in which we should allow children freedom to be themselves. In order to do this, we had to renounce all discipline, all direction, all suggestion, all moral training, all religious instruction. We have been called brave, but it did not require courage. All it required was what we had—a complete belief in the child as a good, not an evil, being. For almost forty years, this belief in the goodness of the child has never wavered; it rather has become a final faith. (p. 4)

For Neill, as for many free school advocates, value relativity does not involve what it did for Bereiter—a questioning of all conceptions of what is good in children and good for them. Neill's statement that the child is "good" is a completely non-relativist conception. It does not, however, refer to an ethical or moral principle or standard used to direct the child's education. Instead, just as in Skinner's cultural transmission ideology, the conception of the good is derived from what we have termed the psychologist's fallacy. Neill's faith in the "goodness of the child" is the belief that what children *do* want, when left to themselves, can be equated with what they *should* want from an ethical standpoint. In one way this faith is a belief that children are wired so as to act and develop compatibly with ethical norms. In another sense, however, it is an ethical postulation that decisions about what is right for children should be derived from what children do desire—that whatever children do is right.

This position begs the open question, "Why is freedom to be oneself good; by what standard is it a good thing?"

The question is raised by Dewey as follows (1938):

The objection made [to identifying the educative process with growing or developing] is that growth might take many different directions: a man, for example, who starts out on a career of burglary may grow in that direction . . . into a highly expert burglar. Hence it is argued that 'growth' is not enough; we must also specify the direction in which growth takes place, the end toward which it tends. (p. 75)

In Neill's view it is not clear whether there is a standard of development, i.e., some standard of goodness which children who grow up freely all meet, or whether children who grow up freely are good only by their own standards, even if they are thieves or villains by some other ethical standards. To the extent that there is a non-relativist criterion employed by Neill, it does not derive from, nor is it justified by, the ethical principles of philosophy. Rather, it is derived from matters of psychological fact about "mental health" and "happiness."

The merits of Summerhill are the merits of healthy free children whose lives are unspoiled by fear and hate. (Neill, 1960, p. 4)

The aim of education, in fact, the aim of life is to work joyfully and to find happiness. (Neill, 1960, p. 297).

Freedom, then, is not justified as an ethical principle but as a matter of psychological fact, leading to "mental health and happiness." These are ultimate terms, as are the terms "maximizing reinforcement" and "cultural survival" for Skinner. For other romantic educators the ultimate value terms are also psychological, e.g., "self-realization," "self-actualization," and "spontaneity." These are defined as "basic human tendencies" and are taken as good in themselves rather than being subject to the scrutiny of moral philosophy.

We have attempted to show that romantic libertarian ideologies are grounded on value-relativism and reliance on the psychologist's fallacy, just as are cultural-transmission ideologies, which see education as behavior control in the service of cultural survival. As a result of these shared premises, both romantic and cultural-transmission ideologies tend to generate a kind of elitism. In the case of Skinner, this elitism is reflected in the vision of the psychologist as a culture-designer, who "educates others" to conform to culture and maintain it but not to develop the values and knowledge which would be required for culture-designing. In the case of the romantic, the elitism is reflected in a refusal to impose intellectual and ethical values of libertarianism, equal justice, intellectual inquiry, and social reconstructionism on the child, even though these values are held to be the most important ones:

. . . Summerhill is a place in which people who have the innate ability and wish to be scholars will be scholars; while those who are only fit to sweep the streets will sweep the streets. But we have not produced a street cleaner so far. Nor do I write this snobbishly, for I would rather see a school produce a happy street cleaner than a neurotic scholar. (Neill, 1960, pp. 4-5)

In summary, in spite of their libertarian and non-indoctrinative emphases, romantic ideologies also have a tendency to be elitist or patronizing. Recalling the role of Dostoievsky's Grand Inquisitor, they see education as a process which only intends the child to be happy and adjusted rather than one which confronts the child with the ethical and intellectual problems and principles which the educator himself confronts. Skinner and Neill agree it is better for the child to be a happy pig than an unhappy Socrates. We may question, however, whether they have the right to withhold that choice.

Value Postulates of Progressivism

Progressive ideology, in turn, rests on the value postulates of ethical liberalism.[2] This position rejects traditional standards and value-relativism in favor of ethical universals. Further, it recognizes that value universals are ethical principles formulated and justified by the method of philosophy, not simply by the method of psychology. The ethical liberal position favors the active stimulation of the development of these principles in children. These principles are presented through a process of critical questioning which creates an awareness of the ground and limits of rational assent; they also are seen as relevant to universal trends in the child's own social and moral development. The liberal recognition of principles as *principles* clears them from confusion with psychological facts. To be concerned about children's happiness is an ethical imperative for the educator without regard to "mental health," "positive reinforcement," or other psychological terms used by educators who commit the "psychologist's fallacy." Rational ethical principles, not the values of parents or culture, are the final value-arbiters in defining educational aims. Such principles may call for consultation with parents, community, and children in formulating aims, but they do not warrant making them final judges of aims.

The liberal school recognizes that ethical principles determine the ends as well as the means of education. There is great concern not only to make schools more just, i.e., to provide equality of educational opportunity and to allow freedom of belief but also to educate so that free and just people emerge from the schools. Accordingly, liberals also conscientiously engage in moral education. It is here that the progressive and romantic diverge, in spite of a common concern for the liberty and rights of the child. For the romantic, liberty means non-interference. For the liberal, the principle of respect for liberty is itself defined as a moral aim of education. Not only are the rights of the child to be respected by the teacher, but the child's development is to be stimulated so that he may come to respect and defend his own rights and the rights of others.

[2] There are two main schools of ethical liberalism. The more naturalistic or utilitarian one is represented in the works of J. S. Mill, Sidgwick, Dewey, and Tufts. The other is represented in the works of Locke, Kant, and Rawls. A modern statement of the liberal ethical tradition in relation to education is provided by R. S. Peters (1968).

Recognition of concern for liberty as a principle leads to an explicit, libertarian conception of moral education. According to Dewey and McLellan (1895),

Summing up, we may say that every teacher requires a sound knowledge of ethical and psychological principles . . . . Only psychology and ethics can take education out of the rule-of-thumb stage and elevate the school to a vital, effective institution in the *greatest of all constructions—the building of a free and powerful character.* (p. 207)

In the liberal view, educational concern for the development of a "free character" is rooted in the principle of liberty. For the romantic or relativist libertarian this means that "everyone has their own bag," which may or may not include liberty; and to actively stimulate the development of regard for liberty or a free character in the child is as much an imposition on the child as any other educational intervention. The progressive libertarians differ on this point. They advocate a strong rather than a weak application of liberal principles to education. Consistent application of ethical principles to education means that education *should* stimulate the development of ethical principles in students.

In regard to ethical values, the progressive ideology adds the postulates of *development* and *democracy* to the postulates of liberalism. The notion of educational democracy is one in which justice between teacher and child means joining in a community in which value decisions are made on a shared and equitable basis, rather than non-interference with the child's value-decisions. Because ethical principles function as principles, the progressive ideology is "democratic" in a sense that romantic and cultural transmission ideologies are not.

In discussing Skinner we pointed to a fundamental problem in the relation between the ideology of the relativist educator and that of the student. Traditional education did not find it a problem to reconcile the role of teacher and the role of student. Both were members of a common culture and the task of the teacher was to transmit that culture and its values to the student. In contrast, modern psychologists advocating cultural transmission ideologies do not hold this position. As social relativists they do not really believe in a common culture; instead they are in the position of transmitting values which are different both from those they believe in and those believed in by the student. At the extreme, as we mentioned earlier, Skinner proposes an ideology for ethically relative psychologist-kings or culture designers who control others. Clearly there is a contradiction between the ideology for the psychologist-king and the ideology for the child.

Romantic or radical ideologies are also unable to solve this problem. The romantic adopts what he assumes are the child's values, or takes as his value premise what is "natural" in the child rather than endorsing the culture's values. But while the adult believes in the child's freedom and creativity and wants a free, more natural society, the child neither fully comprehends nor necessarily adheres to the adult's beliefs. In addition, the romantic must strive to give the child freedom to grow even though such freedom may lead the child to become a reactionary. Like the behavior modifier, then, the romantic has an ideology, but it is different from the one which the student is supposed to develop.

The progressive is non-elitist because he attempts to get all children to develop in the direction of recognizing the principles he holds. But is this not indoctrinative? Here we need to clarify the postulates of development and democracy as they guide education.

For the progressive, the problem of offering a non-indoctrinative education which is based on ethical and epistemological principles is partially resolved by a conception that these principles represent developmentally advanced or mature stages of reasoning, judgment, and action. Because there are culturally universal stages or sequences of moral development (Kohlberg & Turiel, 1971), stimulation of the child's development to the next step in a natural direction is equivalent to a long-range goal of teaching ethical principles.

Because the development of these principles is natural they are not imposed on the child—he chooses them himself. A similar developmental approach is taken toward intellectual values. Intellectual education in the progressive view is not merely a transmission of information and intellectual skills, it is the communication of patterns and methods of "scientific" reflection and inquiry. These patterns correspond to higher stages of logical reasoning, Piaget's formal operations. According to the progressive, there is an important analogy between scientific and ethical patterns of judgment or problem-solving, and there are overlapping rationales for intellectual and ethical education. In exposing the child to opportunities for reflective scientific inquiry, the teacher is guided by the principles of scientific method which the teacher himself accepts as the basis of rational reflection. Reference to such principles is non-indoctrinative if these principles are not presented as formulae to be learned ready-made or as rote patterns grounded in authority. Rather, they are part of a process of reflection by the student and teacher. A similar approach guides the process of reflection on ethical or value problems.

The problem of indoctrination is also resolved for the progressive by the concept of democracy. A concern for the child's freedom from indoctrination is part of a concern for the child's freedom to make decisions and act meaningfully. Freedom, in this context, means democracy, i.e., power and participation in a social system which recognizes basic equal rights. It is impossible for teachers not to engage in value-judgments and decisions. A concern for the liberty of the child does not create a school in which the teacher is value-neutral and any pretense of it creates "the hidden curriculum" (Kohlberg,

1969b). But it can create a school in which the teacher's value-judgments and decisions involve the students democratically.

We turn, now, to the nature and justification of these universal and intrinsically worthy aims and principles. In the next sections we attempt to indicate the way in which the concept of development, rooted in psychological study, can aid in prescribing aims of education without commission of the psychologist's fallacy. We call this the developmental-philosophic strategy for defining educational aims.

Strategies for Defining Educational Objectives and Evaluating Educational Experience

We have considered the core psychological and philosophical assumptions of the three major streams of educational ideology. Now we shall consider these assumptions as they have been used to define objectives in early education.

There appear to be three fundamental strategies for defining educational objectives, which we call "the bag of virtues" or "desirable trait" strategy, the "industrial psychology" or "prediction of success" strategy and the "developmental-philosophic" strategy. These strategies tend to be linked, respectively, with the romantic, the cultural transmission, and the progressive educational ideologies.

The romantic tends to define educational objectives in terms of a "bag of virtues"—a set of traits characterizing an ideal healthy or fully-functioning personality. Such definitions of objectives are justified by a psychiatric theory of a spontaneous, creative, or self-confident personality. This standard of value springs from the romantic form of the psychologist's fallacy. Statements of value (desirability of a character-trait) are derived from psychological propositions of fact, e.g., that a given trait is believed to represent psychological "illness" or "health."

The cultural transmission ideology defines immediate objectives in terms of standards of knowledge and behavior learned in school. It defines the long-range objective as eventual power and status in the social system (e.g., income, success). In Skinner's terms, the objective is to maximize the reinforcement each individual receives from the system, while maintaining the system. In defining objectives, this focus on prediction of later success is common to those whose interest lies in maintaining the system in its present form and those whose interest lies in equalizing opportunity for success in the system.

Within the cultural transmission school there is a second strategy for elaborating objectives which we have called the "industrial psychology" approach (Kohlberg, 1972). Psychologically, this strategy is more explicitly atheoretical than the "bag of virtues" approach; with regard to values it is more socially relativistic. Adopting the stance of the value-free consultant, it evaluates a behavior in terms of its usefulness as a means to the student's or the system's ends, and focuses on the empirical prediction of later successes. In practice, this approach has focused heavily on tests and measurements of achievement as they predict or relate to later success in the educational or social system.

The third strategy, the developmental-philosophic, is linked to the progressive ideology. The progressive believes that a liberal conception of education pursuing intrinsically worthy aims or states is the best one for everyone. Such a conception of objectives must have a psychological component. The progressive defines the psychologically valuable in developmental terms. Implied in the term "development" is the notion that a more developed psychological state is more valuable or adequate than a less developed state.

The developmental-philosophic strategy attempts to clarify, specify, and justify the concept of adequacy implicit in the concept of development. It does so through: a) elaborating a formal psychological theory of development—the cognitive-developmental theory; b) elaborating a formal ethical and epistemological theory of truth and worth linked to the psychological theory; c) relating both of these to the facts of development in a specific area; and d) describing empirical sequences of development worth cultivating.

Now we need to critically examine the three strategies. Our task is both logical and empirical. Logically, the chief question is, "Does the strategy define objectives which are intrinsically valuable or universally desirable? Can it deal with the charge that its value is relative or arbitrary?" Empirically, the major question is, "Does the strategy define objectives predicting to something of long-term value in later life?"

The Bag of Virtues Strategy

The "bag of virtues" strategy for choosing objectives is the approach which comes most naturally to educators. An example is the formulation of a Headstart list of objectives—as cited in Dr. Edith Grotberg's review (1969) offered by a panel of authorities on child development. One goal is "helping the emotional and social development of the child by encouraging self-confidence, spontaneity, curiosity and self-discipline." We may note that development is defined here in terms of trait words. From the point of view of the philosophic-developmentalist, the qualification of the term "social development" by such trait words is superfluous and misleading. The developmentalist would chart universals in preschool social development empirically and theoretically with implications for later development and would indicate the conditions which stimulate such development. Such a charting of development would make trait words like "spontaneity" and "self-confidence" unnecessary.

The justification for using trait words to qualify development as an educational end has usually been that development is too vague a term. We consider this question later. Here we need only note the arbitrariness and vagueness which underlies all efforts to use the positive connotations of ordinary trait terms of personality or character to define educational standards and values. This arbitrariness and vagueness exists in lists of mental health traits such as the Headstart list and also in lists of moral virtues composing moral character, such as the Hartshorne and May (1928-1932) objectives of "honesty, service, and self-control." Arbitrariness exists first in composing the list or "bag" of virtues itself. One member of the committee likes "self-discipline," another "spontaneity"; the committee includes both. While both words sound nice, one wonders whether cultivating "self-discipline" and cultivating "spontaneity" are consistent with one another. Second, we may note that the observable meaning of a virtue-word is relative to a conventional cultural standard which is both psychologically vague and ethically relative. The behavior that one person labels "self-discipline" another calls "lack of spontaneity." Because the observable meaning of a virtue-word is relative to a conventional cultural standard, its meaning is psychologically vague, a fact which was first demonstrated by Hartshorne and May for the virtue-word "honesty." Hartshorne and May were dismayed to discover that they could locate no such stable personality trait as honesty in school children. A child who cheated on one occasion might or might not cheat on another: cheating was for the most part situationally determined. In a factor analysis, there was no clearly identifiable factor or correlation pattern which could be called "honesty." Furthermore, "honesty" measurements did not predict to later behavior. This contradicts the commonsense notion underlying the bag of virtues approach. It turns out that dictionary terms for personality do not describe situationally general personality dispositions which are stable or predictive over development.

Related to the problem of psychological definition and measurement is the problem of the relativity of the standard of value defining "honesty" or any other virtue. Labeling a set of behaviors displayed by a child with positive or negative trait terms does not signify that they are of adaptive or ethical importance. It represents an appeal to particular community conventions, since one person's *"integrity"* is another person's *"stubbornness,"* one person's *"honesty* in expressing your true feelings" is another person's *"insensitivity* to the feelings of others."

We have criticized the "bag of virtues" approach on the grounds of *logical* questions raised by a procedure of sorting through the dictionary for trait terms with positive meaning. We need next to question two "scientific" or *psychological* assumptions, the concept of the personality trait and the concept of mental health, as they relate to the development of children. With regard to the trait assumption, longitudinal research findings lead us to question whether there are positive or adaptive childhood personality traits which are stable or pre-dictive over time and development, even if such traits are defined by psycho-logical rather than lexical methods. The relatively general and longitudinally stable personality traits which have been identified in earlier childhood are traits of temperament—introversion-extroversion, passivity-activity—which have been shown to be in large part hereditary temperamental traits without adaptive significance (research reviewed in Ausubel & Sullivan, 1970; Kohlberg, 1969b; Kohlberg, La Crosse & Ricks, 1971). The longitudinal research indicates that the notions of "mental health" or "mental illness" are even more questionable as concepts defining the meaning and value of personality traits. Unlike develop-ment, the term "mental health" has no clear psychological meaning when ap-plied to children and their education. When the clinician examines a child with reference to mental health, he records the child's lags (and advances) in cognitive, social, and psychomotor development. Occasionally such lags are indicative of "illness," e.g., of an organic brain condition. But, in general, if "illness" means anything beyond retarded development it means a prognosis of continued failure to develop. Considering the child's development as an aim of education, the metaphors of health and illness add little to detailed and adequate conceptions of cognitive and social development. This also is indi-cated by empirical longitudinal findings (Kohlberg, LaCrosse & Ricks, 1971). We are led to ask whether early childhood traits with apparent negative mental health implications like dependency, aggression, or anxiety, have predictive value as indicators of adult difficulties in "life adjustment" or "mental health." The answer at present is no: the mental health traits listed among the Head-start objectives, as well as those commonly included among the goals of other early education programs, have failed to show their predictive value for posi-tive or negative adult life adjustment. Even if the behavior changes sought in such programs were achieved, the child would be no more likely than before to become a well-adjusted adult.

Secondly, from the philosophic point of view, those who espouse the mental health bag of virtues commit the psychologist's fallacy and a related fallacy, that a panel of psychiatrists or child psychiatrists such as the one defining Head-start objectives are "experts" on ethical principles or values.

In educational practice, a concern for mental health has at least meant an ethical concern for the happiness of the child; this was neglected by cultural transmission school. But ethical principles based on a concern for the child's liberty and happiness can stand on their own without a mental health bag of virtues to rationalize them.

The Industrial Psychology Rationale

Translating educational objectives into a "bag of virtues" (skills) in the intellectual domain does not run into all the difficulties which it has encountered in the social-emotional domain. This is because reasonable precision has been attained in defining and measuring intellectual skills and achievements, because there is some degree of predictability over time in these skills, and because the questions of value-relativity raised by concepts of "moral character" and "mental health" as educational objectives are not as obvious when school aims are defined in terms of intellectual skills. But concepts of intellectual skills have only appeared satisfactory because of the high empirical overlap or correlation of these skills with cognitive development (in the developmental-philosophic sense) and because of the overlap with the non-educational or "biological" constant of general intelligence. Once cognitive skills are defined and measured by educational *achievement* measures, they have little clear use in defining educational objectives.

The "achievement skills" conception is a joint product of the "bag of virtues" and "industrial psychology" approach to educational aims. We have noted that the industrial psychology approach rests on identifying and measuring relative individual success in meeting the task demands of a current job or work-position, and on identifying characteristics predicting to later success or mobility in the job-system. Its major application in education has been the development of achievement tests. While not originally developed to define operational educational goals, achievement tests have frequently been used for this purpose. The massive Coleman Report (1966) rested its entire analysis of the quality and effects of schooling on variations in achievement test scores. A number of academic early education programs, including the Bereiter and Engelmann program (1966) previously quoted, essentially define their objective as the improvement of later achievement scores.

From the ethical or philosophic point of view, the use of achievement tests to measure educational objectives rests on a compounding of one type of relativism on another. The items composing an achievement test do not derive from any epistemological principles of adequate patterns of thought and knowledge, but rather represent samples of items taught in the schools. The information taught in the schools is relative and arbitrary: Latin and Greek for one hour, computer programming for another. There is no internal logical or epistemological analysis of these items to justify their worth. Another relativistic aspect of achievement tests is "marking on the curve." This leads to what Zigler has called "defining compensatory education objectives as raising the entire country above the 50th percentile in achievement tests" (unpublished comment).

Finally, and most basically, the relativism underlying achievement tests involves predicting to success in a system without asking whether the system awards success in an ethically justifiable manner, or whether success itself is an ethically justifiable goal. The original ethical impulse in constructing the achievement test was to equalize educational opportunity by a more impartial selection system than teachers' grades, recommendations, and the quality of schools the child has previously attended. This was done with relativistic acceptance that the content and demands of the school serve as social status gating mechanisms. It is hardly surprising that the whole desire to equalize opportunity, or increase educational and occupational justice through raising educational achievement scores, has failed in every possible sense of the word "failure" (Jencks, *et al.*, 1972).

On the psychological and factual side, there have been two basic and related flaws in the assumption that achievement tests represent something of educational value. The first is the notion that correlation or prediction can be substituted for causation. The second, related notion is that success within an arbitrary system, the schools, implies success in other aspects of life. With regard to the first assumption, advocates of the industrial psychology strategy and achievement tests based on it feel that the relation between causation and prediction is unimportant. We can efficiently select those who will do well in college, become successful salesmen, or become juvenile delinquents without facing the causation issue. But if we shift from using a test or a measure of behavior as a selector to using it as the criterion for an educational objective, the problem is quite different. Unless a predictor of later achievement or adjustment is also a causal determinant of it, it cannot be used to define educational objectives.

As an example of the confusion between correlation and causation, we know that grades and achievement scores in elementary school predict to comparable scores in high school which in turn predict to comparable scores in college. The assumption is then made that the *cause* of particular achievement scores is the earlier achievement. It is assumed that a child who does not attain a second grade level of performance on reading achievement will not attain an adequate level of reading later because he is low in reading achievement at second grade.

In fact, the prediction of early to later achievement is mainly due to factors extraneous to achievement itself. Longitudinal studies show that the stability or predictive power of school achievement tests is largely due, first, to a factor of general intelligence and, second, to social class. Achievement scores correlate with I.Q. scores and both measures predict to later school achievement; early elementary achievement does not predict to later achievement any better than does I.Q. alone. In other words, bright children learn what they're taught in school faster, but learning what they're taught in school does not make them brighter nor does it necessarily mean that they will learn later material faster.

Achievement tests also fail to predict to success in later life; in fact, longitudinal studies indicate that school achievement predicts to nothing of value other than itself.

For example, in terms of future job success, high school dropouts do as well as graduates who do not attend college; high school graduates with poor achievement scores and grades do as well as those with good scores; and, college graduates with poor grades do as well as those with good grades (see Kohlberg, LaCrosse & Ricks, 1971; Jencks, *et al*, 1972).

In summary, academic achievement tests have no theoretical rationale. Their practical rationale is primarily an industrial psychology "prediction for selection." But even by industrial psychology standards the tests do not do well since they fail to predict to later life achievement.

These criticisms do not imply that schools should be unconcerned with academic learning. They do suggest: (1) a heavy element of arbitrariness in current school objectives in academic learning; (2) the inability of educational testing methods endorsed by the industrial psychology school to make these objectives less arbitrary; and (3) the invalidity of assuming that if academic achievement is good, early achievement is best. Schools should teach reading, writing, and arithmetic, but their goals and success in teaching these subjects should not be judged by skill or achievement tests.

The Developmental-Philosophic Strategy

The developmental-philosophic strategy, as opposed to the other two, can deal with the ethical question of having a standard of non-relative or universal value and with factual questions of prediction. The concept of development, as elaborated by cognitive-developmental theory, implies a standard of adequacy *internal* to, and governing, the developmental process itself. It is obvious that the notion of development must do more than merely define what comes later in time. It is not clear that what comes later must be better. As an example, if anal interests mature later in time than oral interests, this in itself is no reason for claiming that the anal interests are better than the oral interests.

Cognitive-developmental theory, however, postulates a formal internal standard of adequacy which is not merely an order of events in time. In doing so it elaborates the ordinary-language meaning of the term "development." Webster's Dictionary tells us that to develop means "to make active, to move from the original position to one providing more opportunity for effective use, to cause to grow and differentiate along lines natural of its kind; to go through a process of natural growth, differentiation, or evolution by successive changes." This suggests an internal standard of adequacy governing development; it implies that development is not just any behavior change, but a change toward greater differentiation, integration, and adaptation. Cognitive-developmental psychological theory postulates that movement through a sequential progression represents movement from a less adequate psychological state to a more adequate psychological state. The existence of this "internal standard of adequacy" is suggested by studies which show that the child prefers thinking at the next higher moral or logical stage to thinking at his own stage (or at lower stages) (Rest, 1973), and that he moves in that direction under normal conditions of stimulation.

The concept of development also implies that such an internal standard of adequacy is different from notions of adaptation based on culturally relative success or survival. As a case, we may take stages of morality. Being at the highest moral stage led Socrates and Martin Luther King to be put to death by members of their culture. Obviously, then, moral development cannot be justified as adaptive by standards of survival or of conformity to cultural standards. In terms of developmental psychological theory, however, King's morality was more adequate than the morality of most people who survive longer. Formally, King's morality was a more differentiated and integrated moral system than that of most people. It was more adequate because if all people adopted King's morality, it would resolve for everyone moral problems and conflicts unresolved by lower-stage moralities.

As the example of King suggests, the formal standard of cognitive-developmental psychological theory is not itself ultimate, but must be elaborated as a set of ethical and epistemological principles and justified by the method of philosophy and of ethics. The distinctive feature of the developmental-philosophic approach is that a philosophic conception of adequate principles is coordinated with a psychological theory of development and with the fact of development.

In contrast to "value-free" approaches, the approach suggested by Dewey and Piaget considers questions of value or adequacy at the very start. Piaget begins by establishing epistemological and logical criteria for deciding which thought structures are most adaptive and adequate for coping with complexity. Similarly, our work on ethical stages has taken a philosophic notion of adequate principles of justice (represented especially in the work of Kant and Rawls) to guide us in defining the direction of development. Epistemological and ethical principles guide psychological inquiry from the start. Thus, the strategy attempts to avoid the naturalistic fallacy of directly deriving judgments of value from judgments about the facts of development, although it assumes that the two may be systematically related. It takes as an hypothesis for empirical confirmation or refutation that development is a movement toward greater epistemological or ethical adequacy as defined by philosophic principles of adequacy.

The progressives' philosophical method differs from the approaches of philosophers of other persuasions in that the progressive or developmental method is partly empirical rather than purely analytic. It combines a prior conception of development with a prior notion of an ethical standard of adequacy; but these notions can be revised in light of the facts, including the facts of development. If the facts of development do not indicate that individuals move toward philosophically desired principles of justice, then the initial philosophic definition of the direction of development is in error, and must be revised. The analytic and normative "ought" of the developmental philosopher must take into account the facts of development, but is not simply a translation of these facts.

This method of "empirical" or "experimental" philosophy is especially central for an educational philosophy prescribing educational aims. Philosophical principles cannot be stated as ends of education until they can be stated psychologically. This means translating them into statements about a more adequate stage of development. Otherwise the rationally accepted principles of the philosopher will only be arbitrary concepts and doctrines for the child. Accordingly, to make a genuine statement of an educational end, the educational philosopher must coordinate notions of principles with understanding of the facts of development.

Development as the Aim of Education

We have attempted to clarify and justify the basic claim that developmental criteria are the best ones for defining educationally important behavior changes. We need now to clarify how the psychological study of development can concretely define educational goals. A common criticism is that the concept of development is too vague to genuinely clarify the choice of the curricular content and aims of education. A second, related criticism is that the concept of development, with its connotation of the "natural," is unsuited to determine actual educational policy.

With regard to the issue of vagueness, if the concept of development is to aid in selecting educational aims and content, this assumes that only some behavior changes out of many can be labeled developmental. We need to justify this assumption and to clarify the conditions for developmental change.

Our position has been challenged by Bereiter (1970), who claims that determining whether or not a behavior change is development is a matter of theory, not an empirical issue. For example, Piagetian research shows that fundamental arithmetical reasoning (awareness of one-to-one correspondence, of inclusion of a larger class in a sub-class, of addition and subtraction as inverse operations), usually develops naturally, without formal instruction or schooling, i.e., it constitutes development. Such reasoning can also be explicitly taught, however, following various non-developmental learning theories. Accordingly, says Bereiter, to call fundamental arithmetical reasoning developmental does not define it as a developmental educational objective distinct from non-developmental objectives like rote knowledge of the multiplication tables.

In answer, the cognitive-developmental position claims that developmental behavior change is irreversible, general over a field of responses, sequential, and hierarchical (Kohlberg, 1970). When a set of behavior changes meets all these criteria, changes are termed stages or structural reorganizations. A specific area of behavioral change like fundamental arithmetical reasoning may or may not meet these criteria. Engelmann claims to have artificially taught children the "naturally developing" operation of conservation, but Kamii (1971) found that the children so taught met Engelmann's criteria of conservation without meeting the criteria of development, e.g., the response could be later forgotten or unlearned, it was not generalized, and so forth.

When a set of responses taught artificially do not meet the criteria of natural development this is not because educational intervention is generally incompatible with developmental change. It is because the particular intervention is found to mimic development rather than to stimulate it. The issue of whether an educational change warrants the honorific label "development" is a question for empirical examination, not simply a matter of theory.

We have claimed that development can occur either naturally or as the result of a planned educational program. As was discussed earlier, development depends on experience. It is true, however, that the way in which experience stimulates development (through discrepancy and match between experienced events and information-processing structures) is not the way experience is programmed in many forms of instruction and educational intervention. It is also true that the kinds of experience leading to development must be viewed in terms of a stimulation which is general rather than highly specific in its content or meaning.

Because the experiences necessary for structural development are believed to be *universal,* it is possible for the child to develop the behavior naturally, without planned instruction. But the fact that only about half of the adult American population fully reaches Piaget's stage of formal operational reasoning and only 5% reach the highest moral stage demonstrates that natural or universal forms of development are not inevitable but depend on experience (Kuhn, Langer, Kohlberg & Haan, 1971).

If this argument is accepted, it not only answers the charge that development is a vague concept but helps answer the charge that there are kinds of development (such as growth in skill at burglary) which are not valuable.

Such questionable types of "development" do not constitute development in the sense of a universal sequence or in the sense of growth of some general aspect of personality. As stated by Dewey (1938): "That a man may grow in efficiency as a burglar . . . cannot be doubted. But from the standpoint of growth as education and education as growth the question is whether such growth promotes or retards growth in general" (p. 75).

While a coherent argument has been made for why universal developmental sequences define something of educational value, we need to consider why such sequences comprise the ultimate criteria of educational value. We also need to consider how they relate to competing educational values. How does universal structural development as an educational aim relate to ordinary definitions of information and skills central to the educational curriculum? It seems obvious that many changes or forms of learning are of value which are not universals in development. As an example, while many unschooled persons have learned to read, the capacity and motivation to read does not define a developmental universal; nonetheless, it seems to us a basic educational objective. We cannot dispose of "growth in reading" as an educational objective, as we could "growth in burglary," simply because it is not a universal in development. But we argue that the ultimate importance of learning to read can only be understood in the context of more universal forms of development. Increased capacity to read is not itself a development, although it is an attainment reflecting various aspects of development. The value or importance of reading lies in its potential contribution to further cognitive, social, and aesthetic development. As stated by Dewey (1898):

No one can estimate the benumbing and hardening effect of continued drill in reading as mere form. It should be obvious that what I have in mind is not a Philistine attack upon books and reading. The question is not how to get rid of them, but how to get their value—how to use them to their capacity as servants of the intellectual and moral life. To answer this question, we must consider what is the effect of growth in a special direction upon the attitudes and habits which alone open up avenues for development in other lines. (p. 29)

A developmental definition of educational objectives must not only cope with competing objectives usually defined non-developmentally, but with the fact that the universal aspects of development are multiple. Here, as in the case of evaluating non-developmental objectives, the progressive educator must consider the relation of a particular development to development in general. As an example, Kamii (1971) has defined a program of preschool intervention related to each of the chapter headings of Piaget's books: space, time, causality, number, classification, and so on. Kamii's intent in making use of all the areas of cognitive development discussed by Piaget is not to imply that each constitutes a separate, intrinsic educational objective. Rather, her interest is to make use of all aspects of the child's experience relevant to *general* Piagetian cognitive development. Such a concept of generalized cognitive-stage development is meaningful because Kohlberg and DeVries (1971) and others have shown that there is a general Piagetian cognitive-level factor distinct from psychometric general intelligence.

In contrast to the psychometric concept of intelligence, the developmental level concept of intelligence does provide a standard or a set of aims for preschool education. It does not assume a concept of fixed capacity or "intelligence quotient" constant over development. In this sense, developmental level is more like "achievement" than like "capacity," but developmental level tests differ from achievement tests in several ways. While the developmental level concept does not distinguish between achievement and capacity, it distinguishes between cognitive achievement (performance) and cognitive process (or competence). Developmental tests measure level of thought process, not the difficulty or correctness of thought product. They measure not cognitive performance but cognitive competence, the basic possession of a core concept, not the speed and agility with which the concept is expressed or used under rigid test conditions.

Psychometric and developmental level concepts of intelligence are quite different. In practice, however, the two kinds of measures are highly correlated with one another, explaining why clear theoretical and operational distinctions between the two concepts of intelligence have not been made until recently. Factor-analytic findings now can provide an empirical basis for this distinction (Kohlberg & DeVries, 1971). While psychometric measures of general intelligence and of "primary mental abilities" at mental age six correlate with Piagetian measures of cognitive level, there is also a common factor to all developmental level tests. This factor is independent of general intelligence or of any special psychometric ability. In other words, it is possible to distinguish between psychometric capacity and developmental level concepts or measures of intelligence. Given the empirical distinction, cognitive stage measures provide a rational standard for educational intervention where psychometric intelligence tests do not. This is true for the following reasons:

1. The core structure defined by stage tests is in theory and experiment more amenable to educational intervention—Piagetian theory is a theory of stage movement occurring through *experience* of structural disequilibrium.

2. Piagetian performance predicts later development independent of a fixed biological rate or capacity factor, as demonstrated by evidence for longitudinal stability or prediction independent of I.Q. Because Piaget items define invariant sequences, development to one stage facilitates development to the next.

3. Piagetian test content has cognitive value in its own right. If a child is able to think causally instead of magically about phenomena, for instance, his ability has a cognitive value apart from arbitrary cultural demands—it is not a mere indicator of brightness, like knowing the word "envelope" or "amanuensis." This is reflected in the fact that Piaget test scores are qualitative; they are not arbitrary points on a curve. The capacity to engage in concrete logical reasoning is a definite attainment, being at mental age six is not. We can ask that all children reason in terms of logical operations; we cannot ask that all children have high I.Q.'s.

4. This cognitive value is culturally universal, the sequence of development occurs in every culture and subculture.

The existence of a general level factor in cognitive development allows us to put particular universal sequences of cognitive development into perspective as educational aims. The worth of a development in any particular cognitive sequence is determined by its contribution to the whole of cognitive development.

We must now consider the relation of developmental aims of education to the notion of developmental acceleration as an educational objective. We indicated that a concept of stages as "natural" does not mean that they are inevitable; many individuals fail to attain the higher stages of logical and moral reasoning. Accordingly, the aim of the developmental educator is not the acceleration of development but the eventual adult attainment of the highest stage. In this sense, the developmentalist is not interested in *stage-acceleration,* but in avoiding *stage-retardation.* Moral development research reviewed elsewhere suggests that there is what approaches an optimal period for movement from one stage to the next (Kohlberg & Turiel, 1973). When a child has just attained a given stage, he is unlikely to respond to stimulation toward movement to the next stage. In addition, after a long period of use of a given stage of thought, a child tends to "stabilize" at that stage and develops screening mechanisms for contradictory stimulation. Accordingly, it has been found that both very young and very old children at a given stage (compared to the age-norm for that stage) are less responsive or less able to assimilate stimulation at the next higher stage than children at the age-norm for that stage. The notion of an "open period" is not age-specific, it is individual. A child late in reaching Stage 2 may be "open" to Stage 3 at an age beyond that of another child who reached Stage 2 earlier. Nevertheless, gross age-periods may be defined which are "open periods" for movement from one stage to the next. Avoidance of retardation as an educational aim means presenting stimulation in these periods where the possibility for development is still open.

We need to consider a related distinction between *acceleration* and *decalage* as an aim of education. Piaget distinguishes between the appearance of a stage and its "horizontal *decalage,*" its spread or generalization across the range of basic physical and social actions, concepts, and objects to which the stage potentially applies. As a simple example, concrete logic or conservation is first noted in the concept of mass and only later in weight and volume. Accordingly, acceleration of the stage of concrete operations is one educational enterprise and the encouragement of *decalage* of concrete reasoning to a new concept or phenomenon is another. It is the latter which is most relevant to education. Education is concerned not so much with age of onset of a child's capacity for concrete logical thought, but with the possession of a logical mind—the degree to which he has organized his experience or his world in a logical fashion.

It is likely that the occurrence of such horizontal *decalage,* rather than age of first appearance of concrete operations, predicts to later formal operational thought. Formal reasoning develops because concrete reasoning represents a poor, though partially successful, strategy for solving many problems. The child who has never explored the limits of concrete logical reasoning and lives in a world determined by arbitrary unexplained events and forces, will see the limits of the partial solutions of concrete logic as set by intangible forces, rather than looking for a more adequate logic to deal with unexplained problems.

We have so far discussed development only as general cognitive development. According to cognitive-developmental theory there is always a cognitive component to development, even in social, moral, and aesthetic areas. Development, however, is broader than cognitive-logical development. One central area is moral development, as defined by invariant stages of moral reasoning (Kohlberg & Turiel, 1971, 1973). On the one hand, these stages have a cognitive component; attainment of a given Piaget cognitive stage is a necessary, though not sufficient, condition for the parallel moral stage. On the other hand, moral reasoning stages relate to action; principled moral reasoning has been found to be a precondition for principled moral action (Kohlberg and Turiel, 1973). For reasons elaborated throughout this paper, the stimulation of moral development through the stages represents a rational and ethical focus of education related to, but broadening, an educational focus upon cognitive development as such (Kohlberg & Turiel, 1971). Programs effective in stimulating moral development have been successfully demonstrated (Blatt & Kohlberg, 1973).

While developmental moral education widens the focus of cognitive-developmental education beyond the purely cognitive, there is a still broader unity, called ego-development, of which both cognitive and moral development are part (Loevinger, Wessler & Redmore, 1970). Particularly in the earlier childhood years, it is difficult to distinguish moral development from ego-development. Cognitive development, in the Piagetian sense, is also related to ego development, since both concern the child's core beliefs about the physical and social world. Much recent research demonstrates that the development of the ego, as attitudes and beliefs about the self, involves step-by-step parallel development of attitudes and beliefs about the physical and social world. Further, it indicates definite stages of ego-development, defined by Loevinger *et al.* (1970), van den Daele (1970) and others, which imply step-by-step parallels to Piaget's cognitive stages, although they include more social emotional content. In general, attainment of a Piagetian cognitive stage is a necessary but not sufficient condition for attainment of the parallel ego stage. All children at a given ego stage must have attained the parallel cognitive stage, but not all children at a cognitive stage will have organized their self-concept and social experience at the corresponding ego stage. Thus, a general concept of ego-development as a universal sequential phenomenon is becoming an empirically meaningful guide to defining broad educational objectives. Furthermore, experimental educational programs to stimulate ego-development have been piloted with some definite success at both the preschool and the high school levels (van den Daele, 1970; Sprinthall & Mosher, 1970).

Thus, education for general cognitive development, and perhaps even education for moral development, must be judged by its contribution to a more general concept of ego-development. In saying this, we must remember that "ego-development" is the psychologist's term for a sequence which also must have a philosophic rationale. One pole of ego-development is self-awareness; the parallel pole is awareness of the world. Increasing awareness is not only "cognitive," it is moral, aesthetic, and metaphysical; it is the awareness of new meanings in life.

Finally, we need to note that in the realm of ego-development, a focus upon "horizontal *decalage*" rather than acceleration is especially salient. The distinction reflects in a more precise and viable fashion the concern of maturational or romantic stage-theorists for an educational focus upon "healthy" passage through stages, rather than their acceleration. In maturational theories of personality stages, age leads to a new stage regardless of experience and reorganizations at previous stages. As a result, education and experience become valuable not for movement to a new stage, but for healthy or *successful integration* of the concerns of a stage. Onset of the next stage occurs regardless of experience; it is only healthy integration of the stages which is contingent on experience and which should be the focus for education. Without accepting this contention, cognitive-developmental theory would agree that premature development to a higher ego stage without a corresponding *decalage* throughout the child's world and life presents problems. In psychoanalytic maturational terms, the dangers of uneven or premature ego development are expressed as defects in ego-strength with consequent vulnerability to regression. In cognitive-developmental terms, inadequate "horizontal *decalage*" represents a somewhat similar phenomenon. While the relation of "ego-strength" to logical and moral *decalage* is not well understood, there are many reasons to believe they are related. A child who continues to think in magical or egocentric terms in some areas of cognition and morality is likely to be vulnerable to something like "regression" under stress later in life.

In conclusion, if a broad concept of development, conceived in stage-sequential terms, is still vague as a definer of educational ends, it is not due to the inherent narrowness or vagueness of the concept. Rather, it is due to the fact that researchers have only recently begun the kind of longitudinal and educational research needed to make the concept precise and useable. When Dewey advocated education as development at the turn of the century, most American educational psychologists turned instead to industrial psychology or to the mental health bag of virtues. If the results of the cognitive-developmental research of the last decades are still limited, they indicate real promise for finally translating Dewey's vision into a precise reality.

Summary and Conclusions

The present paper essentially recapitulates the progressive position first formulated by John Dewey. This position has been clarified psychologically by the work of Piaget and his followers; its philosophic premises have been advanced by the work of modern analytic philosophers like Hare, Rawls, and Peters. The progressive view of education makes the following claims:

1. That the aims of education may be identified with development, both intellectual and moral.

2. That education so conceived supplies the conditions for passing through an order of connected stages.

3. That such a developmental definition of educational aims and processes requires both the method of philosophy or ethics and the method of psychology or science. The justification of education as development requires a philosophic statement explaining why a higher stage is a better or a more adequate stage. In addition, before one can define a set of educational goals based on a philosophical statement of ethical, scientific, or logical principles one must be able to translate it into a statement about psychological stages of development.

4. This, in turn, implies that the understanding of logical and ethical principles is a central aim of education. This understanding is the philosophic counterpart of the psychological statement that the aim of education is the development of the individual through cognitive and moral stages. It is characteristic of higher cognitive and moral stages that the child himself constructs logical and ethical principles; these, in turn, are elaborated by science and philosophy.

5. A notion of education as attainment of higher stages of development, involving an understanding of principles, was central to "aristocratic" Platonic doctrines of liberal education. This conception is also central to Dewey's notion of a democratic education. The democratic educational end for all humans must be "the development of a free and powerful character." Nothing less than democratic education will prepare free people for factual and moral choices which they will inevitably confront in society. The democratic educator must be guided by a set of psychological and ethical principles which he openly presents to his students, inviting criticism as well as understanding. The alternative is the "educator-king," such as the behavior-modifier with an ideology of controlling behavior, or the teacher-psychiatrist with

an ideology of "improving" students' mental health. Neither exposes his ideology to the students, allowing them to evaluate its merit for themselves.

6. A notion of education for development and education for principles is liberal, democratic, and non-indoctrinative. It relies on open methods of stimulation through a sequence of stages, in a direction of movement which is universal for all children. In this sense, it is natural.

The progressive position appears idealistic rather than pragmatic, industrial-vocational, or adjustment-orientated, as is often charged by critics of progressivism who view it as ignoring "excellence." But Dewey's idealism is supported by Piagetian psychological findings which indicate that all children, not only well-born college students, are "philosophers" intent on organizing their lives into universal patterns of meaning. It is supported by findings that most students seem to move forward in developmentally oriented educational programs. Furthermore, the idealism of the developmental position is compatible with the notion that the child is involved in a process of both academic and vocational education. Dewey denied that educational experience stimulating intellectual and moral development could be equated with academic schooling. He claimed that practical or vocational education as well as academic education could contribute to cognitive and moral development; it should be for all children, not only for the poor or the "slow." Our educational system currently faces a choice between two forms of injustice, the first an imposition of an arbitrary academic education on all, the second a division into a superior academic track and an inferior vocational track. The developmental conception remains the only rationale for solving these injustices, and for providing the basis for a truly democratic educational process.

References

Ausubel, D., & Sullivan, E. *Theory and problems of child development.* New York: Grune and Stratton, 1970.

Bereiter, C. Educational implications of Kohlberg's cognitive-developmental view. *Interchange,* 1 (2, 1970), 25-32.

Bereiter, C. Moral alternatives to education. *Interchange,* 3 (1, 1972), 25-41.

Bereiter, C. *Must we educate?* Engelwood Cliffs, N. J.: Prentice-Hall, 1973.

Bereiter, C., & Engelmann, S. *Teaching disadvantaged children in the preschool.* Engelwood Cliffs, N. J.: Prentice-Hall, 1966.

Berkowitz, L. *Development of motives and values in a child.* New York: Basic Books, 1964.

Bettelheim, B. On moral education. In T. Sizer (Ed.), *Moral education.* Cambridge, Mass.: Harvard University Press, 1970.

Blatt, M., & Kohlberg, L. Effects of classroom discussion upon children's level of moral judgment. In Kohlberg & Turiel (Eds.), *Recent research in moral development.* New York: Holt, Rinehart and Winston, 1973.

Brandt, R. B. *Ethical theory.* Engelwood Cliffs, N.J.: Prentice-Hall, 1956.

Coleman, J. S. *et al. Equality of educational opportunity.* Washington, D.C.: U. S. Dept. of Health, Education and Welfare, Office of Education, 1966.

Dewey, J. The primary-education fetish. *The Forum.* Washington, D. C.: U. S. Government Printing Office, May, 1898.

Dewey, J. *Experience and education.* New York: Collier, 1963 (originally written in 1938).

Dewey, J. & McLellan, J. The psychology of number. In R. Archambault (Ed.), *John Dewey on education: Selected writings.* New York: Random House, 1964.

Freud, A. The ego and the mechanisms of defense. London: Hogarth Press, 1937.

Grotberg, E. *Review of research, 1965 to 1969.* Office of Economic Opportunity Pamphlet 6108-13. Washington, D.C.: Research and Evaluation Office, Project Head Start, Office of Economic Opportunity, 1969.

Group for the Advancement of Psychiatry. *Psychopathological disorders in childhood: Theoretical considerations and a proposed classification.* Formulated by the Committee on Child Psychiatry, GAP Report, 62 (6, 1966), 173-343.

Hall, G. S. The ideal school based on child study. *The Forum,* 32, 1901.

Hartshorne, H., & May, M. A. *Studies in the nature of character.* Vol. 1. Studies in deceit. Vol. 2. Studies in service and self-control. Vol. 3. Studies in organization of character. New York: Macmillan, 1928-1930.

Jencks, C., *et al. Inequality: A reassessment of the effect of family and schooling in America.* New York: Basic Books, 1972.

Kamii, C. Evaluating pupil learning in preschool education: Socio-emotional, perceptual-motor, and cognitive objectives. In B. S. Bloom, J. T. Hastings, & G. Madaus (Eds.), *Formative and summative evaluation of student learning.* New York: McGraw-Hill, 1971.

Kohlberg, L. Early education: A cognitive-developmental view. *Child Development,* 39 (December, 1968), 1013-1062.

Kohlberg, L. The moral atmosphere of the school. Paper delivered at Association for Supervision and Curriculum Development Conference on the "Unstudied Curriculum." Washington, D.C., January 9, 1969a (printed in A.A.S.C. Yearbook, 1970).

Kohlberg, L. Stage and sequence: The cognitive-developmental approach to socialization. In D. Goslin (Ed.), *Handbook of socialization theory and research.* New York: Rand McNally, 1969b.

Kohlberg, L. Reply to Bereiter's statement on Kohlberg's cognitive-developmental view. *Interchange,* 1 (2, 1970), 40-48.

Kohlberg, L. From is to ought: How to commit the naturalistic fallacy and get away with it in the study of moral development. In T. Mischel (Ed.), *Cognitive development and epistemology.* New York: Academic Press, 1971.

Kohlberg, L., LaCrosse, R., & Ricks, D. The predictability of adult mental health from childhood behavior. In B. Wolman (Ed.), *Handbook of child psychopathology.* New York: McGraw-Hill, 1971.

Kohlberg, L. & DeVries, R. Relations between Piaget and psychometric assessments of intelligence. In C. Lavatelli (Ed.), *The natural curriculum.* E.R.I.C., 1971. Urbana, Ill.:

Kohlberg, L., & Turiel, E. Moral development and moral education. In G. Lesser (Ed.), *Psychology and educational practice.* Chicago: Scott Foresman, 1971.

Kohlberg, L., & Turiel, E. (Eds.). *Recent research in moral development.* New York: Holt, Rinehart and Winston, 1973.

Kuhn, D., Langer, J., Kohlberg, L., & Haan, N. The development of formal operations in logical and moral judgment. Unpublished mimeo monograph. Columbia University, 1971.

Langer, J. *Theories of development.* New York: Holt, Rinehart and Winston, 1969.

Loevinger, J., Wessler, R., & Redmore, C. *Measuring ego development.* San Francisco: Jossey-Bass, 1970.

Mead, G. H. *Movements of thought in the nineteenth century.* Chicago: University of Chicago Press, 1936.

Neill, A. S. *Summerhill.* New York: Hart, 1960.

Peters, R. S. *Ethics and education.* Chicago: Scott Foresman, 1968.

Piaget, J. The general problem of the psychobiological development of the child. In J. M. Tanner & B. Inhelder (Eds.), *Discussion on child development.* Vol. 4. New York: International Universities Press, 1960.

Rawls, J. *A theory of justice.* Cambridge, Mass.: Harvard University Press, 1971.

Rest, J. Comprehension preference and spontaneous usage in moral judgment. In L. Kohlberg & E. Turiel (Eds.), *Recent research in moral development.* New York: Holt, Rinehart and Winston, 1973.

Skinner, B. F. *Beyond freedom and dignity.* New York: Alfred A. Knopf, 1971.

Sprinthall, N. A., & Mosher, R. L. Psychological education in secondary schools: A program to promote individual and human development. *American Psychologist, 25* (October, 1970), 911-924.

Turiel, E. Developmental processes in the child's moral thinking. In P. Mussen, J. Langer, & M. Covington (Eds.), *new Directions in developmental psychology.* New York: Holt, Rinehart and Winston, 1969.

van den Daele, L. Preschool intervention with social learning. *Journal of Negro Education, 39* (Fall, 1970), 296-304.

In a Different Voice:
Women's Conceptions of
Self and of Morality

CAROL GILLIGAN

Carol Gilligan examines the limitations of several models of human development, most notably Kohlberg's stage theory of moral development, and concludes that they have not given adequate expression to the concerns and experiences of women. Through a review of psychological and literary sources, she illustrates the feminine construction of reality. From her interviews with women contemplating abortion, she derives an alternative sequence for the development of women's moral judgments and argues for the integration of the "feminine voice" into an expanded conception of adulthood.

The arc of developmental theory leads from infantile dependence to adult autonomy, tracing a path characterized by an increasing differentiation of self from other and a progressive freeing of thought from contextual constraints. The vision of Luther, journeying from the rejection of a self defined by others to the assertive boldness of "Here I stand" and the image of Plato's allegorical man in the cave, separating at last the shadows from the sun, have taken powerful hold on the psychological understanding of what constitutes development. Thus, the individual, meeting fully the developmental challenges of adolescence as set for him by Piaget, Erikson, and Kohlberg, thinks formally, proceeding from theory to fact, and defines both the self and the moral autonomously, that is, apart from the identifications and conventions that had comprised the particulars of his childhood world. So equipped, he is presumed ready to live as an adult, to love and work in a way that is both intimate and generative, to develop an ethical sense of caring and a genital mode of relating in which giving and taking fuse in the ultimate reconciliation of the tension between self and other.

The research reported here was partially supported by a grant from the Spencer Foundation. I wish to thank Mary Belenky for her collaboration and colleagueship in the abortion decision study and Michael Murphy for his comments and help in preparing this manuscript.

Harvard Educational Review   Vol. 47   No. 4   November 1977, 481–517

Yet the men whose theories have largely informed this understanding of development have all been plagued by the same problem, the problem of women, whose sexuality remains more diffuse, whose perception of self is so much more tenaciously embedded in relationships with others and whose moral dilemmas hold them in a mode of judgment that is insistently contextual. The solution has been to consider women as either deviant or deficient in their development.

That there is a discrepancy between concepts of womanhood and adulthood is nowhere more clearly evident than in the series of studies on sex-role stereotypes reported by Broverman, Vogel, Broverman, Clarkson, and Rosenkrantz (1972). The repeated finding of these studies is that the qualities deemed necessary for adulthood—the capacity for autonomous thinking, clear decision making, and responsible action—are those associated with masculinity but considered undesirable as attributes of the feminine self. The stereotypes suggest a splitting of love and work that relegates the expressive capacities requisite for the former to women while the instrumental abilities necessary for the latter reside in the masculine domain. Yet, looked at from a different perspective, these stereotypes reflect a conception of adulthood that is itself out of balance, favoring the separateness of the individual self over its connection to others and leaning more toward an autonomous life of work than toward the interdependence of love and care.

This difference in point of view is the subject of this essay, which seeks to identify in the feminine experience and construction of social reality a distinctive voice, recognizable in the different perspective it brings to bear on the construction and resolution of moral problems. The first section begins with the repeated observation of difference in women's concepts of self and of morality. This difference is identified in previous psychological descriptions of women's moral judgments and described as it again appears in current research data. Examples drawn from interviews with women in and around a university community are used to illustrate the characteristics of the feminine voice. The relational bias in women's thinking that has, in the past, been seen to compromise their moral judgment and impede their development now begins to emerge in a new developmental light. Instead of being seen as a developmental deficiency, this bias appears to reflect a different social and moral understanding.

This alternative conception is enlarged in the second section through consideration of research interviews with women facing the moral dilemma of whether to continue or abort a pregnancy. Since the research design allowed women to define as well as resolve the moral problem, developmental distinctions could be derived directly from the categories of women's thought. The responses of women to structured interview questions regarding the pregnancy decision formed the basis for describing a developmental sequence that traces progressive differentiations in their understanding and judgment of conflicts between self and other. While the sequence of women's moral development follows the three-level progression of all social developmental theory, from an egocentric through a societal to a universal perspective, this progression takes place within a distinct moral conception. This conception differs from that derived by Kohlberg from his all-male longitudinal research data.

This difference then becomes the basis in the third section for challenging the current assessement of women's moral judgment at the same time that it brings to bear a new perspective on developmental assessment in general. The inclusion in the overall conception of development of those categories derived from the study of women's moral judgment enlarges developmental understanding, enabling it to encompass better the thinking of both sexes. This is particularly true with respect to the construction and resolution of the dilemmas of adult life. Since the conception of adulthood retrospectively shapes the theoretical understanding of the development that precedes it, the changes in that conception that follow from the more central inclusion of women's judgments recast developmental understanding and lead to a reconsideration of the substance of social and moral development.

Characteristics of the Feminine Voice

The revolutionary contribution of Piaget's work is the experimental confirmation and refinement of Kant's assertion that knowledge is actively constructed rather than passively received. Time, space, self, and other, as well as the categories of developmental theory, all arise out of the active interchange between the individual and the physical and social world in which he lives and of which he strives to make sense. The development of cognition is the process of reappropriating reality at progressively more complex levels of apprehension, as the structures of thinking expand to encompass the increasing richness and intricacy of experience.

Moral development, in the work of Piaget and Kohlberg, refers specifically to the expanding conception of the social world as it is reflected in the understanding and resolution of the inevitable conflicts that arise in the relations between self and others. The moral judgment is a statement of priority, an attempt at rational resolution in a situation where, from a different point of view, the choice itself seems to do violence to justice.

Kohlberg (1969), in his extension of the early work of Piaget, discovered six stages of moral judgment, which he claimed formed an invariant sequence, each successive stage representing a more adequate construction of the moral problem, which in turn provides the basis for its more just resolution. The stages divide into three levels, each of which denotes a significant expansion of the moral point of view from an egocentric through a societal to a universal ethical conception. With this expansion in perspective comes the capacity to free moral judgment from the individual needs and social conventions with which it had earlier been confused and anchor it instead in principles of justice that are universal in application. These principles provide criteria upon which both individual and societal claims can be impartially assessed. In Kohlberg's view, at the highest stages of development morality is freed from both psychological and historical constraints, and the individual can judge independently of his own particular needs and of the values of those around him.

That the moral sensibility of women differs from that of men was noted by Freud (1925/1961) in the following by now well-quoted statement:

I cannot evade the notion (though I hesitate to give it expression) that for women the level of what is ethically normal is different from what it is in man. Their superego is never so inexorable, so impersonal, so independent of its emotional origins as we require it to be in men. Character-traits which critics of every epoch have brought up against women—that they show less sense of justice than men, that they are less ready to submit to the great exigencies of life, that they are more often influenced in their judgments by feelings of affection or hostility—all these would be amply accounted for by the modification in the formation of their super-ego which we have inferred above. (pp. 257–258)

While Freud's explanation lies in the deviation of female from male development around the construction and resolution of the Oedipal problem, the same observations about the nature of morality in women emerge from the work of Piaget and Kohlberg. Piaget (1932/1965), in his study of the rules of children's games, observed that, in the games they played, girls were "less explicit about agreement [than boys] and less concerned with legal elaboration" (p. 93). In contrast to the boys' interest in the codification of rules, the girls adopted a more pragmatic attitude, regarding "a rule as good so long as the game repays it" (p. 83). As a result, in comparison to boys, girls were found to be "more tolerant and more easily reconciled to innovations" (p. 52).

Kohlberg (1971) also identifies a strong interpersonal bias in the moral judgments of women, which leads them to be considered as typically at the third of his six-stage developmental sequence. At that stage, the good is identified with "what pleases or helps others and is approved of by them" (p. 164). This mode of judgment is conventional in its conformity to generally held notions of the good but also psychological in its concern with intention and consequence as the basis for judging the morality of action.

That women fall largely into this level of moral judgment is hardly surprising when we read from the Broverman et al. (1972) list that prominent among the twelve attributes considered to be desirable for women are tact, gentleness, awareness of the feelings of others, strong need for security, and easy expression of tender feelings. And yet, herein lies the paradox, for the very traits that have traditionally defined the "goodness" of women, their care for and sensitivity to the needs of others, are those that mark them as deficient in moral development. The infusion of feeling into their judgments keeps them from developing a more independent and abstract ethical conception in which concern for others derives from principles of justice rather than from compassion and care. Kohlberg, however, is less pessimistic than Freud in his assessment, for he sees the development of women as extending beyond the interpersonal level, following the same path toward independent, principled judgment that he discovered in the research on men from which his stages were derived. In Kohlberg's view, women's development will proceed beyond Stage Three when they are challenged to solve moral problems that require them to see beyond the relationships that have in the past generally bound their moral experience.

What then do women say when asked to construct the moral domain; how do we identify the characteristically "feminine" voice? A Radcliffe undergraduate, responding to the question, "If you had to say what morality meant to you, how would you sum it up?," replies:

> When I think of the word morality, I think of obligations. I usually think of it as conflicts between personal desires and social things, social considerations, or personal desires of yourself versus personal desires of another person or people or whatever. Morality is that whole realm of how you decide these conflicts. A moral person is one who would decide, like by placing themselves more often than not as equals, a truly moral person would always consider another person as their equal . . . in a situation of social interaction, something is morally wrong where the individual ends up screwing a lot of people. And it is morally right when everyone comes out better off.[1]

Yet when asked if she can think of someone whom she would consider a genuinely moral person, she replies, "Well, immediately I think of Albert Schweitzer because he has obviously given his life to help others." Obligation and sacrifice override the ideal of equality, setting up a basic contradiction in her thinking.

Another undergraduate responds to the question, "What does it mean to say something is morally right or wrong?," by also speaking first of responsibilities and obligations:

> Just that it has to do with responsibilties and obligations and values, mainly values. . . . In my life situation I relate morality with interpersonal relationships that have to do with respect for the other person and myself. [Why respect other people?] Because they have a consciousness or feelings that can be hurt, an awareness that can be hurt.

The concern about hurting others persists as a major theme in the responses of two other Radcliffe students:

> [Why be moral?] Millions of people have to live together peacefully. I personally don't want to hurt other people. That's a real criterion, a main criterion for me. It underlies my sense of justice. It isn't nice to inflict pain. I empathize with anyone in pain. Not hurting others is important in my own private morals. Years ago, I would have jumped out of a window not to hurt my boyfriend. That was pathological. Even today though, I want approval and love and I don't want enemies. Maybe that's why there is morality—so people can win approval, love and friendship.

> My main moral principle is not hurting other people as long as you aren't going against your own conscience and as long as you remain true to yourself. . . . There are many moral issues such as abortion, the draft, killing, stealing, monogamy, etc. If something is a controversial issue like these, then I always say it is up to the individual. The individual has to decide and then follow his own conscience. There are no moral absolutes. . . . Laws are pragmatic instruments, but they are not absolutes. A viable society can't make exceptions all the time, but I would personally. . . . I'm afraid I'm heading for some big crisis with my boy-

---

[1] The Radcliffe women whose responses are cited were interviewed as part of a pilot study on undergraduate moral development conducted by the author in 1970.

> friend someday, and someone will get hurt, and he'll get more hurt than I will.
> I feel an obligation to not hurt him, but also an obligation to not lie. I don't
> know if it is possible to not lie and not hurt.

The common thread that runs through these statements, the wish not to hurt others and the hope that in morality lies a way of solving conflicts so that no one will get hurt, is striking in that it is independently introduced by each of the four women as the most specific item in their response to a most general question. The moral person is one who helps others; goodness is service, meeting one's obligations and responsibilities to others, if possible, without sacrificing oneself. While the first of the four women ends by denying the conflict she initially introduced, the last woman anticipates a conflict between remaining true to herself and adhering to her principle of not hurting others. The dilemma that would test the limits of this judgment would be one where helping others is seen to be at the price of hurting the self.

The reticence about taking stands on "controversial issues," the willingness to "make exceptions all the time" expressed in the final example above, is echoed repeatedly by other Radcliffe students, as in the following two examples:

> I never feel that I can condemn anyone else. I have a very relativistic position.
> The basic idea that I cling to is the sanctity of human life. I am inhibited about
> impressing my beliefs on others.

> I could never argue that my belief on a moral question is anything that another
> person should accept. I don't believe in absolutes. . . . If there is an absolute for
> moral decisions, it is human life.

Or as a thirty-one-year-old Wellesley graduate says, in explaining why she would find it difficult to steal a drug to save her own life despite her belief that it would be right to steal for another: "It's just very hard to defend yourself against the rules. I mean, we live by consensus, and you take an action simply for yourself, by yourself, there's no consensus there, and that is relatively indefensible in this society now."

What begins to emerge is a sense of vulnerability that impedes these women from taking a stand, what George Eliot (1860/1965) regards as the girl's "susceptibility" to adverse judgments of others, which stems from her lack of power and consequent inability to do something in the world. While relativism in men, the unwillingness to make moral judgments that Kohlberg and Kramer (1969) and Kohlberg and Gilligan (1971) have associated with the adolescent crisis of identity and belief, takes the form of calling into question the concept of morality itself, the women's reluctance to judge stems rather from their uncertainty about their right to make moral statements or, perhaps, the price for them that such judgment seems to entail. This contrast echoes that made by Matina Horner (1972), who differentiated the ideological fear of success expressed by men from the personal conflicts about succeeding that riddled the women's responses to stories of competitive achievement.

Most of the men who responded with the expectation of negative consequences because of success were not concerned about their masculinity but were instead likely to have expressed existential concerns about finding a "non-materialistic happiness and satisfaction in life." These concerns, which reflect changing attitudes toward traditional kinds of success or achievement in our society, played little, if any, part in the female stories. Most of the women who were high in fear of success imagery continued to be concerned about the discrepancy between success in the situation described and feminine identity. (pp. 163–164)

When women feel excluded from direct participation in society, they see themselves as subject to a consensus or judgment made and enforced by the men on whose protection and support they depend and by whose names they are known. A divorced middle-aged woman, mother of adolescent daughters, resident of a sophisticated university community, tells the story as follows:

As a woman, I feel I never understood that I was a person, that I can make decisions and I have a right to make decisions. I always felt that that belonged to my father or my husband in some way or church which was always represented by a male clergyman. They were the three men in my life: father, husband, and clergyman, and they had much more to say about what I should or shouldn't do. They were really authority figures which I accepted. I didn't rebel against that. It only has lately occurred to me that I never even rebelled against it, and my girls are much more conscious of this, not in the militant sense, but just in the recognizing sense. . . . I still let things happen to me rather than make them happen, than to make choices, although I know all about choices. I know the procedures and the steps and all. [Do you have any clues about why this might be true?] Well, I think in one sense, there is less responsibility involved. Because if you make a dumb decision, you have to take the rap. If it happens to you, well, you can complain about it. I think that if you don't grow up feeling that you ever had any choices, you don't either have the sense that you have emotional responsibility. With this sense of choice comes this sense of responsibility.

The essence of the moral decision is the exercise of choice and the willingness to accept responsibility for that choice. To the extent that women perceive themselves as having no choice, they correspondingly excuse themselves from the responsibility that decision entails. Childlike in the vulnerability of their dependence and consequent fear of abandonment, they claim to wish only to please but in return for their goodness they expect to be loved and cared for. This, then, is an "altruism" always at risk, for it presupposes an innocence constantly in danger of being compromised by an awareness of the trade-off that has been made. Asked to describe herself, a Radcliffe senior responds:

I have heard of the onion skin theory. I see myself as an onion, as a block of different layers, the external layers for people that I don't know that well, the agreeable, the social, and as you go inward there are more sides for people I know that I show. I am not sure about the innermost, whether there is a core, or whether I have just picked up everything as I was growing up, these different influences. I think I have a neutral attitude towards myself, but I do think in terms of good and bad. . . . Good—I try to be considerate and thoughtful of other people and I try to be fair in situations and be tolerant. I use the words but I try and work them out practically. . . . Bad things—I am not sure if they are bad, if they are altruistic or I am doing them basically for approval of other people. [Which things are these?] The values I have when I try to act them out. They deal mostly with interpersonal type relations. . . . If I were doing it for approval, it would be a very tenuous thing. If I didn't get the right feedback, there might go all my values.

Ibsen's play, *A Doll House* (1879/1965), depicts the explosion of just such a world through the eruption of a moral dilemma that calls into question the notion of goodness that lies at its center. Nora, the "squirrel wife," living with her husband as she had lived with her father, puts into action this conception of goodness as sacrifice and, with the best of intentions, takes the law into her own hands. The crisis that ensues, most painfully for her in the repudiation of that goodness by the very person who was its recipient and beneficiary, causes her to reject the suicide that she had initially seen as its ultimate expression and chose instead to seek new and firmer answers to the adolescent questions of identity and belief.

The availability of choice and with it the onus of responsibility has now invaded the most private sector of the woman's domain and threatens a similar explosion. For centuries, women's sexuality anchored them in passivity, in a receptive rather than active stance, where the events of conception and childbirth could be controlled only by a withholding in which their own sexual needs were either denied or sacrificed. That such a sacrifice entailed a cost to their intelligence as well was seen by Freud (1908/1959) when he tied the "undoubted intellectual inferiority of so many women" to "the inhibition of thought necessitated by sexual suppression" (p. 199). The strategies of withholding and denial that women have employed in the politics of sexual relations appear similar to their evasion or withholding of judgment in the moral realm. The hesitance expressed in the previous examples to impose even a belief in the value of human life on others, like the reluctance to claim one's sexuality, bespeaks a self uncertain of its strength, unwilling to deal with consequence, and thus avoiding confrontation.

Thus women have traditionally deferred to the judgment of men, although often while intimating a sensibility of their own which is at variance with that judgment. Maggie Tulliver, in *The Mill on the Floss* (Eliot, 1860/1965) responds to the accusations that ensue from the discovery of her secretly continued relationship with Phillip Wakeham by acceding to her brother's moral judgment while at the same time asserting a different set of standards by which she attests her own superiority:

I don't want to defend myself. . . . I know I've been wrong—often continually. But yet, sometimes when I have done wrong, it has been because I have feelings that you would be the better for if you had them. If *you* were in fault ever, if you had done anything very wrong, I should be sorry for the pain it brought you; I should not want punishment to be heaped on you. (p. 188)

An eloquent defense, Kohlberg would argue, of a Stage Three moral position, an assertion of the age-old split between thinking and feeling, justice and mercy, that underlies many of the clichés and stereotypes concerning the difference between the sexes. But considered from another point of view, it is a moment of confrontation, replacing a former evasion, between two modes of judging, two differing constructions of the moral domain—one traditionally associated with masculinity and the public world of social power, the other with femininity and the privacy of domestic interchange. While the developmental ordering of these two points of view has been to consider the masculine as the more adequate and thus as replacing the feminine as the individual moves toward higher stages, their reconciliation remains unclear.

The Development of Women's Moral Judgment

Recent evidence for a divergence in moral development between men and women comes from the research of Haan (Note 1) and Holstein (1976) whose findings lead them to question the possibility of a "sex-related bias" in Kolhberg's scoring system. This system is based on Kohlberg's six-stage description of moral development. Kohlberg's stages divide into three levels, which he designates as preconventional, conventional, and postconventional, thus denoting the major shifts in moral perspective around a center of moral understanding that equates justice with the maintenance of existing social systems. While the preconventional conception of justice is based on the needs of the self, the conventional judgment derives from an understanding of society. This understanding is in turn superseded by a postconventional or principled conception of justice where the good is formulated in universal terms. The quarrel with Kohlberg's stage scoring does not pertain to the structural differentiation of his levels but rather to questions of stage and sequence. Kohlberg's stages begin with an obedience and punishment orientation (Stage One), and go from there in invariant order to instrumental hedonism (Stage Two), interpersonal concordance (Stage Three), law and order (Stage Four), social contract (Stage Five), and universal ethical principles (Stage Six).

The bias that Haan and Holstein question in this scoring system has to do with the subordination of the interpersonal to the societal definition of the good in the transition from Stage Three to Stage Four. This is the transition that has repeatedly been found to be problematic for women. In 1969, Kohlberg and Kramer identified Stage Three as the characteristic mode of women's moral judgments, claiming that, since women's lives were interpersonally based, this stage was not only "functional" for them but also adequate for resolving the moral conflicts that they faced. Turiel (1973) reported that while girls reached Stage Three sooner than did boys, their judgments tended to remain at that stage while the boys' development continued further along Kohlberg's scale. Gilligan, Kohlberg, Lerner, and Belenky (1971) found a similar association between sex and moral-judgment stage in a study of high-school students, with the girls' responses being scored predominantly at Stage Three while the boys' responses were more often scored at Stage Four.

This repeated finding of developmental inferiority in women may, however, have more to do with the standard by which development has been measured than with the quality of women's thinking per se. Haan's data (Note 1) on the Berkeley

Free Speech Movement and Holstein's (1976) three-year longitudinal study of adolescents and their parents indicate that the moral judgments of women differ from those of men in the greater extent to which women's judgments are tied to feelings of empathy and compassion and are concerned more with the resolution of "real-life" as opposed to hypothetical dilemmas (Note 1, p. 34). However, as long as the categories by which development is assessed are derived within a male perspective from male research data, divergence from the masculine standard can be seen only as a failure of development. As a result, the thinking of women is often classified with that of children. The systematic exclusion from consideration of alternative criteria that might better encompass the development of women indicates not only the limitations of a theory framed by men and validated by research samples disproportionately male and adolescent, but also the effects of the diffidence prevalent among women, their reluctance to speak publicly in their own voice, given the constraints imposed on them by the politics of differential power between the sexes.

In order to go beyond the question, "How much like men do women think, how capable are they of engaging in the abstract and hypothetical construction of reality?" it is necessary to identify and define in formal terms developmental criteria that encompass the categories of women's thinking. Such criteria would include the progressive differentiations, comprehensiveness, and adequacy that characterize higher-stage resolution of the "more frequently occurring, real-life moral dilemmas of interpersonal, empathic, fellow-feeling concerns" (Haan, Note 1, p. 34), which have long been the center of women's moral judgments and experience. To ascertain whether the feminine construction of the moral domain relies on a language different from that of men, but one which deserves equal credence in the definition of what constitutes development, it is necessary first to find the places where women have the power to choose and thus are willing to speak in their own voice.

When birth control and abortion provide women with effective means for controlling their fertility, the dilemma of choice enters the center of women's lives. Then the relationships that have traditionally defined women's identities and framed their moral judgments no longer flow inevitably from their reproductive capacity but become matters of decision over which they have control. Released from the passivity and reticence of a sexuality that binds them in dependence, it becomes possible for women to question with Freud what it is that they want and to assert their own answers to that question. However, while society may affirm publicly the woman's right to choose for herself, the exercise of such choice brings her privately into conflict with the conventions of femininity, particularly the moral equation of goodness with self-sacrifice. While independent assertion in judgment and action is considered the hallmark of adulthood and constitutes as well the standard of masculine development, it is rather in their care and concern for others that women have both judged themselves and been judged.

The conflict between self and other thus constitutes the central moral problem for women, posing a dilemma whose resolution requires a reconciliation between femininity and adulthood. In the absence of such a reconciliation, the moral problem cannot be resolved. The "good woman" masks assertion in evasion, denying responsibility by claiming only to meet the needs of others, while the "bad woman" forgoes or renounces the commitments that bind her in self-deception and betrayal. It is precisely this dilemma—the conflict between compassion and autonomy, between virtue and power—which the feminine voice struggles to resolve in its effort to reclaim the self and to solve the moral problem in such a way that no one is hurt.

When a woman considers whether to continue or abort a pregnancy, she contemplates a decision that affects both self and others and engages directly the critical moral issue of hurting. Since the choice is ultimately hers and therefore one for which she is responsible, it raises precisely those questions of judgment that have been most problematic for women. Now she is asked whether she wishes to interrupt that stream of life which has for centuries immersed her in the passivity of dependence while at the same time imposing on her the responsibility for care. Thus the abortion decision brings to the core of feminine apprehension, to what Joan Didion (1972) calls "the irreconcilable difference of it—that sense of living one's deepest life underwater, that dark involvement with blood and birth and death" (p. 14), the adult questions of responsibility and choice.

How women deal with such choices has been the subject of my research, designed to clarify, through considering the ways in which women construct and resolve the abortion decision, the nature and development of women's moral judgment. Twenty-nine women, diverse in age, race, and social class, were referred by abortion and pregnancy counseling services and participated in the study for a variety of reasons. Some came to gain further clarification with respect to a decision about which they were in conflict, some in response to a counselor's concern about repeated abortions, and others out of an interest in and/or willingness to contribute to ongoing research. Although the pregnancies occurred under a variety of circumstances in the lives of these women, certain commonalities could be discerned. The adolescents often failed to use birth control because they denied or discredited their capacity to bear children. Some of the older women attributed the pregnancy to the omission of contraceptive measures in circumstances where intercourse had not been anticipated. Since the pregnancies often coincided with efforts on the part of the women to end a relationship, they may be seen as a manifestation of ambivalence or as a way of putting the relationship to the ultimate test of commitment. For these women, the pregnancy appeared to be a way of testing truth, making the baby an ally in the search for male support and protection or, that failing, a companion victim of his rejection. There were, finally, some women who became pregnant either as a result of a failure of birth control or intentionally as part of a joint decision that later was reconsidered. Of the twenty-nine women, four decided to have the baby, one miscarried, twenty-one chose abortion, and three remained in doubt about the decision.

In the initial part of the interview, the women were asked to discuss the decision that confronted them, how they were dealing with it, the alternatives they were considering, their reasons for and against each option, the people involved, the conflicts entailed, and the ways in which making this decision affected their self-concepts and their relationships with others. Then, in the second part of the interview, moral judgment was assessed in the hypothetical mode by presenting for resolution three of Kohlberg's standard research dilemmas.

While the structural progression from a preconventional through a conventional to a postconventional moral perspective can readily be discerned in the women's responses to both actual and hypothetical dilemmas, the conventions that shape women's moral judgments differ from those that apply to men. The construction of the abortion dilemma, in particular, reveals the existence of a distinct moral language whose evolution informs the sequence of women's development. This is the language of selfishness and responsibility, which defines the moral problem as one of obligation to exercise care and avoid hurt. The infliction of hurt is considered selfish and immoral in its reflection of unconcern, while the expression of care is seen as the fulfillment of moral responsibility. The reiterative use of the language of selfishness and responsibility and the underlying moral orientation it reflects sets the women apart from the men whom Kohlberg studied and may be seen as the critical reason for their failure to develop within the constraints of his system.

In the developmental sequence that follows, women's moral judgments proceed from an initial focus on the self at the *first level* to the discovery, in the transition to the *second level,* of the concept of responsibility as the basis for a new equilibrium between self and others. The elaboration of this concept of responsibility and its fusion with a maternal concept of morality, which seeks to ensure protection for the dependent and unequal, characterizes the *second level* of judgment. At this level the good is equated with caring for others. However, when the conventions of feminine goodness legitimize only others as the recipients of moral care, the logical inequality between self and other and the psychological violence that it engenders creates the disequilibrium that initiates the *second* transition. The relationship between self and others is then reconsidered in an effort to sort out the confusion between conformity and care inherent in the conventional definition of feminine goodness and to establish a new equilibrium, which dissipates the tension between selfishness and responsibility. At the *third level,* the self becomes the arbiter of an independent judgment that now subsumes both conventions and individual needs under the moral principle of nonviolence. Judgment remains psychological in its concern with the intention and consequences of action, but it now becomes universal in its condemnation of exploitation and hurt.

Level I: Orientation to Individual Survival

In its initial and simplest construction, the abortion decision centers on the self. The concern is pragmatic, and the issue is individual survival. At this level, "should" is undifferentiated from "would," and others influence the decision only through their power to affect its consequences. An eighteen-year-old, asked what she thought when she found herself pregnant, replies: "I really didn't think anything except that I didn't want it. [Why was that?] I didn't want it, I wasn't ready for it, and next year will be my last year and I want to go to school."

Asked if there was a right decision, she says, "There is no right decision. [Why?]

213

I didn't want it." For her the question of right decision would emerge only if her own needs were in conflict; then she would have to decide which needs should take precedence. This was the dilemma of another eighteen-year-old, who saw having a baby as a way of increasing her freedom by providing "the perfect chance to get married and move away from home," but also as restricting her freedom "to do a lot of things."

At this first level, the self, which is the sole object of concern, is constrained by lack of power; the wish "to do a lot of things" is constantly belied by the limitations of what, in fact, is being done. Relationships are, for the most part, disappointing: "The only thing you are ever going to get out of going with a guy is to get hurt." As a result, women may in some instances deliberately choose isolation to protect themselves against hurt. When asked how she would describe herself to herself, a nineteen-year-old, who held herself responsible for the accidental death of a younger brother, answers as follows:

> I really don't know. I never thought about it. I don't know. I know basically the outline of a character. I am very independent. I don't really want to have to ask anybody for anything and I am a loner in life. I prefer to be by myself than around anybody else. I manage to keep my friends at a limited number with the point that I have very few friends. I don't know what else there is. I am a loner and I enjoy it. Here today and gone tomorrow.

The primacy of the concern with survival is explicitly acknowledged by a sixteen-year-old delinquent in response to Kohlberg's Heinz dilemma, which asks if it is right for a desperate husband to steal an outrageously overpriced drug to save the life of his dying wife:

> I think survival is one of the first things in life and that people fight for. I think it is the most important thing, more important than stealing. Stealing might be wrong, but if you have to steal to survive yourself or even kill, that is what you should do. . . . Preservation of oneself, I think, is the most important thing; it comes before anything in life.

The First Transition: From Selfishness to Responsibility

In the transition which follows and criticizes this level of judgment, the words selfishness and responsibility first appear. Their reference initially is to the self in a redefinition of the self-interest which has thus far served as the basis for judgment. The transitional issue is one of attachment or connection to others. The pregnancy catches up the issue not only by representing an immediate, literal connection, but also by affirming, in the most concrete and physical way, the capacity to assume adult feminine roles. However, while having a baby seems at first to offer respite from the loneliness of adolescence and to solve conflicts over dependence and independence, in reality the continuation of an adolescent pregnancy generally compounds these problems, increasing social isolation and precluding further steps toward independence.

To be a mother in the societal as well as the physical sense requires the assumption of parental responsibility for the care and protection of a child. However, in

214

order to be able to care for another, one must first be able to care responsibly for oneself. The growth from childhood to adulthood, conceived as a move from selfishness to responsibility, is articulated explicitly in these terms by a seventeen-year-old who describes her response to her pregnancy as follows:

> I started feeling really good about being pregnant instead of feeling really bad, because I wasn't looking at the situation realistically. I was looking at it from my own sort of selfish needs because I was lonely and felt lonely and stuff. . . . Things weren't really going good for me, so I was looking at it that I could have a baby that I could take care of or something that was part of me, and that made me feel good . . . but I wasn't looking at the realistic side . . . about the responsibility I would have to take on . . . I came to this decision that I was going to have an abortion [because] I realized how much responsibility goes with having a child. Like you have to be there, you can't be out of the house all the time which is one thing I like to do . . . and I decided that I have to take on responsibility for myself and I have to work out a lot of things.

Stating her former mode of judgment, the wish to have a baby as a way of combating loneliness and feeling connected, she now criticizes that judgment as both "selfish" and "unrealistic." The contradiction between wishes for a baby and for the freedom to be "out of the house all the time"—that is, for connection and also for independence—is resolved in terms of a new priority, as the criterion for judgment changes. The dilemma now assumes moral definition as the emergent conflict between wish and necessity is seen as a disparity between "would" and "should." In this construction the "selfishness" of willful decision is counterposed to the "responsibility" of moral choice:

> What I want to do is to have the baby, but what I feel I should do which is what I need to do, is have an abortion right now, because sometimes what you want isn't right. Sometimes what is necessary comes before what you want, because it might not always lead to the right thing.

While the pregnancy itself confirms femininity—"I started feeling really good; it sort of made me feel, like being pregnant, I started feeling like a woman"—the abortion decision becomes an opportunity for the adult exercise of responsible choice.

> [How would you describe yourself to yourself?] I am looking at myself differently in the way that I have had a really heavy decision put upon me, and I have never really had too many hard decisions in my life, and I have made it. It has taken some responsibility to do this. I have changed in that way, that I have made a hard decision. And that has been good. Because before, I would not have looked at it realistically, in my opinion. I would have gone by what I wanted to do, and I wanted it, and even if it wasn't right. So I see myself as I'm becoming more mature in ways of making decisions and taking care of myself, doing something for myself. I think it is going to help me in other ways, if I have other decisions to make put upon me, which would take some responsibility. And I would know that I could make them.

In the epiphany of this cognitive reconstruction, the old becomes transformed in terms of the new. The wish to "do something for myself" remains, but the terms of its fulfillment change as the decision affirms both femininity and adulthood in its integration of responsibility and care. Morality, says another adolescent, "is the way you think about yourself . . . sooner or later you have to make up your mind to start taking care of yourself. Abortion, if you do it for the right reasons, is helping yourself to start over and do different things."

Since this transition signals an enhancement in self-worth, it requires a conception of self which includes the possibility for doing "the right thing," the ability to see in oneself the potential for social acceptance. When such confidence is seriously in doubt, the transitional questions may be raised but development is impeded. The failure to make this first transition, despite an understanding of the issues involved, is illustrated by a woman in her late twenties Her struggle with the conflict between selfishness and responsibility pervades but fails to resolve her dilemma of whether or not to have a third abortion.

> I think you have to think about the people who are involved, including yourself. You have responsibilities to yourself . . . and to make a right, whatever that is, decision in this depends on your knowledge and awareness of the responsibilities that you have and whether you can survive with a child and what it will do to your relationship with the father or how it will affect him emotionally.

Rejecting the idea of selling the baby and making "a lot of money in a black market kind of thing . . . because mostly I operate on principles and it would just rub me the wrong way to think I would be selling my own child," she struggles with a concept of responsibility which repeatedly turns back on the question of her own survival. Transition seems blocked by a self-image which is insistently contradictory:

> [How would you describe yourself to yourself?] I see myself as impulsive, practical—that is a contradiction—and moral and amoral, a contradiction. Actually the only thing that is consistent and not contradictory is the fact that I am very lazy which everyone has always told me is really a symptom of something else which I have never been able to put my finger on exactly. It has taken me a long time to like myself. In fact there are times when I don't, which I think is healthy to a point and sometimes I think I like myself too much and I probably evade myself too much, which avoids responsibility to myself and to other people who like me. I am pretty unfaithful to myself. . . I have a hard time even thinking that I am a human being, simply because so much rotten stuff goes on and people are so crummy and insensitive.

Seeing herself as avoiding responsibility, she can find no basis upon which to resolve the pregnancy dilemma. Instead, her inability to arrive at any clear sense of decision only contributes further to her overall sense of failure. Criticizing her parents for having betrayed her during adolescence by coercing her to have an abortion she did not want, she now betrays herself and criticizes that as well. In this light, it is less surprising that she considered selling her child, since she felt herself to have, in effect, been sold by her parents for the sake of maintaining their social status.

The Second Level: Goodness as Self-Sacrifice

The transition from selfishness to responsibility is a move toward social participation. Whereas at the first level, morality is seen as a matter of sanctions imposed by a society of which one is more subject than citizen, at the second level, moral judgment comes to rely on shared norms and expectations. The woman at this level validates her claim to social membership through the adoption of societal values. Consensual judgment becomes paramount and goodness the overriding concern as survival is now seen to depend on acceptance by others.

Here the conventional feminine voice emerges with great clarity, defining the self and proclaiming its worth on the basis of the ability to care for and protect others. The woman now constructs the world perfused with the assumptions about feminine goodness reflected in the stereotypes of the Broverman et al. (1972) studies. There the attributes considered desirable for women all presume an other, a recipient of the "tact, gentleness and easy expression of feeling" which allow the woman to respond sensitively while evoking in return the care which meets her own "very strong need for security" (p. 63). The strength of this position lies in its capacity for caring; its limitation is the restriction it imposes on direct expression. Both qualities are elucidated by a nineteen-year-old who contrasts her reluctance to criticize with her boyfriend's straightforwardness:

> I never want to hurt anyone, and I tell them in a very nice way, and I have respect for their own opinions, and they can do the things the way that they want, and he usually tells people right off the bat. . . . He does a lot of things out in public which I do in private. . . . it is better, the other [his way], but I just could never do it.

While her judgment clearly exists, it is not expressed, at least not in public. Concern for the feelings of others imposes a deference which she nevertheless criticizes in an awareness that, under the name of consideration, a vulnerability and a duplicity are concealed.

At the second level of judgment, it is specifically over the issue of hurting that conflict arises with respect to the abortion decision. When no option exists that can be construed as being in the best interest of everyone, when responsibilities conflict and decision entails the sacrifice of somebody's needs, then the woman confronts the seemingly impossible task of choosing the victim. A nineteen-year-old, fearing the consequences for herself of a second abortion but facing the opposition of both her family and her lover to the continuation of the pregnancy, describes the dilemma as follows:

> I don't know what choices are open to me; it is either to have it or the abortion; these are the choices open to me. It is just that either way I don't . . . I think what confuses me is it is a choice of either hurting myself or hurting other people around me. What is more important? If there could be a happy medium, it would be fine, but there isn't. It is either hurting someone on this side or hurting myself.

While the feminine identification of goodness with self-sacrifice seems clearly to dictate the "right" resolution of this dilemma, the stakes may be high for the woman herself, and the sacrifice of the fetus, in any event, compromises the altruism of an abortion motivated by a concern for others. Since femininity itself is in conflict in an abortion intended as an expression of love and care, this is a resolution which readily explodes in its own contradiction.

"I don't think anyone should have to choose between two things that they love," says a twenty-five-year-old woman who assumed responsibility not only for her lover but also for his wife and children in having an abortion she did not want:

> I just wanted the child and I really don't believe in abortions. Who can say when life begins. I think that life begins at conception and . . . I felt like there were changes happening in my body and I felt very protective . . . [but] I felt a responsibility, my responsibility if anything ever happened to her [his wife]. He made me feel that I had to make a choice and there was only one choice to make and that was to have an abortion and I could always have children another time and he made me feel if I didn't have it that it would drive us apart.

The abortion decision was, in her mind, a choice not to choose with respect to the pregnancy—"That was my choice, I had to do it." Instead, it was a decision to subordinate the pregnancy to the continuation of a relationship that she saw as encompassing her life—"Since I met him, he has been my life. I do everything for him; my life sort of revolves around him." Since she wanted to have the baby and also to continue the relationship, either choice could be construed as selfish. Furthermore, since both alternatives entailed hurting someone, neither could be considered moral. Faced with a decision which, in her own terms, was untenable, she sought to avoid responsibility for the choice she made, construing the decision as a sacrifice of her own needs to those of her lover. However, this public sacrifice in the name of responsibility engendered a private resentment that erupted in anger, compromising the very relationship that it had been intended to sustain.

> Afterwards we went through a bad time because I hate to say it and I was wrong, but I blamed him. I gave in to him. But when it came down to it, I made the decision. I could have said, 'I am going to have this child whether you want me to or not,' and I just didn't do it.

Pregnant again by the same man, she recognizes in retrospect that the choice in fact had been hers, as she returns once again to what now appears to have been missed opportunity for growth. Seeking, this time, to make rather than abdicate the decision, she sees the issue as one of "strength" as she struggles to free herself from the powerlessness of her own dependence:

> I think that right now I think of myself as someone who can become a lot stronger. Because of the circumstances, I just go along like with the tide. I never really had anything of my own before . . . [this time] I hope to come on strong and make a big decision, whether it is right or wrong.

Because the morality of self-sacrifice had justified the previous abortion, she now must suspend that judgment if she is to claim her own voice and accept responsibility for choice.

She thereby calls into question the underlying assumption of Level Two, which leads the woman to consider herself responsible for the actions of others, while holding others responsible for the choices she makes. This notion of reciprocity, backwards in its assumptions about control, disguises assertion as response. By reversing responsibility, it generates a series of indirect actions, which leave everyone feeling manipulated and betrayed. The logic of this position is confused in that the morality of mutual care is embedded in the psychology of dependence. Assertion becomes personally dangerous in its risk of criticism and abandonment, as well as potentially immoral in its power to hurt. This confusion is captured by Kohlberg's (1969) definition of Stage Three moral judgment, which joins the need for approval with the wish to care for and help others.

When thus caught between the passivity of dependence and the activity of care, the woman becomes suspended in an immobility of both judgment and action. "If I were drowning, I couldn't reach out a hand to save myself, so unwilling am I to set myself up against fate" (p. 7), begins the central character of Margaret Drabble's novel, *The Waterfall* (1971), in an effort to absolve herself of responsibility as she at the same time relinquishes control. Facing the same moral conflict which George Eliot depicted in *The Mill on the Floss,* Drabble's heroine proceeds to relive Maggie Tulliver's dilemma but turns inward in her search for the way in which to retell that story. What is initially suspended and then called into question is the judgment which "had in the past made it seem better to renounce myself than them" (Drabble, p. 50).

The Second Transition: From Goodness to Truth

The second transition begins with the reconsideration of the relationship between self and other, as the woman starts to scrutinize the logic of self-sacrifice in the service of a morality of care. In the interview data, this transition is announced by the reappearance of the word selfish. Retrieving the judgmental initiative, the woman begins to ask whether it is selfish or responsible, moral or immoral, to include her own needs within the compass of her care and concern. This question leads her to reexamine the concept of responsibility, juxtaposing the outward concern with what other people think with a new inner judgment.

In separating the voice of the self from those of others, the woman asks if it is possible to be responsible to herself as well as to others and thus to reconcile the disparity between hurt and care. The exercise of such responsibility, however, requires a new kind of judgment whose first demand is for honesty. To be responsible, it is necessary first to acknowledge what it is that one is doing. The criterion for judgment thus shifts from "goodness" to "truth" as the morality of action comes to be assessed not on the basis of its appearance in the eyes of others, but in terms of the realities of its intention and consequence.

A twenty-four-year-old married Catholic woman, pregnant again two months following the birth of her first child, identifies her dilemma as one of choice: "You have to now decide; because it is now available, you have to make a decision. And if it wasn't available, there was no choice open; you just do what you have to do." In the absence of legal abortion, a morality of self-sacrifice was necessary in order to insure protection and care for the dependent child. However, when such sacrifice becomes optional, the entire problem is recast.

The abortion decision is framed by this woman first in terms of her responsibilities to others: having a second child at this time would be contrary to medical advice and would strain both the emotional and financial resources of the family. However, there is, she says, a third reason for having an abortion, "sort of an emotional reason. I don't know if it is selfish or not, but it would really be tying myself down and right now I am not ready to be tied down with two."

Against this combination of selfish and responsible reasons for abortion is her Catholic belief that

> . . . it is taking a life, and it is. Even though it is not formed, it is the potential, and to me it is still taking a life. But I have to think of mine, my son's and my husband's, to think about, and at first I think that I thought it was for selfish reasons, but it is not. I believe that too, some of it is selfish. I don't want another one right now; I am not ready for it.

The dilemma arises over the issue of justification for taking a life: "I can't cover it over, because I believe this and if I do try to cover it over, I know that I am going to be in a mess. It will be denying what I am really doing." Asking "Am I doing the right thing; is it moral?," she counterposes to her belief against abortion her concern with the consequences of continuing the pregnancy. While concluding that "I can't be so morally strict as to hurt three other people with a decision just because of my moral beliefs," the issue of goodness still remains critical to her resolution of the dilemma:

> The moral factor is there. To me it is taking a life, and I am going to take that upon myself, that decision upon myself and I have feelings about it, and talked to a priest . . . but he said it is there and it will be from now on, and it is up to the person if they can live with the idea and still believe they are good.

The criteria for goodness, however, move inward as the ability to have an abortion and still consider herself good comes to hinge on the issue of selfishness with which she struggles to come to terms. Asked if acting morally is acting according to what is best for the self or whether it is a matter of self-sacrifice, she replies:

> I don't know if I really understand the question. . . . Like in my situation where I want to have the abortion and if I didn't it would be self-sacrificing, I am really in the middle of both those ways . . . but I think that my morality is strong and if these reasons—financial, physical reality and also for the whole family involved—were not here, that I wouldn't have to do it, and then it would be a self-sacrifice.

The importance of clarifying her own participation in the decision is evident in her attempt to ascertain her feelings in order to determine whether or not she was "putting them under" in deciding to end the pregnancy. Whereas in the first transition, from selfishness to responsibility, women made lists in order to bring to their consideration needs other than their own, now, in the second transition, it is the needs of the self which have to be deliberately uncovered. Confronting the reality of her own wish for an abortion, she now must deal with the problem of selfishness and the qualification that she feels it imposes on the "goodness" of her decision. The primacy of this concern is apparent in her description of herself:

> I think in a way I am selfish for one thing, and very emotional, very . . . and I think that I am a very real person and an understanding person and I can handle life situations fairly well, so I am basing a lot of it on my ability to do the things that I feel are right and best for me and whoever I am involved with. I think I was very fair to myself about the decision, and I really think that I have been truthful, not hiding anything, bringing out all the feelings involved. I feel it is a good decision and an honest one, a real decision.

Thus she strives to encompass the needs of both self and others, to be responsible to others and thus to be "good" but also to be responsible to herself and thus to be "honest" and "real."

While from one point of view, attention to one's own needs is considered selfish, when looked at from a different perspective, it is a matter of honesty and fairness. This is the essence of the transitional shift toward a new conception of goodness which turns inward in an acknowledgement of the self and an acceptance of responsibility for decision. While outward justification, the concern with "good reasons," remains critical for this particular woman: "I still think abortion is wrong, and it will be unless the situation can justify what you are doing." But the search for justification has produced a change in her thinking, "not drastically, but a little bit." She realizes that in continuing the pregnancy she would punish not only herself but also her husband, toward whom she had begun to feel "turned off and irritated." This leads her to consider the consequences self-sacrifice can have both for the self and for others. "God," she says, "can punish, but He can also forgive." What remains in question is whether her claim to forgiveness is compromised by a decision that not only meets the needs of others but that also is "right and best for me."

The concern with selfishness and its equation with immorality recur in an interview with another Catholic woman whose arrival for an abortion was punctuated by the statement, "I have always thought abortion was a fancy word for murder." Initially explaining this murder as one of lesser degree—"I am doing it because I have to do it. I am not doing it the least bit because I want to," she judges it "not quite as bad. You can rationalize that it is not quite the same." Since "keeping the child for lots and lots of reasons was just sort of impractical and out," she considers her options to be either abortion or adoption. However, having previously given up one child for adoption, she says: "I knew that psychologically there was no way that I could hack another adoption. It took me about four-and-a-half years to get my head on straight; there was just no way I was going to go through it again." The decision thus reduces in her eyes to a choice between murdering the fetus or damaging herself. The choice is further complicated by the fact that by continuing the pregnancy she would hurt not only herself but also her parents, with whom she lived. In the face of these manifold moral contradictions, the psychological demand for honesty that arises in counseling finally allows decision:

> On my own, I was doing it not so much for myself; I was doing it for my parents.
> I was doing it because the doctor told me to do it, but I had never resolved in my
> mind that I was doing it for me. Because it goes right back to the fact that I never
> believed in abortions. . . . Actually, I had to sit down and admit, no, I really don't
> want to go the mother route now. I honestly don't feel that I want to be a mother,
> and that is not really such a bad thing to say after all. But that is not how I felt
> up until talking to Maureen [her counselor]. It was just a horrible way to feel, so
> I just wasn't going to feel it, and I just blocked it right out.

As long as her consideration remains "moral," abortion can be justified only as
an act of sacrifice, a submission to necessity where the absence of choice precludes
responsibility. In this way, she can avoid self-condemnation, since, "When you get
into moral stuff then you are getting into self-respect and that stuff, and at least
if I do something that I feel is morally wrong, then I tend to lose some of my self-
respect as a person." Her evasion of responsibility, critical to maintaining the
innocence necessary for self-respect, contradicts the reality of her own participation
in the abortion decision. The dishonesty in her plea of victimization creates the
conflict that generates the need for a more inclusive understanding. She must now
resolve the emerging contradiction in her thinking between two uses of the term
right: "I am saying that abortion is morally wrong, but the situation is right, and I
am going to do it. But the thing is that eventually they are going to have to go
together, and I am going to have to put them together somehow." Asked how this
could be done, she replies:

> I would have to change morally wrong to morally right. [How?] I have no idea.
> I don't think you can take something that you feel is morally wrong because the
> situation makes it right and put the two together. They are not together, they are
> opposite. They don't go together. Something is wrong, but all of a sudden because
> you are doing it, it is right.

This discrepancy recalls a similar conflict she faced over the question of euthanasia, also considered by her to be morally wrong until she "took care of a couple of
patients who had flat EEGs and saw the job that it was doing on their families."
Recalling that experience, she says:

> You really don't know your black and whites until you really get into them and are
> being confronted with it. If you stop and think about my feelings on euthanasia
> until I got into it, and then my feelings about abortion until I got into it, I
> thought both of them were murder. Right and wrong and no middle but there
> is a gray.

In discovering the gray and questioning the moral judgments which formerly
she considered to be absolute, she confronts the moral crisis of the second transition. Now the conventions which in the past had guided her moral judgment become subject to a new criticism, as she questions not only the justification for hurting others in the name of morality but also the "rightness" of hurting herself.
However, to sustain such criticism in the face of conventions that equate goodness

with self-sacrifice, the woman must verify her capacity for independent judgment and the legitimacy of her own point of view.

Once again transition hinges on self-concept. When uncertainty about her own worth prevents a woman from claiming equality, self-assertion falls prey to the old criticism of selfishness. Then the morality that condones self-destruction in the name of responsible care is not repudiated as inadequate but rather is abandoned in the face of its threat to survival. Moral obligation, rather than expanding to include the self, is rejected completely as the failure of conventional reciprocity leaves the woman unwilling any longer to protect others at what is now seen to be her own expense. In the absence of morality, survival, however "selfish" or "immoral," returns as the paramount concern.

A musician in her late twenties illustrates this transitional impasse. Having led an independent life which centered on her work, she considered herself "fairly strong-willed, fairly in control, fairly rational and objective" until she became involved in an intense love affair and discovered in her capacity to love "an entirely new dimension" in herself. Admitting in retrospect to "tremendous naiveté and idealism," she had entertained "some vague ideas that some day I would like a child to concretize our relationship . . . having always associated having a child with all the creative aspects of my life." Abjuring, with her lover, the use of contraceptives because, "as the relationship was sort of an ideal relationship in our minds, we liked the idea of not using foreign objects or anything artificial," she saw herself as having relinquished control, becoming instead "just simply vague and allowing events to just carry me along." Just as she began in her own thinking to confront "the realities of that situation"—the possibility of pregnancy and the fact that her lover was married—she found herself pregnant. "Caught" between her wish to end a relationship that "seemed more and more defeating" and her wish for a baby, which "would be a connection that would last a long time," she is paralyzed by her inability to resolve the dilemma which her ambivalence creates.

The pregnancy poses a conflict between her "moral" belief that "once a certain life has begun, it shouldn't be stopped artificially" and her "amazing" discovery that to have the baby she would "need much more [support] than I thought." Despite her moral conviction that she "should" have the child, she doubts that she could psychologically deal with "having the child alone and taking the responsibility for it." Thus a conflict erupts between what she considers to be her moral obligation to protect life and her inability to do so under the circumstances of this pregnancy. Seeing it as "my decision and my responsibility for making the decision whether to have or have not the child," she struggles to find a viable basis on which to resolve the dilemma.

Capable of arguing either for or against abortion "with a philosophical logic," she says, on the one hand, that in an overpopulated world one should have children only under ideal conditions for care but, on the other, that one should end a life only when it is impossible to sustain it. She describes her impasse in response to the question of whether there is a difference between what she wants to do and what she thinks she should do:

Yes, and there always has. I have always been confronted with that precise situation in a lot of my choices, and I have been trying to figure out what are the things that make me believe that these are things I should do as opposed to what I feel I want to do. [In this situation?] It is not that clear cut. I both want the child and feel I should have it, and I also think I should have the abortion and want it, but I would say it is my stronger feeling, and that I don't have enough confidence in my work yet and that is really where it is all hinged, I think . . . [the abortion] would solve the problem and I know I can't handle the pregnancy.

Characterizing this solution as "emotional and pragmatic" and attributing it to her lack of confidence in her work, she contrasts it with the "better thought out and more logical and more correct" resolution of her lover who thinks that she should have the child and raise it without either his presence or financial support. Confronted with this reflected image of herself as ultimately giving and good, as self-sustaining in her own creativity and thus able to meet the needs of others while imposing no demands of her own in return, she questions not the image itself but her own adequacy in filling it. Concluding that she is not yet capable of doing so, she is reduced in her own eyes to what she sees as a selfish and highly compromised fight

for my survival. But in one way or another, I am going to suffer. Maybe I am going to suffer mentally and emotionally having the abortion, or I would suffer what I think is possibly something worse. So I suppose it is the lesser of two evils. I think it is a matter of choosing which one I know that I can survive through. It is really. I think it is selfish, I suppose, because it does have to do with that. I just realized that. I guess it does have to do with whether I would survive or not. [Why is this selfish?] Well, you know, it is. Because I am concerned with my survival first, as opposed to the survival of the relationship or the survival of the child, another human being . . . I guess I am setting priorities, and I guess I am setting my needs to survive first. . . . I guess I see it in negative terms a lot . . . but I do think of other positive things; that I am still going to have some life left, maybe. I don't know.

In the face of this failure of reciprocity of care, in the disappointment of abandonment where connection was sought, survival is seen to hinge on her work which is "where I derive the meaning of what I am. That's the known factor." While uncertainty about her work makes this survival precarious, the choice for abortion is also distressing in that she considers it to be "highly introverted—that in this one respect, having an abortion would be going a step backward; going outside to love someone else and having a child would be a step forward." The sense of retrenchment that the severing of connection signifies is apparent in her anticipation of the cost which abortion would entail:

Probably what I will do is I will cut off my feelings, and when they will return or what would happen to them after that, I don't know. So that I don't feel anything at all, and I would probably just be very cold and go through it very coldly. . . . The more you do that to yourself, the more difficult it becomes to love again or to trust again or to feel again. . . . Each time I move away from that, it becomes easier, not more difficult, but easier to avoid committing myself to a relationship. And I am really concerned about cutting off that whole feeling aspect.

Caught between selfishness and responsibility, unable to find in the circumstances of this choice a way of caring which does not at the same time destroy, she confronts a dilemma which reduces to a conflict between morality and survival. Adulthood and femininity fly apart in the failure of this attempt at integration as the choice to work becomes a decision not only to renounce this particular relationship and child but also to obliterate the vulnerability that love and care engender.

The Third Level: The Morality of Nonviolence

In contrast, a twenty-five-year-old woman, facing a similar disappointment, finds a way to reconcile the initially disparate concepts of selfishness and responsibility through a transformed understanding of self and a corresponding redefinition of morality. Examining the assumptions underlying the conventions of feminine self-abnegation and moral self-sacrifice, she comes to reject these conventions as immoral in their power to hurt. By elevating nonviolence—the injunction against hurting—to a principle governing all moral judgment and action, she is able to assert a moral equality between self and other. Care then becomes a universal obligation, the self-chosen ethic of a postconventional judgment that reconstructs the dilemma in a way that allows the assumption of responsibility for choice.

In this woman's life, the current pregnancy brings to the surface the unfinished business of an earlier pregnancy and of the relationship in which both pregnancies occurred. The first pregnancy was discovered after her lover had left and was terminated by an abortion experienced as a purging expression of her anger at having been rejected. Remembering the abortion only as a relief, she nevertheless describes that time in her life as one in which she "hit rock bottom." Having hoped then to "take control of my life," she instead resumed the relationship when the man reappeared. Now, two years later, having once again "left my diaphragm in the drawer," she again becomes pregnant. Although initially "ecstatic" at the news, her elation dissipates when her lover tells her that he will leave if she chooses to have the child. Under these circumstances, she considers a second abortion but is unable to keep the repeated appointments she makes because of her reluctance to accept the responsibility for that choice. While the first abortion seemed an "honest mistake," she says that a second would make her feel "like a walking slaughter-house." Since she would need financial support to raise the child, her initial strategy was to take the matter to "the welfare people" in the hope that they would refuse to provide the necessary funds and thus resolve her dilemma:

> In that way, you know, the responsibility would be off my shoulders, and I could say, it's not my fault, you know, the state denied me the money that I would need to do it. But it turned out that it was possible to do it, and so I was, you know, right back where I started. And I had an appointment for an abortion, and I kept calling and cancelling it and then remaking the appointment and cancelling it, and I just couldn't make up my mind.

Confronting the need to choose between the two evils of hurting herself or ending the incipient life of the child, she finds, in a reconstruction of the dilemma itself, a basis for a new priority that allows decision. In doing so, she comes to see the conflict as arising from a faulty construction of reality. Her thinking recapitulates the developmental sequence, as she considers but rejects as inadequate the components of earlier-stage resolutions. An expanded conception of responsibility now reshapes moral judgment and guides resolution of the dilemma, whose pros and cons she considers as follows:

> Well, the pros for having the baby are all the admiration that you would get from, you know, being a single woman, alone, martyr, struggling, having the adoring love of this beautiful Gerber baby . . . just more of a home life than I have had in a long time, and that basically was it, which is pretty fantasyland; it is not very realistic. . . . Cons against having the baby: it was going to hasten what is looking to be the inevitable end of the relationship with the man I am presently with. . . . I was going to have to go on welfare, my parents were going to hate me for the rest of my life, I was going to lose a really good job that I have, I would lose a lot of independence . . . solitude . . . and I would have to be put in a position of asking help from a lot of people a lot of the time. Cons against having the abortion is having to face up to the guilt . . . and pros for having the abortion are I would be able to handle my deteriorating relation with S. with a lot more capability and a lot more responsibility for him and for myself . . . and I would not have to go through the realization that for the next twenty-five years of my life I would be punishing myself for being foolish enough to get pregnant again and forcing myself to bring up a kid just because I did this. Having to face the guilt of a second abortion seemed like, not exactly, well, exactly the lesser of the two evils but also the one that would pay off for me personally in the long run because by looking at why I am pregnant again and subsequently have decided to have a second abortion, I have to face up to some things about myself.

Although she doesn't "feel good about having a second abortion," she nevertheless concludes,

> I would not be doing myself or the child or the world any kind of favor having this child. . . . I don't need to pay off my imaginary debts to the world through this child, and I don't think that it is right to bring a child into the world and use it for that purpose.

Asked to describe herself, she indicates how closely her transformed moral understanding is tied to a changing self-concept:

> I have been thinking about that a lot lately, and it comes up different than what my usual subconscious perception of myself is. Usually paying off some sort of debt, going around serving people who are not really worthy of my attentions because somewhere in my life I think I got the impression that my needs are really secondary to other people's, and that if I feel, if I make any demands on other people to fulfill my needs, I'd feel guilty for it and submerge my own in favor of other people's, which later backfires on me, and I feel a great deal of resentment for other people that I am doing things for, which causes friction and the eventual

deterioration of the relationship. And then I start all over again. How would I describe myself to myself? Pretty frustrated and a lot angrier than I admit, a lot more aggressive than I admit.

Reflecting on the virtues which comprise the conventional definition of the feminine self, a definition which she hears articulated in her mother's voice, she says, "I am beginning to think that all these virtues are really not getting me anywhere. I have begun to notice." Tied to this recognition is an acknowledgement of her power and worth, both previously excluded from the image she projected:

> I am suddenly beginning to realize that the things that I like to do, the things I am interested in, and the things that I believe and the kind of person I am is not so bad that I have to constantly be sitting on the shelf and letting it gather dust. I am a lot more worthwhile than what my past actions have led other people to believe.

Her notion of a "good person," which previously was limited to her mother's example of hard work, patience and self-sacrifice, now changes to include the value that she herself places on directness and honesty. Although she believes that this new self-assertion will lead her "to feel a lot better about myself" she recognizes that it will also expose her to criticism:

> Other people may say, 'Boy, she's aggressive, and I don't like that,' but at least, you know, they will know that they don't like that. They are not going to say, 'I like the way she manipulates herself to fit right around me.' . . . What I want to do is just be a more self-determined person and a more singular person.

While within her old framework abortion had seemed a way of "copping out" instead of being a "responsible person [who] pays for his mistakes and pays and pays and is always there when she says she will be there and even when she doesn't say she will be there is there," now, her "conception of what I think is right for myself and my conception of self-worth is changing." She can consider this emergent self "also a good person," as her concept of goodness expands to encompass "the feeling of self-worth; you are not going to sell yourself short and you are not going to make yourself do things that, you know, are really stupid and that you don't want to do." This reorientation centers on the awareness that:

> I have a responsibility to myself, and you know, for once I am beginning to realize that that really matters to me . . . instead of doing what I want for myself and feeling guilty over how selfish I am, you realize that that is a very usual way for people to live . . . doing what you want to do because you fee. that your wants and your needs are important, if to no one else, then to you, and that's reason enough to do something that you want to do.

Once obligation extends to include the self as well as others, the disparity between selfishness and responsibility is reconciled. Although the conflict between self and other remains, the moral problem is restructured in an awareness that the occurrence of the dilemma itself precludes non-violent resolution. The abortion decision is now seen to be a "serious" choice affecting both self and others: "This is a life that I have taken, a conscious decision to terminate, and that is just very heavy, a very heavy thing." While accepting the necessity of abortion as a highly compromised resolution, she turns her attention to the pregnancy itself, which she now considers to denote a failure of responsibility, a failure to care for and protect both self and other.

As in the first transition, although now in different terms, the conflict precipitated by the pregnancy catches up the issues critical to development. These issues now concern the worth of the self in relation to others, the claiming of the power to choose, and the acceptance of responsibility for choice. By provoking a confrontation with these issues, the crisis can become "a very auspicious time; you can use the pregnancy as sort of a learning, teeing-off point, which makes it useful in a way." This possibility for growth inherent in a crisis which allows confrontation with a construction of reality whose acceptance previously had impeded development was first identified by Coles (1964) in his study of the children of Little Rock. This same sense of possibility is expressed by the women who see, in their resolution of the abortion dilemma, a reconstructed understanding which creates the opportunity for "a new beginning," a chance "to take control of my life."

For this woman, the first step in taking control was to end the relationship in which she had considered herself "reduced to a nonentity," but to do so in a responsible way. Recognizing hurt as the inevitable concomitant of rejection, she strives to minimize that hurt "by dealing with [his] needs as best I can without compromising my own . . . that's a big point for me, because the thing in my life to this point has been always compromising, and I am not willing to do that any more." Instead, she seeks to act in a "decent, human kind of way . . . one that leaves maybe a slightly shook but not totally destroyed person." Thus the "nonentity" confronts her power to destroy which formerly had impeded any assertion, as she consider the possibility for a new kind of action that leaves both self and other intact.

The moral concern remains a concern with hurting as she considers Kohlberg's Heinz dilemma in terms of the question, "who is going to be hurt more, the druggist who loses some money or the person who loses their life?" The right to property and right to life are weighed not in the abstract, in terms of their logical priority, but rather in the particular, in terms of the actual consequences that the violation of these rights would have in the lives of the people involved. Thinking remains contextual and admixed with feelings of care, as the moral imperative to avoid hurt begins to be informed by a psychological understanding of the meaning of nonviolence.

Thus, release from the intimidation of inequality finally allows the expression of a judgment that previously had been withheld. What women then enunciate is not a new morality, but a moral conception disentangled from the constraints that formerly had confused its perception and impeded its articulation. The willingness to express and take responsibility for judgment stems from the recognition of the psychological and moral necessity for an equation of worth between self and other. Responsibility for care then includes both self and other, and the obligation not to hurt, freed from conventional constraints, is reconstructed as a universal guide to moral choice.

The reality of hurt centers the judgment of a twenty-nine-year-old woman, married and the mother of a preschool child, as she struggles with the dilemma posed by a second pregnancy whose timing conflicts with her completion of an advanced degree. Saying that "I cannot deliberately do something that is bad or would hurt another person because I can't live with having done that," she nevertheless confronts a situation in which hurt has become inevitable. Seeking that solution which would best protect both herself and others, she indicates, in her definition of morality, the ineluctable sense of connection which infuses and colors all of her thinking:

> [Morality is] doing what is appropriate and what is just within your circumstances, but ideally it is not going to affect—I was going to say, ideally it wouldn't negatively affect another person, but that is ridiculous, because decisions are always going to affect another person. But you see, what I am trying to say is that it is the person that is the center of the decision making, of that decision making about what's right and what's wrong.

The person who is the center of this decision making begins by denying, but then goes on to acknowledge, the conflicting nature both of her own needs and of her various responsibilities. Seeing the pregnancy as a manifestation of the inner conflict between her wish, on the one hand, "to be a college president" and, on the other, "to be making pottery and flowers and having kids and staying at home," she struggles with contradiction between femininity and adulthood. Considering abortion as the "better" choice—because "in the end, meaning this time next year or this time two weeks from now, it will be less of a personal strain on us individually and on us as a family for me not to be pregnant at this time," she concludes that the decision has

> got to be, first of all, something that the woman can live with—a decision that the woman can live with, one way or another, or at least try to live with, and that it be based on where she is at and other people, significant people in her life, are at.

At the beginning of the interview she had presented the dilemma in its conventional feminine construction, as a conflict between her own wish to have a baby and the wish of others for her to complete her education. On the basis of this construction she deemed it "selfish" to continue the pregnancy because it was something "I want to do." However, as she begins to examine her thinking, she comes to abandon as false this conceptualization of the problem, acknowledging the truth of her own internal conflict and elaborating the tension which she feels between her femininity and the adulthood of her work life. She describes herself as "going in two directions" and values that part of herself which is "incredibly passionate and sensitive"—her capacity to recognize and meet, often with anticipation, the needs of others. Seeing her "compassion" as "something I don't want to lose" she regards it as endangered by her pursuit of professional advancement. Thus the self-deception of her initial presentation, its attempt to sustain the fiction of her own innocence, stems from her fear that to say that *she* does not want to have another baby at this time would be

> an acknowledgement to me that I am an ambitious person and that I want to

have power and responsibility for others and that I want to live a life that extends from 9 to 5 every day and into the evenings and on weekends, because that is what the power and responsibility means. It means that my family would necessarily come second . . . there would be such an incredible conflict about which is tops, and I don't want that for myself.

Asked about her concept of "an ambitious person" she says that to be ambitious means to be

power hungry [and] insensitive. [Why insensitive?] Because people are stomped on in the process. A person on the way up stomps on people, whether it is family or other colleagues or clientele, on the way up. [Inevitably?] Not always, but I have seen it so often in my limited years of working that it is scary to me. It is scary because I don't want to change like that.

Because the acquisition of adult power is seen to entail the loss of feminine sensitivity and compassion, the conflict between femininity and adulthood becomes construed as a moral problem. The discovery of the principle of nonviolence begins to direct attention to the moral dilemma itself and initiates the search for a resolution that can encompass both femininity and adulthood.

Developmental Theory Reconsidered

The developmental conception delineated at the outset, which has so consistently found the development of women to be either aberrant or incomplete, has been limited insofar as it has been predominantly a male conception, giving lip-service, a place on the chart, to the interdependence of intimacy and care but constantly stressing, at their expense, the importance and value of autonomous judgment and action. To admit to this conception the truth of the feminine perspective is to recognize for both sexes the central importance in adult life of the connection between self and other, the universality of the need for compassion and care. The concept of the separate self and of the moral principle uncompromised by the constraints of reality is an adolescent ideal, the elaborately wrought philosophy of a Stephen Daedalus, whose flight we know to be in jeopardy. Erikson (1964), in contrasting the ideological morality of the adolescent with the ethics of adult care, attempts to grapple with this problem of integration, but is impeded by the limitations of his own previous developmental conception. When his developmental stages chart a path where the sole precursor to the intimacy of adult relationships is the trust established in infancy and all intervening experience is marked only as steps toward greater independence, then separation itself becomes the model and the measure of growth. The observation that for women, identity has as much to do with connection as with separation led Erikson into trouble largely because of his failure to integrate this insight into the mainstream of his developmental theory (Erikson, 1968).

The morality of responsibility which women describe stands apart from the morality of rights which underlies Kohlberg's conception of the highest stages of moral judgment. Kohlberg (Note 3) sees the progression toward these stages as resulting from the generalization of the self-centered adolescent rejection of societal morality into a principled conception of individual natural rights. To illustrate this progression, he cites as an example of integrated Stage Five judgment, "possibly moving to Stage Six," the following response of a twenty-five-year-old subject from his male longitudinal sample:

> [What does the word morality mean to you?] Nobody in the world knows the answer. I think it is recognizing the right of the individual, the rights of other individuals, not interfering with those rights. Act as fairly as you would have them treat you. I think it is basically to preserve the human being's right to existence. I think that is the most important. Secondly, the human being's right to do as he pleases, again without interfering with somebody else's rights. (p. 29)

Another version of the same conception is evident in the following interview response of a male college senior whose moral judgment also was scored by Kohlberg (Note 4) as at Stage Five or Six:

> [Morality] is a prescription, it is a thing to follow, and the idea of having a concept of morality is to try to figure out what it is that people can do in order to make life with each other livable, make for a kind of balance, a kind of equilibrium, a harmony in which everybody feels he has a place and an equal share in things, and it's doing that—doing that is kind of contributing to a state of affairs that go beyond the individual in the absence of which, the individual has no chance for self-fulfillment of any kind. Fairness; morality is kind of essential, it seems to me, for creating the kind of environment, interaction between people, that is prerequisite to this fulfillment of most individual goals and so on. If you want other people to not interfere with your pursuit of whatever you are into, you have to play the game.

In contrast, a woman in her late twenties responds to a similar question by defining a morality not of rights but of responsibility:

> [What makes something a moral issue?] Some sense of trying to uncover a right path in which to live, and always in my mind is that the world is full of real and recognizable trouble, and is it heading for some sort of doom and is it right to bring children into this world when we currently have an overpopulation problem, and is it right to spend money on a pair of shoes when I have a pair of shoes and other people are shoeless. . . . It is part of a self-critical view, part of saying, how am I spending my time and in what sense am I working? I think I have a real drive to, I have a real maternal drive to take care of someone. To take care of my mother, to take care of children, to take care of other people's children, to take care of my own children, to take care of the world. I think that goes back to your other question, and when I am dealing with moral issues, I am sort of saying to myself constantly, are you taking care of all the things that you think are important and in what ways are you wasting yourself and wasting those issues?

While the postconventional nature of this woman's perspective seems clear, her judgments of Kohlberg's hypothetical moral dilemmas do not meet his criteria for scoring at the principled level. Kohlberg regards this as a disparity between normative and metaethical judgments which he sees as indicative of the transition between conventional and principled thinking. From another perspective, however, this judgment represents a different moral conception, disentangled from societal conventions and raised to the principled level. In this conception, moral judgment is oriented toward issues of responsibility. The way in which the responsibility orientation guides moral decision at the postconventional level is described by the following woman in her thirties:

> [Is there a right way to make moral decisions?] The only way I know is to try to be as awake as possible, to try to know the range of what you feel, to try to consider all that's involved, to be as aware as you can be to what's going on, as conscious as you can of where you're walking. [Are there principles that guide you?] The principle would have something to do with responsibility, responsibility and caring about yourself and others. . . . But it's not that on the one hand you choose to be responsible and on the other hand you choose to be irresponsible—both ways you can be responsible. That's why there's not just a principle that once you take hold of you settle—the principle put into practice here is still going to leave you with conflict.

The moral imperative that emerges repeatedly in the women's interviews is an injunction to care, a responsibility to discern and alleviate the "real and recognizable trouble" of this world. For the men Kohlberg studied, the moral imperative appeared rather as an injunction to respect the rights of others and thus to protect from interference the right to life and self-fulfillment. Women's insistence on care is at first self-critical rather than self-protective, while men initially conceive obligation to others negatively in terms of noninterference. Development for both sexes then would seem to entail an integration of rights and responsibilities through the discovery of the complementarity of these disparate views. For the women I have studied, this integration between rights and responsibilities appears to take place through a principled understanding of equity and reciprocity. This understanding tempers the self-destructive potential of a self-critical morality by asserting the equal right of all persons to care. For the men in Kohlberg's sample as well as for those in a longitudinal study of Harvard undergraduates (Gilligan & Murphy, Note 5) it appears to be the recognition through experience of the need for a more active responsibility in taking care that corrects the potential indifference of a morality of noninterference and turns attention from the logic to the consequences of choice. In the development of a postconventional ethic understanding, women come to see the violence generated by inequitable relationships, while men come to realize the limitations of a conception of justice blinded to the real inequities of human life.

Kohlberg's dilemmas, in the hypothetical abstraction of their presentation, divest the moral actors from the history and psychology of their individual lives and separate the moral problem from the social contingencies of its possible occurrence. In doing so, the dilemmas are useful for the distillation and refinement of the "objective principles of justice" toward which Kohlberg's stages strive. However, the reconstruction of the dilemma in its contextual particularity allows the understanding of cause and consequence which engages the compassion and tolerance considered by previous theorists to qualify the feminine sense of justice. Only when substance is given to the skeletal lives of hypothetical people is it possible to consider the social injustices which their moral problems may reflect and to imagine the individual suffering their occurrence may signify or their resolution engender.

The proclivity of women to reconstruct hypothetical dilemmas in terms of the real, to request or supply the information missing about the nature of the people and the places where they live, shifts their judgment away from the hierarchical ordering of principles and the formal procedures of decision making that are critical for scoring at Kohlberg's highest stages. This insistence on the particular signifies an orientation to the dilemma and to moral problems in general that differs from any of Kohlberg's stage descriptions. Given the constraints of Kohlberg's system and the biases in his research sample, this different orientation can only be construed as a failure in development. While several of the women in the research sample clearly articulated what Kohlberg regarded as a postconventional metaethical position, none of them were considered by Kohlberg to be principled in their normative moral judgments of his hypothetical moral dilemmas (Note 4). Instead, the women's judgments pointed toward an identification of the violence inherent in the dilemma itself which was seen to compromise the justice of any of its possible resolutions. This construction of the dilemma led the women to recast the moral judgment from a consideration of the good to a choice between evils.

The woman whose judgment of the abortion dilemma concluded the developmental sequence presented in the preceding section saw Kohlberg's Heinz dilemma in these terms and judged Heinz's action in terms of a choice between selfishness and sacrifice. For Heinz to steal the drug, given the circumstances of his life (which she inferred from his inability to pay two thousand dollars), he would have "to do something which is not in his best interest, in that he is going to get sent away, and that is a supreme sacrifice, a sacrifice which I would say a person truly in love might be willing to make." However, not to steal the drug "would be selfish on his part . . . he would just have to feel guilty about not allowing her a chance to live longer." Heinz's decision to steal is considered not in terms of the logical priority of life over property which justifies its rightness, but rather in terms of the actual consequences that stealing would have for a man of limited means and little social power.

Considered in the light of its probable outcomes—his wife dead, or Heinz in jail, brutalized by the violence of that experience and his life compromised by a record of felony—the dilemma itself changes. Its resolution has less to do with the relative weights of life and property in an abstract moral conception than with the collision it has produced between two lives, formerly conjoined but now in opposition, where the continuation of one life can now occur only at the expense of the other. Given this construction, it becomes clear why consideration revolves around the issue of sacrifice and why guilt becomes the inevitable concomitant of either resolution.

Demonstrating the reticence noted in the first section about making moral judgments, this woman explains her reluctance to judge in terms of her belief that everybody's existence is so different that I kind of say to myself, that might be something that I wouldn't do, but I can't say that it is right or wrong for that person. I can only deal with what is appropriate for me to do when I am faced with specific problems.

Asked if she would apply to others her own injunction against hurting, she says:

See, I can't say that it is wrong. I can't say that it is right or that it's wrong because I don't know what the person did that the other person did something to hurt him . . . so it is not right that the person got hurt, but it is right that the person who just lost the job has got to get that anger up and out. It doesn't put any bread on his table, but it is released. I don't mean to be copping out. I really am trying to see how to answer these questions for you.

Her difficulty in answering Kohlberg's questions, her sense of strain with the construction which they impose on the dilemma, stems from their divergence from her own frame of reference:

I don't even think I use the words right and wrong anymore, and I know I don't use the word moral, because I am not sure I know what it means. . . . We are talking about an unjust society, we are talking about a whole lot of things that are not right, that are truly wrong, to use the word that I don't use very often, and I have no control to change that. If I could change it, I certainly would, but I can only make my small contribution from day to day, and if I don't intentionally hurt somebody, that is my contribution to a better society. And so a chunk of that contribution is also not to pass judgment on other people, particularly when I don't know the circumstances of why they are doing certain things.

The reluctance to judge remains a reluctance to hurt, but one that stems now not from a sense of personal vulnerability but rather from a recognition of the limitations of judgment itself. The deference of the conventional feminine perspective can thus be seen to continue at the postconventional level, not as moral relativism but rather as part of a reconstructed moral understanding. Moral judgment is renounced in an awareness of the psychological and social determinism of all human behavior at the same time as moral concern is reaffirmed in recognition of the reality of human pain and suffering.

I have a real thing about hurting people and always have, and that gets a little complicated at times, because, for example, you don't want to hurt your child. I don't want to hurt my child but if I don't hurt her sometimes, then that's hurting her more, you see, and so that was a terrible dilemma for me.

Moral dilemmas are terrible in that they entail hurt; she sees Heinz's decision as "the result of anguish, who am I hurting, why do I have to hurt them." While the morality of Heinz's theft is not in question, given the circumstances which necessitated it, what is at issue is his willingness to substitute himself for his wife and become, in her stead, the victim of exploitation by a society which breeds and legitimizes the druggist's irresponsibility and whose injustice is thus manifest in the very occurrence of the dilemma.

234

The same sense that the wrong questions are being asked is evident in the response of another woman who justified Heinz's action on a similar basis, saying "I don't think that exploitation should really be a right." When women begin to make direct moral statements, the issues they repeatedly address are those of exploitation and hurt. In doing so, they raise the issue of nonviolence in precisely the same psychological context that brought Erikson (1969) to pause in his consideration of the truth of Gandhi's life.

In the pivotal letter, around which the judgment of his book turns, Erikson confronts the contradiction between the philosophy of nonviolence that informed Gandhi's dealing with the British and the psychology of violence that marred his relationships with his family and with the children of the ashram. It was this contradiction, Erikson confesses,

> which almost brought *me* to the point where I felt unable to continue writing *this* book because I seemed to sense the presence of a kind of untruth in the very protestation of truth; of something unclean when all the words spelled out an unreal purity; and, above all, of displaced violence where nonviolence was the professed issue. (p. 231)

In an effort to untangle the relationship between the spiritual truth of Satyagraha and the truth of his own psychoanalytic understanding, Erikson reminds Gandhi that "Truth, you once said, 'excludes the use of violence because man is not capable of knowing the absolute truth and therefore is not competent to punish'" (p. 241). The affinity between Satyagraha and psychoanalysis lies in their shared commitment to seeing life as an "experiment in truth," in their being

> somehow joined in a universal "therapeutics," committed to the Hippocratic principle that one can test truth (or the healing power inherent in a sick situation) only by action which avoids harm—or better, by action which maximizes mutuality and minimizes the violence caused by unilateral coercion or threat. (p. 247)

Erikson takes Gandhi to task for his failure to acknowledge the relativity of truth. This failure is manifest in the coercion of Gandhi's claim to exclusive possession of the truth, his "unwillingness to learn from *anybody anything* except what was approved by the 'inner voice'" (p. 236). This claim led Gandhi, in the guise of love, to impose his truth on others without awareness or regard for the extent to which he thereby did violence to their integrity.

The moral dilemma, arising inevitably out of a conflict of truths, is by definition a "sick situation" in that its either/or formulation leaves no room for an outcome that does not do violence. The resolution of such dilemmas, however, lies not in the self-deception of rationalized violence—"I was" said Gandhi, "a cruelly kind husband. I regarded myself as her teacher and so harassed her out of my blind love for her" (p. 233)—but rather in the replacement of the underlying antagonism with a mutuality of respect and care.

Gandhi, whom Kohlberg has mentioned as exemplifying Stage Six moral judgment and whom Erikson sought as a model of an adult ethical sensibility, instead is criticized by a judgment that refuses to look away from or condone the infliction of harm. In denying the validity of his wife's reluctance to open her home to strangers and in his blindness to the different reality of adolescent sexuality and temptation, Gandhi compromised in his everyday life the ethic of nonviolence to which in principle and in public he was so steadfastly committed.

The blind willingness to sacrifice people to truth, however, has always been the danger of an ethics abstracted from life. This willingness links Gandhi to the biblical Abraham, who prepared to sacrifice the life of his son in order to demonstrate the integrity and supremacy of his faith. Both men, in the limitations of their fatherhood, stand in implicit contrast to the woman who comes before Solomon and verifies her motherhood by relinquishing truth in order to save the life of her child. It is the ethics of an adulthood that has become principled at the expense of care that Erikson comes to criticize in his assessment of Gandhi's life.

This same criticism is dramatized explicitly as a contrast between the sexes in *The Merchant of Venice* (1598/1912), where Shakespeare goes through an extraordinary complication of sexual identity (dressing a male actor as a female character who in turn poses as a male judge) in order to bring into the masculine citadel of justice the feminine plea for mercy. The limitation of the contractual conception of justice is illustrated through the absurdity of its literal execution, while the "need to make exceptions all the time" is demonstrated contrapuntally in the matter of the rings. Portia, in calling for mercy, argues for that resolution in which no one is hurt, and as the men are forgiven for their failure to keep both their rings and their word, Antonio in turn foregoes his "right" to ruin Shylock.

The research findings that have been reported in this essay suggest that women impose a distinctive construction on moral problems, seeing moral dilemmas in terms of conflicting responsibilities. This construction was found to develop through a sequence of three levels and two transitions, each level representing a more complex understanding of the relationship between self and other and each transition involving a critical reinterpretation of the moral conflict between selfishness and responsibility. The development of women's moral judgment appears to proceed from an initial concern with survival, to a focus on goodness, and finally to a principled understanding of nonviolence as the most adequate guide to the just resolution of moral conflicts.

In counterposing to Kohlberg's longitudinal research on the development of hypothetical moral judgment in men a cross-sectional study of women's responses to actual dilemmas of moral conflict and choice, this essay precludes the possibility of generalization in either direction and leaves to further research the task of sorting out the different variables of occasion and sex. Longitudinal studies of women's moral judgments are necessary in order to validate the claims of stage and sequence presented here. Similarly, the contrast drawn between the moral judgments of men and women awaits for its confirmation a more systematic comparison of the responses of both sexes. Kohlberg's research on moral development has confounded the variables of age, sex, type of decision, and type of dilemma by presenting a single configuration (the responses of adolescent males to hypothetical dilemmas of conflicting rights) as the basis for a universal stage sequence. This paper underscores the need for systematic treatment of these variables and points toward their study as a critical task for future moral development research.

For the present, my aim has been to demonstrate the centrality of the concepts of responsibility and care in women's constructions of the moral domain, to indicate the close tie in women's thinking between conceptions of the self and conceptions of morality, and, finally, to argue the need for an expanded developmental theory that would include, rather than rule out from developmental consideration, the difference in the feminine voice. Such an inclusion seems essential, not only for explaining the development of women but also for understanding in both sexes the characteristics and precursors of an adult moral conception.

Reference Notes

1. Haan, N. *Activism as moral protest: Moral judgments of hypothetical dilemmas and an actual situation of civil disobedience.* Unpublished manuscript, University of California at Berkeley, 1971.
2. Turiel, E. *A comparative analysis of moral knowledge and moral judgment in males and females.* Unpublished manuscript, Harvard University, 1973.
3. Kohlberg, L. *Continuities and discontinuities in childhood and adult moral development revisited.* Unpublished paper, Harvard University, 1973.
4. Kohlberg, L. Personal communication, August, 1976.
5. Gilligan, C., & Murphy, M. *The philosopher and the "dilemma of the fact": Moral development in late adolescence and adulthood.* Unpublished manuscript, Harvard University, 1977.

References

Broverman, I., Vogel, S., Broverman, D., Clarkson, F., & Rosenkrantz, P. Sex-role stereotypes: A current appraisal. *Journal of Social Issues*, 1972, **28**, 59–78.

Coles, R. *Children of crisis.* Boston: Little, Brown, 1964.

Didion, J. The women's movement. *New York Times Book Review*, July 30, 1972, pp. 1–2; 14.

Drabble, M. *The waterfall.* Hammondsworth, Eng.: Penguin Books, 1969.

Eliot, G. *The mill on the floss.* New York: New American Library, 1965. (Originally published, 1860.)

Erikson, E. H. *Insight and responsibility.* New York: W. W. Norton, 1964.

Erikson, E. H. *Identity: Youth and crisis.* New York: W. W. Norton, 1968.

Erikson, E. H. *Gandhi's truth.* New York: W. W. Norton, 1969.

Freud, S. "Civilized" sexual morality and modern nervous illness. In J. Strachey (Ed.), *The standard edition of the complete psychological works of Sigmund Freud* (Vol. 9). London: Hogarth Press, 1959. (Originally published, 1908.)

Freud, S. Some psychical consequences of the anatomical distinction between the sexes. In J. Strachey (Ed.), *The standard edition of the complete psychological works of Sigmund Freud* (Vol. 19). London: Hogarth Press, 1961. (Originally published, 1925.)

Gilligan, C., Kohlberg, L., Lerner, J., & Belenky, M. Moral reasoning about sexual dilemmas: The development of an interview and scoring system. *Technical Report of the President's Commission on Obscenity and Pornography* (Vol. 1) [415 060–137]. Washington, D.C.: U.S. Government Printing Office, 1971.

Haan, N. Hypothetical and actual moral reasoning in a situation of civil disobedience. *Journal of Personality and Social Psychology*, 1975, **32**, 255–270.

Holstein, C. Development of moral judgment: A longitudinal study of males and females. *Child Development*, 1976, **47**, 51–61.

Horner, M. Toward an understanding of achievement-related conflicts in women. *Journal of Social Issues,* 1972, **29,** 157–174.

Ibsen, H. *A doll's house.* In *Ibsen plays.* Hammondsworth, Eng.: Penguin Books, 1965. (Originally published, 1879.)

Kohlberg, L. From is to ought: How to commit the naturalistic fallacy and get away with it in the study of moral development. In T. Mischel (Ed.), *Cognitive development and epistemology.* New York: Academic Press, 1971.

Kohlberg, L., & Gilligan, C. The adolescent as a philosopher: The discovery of the self in a postconventional world. *Daedalus,* 1971, **100,** 1051–1056.

Kohlberg, L., & Kramer, R. Continuities and discontinuities in childhood and adult moral development. *Human Development,* 1969, **12,** 93–120.

Piaget, J. *The moral judgment of the child.* New York: The Free Press, 1965. (Originally published, 1932.)

Shakespeare, W. *The merchant of Venice.* In *The comedies of Shakespeare.* London: Oxford University Press, 1912. (Originally published, 1598.)

PART II

Education and Social Equality

Selection and Guidance in the Secondary School

JAMES BRYANT CONANT

According to James Bryant Conant, educators must provide a closer fit between school-ing and the economy's needs for professional and occupational skills. He presents a model of a perfect meritocracy as the ideal toward which United States society should strive. Within such a society, Conant argues, the school's role is to guide students toward occupations best suited to their individual skills. Length and type of schooling should be determined by individual capacities and by the training requirements of particular jobs. Equality of educational opportunity, in Conant's view, would provide the necessary resources for advanced training to students of talent, regardless of social class. The paper was presented at a symposium in honor of the 300th anniversary of the founding of Boston Latin School, a public examination school.

Education is a social process. Neither our schools nor our colleges operate in a vacuum. To anyone who has studied the cultural history of a modern nation the inter-relation of education to economic, political, and other cultural forces, including those generated by organized religions, is very clear. There is nothing new about our present tendency to analyze educational problems with reference to the needs of the society which education serves. What is new, however, is the relative importance of education as one of the factors influencing the future of the nation. The expansion of universal education in the United States to include the high school grades is the culmination of a social revolution of great import for our future. There is no need for me to remind this audience of how greatly the national educational scene as well as the local picture has altered since the Roxbury Latin School celebrated its 250th anniversary. Nor has the process reached an end. Unless all signs fail, by 1995 universal education will have spread to include the last years of high school for a large percentage of boys and girls, and two years at least of further instruction for a considerable proportion.

Now these high school years and the post high school education have potent effects on the subsequent life of a young man or woman. The subsequent occupation is today in no small measure determined by these years. And since the proper distribution of occupations in a modern society is almost the central core of the welfare of that soci-ety, we recognize with what terrific social forces we educators are today concerned. No matter how few boys any of us may instruct, how large or small a school, to a certain

Harvard Educational Review   Vol. 18   No. 2   Spring 1948, 61-67

degree each of us each day shapes the future of the country. And we do so not only in the sense of influencing for better or worse the moral qualities of our future citizens (though this is of the first importance), but in determining whether we shall have a large or a small percent of our future adults in satisfying occupations or spending their lives vainly trying to find an outlet for their ambitions.

Both the secondary schools and the colleges, I think, have often failed to face squarely the social implications of the education which they give. We have talked too often as though education did proceed in a vacuum and that the general or liberal education of a future citizen could be considered apart from his future role in society as an adult. Now I do not believe you can divorce a consideration of a general or liberal education from the eventual occupational status of the boy or girl in question; no more can you divorce it from a consideration of the local situation or the place of his family in a social group as determined by the interaction of a variety of social forces.

To me there is nothing inconsistent in maintaining our ideal of an American society of high fluidity — great social mobility up and down — and at the same time viewing in the cold light of hard analysis the relation of education to society. In fact, I do not believe that we can succeed in approaching our goal of a nation with a maximum of social fluidity unless we do face in a realistic fashion the problem of connecting the general education of a boy or girl with occupational or professional training. We must likewise recognize the importance of providing highly diversified types of education during the later years of high school and at the more advanced level. We must not only provide many diverse educational channels, but likewise endeavor to lower the social barriers which separate them. False snobbery between various occupations we must seek to minimize as best we can. This we can do in part by the atmosphere created in the school and by wise guidance through each succeeding year.

Now it would be my contention that we as educators have a task to do, not only in providing adequate selection and guidance in our own schools and colleges, but in informing the public of the role of guidance in our modern system of education. To this end I believe we should be ready to answer the question, "Shall everyone go to college (that is a four-year college)?" by the counter question, "What is the minimum length of formal education required for each occupation?"

The time has come, it seems to me, when we must recognize clearly that in a modern society a great variety of talents can be usefully employed. Depending on the talent and the type of employment, shorter or longer periods of formal education are required. There is nothing magic about four years. Indeed, I believe that for many occupations a two-year terminal education beyond high school provides the proper answer. Such education can be given locally at minimum expense to the taxpayer. In these new types of local institutions (I do not call them junior colleges for I think they should be quite different from most of the institutions which now go by that name), in these terminal two-year institutions, a combination of vocational training and general education should be given. If this were done, the four-year liberal arts colleges and universities would be left to work out the problem of equipping young people for certain occupations. These are the professions (using that word in its modern and most generous sense), careers in the management of business and public service. I am not going into the question of how long that advanced education should be and in what way the colleges and the university professional schools at the graduate level should cooperate. That subject is both confused and controversial.

Educational guidance is to me the key which will solve the problem posed by the question, "Shall everyone go to college, and if not, how shall we select those who are to be denied the privilege?" The less we talk about the *privilege* of advanced education the better. As a matter of fact, as pecuniary rewards are now moving, in the not too distant future a college education will be less and less of a privilege unless the education leads to definite occupations.

Depending on the local situations — and I emphasize those words — depending on the local situations, some degree of selection will certainly be required in various types of secondary schools. I have already pointed out that I think the Roxbury Latin School has for a long time past exercised wise selections and concentrated on one task, namely, that of a preparatory school for college for boys, from whatever economic background, and boys of superior scholastic ability. Now in emphasizing this particular role of the Roxbury Latin School, which I hope it will continue to play in the future, I should like to make it plain that I do not wish to place this type of school at the top of an educational hierarchy. Quite the contrary, for to do so would be to negate one of my basic propositions, namely, that we should move in the United States further in the direction of recognizing the social equality of all useful labor. To that end the establishment of special high schools for those with musical or artistic talent as well as for those with high scientific talent (as in New York City) is surely to be commended. Not that complete separation of all youths with different talents is the answer; again, the local situation must control. But as pacemakers separate schools can often be of great value in the progress of education as a whole.

In all that I have said thus far I have spoken of talent, diversified talent. Now I must admit that American public opinion as voiced by the press and translated into action by elected representatives has been very loath until recently to admit the reality of talent. Only in matters connected with organized sport does the average American think clearly and realistically about the significance of innate ability. Countless parents condemn schools, colleges, and universities because their offspring are not being transformed into doctors and lawyers of great promise; but very few condemn the athletic director and his coaches because a son failed to develop into an All-American football player; and fewer still expect the college to make an average athlete out of a frail and badly coordinated youth. Yet when it comes to studies, parents and children often expect the school and college to accomplish the equivalent of turning a cripple into a football player. And for this attitude the educational fraternity must take its share of blame. Every teacher worth his or her salt has to take a roseate view of both the potentialities of the pupils and the transforming power of education. Furthermore, friends and supporters of various schools and colleges, who in this century have wanted either more public funds, or more students, or more gifts (or all three), have quite consciously fostered the idea that education can work miracles. As a result of all this muddy thinking, the reality of talent is all too often denied by the average American citizen.

What has been called the "Jacksonian tradition" in American thinking, combined with the propaganda of certain educators, has spread the idea that any American child can, if he wants, with the aid of proper education become anything he desires. The very fact that so-called higher education, particularly in the institutions with the highest standards and greatest reputation, has been available to a large degree only to the children of the upper-income groups has made suspect the whole process of professional education. By denying the reality of intellectual talent, the "Jacksonian democrat" can also minimize the significance of professional training. Neither "brains" nor wealth determines which men get ahead in this American democracy, he declares; the only thing that counts, this sturdy individualist would maintain, is will power. And in spite of the historic connection between the mores of the U.S.A. and the doctrine of predestination, most Americans are quite convinced that each man's will is free.

We meet here a social phenomenon of great interest and one that has played an important role in the development of the United States. One of the most baffling experiences for a foreigner is to encounter this strain in our thinking; it seems to him the democracy of the "levellers" of three centuries ago; it seems equalitarianism gone wild. To assume that the graduate of a night law school is just as well trained as one who has won honors at a famous university school of law seems to a foreign scholar either ludicrous or disastrous. Yet, while admitting that this American blindness to differences in ability and training along professional lines has worked much evil in the past, I believe it has been a healthy symptom of the vitality of our democratic life. Such leveling doctrines were the antibodies supplied unconsciously by the body politic to counteract the claims of those who had enjoyed "the privileges of a higher education." Here we have one of the instinctive defense mechanisms of American democracy at work to guard against the ascendancy of a privileged group.

There may be some who think I am stretching a long bow in thus ascribing to the American electorate a prejudice against high standards of professional training and breaking the bow perhaps in relating this prejudice to a general social and political philosophy. If so, I only ask the skeptics to try to persuade a legislative group in Washington or a number of state capitals as to the desirability of finding intellectual talent and educating this talent at government expense. I ask the same skeptics to look at the recorded debates on the state approval of medical schools with inadequate staffs and low standards. The fact that so many of our elected representatives are lawyers has had an important bearing on educational legislation. Because some men of great native ability have been successful in the practice of law even on the basis of very poor preparation, the false conclusion has been drawn that law schools with high standards are either unimportant or a positive evil. And by analogy the same argument has been advanced regarding medical and scientific training.

Clearly the remedy for the evil which has evoked this democratic defense response — the evil of inequality of educational opportunity — is not to deny the reality of talent or the significance of superior advanced education, but to provide funds so that the boy of real talent may get as good an education as he needs. And to meet the argument that the job of the colleges and universities is to make anyone who has the "will power" a first-rate lawyer, doctor, engineer, or scientist, one must daily educate the American people about the realities of human nature.

Just to emphasize the importance of guidance and selection, I should like to conclude my remarks by asking certain of the school men here, namely those from the private schools, or the suburban schools in well-to-do areas, whether their chief preoccupation should not be with keeping boys away from four-year colleges instead of trying to get them in. I put this question in a somewhat unorthodox form, I admit, to challenge your attention. But I would be inclined to think, on the whole, the so-called preparatory schools are to be criticized not for the boys they fail to get into college, but for the boys they send to college who would have been better off not to have gone to a four-year type of institution.

To those educators from high schools where only a fraction of the graduating class now goes on to a four-year college, I would ask the opposite question. "Are you sure you are doing all you can to find potential professional talent for the country? Are you finding the talent and providing the proper environment for its growth?" In short, to both groups of school men I would say, "Are you thinking as educational statesmen of education as a social process? Are you employing all the devices now available and mustering the highest wisdom at your command to provide good educational guidance?"

Now you may well reply that I have spoken in very general terms. As an ideal, diversified channels of education freely open to all economic groups may be fine indeed. But in practice how can you possibly tell in advance what boys and girls are going to be in fact happy and useful in a given occupaton?

I agree that I have spoken in very general terms, but at least I trust I have left in no one's mind any misunderstanding about my firm conviction that only through the further development of education guidance can we utilize our educational system to the best advantage of the country. Educational guidance is no mechanical process. It involves a very personal relation of teacher to pupil, but the teacher can be guided by the new tests which are now available and which are certain to be greatly improved in the near future. I like to think of these tests as fulfilling the same function for a teacher that a chemical and bacteriological laboratory fulfills for a physician who is a good diagnostician.

The English Adolescent

STEPHEN SPENDER

In an essay that fuses personal experience with accounts of his contemporaries, Stephen Spender, noted poet and playwright, describes how British schools and cultural traditions have affected adolescents and perpetuated a profoundly class-divided society. Attitudes about sex, the individual's responsibility to society, and differences in political and social values are shaped by class and are reinforced by the socializing processes of the schools. Although Spender is highly critical of British schools, he recognizes that they have nevertheless contributed to the strengths of British society.

Let me recall that an aim of this Seminar is "to prepare a publication on *education in many societies*, which will set forth the facts of adolescent experience as modified by various cultures and show something of the differences in the human material from which the future world citizens will be made."

As an English representative here, I should try therefore to describe the English adolescent as he is affected through his education by the English social background and cultural tradition. I shall have to consider what there is of value in the English adolescent experience which could be a contribution to the experience of the young world citizen of the future, and I must consider also whether there are not experiences elsewhere which would be valuable to the English adolescent. I may as well say at once that here I am confronted by a characteristically English paradox. When one considers the experience of English adolescents of whatever class in detail, one is struck more by what can be criticized adversely than by what can be praised; and yet, when one considers the result of the best type of personality moulded by the English educational system, one is bound to admit that here is something very valuable indeed. I think I shall find myself therefore being destructive in detail of the kind of experiences which are offered to or withheld from English boys and girls but constructive when I come to examine values and attitudes.

I must warn you, though, that I am no expert in these matters. My own adolescent experience was that of a boy who went to a big London day school which was one of the very few English minor public schools[1] which offered scholarships to boys coming

---

This article was originally presented as a lecture at the Summer Seminar in Education for International Understanding, Paris, 1947, under the auspices of UNESCO.

[1] In England a "public school" is one that would be referred to in this country as independent, private, or non-tax supported. — ED.

Harvard Educational Review   Vol. 18   No. 4   Fall 1948, 228–239

from working-class homes and schools. After that, I was at Oxford. I have also taught for a term at a minor public school. I have met, of course, many public school boys, and discussed their schooling with them. During the war I was a member of the London Fire Service, and there I had a good deal of opportunity to discuss their education with many men who had been sent to the Elementary and Secondary schools, where those are educated who cannot afford to continue their education beyond the governmentally fixed school-leaving age. Most of these stopped being educated and went to work at the age of fourteen, though some of them studied at Evening Classes afterwards. I also know a little about the kind of education which is provided for rich girls and for poor girls. But, on the whole, since in any case, I must limit myself, I shall be speaking of the adolescent experience of members of my own sex, and also I shall be speaking with real experience only of my own class.

I am not asked to speak about schools, but about the adolescent. One cannot think of the English adolescent without thinking of a little fragment of human material confronted by a great hierarchy of educational machines through which his young life is going to pass, and from which he will emerge as a member of a community. And the first point to make is that those machines select their material. There are the elementary schools, the secondary schools, the private preparatory schools, the grammar schools, the minor public schools, the great public schools, like Eton and Winchester, Harrow and Charterhouse, and then there are the universities, Oxford and Cambridge, and what are called, I believe, the provincial universities. Then, also, a class apart, there are the Girls' Public Schools. There are also the small progressive schools for rich children, which are in revolt against the Public School system.

And Eton and Harrow do not select the boy who goes to the Elementary School. English education is on a class basis. Indeed class feeling is more deeply ingrained in our educational system than anywhere else. I can illustrate this by drawing attention to what I know to be a fact; that many middle-class parents who consider that in their own lives they have shed all traces of class feeling, and who may even wish to belong to the working class, yet, when it comes to educating their own children, send them to the public school against whose values they have rebelled themselves. The reason for this is not merely, I think, that such parents consider the public school the best possible education; they also feel that having a public school education is the sign of belonging to a social class, and they do not feel entitled, just because they have withdrawn from spiritual membership of that class themselves, to impose the choice which they have made for themselves on their children.

I

Thus, the main social experience of the English child and adolescent is that he belongs to a social class. The child of poor parents is forced continually to think of the job which he will do when he leaves school, the job that will grade him for life. He can only obtain the higher education which will make it possible for him to enter a profession by winning scholarship after scholarship, which will take him to the secondary school and finally to the University. If he wins sufficient scholarships to get to a University and then to pass beyond the University into a profession, he will then be absorbed into the broad middle class which is the main stream of English social and cultural life.

The poor are thus in a practical and empirical way made conscious of their place in society during their adolescence by their education. This does not mean that they recognize the superiority of the rich, but it does mean that they realize their own limitations. The social history of the poor man or woman is his or her education. The sons of those who can afford and who do send their children to public schools are conscious of their social position in quite a different way. They know that they belong to a privileged class, and they are conscious of social superiority. In between the public schools and the completely state-supported schools, there is a kind of limbo of minor public schools, day schools and grammar schools, which, unlike the genuine working-class schools, have a real consciousness of social inferiority. This attitude is very noticeable amongst those grammar school boys who come up to Oxford and Cambridge: they feel ill-at-ease with the public school boys. The sense of social superiority of public school boys is only equalled by the energy with which members of the upper-middle class in England sometimes pretend that it does not exist. Here are two examples. In 1928, I went to visit a friend who had just arrived at New College from Oxford. He was giving a tea party to six or eight other Etonians all of whom had also just come up to Oxford. They were all convulsed with amusement for a reason which they quickly divulged to me. To their amazement one of their contemporaries, who had come up with them to New College, was a boy—I shall call X—whom they had known and laughed at all their time at Eton, because he was the son of the school grocer; he often waited on them behind the counter of his father's shop.

The year, 1928, may seem very long ago, but the second story is more recent. In the autumn of 1940, before I was called up for military service, I taught for a term in a West-country public school. The boys at this school were mostly the sons of clergy, doctors, and other professional men. This school, in common with several other public schools, supported, as an act of charity, a mission which did good work amongst poor boys in one of the large neighbouring towns. It was suggested that as a revolutionary measure which fitted in with the mood of a country fighting a war alone for the salvation of world democracy, the school should offer two scholarships to be given to two working-class boys so that they might be educated together with the sons of the parsons, doctors, and schoolmasters. As an experiment, another master and myself asked all the boys in a certain house of the school to write a short essay on their reactions to this proposal. The results of this inquiry amazed me. There was not a single boy who treated the suggestion as simply an invitation to two other boys, with a rather different background perhaps, to enter the school. To all of them it seemed outrageous and revolutionary. The answers were divided between (a) those who thought that it would lower and vitiate the school to have these two working-class boys and (b) those who thought that the shock of such a social environment as that of our school on the working-class boys would be such that they would never find their places in their own world again, would never be happy, and would probably be ruined in their later lives.

There is a saving grace in both these illustrations. Neither the undergraduates at Eton nor the boys at the school showed hatred or intolerance of the working-class boys. Their attitude was, rather, one of surprise to find that such people existed in the same sense, with the same ambitions and potentialities as themselves. And as a matter of fact the Etonians took well to X, the school grocer's son, when they had got over the shock of discovering that he was rather cleverer than themselves.

This is important, because English class feeling is deep rather than narrow. It derives from profound and utmost self-confidence of the ruling classes in themselves, and it has a depth which can absorb newcomers when they have proved that they can also belong to the middle class. This depth and breadth rather than narrowness derives from the fact that we are in a middle-class society with a middle-class culture. The working-class boy who wins scholarships makes his way up until he enters the middle class. Of course, politically, he may remain a revolutionary proletarian, but even such a political attitude does not alter the fact that the revolutionary writer or the trade-union leader inevitably enters into the middle class of traditional England. The trade unionist and socialist leaders who now appear to be in power in England have worked their way up through the educational system through self-education, into the middle class, which to some extent has broadened itself, by becoming aware of their existence, and absorbing them.

Perhaps I may seem to have strayed from the subject of the adolescent. But I think it is essential to bear in mind that there is a great difference between the experience of the adolescent of working-class parents in England and that of parents who can afford to send their children to the schools where one pays for an expensive education. This difference goes to the very depths of English life. In experiencing this class difference the adolescent experiences a social reality in effective action, which is more or less concealed in adult life. When I say that the poor child who has only a primary education is experiencing the class system, I mean that he is excluded by it from the middle-class tradition which is the main social and cultural stream of English life. And if the poor child gets scholarships and educates himself into one of the professions, into the arts or into politics, he enters culturally into the middle class, and is accepted by it. So we have in England this situation: that class counts very much in so far as the poor and the uneducated are excluded by poverty or ignorance from the middle class, and very little in so far as the middle class has a broad and deep culture which is capable of absorbing into itself every explicit and educated point of view even when it appears to be politically opposed to it. England is an evolutionary rather than a revolutionary country because it has a protean middle class.

Thus, also, we find that the class difference leads to entirely different forms of characteristic adolescent experiences of children of different classes. When we come to physical and physiological development, we find that the difference is very striking, because the public schools take the children away from their homes for nine months in the year and board them. The boarding-school life is undoubtedly healthy, rather spartan-like, and toughening. The poor children do not leave their homes where, though they may be very poor, they may nevertheless be pampered and spoiled far more than richer children. Sometimes periods of pampering alternate with periods of poverty.

The atmosphere of the English working-class or lower-middle-class home, especially in large towns, cannot be said to be conducive to good physical and physiological development. During the early part of the war, as a nation, we were shocked into awareness of this. In the first place the medical examination of hundreds of thousands of young men and women for the services showed how deplorable the physical condition of the poor was. In the second place, people in the country became aware of the often verminous and nearly always unhealthy condition of children from the towns, when the towns-children were billeted on them during the period of evacuation of towns for fear of air raids. A report on the condition of these children was published by the Women's Institutes Association of Great Britain. This is an appalling document, containing a great deal of information for whomever wants to read it.

When I asked my fellow-firemen how they brought up their children, nearly always I found that they preferred giving them tinned to fresh milk, that their children drank large quantities of beer and of tea, and that their most frequent meal was fried fish and chips. The elementary and secondary schools can hardly fight more than a losing battle against such conditions at home. The boarding schools, however, with their simple diet and their emphasis on the importance of games can certainly claim that physically, if not mentally, they produce a healthy type of adolescent.

II

Another great difference between the education of the upper- and lower-class adolescent is in the development of his attitude towards courtship, marriage, and sexual problems. Here again the child of poor parents takes his or her attitude from the home. The problem for the children who go to boarding schools is that, except in a few schools such as Bedales, where there are both girls and boys, the sexes are artificially separated from each other, at an age when the poor boy is probably walking out with his first girl.

In the English public schools there is no training for courtship and marriage; there is simply a problem called sex, of which everyone is uncomfortably aware. In so far as there is an attempt to deal with this problem, it is pushed on to the science master, who is supposed to explain the biological functioning of sex to the boys, probably by a process of first explaining to them the amours of flowers, then frogs, and so on through the animal kingdom, until the possibility of such a relationship between human beings is indicated. The housemaster, or even the headmaster may be called in, if the sexual problem threatens to break out of this scientific test tube, where the school likes to keep it, and infect the emotional atmosphere of a boy's mind. It is no exaggeration to say that the attitude of most English school masters to sex is simply that it is not a question that should arise in a public school. It should do so after the boy has left school, and then it should solve itself without any previous training through a miracle of love.

The attitude of a headmaster of a minor public school is illustrated by the following story, which he told me himself. He said that one day he had walked down a lane near the school and he had seen two of the older boys sitting on a bench with their arms around the waists of two girls. I asked him what he had done. He said that he had sent for the two boys the following day and had said: "I saw you two boys with two girls yesterday. Now in certain countries, such as France, it would be thought that there was nothing wrong with the idea of two boys aged sixteen and seventeen sitting on a bench with their arms round the waists of two girls. However, we in England do not believe in that sort of thing. And on the whole, I think that the English way is best." He seemed very proud of this reply, and no doubt it cowed the two boys. The only trouble is that the English way has met with the criticism that in some cases it perverts the normal development of the relations between the sexes; and that the English public school boy, untrained in courtship and marriage, is a gauche and even a cold husband, unless he revolts against the deficiency in his training and nature and becomes a rake, or even a pervert. Often the frustrated emotions of English adolescents of the public schools become directed onto other boys.

Public school masters vary greatly in their attitude towards homosexual relations between boys under their care. There are some masters who spend a great deal of their time writing notes to other masters suggesting that some particular boy should be restrained from seeing another boy. Other masters are more tolerant, but every master knows that there is always the danger of a scandal, and a scandal which might do the school harm cannot be tolerated. Masters and boys are trapped in a public school by the fact that ultimately the only attitude to these problems is to say, "No! They must not happen at school. There is no really satisfactory way of diverting them into positive channels. They must be postponed or repressed."

A young woman who went to one of the "Girls' Public Schools," and to whom I have shown this paper, commented: "Sex education for girls, as far as I know or have experienced, is pretty well parallel with that of boys. The botany mistress drops embarrassed hints, or the biology mistress makes a better job of it. Games, hobbies, and all the rest are terrifically encouraged to counteract any nascent interest in boys. At the same time *schwaermerei* on other girls is persecuted by authority—a fact which I am sure does much to stimulate it. . . . In the upper-middle classes I think the education of girls, with its emphases on games, Girl Guides, heartiness and unsentimentality, does tend to produce much too high a percentage of gawky and frigid women who—now that arranged marriages are no longer the fashion—have not the slightest idea how to approach the other sex. 'The English spinster' is, of course, proverbial abroad and is largely the product of bad education in adolescence, which still goes on.

"On the other hand this only applies to the middle class. The working-class girl does not seem to have the same difficulties, probably because she imbibes the facts of life and a natural attitude in her more congested home life and while 'helping mother.'

"Against this I think that English middle-class women have in a very high degree the same attitude of responsibility as English men and are—in spite of these inadequacies as *women*—better citizens than most European women, because more generally emancipated, and taught from childhood to think themselves in no way inferior to the opposite sex."

It seems to me that our trouble in England in these matters is that we do not have an ideal of chastity or even restraint; we insist simply on a complete negation of the instinctual life of children, which often we succeed in killing or perverting. We do not accept the senses and then discipline them: we simply deny them and the consequence of this denial is to drive some English men and women into a pursuit of sensual reality which they have lost. Here we pay the price of belonging to a Protestant tradition, and there is no doubt a great deal that we have to learn from the Latin and Catholic countries, as well as from the psychologists.

III

The English public school is really a kind of small city state, and I think it is only if one sees it in this way that one can really understand its weaknesses and its merits. Like the city state, it is a community small enough and old enough for public opinion to be regarded as impersonal and almost sacred. The floggings, lines, and other sensational punishments for which public schools are famous are only really border-line penalties for those who run outside the boundaries of the discipline of the inner city which is created by the extraordinary seriousness with which masters and boys take the school and themselves. A public schoolboy from Winchester who will soon, I am sure, be a cabinet minister, once said to me: "At Winchester, when I was head of my house, I was a greater man than I shall ever be again in my life, even if I live to be Prime Minister." An appalling remark, from an appalling man, I thought at the time, but he will certainly be an excellent prime minister!

Thus the important thing about the public school is that the boys regard all its institutions, all its offices, as sacred; and the masters and parents do also. For a housemaster the choice of prefects and of the boy who will be head of the house is as serious as the choice of a new cabinet for a country, and the boys chosen for these functions take them as seriously as any task they will undertake in the rest of their lives. Of course, there are prefects and head boys who fail, but such failure is parallel to the scandal attaching to a cabinet minister who reveals to his friends the secrets of the Budget.

If one teaches at a public school, one finds it difficult to regard the boys just as boys: they are carried along, as on invisible lines, by the inner discipline of the school-state: if one punishes them, that is just like putting them back onto the lines from which they may have slipped.

I think that the explanation of the extraordinary civic sense of responsibility of England is to be found in the English education which teaches boys to take themselves seriously as functions of an institution, before they take themselves seriously as persons or as individuals. This really explains a great deal, both of the merits and defects of the English. It explains why the English are so suspicious of anyone who takes himself seriously as a person, why they mistrust any machinery of thought, such as psychoanalysis, which directs the attentions of the individual too much onto himself and yet why, as responsible members of a community, they show a deadly earnestness about their own positions which leaves no room for cynicism.

The schoolmasters who persuaded a boy of sixteen at Winchester that he was a great man, were, in a sense, taking him far too seriously, or letting him take himself so; and in another sense they were not taking him seriously enough, because they were ignoring the fact that his psychological development at this time could not have been that of a Pericles. Perhaps they were doing him an injury, and yet they were giving him qualities which the ruling class of a society, such as the British Empire has been until now, undoubtedly needs.

Thus, I think that the English civic sense is not learned by giving children lessons in how local government works, but in forcing onto them in their youth the responsibilities of a very old tradition.

IV

The upper-class English adolescent, who is looked upon sometimes by the outside world as cold and impassive, often has nevertheless a tormented adolescence, which may be followed by a permanent inability to grow up in certain ways, or by a stifling of his emotional life, or by a rare capacity to learn and to develop throughout the whole of his life. The chief problems which may disturb him are sexual ones — which I have discussed — or a religious crisis, or a crisis in his relationship with his parents. In none of these things is he really helped in his upbringing, which tells him to suppress his sexual life, which cuts him off from his parents at a time when he should be getting to know and adjust himself to them in a mature relationship, and which teaches him a conventionalized tepid religious faith which seems only to be taught in order that it may be blown away by the first fresh winds of scientific knowledge.

As I have suggested, the strength of the public school is its power to make boys take their activities, which help the life of the school and live out its traditions, very seriously. The effect of the school city-state is to produce a type, what most public school-masters would call 'the public school type.' The characteristic of this type is that mixture of good qualities summed up in the minds of schoolmasters by the phrase: *Mens sana in corpore sano.*

The weakness of the system is that it becomes too easy for the masters and the boys themselves to value every activity of the members of the school in so far as it contributes or fails to contribute to the school state and school type. Games can be regarded in this way. The school team, if it wins matches, contributes to the glory of the school; the discipline of games is a sacred rite within the school tradition; and, moreover, games are supposed to help the boys to lead asexual lives. It will be noticed here that games are not regarded, as they might well be, in part at least, as being valuable because they provide an escape from school ritual. The result of this attitude has been that a good many boys have revolted against games, precisely because they realize that they are being used as a means of preaching and practicing the school dogmas instead of as play.

Religion, just as much as games, tends to become a part of the school ritual, instead of a window on to a wider, more universally valid order outside it. I am sure that head-masters do not intend this to happen, but nevertheless it does happen. The boy who shows an interest in religion which threatens to take him beyond the spiritual boundaries of the city state is regarded as unhealthy, dangerous, just as much as the boy who takes too great an interest in the arts. The religion that is taught in school strengthens the school code, which may give a boy certain ethical standards that will last him all his life, but it does not give him an understanding of Christian charity or the faith in an invisible world which will last him for a week after he has left school, if he is brought in touch with the violence and crudity and passion of the real world.

If my analysis is even partly correct, it will be seen that our public school education, whilst it instils us with a sense of responsibility to the community, does so at considerable cost to our personal psychology and relationship. In fact, it tends to perpetuate the adolescence of the Englishman by discouraging the interest in spiritual life for its own sake which leads to spiritual maturity, by teaching us to treat as irrelevant physical instincts which lead men and women to understand each other in a mature and full relationship, and by neglecting the problem of the relationship of the growing child with his parents.

Our greatest novelists and poets bear witness that the English middle classes are people of the "undisciplined heart" as Dickens showed in *David Copperfield* or of the "undeveloped heart" which is the theme of the novels of the greatest living English novelist, E. M. Forster. At the same time, if we are a people who never recover from certain adolescent weaknesses, we also acquire in adolescence certain virtues, such as reasonableness, adaptability, generosity, adventurousness, and an astonishingly open mind, combined with a pious attitude towards our institutions. England is supremely the country where the people respond to a national emergency and are capable of that kind of illumination which can see beyond self-interest to the need of the whole country, when it is explained to them, or which can reverse a long-established national policy towards some part of the empire within a few days. Most surprisingly of all, the very class of people who, according to a materialist view, should be most tied up with their own interests, the wealthy public school boys, are the first to sacrifice their lives in a war. Probably, if, in addition to having material interests, they were capable also of developing deep relationships with other people and their families, this capacity for sacrifice would not be so great. The philistines of the undisciplined and undeveloped heart have been among the first to save England in two wars.

V

In this sketch, nearly everything I have said has tended to emphasize the difference between the adolescent experience of the social classes in England. On the one hand, there are the public school boys, artificially withdrawn from parental affection, and indeed from nearly all affection, during the long years of adolescence; on the other hand, there is the poor boy who is a home boy, who is often surrounded by an almost stifling family affection, and who regards 'leaving mum' as the most supremely difficult decision of his life. If I may appeal to the English novelists again, D. H. Lawrence, who was himself the son of a Nottingham miner, shows in his novels a classic picture of his own transition from his working-class origins to his later middle-class environment as a literary artist. His early novel, *Sons and Lovers*, is a heart-rending account of a working-class boy (Lawrence himself) breaking away from his mother's love; whilst his later novels show him lost in a world of the upper classes and trying to recreate the passionate atmosphere of the clinging relationship with his mother in a febrile sexuality.

Perhaps it would be true to say that if the English adolescent who goes to the boarding public school suffers from lack of affection, the working-class boy (the boy more than the girl) suffers from an excess of it. In the difficult lives of the poor, the home, unless it is a complete failure, as may happen, becomes the centre and supreme compensation for all the disappointments of life. And often there is a touching and perhaps rather oppressive emotional dependence of the parents on the children. With the girls this takes the practical form of loading them heavily with responsibilities, making them become, for example, at an early age, the mother of the younger children; with the boys it is more likely to be an emotional burden of the kind so poignantly described by D. H. Lawrence.

I think that many witnesses who have been in the services during World Wars I and II would agree that, on the whole, the public-school boys are tougher than the working-class stay-at-home boys, and that this was very evident between 1914 and 1918, and still evident, though less so, between 1939 and 1945. Perhaps here we have a clue to the unity of English morale: that the upper-class adolescents have retained, to a considerable extent, their toughness and their capacity for leadership. However, toughness is not in itself a sufficient explanation. One has to add to it a few character-istics which really, I think, make the English adolescent exceptional, and which are certainly of value as an experience not to be submerged under the social changes which are taking place all over the world.

The first characteristic, I should call innocence! The English public schoolboy is set aside from the experience of the world during his growing years, and plunged into a tradition which has to a great extent remained islanded from the surrounded world. The result is that, with all his faults, he remains to some extent an innocent, and his very defects are based on this innocence. Thus, as I have explained, his snobbishness is based on an almost incredible unawareness of the conditions and existence of the working populations in an industrial civilization. Now snobbishness is certainly not a virtue, but the fact that this fault is one of innocence instead of one of narrowness and self-opinionatedness means that it can be remedied. So that there exists side by side with the English narrow-mindedness an equally strong open-mindedness, a capacity to see the other person's point of view.

This innocence is not a specially public school virtue. It is a virtue of other centuries, a country virtue of the country-side. But perhaps because the public schools are situ-ated in the country-side, they have become, almost accidentally, transmitters of this quality of saving youth from the corruption of the towns. And the other virtues — toler-ance, courage, modesty, adaptability, and the rest — are only consequences of this fun-damental innocence.

Toughness and an integrity which, with all the faults of the English educational sys-tem have not been betrayed, are the contributions of the upper classes to the unity which has enabled English youth to unite for the desperate struggles of two wars. And with all the differences of background and training, the poor recognize and have, themselves, these values. Different as their experiences and environment are, they are given a schooling based on the same idea that education is a training which can create good citizens and strengthen character, and not just a machine for making youths pass examinations. The teacher is responsible, not just for the learning of his pupil, but for his whole development, his physical and moral well-being.

The contribution of the English adolescent experience to the planning of an adoles-cent experience of a world citizen, might well be the idea that a certain isolation of the adolescent from the modern industrial civilization is necessary. The problem is to iso-late him, without at the same time making him unable to deal with the harshest reali-ties of our existence, and of giving him the strength of his virtues. As I have suggested, a weakness of the English public school system is that the energies of the boys are too often only directed towards the school itself. This has the result that emotional prob-lems of adolescence which conflict with the discipline of the school-state are treated as though they do not exist; and the result of *that* is the protraction throughout the life of many Englishmen of unsolved emotional problems of adolescence. Again, the school chapel, which, like the school football field, produces a self-worshipping kind of pub-lic school religion corresponding to public school games, neglects the fundamental ed-ucational problem of our time: that is, how, during the period of adolescence, to strengthen in the mind of youth a faith in spiritual values and in human values cap-able of resisting the materialism and the power policies of the world of enormous con-flicting social interests in which we live.

I cannot introduce phrases such as *spiritual values* and *human values* without attempting more precise definitions. By spiritual values I mean the sense that the structure of society exists for the sake of a purpose which is a spiritual purpose, and not just for its own sake. It is simply the sense that all material and social structures exist for the sake of an aim, and that that aim cannot be simply the structure and the material well-being of the society itself, but its vision of a purpose in life. It is the recognition that no civilization is judged good because its members were of a certain social class or a certain race, but by the values which that civilization produced; and those values are not just the material conditions within which members of that civilization lived their lives.

By human values, I mean the realization that human beings, human individuals, are each one of them sacred. A business, or a nation, or a political party, or a world organization, which treats human lives as though they are chattels that can be moved about or cast aside or destroyed without regard for their sacred nature, or as though they were the mud which is dug out of a river bed when the course of the river is altered, is dehumanizing the human spirit, because the whole of humanity, even the humanity of the people who commit crimes against humanity, is involved in acts directed against any section of humanity.

Therefore, I believe that, in the world of today, it is necessary that the adolescent have a far greater degree of realization of himself as a spiritual and also as a physical individual being than exists within the English adolescent experience. At the same time, I think that during this period of transition, the English experience has much from which people in other countries may learn.

Educational and Occupational Aspirations of "Common Man" Boys

JOSEPH A. KAHL

In this article Joseph A. Kahl explores the social influences on working-class high school boys that account for differences in the motivation to go to college. He finds that parental pressure is closely associated with these differences. Although, as the author himself observes, this finding is obvious, it points out that social class has a powerful effect on parents' and students' aspirations and on their attitudes toward social mobility.

This article is concerned with the ambitions of high school boys. It reports an interview study of 24 boys of the "common man" or "working" class. They all had enough intelligence to go to college and thereby get a good start toward the higher levels of occupational life, yet one-half of the boys chose not to strive for such success. Instead, they planned little or no schooling beyond high school and said they would be content with the lesser jobs that would likely be open to them. The aim of the study was to explore the social influences which helped to explain the choices of these boys, with particular focus on the question: why were 12 boys striving to "better" themselves while 12 were not?

The study was part of a larger one called "The Mobility Project" underway at Harvard's Laboratory of Social Relations.[1] The sample of 24 for interview analysis was drawn from a larger sample of 3971 boys on whom questionnaire data were available. A brief discussion of the questionnaire data is necessary in order to establish a framework for the interview material.

The Questionnaire Study

It has long been known that occupational success is highly related to educational achievement. On the average, those with the most education get the best jobs (defined

[1] The project is under the direction of Drs. Talcott Parsons, Samuel A. Stouffer, and Florence R. Kluckhohn. I am highly indebted to them and to Research Assistants Dr. Norman Boyan and Mr. Stuart Cleveland. The statistical computations are the work of Stouffer, Boyan and Cleveland; I merely summarize their results. Stouffer has prepared a detailed report on those data for early publication. The interviewing was under the supervision of Kluckhohn, with the cooperation of many graduate students. Of the total of approximately 160 hours of interviews with the 24 boys and their families, I conducted about 60. I alone am responsible for the interpretation of the interview data.

Harvard Educational Review   Vol. 23   No. 3   Summer 1953, 186-209

TABLE 1
*Distribution of Fathers' Occupations and Sons' Occupational Aspirations:
3971 Cases*

Occupational Level	Percent of Fathers at this Level	Percent of Sons who Aspire to this Level
Major white collar (e.g. doctor, lawyer, dept. store executive)	4	15
Middle white collar (e.g. office manager, school teacher, CPA)	14	29
Minor white collar (e.g. small store owner, bookkeeper, postal clerk)	20	10
Skilled labor & service (e.g. highly skilled trades, policeman)	32	23
Other labor & service (e.g. semiskilled and unskilled factory workers, waiter)	21	5
Others:		
Indeterminate	9	7
Fantasy (baseball, FBI)	—	8
Military service only	—	3
TOTAL	100	100

in terms of both income and prestige). Occupation, in turn, is at the center of the complex we call "social class." Thus if we learn more about the determinants of occupational placement, we learn more about social class placement. Yet the argument chases its tail, for we also know that social class of parents influences educational achievement of sons.[2]

It seemed convenient to break into this circle of causation by studying large numbers of people who were readily available: boys in school. Their current educational plans would be predictors of their future occupational success. And their IQ scores plus their family class (status) backgrounds should divulge major determinants of their educational aspirations. Therefore a questionnaire was distributed to boys in public high schools in eight towns that are part of the Boston metropolitan area. (The omission of Catholic parochial schools was the major deficiency in the data.) All the boys in the sophomore and junior classes of those schools filled out a form, regardless of their curriculum. If occupations of fathers are used as a guide to social class, then it can be said that the boys' families duplicated rather closely the class composition of the metropolitan area as disclosed by census figures. The distribution of fathers' occupations is shown in Table 1, along with the distribution of sons' aspirations. It is worth noting that if the job system remains constant, many boys will become dissatisfied, for more boys were aiming at high level jobs than can be absorbed by available openings.

[2] For theoretical discussion and empirical data on the problem, consult the following works: August B. Hollingshead, *Elmtown's Youth* (New York: Wiley, 1947); Talcott Parsons, "An Analytical Approach to the Theory of Social Stratification," *American Journal of Sociology*, 45 (May 1940), 841–862; H.T. Himmelweit, et al., "The Views of Adolescents on Some Aspects of the Social Class Structure," *British Journal of Sociology*, 3 (June 1952), 148–172; Elbridge Sibley, "Some Demographic Clues to Stratification," *American Sociological Review*, 7 (June 1942) 322–330; W. Lloyd Warner, et al., *Who Shall be Educated?* (New York: Harper, 1944).

TABLE 2
Percentage of Boys Who Expect to Go to College, by IQ and Father's Occupation: 3348 Cases

| Father's Occupation | IQ Quintile (Boys) | | | | | All Quintiles |
	(Low) 1	2	3	4	(High) 5	
Major white collar	56%	72%	79%	82%	89%	80%
Middle white collar	28	36	47	53	76	52
Minor white collar	12	20	22	29	55	26
Skilled labor and service	4	15	19	22	40	19
Other labor and service	9	6	10	14	29	12
All Occupations	11	17	24	30	52	27

The questionnaire showed that the boys who had fairly clear occupational aims also had plans for an education that would appropriately prepare them for the jobs of their choice. About one fourth of the boys were in the college preparatory course *and* were definitely planning a college career (and a later follow-up disclosed that most of them actually did go on to college). The IQ scores of the boys and the occupations of their fathers turned out to be of practically equal utility as predictors of the boys' educational ambitions. Most boys with high intelligence or from high status homes planned a college career, whereas most boys with low intelligence or from low status homes did not aspire to higher education. But IQ scores and social class level are known to be related; consequently, the data were arranged in the form of Table 2 to show the independent operation of these two factors. It indicates the percentage of boys who aim toward college in various IQ and status categories. At the extremes, the prediction was very good: boys from "major white collar" families who were among the top quintile of their classmates in intelligence strove for college 89 percent of the time, whereas boys from "other labor and service" families who were among the bottom quintile of their classmates in intelligence strove for college only 9 percent of the time (623 cases where father's occupation or son's IQ were unknown have been eliminated from Table 2).

Although prediction was good at the extremes, it was not good in the middle of the distribution. Of particular interest was the fact that if a boy had high intelligence and came from the most populous part of the status range — its lower middle section — one could not well predict his aspiration. Thus a boy from the top quintile of intelligence whose father was a minor white collar worker or a skilled laborer had almost a fifty-fifty chance of aiming at a college career.

It was found that the predicting variables could be used, though less adequately, for grammar school as well as high school accomplishment. Boys with high IQ scores usually had good marks starting with the first grade, but more especially boys with low IQ scores had poor marks. Social status was not an important factor in the earliest grades; it began to take effect around the 4th grade and had increasing effect as each year passed. By the time they chose from among the separate curricula in the 9th grade, boys from low status families both performed at and aspired to much lower levels than high status boys of equal intelligence, even though they had been similar in early school accomplishment.

TABLE 3
Relation Between Parental Pressure and Son's Aspiration: 24 Boys

Son's Aspiration	Parental Pressure toward College	
	No	Yes
College	4	8
No College	11	1

Note. Chi square = 6.4; p < .02

The Interviews

The answers to the questionnaires raised an important problem: *what influences the aspirations of the boys in the lower middle levels of the status range whose environment gives them a wide choice?* Many of these boys have sufficient intelligence to aim high. They will not necessarily be isolated if they look up, for some of their friends do, yet it is not taken for granted by their families and neighbors that *all* boys should go to college. Therefore these boys must make a conscious and pointed decision at some stage of their careers.

In order to explore the decision-making of such boys, 24 of them were chosen for interview analysis. They fell into two groups: 12 boys were in the college preparatory course, had marks in the top half of their class, and definitely planned to go to a regular academic college after high school. The other 12 were not in the college preparatory course and did not plan to go to college. All 24 had IQ scores in the top three deciles of their schools; they had the intelligence to go to college if they chose to go. And all the boys had fathers who were petty white collar, skilled, or semi-skilled workers. The demographic variables of the larger study could not explain the differences in aspiration among these boys; the interviews were designed to begin where the statistics left off.

The interview material did disclose an additional factor which accounted for some of the remaining variation in aspiration: parental pressure, by which is meant a clear and overt attempt by either or both parents to influence their son to go to college. It was found that within a certain social class level to be defined and described below, namely, the "common man" group, some parents were satisfied with their own lot in life and did not attempt to push their sons up the status ladder, whereas other parents clearly encouraged their sons to strive for a "better" life. When the parents were rated on this factor on the basis of their interviews, its strong relationship with aspiration was clear. The results are shown in Table 3.[3] These results fit the standard jibe that "sociologists spend a lot of money to prove the obvious." Everybody knows that parents influence their children. Yet the processes through which that influence is transmitted

[3] Some of the relationship between parental pressure and son's aspiration shown in Table 3 may be from contamination in the ratings: in most, though not all cases, I knew the aspiration of the son at the time I rated the pressure of his parents. The same problem occurred when Mr. Cleveland rated the cases. We disagreed on 4 out of the total 48 ratings; the association between pressure and aspiration in his ratings was higher than in mine. The Mobility Project is now working on a questionnaire for boys to measure their perceptions of pressure from their parents. Thus the interview study was not aimed at "proof"—it fulfilled its purpose of exploring a confusing questionnaire result and offering a new hypothesis which can be tested by further questionnaire data.

are perhaps worthy of study. The remainder of this article will summarize that part of the extensive case material which throws light on the relationship between parental pressure and son's aspiration.

The boys who were interviewed came from two industrial-residential suburbs of Boston with populations between 50,000 and 100,000. Both towns have some wage earners who commute to work in central Boston, but the majority of them work in the industries of their own town. The boys were interviewed during school hours in repeated sessions which totaled about 5 hours per boy. The parents were interviewed for an hour or two in their homes. The interviews did not follow a fixed schedule, but were focused on attitudes toward school and work; many were mechanically recorded.

The Common Man Class

The cases were chosen from the minor white collar, skilled and semi-skilled occupational groups. Preliminary interviews indicated that most of these families thought of themselves as belonging to a status level which I shall call the "common man" class. A few families in the sample as it was first chosen fell outside the common man class, and they were eliminated in picking the final 24 for analysis.[4]

Most parents spoke about a three class system with themselves in the middle. But they did not call themselves middle class; they used such phrases as "common man," "average sort," "ordinary folks," "working people." They saw a "lower class" beneath them — people who lived in slums, had rough manners and morals, and had tough kids who were a bad influence on their own children. And they saw a group of "rich people," "business class" or "professionals" above them; I shall call this the "middle" class. A few respondents detected a fourth level, "the very rich," but their understanding of this group was hazy, for, as many studies have indicated, people make subtle distinctions at levels close to themselves but merge people who are far from themselves into indistinct clusters.

The respondents used two main criteria for making status distinctions between people: prestige and consumption. The prestige ratings did not refer to personal reputation in the community, perhaps because these are big towns where people do not know many of their fellows by name. Instead, the ratings referred to the moral repute of people who lived a certain way. The respondents thought in terms of prestige categories which were based essentially on consumption behavior or general "style of life," and they recognized that consumption depends on income, which in turn depends on occupation. But the ranking of occupations was derivative — a halo effect from the consumption privileges they bought.

---

[4] The scores of the 24 families on the Warner Index of Status Characteristics ranged from 43 to 71, with 57.5 as the median — right in the center of his "upper-lower" class. Warner writes that the upper-lower is the "least differentiated from the adjacent levels and hardest to distinguish in the hierarchy," and so he often combines it with the lower-middle and calls the combination the level of the "Common Man." See W. Lloyd Warner et al., *Social Class in America* (Chicago: Science Research Associates, 1949), chap. 1. My data indicate that in the urban scene the line between lower-middle and upper-lower cannot usefully be distinguished. The overlap between the lower levels of the white collar world and the upper levels of the blue collar world is pronounced and growing. For additional evidence see Survey No. 244 (Chicago: National Opinion Research Center, March 1947).

No symbol better represents the common man in these communities (and of course it is a local symbol) than the two-family wooden frame house in good condition. These houses stretch out mile after mile all over the metropolitan area. They are crowded rather closely together; there is little lawn space except, perhaps, for a small yard in the rear. The houses have a living room, dining room, kitchen, two or three bedrooms and a bathroom. They are furnished for comfort, not for conspicuous style: furniture is not remodeled just to "bring it up to date." The furnishings are in the Sears-Roebuck tradition, usually 10 to 20 years old, and not necessarily conforming to any matched pattern. The walls are usually covered with flowered paper, and often the dining room has a linoleum rug. There is a small TV set, and in front is parked a second-hand Ford or Chevrolet. Most of the upkeep of the house is taken care of by father, who is "handy with tools."

The subjects thought themselves well off because nowadays father had a steady job, and they remembered well when jobs were scarce. But they faced a constant struggle with inflation, and often mother or older children worked part time to help balance the weekly budget. Savings accounts with more than a couple of hundred dollars were rare.

There were rather wide variations in income among these families, coming from differences in father's paycheck and from the number of family members who worked. But these variations were often matched by variations in the size of the family. A policeman who earned $3,600 a year and had two young children lived approximately the same way as a milkman who earned $5,000 and had nine children, including an older daughter who contributed $5 a week from her secretarial earnings. The respondents recognized the variations in income, even to the extent of noting that some neighbors could afford a two-week vacation in the country; yet they considered all people who lived about as they did, just getting by on a weekly paycheck, as similar to themselves. They readily distinguished themselves from slumdwellers and from people who could afford a large single family house with a yard.

They did not make sharp distinctions between white and blue collar work. Often the fathers had had both types of jobs during their careers, and quite common was the family where one son worked in a factory while another was a clerk. Prestige was based on income and style of life, not on the color of one's work collar.

About half of the parents had gone at least part way through high school; only one had attended a liberal arts college; and a few fathers had gone to a business college or technical trade school for a year or less after high school. Most of the parents were native-born; they came predominantly from Yankee, Irish, Italian, and French-Canadian stock.

This sample of common man families had a style of life, a set of value-attitudes about it, and a class-consciousness which distinguished people like themselves from others who lived differently. (The class-consciousness concerned a definition of social space and not an idea of joint action.) They felt that they were ordinary people who were respectable but unimportant; who were decent but powerless; who lived comfortably but without the flamboyance, the freedom and the fun of conspicuous consumption; who, compared to the middle class, had inadequate income, inadequate education, inadequate understanding of the way things *really* worked, inadequate social and technical skills.[5]

The parents were articulate in varying degrees about these matters; a few seemed to live the daily routine without much awareness of their place in the social scheme of things, but most had at least some perceptions of social space and some way of placing themselves within it. Fifteen of the 24 families tended toward the view that the social scheme and their own place in it were morally proper and legitimate. They believed that people like themselves who were not overly bright or ambitious had, as a matter of course, a certain style of life which might be questioned in detail but not in substance. Some said this way of life was not only to be accepted but to be preferred — the competitive game to rise higher was not worth the candle. These 15 families could be said to espouse the core value of "getting by."

Eight families felt that the general social scheme was not bad, but that they had not risen quite as high as they should have. And one man raised serious questions about the moral justice of the scheme itself — he had flirted with radicalism in his youth, but lacked the courage to stick to it in the face of social ostracism. These 9 families could be said to believe in the core value of "getting ahead."

The distinctions just made were based on the fathers' attitudes toward their own success in life. In a few instances the fathers were considerably more satisfied with their achievements than were their wives, but usually both spouses told the same story.

Let us first examine the attitudes of those who accepted the scheme of things and their own place within it — who believed in just "getting by."[6] They were concerned with balancing the budget each week, with living for the moment in a smooth manner. They looked neither to the past nor the future. Father wanted a job which offered congenial workmates, an easy boss, a regular paycheck. Mother would work occasionally if current bills demanded it or if she enjoyed it — she generally had no strong principles for or against women working. The children were encouraged to enjoy themselves while they were young and before the burdens of life bound them to regular work — sometimes the school-age children were encouraged to work part-time to bring in a little extra money to the family purse, but the pressure was weak. The children were told to stay in high school because a diploma was pretty important in getting jobs nowadays, but they were allowed to pick their own curriculum according to taste. The value "doing what you like to do" was applied to schoolwork, to part-time jobs, and to career aspirations. Rarely was the possibility of a college education seriously considered: "we can't afford such things," or "we aren't very bright in school." Indeed, their perception of college and the kind of jobs college-trained people held were exceedingly vague; they understood that such people were professionals and made a lot of money, but they

[5] For a vivid description of the attitudes of similar industrial workers, see Ely Chinoy, "The Tradition of Opportunity and the Aspirations of Automobile Workers," *American Journal of Sociology*, 42 (March 1952), 453–459.

[6] For another way of phrasing the same observations, see Florence R. Kluckhohn, "Dominant and Substitute Profiles of Cultural Orientations: Their Significance for the Analysis of Social Stratification," *Social Forces*, 28 (May, 1950), 376–393. See also Clyde Kluckhohn and Florence R. Kluckhohn, "American Culture: Generalized Orientations and Class Patterns," in *Conflicts of Power in Modern Culture*, ed. by Lyman Bryson, et al. (New York: Harper, 1948).

did not know any such people socially and had no concrete images of what such a life might be. In sum, they felt that common people like themselves were lucky to have a regular job, that the sons would be as the fathers, that such was life and why think about it.

By contrast, the parents who believed in "getting ahead" were more sensitive to social hierarchies and thought more about the subject than those who were satisfied with their lot. They used the middle class as a reference group that was close enough to have meaning, though far enough away to be different. They kept thinking: "There, but for a few small difficulties, go I." The difficulty they usually referred to was lack of education. These people spoke with monotonous regularity about their handicap of poor education. Sometimes they blamed themselves for not taking advantage of their opportunities when young; they said that they did not realize when they still had time how important it was to get advanced training. Others merely shrugged their shoulders with the comment that they came from large families without much money; everyone had to go to work.

Often fathers pointed to the men immediately above themselves in the work hierarchy: machinists to mechanical engineers, carpenters to architects, clerks to office managers. Comparing themselves to those from whom they took orders, the fathers would say: "Those fellows are better trained than I and can do things I can't do." Rarely did they complain that the people who got ahead were the sons of the bosses or people with good connections. Instead, they saw an occupational world stratified according to the basic principle of education, and education was something you got when you were young. These people felt vaguely guilty: they accepted the middle class value of getting ahead, they knew they had not gotten ahead, and thus they felt they were to some degree inadequate. They rationalized that it may not have been their fault that they had not received a good education, but nevertheless they felt themselves at least partial failures. Yet if they were blocked, their sons were not. Consequently, they encouraged their sons to take school seriously and to aim for college. By way of contrast, it is interesting to observe that two middle-class fathers, though admitting that education was important, denied it was crucial. They pointed to "self-made" men who got up because they were smart and worked hard, and they pointed to educated men who were loafers or stuffed with useless book-learning and were not successful in business. Thus it seems that a sense of failure seeks to excuse itself by an external factor like education, whereas a sense of success seeks to glorify itself by an internal factor like brains or "push."

Here are some witnesses to support the general statements made above about the values of these common men:

Case A

The father went to work as a machinist right after high school graduation. Two years later his parents talked him into going to Business College. After that training, he did very well as a sales manager but didn't like the work. He returned to the machine shop, and has been happy for 30 years. His wife points to the moral of his story: "I want my boy to do what he likes. Now take my husband. He was very smart in school. He graduated a year young; he skipped a grade. Then his mother wanted him to go to the Business College and he did and he took a job selling, but he wasn't happy with it and so he went back to the machinist work that he had done. You know, he has been told several times that with all of that schooling he should have a better job but he likes what he is doing and I think if that makes him happy that is all that is important. I don't think a person should be made to do something he doesn't like. I don't like housework, and I know I would just have hated it if I had had to do housework for somebody else; why, I would be the most unhappy woman in the world. . . . During the war my husband made a lot of money working overtime, but you had to work extra for it and I don't think it is good for them to have to work too hard. If you do you come home all tired out and it just doesn't seem worth it, so I'd just as soon have him work the regular day and get the regular day's pay."

Case B

The father is a bread salesman; he has five children. He is a high school graduate. "I was never a bright one myself, I must say. The one thing I've had in mind is making enough to live on from day to day; I've never had much hope of a lot of it piling up. However, I'd rather see my son make an improvement over what I'm doing and I'm peddling bread. . . . I think he's lazy. Maybe I am too, but I gotta get out and hustle. . . . I don't keep after him. I have five kiddos. When you have a flock like that it is quite a job to keep your finger on this and the other thing. . . . I really don't know what he would like to do. Of course, no matter what I would like him to do, it isn't my job to say so as he may not be qualified. I tried to tell him where he isn't going to be a doctor or lawyer or anything like that, I told him he should learn English and learn to meet people. Then he could go out and sell something worth while where a sale would amount to something for him. That is the only suggestion that I'd make to him. . . . I took typing, shorthand, bookkeeping and we had Latin, French, Geometry. We had everything. But anything I would know then I've forgotten now. . . . I suppose there are some kids who set their mind to some goal and plug at it, but the majority of kids I have talked to take what comes. Just get along. . . . I don't think a high school diploma is so important. I mean only in so far as you might apply for a job and if you can say, 'I have a diploma,' it might help get the job, but other than that I don't see that it ever did me any good."

Case C

The father is a baker; the mother works in a chainstore. Both parents have had some high school. They have eight children. She said: "I don't go to see the teachers. I figure the teachers know what they're doing. When I go up there I can't talk good enough. Some women go up there, and I don't know, they're so la-ti-ta. But I can't talk that way. Me, I'm just plain words of one syllable and that's all. And the teachers, they'd just as soon not have you get in their way, I figure. They know what they're doing. . . . I hate to push the kid. I figure he'll get his knocks later on, and he should do what he wants to now. . . . College would be out of the question. We figure we're lucky to be able to put them through high school. When they get out of school, I try to make them get a job as soon as they can. . . . I don't make them do homework or anything. I figure they're old enough to know what they want to do and they'll get their work done by and by. . . . If I didn't go to work, the boy would have had to leave school and go to work, and I didn't want that. It's better to have me working, so it all isn't on one kiddo. . . . They're not very friendly here. I don't really know the neighbors at all. It was different where we used to live. Of course, it wasn't as good a neighborhood as it is here, but I liked it better. Everybody was friendly. We'd all be in each other's house for tea all the time. And we were always having babies. There was about ten women always pregnant. And we'd always be sitting out on the steps talking to each other. . . . I'm not very deep-minded. We don't talk about things like that [the future]."

Case D

The father is a petty foreman in a factory with about 20 men under him. He had three years of high school, and is convinced he would have gotten further ahead if he had had more education. "Down at the shop we see a lot of men come in and try to make their way. The ones with the college education seem to succeed better. They seem better able to handle jobs of different sorts. They may not know any more than the other fellows but they know how to learn. Somehow they've learned how to learn more easily. Not only that, they know how to find out about things. If they don't know the answer to a question, they know how to find out about it. They know where to go to look it up. . . . If they get a job and see that they aren't going to get anywhere they know enough to get out of it or to switch. They know enough to quit. I don't blame them either. After they've sacrificed to go to college and had that training. So that's why I hope my boy will go to college. . . . The college men seem also better able to handle themselves socially. They seem smoother in getting along with people and more adaptable to new situations. I think that I would have gotten along a lot better myself if I had had that sort of an education.

Boys' Attitudes Toward School and Work

School and the possibility of college were viewed by all the boys solely as steps to jobs. None was interested in learning for the subtle pleasures it can offer; none craved intellectual understanding for its own sake. The most common phrase in the entire body of interviews was "nowadays you need a high school diploma (or a college degree) to get a good job." Often a distinction was drawn between the diploma and the education it symbolized; the boys wanted the parchment, not the learning. In this pragmatic approach toward schooling, the boys reflected the views of their parents (and of most of their teachers).

All the boys who were convinced that a college degree was the basic essential for a job were seeking middle-class jobs. Often they had a specific occupation in mind, such as engineering or accounting. Sometimes they just knew the level of job which they wanted, and talked more about the style of life that the income would buy than the details of the work itself. By contrast, the boys who were not aiming toward college occasionally had a specific common man job as their goal, but more often had no firm goal at all—they would "take anything that comes along."

It was not always clear which came first: the job ambition or the school performance. Sometimes the desire for the job did seem to be the base for the school motivation, yet sometimes a boy who did well in school became slowly convinced that he was good enough to think of a middle-class job and sought for one that would be suitable without knowing in advance what it might be. Here are two contrasting examples: One boy had always wanted to be an architect. His hobby was drawing, and he proudly showed me the plans for many homes he had designed in his spare time. He wanted to go to the Massachusetts Institute of Technology, and was taking the technical college preparatory course. Another boy, who had always done very well in school, planned to be a high school teacher because everyone told him that a boy who did well with books would be a good teacher—but he had no special subject in mind and wasn't sure he would like teaching.

The attitudes of the boys toward schoolwork itself ranged from mild interest in a few courses that seemed to have the closest connection with future work, through tolerance for an activity that was simply a part of life to be taken for granted, through boredom, to active dislike of a dull and difficult task that distracted from more important activity. The mode was somewhere between taking it for granted and boredom. For example:

> I don't hate school, but I don't think there are many who are dying to go. [This boy gets the best marks in his class.]

> Yes, I think school is important. If you don't know anything you won't be anything is the way I look at it. If you are going to make a name for yourself in the world you have to know something.

> I'd much rather be working and earning money than going to school and spending it. I'll be glad when I get through. . . . I'll stay until I graduate. . . . I might be trying to get a job sometime and they'd want to know how good I was. Then I could show them my high school diploma, and I might want to set up a small business, too. And then I'd want to know bookkeeping and how to type and how to spell.

> You do well in things you like.

> I don't see why you have to take English if you want to be a mechanic. I suppose it broadens your mind.

> I like school but not schoolwork.

> I think English is a lot of bunk. I don't mean it that way but I mean that we spend a lot of time reading books and poetry. I just don't see it. Then there's stuff like Trig. I can't see taking that unless you are going after a high position—like a doctor or scientist. If you've high ideals, have set high standards, it's O.K., but otherwise I can't see it's any help.

The boys, like their parents, can be divided into two groups: those who believed in "getting by" and those who believed in "getting ahead." This basic split was reflected in their more specific attitudes towards the details of schoolwork, after school recreation and jobs. The boys who believed in just "getting by" generally were bored with school, anticipated some sort of common man job, and found peer group activity to be the most important thing in life. They were gayer than those who felt a driving ambition to do things and be successful. By contrast, the strivers who believed in "getting ahead" seemed to take schoolwork more seriously than recreational affairs. Each group noticed the difference in the behavior of the other. The strivers "didn't know how to have any fun." The strivers said that the non-strivers were "irresponsible; didn't know what was good for them."

It is interesting to speculate about the development of those attitudes in the future, using the fathers as indicators of how the boys might feel when they are further along in the life cycle. The fathers all had common man jobs, and with the exception of a few skilled workers they found work a dull routine, not a creative activity. Their sons did not know from direct experience the monotony of work; instead many boys looked forward to a job in romantic terms. It symbolized to them an escape from childhood, an end to the school routine, a freedom from dependency on father's pocketbook, a chance to get money for cars and girls. But the boys who went into common man jobs would, if they repeated their fathers' experiences, suffer at least some disillusionment. Not only would they learn that work can be duller and more empty than school, but many would feel some pangs of failure, for even though they did not all embrace the middle-class norm of getting ahead, they were aware that it existed and was to some degree the dominant norm of their society. They would feel just a little on the outside of things. Many fathers and sons who perceived this value conflict comforted themselves with the philosophy of just getting by—enjoy what you can and don't bother to worry or plan because there's nothing you can do about it. The irony of the situation lay in the fact that the sons looked forward to adulthood as their greatest chance to live according to this philosophy, while the fathers looked back on adolescence as their period of greatest glory. It may well be that the boys' gang is the one institution of our culture which best transforms the values of getting by into organized interaction and satisfying ceremony, yet the boys did not know it.

Those boys who were aiming at middle-class jobs were sacrificing some adolescent freedom and fun in order to channel more energy into schoolwork; for some, the sacrifice would lead to professional careers that would have creative meaning. At any rate, while in school they felt that their books were tied in with important aspects of their future lives, even though the books were not very exciting in themselves. Both of these ways of life contained satisfactions and dissatisfactions; the important thing to notice is that they were different.

Let us turn to a consideration of the development through time of the boys' attitudes toward school and work. In many ways, the grammar school years were crucial in "defining the situation." From his experiences in those years, each boy gradually formed a conception of himself as a pupil based on his estimate of his intelligence and his interest in books.

Each boy's performance defined the situation for his parents as well as for himself. The parents in this sample had not studied Gesell; they had no scientific standards for estimating the intelligence of their children. Yet, intelligence is a basic value in American culture; people who are "smart" are expected to act differently from those who are "dumb." Parents used early school performance as their main criterion for placing their children. If a boy did well, his parents expected him to continue doing well; if he did poorly, they usually decided that he was just one of those who was not smart and good at books and often emphasized his other qualities, such as skill with his hands or ability to get on well with people. The boy who was defined as smart and then later began to slip seriously in his schoolwork often got into trouble with his parents. They would assume he had gotten lazy or had started to run around with bad companions who were ruining him.

These common man parents seemed to have more tolerance for individual differences than do middle class parents. Often they themselves had done poorly in school and felt that they could not expect all their children to be brilliant. Consequently, they paid much attention to their sons' demonstration of ability in grammar school. There was a feed-back situation: the better a boy did in school, the better he was expected to do. Said a father of nine:

> John and his sister are the only two that have talent — I think those are the only two that are college timber. One of the boys is going to work with his hands — he hasn't said anything about it, but I can watch him, I can see that he wants to do carpentry or mechanical work, machine work of some kind. Couple of the children have been held back in school — none of them are as good as John. You know, I try and keep him from being too much a model for them to follow. I think it's good, but I don't want them to feel that they have to do as well as he can because I know they can't — he's exceptional.

A boy from another family echoed the sentiments in the terse remark: "I suppose they figure: if ya got it, ya got it; if ya haven't, ya haven't."

The average marks for the first six years of school were significantly higher for the 12 boys who were college oriented than for the 12 who did not plan further education after high school. But the difference was not great; the first group averaged just above "B," the second group just below it. As has been remarked, the causal direction was not always the same; some boys had ambitions for college while in high school because they had done well in grammar school; some boys did well in grammar school in order to prepare themselves for college (probably more because their parents pushed them than because they understood the connection.)

By the time a boy entered junior high school in 7th grade he had a conception of himself as a scholar: he knew how he *ought* to behave. But his behavior did not always match his own norms, for the situation contained cross-pressures. When homework first appeared (around 8th grade), it became a question of homework versus baseball, homework versus daydreaming, homework versus after school job that brought in precious money and independence from father's pocketbook. Before this time, it was easy for a bright boy to do well: spontaneous intellectual curiosity was all the teacher asked. Homework was a different matter.

Other difficulties arose about the same time. The boys had to choose their curricula and it was known to all that the four programs increased in difficulty as follows: trade, general, commercial, and college preparatory. The unanimity on this rank order was complete, even to those boys who admitted they were more interested in mechanical than verbal activity but wouldn't go to trade school because the trade diploma was not as "good" as the regular one. As one boy put it, and his words were repeated almost verbatim by many others:

> I chose commercial because it was sort of in-between the general and the college course. I didn't want to take the general course, figuring, oh, you know, people would say, "oh, he must be failing." I didn't want to go to college; I don't have a brilliant mind.

There is another factor that became important about the same time: peer group pressures. If a boy wanted to aim higher than his friends, he had to accept derision or isolation from those who thought it was stupid and sissified to join the "fruits" in the college course who carried books home at night. An occasional boy of exceptional social skill was able to stick with the old gang even though he followed a higher curriculum than they did; others gave up their aspirations; still others became isolates or managed to switch into a college-oriented peer group. This problem was of course more acute for ambitious boys from the common man than the middle class, for in the lower status neighborhoods the majority of boys were not oriented toward college, whereas the reverse was true in the upper status areas.

The questionnaire study discussed at the beginning of this article indicated that IQ was the one factor which best accounted for marks received in early grammar school, though the correlation was not very high. It also indicated that social status of family became an important explanatory variable *after* grammar school. For common man boys, the interviews seem to have given some of the reasons why status became important only in the later years. It was in junior high that school became a problem to the boys: homework, the increased difficulties of the work in the college preparatory curriculum (and the much greater competition therein which followed from the selection procedures for entering it), and peer group pressures all combined to make it harder for a bright common man boy to continue doing well in school — natural intelligence was no longer enough. In addition, he then began to worry about the availability of money for college — and college was the reason for doing well in high school. Some boys surmounted these difficulties and continued to do well. But this occurred because they had specific motivation that was strong enough to carry them over the hurdles — motivation which was more rare in the common man than the middle class. The interviews suggested that such motivation came from four directions:

> 1) If a boy had done well in the early years, *and* had built up a self-conception in which good school performance was vital, he would work hard to keep up his record. But an idea that school was vital occurred only when that early performance was truly exceptional, or if the importance of his standing to him was reinforced by one or more of the other factors listed below.

> 2) A boy would sacrifice other pleasures for homework when they weren't important to him. If a boy was not good at sports, if he did not have close and satisfying peer contacts, or if he had no hobby that was strongly rewarding as well as distracting, then the cost of homework was less and the balance more in its favor. In extreme cases frustrations in these alternative spheres motivated a boy to good school performance as compensation.

> 3) If a boy's family rewarded good school performance and punished poor performance, and the boy was not in rebellion against the family for emotional reasons, he was more likely to give up some play for homework.

> 4) If a boy had a rational conviction about the importance of schoolwork for his future career, he would strive to keep up his performance. But that conviction never appeared unless the parents emphasized it.

There were no cases in which the boy found in schoolwork sufficient intellectual satisfactions to supply its own motivation. And there were no cases where a sympathetic and encouraging teacher had successfully stimulated a boy to high aspirations.

As a result of the four motivational factors in combination, each boy chose his curriculum and reacted to homework in his own way. Sometimes the balance of factors shifted after the first decision. About one-fifth of the boys moved down from one curriculum to a lower one; one boy moved up a step. These adjustments resulted from a difference between a boy's anticipation of what the college preparatory work would be like and his discovery of the facts.

The argument so far is that an intelligent common man boy was not college-oriented in high school unless he had a very special reason for so being. Behind all the reasons stood one pre-eminent force: parental pressure.

Parents who believed in the value of "getting ahead" started to apply pressure from the beginning of the school career. They encouraged high marks, they paid attention to what was happening at school, they stressed that good performance was necessary for occupational success, they suggested various occupations that would be good for their sons. Their boys reached high school with a markedly different outlook from those who were not pushed. The strivers tended to have more specific occupational goals, they had educational aims to match, they worked harder in school, they thought more of the future, they were more sensitive to status distinctions, and they believed they could somehow manage to pay their way through college and reach the middle class.

The reader is referred back to Table 3. In all the cases therein, except two, families who applied pressure were families who believed in "getting ahead." That usually meant that the father was dissatisfed with his own occupational success. In the two exceptional cases where the father was satisfied, the pressure came from the mother, who was less content than her husband.

Two of the four boys who were aiming for college without pressure from home were instances of the "feed-back" phenomenon. They came from large families where the parents would support any aims of children without expecting them all to be alike. The boys had always done exceptionally well in school, and came to think of themselves as the kind of people who "ought" to go to college. The parents fully supported the high ambitions but did not initiate them. The other two boys who were aiming for college without pressure came from homes that were ambivalent: the father was more satisfied with his job than was the mother. The mother did not desire to repudiate her husband, so offered only the softest of suggestions that her son should try to do better.

The connection between parental pressure and sons' response was not just in the mind of the outsider who rated the cases; the boys were aware of it. One boy expressed clearly the relation between his views and those of his parents in these words:

> I'd like to learn to specialize in college. My folks want me to go to college too. My father didn't get through high school, and he wishes he'd gone to college. He has a good job now but he says if he had just a little bit of college he could have gone much higher. He's got a good job but he's gone as high as he can without a college education. . . . My mother and father don't want me to be a hired man. They want me to be in the upper bracket. They want me to learn by going to school and college, to go ahead by getting a higher education.

A boy who was not being pushed by his parents took an entirely different approach:

> I'm not definite what I'd like to do. Any kind of job. Anything as long as I get a little cash. . . . My folks tell me to go out and get a job, anything, just as long as it's a job. They say I'm old enough to start turning in board. . . . I haven't got much brain for all that college stuff. . . . You know, nobody would believe me now, but I was an "A" student in grammar school. I dunno what happened; just started dropping gradually.

. . . I guess the work just started getting harder. . . . I could do better work if I wanted to. As long as I pass I don't care. What the hell? I got nothin' to look forward to. . . . I was told to take the college course by the teachers. But I didn't want to. I wanted to take it easy.

The interviews indicated that the boys learned to an extraordinary degree to view the occupational system from their parents' perspective. They took over their parents' view of the opportunities available, the desirability and possibility of change of status, the techniques to be used if change was desired, and the appropriate goals for boys who performed as they did in school. The occasional boy who differed from his parents had gotten his ideas from a friend — never from an abstract medium of communication, such as books or movies.

Summary and Conclusions

This article began with a report of a questionnaire study which indicated that IQ and family status were useful predictors of the educational and occupational ambitions of high school boys. Yet those two variables left unexplained a considerable variance, which was particularly great for boys of high intelligence who came from homes of lower middle status. Consequently, a small sample was chosen from that group for interview analysis; half of the boys in the sample aspired to go to college and prepare for middle class occupations, and the other half of the boys did not desire to go to college and looked forward to common man occupations. The interviews disclosed that although there was a general way of life which identified the common man class, some members were content with that way of life while others were not. Parents who were discontented tended to train their sons from the earliest years of grammar school to take school seriously and use education as the means to climb into the middle class. Only sons who internalized such values were sufficiently motivated to overcome the obstacles which faced the common man boys in school; only they saw a reason for good school performance and college aspirations.

The American creed is supposed to teach everyone that he can become President — if not of the United States, then of United States Steel. Yet these interviews showed that the Creed is by no means universal. Some common man families do not think in such terms, and do not try to push their children up the ladder. The Horatio Alger myth is a middle class myth which percolates down to some, but not all, members of the common man class. If a common man family does accept the myth and has sons who show in their early school performance signs of talent, then they push them forward and encourage them to climb. The schools are more a means than an initiator of ascent.

If a boy does not take advantage of the schools to climb, his later chances will be slim. Many observers have noted that in recent decades the opportunities for getting ahead through owning independent business, or of ascending in the factory from apprentice to boss, are declining.[7] We seem to have approached a bureaucratized class system that has a fundamental split into two halves: the educated and the ignorant.

[7] See, for example, C. Wright Mills, *White Collar: The American Middle Classes* (New York: Oxford University Press, 1951), chaps. 1, 2, 4, and 12.

The educated begin at a higher level than the ignorant ever reach. Ownership of property is far less significant than education as a dividing force for all except the very few at the top who own so much. In the early days of the Republic few men had a higher education but many owned productive property. Now the proportions are reversed; even most of the educated work for salaries. Therefore the fathers of the boys in this sample were realists; they were correct in teaching their sons that what they did in school would determine their whole lives. Some sons would not fully understand their fathers until they were out in the work world and could see for themselves. By then it would be too late to change.[8]

[8] For a contrasting description of the training of middle class children, see David F. Aberle and Kaspar D. Naegele, "Middle Class Fathers' Occupational Role and Attitudes Toward Children" *American Journal of Orthopsychiatry*, **22** (April, 1952), 366–378.

The School Class as a Social System: Some of Its Functions in American Society

TALCOTT PARSONS

Talcott Parsons examines the role of the school in performing the functions of socialization and selection. Socialization involves the student's internalization of the "capacity for successful performance" in adult society; selection provides a means of allocating "human resources within the role structure of adult society." Parsons approaches the study of these processes through a detailed analysis of classroom interactions and shows how teachers influence a student's cognitive and social development.

THIS ESSAY WILL ATTEMPT TO OUTLINE, if only sketchily, an analysis of the elementary and secondary school class as a social system, and the relation of its structure to its primary functions in the society as an agency of socialization and allocation. While it is important that the school class is normally part of the larger organization of a school, the class rather than the whole school will be the unit of analysis here, for it is recognized both by the school system and by the individual pupil as the place where the "business" of formal education actually takes place. In elementary schools, pupils of one grade are typically placed in a single "class" under one main teacher, but in the secondary school, and sometimes in the upper elementary grades, the pupil works on different subjects under different teachers; here the complex of classes participated in by the same pupil is the significant unit for our purposes.

THE PROBLEM: SOCIALIZATION AND SELECTION

Our main interest, then, is in a dual problem: first of how the school class functions to internalize in its pupils both the commitments and capacities for

* I am indebted to Mrs. Carolyn Cooper for research assistance in the relevant literature and for editorial work on the first draft of this paper.

Harvard Educational Review   Vol. 29   No. 4   Fall 1959, 297-318

successful performance of their future adult roles, and second of how it functions to allocate these human resources within the role-structure of the adult society. The primary ways in which these two problems are inter-related will provide our main points of reference.

First, from the functional point of view the school class can be treated as an agency of socialization. That is to say, it is an agency through which individual personalities are trained to be motivationally and technically adequate to the performance of adult roles. It is not the sole such agency; the family, informal "peer groups," churches, and sundry voluntary organizations all play a part, as does actual on-the-job training. But, in the period extending from entry into first grade until entry into the labor force or marriage, the school class may be regarded as the focal socializing agency.

The socialization function may be summed up as the development in individuals of the commitments and capacities which are essential prerequisites of their future role-performance. Commitments may be broken down in turn into two components: commitment to the implementation of the broad *values* of society, and commitment to the performance of a specific type of role within the *structure* of society. Thus a person in a relatively humble occupation may be a "solid citizen" in the sense of commitment to honest work in that occupation, without an intensive and sophisticated concern with the implementation of society's higher-level values. Or conversely, someone else might object to the anchorage of the feminine role in marriage and the family on the grounds that such anchorage keeps society's total talent resources from being distributed equitably to business, government, and so on. Capacities can also be broken down into two components, the first being competence, or the skill to perform the tasks involved in the individual's roles, and the second being "role-responsibility" or the capacity to live up to other people's expectations of the interpersonal behavior appropriate to these roles. Thus a mechanic as well as a doctor needs to have not only the basic "skills of his trade," but also the ability to behave responsibly toward those people with whom he is brought into contact in his work.

While on the one hand, the school class may be regarded as a primary agency by which these different components of commitments and capacities are generated, on the other hand, it is, from the point of view of the society, an agency of "manpower" allocation. It is well known that in American society there is a very high, and probably increasing, correlation between one's status level in the society and one's level of educational attainment. Both social status and educational level are obviously related to the occupational status which is attained. Now, as a result of the general process of both educational and occupational upgrading, completion of high school is increasingly coming to be the norm for minimum satisfactory educational attainment, and the most significant line for future occupational status has come to be drawn between members of an age-cohort who do and do not go to college.

We are interested, then, in what it is about the school class in our society that determines the distinction between the contingents of the age-cohort which do and do not go to college. Because of a tradition of localism and a rather pragmatic pluralism, there is apparently considerable variety among school systems of various cities and states. Although the situation in metropolitan Boston probably represents a more highly structured pattern than in many other parts of the country, it is probably not so extreme as to be misleading in its main features. There, though of course actual entry into college does not come until after graduation from high school, the main dividing line is between those who are and are not enrolled in the college preparatory course in high school; there is only a small amount of shifting either way after about the ninth grade when the decision is normally made. Furthermore, the evidence seems to be that by far the most important criterion of selection is the record of school performance in elementary school. These records are evaluated by teachers and principals, and there are few cases of entering the college preparatory course against their advice. It is therefore not stretching the evidence too far to say broadly that the primary selective process occurs through differential school performance in elementary school, and that the "seal" is put on it in junior high school.[1]

The evidence also is that the selective process is genuinely assortative. As in virtually all comparable processes, ascriptive as well as achieved factors influence the outcome. In this case, the ascriptive factor is the socio-economic status of the child's family, and the factor underlying his opportunity for achievement is his individual ability. In the study of 3,348 Boston high school boys on which these generalizations are based, each of these factors was quite highly correlated with planning college. For example, the percentages planning college, by father's occupation, were: 12 per cent for semi-skilled and unskilled, 19 per cent for skilled, 26 per cent for minor white collar, 52 per cent for middle white collar, and 80 per cent for major white collar. Likewise, intentions varied by ability (as measured by IQ), namely, 11 per cent for the lowest quintile, 17 per cent for the next, 24 per cent for the middle, 30 per cent for the next to the top, and 52 per cent for the highest. It should be noted also that within any ability quintile, the

[1] The principal source for these statements is a study of social mobility among boys in ten public high schools in the Boston metropolitan area, conducted by Samuel A. Stouffer, Florence R. Kluckhohn, and the present author. Unfortunately the material is not available in published form.

relationship of plans to father's occupation is seen. For example, within the very important top quintile in ability as measured, the range in college intentions was from 29 per cent for sons of laborers to 89 per cent for sons of major white collar persons.[2]

The essential points here seem to be that there is a relatively uniform criterion of selection operating to differentiate between the college and the non-college contingents, and that for a very important part of the cohort the operation of this criterion is not a "put-up job"—it is not simply a way of affirming a previously determined ascriptive status. To be sure, the high-status, high-ability boy is very likely indeed to go to college, and the low-status, low-ability boy is very unlikely to go. But the "cross-pressured" group for whom these two factors do not coincide[3] is of considerable importance.

Considerations like these lead me to conclude that the main process of differentiation (which from another point of view is selection) that occurs during elementary school takes place on a single main axis of *achievement*. Broadly, moreover, the differentiation leads up through high school to a bifurcation into college-goers and non-college-goers.

To assess the significance of this pattern, let us look at its place in the socialization of the individual. Entering the system of formal education is the child's first major step out of primary involvement in his family of orientation. Within the family certain foundations of his motivational system have been laid down. But the only characteristic fundamental to later roles which has clearly been "determined" and psychologically stamped in by that time is sex role. The postoedipal child enters the system of formal education clearly categorized as boy or girl, but beyond that his *role* is not yet differentiated. The process of selection, by which persons will select and be selected for categories of roles, is yet to take place.

On grounds which cannot be gone into here, it may be said that the most

[2] See table from this study in J. A. Kahl, *The American Class Structure* (New York: Rinehart & Co., 1953), p. 283. Data from a nationwide sample of high school students, published by the Educational Testing Service, show similar patterns of relationships. For example, the ETS study shows variation, by father's occupation, in proportion of high school seniors planning college, of from 35 per cent to 80 per cent for boys and 27 per cent to 79 per cent for girls. (From *Background Factors Related to College Plans and College Enrollment among High School Students* [Princeton, N. J.: Educational Testing Service, 1957]).

[3] There seem to be two main reasons why the high-status, low-ability group is not so important as its obverse. The first is that in a society of expanding educational and occupational opportunity the general trend is one of upgrading, and the social pressures to downward mobility are not as great as they would otherwise be. The second is that there are cushioning mechanisms which tend to protect the high status boy who has difficulty "making the grade." He may be sent to a college with low academic standards, he may go to schools where the line between ability levels is not rigorously drawn, etc.

important single predispositional factor with which the child enters the school is his level of *independence*. By this is meant his level of self-sufficiency relative to guidance by adults, his capacity to take responsibility and to make his own decisions in coping with new and varying situations. This, like his sex role, he has as a function of his experience in the family.

The family is a collectivity within which the basic status-structure is ascribed in terms of biological position, that is, by generation, sex, and age. There are inevitably differences of performance relative to these, and they are rewarded and punished in ways that contribute to differential character formation. But these differences are not given the sanction of institutionalized social status. The school is the first socializing agency in the child's experience which institutionalizes a differentiation of status on nonbiological bases. Moreover, this is not an ascribed but an achieved status; it is the status "earned" by differential performance of the tasks set by the teacher, who is acting as an agent of the community's school system. Let us look at the structure of this situation.

THE STRUCTURE OF THE ELEMENTARY SCHOOL CLASS

In accord with the generally wide variability of American institutions, and of course the basically local control of school systems, there is considerable variability of school situations, but broadly they have a single relatively well-marked framework.[4] Particularly in the primary part of the elementary grades, i.e., the first three grades, the basic pattern includes one main teacher for the class, who teaches all subjects and who is in charge of the class generally. Sometimes this early, and frequently in later grades, other teachers are brought in for a few special subjects, particularly gym, music, and art, but this does not alter the central position of the main teacher. This teacher is usually a woman.[5] The class is with this one teacher for the school year, but usually no longer.

The class, then, is composed of about 25 age-peers of both sexes drawn from a relatively small geographical area—the neighborhood. Except for sex in certain respects, there is initially no formal basis for differentiation of status within the school class. The main structural differentiation develops gradually, on the single main axis indicated above as achievement.

[4] This discussion refers to public schools. Only about 13 per cent of all elementary and secondary school pupils attend non-public schools, with this proportion ranging from about 22 per cent in the Northeast to about 6 per cent in the South. U. S. Office of Education, *Biennial Survey of Education in the United States, 1954-56* (Washington: U. S. Government Printing Office, 1959), chap. ii, "Statistics of State School Systems, 1955-56," Table 44, p. 114.

[5] In 1955-56, 13 per cent of the public elementary school instructional staff in the United States were men. *Ibid.*, p. 7.

That the differentiation should occur on a single main axis is insured by four primary features of the situation. The first is the initial equalization of the "contestants' " status by age and by "family background," the neighborhood being typically much more homogeneous than is the whole society. The second circumstance is the imposition of a common set of tasks which is, compared to most other task-areas, strikingly undifferentiated. The school situation is far more like a race in this respect than most role-performance situations. Third, there is the sharp polarization between the pupils in their initial equality and the *single* teacher who is an adult and "represents" the adult world. And fourth, there is a relatively systematic process of evaluation of the pupils' performances. From the point of view of a pupil, this evaluation, particularly (though not exclusively) in the form of report card marks, constitutes reward and/or punishment for past performance; from the viewpoint of the school system acting as an allocating agency, it is a basis of *selection* for future status in society.

Two important sets of qualifications need to be kept in mind in interpreting this structural pattern, but I think these do not destroy the significance of its main outline. The first qualification is for variations in the formal organization and procedures of the school class itself. Here the most important kind of variation is that between relatively "traditional" schools and relatively "progressive" schools. The more traditional schools put more emphasis on discrete units of subject-matter, whereas the progressive type allows more "indirect" teaching through "projects" and broader topical interests where more than one bird can be killed with a stone. In progressive schools there is more emphasis on groups of pupils working together, compared to the traditional direct relation of the individual pupil to the teacher. This is related to the progressive emphasis on co-operation among the pupils rather than direct competition, to greater permissiveness as opposed to strictness of discipline, and to a de-emphasis on formal marking.[6] In some schools one of these components will be more prominent, and in others, another. That it is, however, an important range of variation is clear. It has to do, I think, very largely with the independence-dependence training which is so important to early socialization in the family. My broad interpretation is that those people who emphasize independence training will tend to be those who favor relatively progressive education. The relation of support for progressive education to relatively high socioeconomic status and to "intellectual" interests and the like is well known. There is no contradiction between these emphases both on independence

[6] This summary of some contrasts between traditional and progressive patterns is derived from general reading in the literature rather than any single authoritative account.

and on co-operation and group solidarity among pupils. In the first instance this is because the main focus of the independence problem at these ages is vis-à-vis adults. However, it can also be said that the peer group, which here is built into the school class, is an indirect field of expression of dependency needs, displaced from adults.

The second set of qualifications concerns the "informal" aspects of the school class, which are always somewhat at variance with the formal expectations. For instance, the formal pattern of nondifferentiation between the sexes may be modified informally, for the very salience of the one-sex peer group at this age period means that there is bound to be considerable implicit recognition of it—for example, in the form of teachers' encouraging group competition between boys and girls. Still, the fact of coeducation and the attempt to treat both sexes alike in all the crucial formal respects remain the most important. Another problem raised by informal organization is the question of how far teachers can and do treat pupils particularistically in violation of the universalistic expectations of the school. When compared with other types of formal organizations, however, I think the extent of this discrepancy in elementary schools is seen to be not unusual. The school class is structured so that opportunity for particularistic treatment is severely limited. Because there are so many more children in a school class than in a family, and they are concentrated in a much narrower age range, the teacher has much less chance than does a parent to grant particularistic favors.

Bearing in mind these two sets of qualifications, it is still fair, I think, to conclude that the major characteristics of the elementary school class in this country are such as have been outlined. It should be especially emphasized that more or less progressive schools, even with their relative lack of emphasis on formal marking, do not constitute a separate pattern, but rather a variant tendency within the same pattern. A progressive teacher, like any other, will form opinions about the different merits of her pupils relative to the values and goals of the class and will communicate these evaluations to them, informally if not formally. It is my impression that the extremer cases of playing down relative evaluation are confined to those upper-status schools where going to a "good" college is so fully taken for granted that for practical purposes it is an ascribed status. In other words, in interpreting these facts the selective function of the school class should be kept continually in the forefront of attention. Quite clearly its importance has not been decreasing; rather the contrary.

THE NATURE OF SCHOOL ACHIEVEMENT

What, now, of the content of the "achievement" expected of elementary school children? Perhaps the best broad characterization which can be given is that it involves the types of performance which are, on the one hand, appropriate to the school situation and, on the other hand, are felt by adults to be important in themselves. This vague and somewhat circular characterization may, as was mentioned earlier, be broken down into two main components. One of these is the more purely "cognitive" learning of information, skills, and frames of reference associated with empirical knowledge and technological mastery. The *written* language and the early phases of mathematical thinking are clearly vital; they involve cognitive skills at altogether new levels of generality and abstraction compared to those commanded by the pre-school child. With these basic skills goes assimilation of much factual information about the world.

The second main component is what may broadly be called a "moral" one. In earlier generations of schooling this was known as "deportment." Somewhat more generally it might be called responsible citizenship in the school community. Such things as respect for the teacher, consideration and co-operativeness in relation to fellow-pupils, and good "work-habits" are the fundamentals, leading on to capacity for "leadership" and "initiative."

The striking fact about this achievement content is that in the elementary grades these two primary components are not clearly differentiated from each other. Rather, the pupil is evaluated in diffusely general terms; a *good* pupil is defined in terms of a fusion of the cognitive and the moral components, in which varying weight is given to one or the other. Broadly speaking, then, we may say that the "high achievers" of the elementary school are both the "bright" pupils, who catch on easily to their more strictly intellectual tasks, and the more "responsible" pupils, who "behave well" and on whom the teacher can "count" in her difficult problems of managing the class. One indication that this is the case is the fact that in elementary school the purely intellectual tasks are relatively easy for the pupil of high intellectual ability. In many such cases, it can be presumed that the primary challenge to the pupil is not to his intellectual, but to his "moral," capacities. On the whole, the progressive movement seems to have leaned in the direction of giving enhanced emphasis to this component, suggesting that of the two, it has tended to become the more problematical.[7]

The essential point, then, seems to be that the elementary school, re-

---

[7] This account of the two components of elementary school achievement and their relation summarizes impressions gained from the literature, rather than being based on the opinions of particular authorities. I have the impression that achievement in this sense corresponds closely to what is meant by the term as used by McClelland and his associates. Cf. D. C. McClelland *et al.*, *The Achievement Motive* (New York: Appleton-Century-Crofts, Inc., 1953).

garded in the light of its socialization function, is an agency which differentiates the school class broadly along a single continuum of achievement, the content of which is relative excellence in living up to the expectations imposed by the teacher as an agent of the adult society. The criteria of this achievement are, generally speaking, undifferentiated into the cognitive or technical component and the moral or "social" component. But with respect to its bearing on societal values, it is broadly a differentiation of *levels* of capacity to act in accord with these values. Though the relation is far from neatly uniform, this differentiation underlies the processes of selection for levels of status and role in the adult society.

Next, a few words should be said about the out-of-school context in which this process goes on. Besides the school class, there are clearly two primary social structures in which the child participates: the family and the child's informal "peer group."

FAMILY AND PEER GROUP IN RELATION TO THE SCHOOL CLASS

The school-age child, of course, continues to live in the parental household and to be highly dependent, emotionally as well as instrumentally, on his parents. But he is now spending several hours a day away from home, subject to a discipline and a reward system which are essentially independent of that administered by the parents. Moreover, the range of this independence gradually increases. As he grows older, he is permitted to range further territorially with neither parental nor school supervision, and to do an increasing range of things. He often gets an allowance for personal spending and begins to earn some money of his own. Generally, however, the emotional problem of dependence-independence continues to be a very salient one through this period, frequently with manifestations by the child of compulsive independence.

Concomitantly with this, the area for association with age-peers without detailed adult supervision expands. These associations are tied to the family, on the one hand, in that the home and yards of children who are neighbors and the adjacent streets serve as locations for their activities; and to the school, on the other hand, in that play periods and going to and from school provide occasions for informal association, even though organized extracurricular activities are introduced only later. Ways of bringing some of this activity under another sort of adult supervision are found in such organizations as the boy and girl scouts.

Two sociological characteristics of peer groups at this age are particularly striking. One is the fluidity of their boundaries, with individual children drifting into and out of associations. This element of "voluntary association" contrasts strikingly with the child's ascribed membership in the family and the school class, over which he has no control. The second characteristic is the peer group's sharp segregation by sex. To a striking degree this is enforced by the children themselves rather than by adults.

The psychological functions of peer association are suggested by these two characteristics. On the one hand, the peer group may be regarded as a field for the exercise of independence from adult control; hence it is not surprising that it is often a focus of behavior which goes beyond independence from adults to the range of adult-*disapproved* behavior; when this happens, it is the seed bed from which the extremists go over into delinquency. But another very important function is to provide the child a source of non-adult approval and acceptance. These depend on "technical" and "moral" criteria as diffuse as those required in the school situation. On the one hand, the peer group is a field for acquiring and displaying various types of "prowess"; for boys this is especially the physical prowess which may later ripen into athletic achievement. On the other hand, it is a matter of gaining acceptance from desirable peers as "belonging" in the group, which later ripens into the conception of the popular teen-ager, the "right guy." Thus the adult parents are augmented by age-peers as a source of rewards for performance and of security in acceptance.

The importance of the peer group for socialization in our type of society should be clear. The motivational foundations of character are inevitably first laid down through identification with parents, who are generation-superiors, and the generation difference is a type example of a hierarchical status difference. But an immense part of the individual's adult role performance will have to be in association with status-equals or near-equals. In this situation it is important to have a reorganization of the motivational structure so that the original dominance of the hierarchical axis is modified to strengthen the egalitarian components. The peer group plays a prominent part in this process.

Sex segregation of latency period peer groups may be regarded as a process of reinforcement of sex-role identification. Through intensive association with sex-peers and involvement in sex-typed activities, they strongly reinforce belongingness with other members of the same sex and contrast with the opposite sex. This is the more important because in the coeducational school a set of forces operates which specifically plays down sex-role differentiation.

It is notable that the latency period sex-role pattern, instead of institutionalizing relations to members of the opposite sex, is characterized by an avoidance of such relations, which only in adolescence gives way to dating. This avoidance is clearly associated with the process of reorganization of the erotic components of motivational structure. The pre-oedipal objects of erotic attachment were both intra-familial and generation-superior. In both respects there must be a fundamental shift by the time the child reaches adulthood. I would suggest that one of the main functions of the avoidance pattern is to help cope with the psychological difficulty of over-coming the earlier incestuous attachments, and hence to prepare the child for assuming an attachment to an age-mate of opposite sex later.

Seen in this perspective, the socialization function of the school class assumes a particular significance. The socialization functions of the family by this time are relatively residual, though their importance should not be underestimated. But the school remains adult-controlled and, moreover, induces basically the same kind of identification as was induced by the family in the child's pre-oedipal stage. This is to say that the learning of achievement-motivation is, psychologically speaking, a process of identifi-cation with the teacher, of doing well in school in order to please the teacher (often backed by the parents) in the same sense in which a pre-oedipal child learns new skills in order to please his mother.

In this connection I maintain that what is internalized through the pro-cess of identification is a reciprocal pattern of role-relationships.[8] Unless there is a drastic failure of internalization altogether, not just one, but both sides of the interaction will be internalized. There will, however, be an emphasis on one or the other, so that some children will more nearly identify with the socializing agent, and others will more nearly identify with the opposite role. Thus, in the pre-oedipal stage, the "independent" child has identified more with the parent, and the "dependent" one with the child-role vis-à-vis the parent.

In school the teacher is institutionally defined as superior to any pupil in knowledge of curriculum subject-matter and in responsibility as a good citizen of the school. In so far as the school class tends to be bifurcated (and of course the dichotomization is far from absolute), it will broadly be on the basis, on the one hand, of identification with the teacher, or ac-ceptance of her role as a model; and, on the other hand, of identification with the pupil peer group. This bifurcation of the class on the basis of identification with teacher or with peer group so strikingly corresponds with the bifurcation into college-goers and non-college-goers that it would be hard to avoid the hypothesis that this structural dichotomization in the school system is the primary source of the selective dichotomization. Of course in detail the relationship is blurred, but certainly not more so than in a great many other fields of comparable analytical complexity.

---

[8] On the identification process in the family see my paper, "Social Structure and the Development of Personality," *Psychiatry*, XXI (November, 1958), pp. 321-40.

These considerations suggest an interpretation of some features of the elementary teacher role in American society. The first major step in socialization, beyond that in the family, takes place in the elementary school, so it seems reasonable to expect that the teacher-figure should be characterized by a combination of similarities to and differences from parental figures. The teacher, then, is an adult, characterized by the generalized superiority, which a parent also has, of adult status relative to children. She is not, however, ascriptively related to her pupils, but is performing an occupational role—a role, however, in which the recipients of her services are tightly bound in solidarity to her and to each other. Furthermore, compared to a parent's, her responsibility to them is much more universalistic, this being reinforced, as we saw, by the size of the class; it is also much more oriented to performance rather than to solicitude for the emotional "needs" of the children. She is not entitled to suppress the distinction between high and low achievers, just because not being able to be included among the high group would be too hard on little Johnny—however much tendencies in this direction appear as deviant patterns. A mother, on the other hand, must give *first* priority to the needs of her child, regardless of his capacities to achieve.

It is also significant for the parallel of the elementary school class with the family that the teacher is normally a woman. As background it should be noted that in most European systems until recently, and often today in our private parochial and non-sectarian schools, the sexes have been segregated and each sex group has been taught by teachers of their own sex. Given coeducation, however, the woman teacher represents continuity with the role of the mother. Precisely the lack of differentiation in the elementary school "curriculum" between the components of subject-matter competence and social responsibility fits in with the greater diffuseness of the feminine role.

But at the same time, it is essential that the teacher is not a mother to her pupils, but must insist on universalistic norms and the differential reward of achievement. Above all she must be the agent of bringing about and legitimizing a differentiation of the school class on an achievement axis. This aspect of her role is furthered by the fact that in American society the feminine role is less confined to the familial context than in most other societies, but joins the masculine in occupational and associational concerns, though still with a greater relative emphasis on the family. Through identification with their teacher, children of both sexes learn that the category "woman" is not co-extensive with "mother" (and future wife), but that the feminine role-personality is more complex than that.

In this connection it may well be that there is a relation to the once-controversial issue of the marriage of women teachers. If the differentiation between what may be called the maternal and the occupational components of the feminine role is incomplete and insecure, confusion between them may be avoided by insuring that both are not performed by the same persons. The "old maid" teacher of American tradition may thus be thought of as having renounced the maternal role in favor of the occupational.[9] Recently, however, the highly affective concern over the issue of married women's teaching has conspicuously abated, and their actual participation has greatly increased. It may be suggested that this change is associated with a change in the feminine role, the most conspicuous feature of which is the general social sanctioning of participation of women in the labor force, not only prior to marriage, but also after marriage. This I should interpret as a process of structural differentiation in that the same category of persons is permitted and even expected to engage in a more complex set of role-functions than before.

The process of identification with the teacher which has been postulated here is furthered by the fact that in the elementary grades the child typically has one teacher, just as in the pre-oedipal period he had one parent, the mother, who was the focus of his object-relations. The continuity between the two phases is also favored by the fact that the teacher, like the mother, is a woman. But, if she acted only like a mother, there would be no genuine reorganization of the pupil's personality system. This reorganization is furthered by the features of the teacher role which differentiate it from the maternal. One further point is that while a child has one main teacher in each grade, he will usually have a new teacher when he progresses to the next higher grade. He is thus accustomed to the fact that teachers are, unlike mothers, "interchangeable" in a certain sense. The school year is long enough to form an important relationship to a particular teacher, but not long enough for a highly particularistic attachment to crystallize. More than in the parent-child relationship, in school the child must internalize his relation to the teacher's *role* rather than her particular personality; this is a major step in the internalization of universalistic patterns.

SOCIALIZATION AND SELECTION IN THE ELEMENTARY SCHOOL

To conclude this discussion of the elementary school class, something should be said about the fundamental conditions underlying the process which is, as we have seen, simultaneously (1) an emancipation of the child

---

[9] It is worth noting that the Catholic parochial school system is in line with the more general older American tradition, in that the typical teacher is a nun. The only difference in this respect is the sharp religious symbolization of the difference between mother and teacher.

from primary emotional attachment to his family, (2) an internalization of a level of societal values and norms that is a step higher than those he can learn in his family alone, (3) a differentiation of the school class in terms both of actual achievement and of differential *valuation* of achievement, and (4) from society's point of view, a selection and allocation of its human resources relative to the adult role system.[10]

Probably the most fundamental condition underlying this process is the sharing of common values by the two adult agencies involved—the family and the school. In this case the core is the shared valuation of *achievement*. It includes, above all, recognition that it is fair to give differential rewards for different levels of achievement, so long as there has been fair access to opportunity, and fair that these rewards lead on to higher-order opportunities for the successful. There is thus a basic sense in which the elementary school class is an embodiment of the fundamental American value of equality of opportunity, in that it places value *both* on initial equality and on differential achievement.

As a second condition, however, the rigor of this valuational pattern must be tempered by allowance for the difficulties and needs of the young child. Here the quasi-motherliness of the woman teacher plays an important part. Through her the school system, assisted by other agencies, attempts to minimize the insecurity resulting from the pressures to learn, by providing a certain amount of emotional support defined in terms of what is due to a child of a given age level. In this respect, however, the role of the school is relatively small. The underlying foundation of support is given in the home, and as we have seen, an important supplement to it can be provided by the informal peer associations of the child. It may be suggested that the development of extreme patterns of alienation from the school is often related to inadequate support in these respects.

Third, there must be a process of selective rewarding of valued performance. Here the teacher is clearly the primary agent, though the more progressive modes of education attempt to enlist classmates more systematically than in the traditional pattern. This is the process that is the direct source of intra-class differentiation along the achievement axis.

The final condition is that this initial differentiation tends to bring about a status system in the class, in which not only the immediate results of school work, but a whole series of influences, converge to consolidate different expectations which may be thought of as the children's "levels of aspiration." Generally some differentiation of friendship groups along this

---

[10] The following summary is adapted from T. Parsons, R. F. Bales *et al.*, *Family, Socialization and Interaction Process* (Glencoe, Ill.: The Free Press, 1955), esp. chap. iv.

line occurs, though it is important that it is by no means complete, and that children are sensitive to the attitudes not only of their own friends, but of others.

Within this general discussion of processes and conditions, it is important to distinguish, as I have attempted to do all along, the socialization of the individual from the selective allocation of contingents to future roles. For the individual, the old familial identification is broken up (the family of orientation becomes, in Freudian terms, a "lost object") and a new identification is gradually built up, providing the first-order structure of the child's identity apart from his originally ascribed identity as son or daughter of the "Joneses." He both transcends his familial identification in favor of a more independent one and comes to occupy a differentiated status within the new system. His personal status is inevitably a direct function of the position he achieves, primarily in the formal school class and secondarily in the informal peer group structure. In spite of the sense in which achievement-ranking takes place along a continuum, I have put forward reasons to suggest that, with respect to this status, there is an important differentiation into two broad, relatively distinct levels, and that his position on one or the other enters into the individual's definition of his own identity. To an important degree this process of differentiation is independent of the socio-economic status of his family in the community, which to the child is a prior ascribed status.

When we look at the same system as a selective mechanism from the societal point of view, some further considerations become important. First, it may be noted that the valuation of achievement and its sharing by family and school not only provides the appropriate values for internalization by individuals, but also performs a crucial integrative function for the system. Differentiation of the class along the achievement axis is inevitably a source of strain, because it confers higher rewards and privileges on one contingent than on another within the same system. This common valuation helps make possible the acceptance of the crucial differentiation, especially by the losers in the competition. Here it is an essential point that this *common* value on achievement is shared by units with different statuses in the system. It cuts across the differentiation of families by socioeconomic status. It is necessary that there be realistic opportunity and that the teacher can be relied on to implement it by being "fair" and rewarding achievement by whoever shows capacity for it. The fact is crucial that the distribution of abilities, though correlated with family status, clearly does not coincide with it. There can then be a genuine selective process within a set of "rules of the game."

This commitment to common values is not, however, the sole integrative mechanism counteracting the strain imposed by differentiation. Not only does the individual pupil enjoy familial support, but teachers also like and indeed "respect" pupils on bases independent of achievement-status, and peer-group friendship lines, though correlated with position on the achievement scale, again by no means coincide with it, but cross-cut it. Thus there are cross-cutting lines of solidarity which mitigate the strains generated by rewarding achievement differentially.[11]

It is only *within* this framework of institutionalized solidarity that the crucial selective process goes on through selective rewarding and the consolidation of its results into a status-differentiation within the school class. We have called special attention to the impact of the selective process on the children of relatively high ability but low family status. Precisely in this group, but pervading school classes generally, is another parallel to what was found in the studies of voting behavior.[12] In the voting studies it was found that the "shifters"—those voters who were transferring their allegiance from one major party to the other—tended, on the one hand, to be the "cross-pressured" people, who had multiple status characteristics and group allegiances which predisposed them simultaneously to vote in opposite directions. The analogy in the school class is clearly to the children for whom ability and family status do not coincide. On the other hand, it was precisely in this group of cross-pressured voters that political "indifference" was most conspicuous. Non-voting was particularly prevalent in this group, as was a generally cool emotional tone toward a campaign. The suggestion is that some of the pupil "indifference" to school performance may have a similar origin. This is clearly a complex phenomenon and cannot be further analyzed here. But rather than suggesting, as is usual on common sense grounds, that indifference to school work represents an "alienation" from cultural and intellectual values, I would suggest exactly the opposite: that

[11] In this, as in several other respects, there is a parallel to other important allocative processes in the society. A striking example is the voting process by which political support is allocated between party candidates. Here, the strain arises from the fact that one candidate and his party will come to enjoy all the perquisites—above all the power—of office, while the other will be excluded for the time being from these. This strain is mitigated, on the one hand, by the common commitment to constitutional procedure, and, on the other hand, by the fact that the nonpolitical bases of social solidarity, which figure so prominently as determinants of voting behavior, still cut across party lines. The average person is, in various of his roles, associated with people whose political preference is different from his own; he therefore could not regard the opposite party as composed of unmitigated scoundrels without introducing a rift within the groups to which he is attached. This feature of the electorate's structure is brought out strongly in B. R. Berelson, P. F. Lazarsfeld and W. N. McPhee, *Voting* (Chicago: University of Chicago Press, 1954). The conceptual analysis of it is developed in my own paper, " 'Voting' and the Equilibrium of the American Political System" in E. Burdick and A. J. Brodbeck (eds.), *American Voting Behavior* (Glencoe, Ill.: The Free Press, 1959).

[12] *Ibid.*

an important component of such indifference, including in extreme cases overt revolt against school discipline, is connected with the fact that the stakes, as in politics, are very high indeed. Those pupils who are exposed to contradictory pressures are likely to be ambivalent; at the same time, the personal stakes for them are higher than for the others, because what happens in school may make much more of a difference for their futures than for the others, in whom ability and family status point to the same expectations for the future. In particular for the upwardly mobile pupils, too much emphasis on school success would pointedly suggest "burning their bridges" of association with their families and status peers. This phenomenon seems to operate even in elementary school, although it grows somewhat more conspicuous later. In general I think that an important part of the anti-intellectualism in American youth culture stems from the *importance* of the selective process through the educational system rather than the opposite.

One further major point should be made in this analysis. As we have noted, the general trend of American society has been toward a rapid upgrading in the educational status of the population. This means that, relative to past expectations, with each generation there is increased pressure to educational achievement, often associated with parents' occupational ambitions for their children.[13] To a sociologist this is a more or less classical situation of anomic strain, and the youth-culture ideology which plays down intellectual interests and school performance seems to fit in this context. The orientation of the youth culture is, in the nature of the case, ambivalent, but for the reasons suggested, the anti-intellectual side of the ambivalence tends to be overtly stressed. One of the reasons for the dominance of the anti-school side of the ideology is that it provides a means of protest against adults, who are at the opposite pole in the socialization situation. In certain respects one would expect that the trend toward greater emphasis on independence, which we have associated with progressive education, would accentuate the strain in this area and hence the tendency to decry adult expectations. The whole problem should be subjected to a thorough analysis in the light of what we know about ideologies more generally.

The same general considerations are relevant to the much-discussed problem of juvenile delinquency. Both the general upgrading process and the pressure to enhanced independence should be expected to increase strain on the lower, most marginal groups. The analysis of this paper has been concerned with the line between college and non-college contingents; there

---

[13] J. A. Kahl, "Educational and Occupational Aspirations of 'Common Man' Boys," *Harvard Educational Review*, XXIII (Summer, 1953), pp. 186–203; also in this volume on pp.

is, however, another line between those who achieve solid non-college educational status and those for whom adaptation to educational expectations at *any* level is difficult. As the acceptable minimum of educational qualification rises, persons near and below the margin will tend to be pushed into an attitude of repudiation of these expectations. Truancy and delinquency are ways of expresing this repudiation. Thus the very *improvement* of educational standards in the society at large may well be a major factor in the failure of the educational process for a growing number at the lower end of the status and ability distribution. It should therefore not be too easily assumed that delinquency is a symptom of a *general* failure of the educational process.

DIFFERENTIATION AND SELECTION IN THE SECONDARY SCHOOL

It will not be possible to discuss the secondary school phase of education in nearly as much detail as has been done for the elementary school phase, but it is worthwhile to sketch its main outline in order to place the above analysis in a wider context. Very broadly we may say that the elementary school phase is concerned with the internalization in children of motivation to achievement, and the selection of persons on the basis of differential capacity for achievement. The focus is on the *level* of capacity. In the secondary school phase, on the other hand, the focus is on the differentiation of *qualitative types* of achievement. As in the elementary school, this differentiation cross-cuts sex role. I should also maintain that it cross-cuts the levels of achievement which have been differentiated out in the elementary phase.

In approaching the question of the types of capacity differentiated, it should be kept in mind that secondary school is the principal springboard from which lower-status persons will enter the labor force, whereas those achieving higher status will continue their formal education in college, and some of them beyond. Hence for the lower-status pupils the important line of differentiation should be the one which will lead into broadly different categories of jobs; for the higher-status pupils the differentiation will lead to broadly different roles in college.

My suggestion is that this differentiation separates those two components of achievement which we labelled "cognitive" and "moral" in discussing the elementary phase. Those relatively high in "cognitive" achievement will fit better in specific-function, more or less technical roles; those relatively high in "moral" achievement will tend toward diffuser, more "socially" or "humanly" oriented roles. In jobs not requiring college training, the one category may be thought of as comprising the more impersonal and technical occupations, such as "operatives," mechanics, or clerical workers; the other, as occupations where "human relations" are prominent, such as salesmen and agents of various sorts. At the college level, the differentiation certainly relates to concern, on the one hand, with the specifically intellectual curricular work of college and, on the other hand, with various types of diffused responsibility in human relations, such as leadership roles in student government and extracurricular activities. Again, candidates for post-graduate professional training will probably be drawn mainly from the first of these two groups.

In the structure of the school, there appears to be a gradual transition from the earliest grades through high school, with the changes timed differently in different school systems. The structure emphasized in the first part of this discussion is most clearly marked in the first three "primary" grades. With progression to the higher grades, there is greater frequency of plural teachers, though very generally still a single main teacher. In the sixth grade and sometimes in the fifth, a man as main teacher, though uncommon, is by no means unheard of. With junior high school, however, the shift of pattern becomes more marked, and still more in senior high.

By that time the pupil has several different teachers of both sexes[14] teaching him different subjects, which are more or less formally organized into different courses—college preparatory and others. Furthermore, with the choice of "elective" subjects, the members of the class in one subject no longer need be exactly the same as in another, so the pupil is much more systematically exposed to association with different people, both adults and age-peers, in different contexts. Moreover, the school he attends is likely to be substantially larger than was his elementary school, and to draw from a wider geographical area. Hence the child is exposed to a wider range of statuses than before, being thrown in with more age-peers whom he does not encounter in his neighborhood; it is less likely that his parents will know the parents of any given child with whom he associates. It is thus my impression that the transitions to junior high and senior high school are apt to mean a considerable reshuffling of friendships. Another conspicuous difference between the elementary and secondary levels is the great increase in high school of organized extracurricular activities. Now, for the first time, organized athletics become important, as do a variety of clubs and associations which are school-sponsored and supervised to varying degrees.

Two particularly important shifts in the patterning of youth culture occur in this period. One, of course, is the emergence of more positive cross-sex relationships outside the classroom, through dances, dating, and the like.

[14] Men make up about half (49 per cent) of the public secondary school instructional staff. *Biennial Survey of Education in the United States, 1954-56, op. cit.,* chap. ii, p. 7.

The other is the much sharper prestige-stratification of informal peer group-ings,. with indeed an element of snobbery which often exceeds that of the adult community in which the school exists.[15] Here it is important that though there is a broad correspondence between the prestige of friendship groups and the family status of their members, this, like the achievement order of the elementary school, is by no means a simple "mirroring" of the community stratification scale, for a considerable number of lower-status children get accepted into groups including members with higher family status than themselves. This stratified youth system operates as a genuine assortative mechanism; it does not simply reinforce ascribed status.

The prominence of this youth culture in the American secondary school is, in comparison with other societies, one of the hallmarks of the American educational system; it is much less prominent in most European systems. It may be said to constitute a kind of structural fusion between the school class and the peer-group structure of the elementary period. It seems clear that what I have called the "human relations"-oriented contingent of the secondary school pupils is more active and prominent in extracurricular activities, and that this is one of the main foci of their differentiation from the more impersonally- and technically-oriented contingent. The personal qualities figuring most prominently in the human relations contingent can perhaps be summed up as the qualities that make for "popularity." I sug-gest that, from the point of view of the secondary school's selective function, the youth culture helps to differentiate between types of personalities which will, by and large, play different kinds of roles as adults.

The stratification of youth groups has, as noted, a selective function; it is a bridge between the achievement order and the adult stratification system of the community. But it also has another function. It is a focus of prestige which exists along side of, and is to a degree independent of, the achieve-ment order focussing on school work as such. The attainment of prestige in the informal youth group is itself a form of valued achievement. Hence, among those individuals destined for higher status in society, one can dis-cern two broad types: those whose school work is more or less outstanding and whose informal prestige is relatively satisfactory; and vice versa—those whose informal prestige is outstanding, and school performance satisfactory. Falling below certain minima in either respect would jeopardize the child's claim to belong in the upper group.[16] It is an important point here that

[15] See, for instance, C. W. Gordon, *The Social System of the High School: A Study in the Sociology of Adolescence* (Glencoe, Ill.: The Free Press, 1957).
[16] J. Riley, M. Riley, and M. Moore, "Adolescent Values and the Riesman Typology" in S. M. Lipset and L. Lowenthal (eds.), *The Sociology of Culture and the Analysis of Social Character* (Glencoe, Ill.: The Free Press, to be published in 1960).

those clearly headed for college belong to peer groups which, while often depreciative of intensive concern with studies, also take for granted and reinforce a level of scholastic attainment which is necessary for admission to a good college. Pressure will be put on the individual who tends to fall below such a standard.

In discussing the elementary school level it will be remembered that we emphasized that the peer group served as an object of emotional dependency displaced from the family. In relation to the pressure for school achievement, therefore, it served at least partially as an expression of the lower-order motivational system *out* of which the child was in process of being socialized. On its own level, similar things can be said of the adolescent youth culture; it is in part an expression of regressive motivations. This is true of the emphasis on athletics despite its lack of relevance to adult roles, of the "homosexual" undertones of much intensive same-sex friendship, and of a certain "irresponsibility" in attitudes toward the opposite sex—e.g., the exploitative element in the attitudes of boys toward girls. This, however, is by no means the whole story. The youth culture is also a field for practicing the assumption of higher-order responsibilities, for conducting delicate human relations without immediate supervision and learning to accept the consequences. In this connection it is clearly of particular importance to the contingent we have spoken of as specializing in "human relations."

We can, perhaps, distinguish three different levels of crystallization of these youth-culture patterns. The middle one is that which may be considered age-appropriate without clear status-differentiation. The two keynotes here seem to be "being a good fellow" in the sense of general friendliness and being ready to take responsibility in informal social situations where something needs to be done. Above this, we may speak of the higher level of "outstanding" popularity and qualities of "leadership" of the person who is turned to where unusual responsibilities are required. And below the middle level are the youth patterns bordering on delinquency, withdrawal, and generally unacceptable behavior. Only this last level is clearly "regressive" relative to expectations of appropriate behavior for the age-grade. In judging these three levels, however, allowance should be made for a good many nuances. Most adolescents do a certain amount of experimenting with the borderline of the unacceptable patterns; that they should do so is to be expected in view of the pressure toward independence from adults, and of the "collusion" which can be expected in the reciprocal stimulation of age-peers. The question is whether this regressive behavior comes to be confirmed into a major pattern for the personality as a whole. Seen in this perspective, it seems legitimate to maintain that the middle and the higher patterns indicated are the major ones, and that only a minority of adolescents comes to be confirmed in a truly unacceptable pattern of living. This minority may well be a relatively constant proportion of the age cohort, but apart from situations of special social disorganization, the available evidence does not suggest that it has been a progressively growing one in recent years.

The patterning of cross-sex relations in the youth culture clearly foreshadows future marriage and family formation. That it figures so prominently in school is related to the fact that in our society the element of ascription, including direct parental influence, in the choice of a marriage partner is strongly minimized. For the girl, it has the very important significance of reminding her that her adult status is going to be very much concerned with marriage and a family. This basic expectation for the girl stands in a certain tension to the school's curricular coeducation with its relative lack of differentiation by sex. But the extent to which the feminine role in American society continues to be anchored in marriage and the family should not be allowed to obscure the importance of coeducation. In the first place, the contribution of women in various extra-familial occupations and in community affairs has been rapidly increasing, and certainly higher levels of education have served as a prerequisite to this contribution. At the same time, it is highly important that the woman's familial role should not be regarded as drastically segregated from the cultural concerns of the society as a whole. The educated woman has important functions *as wife and mother,* particularly as an influence on her children in backing the schools and impressing on them the importance of education. It is, I think, broadly true that the immediate responsibility of women for family management has been increasing, though I am very skeptical of the alleged "abdication" of the American male. But precisely in the context of women's increased family responsibility, the influence of the mother both as agent of socialization and as role model is a crucial one. This influence should be evaluated in the light of the general upgrading process. It is very doubtful whether, apart from any other considerations, the motivational prerequisites of the general process could be sustained without sufficiently high education of the women who, as mothers, influence their children.

Conclusion

With the general cultural upgrading process in American society which has been going on for more than a century, the educational system has come to play an increasingly vital role. That this should be the case is, in my opinion, a consequence of the general trend to structural differentiation in the society. Relatively speaking, the school is a specialized agency. That it should increasingly have become the principal channel of selection as well as agency of socialization is in line with what one would expect in an increasingly differentiated and progressively more upgraded society. The legend of the "self-made man" has an element of nostalgic romanticism and is destined to become increasingly mythical, if by it is meant not just mobility from humble origins to high status, which does indeed continue to occur, but that the high status was attained through the "school of hard knocks" without the aid of formal education.

The structure of the public school system and the analysis of the ways in which it contributes both to the socialization of individuals and to their allocation to roles in society is, I feel, of vital concern to all students of American society. Notwithstanding the variegated elements in the situation, I think it has been possible to sketch out a few major structural patterns of the public school system and at least to suggest some ways in which they serve these important functions. What could be presented in this paper is the merest outline of such an analysis. It is, however, hoped that it has been carried far enough to suggest a field of vital mutual interest for social scientists on the one hand and those concerned with the actual operation of the schools on the other.

The Concept of Equality of Educational Opportunity

JAMES S. COLEMAN

Although there is wide agreement in the United States that our society accepts and supports the fundamental value of equal opportunity, when it comes to areas of specific application there is considerable disagreement over its meaning. In this article, the author traces the evolutionary shifts in interpretation of the concept of equality of educational opportunity, not only putting into perspective the different views which form the basis for disagreement today but also indicating how the current direction of change may influence the interpretation of this concept in the future.

The concept of "equality of educational opportunity" as held by members of society has had a varied past. It has changed radically in recent years, and is likely to undergo further change in the future. This lack of stability in the concept leads to several questions. What has it meant in the past, what does it mean now, and what will it mean in the future? Whose obligation is it to provide such equality? Is the concept a fundamentally sound one, or does it have inherent contradictions or conflicts with social organization? But first of all, and above all, what is and has been meant in society by the idea of equality of educational opportunity?

To answer this question, it is necessary to consider how the child's position in society has been conceived in different historical periods. In pre-industrial Europe, the child's horizons were largely limited by his family. His station in life was likely to be the same as his father's. If his father was a serf, he would likely live his own life as a serf; if his father was a shoemaker, he would likely become a shoemaker. But even this immobility was not the crux of the matter; he was a part of the family production enterprise and would likely remain within this enterprise throughout his life. The extended family, as the basic unit of social organization, had complete authority over the child, and complete responsibility for him. This responsibility ordinarily did not end when the child became an adult because he remained a part of the same economic unit and carried on this tradition of re-

Harvard Educational Review   Vol. 38   No. 1   Winter 1968, 7–22

297

sponsibility into the next generation. Despite some mobility out of the family, the general pattern was family continuity through a patriarchal kinship system.

There are two elements of critical importance here. First, the family carried responsibility for its members' welfare from cradle to grave. It was a "welfare society," with each extended family serving as a welfare organization for its own members. Thus it was to the family's interest to see that its members became productive. Conversely, a family took relatively small interest in whether someone in *another* family became productive or not—merely because the mobility of productive labor between family economic units was relatively low. If the son of a neighbor was allowed to become a ne'er-do-well, it had little real effect on families other than his own.

The second important element is that the family, as a unit of economic production, provided an appropriate context in which the child could learn the things he needed to know. The craftsman's shop or the farmer's fields were appropriate training grounds for sons, and the household was an appropriate training ground for daughters.

In this kind of society, the concept of equality of educational opportunity had no relevance at all. The child and adult were embedded within the extended family, and the child's education or training was merely whatever seemed necessary to maintain the family's productivity. The fixed stations in life which most families occupied precluded any idea of "opportunity" and, even less, equality of opportunity.

With the industrial revolution, changes occurred in both the family's function as a self-perpetuating economic unit and as a training ground. As economic organizations developed outside the household, children began to be occupationally mobile outside their families. As families lost their economic production activities, they also began to lose their welfare functions, and the poor or ill or incapacitated became more nearly a community responsibility. Thus the training which a child received came to be of interest to all in the community, either as his potential employers or as his potential economic supports if he became dependent. During this stage of development in eighteenth-century England, for instance, communities had laws preventing immigration from another community because of the potential economic burden of immigrants.

Further, as men came to employ their own labor outside the family in the new factories, their families became less useful as economic training grounds for their children. These changes paved the way for public education. Families needed a context within which their children could learn some general skills which would be useful for gaining work outside the family; and men of influence in the community began to be interested in the potential productivity of other men's children.

It was in the early nineteenth century that public education began to appear in Europe and America. Before that time, private education had grown with the

298

expansion of the mercantile class. This class had both the need and resources to have its children educated outside the home, either for professional occupations or for occupations in the developing world of commerce. But the idea of general educational opportunity for all children arose only in the nineteenth century.

The emergence of public, tax-supported education was not solely a function of the stage of industrial development. It was also a function of the class structure in the society. In the United States, without a strong traditional class structure, universal education in publicly-supported free schools became widespread in the early nineteenth century; in England, the "voluntary schools," run and organized by churches with some instances of state support, were not supplemented by a state-supported system until the Education Act of 1870. Even more, the character of educational opportunity reflected the class structure. In the United States, the public schools quickly became the common school, attended by representatives of all classes; these schools provided a common educational experience for most American children—excluding only those upper-class children in private schools, those poor who went to no schools, and Indians and Southern Negroes who were without schools. In England, however, the class system directly manifested itself through the schools. The state-supported, or "board schools" as they were called, became the schools of the laboring lower classes with a sharply different curriculum from those voluntary schools which served the middle and upper classes. The division was so sharp that two government departments, the Education Department and the Science and Art Department, administered external examinations, the first for the products of the board schools, and the second for the products of the voluntary schools as they progressed into secondary education. It was only the latter curricula and examinations that provided admission to higher education.

What is most striking is the duration of influence of such a dual structure. Even today in England, a century later (and in different forms in most European countries), there exists a dual structure of public secondary education with only one of the branches providing the curriculum for college admission. In England, this branch includes the remaining voluntary schools which, though retaining their individual identities, have become part of the state-supported system.

This comparison of England and the United States shows clearly the impact of the class structure in society upon the concept of educational opportunity in that society. In nineteenth-century England, the idea of *equality* of educational opportunity was hardly considered; the system was designed to provide *differentiated* educational opportunity appropriate to one's station in life. In the United States as well, the absence of educational opportunity for Negroes in the South arose from the caste and feudal structure of the largely rural society. The idea of differentiated educational opportunity, implicit in the Education Act of 1870 in England, seems to derive from dual needs: the needs arising from industrialization for a basic education for the labor force, and the interests of parents in having one's own child receive a good education. The middle classes could meet both these needs by providing a free system for the children of laboring classes, and a tuition system (which soon came to be supplemented by state grants) for their own. The long survival of this differentiated system depended not only on the historical fact that the voluntary schools existed before a public system came into existence but on the fact that it allows both of these needs to be met: the community's collective need for a trained labor force, and the middle-class individual's interest in a better education for his own child. It served a third need as well: that of maintaining the existing social order—a system of stratification that was a step removed from a feudal system of fixed estates, but designed to prevent a wholesale challenge by the children of the working class to the positions held for children of the middle classes.

The similarity of this system to that which existed in the South to provide differential opportunity to Negroes and whites is striking, just as is the similarity of class structures in the second half of nineteenth-century England to the white-Negro caste structure of the southern United States in the first half of the twentieth century.

In the United States, nearly from the beginning, the concept of educational opportunity had a special meaning which focused on equality. This meaning included the following elements:

(1) Providing a *free* education up to a given level which constituted the principal entry point to the labor force.

(2) Providing a *common curriculum* for all children, regardless of background.

(3) Partly by design and partly because of low population density, providing that children from diverse backgrounds attend the *same school*.

(4) Providing equality within a given *locality*, since local taxes provided the source of support for schools.

This conception of equality of opportunity is still held by many persons; but there are some assumptions in it which are not obvious. First, it implicitly assumes that the existence of free schools eliminates economic sources of inequality of opportunity. Free schools, however, do not mean that the costs of a child's education become reduced to zero for families at all economic levels. When free education was introduced, many families could not afford to allow the child to attend school beyond an early age. His labor was necessary to the family—whether in rural or urban areas. Even after the passage of child labor laws, this remained true on the farm. These economic sources of inequality of opportunity have become small indeed (up through secondary education); but at one time they were a major source of inequality. In some countries they remain so; and certainly for higher education they remain so.

Apart from the economic needs of the family, problems inherent in the social structure raised even more fundamental questions about equality of educational opportunity. Continued school attendance prevented a boy from being trained in his father's trade. Thus, in taking advantage of "equal educational opportunity," the son of a craftsman or small tradesman would lose the opportunity to enter those occupations he would most likely fill. The family inheritance of occupation at all social levels was still strong enough, and the age of entry into the labor force was still early enough, that secondary education interfered with opportunity for working-class children; while it opened up opportunities at higher social levels, it closed them at lower ones.

Since residue of this social structure remains in present American society, the dilemma cannot be totally ignored. The idea of a common educational experience implies that this experience has only the effect of widening the range of opportunity, never the effect of excluding opportunities. But clearly this is never precisely true so long as this experience prevents a child from pursuing certain occupational paths. This question still arises with the differentiated secondary curriculum: an academic program in high school has the effect not only of keeping open the opportunities which arise through continued education, but also of closing off opportunities which a vocational program keeps open.

A second assumption implied by this concept of equality of opportunity is that opportunity lies in *exposure* to a given curriculum. The amount of opportunity is then measured in terms of the level of curriculum to which the child is exposed. The higher the curriculum made available to a given set of children, the greater their opportunity.

The most interesting point about this assumption is the relatively passive role of the school and community, relative to the child's role. The school's obligation is to "provide an opportunity" by being available, within easy geographic access of the child, free of cost (beyond the value of the child's time), and with a curriculum that would not exclude him from higher education. The obligation to "use the opportunity" is on the child or the family, so that his role is defined as the active one: the responsibility for achievement rests with him. Despite the fact that the school's role was the relatively passive one and the child's or family's role the active one, the use of this social service soon came to be no longer a choice of the parent or child, but that of the state. Since compulsory attendance laws appeared in the nineteenth century, the age of required attendance has been periodically moved upward.

This concept of equality of educational opportunity is one that has been implicit in most educational practice throughout most of the period of public education in the nineteenth and twentieth centuries. However, there have been several challenges to it; serious questions have been raised by new conditions in public education. The first of these in the United States was a challenge to assumption two, the common curriculum. This challenge first occurred in the early years of the twentieth century with the expansion of secondary education. Until the report of the committee of the National Education Association, issued in 1918, the standard curriculum in secondary schools was primarily a classical one appropriate for college entrance. The greater influx of noncollege-bound adolescents into the high school made it necessary that this curriculum be changed into one more appropriate to the new majority. This is not to say that the curriculum changed immediately in the schools, nor that all schools changed equally, but rather that the seven "cardinal principles" of the N.E.A. report became a powerful influence in the movement toward a less academically rigid curriculum. The introduction of the new nonclassical curriculum was seldom if ever couched in terms of a conflict between those for whom high school was college preparation, and those for whom it was terminal education; nevertheless, that was the case. The "inequality" was seen as the use of a curriculum that served a minority and was not designed to fit the needs of the majority; and the shift of curriculum was intended to fit the curriculum to the needs of the new majority in the schools.

In many schools, this shift took the form of *diversifying* the curriculum, rather than supplanting one by another; the college-preparatory curriculum remained though watered down. Thus the kind of equality of opportunity that emerged from the newly-designed secondary school curriculum was radically different from the elementary-school concept that had emerged earlier. The idea inherent in the new secondary school curriculum appears to have been to take as given the diverse occupational paths into which adolescents will go after secondary school, and to say (implicitly): there is greater equality of educational opportunity for a boy who is not going to attend college if he has a specially-designed curriculum than if he must take a curriculum designed for college entrance.

There is only one difficulty with this definition: it takes as *given* what should be problematic—that a given boy is going into a given post-secondary occupational or educational path. It is one thing to take as given that approximately 70 per cent of an entering high school freshman class will not attend college; but to assign a *particular child* to a curriculum designed for that 70 per cent closes off for that child the opportunity to attend college. Yet to assign all children to a curriculum designed for the 30 per cent who will attend college creates inequality for those who, at the end of high school, fall among the 70 per cent who do not attend college. This is a true dilemma, and one which no educational system has fully solved. It is more general than the college/noncollege dichotomy, for there is a wide variety of different paths that adolescents take on the completion of secondary school. In England, for example, a student planning to attend a university must specialize in the arts or the sciences in the later years of secondary school. Similar specialization occurs in the German gymnasium; and this is wholly within the group planning to attend university. Even greater specialization can be found among noncollege curricula, especially in the vocational, technical, and commercial high schools.

The distinguishing characteristic of this concept of equality of educational opportunity is that it accepts as given the child's expected future. While the concept discussed earlier left the child's future wholly open, this concept of differentiated curricula uses the expected future to match child and curriculum. It should be noted that the first and simpler concept is easier to apply in elementary schools where fundamental tools of reading and arithmetic are being learned by all children; it is only in secondary school that the problem of diverse futures arises. It should also be noted that the dilemma is directly due to the social structure itself: if there were a virtual absence of social mobility with everyone occupying a fixed estate in life, then such curricula that take the future as given would provide equality of opportunity relative to that structure. It is only because of the high degree of occupational mobility between generations—that is, the greater degree of equality of *occupational* opportunity—that the dilemma arises.

The first stage in the evolution of the concept of equality of educational opportunity was the notion that all children must be exposed to the same curriculum in the same school. A second stage in the evolution of the concept assumed that different children would have different occupational futures and that equality of opportunity required providing different curricula for each type of student. The third and fourth stages in this evolution came as a result of challenges to the basic idea of equality of educational opportunity from opposing directions. The third stage can be seen at least as far back as 1896 when the Supreme Court upheld the southern states' notion of "separate but equal" facilities. This stage ended in 1954 when the Supreme Court ruled that legal separation by race inherently constitutes inequality of opportunity. By adopting the "separate but equal" doctrine, the southern states rejected assumption three of the original concept, the assumption that equality depended on the opportunity to attend the same school. This rejection was, however, consistent with the overall logic of the original concept since attendance at the same school was not an inherent part of that logic. The underlying idea was that opportunity resided in exposure to a curriculum; the community's responsibility was to provide that exposure, the child's to take advantage of it.

It was the pervasiveness of this underlying idea which created the difficulty for the Supreme Court. For it was evident that even when identical facilities and identical teacher salaries existed for racially separate schools, "equality of educational opportunity" in some sense did not exist. This had also long been evident to Englishmen as well, in a different context, for with the simultaneous existence of the "common school" and the "voluntary school," no one was under the illusion that full equality of educational opportunity existed. But the source of this inequality remained an unarticulated feeling. In the decision of the Supreme Court, this unarticulated feeling began to take more precise form. The essence of it was that the *effects* of such separate schools were, or were likely to be, different. Thus a concept of equality of opportunity which focused on *effects* of schooling began to take form. The actual decision of the Court was in fact a confusion of two unrelated premises: this new concept, which looked at results of schooling, and the legal premise that the use of race as a basis for school assignment violates fundamental freedoms. But what is important for the evolution of the concept of equality of opportunity is that a new and different assumption was introduced, the assumption that equality of opportunity depends in some fashion upon effects of schooling. I believe the decision would have been more soundly based had it not depended on the effects of schooling, but only on the violation of freedom; but by introducing the question of effects of schooling, the Court brought into the open the implicit goals of equality of educational opportunity—that is, goals having to do with the *results* of school—to which the original concept was somewhat awkwardly directed.

That these goals were in fact behind the concept can be verified by a simple mental experiment. Suppose the early schools had operated for only one hour a week and had been attended by children of all social classes. This would have met the explicit assumptions of the early concept of equality of opportunity since the school is free, with a common curriculum, and attended by all children in the locality. But it obviously would not have been accepted, even at that time, as providing equality of opportunity, because its effects would have been so minimal. The additional educational resources provided by middle- and upper-class families, whether in the home, by tutoring, or in private supplementary schools, would have created severe inequalities in results.

Thus the dependence of the concept upon results or effects of schooling, which had remained hidden until 1954, came partially into the open with the Supreme Court decision. Yet this was not the end, for it created more problems than it solved. It might allow one to assess gross inequalities, such as that created by dual school systems in the South, or by a system like that in the mental experiment I just described. But it allows nothing beyond that. Even more confounding, because the decision did not use effects of schooling as a criterion of inequality but only as justification for a criterion of racial integration, integration itself emerged as the basis for still a new concept of equality of educational opportunity. Thus the idea of effects of schooling as an element in the concept was introduced but immediately overshadowed by another, the criterion of racial integration.

The next stage in the evolution of this concept was, in my judgment, the Office of Education Survey of Equality of Educational Opportunity. This survey was carried out under a mandate in the Civil Rights Act of 1964 to the Commissioner of Education to assess the "lack of equality of educational opportunity" among racial and other groups in the United States. The evolution of this concept, and the conceptual disarray which this evolution had created, made the very definition of the task exceedingly difficult. The original concept could be examined by determining the degree to which all children in a locality had access to the same schools and the same curriculum, free of charge. The existence of diverse secondary curricula appropriate to different futures could be assessed relatively easily. But the very assignment of a child to a specific curriculum implies acceptance of the concept of equality which takes futures as given. And the introduction of the new interpretations, equality as measured by results of schooling and equality defined by racial integration, confounded the issue even further.

As a consequence, in planning the survey it was obvious that no single concept of equality of educational opportunity existed and that the survey must give information relevant to a variety of concepts. The basis on which this was done can be seen by reproducing a portion of an internal memorandum that determined the design of the survey:

The point of second importance in design [second to the point of discovering the intent of Congress, which was taken to be that the survey was not for the purpose of locating willful discrimination, but to determine educational inequality without regard to intention of those in authority] follows from the first and concerns the definition of inequality. One type of inequality may be defined in terms of differences of the community's input to the school, such as per-pupil expenditure, school plants, libraries, quality of teachers, and other similar quantities.

A second type of inequality may be defined in terms of the racial composition of the school, following the Supreme Court's decision that segregated schooling is inherently unequal. By the former definition, the question of inequality through segregation is excluded, while by the latter, there is inequality of education within a school system so long as the schools within the system have different racial composition.

A third type of inequality would include various intangible characteristics of the school as well as the factors directly traceable to the community inputs to the school. These intangibles are such things as teacher morale, teachers' expectations of students, level of interest of the student body in learning, or others. Any of these factors may affect the impact of the school upon a given student within it. Yet such a definition gives no suggestion of where to stop, or just how relevant these factors might be for school quality.

Consequently, a fourth type of inequality may be defined in terms of consequences of the school for individuals with equal backgrounds and abilities. In this definition, equality of educational opportunity is equality of results, given the same individual input. With such a definition, inequality might come about from differences in the school inputs and/or racial composition and/or from more intangible things as described above.

Such a definition obviously would require that two steps be taken in the determination of inequality. First, it is necessary to determine the effect of these various factors upon educational results (conceiving of results quite broadly, including not only achievement but attitudes toward learning, self-image, and perhaps other variables). This provides various measures of the school's quality in terms of its effect upon its students. Second, it is necessary to take these measures of quality, once determined, and determine the differential exposure of Negroes (or other groups) and whites to schools of high and low quality.

A fifth type of inequality may be defined in terms of consequences of the school for individuals of unequal backgrounds and abilities. In this definition, equality of educational opportunity is equality of results given *different* individual inputs. The most striking examples of inequality here would be children from households in which a language other than English, such as Spanish or Navaho, is spoken. Other examples would be low-achieving children from homes in which there is a poverty of verbal expression or an absence of experiences which lead to conceptual facility.

Such a definition taken in the extreme would imply that educational equality is reached only when the results of schooling (achievement and attitudes) are the same for racial and religious minorities as for the dominant group.

The basis for the design of the survey is indicated by another segment of this memorandum:

Thus, the study will focus its principal effort on the fourth definition, but will also provide information relevant to all five possible definitions. This insures the pluralism which is obviously necessary with respect to a definition of inequality. The major justification for this focus is that the results of this approach can best be translated into policy which will improve education's effects. The results of the first two approaches (tangible inputs to the school, and segregation) can certainly be translated into policy, but there is no good evidence that these policies will improve education's effects; and while policies to implement the fifth would certainly improve education's effects, it seems hardly possible that the study could provide information that would direct such policies.

Altogether, it has become evident that it is not our role to define what constitutes equality for policy-making purposes. Such a definition will be an outcome of the interplay of a variety of interests, and will certainly differ from time to time as these interests differ. It should be our role to cast light on the state of inequality defined in the variety of ways which appear reasonable at this time.

The survey, then, was conceived as a pluralistic instrument, given the variety of concepts of equality of opportunity in education. Yet I suggest that despite the avowed intention of not adjudicating between these different ideas, the survey has brought a new stage in the evolution of the concept. For the definitions of equality which the survey was designed to serve split sharply into two groups. The first three definitions concerned input resources: first, those brought to the school by the actions of the school administration (facilities, curriculum, teachers); second, those brought to the school by the other students, in the educational backgrounds which their presence contributed to the school; and third, the intangible characteristics such as "morale" that result from the interaction of all these factors. The fourth and fifth definitions were concerned with the effects of schooling. Thus the five definitions were divided into three concerned with inputs to school and two concerned with effects of schooling. When the Report emerged, it did not give five different measures of equality, one for each of these definitions; but it did focus sharply on this dichotomy, giving in Chapter Two information on inequalities of input relevant to definitions one and two, and in Chapter Three information on inequalities of results relevant to definitions four and five, and also in Chapter Three information on the relation of input to results again relevant to definitions four and five.

Although not central to our discussion here, it is interesting to note that this examination of the relation of school inputs to effects on achievement showed that those input characteristics of schools that are most alike for Negroes and whites have least effect on their achievement. The magnitudes of differences between schools attended by Negroes and those attended by whites were as follows: least, facilities and curriculum; next, teacher quality; and greatest, educational backgrounds of fellow students. The order of importance of these inputs on the achievement of Negro students is precisely the same: facilities and curriculum least, teacher quality next, and backgrounds of fellow students, most.

By making the dichotomy between inputs and results explicit, and by focusing attention not only on inputs but on results, the Report brought into the open what had been underlying all the concepts of equality of educational opportunity but had remained largely hidden: that the concept implied *effective* equality of opportunity, that is, equality in those elements that are effective for learning. The reason this had remained half-hidden, obscured by definitions that involve inputs is, I suspect, because educational research has been until recently unprepared to demonstrate what elements are effective. The controversy that has surrounded the Report indicates that measurement of effects is still subject to sharp disagreement; but the crucial point is that *effects* of inputs have come to constitute the basis for assessment of school quality (and thus equality of opportunity) in place of using certain inputs by definition as measures of quality (e.g., small classes are better than large, higher-paid teachers are better than lower-paid ones, by definition).

It would be fortunate indeed if the matter could be left to rest there--if merely by using effects of school rather than inputs as the basis for the concept, the problem were solved. But that is not the case at all. The conflict between definitions four and five given above shows this. The conflict can be illustrated by resorting again to the mental experiment discussed earlier—providing a standard education of one hour per week, under identical conditions, for all children. By definition four, controlling all background differences of the children, results for Negroes and whites would be equal, and thus by this definition equality of opportunity would exist. But because such minimal schooling would have minimal effect, those children from educationally strong families would enjoy educational opportunity far surpassing that of others. And because such educationally strong backgrounds are found more often among whites than among Negroes, there would be very large overall Negro-white achievement differences—and thus inequality of opportunity by definition five.

It is clear from this hypothetical experiment that the problem of what constitutes equality of opportunity is not solved. The problem will become even clearer by showing graphs with some of the results of the Office of Education Survey. The highest line in Figure 1 shows the achievement in verbal skills by whites in the urban Northeast at grades 1, 3, 6, 9, and 12. The second line shows the achievement at each of these grades by whites in the rural Southeast. The third shows the achievement of Negroes in the urban Northeast. The fourth shows the achievement of Negroes in the rural Southeast.

When compared to the whites in the urban Northeast, each of the other three

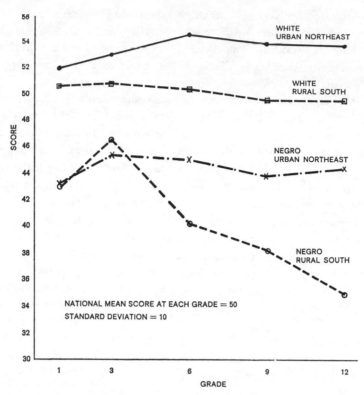

FIGURE 1

Patterns of Achievement in Verbal Skills at Various Grade Levels by Race and Region

groups shows a different pattern. The comparison with whites in the rural South shows the two groups beginning near the same point in the first grade, and diverging over the years of school. The comparison with Negroes in the urban Northeast shows the two groups beginning farther apart at the first grade and remaining about the same distance apart. The comparison with Negroes in the rural South shows the two groups beginning far apart and moving much farther apart over the years of school.

Which of these, if any, shows equality of educational opportunity between regional and racial groups? Which shows greatest inequality of opportunity? I think the second question is easier to answer than the first. The last comparison showing both initial difference and the greatest increase in difference over grades 1 through 12 appears to be the best candidate for the greatest inequality. The first comparison, with whites in the rural South, also seems to show inequality of opportunity, because of the increasing difference over the twelve years. But what about the second comparison, with an approximately constant difference between Negroes and whites in the urban Northeast? Is this equality of opportunity? I suggest not. It means, in effect, only that the period of school has left the average Negro at about the same level of achievement relative to whites as he began—in this case, achieving higher than about 15 per cent of the whites, lower than about 85 per cent of the whites. It may well be that in the absence of school those lines of achievement would have diverged due to differences in home environments; or perhaps they would have remained an equal distance apart, as they are in this graph (though at lower levels of achievement for both groups, in the absence of school). If it were the former, we could say that school, by keeping the lines parallel, has been a force toward the equalization of opportunity. But in the absence of such knowledge, we cannot say even that.

What would full equality of educational opportunity look like in such graphs? One might persuasively argue that it should show a convergence, so that even though two population groups begin school with different levels of skills on the average, the average of the group that begins lower moves up to coincide with that of the group that begins higher. Parenthetically, I should note that this does *not* imply that all students' achievement comes to be identical, but only that the *averages* for two population groups that begin at different levels come to be identical. The diversity of individual scores could be as great as, or greater than, the diversity at grade 1.

Yet there are serious questions about this definition of equality of opportunity. It implies that over the period of school there are no other influences, such as the family environment, which affect achievement over the twelve years of school, even though these influences may differ greatly for the two population groups. Concretely, it implies that white family environments, predominantly middle class, and Negro family environments, predominantly lower class, will produce no effects on achievement that would keep these averages apart. Such an assumption seems highly unrealistic, especially in view of the general importance of family background for achievement.

However, if such possibilities are acknowledged, then how far can they go before there is inequality of educational opportunity? Constant difference over school? Increasing differences? The unanswerability of such questions begins to give a sense of a new stage in the evolution of the concept of equality of educational opportunity. These questions concern the *relative intensity* of two sets of influences: those which are alike for the two groups, principally in school, and those which are different, principally in the home or neighborhood. If the school's influences are not only alike for the two groups, but very strong relative to the divergent influences, then the two groups will move together. If school influences are very weak, then the two groups will move apart. Or more generally, the relative intensity of the convergent school influences and the divergent out-of-school influences determines the effectiveness of the educational system in providing equality of educational opportunity. In this perspective, complete equality of opportunity can be reached only if all the divergent out-of-school influences vanish, a condition that would arise only in the advent of boarding schools; given the existing divergent influences, equality of opportunity can only be approached and never fully reached. The concept becomes one of degree of proximity to equality of opportunity. This proximity is determined, then, not merely by the *equality* of educational inputs, but by the *intensity* of the school's influences relative to the external divergent influences. That is, equality of output is not so much determined by equality of the resource inputs, but by the power of these resources in bringing about achievement.

Here, then, is where the concept of equality of educational opportunity presently stands. We have observed an evolution which might have been anticipated a century and a half ago when the first such concepts arose, yet one which is very different from the concept as it first developed. This difference is sharpened if we examine a further implication of the current concept as I have described it. In describing the original concept, I indicated that the role of the community and the educational institution was relatively passive; they were expected to provide a set of free public resources. The responsibility for profitable use of those resources lay with the child and his family. But the evolution of the concept has reversed these roles. The implication of the most recent concept, as I have described it, is that the responsibility to create achievement lies with the educational institution, not the child. The difference in achievement at grade 12 between the average Negro and the average white is, in effect, the degree of inequality of opportunity, and the reduction of that inequality is a responsibility of the school. This shift in responsibility follows logically from the change in the concept of equality of educational opportunity from school resource inputs to effects of schooling. When that change occurred, as it has in the past few years, the school's responsibility shifted from increasing and distributing equally *its* "quality" to increasing the quality of its *students'* achievements. This is a notable shift, and one which should have strong consequences for the practice of education in future years.

Race and Education:
A Search for Legitimacy

CHARLES V. HAMILTON

The author asserts that the educational questions and issues being raised by many black parents, students, and teachers today are substantially different from the traditional concerns of experts. The black spokesmen are questioning the legitimacy of the educational institutions; they no longer believe that it is sufficient to try to increase the effectiveness of those institutions. This difference has caused a tension between those who have been victims of indifferent and inefficient policies and practices and those who believe it is still possible to make the existing institutions operable. Black people are calling for community control, not for integration. They are focusing as much on Afro-American culture and awareness as they are on verbal and arithmetic skills. Some black people are thinking of entirely new, comprehensive forms of education, based on substantially different normative values.

An article on public policy, race, and education in the United States in the late 1960's cannot overlook the clear existence of tremendous ferment taking place in the various black communities in this country. The nature of that ferment is such that, if we would devise relevant policy for educating vast numbers of black people today, we cannot focus merely, or even primarily, on achievement in verbal and mathematical skills as criteria for educational improvement. At one time, possibly to the mid-1960's, it was possible to talk about educational policy largely in terms of "integration" (or at least, desegregation) and assume that plans to implement integration would be dealing with the core of the problem of educational deficiency. This is no longer the case.

Today, one hears wholly different demands being raised in the black community. These demands are better represented by the kinds of resolutions coming out of the workshops of the newly formed (June, 1968) National Association of Afro-American Educators than by the conclusions reached by the report on *Equality of Educational Opportunity* (Coleman Report). These demands are reflected more clearly in the demonstrations of black high school students in

Harvard Educational Review   Vol. 38   No. 4   Fall 1968, 669-684

many cities for more emphasis on Afro-American history and culture and for better science lab facilities than by the findings of the United States Commission on Civil Rights (*Racial Isolation in the Public Schools*). These demands are more clearly illustrated in the positions taken by the Harlem chapter of the Congress of Racial Equality (CORE), calling for an independent school system for Harlem, and by many of the Concerned Black Parents groups than in policy recommendations found in the statement issued by the Board of Education of Chicago, Illinois in August, 1967 (Redmond Report).

First, I would like to indicate why it is more important at this time, from a socio-political point of view, to put more credence in the wishes of the black community than in the statements and findings of the experts. Second, I would like to give examples of the kinds of things on the minds of some of those black people taking an active interest in new directions for education in the black community. Third, I want to present a sketch of a proposal for dealing with some of the problems in some of the large, urban areas. I am not sanguine that the proposal will be applicable in all places (I assume it will not be), but neither do I believe it possible or necessary to develop one model to fit all occasions. My proposal attempts to combine some of the fervent wishes of a growing number of black people with the clear need to think in wholly new institutional terms. I am fully aware that public policy in this area has been influenced by such dichotomies as "integration vs. segregation" (*de jure* and *de facto*) and "integrated education vs. quality (compensatory) education." My presentation will not use these terms as primary focal points, but it is clear that the main thrust of my proposal will support the involvement of more parents in the school system and the improvement of educational opportunities within the black community. Some critics will view this as an "enrichment" proposal, or as an effort at "compensatory" education, or even as a black power move to maintain and further divisiveness in the society. I simply acknowledge these criticisms at the outset and intend to let my proposal stand on its own merits.

A Crisis of Educational Legitimacy

It is absolutely crucial to understand that the society cannot continue to write reports accurately describing the failure of the educational institutions *vis-à-vis* black people without ultimately taking into account the impact those truths will have on black Americans. There comes a point when it is no longer possible to recognize institutional failure and then merely propose more stepped-up measures to overcome those failures—especially when the proposals come from the same kinds of people who administered for so long the present unacceptable and dysfunctional policies and systems. Professor Seymour Martin Lipset once wrote:

Legitimacy involves the capacity of the system to engender and maintain the belief that the existing political institutions are the most appropriate ones for the society. The extent to which contemporary democratic political systems are legitimate depends in large measure upon the ways in which the key issues which have historically divided the society have been resolved.

While effectiveness is primarily instrumental, legitimacy is evaluative. Groups regard a political system as legitimate or illegitimate according to the way in which its values fit with theirs.[1]

And in another place, he has written:

All claims to a legitimate title to rule in new states must ultimately win acceptance through demonstrating effectiveness. The loyalty of the different groups to the system must be won through developing *in them* the conviction that this system is the best—or at least an excellent—way to accomplish their objectives. And even claims to legitimacy of a supernatural sort, such as "the gift of grace," are subjected on the part of the populace to a highly pragmatic test—that is, what is the payoff?[2]

The United States gradually acquired legitimacy as a result of being *effective*.[3]

The important point here is that loyalty, allegiance, is predicated on performance. What decision-makers *say* is not of primary importance, but it is important what black people *believe*. Do they *believe* that the school systems are operating in their behalf? Do they *believe* that the schools are *legitimate* in terms of educating their children and inculcating in them a proper sense of values? With the end product (i.e., their children graduating from high school as functional illiterates) clearly before their eyes at home and with volumes of reports documenting lack of payoff, it is not difficult to conclude that black people have good reason to question the legitimacy of the educational systems.

They begin to question the entire process, because they are aware that the schools, while not educating their children, are at the same time supporting a particularly unacceptable situation. They know that the schools are one of the major institutions for socializing their children into the dominant value structure of the society. Professor V. O. Key, Jr. concluded in his book, *Politics, Parties and Pressure Groups:*

In modern societies the school system, in particular, functions as a formidable instrument of political power in its role as a transmitter of the goals, values, and attitudes of the polity. In the selection of values and attitudes to be inculcated, it chooses those cherished by the dominant elements in the political order. By and large the

---

[1] Seymour Martin Lipset, *Political Man: The Social Bases of Politics* (New York: Doubleday, 1963), p. 64.

[2] Seymour Martin Lipset, *The First New Nation: The United States in Historical and Comparative Perspective* (New York: Basic Books, 1963), pp. 45-46. (Emphasis added.)

[3] *Ibid.*, p. 59. (Emphasis in original.)

impact of widely accepted goals, mores, and social values fixes the programs of American schools. When schools diverge from this vaguely defined directive and collide with potent groups in the political system, they feel a pressure to conform.[4]

The relevance of all this is that makers of policy and their advisers must recognize that there is a point beyond which vast numbers of black people *will* become alienated and will no longer view efforts on their behalf, however well-intentioned, as legitimate. When this happens, it behooves decision-makers, if they would search for ways of restoring faith, trust, and confidence, to listen to the demands of the alienated. The "experts" might see integration as socially and educationally sound and desirable, but *their* vision and empirical data might well be, at this juncture, irrelevant. Unless this is understood, I am suggesting that public policy might well find itself in the position of attempting to force its programs on a reluctant black community. And this is hardly a formula for the development of a viable body politic.

A clear example of a paternalistic, objectionable policy is contained in the report of the Chicago Board of Education, *Increasing Desegregation of Faculties, Students, and Vocational Education Programs,* issued August 23, 1967. The Report called for busing black children into all- or predominantly white schools. It contains the very revealing paragraph:

The assignment of students outside their neighborhood may be objected to by Negro parents who prefer that their children attend the segregated neighborhood school. This viewpoint cannot be ignored. Prior to implementation of such a transfer policy the administration must take steps to reassure apprehensive sending area parents that transfer will be beneficial not only in terms of integration but of improved education for their children. The generation of a favorable consensus in the designated sending area is important. *If such a consensus is unobtainable, the transfer program would have to proceed without a popular base.* In the light of the dismal alternatives such a program perhaps should proceed even without consensus, but every effort should be made to attain it.[5]

This is a perpetuation of the pattern of telling the black community what is best for it. My point is that this position will only increase alienation, not alleviate it. At the present time, when the educational systems are perceived as illegitimate, it is highly unlikely that such a policy could lead to success. In order for the program to work, support *must* be obtained from the black community. This means that educational achievement must be conceived more broadly than as the mere acquisition of verbal and mathematical skills. Very many black parents are (for good reason) quite concerned about what happens to the self-image of their black children in predominantly white schools—schools

[4] V. O. Key, Jr., *Politics, Parties and Pressure Groups* (New York: Thomas Y. Crowell Company, 1964), pp. 12-13.
[5] *Increasing Desegregation of Faculties, Students, and Vocational Education Programs* (Board of Education, City of Chicago, August 23, 1967), p. B-20. (Emphasis added.)

which reflect dominant white values and mores. Are these schools prepared to deal with their own white racism? Probably not, and a few summer institutes for white, middle-class teachers cannot prepare them. Are these schools prepared to come to terms with a young black child's search for identity? Will the black child indeed acquire certain skills which show up favorably on standardized tests, but at the same time avoid coming to grips with the fact that he or she should not attempt to be a carbon copy of the culture and ethos of another racial and ethnic group? Virtually all the social scientists, education experts, and public policy-makers who emphasize integration overlook this crucial, intangible, psychological factor. Many concerned black parents and teachers do not overlook it, however. And their viewpoint has nothing to do with black people wanting to perpetuate "separate but unequal" facilities, or with attitudes of "hate whitey." This concern is simply a necessary reaction to the fact that many white (and black) liberal, integration-oriented spokesmen are tuned in to a particular result and overlook other phenomena. They fail to understand that their criteria for "educational achievement" simply might not be relevant anymore.

What I am stating (in as kind a way as possible) is that setting criteria for measuring equal educational opportunity can no longer be the province of the established "experts." The policy-makers must now listen to those for whom they say they are operating; which means of course that they must be willing to share the powers of policy-making. The experts must understand that what is high on the liberal social scientist's agenda does not coincide with the agenda of many black people. The experts are still focusing on the effectiveness of existing educational institutions. Many black people have moved to the evaluation of the legitimacy of these institutions.

American social scientists generally are unable to grasp the meaning of alienation when applied to certain groups in this country. (Most of the recent perceptive literature on alienation and modernization deals with new nations of Africa and Asia.)[6]

Consequently, Grant McConnell, in an important book, *Private Power and American Democracy,* could write:

[6] See: Myron Weiner, ed., *Modernization, The Dynamics of Growth* (New York: Basic Books, 1966);
David Apter, *The Politics of Modernization* (Chicago: University of Chicago Press, 1965);
S. N. Eisenstadt, *Modernization: Protest and Change* (Englewood Cliffs, N. J.: Prentice-Hall, Inc., 1966);
Edward Shils, *Political Development in the New States* (New York: Humanities Press, 1964);
Thomas Hodgkin, *Nationalism in Colonial Africa* (New York: New York University Press, 1957);
K. H. Silvert, *Expectant Peoples: Nationalism and Development* (New York: Random House, 1964);
Lucian W. Pye, *Politics, Personality and Nation Building: Burma's Search for Identity* (New Haven: Yale University Press, 1962).

In general the use of government has depended on a particular group's capacity to isolate the relevant governmental agency from influences other than its own and to establish itself as the agency's constituency—at once giving an air of validity to its own ends and endowing it with the added disciplinary power of public authority over its own members.[7]

And later:

...farm migrant workers, Negroes, and the urban poor have not been included in the system of "pluralist" representation so celebrated in recent years.[8]

Then finally:

It can be readily agreed that if explosive mass movements are a genuine threat to America, a politics of narrow constituencies might be desirable to counter the danger. Small associations probably do provide order and stability for any society. In the United States some associations may serve in this manner to a greater degree than others. The American Civil Liberties Union and the League of Woman Voters have given notable service to American democracy. Trade unions and farm organizations have undoubtedly also been similarly useful at various times. Nevertheless, it should be clear that a substantial price is paid for any guarantee against mass movements provided by a pattern of small constituencies. That price is paid in freedom and equality. Although the price would be worth paying if the danger were grave, it can hardly be argued that such an extremity is present.[9]

There are voices in the black community (accompanied, as we well know, by acts of expressive violence) saying precisely that the danger *is* grave and that the extremity *is* present. The educational systems are particularly vulnerable, because of their very conspicuous inability to "pay-off."

An Alternative Agenda

It is instructive, then, to examine some of the major items presented by certain voices in the black community. Clearly, one source of constructive ideas would be black teachers, those persons who not only teach in ghetto schools, but whose children attend those schools (in most instances), who, themselves, grew up in the black community, and who, for the most part, still live in black communities.[10] Approximately 800 such teachers met in Chicago, June 6-9, 1968, in

[7] Grant McConnell, *Private Power and American Democracy* (New York: Random House, 1965), pp. 346-347.
[8] *Ibid.*, p. 349.
[9] *Ibid.*, pp. 355-356.
[10] In a column entitled "Quality Teaching in Decentralized Slum Schools," Fred M. Hechinger, education editor of *The New York Times*, wrote: "It seems more realistic and, for the long pull, more constructive to face the fact that part of the answer to the crisis must come through the efforts of Negro teachers. If young Negro college graduates can be channeled into these schools and if their greater identification with the children's and the parents' own background can more easily gain the pupils' confidence and attention, then to sacrifice some of the present licensing requirements may be a small price to pay" (*The New York Times*, April 29, 1968).

a national conference and formed the National Association of Afro-American Educators. They did not spend the four days discussing the Coleman Report or the report of the U.S. Civil Rights Commission. One could identify four particular areas of concern at that conference, and these areas coincide to a great extent with the issues raised by associations of Concerned Black Parents as well as various Afro-American History clubs in the high schools around the country.

(1) Control

It was generally concluded that the existing educational systems were not responsive to the wishes of the black community. Therefore, those structural arrangements now operating should be changed substantially. The decision-making process in most ghetto school systems was challenged. The workshop on the black school and the black community issued the following statement:

—Whereas, the educational systems of this nation have criminally failed the Black youth of this country,
—Whereas, Black parents have not had a voice in determining the educational destiny of their youth,
—Whereas, the Black youth and Black parents are demanding relevant education to meet their needs,
—Therefore, be it resolved that we encourage, support and work to organize local communities to control their own schools through local or neighborhood school boards and further that this organization go on record to immediately implement such plans.
—The goal of the National Association of Afro-American Educators should be Black control of the Black Community schools.[11]

One hears these kinds of statements increasingly among newly politicized people in the black communities. The focus has shifted; emphasis is now on viable ways to gain enough leverage to drastically revise a system. Black people, having moved to the stage of questioning the system's very legitimacy, are seeking ways to create a new system. This is difficult for most Americans to understand precisely because they have assumed the continuing legitimacy of the present educational system.

(2) Parent Involvement and Alliance with Black Teachers

It is becoming clearer and clearer that the major agents of control should be black parents in the community working closely with the teachers in the school. For this reason, if no other, many black spokesmen do not favor various compulsory plans for busing black children out of their commmunities into white schools, in some instances, miles away from home. Are we to assume that black parents, like-

---

[11] Excerpt from notes of discussion and reports of workshops of National Association of Afro-American Educators (Chicago, Illinois, 1968). (Mimeographed).

wise, will travel miles across town in the evenings to attend PTA meetings—frequently to be surrounded by a sea of white faces, more articulate and with more organized voting strength? The principle of busing overlooks the very important factor of facilitating black parent participation in the child's schooling. If in fact the home has a critical role to play in the educational process, then we would be well advised not to pursue policies which would make that role more difficult.

The participation of black parents in the child's schooling is one of the points high on the agenda of some black people. And it is clearly at odds with one of the stated objectives of the Redmond Report: to bus black children into white schools, but to maintain a quota (no white elementary school would be over 15 percent black; no high school over 25 percent black), in order to guard against the possibility of a white exodus. James Redmond, Superintendent of Schools in Chicago, said: "Chicago will become a predominantly Negro city unless dramatic action is taken soon ... School authorities (must) quickly achieve and maintain stable racial proportions in changing fringe areas."[12] Trying to placate whites simply is not a matter of top (or high) priority to many black people, especially if it must be done by manipulating black children.

Discussion of parental involvement and control has serious implications for the standards of professionalism we adopt. Black parents might well have different notions about what is methodologically sound, what is substantively valuable. They might well be impatient with some of the theories about teaching reading and writing. And at this stage who is to say that their doubts are not valid? The present approaches have hardly proved efficacious. Therefore, when we get sizeable black parental participation, we are opening up the profession to question and challenge about what constitutes educational legitimacy. No profession welcomes such intrusion from laymen. This is quite understandable; professionals have a vested self-interest. All those years of college courses and practice teaching and certifying exams, all those credentials of legitimacy may be going by the board. But that is precisely what happens in societies which are modernizing, in societies where new groupings—alienated from traditional norms—rise to make new normative demands. It is disturbing, disruptive, painful. It is change. And this is the phenomenon American social science has been unable to come to terms with in the latter half of the twentieth century—especially with reference to the issue of race relations.

[12] Quoted in an editorial in *Chicago Sun-Times*, January 12, 1968, p. 27. The editorial, which favored the Redmond Plan, further stated: "That part of the Redmond Plan that has excited opposition calls for fixing immediately a balanced racial enrollment in those all-white schools that are in the way of the Negro expansion. It would be roughly 90 per cent white, 10 per cent Negro. The Negro pupils (who are from middle-class families) would be acceptable to white families and keep them anchored in the neighborhood, whereas they would flee to the suburbs if the Negro proportion became greater than 25 per cent. The plan may not work. If it does it is at best only a holding action until the entire metropolitan area faces up to the demographic realities of our time. But it should be tried."

(3) Psychological Impact

A third matter of concern to these new black voices is the psychological impact of educational institutions on the black children. Many black people are demanding more black principals in predominantly black schools, if only because they serve as positive role models for the children. Children should be able to see black people in positions of day-to-day power and authority. There is a demand to have the schools recognize *black* heroes with national holidays. There is concern for emphasizing group solidarity and pride, which is crucial for the development of black Americans. And there is very serious question whether a predominantly white, middle-class ethos can perform this function. Again, the Coleman data measure verbal skills and mathematical abilities, but there are other areas of equal importance. One should not assume that symbols of cultural pride are unimportant. Professor Lipset was correct when he described the impact of these symbols, but he was incomplete when he applied them to the United States—when the growing awareness of black Americans is taken into account. He wrote:

A major test of legitimacy is the extent to which given nations have developed a common "secular political culture," mainly national rituals and holidays. The United States has developed a common homogeneous culture in the veneration accorded the Founding Fathers, Abraham Lincoln, Theodore Roosevelt, and their principles.[13]

The schools serve as a major instrument to transmit such a common homogeneous culture. And yet, we are beginning to see black Americans call for the recognition of other heroes: Frederick Douglass, Martin Luther King, Jr., Malcolm X, and so forth. Students are demanding that the traditional Awards Day programs at their schools include such awards as a Malcolm X Manliness Award, a Marcus Garvey Citizenship Award, and Frederick Douglass and Martin Luther King, Jr. Human Rights Awards. We see black writers challenging the idea of a common secular political culture. John Oliver Killens and Lerone Bennett, Jr. are two prominent examples. Killens captured the mood when he wrote:

We (black Americans) even have a different historical perspective. Most white Americans, even today, look upon the Reconstruction period as a horrible time of "carpet-bagging," and "black politicians," and "black corruption," the absolutely lowest ebb in the Great American Story . . .

We black folk, however, look upon Reconstruction as the most democratic period in the history of this nation; a time when the dream the founders dreamed was almost within reach and right there for the taking; a time of democratic fervor the like of which was never seen before and never since . . .

For us, Reconstruction was the time when two black men were Senators in the Congress of the United States from the State of Mississippi; when black men served in the legis-

---

[13] Lipset, *Political Man*, p. 68.

319

latures of all the states in Dixie; and when those "corrupt" legislatures gave to the South its first public-school education . . .[14]

Even our white hero symbols are different from yours. You give us moody Abe Lincoln, but many of us prefer John Brown, whom most of you hold in contempt as a fanatic; meaning, of course, that the firm dedication of any white man to the freedom of the black man is *prima-facie* evidence of perversion or insanity.[15]

And Lerone Bennett, Jr. challenged much of American historical scholarship when he challenged the role and image of Abraham Lincoln:

Abraham Lincoln was *not* the Great Emancipator. As we shall see, there is abundant evidence to indicate that the Emancipation Proclamation was not what people think it is and that Lincoln issued it with extreme misgivings and reservations.[16]

A growing number of black Americans are insisting that the schools begin to reflect this new concern, this new tension. We simply cannot assume a common secular political culture. If we continue to operate on such false assumptions, we will continue to misunderstand the very deep feeling of alienation in the black community. And misunderstanding cannot be a viable basis for enlightened public policy. Likewise, it is not only important that Afro-American history be taught in the black schools, but that it also be incorporated into the curriculum of white schools throughout this country. It is not sufficient that only black children be given an accurate historical picture of the race; all Americans must have this exposure—in the inner city, the suburbs, the rural schools.

Who can predict what the "tests" will show when we begin to expose black children to these kinds of innovations? What sort of impact will this have on the motivation of those "slow learners," those "high risks," those (and here is the misnomer of them all) "culturally deprived?" The legitimacy of the "standardized tests" must be questioned as long as they overlook these very essential components.

(4) Curricula and Instructional Materials

Closely related to the third point is a concern with the kinds and content of materials used, especially in black schools. How are black people portrayed? Do the textbooks reflect the real experience of black Americans in history and in contemporary society? The workshop on instructional materials at the Afro-American Educators Conference concluded:

In each local community black educators must develop criteria for selection of materials which will be presented to the Board of Education, to local textbook committees,

---

[14] John Oliver Killens, *Black Man's Burden* (New York: Trident Press, 1965), pp. 14-15.
[15] *Ibid.*, p. 17.
[16] Lerone Bennett, Jr., "Was Abe Lincoln a White Supremacist?" *Ebony*, 23, No. 4 (February, 1968), p. 35.

and to the major publishing houses which provide text and supplemental materials to that community. It is incumbent upon us, if we are to serve this society, that instructional material which we select be both educationally sound and incorporate a strong black orientation.

Black classroom teachers must help black students to speak the language of the market place and assist them as they move back and forth between "their own thing and a white American thing." Since all groups usually speak two languages, one at home and within their group and another in the economic world; by nurturing and respecting our own language and effectively manipulating the other we will become a truly bilingual people. This is necessary to achieve a viable economic base . . .

Black teachers must become connected with major textbook publishing firms as authors, editors and consultants to create the materials available on the market. We must pressure major publishers to reflect the needs of black children in schools. We will work for a factual inclusion of the scientific contribution of black scientists to medical and scientific advancement. For example, Dr. Daniel Hale Williams (open heart surgery) and Dr. Charles Drew (developer of blood plasma) must receive their rightful place in elementary and secondary science texts.[17]

These are some of the things on the agenda of many black people as they consider possible solutions of our vast educational problems. It is far too soon to evaluate the results of most of these proposals—in some instances they have not even been implemented. And in most cases they are in the embryonic stage. We are without precedent in these matters, and it would be presumptuous of American social scientists to attempt to prejudge results, or even to suppose that they could. Black people are searching for new forms of educational legitimacy, and in that kind of modernizing atmosphere the traditional criteria for measuring effectiveness might well be irrelevant and anachronistic.

An Alternative Model

The rhetoric of race and education, as stated earlier, is prolific with dichotomies of segregation vs. integration, quality education vs. integrated education, compensatory programs vs. busing, and so forth. Too much is assumed by these simplistic terms, and a superficial use of these labels frequently restricts and predetermines discussion at the outset. While this is unfortunate, it is probably unavoidable, given the historical context and the highly emotional atmosphere. Those persons favoring "neighborhood" schools and opposing busing have traditionally been, in the North, white parents and taxpayer groups, usually identified as anti-Negro in their basic racial views. These groups would normally be found opposing open housing laws as well. Therefore their motivations are

[17] Excerpt from notes and discussion and reports of workshops of National Association of Afro-American Educators. (Chicago, Illinois, 1968). (Mimeographed.)

questioned when they argue that they are essentially concerned about "educational standards" and property values. When it is pointed out to them that white students do not suffer academically and (if panic selling is avoided) property values do not go down, they do not listen. And their intransigence leads their opponents to label them as racial bigots and segregationists.

Proponents of busing and integration see a positive academic and social value in racially heterogeneous classrooms. Integration to these people is virtually synonymous with quality. And black people who once worked for desegregated schools but who no longer do so are viewed as having given up the fight, as having joined the white racists, and, indeed, as having become black racists and advocates of "Black Power separatism."[18]

I state this simply to acknowledge an awareness of some of the positions taken before I proceed to suggest an alternative educational plan. The fact that my ideas would appear more closely akin to the views of some white segregationists whose ultimate goal is to deny educational opportunity to black people is an *appearance* I cannot avoid. It is important however to point out that a close examination of the ultimate goals of my suggestions will indicate a clear divergence from views held by the segregationists. In other words I am motivated by an attempt to find an educational approach which is relevant to black people, not one that perpetuates racism. The plan I am suggesting is not a universal panacea; it is not applicable in all black ghettos. Where it is feasible—particularly in the large urban communities—I strongly propose it for consideration.

This is a model which views the ghetto school as the focal point of community life. The educational system should be concerned with the entire family, not simply with the children. We should think in terms of a Comprehensive Family-Community-School Plan with black parents attending classes, taking an active, day-to-day part in the operation of the school. Parents could be students, teachers, and legitimate members of the local school governing board. A similar plan is already in operation in Chicago: the Family Education Center. There are two centers, the Westinghouse and Doolittle Centers, which provide basic adult education, prevocational and vocational training, and work experience programs.

Mr. William H. Robinson, Director of the Cook County Department of Public Aid, has stated:

The Center's most unique feature is the Child Development Program for the students' (parents') pre-school children, who come to school with their mothers and spend the

---

[18] An example of this attitude was contained in the report of the President's civil disorders commission (Kerner Commission). "The Black Power advocates of today consciously feel that they are the most militant group in the Negro protest movement. Yet they have retreated from a direct confrontation with American society on the issue of integration and, by preaching separatism, unconsciously function as an accommodation to white racism" (*Report of the National Advisory Commission on Civil Disorders* [New York: E. P. Dutton & Company, 1968], p. 235).

day in a well-equipped, professionally staffed nursery school. Mothers can attend classes with the assurance that their children are receiving proper care and mental stimulation. Thus, the program makes participation in an educational program possible for many recipients who were prevented previously because they could not obtain adequate child care services.[19]

Since the inception of the program two years ago, 1,300 adults and 500 children have been involved in the centers.

This concept should be expanded to include fathers as well, those unemployed and willing to obtain skills. Many of these parents could serve as teachers, along with a professional staff. They could teach courses in a number of areas (child care, auto mechanics, art, music, home economics, sewing, etc.) for which they are obviously now trained. The Comprehensive Plan would extend the school program to grades through high school—for adults and children—and it would eliminate the traditional calendar year of September to June. (There is no reason why the educational system could not be revised to take vacations for one month, say in December of post-Christmas, and another month in August. The community educational program would be a year-round function, day and evening.)

The school would belong to the community. It would be a union of children, parents, teachers (specially trained to teach in such communities), social workers, psychologists, doctors, lawyers, and community planners. Parent and community participation and control would be crucial in the hiring and firing of personnel, the selection of instructional materials, and the determination of curriculum content. Absolutely everything must be done to make the system a functioning, relevant part of the lives of the local people. Given the present situation of existing and growing alienation, such involvement is essential.

If it can be demonstrated that such a comprehensive educational institution can gain the basic trust and participation of the black community, it should become the center of additional vital community functions. Welfare, credit unions, health services, law enforcement, and recreational programs—all working under the control of the community—could be built around it. Enlightened private industry would find it a place from which to recruit trained, qualified people and could donate equipment and technical assistance. The several advantages of such a plan are obvious. It deals with the important agencies which are in daily, intimate contact with black people; it reduces a vast, fragmented service bureaucracy which now descends on the black community from many different directions, with cumbersome rules and regulations, uncontrolled by and unaccountable to the community. It provides the black people with a meaningful chance for participation in the very important day-to-day processes

---

[19] Cook County Department of Public Aid, *The Challenge of Change* (Annual report, Chicago, 1967), p. 11.

affecting their lives; it gives them educational and vocational tools for the future. All these things reflect the yearnings and aspirations of masses of black people today.

The Comprehensive Plan envisions the local school as a central meeting place to discuss and organize around community issues, political and economic. All of the establishments functioning under the plan would provide relevant intermediary groups to which the people could relate. The size of the community involved would vary, with several factors to be considered: geography, number of participating agencies, available funds (from federal, state, and local governmental sources), and manageability. At all times, the primary concern would be about the active involvement of people and about their possession of real power to make decisions affecting the Comprehensive Plan. They would hire consultants and experts whose legitimacy would be determined by their relevance to the community, not by a predetermined set of criteria superimposed from outside.

The proposed Comprehensive Plan attempts to come to grips with the understandable alienation discussed in the first section and with the appropriateness of the agenda items described in the second section of the paper. This plan is better understood when one keeps in mind the premise presented earlier: black people are questioning, evaluating the *legitimacy* of existing educational institutions, not simply searching for ways to make those institutions more *effective*. I am suggesting that we are at a point in the process of modernization and social transformation when we must begin to think and act in wholly new normative and structural terms.

The Adult Literacy Process
as Cultural Action for Freedom

PAULO FREIRE

Paulo Freire writes from a Third World perspective, but with obvious implications for education in general. He rejects mechanistic conceptions of the adult literacy process, advocating instead a theory and practice based upon authentic dialogue between teachers and learners. Such dialogue, in Freire's approach, centers upon codified representations of the learners' existential situations and leads not only to their acquisition of literacy skills, but more importantly to their awareness of their right and capacity as human beings to transform reality. Becoming literate, then, means far more than learning to decode the written representation of a sound system. It is truly an act of knowing, through which a person is able to look critically at the culture which has shaped him, and to move toward reflection and positive action upon his world.

Every Educational Practice Implies a Concept of Man and the World

Experience teaches us not to assume that the obvious is clearly understood. So it is with the truism with which we begin: All educational practice implies a theoretical stance on the educator's part. This stance in turn implies—sometimes more, sometimes less explicitly—an interpretation of man and the world. It could not be otherwise. The process of men's orientation in the world involves not just the association of sense images, as for animals. It involves, above all, thought-language; that is, the possibility of the act of knowing through his praxis, by which man transforms reality. For man, this process of orientation in the world can be

This article is part of a longer essay by Paulo Freire, *Cultural Action for Freedom,* Harvard Educational Review Monograph Series, No. 1 (Cambridge, Mass.: Harvard Educational Review, 1970). Copyright © 1970 by Paulo Freire.

The author gratefully acknowledges the contributions of Loretta Slover, who translated this essay, and João da Veiga Coutinho and Robert Riordan, who assisted in the preparation of the manuscript.

Harvard Educational Review   Vol. 40   No. 3   August 1970, 452–477

understood neither as a purely subjective event, nor as an objective or mechanistic one, but only as an event in which subjectivity and objectivity are united. Orientation in the world, so understood, places the question of the purposes of action at the level of critical perception of reality.

If, for animals, orientation in the world means adaptation to the world, for man it means humanizing the world by transforming it. For animals there is no historical sense, no options or values in their orientation in the world; for man there is both an historical and a value dimension. Men have the sense of "project," in contrast to the instinctive routines of animals.

The action of men without objectives, whether the objectives are right or wrong, mythical or demythologized, naive or critical, is not praxis, though it may be orientation in the world. And not being praxis, it is action ignorant both of its own process and of its aim. The interrelation of the awareness of aim and of process is the basis for planning action, which implies methods, objectives, and value options.

Teaching adults to read and write must be seen, analyzed, and understood in this way. The critical analyst will discover in the methods and texts used by educators and students practical value options which betray a philosophy of man, well or poorly outlined, coherent or incoherent. Only someone with a mechanistic mentality, which Marx would call "grossly materialistic," could reduce adult literacy learning to a purely technical action. Such a naive approach would be incapable of perceiving that technique itself as an instrument of men in their orientation in the world is not neutral.

We shall try, however, to prove by analysis the self-evidence of our statement. Let us consider the case of primers used as the basic texts for teaching adults to read and write. Let us further propose two distinct types: a poorly done primer and a good one, according to the genre's own criteria. Let us even suppose that the author of the good primer based the selection of its generative words[1] on a prior knowledge of which words have the greatest resonance for the learner (a practice not commonly found, though it does exist).

Doubtlessly, such an author is already far beyond the colleague who composes his primer with words he himself chooses in his own library. Both authors, however, are identical in a fundamental way. In each case they themselves decompose the given generative words and from the syllables create new words. With these words, in turn, the authors form simple sentences and, little by little, small stories, the so-called reading lessons.

[1] In languages like Portuguese or Spanish, words are composed syllabically. Thus, every non-monosyllabic word is, technically, *generative,* in the sense that other words can be constructed from its de-composed syllables. For a word to be authentically generative, however, certain conditions must be present which will be discussed in a later section of this essay. [At the phonetic level the term *generative word* is properly applicable only with regard to a sound-syllabic reading methodology, while the thematic application is universal. See Sylvia Ashton-Warner's *Teacher* for a different treatment of the concept of generative words at the thematic level.—Editor]

Let us say that the author of the second primer, going one step further, suggests that the teachers who use it initiate discussions about one or another word, sentence, or text with their students.

Considering either of these hypothetical cases we may legitimately conclude that there is an implicit concept of man in the primer's method and content, whether it is recognized by the authors or not. This concept can be reconstructed from various angles. We begin with the fact, inherent in the idea and use of the primer, that it is the teacher who chooses the words and proposes them to the learner. Insofar as the primer is the mediating object between the teacher and students, and the students are to be "filled" with words the teachers have chosen, one can easily detect a first important dimension of the image of man which here begins to emerge. It is the profile of a man whose consciousness is "spatialized," and must be "filled" or "fed" in order to know. This same conception led Sartre, criticizing the notion that "to know is to eat," to exclaim: *"O philosophie alimentaire!"*[2]

This "digestive" concept of knowledge, so common in current educational practice, is found very clearly in the primer.[3] Illiterates are considered "undernourished," not in the literal sense in which many of them really are, but because they lack the "bread of the spirit." Consistent with the concept of knowledge as food, illiteracy is conceived of as a "poison herb," intoxicating and debilitating persons who cannot read or write. Thus, much is said about the "eradication" of illiteracy to cure the disease.[4] In this way, deprived of their character as linguistic signs constitutive of man's thought-language, words are transformed into mere "deposits of vocabulary"—the bread of the spirit which the illiterates are to "eat" and "digest."

This "nutritionist" view of knowledge perhaps also explains the humanitarian character of certain Latin American adult literacy campaigns. If millions of men are illiterate, "starving for letters," "thirsty for words," the word must be *brought* to them to save them from "hunger" and "thirst." The word, according to the naturalistic concept of consciousness implicit in the primer, must be "deposited," not born of the creative effort of the learners. As understood in this concept, man is a passive being, the object of the process of learning to read and write, and not its subject. As object his task is to "study" the so-called reading lessons, which in fact are almost completely alienating and alienated, having so little, if anything, to do with the student's socio-cultural reality.[5]

[2] Jean Paul Sartre, *Situations I* (Paris: Librairie Gallimard, 1947), p. 31.

[3] The digestive concept of knowledge is suggested by "controlled readings," by classes which consist only in lectures; by the use of memorized dialogues in language learning; by bibliographical notes which indicate not only which chapter, but which lines and words are to be read; by the methods of evaluating the students' progress in learning.

[4] See Paulo Freire, "La alfabetizacion de adultos, critica de su vision ingenua; compreension de su vision critica," in *Introducción a la Acción Cultural* (Santiago: ICIRA, 1969).

[5] There are two noteworthy exceptions among these primers: (1) in Brazil, *Viver e Lutar*, developed by a team of specialists of the Basic Education Movement, sponsored by the National

It would be a truly interesting study to analyze the reading texts being used in private or official adult literacy campaigns in rural and urban Latin America. It would not be unusual to find among such texts sentences and readings like the following random samples:[6]

> *A asa é da ave*—"The wing is of the bird."
> *Eva viu a uva*—"Eva saw the grape."
> *O galo canta*—"The cock crows."
> *O cachorro ladra*—"The dog barks."
> *Maria gosta dos animais*—"Mary likes animals."
> *João cuida das arvores*—"John takes care of the trees."

O pai de Carlinhos se chama Antonio. Carlinhos é um bom menino, bem comportado e estudioso—"Charles's father's name is Antonio. Charles is a good, well-behaved, and studious boy."

Ada deu o dedo ao urubu? Duvido, Ada deu o dedo a arara. . . .[7]

Se você trabalha com martelo e prego, tenha cuidado para nao furar o dedo.—"If you hammer a nail, be careful not to smash your finger."[8]

* * * *

"Peter did not know how to read. Peter was ashamed. One day, Peter went to school and registered for a night course. Peter's teacher was very good. Peter knows how to read now. Look at Peter's face. [These lessons are generally illustrated.] Peter is smiling. He is a happy man. He already has a good job. Everyone ought to follow his example."

In saying that Peter is smiling because he knows how to read, that he is happy because he now has a good job, and that he is an example for all to follow, the authors establish a relationship between knowing how to read and getting good jobs which, in fact, cannot be borne out. This naiveté reveals, at least, a failure to perceive the structure not only of illiteracy, but of social phenomena in general. Such an approach may admit that these phenomena exist, but it cannot perceive their relationship to the structure of the society in which they are found. It is as if these phenomena were mythical, above and beyond concrete situations, or the results of the intrinsic inferiority of a certain class of men. Unable to grasp

---

Conference of Bishops. (This reader became the object of controversy after it was banned as subversive by the then governor of Guanabara, Mr. Carlos Lacerda, in 1963.) (2) in Chile, the ESPIGA collection. despite some small defects. The collection was organized by Jefatura de Planes Extraordinarios de Educación de Adultos, of the Public Education Ministry.

[6] Since at the time this essay was written the writer did not have access to the primers, and was, therefore, vulnerable to recording phrases imprecisely or to confusing the author of one or another primer, it was thought best not to identify the authors or the titles of the books.

[7] The English here would be nonsensical, as is the Portuguese, the point being the emphasis on the consonant *d.*—Editor

[8] The author may even have added here, ". . . If, however, this should happen, apply a little mercurochrome."

contemporary illiteracy as a typical manifestation of the "culture of silence," directly related to underdeveloped structures, this approach cannot offer an objective, critical response to the challenge of illiteracy. Merely teaching men to read and write does not work miracles; if there are not enough jobs for men able to work, teaching more men to read and write will not create them.

One of these readers presents among its lessons the following two texts on consecutive pages without relating them. The first is about May 1st, the Labor Day holiday, on which workers commemorate their struggles. It does not say how or where these are commemorated, or what the nature of the historical conflict was. The main theme of the second lesson is *holidays*. It says that "on these days people ought to go to the beach to swim and sunbathe..." Therefore, if May 1st is a holiday, and if on holidays people should go to the beach, the conclusion is that the workers should go swimming on Labor Day, instead of meeting with their unions in the public squares to discuss their problems.

Analysis of these texts reveals, then, a simplistic vision of men, of their world, of the relationship between the two, and of the literacy process which unfolds in that world.

A asa é da ave, Eva viu a uva, o galo canta, and *o cachorro late,* are linguistic contexts which, when mechanically memorized and repeated, are deprived of their authentic dimension as thought-language in dynamic interplay with reality. Thus impoverished, they are not authentic expressions of the world.

Their authors do not recognize in the poor classes the ability to know and even create the texts which would express their own thought-language at the level of their perception of the world. The authors repeat with the texts what they do with the words, i.e., they introduce them into the learners' consciousness as if it were empty space—once more, the "digestive" concept of knowledge.

Still more, the a-structural perception of illiteracy revealed in these texts exposes the other false view of illiterates as marginal men.[9] Those who consider them marginal must, nevertheless, recognize the existence of a reality to which they are marginal—not only physical space, but historical, social, cultural, and economic realities—i.e., the structural dimension of reality. In this way, illiterates have to be recognized as beings "outside of," "marginal to" something, since it is impossible to be marginal to nothing. But being "outside of" or "marginal to" necessarily implies a movement of the one said to be marginal from the center, where he was, to the periphery. This movement, which is an action, presupposes in turn not only an agent but also his reasons. Admitting the existence of men "outside of" or "marginal to" structural reality, it seems legitimate to ask: Who is the author of this movement from the center of the structure to its margin? Do so-called marginal men, among them the illiterates, make the decision to move

[9] [The Portuguese word here translated as *marginal man* is *marginado.* This has a passive sense: he who has been made marginal, or sent outside society; as well as the sense of a state of existence on the fringe of society.—Translator.]

out to the periphery of society? If so, marginality is an option with all that it involves: hunger, sickness, rickets, pain, mental deficiencies, living death, crime, promiscuity, despair, the impossibility of being. In fact, however, it is difficult to accept that 40% of Brazil's population, almost 90% of Haiti's, 60% of Bolivia's, about 40% of Peru's, more than 30% of Mexico's and Venezuela's, and about 70% of Guatemala's would have made the tragic *choice* of their own marginality as illiterates.[10] If, then, marginality is not by choice, marginal man has been expelled from and kept outside of the social system and is therefore the object of violence.

In fact, however, the social structure as a whole does not "expel," nor is marginal man a "being outside of." He is, on the contrary, a "being inside of," within the social structure, and in a dependent relationship to those whom we call falsely autonomous beings, inauthentic beings-for-themselves.

A less rigorous approach, one more simplistic, less critical, more technicist, would say that it was unnecessary to reflect about what it would consider unimportant questions such as illiteracy and teaching adults to read and write. Such an approach might even add that the discussion of the concept of marginality is an unnecessary academic exercise. In fact, however, it is not so. In accepting the illiterate as a person who exists on the fringe of society, we are led to envision him as a sort of "sick man," for whom literacy would be the "medicine" to cure him, enabling him to "return" to the "healthy" structure from which he has become separated. Educators would be benevolent counsellors, scouring the outskirts of the city for the stubborn illiterates, runaways from the good life, to restore them to the forsaken bosom of happiness by giving them the gift of the word.

In the light of such a concept—unfortunately, all too widespread—literacy programs can never be efforts toward freedom; they will never question the very reality which deprives men of the right to speak up—not only illiterates, but all those who are treated as objects in a dependent relationship. These men, illiterate or not, are, in fact, not marginal. What we said before bears repeating: They are not "beings outside of"; they are "beings for another." Therefore the solution to their problem is not to become "beings inside of," but men freeing themselves; for, in reality, they are not marginal to the structure, but oppressed men within it. Alienated men, they cannot overcome their dependency by "incorporation" into the very structure responsible for their dependency. There is no other road to humanization—theirs as well as everyone else's—but authentic transformation of the dehumanizing structure.

From this last point of view, the illiterate is no longer a person living on the fringe of society, a marginal man, but rather a representative of the dominated strata of society, in conscious or unconscious opposition to those who, in the same structure, treat him as a thing. Thus, also, teaching men to read and write is no

[10] UNESCO: La situación educativa en América Latina, Cuadro no. 20, page 263 (Paris, 1960).

longer an inconsequential matter of *ba, be, bi, bo, bu,* of memorizing an alienated word, but a difficult apprenticeship in naming the world.

In the first hypothesis, interpreting illiterates as men marginal to society, the literacy process reinforces the mythification of reality by keeping it opaque and by dulling the "empty consciousness" of the learner with innumerable alienating words and phrases. By contrast, in the second hypothesis—interpreting illiterates as men oppressed within the system—the literacy process, as cultural action for freedom, is an act of knowing in which the learner assumes the role of knowing subject in dialogue with the educator. For this very reason, it is a courageous endeavor to demythologize reality, a process through which men who had previously been submerged in reality begin to emerge in order to re-insert themselves into it with critical awareness.

Therefore the educator must strive for an ever greater clarity as to what, at times without his conscious knowledge, illumines the path of his action. Only in this way will he truly be able to assume the role of one of the subjects of this action and remain consistent in the process.

The Adult Literacy Process as an Act of Knowing

To be an act of knowing the adult literacy process demands among teachers and students a relationship of authentic dialogue. True dialogue unites subjects together in the cognition of a knowable object which mediates between them.

If learning to read and write is to constitute an act of knowing, the learners must assume from the beginning the role of creative subjects. It is not a matter of memorizing and repeating given syllables, words, and phrases, but rather of reflecting critically on the process of reading and writing itself, and on the profound significance of language.

Insofar as language is impossible without thought, and language and thought are impossible without the world to which they refer, the human word is more than mere vocabulary—it is word-and-action. The cognitive dimensions of the literacy process must include the relationships of men with their world. These relationships are the source of the dialectic between the products men achieve in transforming the world and the conditioning which these products in turn exercise on men.

Learning to read and write ought to be an opportunity for men to know what *speaking the word* really means: a human act implying reflection and action. As such it is a primordial human right and not the privilege of a few.[11] Speaking the word is not a true act if it is not at the same time associated with the right of self-expression and world-expression, of creating and re-creating, of deciding and choosing and ultimately participating in society's historical process.

[11] Paulo Freire, "La alfabetizacion de adultos."

In the culture of silence the masses are "mute," that is, they are prohibited from creatively taking part in the transformations of their society and therefore prohibited from being. Even if they can occasionally read and write because they were "taught" in humanitarian—but not humanist—literacy campaigns, they are nevertheless alienated from the power responsible for their silence.

Illiterates know they are concrete men. They know that they do things. What they do not know in the culture of silence—in which they are ambiguous, dual beings—is that men's actions as such are transforming, creative, and re-creative. Overcome by the myths of this culture, including the myth of their own "natural inferiority," they do not know that *their* action upon the world is also transforming. Prevented from having a "structural perception" of the facts involving them, they do not know that they cannot "have a voice," i.e., that they cannot exercise the right to participate consciously in the socio-historical transformation of their society, because their work does not belong to them.

It could be said (and we would agree) that it is not possible to recognize all this apart from praxis, that is, apart from reflection and action, and that to attempt it would be pure idealism. But it is also true that action upon an object must be critically analyzed in order to understand both the object itself and the understanding one has of it. The act of knowing involves a dialectical movement which goes from action to reflection and from reflection upon action to a new action. For the learner to know what he did not know before, he must engage in an authentic process of abstraction by means of which he can reflect on the action-object whole, or, more generally, on forms of orientation in the world. In this process of abstraction, situations representative of how the learner orients himself in the world are proposed to him as the objects of his critique.

As an event calling forth the critical reflection of both the learners and educators, the literacy process must relate *speaking the word* to *transforming reality,* and to man's role in this transformation. Perceiving the significance of that relationship is indispensable for those learning to read and write if we are really committed to liberation. Such a perception will lead the learners to recognize a much greater right than that of being literate. They will ultimately recognize that, as men, they have the right to have a voice.

On the other hand, as an act of knowing, learning to read and write presupposes not only a theory of knowing but a method which corresponds to the theory.

We recognize the indisputable unity between subjectivity and objectivity in the act of knowing. Reality is never just simply the objective datum, the concrete fact, but is also men's perception of it. Once again, this is not a subjectivistic or idealistic affirmation, as it might seem. On the contrary, subjectivism and idealism come into play when the subjective-objective unity is broken.[12]

---

[12] There are two ways to fall into idealism: The one consists of dissolving the real in subjectivity; the other in denying all real subjectivity in the interests of objectivity." Jean Paul Sartre, *Search for a Method,* trans. Hazel E. Barnes (New York: Vintage Books, 1968), p. 33.

The adult literacy process as an act of knowing implies the existence of two interrelated contexts. One is the context of authentic dialogue between learners and educators as equally knowing subjects. This is what schools should be—the theoretical context of dialogue. The second is the real, concrete context of facts, the social reality in which men exist.[13]

In the theoretical context of dialogue, the facts presented by the real or concrete context are critically analyzed. This analysis involves the exercise of abstraction, through which, by means of representations of concrete reality, we seek knowledge of that reality. The instrument for this abstraction in our methodology is codification,[14] or representation of the existential situations of the learners.

Codification, on the one hand, mediates between the concrete and theoretical contexts (of reality). On the other hand, as knowable object, it mediates between the knowing subjects, educators and learners, who seek in dialogue to unveil the "action-object wholes."

This type of linguistic discourse must be "read" by anyone who tries to interpret it, even when purely pictorial. As such, it presents what Chomsky calls "surface structure" and "deep structure."

The "surface structure" of codification makes the "action-object whole" explicit in a purely taxonomic form. The first stage of decodification[15]—or reading—is descriptive. At this stage, the "readers"—or decodifiers—focus on the relationship between the categories constituting the codification. This preliminary focus on the surface structure is followed by problematizing the codified situation. This leads the learner to the second and fundamental stage of decodification, the comprehension of the codification's "deep structure." By understanding the codification's "deep structure" the learner can then understand the dialectic which exists between the categories presented in the "surface structure," as well as the unity between the "surface" and "deep" structures.

In our method, the codification initially takes the form of a photograph or sketch which represents a real existent, or an existent constructed by the learners. When this representation is projected as a slide, the learners effect an operation basic to the act of knowing: they gain distance from the knowable object. This experience of distance is undergone as well by the educators, so that educators and learners together can reflect critically on the knowable object which mediates between them. The aim of decodification is to arrive at the critical level of knowing, beginning with the learner's experience of the situation in the "real context."

[13] See Karel Kosik, *Dialectica de lo Concreto* (Mexico: Grijalbo, 1967).

[14] [*Codification* refers alternatively to the imaging, or the image itself, of some significant aspect of the learner's concrete reality (of a slum dwelling, for example). As such, it becomes both the object of the teacher-learner dialogue and the context for the introduction of the generative word.—Editor]

[15] [Decodification refers to a process of description and interpretation, whether of printed words, pictures, or other "codifications." As such, decodification and decodifying are distinct from the process of decoding, or word-recognition.—Editor.]

Whereas the codified representation is the knowable object mediating between knowing subjects, decodification—dissolving the codification into its constituent elements—is the operation by which the knowing subjects perceive relationships between the codification's elements and other facts presented by the real context —relationships which were formerly unperceived. Codification represents a given dimension of reality as individuals live it, and this dimension is proposed for their analysis in a context other than that in which they live it. Codification thus transforms what was a way of life in the real context into "objectum" in the theoretical context. The learners, rather than receive information about this or that fact, analyze aspects of their own existential experience represented in the codification.

Existential experience is a whole. In illuminating one of its angles and perceiving the inter-relation of that angle with others, the learners tend to replace a fragmented vision of reality with a total vision. From the point of view of a theory of knowledge, this means that the dynamic between codification of existential situations and decodification involves the learners in a constant re-construction of their former "ad-miration" of reality.

We do not use the concept "ad-miration" here in the usual way, or in its ethical or esthetic sense, but with a special philosophical connotation.

To "ad-mire" is to objectify the "not-I." It is a dialectical operation which characterizes man as man, differentiating him from the animal. It is directly associated with the creative dimension of his language. To "ad-mire" implies that man stands over against his "not-I" in order to understand it. For this reason, there is no act of knowing without "ad-miration" of the object to be known. If the act of knowing is a dynamic act—and no knowledge is ever complete—then in order to know, man not only "ad-mires" the object, but must always be "re-ad-miring" his former "ad-miration." When we "re-ad-mire" our former "ad-miration" (always an "ad-miration of") we are simultaneously "ad-miring" the act of "ad-miring" and the object "ad-mired," so that we can overcome the errors we made in our former "ad-miration." This "re-ad-miration" leads us to a perception of an anterior perception.

In the process of decodifying representations of their existential situations and perceiving former perceptions, the learners gradually, hesitatingly, and timorously place in doubt the opinion they held of reality and replace it with a more and more critical knowledge thereof.

Let us suppose that we were to present to groups from among the dominated classes codifications which portray their imitation of the dominators' cultural models—a natural tendency of the oppressed consciousness at a given moment.[16] The dominated persons would perhaps, in self-defense, deny the truth of the

[16] Re the oppressed consciousness, see: Frantz Fanon, *The Wretched of the Earth* (New York: Grove Press, 1968); Albert Memmi, *Colonizer and the Colonized* (New York: Orion Press, 1965); and Paulo Freire, *Pedagogy of the Oppressed* (New York: Seabury Press, 1970).

codification. As they deepened their analysis, however, they would begin to perceive that their apparent imitation of the dominators' models is a result of their interiorization of these models and, above all, of the myths of the "superiority" of the dominant classes which cause the dominated to feel inferior. What in fact is pure interiorization appears in a naive analysis to be imitation. At bottom, when the dominated classes reproduce the dominators' style of life, it is because the dominators live "within" the dominated. The dominated can eject the dominators only by getting distance from them and objectifying them. Only then can they recognize them as their antithesis.[17]

To the extent, however, that interiorization of the dominators' values is not only an individual phenomenon, but a social and cultural one, ejection must be achieved by a type of cultural action in which culture negates culture. That is, culture, as an interiorized product which in turn conditions men's subsequent acts, must become the object of men's knowledge so that they can perceive its conditioning power. Cultural action occurs at the level of superstructure. It can only be understood by what Althusser calls "the dialectic of overdetermination."[18] This analytic tool prevents us from falling into mechanistic explanations or, what is worse, mechanistic action. An understanding of it precludes surprise that cultural myths remain after the infrastructure is transformed, even by revolution.

When the creation of a new culture is appropriate but impeded by interiorized cultural "residue," this residue, these myths, must be expelled by means of culture. Cultural action and cultural revolution, at different stages, constitute the modes of this expulsion.

The learners must discover the reasons behind many of their attitudes toward cultural reality and thus confront cultural reality in a new way. "Re-ad-miration" of their former "ad-miration" is necessary in order to bring this about. The learners' capacity for critical knowing—well beyond mere opinion—is established in the process of unveiling their relationships with the historical-cultural world *in* and *with* which they exist.

We do not mean to suggest that critical knowledge of man-world relationships arises as a verbal knowledge outside of praxis. Praxis is involved in the concrete situations which are codified for critical analysis. To analyze the codification in its "deep structure" is, for this very reason, to reconstruct the former praxis and to become capable of a new and different praxis. The relationship between the *theoretical context,* in which codified representations of objective facts are analyzed, and the *concrete context,* where these facts occur, has to be made real.

Such education must have the character of commitment. It implies a movement

---

[17] See Fanon, *The Wretched;* Freire, *Pedagogy.*

[18] See Louis Althusser, *Pour Marx* (Paris: Librairie François Maspero, 1965); and Paulo Freire, *Annual Report: Activities for 1968, Agrarian Reform, Training and Research Institute ICIRA, Chile,* trans. John Dewitt, Center for the Study of Development and Social Change, Cambridge, Mass., 1969 (mimeographed).

from the *concrete context* which provides objective facts, to the *theoretical context* where these facts are analyzed in depth, and back to the *concrete context* where men experiment with new forms of praxis.

It might seem as if some of our statements defend the principle that, whatever the level of the learners, they ought to reconstruct the process of human knowing in absolute terms. In fact, when we consider adult literacy learning or education in general as an act of knowing, we are advocating a synthesis between the educator's maximally systematized knowing and the learners' minimally systematized knowing—a synthesis achieved in dialogue. The educator's role is to propose problems about the codified existential situations in order to help the learners arrive at a more and more critical view of their reality. The educator's responsibility as conceived by this philosophy is thus greater in every way than that of his colleague whose duty is to transmit information which the learners memorize. Such an educator can simply repeat what he has read, and often misunderstood, since education for him does not mean an act of knowing.

The first type of educator, on the contrary, is a knowing subject, face to face with other knowing subjects. He can never be a mere memorizer, but a person constantly readjusting his knowledge, who calls forth knowledge from his students. For him, education is a pedagogy of knowing. The educator whose approach is mere memorization is anti-dialogic; his act of transmitting knowledge is inalterable. For the educator who experiences the act of knowing together with his students, in contrast, dialogue is the seal of the act of knowing. He is aware, however, that not all dialogue is in itself the mark of a relationship of true knowledge.

Socratic intellectualism—which mistook the definition of the concept for knowledge of the thing defined and this knowledge as virtue—did not constitute a true pedagogy of knowing, even though it was dialogic. Plato's theory of dialogue failed to go beyond the Socratic theory of the definition as knowledge, even though for Plato one of the necessary conditions for knowing was that man be capable of a *"prise de conscience,"* and though the passage from *doxa* to *logos* was indispensable for man to achieve truth. For Plato, the *"prise de conscience"* did not refer to what man knew or did not know or knew badly about his dialectical relationship with the world; it was concerned rather with what man once knew and forgot at birth. To know was to remember or recollect forgotten knowledge. The apprehension of both *doxa* and *logos,* and the overcoming of *doxa* by *logos* occurred not in the man-world relationship, but in the effort to remember or rediscover a forgotten *logos.*

For dialogue to be a method of true knowledge, the knowing subjects must approach reality scientifically in order to seek the dialectical connections which explain the form of reality. Thus, to know is not to remember something previously known and now forgotten. Nor can *doxa* be overcome by *logos* apart from the dialectical relationship of man with his world, apart from men's reflective action upon the world.

To be an act of knowing, then, the adult literacy process must engage the learners in the constant problematizing of their existential situations. This problematizing employs "generative words" chosen by specialized educators in a preliminary investigation of what we call the "minimal linguistic universe" of the future learners. The words are chosen (a) for their pragmatic value, *i.e.,* as linguistic signs which command a common understanding in a region or area of the same city or country (in the United States, for instance, the word *soul* has a special significance in black areas which it does not have among whites), and (b) for their phonetic difficulties which will gradually be presented to those learning to read and write. Finally, it is important that the first generative word be tri-syllabic. When it is divided into its syllables, each one constituting a syllabic family, the learners can experiment with various syllabic combinations even at first sight of the word.

Having chosen seventeen generative words,[19] the next step is to codify seventeen existential situations familiar to the learners. The generative words are then worked into the situations one by one in the order of their increasing phonetic difficulty. As we have already emphasized, these codifications are knowable objects which mediate between the knowing subjects, educator-learners, learner-educators. Their act of knowing is elaborated in the *circulo de cultura* (cultural discussion group) which functions as the theoretical context.

In Brazil, before analyzing the learners' existential situations and the generative words contained in them, we proposed the codified theme of man-world relationships in general.[20] In Chile, at the suggestion of Chilean educaors, this important dimension was discussed concurrently with learning to read and write. What is important is that the person learning words be concomitantly engaged in a critical analysis of the social framework in which men exist. For example, the word *favela* in Rio de Janeiro, Brazil, and the word *callampa* in Chile, represent, each with its own nuances, the same social, economic, and cultural reality of the vast numbers of slum dwellers in those countries. If *favela* and *callampa* are used as generative words for the people of Brazilian and Chilean slums, the codifications will have to represent slum situations.

There are many people who consider slum dwellers marginal, intrinsically wicked and inferior. To such people we recommend the profitable experience of discussing the slum situation with slum dwellers themselves. As some of these

[19] We observed in Brazil and Spanish America, especially Chile, that no more than seventeen words were necessary for teaching adults to read and write syllabic languages like Portuguese and Spanish.
[20] See Paulo Freire, *Educacao como Pratica da Liberdade* (Rio de Janeiro: Paz e Terra, 1967). Chilean Edition (Santiago: ICIRA, 1969).

critics are often simply mistaken, it is possible that they may rectify their mythical clichés and assume a more scientific attitude. They may avoid saying that the illiteracy, alcoholism, and crime of the slums, that its sickness, infant mortality, learning deficiencies, and poor hygiene reveal the "inferior nature" of its inhabitants. They may even end up realizing that if intrinsic evil exists it is part of the structures, and that it is the structures which need to be transformed.

It should be pointed out that the Third World as a whole, and more in some parts than in others, suffers from the same misunderstanding from certain sectors of the so-called metropolitan societies. They see the Third World as the incarnation of evil, the primitive, the devil, sin and sloth—in sum, as historically unviable without the director societies. Such a manichean attitude is at the source of the impulse to "save" the "demon-possessed" Third World, "educating it" and "correcting its thinking" according to the director societies' own criteria.

The expansionist interests of the director societies are implicit in such notions. These societies can never relate to the Third World as partners, since partnership presupposes equals, no matter how different the equal parties may be, and can never be established between parties antagonistic to each other.

Thus, "salvation" of the Third World by the director societies can only mean its domination, whereas in its legitimate aspiration to independence lies its utopian vision: to save the director societies in the very act of freeing itself.

In this sense the pedagogy which we defend, conceived in a significant area of the Third World, is itself a utopian pedagogy. By this very fact it is full of hope, for to be utopian is not to be merely idealistic or impractical but rather to engage in denunciation and annunciation. Our pedagogy cannot do without a vision of man and of the world. It formulates a scientific humanist conception which finds its expression in a dialogical praxis in which the teachers and learners together, in the act of analyzing a dehumanizing reality, denounce it while announcing its transformation in the name of the liberation of man.

For this very reason, denunciation and annunciation in this utopian pedagogy are not meant to be empty words, but an historic commitment. Denunciation of a dehumanizing situation today increasingly demands precise scientific understanding of that situation. Likewise, the annunciation of its transformation increasingly requires a theory of transforming action. However, neither act by itself implies the transformation of the denounced reality or the establishment of that which is announced. Rather, as a moment in an historical process, the announced reality is already present in the act of denunciation and annunciation.[21]

That is why the utopian character of our educational theory and practice is as permanent as education itself which, for us, is cultural action. Its thrust toward denunciation and annunciation cannot be exhausted when the reality denounced today cedes its place tomorrow to the reality previously announced in the de-

[21] Re the utopian dimension of denunciation and proclamation, see Leszek Kolakowski, *Toward a Marxist Humanism* (New York: Grove Press, 1969).

nunciation. When education is no longer utopian, *i.e.,* when it no longer embodies the dramatic unity of denunciation and annunciation, it is either because the future has no more meaning for men, or because men are afraid to risk living the future as creative overcoming of the present, which has become old.

The more likely explanation is generally the latter. That is why some people today study all the possibilities which the future contains, in order to "domesticate" it and keep it in line with the present, which is what they intend to maintain. If there is any anguish in director societies hidden beneath the cover of their cold technology, it springs from their desperate determination that their metropolitan status be preserved in the future. Among the things which the Third World may learn from the metropolitan societies there is this that is fundamental: not to replicate those societies when its current utopia becomes actual fact.

When we defend such a conception of education—realistic precisely to the extent that it is utopian—that is, to the extent that it denounces what in fact is, and finds therefore between denunciation and its realization the time of its praxis —we are attempting to formulate a type of education which corresponds to the specifically human mode of being, which is historical.

There is no annunciation without denunciation, just as every denunciation generates annunciation. Without the latter, hope is impossible. In an authentic utopian vision, however, hoping does not mean folding one's arms and waiting. Waiting is only possible when one, filled with hope, seeks through reflective action to achieve that announced future which is being born within the denunciation.

That is why there is no genuine hope in those who intend to make the future repeat their present, nor in those who see the future as something predetermined. Both have a "domesticated" notion of history: the former because they want to stop time; the latter because they are certain about a future they already "know." Utopian hope, on the contrary, is engagement full of risk. That is why the dominators, who merely denounce those who denounce them, and who have nothing to announce but the preservation of the status quo, can never be utopian nor, for that matter, prophetic.[22]

A utopian pedagogy of denunciation and annunciation such as ours will have to be an act of knowing the denounced reality at the level of alphabetization and post-alphabetization, which are in each case cultural action. That is why there is such emphasis on the continual problematization of the learners' existential situations as represented in the codified images. The longer the problematization proceeds, and the more the subjects enter into the "essence" of the problematized object, the more they are able to unveil this "essence." The more they

---

[22] "The right, as a conservative force, needs no utopia; its essence is the affirmation of existing conditions—a fact and not a utopia—or else the desire to revert to a state which was once an accomplished fact. The Right strives to idealize actual conditions, not to change them. What it needs is fraud not utopia." Kolakowski, *Toward a Marxist Humanism,* pp. 71-72.

unveil it, the more their awakening consciousness deepens, thus leading to the "conscientization" of the situation by the poor classes. Their critical self-insertion into reality, *i.e.*, their conscientization, makes the transformation of their state of apathy into the utopian state of *denunciation* and *annunciation* a viable project.

One must not think, however, that learning to read and write precedes "conscientization," or vice-versa. Conscientization occurs simultaneously with the literacy or post-literacy process. It must be so. In our educational method, the word is not something static or disconnected from men's existential experience, but a dimension of their thought-language about the world. That is why, when they participate critically in analyzing the first generative words linked with their existential experience; when they focus on the syllabic families which result from that analysis; when they perceive the mechanism of the syllabic combinations of their language, the learners finally discover, in the various possibilities of combination, their own words. Little by little, as these possibilities multiply, the learners, through mastery of new generative words, expand both their vocabulary and their capacity for expression by the development of their creative imagination.[23]

In some areas in Chile undergoing agrarian reform, the peasants participating in the literacy programs wrote words with their tools on the dirt roads where they were working. They composed the words from the syllabic combinations they were learning. "These men are sowers of the word," said Maria Edi Ferreira, a sociologist from the Santiago team working in the Institute of Training and Research in Agrarian Reform. Indeed, they were not only sowing words, but discussing ideas, and coming to understand their role in the world better and better.

We asked one of these "sowers of words," finishing the first level of literacy classes, why he hadn't learned to read and write before the agrarian reform.

"Before the agrarian reform, my friend," he said, "I didn't even think. Neither did my friends."

"Why?" we asked.

"Because it wasn't possible. We lived under orders. We only had to carry out orders. We had nothing to say," he replied emphatically.

The simple answer of this peasant is a very clear analysis of "the culture of silence." In "the culture of silence," to exist is only to live. The body carries out orders from above. Thinking is difficult, speaking the word, forbidden.

"When all this land belonged to one *latifundio*," said another man in the same conversation, "there was no reason to read and write. We weren't responsible for anything. The boss gave the orders and we obeyed. Why read and write? Now it's a different story. Take me, for example. In the *asentiamiento*,[24] I am respon-

---

[23] "We have observed that the study of the creative aspect of language use develops the assumption that linguistic and mental process are virtually identical, language providing the primary means for free expansion of thought and feeling, as well as for the functioning of creative imagination." Noam Chomsky, *Cartesian Linguistics* (New York: Harper & Row, 1966), p. 31.

[24] After the disappropriation of lands in the agrarian reform in Chile, the peasants who were salaried workers on the large latifundia become "settlers" (*asentados*) during a three-year period

sible not only for my work like all the other men, but also for tool repairs. When I started I couldn't read, but I soon realized that I needed to read and write. You can't imagine what it was like to go to Santiago to buy parts. I couldn't get orientated. I was afraid of everything—afraid of the big city, of buying the wrong thing, of being cheated. Now it's all different."

Observe how precisely this peasant described his former experience as an illiterate: his mistrust, his magical (though logical) fear of the world; his timidity. And observe the sense of security with which he repeats, "Now it's all different."

"What did you feel, my friend," we asked another "sower of words" on a different occasion, "when you were able to write and read your first word?"

"I was happy because I discovered I could make words speak," he replied.

Dario Salas reports,[25] "In our conversations with peasants we were struck by the images they used to express their interest and satisfaction about becoming literate. For example, 'Before we were blind, now the veil has fallen from our eyes'; 'I came only to learn how to sign my name. I never believed I would be able to read, too, at my age', 'Before, letters seemed like little puppets. Today they say something to me, and I can make them talk.'

"It is touching," continues Salas, "to observe the delight of the peasants as the world of words opens to them. Sometimes they would say, 'We're so tired our heads ache, but we don't want to leave here without learning to read and write.' "[26]

The following words were taped during research on "generative themes."[27] They are an illiterate's decodification of a codified existential situation.

"You see a house there, sad, as if it were abandoned. When you see a house with a child in it, it seems happier. It gives more joy and peace to people passing by. The father of the family arrives home from work exhausted, worried, bitter, and his little boy comes to meet him with a big hug, because a little boy is not stiff like a big person. The father already begins to be happier just from seeing his children. Then he really enjoys himself. He is moved by his son's wanting to please him. The father becomes more peaceful, and forgets his problems."

Note once again the simplicity of expression, both profound and elegant, in

---

in which they receive varied assistance from the government through the Agrarian Reform Corporation. This period of "settlement" (*asentamiento*) precedes that of assigning lands to the peasants. This policy is now changing. The phase of "settlement" of the lands is being abolished, in favor of an immediate distribution of lands to the peasants. The Agrarian Reform Corporation will continue, nevertheless, to aid the peasants.

[25] Dario Salas, "Algumas experiencias vividas na Supervisao de Educacao basica," in *A alfabetizacao funcional no Chile*. Report to UNESCO, November, 1968. Introduction: Paulo Freire.

[26] Dario Salas refers here to one of the best adult education programs organized by the Agrarian Reform Corporation in Chile, in strict collaboration with the Ministry of Education and ICIRA. Fifty peasants receive boarding and instruction scholarships for a month. The courses center on discussions of the local, regional, and national situations.

[27] An analysis of the objectives and methodology of the investigation of generative themes lies outside the scope of this essay, but is dealt with in the author's work, *Pedagogy of the Oppressed*.

the peasant's language. These are the people considered absolutely ignorant by the proponents of the "digestive" concept of literacy.

In 1968, an Uruguayan team published a small book, *You Live as You Can* (*Se Vive como se Puede*), whose contents are taken from the tape recordings of literacy classes for urban dwellers. Its first edition of three thousand copies was sold out in Montevideo in fifteen days, as was the second edition. The following is an excerpt from this book.

THE COLOR OF WATER

Water? Water? What is water used for?

"Yes, yes, we saw it (in the picture)."

"Oh, my native village, so far away. . . ."

"Do you remember that village?"

"The stream where I grew up, called Dead Friar . . . you know, I grew up there, a childhood moving from one place to another . . . the color of the water brings back good memories, beautiful memories."

"What is the water used for?"

"It is used for washing. We used it to wash clothes, and the animals in the fields used to go there to drink, and we washed ourselves there, too."

"Did you also use the water for drinking?"

"Yes, when we were at the stream and had no other water to drink, we drank from the stream. I remember once in 1945 a plague of locusts came from somewhere, and we had to fish them out of the water . . . I was small, but I remember taking out the locusts like this, with my two hands—and I had no others. And I remember how hot the water was when there was a drought and the stream was almost dry . . . the water was dirty, muddy, and hot, with all kinds of things in it. But we had to drink it or die of thirst."

The whole book is like this, pleasant in style, with great strength of expression of the world of its authors, those anonymous people, "sowers of words," seeking to emerge from "the culture of silence."

Yes, these ought to be the reading texts for people learning to read and write, and not "Eva saw the grape," "The bird's wing," "If you hammer a nail, be careful not to hit your fingers." Intellectualist prejudices and above all class prejudices are responsible for the naive and unfounded notions that the people cannot write their own texts, or that a tape of their conversations is valueless since their conversations are impoverished of meaning. Comparing what the "sowers of words" said in the above references with what is generally written by specialist authors of reading lessons, we are convinced that only someone with very pronounced lack of taste or a lamentable scientific incompetency would choose the specialists' texts.

Imagine a book written entirely in this simple, poetic, free, language of the people, a book on which inter-disciplinary teams would collaborate in the spirit of true dialogue. The role of the teams would be to elaborate specialized sections of the book in problematic terms. For example, a section on linguistics would deal simply, though not simplistically, with questions fundamental to the learners' critical understanding of language. Let me emphasize again that since one of the important aspects of adult literacy work is the development of the capacity for expression, the section on linguistics would present themes for the learners to discuss, ranging from the increase of vocabulary to questions about communication—including the study of synonyms and antonyms, with its analysis of words in the linguistic context, and the use of metaphor, of which the people are such masters. Another section might provide the tools for a sociological analysis of the content of the texts.

These texts would not, of course, be used for mere mechanical reading, which leaves the readers without any understanding of what is real. Consistent with the nature of this pedagogy, they would become the object of analysis in reading seminars.

Add to all this the great stimulus it would be for those learning to read and write, as well as for students on more advanced levels, to know that they were reading and discussing the work of their own companions. . . .

To undertake such a work, it is necessary to have faith in the people, solidarity with them. It is necessary to be utopian, in the sense in which we have used the word.

Student Social Class and Teacher Expectations: The Self-Fulfilling Prophecy in Ghetto Education

RAY C. RIST

Many studies have shown that academic achievement is highly correlated with social class. Few, however, have attempted to explain exactly how the school helps to reinforce the class structure of the society. In this article Dr. Rist reports the results of an observational study of one class of ghetto children during their kindergarten, first- and second-grade years. He shows how the kindergarten teacher placed the children in reading groups which reflected the social class composition of the class, and how these groups persisted throughout the first several years of elementary school. The way in which the teacher behaved toward the different groups became an important influence on the children's achievement. Dr. Rist concludes by examining the relationship between the "caste" system of the classroom and the class system of the larger society.

A dominant aspect of the American ethos is that education is both a necessary and a desirable experience for all children. To that end, compulsory attendance at some type of educational institution is required of all youth until somewhere in the middle teens. Thus on any weekday during the school year, one can expect slightly over 35,000,000 young persons to be distributed among nearly 1,100,000 classrooms throughout the nation (Jackson, 1968).

There is nothing either new or startling in the statement that there exist gross variations in the educational experience of the children involved. The scope of analysis one utilizes in examining these educational variations will reveal different

This paper is based on research aided by a grant from the United States Office of Education, Grant No. 6-2771. Original Principal Investigator, Jules Henry (deceased) Professor of Anthropology, Washington University. Current Principal Investigators, Helen P. Gouldner, Professor of Sociology, Washington University, and John W. Bennett, Professor of Anthropology, Washington University. The author is grateful for substantive criticism and comments from John Bennett, Marshal Durbin and Helen Gouldner on an earlier draft of this paper.

Harvard Educational Review Vol. 40 No. 3 August 1970, 411–451

variables of importance. There appear to be at least three levels at which analysis is warranted. The first is a macro-analysis of structural relationships where governmental regulations, federal, state, and local tax support, and the presence or absence of organized political and religious pressure all affect the classroom experience. At this level, study of the policies and politics of the Board of Education within the community is also relevant. The milieu of a particular school appears to be the second area of analysis in which one may examine facilities, pupil-teacher ratios, racial and cultural composition of the faculty and students, community and parental involvement, faculty relationships, the role of the principal, supportive services such as medical care, speech therapy, and library facilities—all of which may have a direct impact on the quality as well as the quantity of education a child receives.

Analysis of an individual classroom and the activities and interactions of a specific group of children with a single teacher is the third level at which there may be profitable analysis of the variations in the educational experience. Such micro-analysis could seek to examine the social organization of the class, the development of norms governing interpersonal behavior, and the variety of roles that both the teacher and students assume. It is on this third level—that of the individual classroom—that this study will focus. Teacher-student relationships and the dynamics of interaction between the teacher and students are far from uniform. For any child within the classroom, variations in the experience of success or failure, praise or ridicule, freedom or control, creativity or docility, comprehension or mystification, may ultimately have significance far beyond the boundaries of the classroom situation (Henry, 1955, 1959, 1963).

It is the purpose of this paper to explore what is generally regarded as a crucial aspect of the classroom experience for the children involved—the process whereby expectations and social interactions give rise to the social organization of the class. There occurs within the classroom a social process whereby, out of a large group of children and an adult unknown to one another prior to the beginning of the school year, there emerge patterns of behavior, expectations of performance, and a mutually accepted stratification system delineating those doing well from those doing poorly. Of particular concern will be the relation of the teacher's expectations of potential academic performance to the social status of the student. Emphasis will be placed on the initial presuppositions of the teacher regarding the intellectual ability of certain groups of children and their consequences for the children's socialization into the school system. A major goal of this analysis is to ascertain the importance of the initial expectations of the teacher in relation to the child's chances for success or failure within the public school system. (For previous studies of the significance of student social status to variations in educational experience, cf. Becker, 1952; Hollingshead, 1949; Lynd, 1937; Warner, et al., 1944).

Increasingly, with the concern over intellectual growth of children and the long and close association that children experience with a series of teachers, attention is centering on the role of the teacher within the classroom (Sigel, 1969). A long series of studies have been conducted to determine what effects on children a teacher's values, beliefs, attitudes, and, most crucial to this analysis, a teacher's expectations may have. Asbell (1963), Becker (1952), Clark (1963), Gibson 1965), Harlem Youth Opportunities Unlimited (1964), Katz (1964), Kvaraceus (1965), MacKinnon (1962), Riessman (1962, 1965), Rose (1956), Rosenthal and Jacobson (1968), and Wilson (1963) have all noted that the teacher's expectations of a pupil's academic performance may, in fact, have a strong influence on the actual performance of that pupil. These authors have sought to validate a type of educational self-fulfilling prophecy: if the teacher expects high performance, she receives it, and vice versa. A major criticism that can be directed at much of the research is that although the studies may establish that a teacher has differential expectations and that these influence performance for various pupils, they have not elucidated either the basis upon which such differential expectations are formed or how they are directly manifested within the classroom milieu. It is a goal of this paper to provide an analysis both of the factors that are critical in the teacher's development of expectations for various groups of her pupils and of the process by which such expectations influence the classroom experience for the teacher and the students.

The basic position to be presented in this paper is that the development of expectations by the kindergarten teacher as to the differential academic potential and capability of any student was significantly determined by a series of subjectively interpreted attributes and characteristics of that student. The argument may be succinctly stated in five propositions. First, the kindergarten teacher possessed a roughly constructed "ideal type" as to what characteristics were necessary for any given student to achieve "success" both in the public school and in the larger society. These characteristics appeared to be, in significant part, related to social class criteria. Secondly, upon first meeting her students at the beginning of the school year, subjective evaluations were made of the students as to possession or absence of the desired traits necessary for anticipated "success." On the basis of the evaluation, the class was divided into groups expected to succeed (termed by the teacher "fast learners") and those anticipated to fail (termed "slow learners"). Third, differential treatment was accorded to the two groups in the classroom, with the group designated as "fast learners" receiving the majority of the teaching time, reward-directed behavior, and attention from the teacher. Those designated as "slow learners" were taught infrequently, subjected to more frequent control-oriented behavior, and received little if any supportive behavior from the teacher. Fourth, the interactional patterns between the teacher and the various groups in her class became rigidified, taking on castelike characteristics, during the course of the school year, with the gap in completion of academic material between the two groups widening as the school year progressed. Fifth, a similar process occurred in later years of schooling, but the teachers no longer relied on subjectively interpreted data as the basis for ascertaining differences in students. Rather, they were able to utilize a variety of informational sources related to past performance as the basis for classroom grouping.

Though the position to be argued in this paper is based on a longitudinal study spanning two and one-half years with a single group of black children, additional studies suggest that the grouping of children both between and within classrooms is a rather prevalent situation within American elementary classrooms. In a report released in 1961 by the National Education Association related to data collected during the 1958-1959 school year, an estimated 77.6% of urban school districts (cities with a population above 2500) indicated that they practiced between-classroom ability grouping in the elementary grades. In a national survey of elementary schools, Austin and Morrison (1963) found that "more than 80% reported that they 'always' or 'often' use readiness tests for pre-reading evaluation [in first grade]." These findings would suggest that within-classroom grouping may be an even more prevalent condition than between-classroom grouping. In evaluating data related to grouping within American elementary classrooms, Smith (1971, in press) concludes, "Thus group assignment on the basis of measured 'ability' or 'readiness' is an accepted and widespread practice."

Two grouping studies which bear particular mention are those by Borg (1964) and Goldberg, Passow, and Justman (1966). Lawrence (1969) summarizes the import of these two studies as "the two most carefully designed and controlled studies done concerning ability grouping during the elementary years. . . ." Two school districts in Utah, adjacent to one another and closely comparable in size, served as the setting for the study conducted by Borg. One of the two districts employed random grouping of students, providing all students with "enrichment," while the second school district adopted a group system with acceleration mechanisms present which sought to adapt curricular materials to ability level and also to enable varying rates of presentation of materials. In summarizing Borg's findings, Lawrence states:

In general, Borg concluded that the grouping patterns had no consistent, general effects on achievement at any level . . . . Ability grouping may have motivated bright pupils to realize their achievement potential more fully, but it seemed to have little effect on the slow or average pupils. (p. 1)

The second study by Goldberg, Passow, and Justman was conducted in the New York City Public Schools and represents the most comprehensive study to date on elementary school grouping. The findings in general show results similar to those of Borg indicating that narrowing the ability range within a classroom on some basis of academic potential will in itself do little to produce positive academic change. The most significant finding of the study is that "variability in achievement from classroom to classroom was generally greater than the variability resulting from grouping pattern or pupil ability" (Lawrence, 1969). Thus one may tentatively conclude that teacher differences were at least as crucial to academic performance as were the effects of pupil ability or methods of classroom grouping. The study, however, fails to investigate within-class grouping.

Related to the issue of within-class variability are the findings of the Coleman Report (1966) which have shown achievement highly correlated with individual social class. The strong correlation present in the first grade does not decrease during the elementary years, demonstrating, in a sense, that the schools are not able effectively to close the achievement gap initially resulting from student social class (pp. 290-325). What variation the Coleman Report does find in achievement in the elementary years results largely from within- rather than between-school variations. Given that the report demonstrates that important differences in achievement do not arise from variations in facilities, curriculum, or staff, it concludes:

One implication stands out above all: That schools bring little influence to bear on a child's achievement that is independent of his background and general social context; and that this very lack of independent effect means that the inequalities imposed on children by their home, neighborhood, and peer environment are carried along to become the inequalities with which they confront adult life at the end of school. For equality of educational opportunity through the schools must imply a strong effect of schools that is independent of the child's immediate social environment, and that strong independent effect is not present in American Schools. (p. 325)

It is the goal of this study to describe the manner in which such "inequalities imposed on children" become manifest within an urban ghetto school and the resultant differential educational experience for children from dissimilar social-class backgrounds.

Methodology

Data for this study were collected by means of twice weekly one and one-half hour observations of a single group of black children in an urban ghetto school who began kindergarten in September of 1967. Formal observations were conducted throughout the year while the children were in kindergarten and again in 1969 when these same children were in the first half of their second-grade year. The children were also visited informally four times in the classroom during their first-grade year.[1] The difference between the formal and informal observations consisted in the fact that during formal visits, a continuous handwritten account was taken of classroom interaction and activity as it occurred. Smith and Geoffrey (1968) have labeled this method of classroom observation "microethnography."

---

[1] The author, due to a teaching appointment out of the city, was unable to conduct formal observations of the children during their first-grade year.

The informal observations did not include the taking of notes during the classroom visit, but comments were written after the visit. Additionally, a series of interviews were conducted with both the kindergarten and the second-grade teachers. No mechanical devices were utilized to record classroom activities or interviews.[2]

I believe it is methodologically necessary, at this point, to clarify what benefits can be derived from the detailed analysis of a single group of children. The single most apparent weakness of the vast majority of studies of urban education is that they lack any longitudinal perspective. The complexities of the interactional processes which evolve over time within classrooms cannot be discerned with a single two- or three-hour observational period. Secondly, education is a *social process* that cannot be reduced to variations in IQ scores over a period of time. At best, IQ scores merely give indications of potential, not of process. Third, I do not believe that this school and the classrooms within it are atypical from others in urban black neighborhoods (cf. both the popular literature on urban schools: Kohl, 1967; and Kozol, 1967; as well as the academic literature: Eddy, 1967; Fuchs, 1969; Leacock, 1969; and Moore, 1967). The school in which this study occurred was selected by the District Superintendent as one of five available to the research team. All five schools were visited during the course of the study and detailed observations were conducted in four of them. The principal at the school reported upon in this study commented that I was very fortunate in coming to his school since his staff (and kindergarten teacher in particular) were equal to "any in the city." Finally, the utilization of longitudinal study as a research method in a ghetto school will enhance the possibilities of gaining further insight into mechanisms of adaptation utilized by black youth to what appears to be a basically white, middle-class, value-oriented institution.

The School

The particular school which the children attend was built in the early part of the 1960's. It has classes from kindergarten through the eighth grade and a single special education class. The enrollment fluctuates near the 900 level while the teaching staff consists of twenty-six teachers, in addition to a librarian, two physical education instructors, the principal, and an assistant principal. There are also at the school, on a part-time basis, a speech therapist, social worker, nurse, and doctor, all employed by the Board of Education. All administrators, teachers, staff, and pupils are black. (The author is caucasian.) The school is located in a blighted urban area that has 98% black population within its census district. Within the school itself, nearly 500 of the 900 pupils (55%) come from families supported by funds from Aid to Dependent Children, a form of public welfare.

---

[2] The sections on the observations of the second- and third-grade classrooms have been omitted in this edition.

The Kindergarten Class

Prior to the beginning of the school year, the teacher possessed several different kinds of information regarding the children that she would have in her class. The first was the pre-registration form completed by 13 mothers of children who would be in the kindergarten class. On this form, the teacher was supplied with the name of the child, his age, the name of his parents, his home address, his phone number, and whether he had had any pre-school experience. The second source of information for the teacher was supplied two days before the beginning of school by the school social worker who provided a tentative list of all children enrolled in the kindergarten class who lived in homes that received public welfare funds.

The third source of information on the child was gained as a result of the initial interview with the mother and child during the registration period, either in the few days prior to the beginning of school or else during the first days of school. In this interview, a major concern was the gathering of medical information about the child as well as the ascertaining of any specific parental concern related to the child. This latter information was noted on the "Behavioral Questionnaire" where the mother was to indicate her concern, if any, on 28 different items. Such items as thumb-sucking, bed-wetting, loss of bowel control, lying, stealing, fighting, and laziness were included on this questionnaire.

The fourth source of information available to the teacher concerning the children in her class was both her own experiences with older siblings, and those of other teachers in the building related to behavior and academic performance of children in the same family. A rather strong informal norm had developed among teachers in the school such that pertinent information, especially that related to discipline matters, was to be passed on to the next teacher of the student. The teachers' lounge became the location in which they would discuss the performance of individual children as well as make comments concerning the parents and their interests in the student and the school. Frequently, during the first days of the school year, there were admonitions to a specific teacher to "watch out" for a child believed by a teacher to be a "trouble-maker." Teachers would also relate techniques of controlling the behavior of a student who had been disruptive in the class. Thus a variety of information concerning students in the school was shared, whether that information regarded academic performance, behavior in class, or the relation of the home to the school.

It should be noted that not one of these four sources of information to the teacher was related directly to the academic potential of the incoming kindergarten child. Rather, they concerned various types of social information revealing such facts as the financial status of certain families, medical care of the child, presence or absence of a telephone in the home, as well as the structure of the family in which the child lived, *i.e.*, number of siblings, whether the child lived with both, one, or neither of his natural parents.

The Teacher's Stimulus

When the kindergarten teacher made the permanent seating assignments on the eighth day of school, not only had she the above four sources of information concerning the children, but she had also had time to observe them within the classroom setting. Thus the behavior, degree and type of verbalization, dress, mannerisms, physical appearance, and performance on the early tasks assigned during class were available to her as she began to form opinions concerning the capabilities and potential of the various children. That such evaluation of the children by the teacher was beginning, I believe, there is little doubt. Within a few days, only a certain group of children were continually being called on to lead the class in the Pledge of Allegiance, read the weather calendar each day, come to the front for "show and tell" periods, take messages to the office, count the number of children present in the class, pass out materials for class projects, be in charge of equipment on the playground, and lead the class to the bathroom, library, or on a school tour. This one group of children, that were continually physically close to the teacher and had a high degree of verbal interaction with her, she placed at Table 1.

As one progressed from Table 1 to Table 2 and Table 3, there was an increasing dissimilarity between each group of children at the different tables by at least four major criteria. The first criterion appeared to be the physical appearance of the child. While the children at Table 1 were all dressed in clean clothes that were relatively new and pressed, most of the children at Table 2, and with only one exception at Table 3, were all quite poorly dressed. The clothes were old and often quite dirty. The children at Tables 2 and 3 also had a noticeably different quality and quantity of clothes to wear, especially during the winter months. Whereas the children at Table 1 would come on cold days with heavy coats and sweaters, the children at the other two tables often wore very thin spring coats and summer clothes. The single child at Table 3 who came to school quite nicely dressed came from a home in which the mother was receiving welfare funds, but was supplied with clothing for the children by the families of her brother and sister.

An additional aspect of the physical appearance of the children related to their body odor. While none of the children at Table 1 came to class with an odor of urine on them, there were two children at Table 2 and five children at Table 3 who frequently had such an odor. There was not a clear distinction among the children at the various tables as to the degree of "blackness" of their skin, but there were more children at the third table with very dark skin (five in all) than there were at the first table (three). There was also a noticeable distinction among the various groups of children as to the condition of their hair. While the three boys at Table 1 all had short hair cuts and the six girls at the same table had their hair "processed" and combed, the number of children with either matted or unprocessed hair increased at Table 2 (two boys and three girls) and eight of the children at Table 3 (four boys and four girls). None of the children in the kindergarten class wore their hair in the style of a "natural."

A second major criterion which appeared to differentiate the children at the various tables was their interactional behavior, both among themselves and with the teacher. The several children who began to develop as leaders within the class by giving directions to other members, initiating the division of the class into teams on the playground, and seeking to speak for the class to the teacher ("We want to color now"), all were placed by the teacher at Table 1. This same group of children displayed considerable ease in their interaction with her. Whereas the children at Tables 2 and 3 would often linger on the periphery of groups surrounding the teacher, the children at Table 1 most often crowded close to her.

The use of language within the classroom appeared to be the third major differentiation among the children. While the children placed at the first table were quite verbal with the teacher, the children placed at the remaining two tables spoke much less frequently with her. The children placed at the first table also displayed a greater use of Standard American English within the classroom. Whereas the children placed at the last two tables most often responded to the teacher in black dialect, the children at the first table did so very infrequently. In other words, the children at the first table were much more adept at the use of "school language" than were those at the other tables. The teacher utilized standard American English in the classroom and one group of children was able to respond in a like manner. The frequency of a "no response" to a question from the teacher was recorded at a ratio of nearly three to one for the children at the last two tables as opposed to Table 1. When questions were asked, the children who were placed at the first table most often gave a response.

The final apparent criterion by which the children at the first table were quite noticeably different from those at the other tables consisted of a series of social factors which were known to the teacher prior to her seating the children. Though it is not known to what degree she utilized this particular criterion when she assigned seats, it does contribute to developing a clear profile of the children at the various tables. Table 1 gives a summary of the distribution of the children at the three tables on a series of variables related to social and family conditions. Such variables may be considered to give indication of the relative status of the children within the room, based on the income, education and size of the family. (For a discussion of why these three variables of income, education, and family size may be considered as significant indicators of social status, cf. Frazier, 1962;

TABLE 1

Distribution of Socio-Economic Status Factors by
Seating Arrangement at the Three Tables
in the Kindergarten Classroom

| | Seating Arrangement* | | |
Factors	Table 1	Table 2	Table 3
Income			
1) Families on welfare	0	2	4
2) Families with father employed	6	3	2
3) Families with mother employed	5	5	5
4) Families with both parents employed	5	3	2
5) Total family income below $3,000. /yr**	0	4	7
6) Total family income above $12,000. /yr**	4	0	0
Education			
1) Father ever grade school	6	3	2
2) Father ever high school	5	2	1
3) Father ever college	1	0	0
4) Mother ever grade school	9	10	8
5) Mother ever high school	7	6	5
6) Mother ever college	4	0	0
7) Children with pre-school experience	1	1	0
Family Size			
1) Families with one child	3	1	0
2) Families with six or more children	2	6	7
3) Average number of siblings in family	3-4	5-6	6-7
4) Families with both parents present	6	3	2

* There are nine children at Table 1, eleven at Table 2, and ten children at Table 3.
** Estimated from stated occupation.

Freeman, *et al.*, 1959; Gebhard, *et al.*, 1958; Kahl, 1957; Notestein, 1953; Reiss-man, 1959; Rose, 1956; Simpson and Yinger, 1958.)

Believing, as I do, that the teacher did not randomly assign the children to the various tables, it is then necessary to indicate the basis for the seating arrangement. I would contend that the teacher developed, utilizing some combination of the four criteria outlined above, a series of expectations about the potential performance of each child and then grouped the children according to perceived similarities in expected performance. The teacher herself informed me that the first table consisted of her "fast learners" while those at the last two tables "had no idea of what was going on in the classroom." What becomes crucial in this discussion is to ascertain the basis upon which the teacher developed her criteria of "fast learner" since there had been no formal testing of the children as to their academic potential or capacity for cognitive development. She made evaluative judgments of the expected capacities of the children to perform academic tasks after eight days of school.

Certain criteria became indicative of expected success and others became indicative of expected failure. Those children who closely fit the teacher's "ideal type" of the successful child were chosen for seats at Table 1. Those children that had the least "goodness of fit" with her ideal type were placed at the third table. The criteria upon which a teacher would construct her ideal type of the successful student would rest in her perception of certain attributes in the child that she believed would make for success. To understand what the teacher considered as "success," one would have to examine her perception of the larger society and whom in that larger society she perceived as successful. Thus, in the terms of Merton (1957), one may ask which was the "normative reference group" for Mrs. Caplow that she perceived as being successful.[3] I believe that the reference group utilized by Mrs. Caplow to determine what constituted success was a mixed black-white, well-educated middle class. Those attributes most desired by educated members of the middle class became the basis for her evaluation of the children. Those who possessed these particular characteristics were expected to succeed while those who did not could be expected not to succeed. Highly prized middle-class status for the child in the classroom was attained by demonstrating ease of interaction among adults; high degree of verbalization in Standard American English; the ability to become a leader; a neat and clean appearance; coming from a family that is educated, employed, living together, and interested in the child; and the ability to participate well as a member of a group.

The kindergarten teacher appeared to have been raised in a home where the above values were emphasized as important. Her mother was a college graduate, as were her brother and sisters. The family lived in the same neighborhood for many years, and the father held a responsible position with a public utility company in the city. The family was devoutly religious and those of the family still in the city attend the same church. She and other members of her family were active in a number of civil rights organizations in the city. Thus, it appears that the kindergarten teacher's "normative reference group" coincided quite closely with those groups in which she did participate and belong. There was little discrepancy between the normative values of the mixed black-white educated middle-class and the values of the groups in which she held membership. The attributes indicative of "success" among those of the educated middle class had been attained by the teacher. She was a college graduate, held positions of respect and responsibility in the black community, lived in a comfortable middle-class section of the city in a well-furnished and spacious home, together with her husband earned over $20,000 per year, was active in a number of community organizations, and

[3] The names of all staff and students are pseudonyms. Names are provided to indicate that the discussion relates to living persons, and not to fictional characters developed by the author.

had parents, brother, and sisters similar in education, income, and occupational positions.

The teacher ascribed high status to a certain group of children within the class who fit her perception of the criteria necessary to be among the "fast learners" at Table 1. With her reference group orientation as to what constitute the qualities essential for "success," she responded favorably to those children who possessed such necessary attributes. Her resultant preferential treatment of a select group of children appeared to be derived from her belief that certain behavioral and cultural characteristics are more crucial to learning in school than are others. In a similar manner, those children who appeared not to possess the criteria essential for success were ascribed low status and described as "failures" by the teacher. They were relegated to positions at Table 2 and 3. The placement of the children then appeared to result from their possessing or lacking the certain desired cultural characteristics perceived as important by the teacher.

The organization of the kindergarten classroom according to the expectation of success or failure after the eighth day of school became the basis for the differential treatment of the children for the remainder of the school year. From the day that the class was assigned permanent seats, the activities in the classroom were perceivably different from previously. The fundamental division of the class into those expected to learn and those expected not to permeated the teacher's orientation to the class.

The teacher's rationalization for narrowing her attention to selected students was that the majority of the remainder of the class (in her words) "just had no idea of what was going on in the classroom." Her reliance on the few students of ascribed high social status reached such proportions that on occasion the teacher would use one of these students as an exemplar that the remainder of the class would do well to emulate.

(It is Fire Prevention Week and the teacher is trying to have the children say so. The children make a number of incorrect responses, a few of which follow:) Jim, who had raised his hand, in answer to the question, "Do you know what week it is?" says, "October." The teacher says "No, that's the name of the month. Jane, do you know what special week this is?" and Jane responds, "It cold outside." Teacher says, "No, that is not it either. I guess I will have to call on Pamela. Pamela, come here and stand by me and tell the rest of the boys and girls what special week this is." Pamela leaves her chair, comes and stands by the teacher, turns and faces the rest of the class. The teacher puts her arm around Pamela, and Pamela says, "It fire week." The teacher responds, "Well Pamela, that is close. Actually it is Fire Prevention Week."

On another occasion, the Friday after Hallowe'en, the teacher informed the class that she would allow time for all the students to come to the front of the class and tell of their experiences. She, in reality, called on six students, five of whom sat at Table 1 and the sixth at Table 2. Not only on this occasion, but on others, the teacher focused her attention on the experiences of the higher status students.[4]

(The students are involved in acting out a skit arranged by the teacher on how a family should come together to eat the evening meal.) The students acting the roles of mother, father, and daughter are all from Table 1. The boy playing the son is from Table 2. At the small dinner table set up in the center of the classroom, the four children are supposed to be sharing with each other what they had done during the day—the father at work, the mother at home, and the two children at school. The Table 2 boy makes few comments. (In real life he has no father and his mother is supported by ADC funds.) The teacher comments, "I think that we are going to have to let Milt (Table 1) be the new son. Sam, why don't you go and sit down. Milt, you seem to be one who would know what a son is supposed to do at the dinner table. You come and take Sam's place."

In this instance, the lower-status student was penalized, not only for failing to have verbalized middle-class table talk, but more fundamentally, for lacking middle-class experiences. He had no actual father to whom he could speak at the dinner table, yet he was expected to speak fluently with an imaginary one.

Though the blackboard was long enough to extend parallel to all three tables, the teacher wrote such assignments as arithmetic problems and drew all illustrations on the board in front of the students at Table 1. A rather poignant example of the penalty the children at Table 3 had to pay was that they often could not see the board material.

Lilly stands up out of her seat. Mrs. Caplow asks Lilly what she wants. Lilly makes no verbal response to the question. Mrs. Caplow then says rather firmly to Lilly, "Sit down." Lilly does. However, Lilly sits down sideways in the chair (so she is still facing the teacher). Mrs. Caplow instructs Lilly to put her feet under the table. This Lilly does. Now she is facing directly away from the teacher and the blackboard where the teacher is demonstrating to the students how to print the letter, "O."

The realization of the self-fulfilling prophecy within the classroom was in its final stages by late May of the kindergarten year. Lack of communication with the teacher, lack of involvement in the class activities and infrequent instruction all characterized the situation of the children at Tables 2 and 3. During one observational period of an hour in May, not a single act of communication was directed towards any child at either Table 2 or 3 by the teacher except for twice commanding "sit down." The teacher devoted her attention to teaching those children at Table 1. Attempts by the children at Table 2 and 3 to elicit the attention of the teacher were much fewer than earlier in the school year.

In June, after school had ended for the year, the teacher was asked to comment on the children in her class. Of the children at the first table, she noted:

[4] Through the remainder of the paper, reference to "high" or "low" status students refers to status ascribed to the student by the teacher. Her ascription appeared to be based on perceptions of valued behavioral and cultural characteristics present or absent in any individual student.

I guess the best way to describe it is that very few children in my class are exceptional. I guess you could notice this just from the way the children were seated this year. Those at Table 1 gave consistently the most responses throughout the year and seemed most interested and aware of what was going on in the classroom.

Of those children at the remaining two tables, the teacher commented:

It seems to me that some of the children at Table 2 and most all the children at Table 3 at times seem to have no idea of what is going on in the classroom and were off in another world all by themselves. It just appears that some can do it and some cannot. I don't think that it is the teaching that affects those that cannot do it, but some are just basically low achievers.

The Students' Response

The students in the kindergarten classroom did not sit passively, internalizing the behavior the teacher directed towards them. Rather, they responded to the stimuli of the teacher, both in internal differentiations within the class itself and also in their response to the teacher. The type of response a student made was highly dependent upon whether he sat at Table 1 or at one of the two other tables. The single classroom of black students did not respond as a homogenous unit to the teacher-inspired social organization of the room.

For the high-status students at Table 1, the response to the track system of the teacher appeared to be at least three-fold. One such response was the directing of ridicule and belittlement towards those children at Tables 2 and 3. At no point during the entire school year was a child from Table 2 or 3 ever observed directing such remarks at the children at Table 1.

Mrs. Caplow says, "Raise your hand if you want me to call on you. I won't call on anyone who calls out." She then says, "All right, now who knows that numeral? What is it, Tony?" Tony makes no verbal response but rather walks to the front of the classroom and stands by Mrs. Caplow. Gregory calls out, "He don't know. He scared." Then Ann calls out, "It sixteen, stupid." (Tony sits at Table 3, Gregory and Ann sit at Table 1.)

Jim starts to say out loud that he is smarter than Tom. He repeats it over and over again, "I smarter than you. I smarter than you." (Jim sits at Table 1, Tom at Table 3.)

Milt came over to the observer and told him to look at Lilly's shoes. I asked him why I should and he replied, "Because they so ragged and dirty." (Milt is at Table 1, Lilly at Table 3.)

When I asked Lilly what it was that she was drawing, she replied, "A parachute." Gregory interrupted and said, "She can't draw nothin'."

The problems of those children who were of lower status were compounded, for not only had the teacher indicated her low esteem of them, but their peers had also turned against them. The implications for the future schooling of a child who lacks the desired status credentials in a classroom where the teacher places high value on middle-class "success" values and mannerisms are tragic.

It must not be assumed, however, that though the children at Tables 2 and 3 did not participate in classroom activities and were systematically ignored by the teacher, they did not learn. I contend that in fact they did learn, but in a fundamentally different way from the way in which the high-status children at Table 1 learned. The children at Table 2 and 3 who were unable to interact with the teacher began to develop patterns of interaction among themselves whereby they would discuss the material that the teacher was presenting to the children at Table 1. Thus I have termed their method of grasping the material "secondary learning" to imply that knowledge was not gained in direct interaction with the teacher, but through the mediation of peers and also through listening to the teacher though she was not speaking to them. That the children were grasping, in part, the material presented in the classroom, was indicated to me in home visits when the children who sat at Table 3 would relate material specifically taught by the teacher to the children at Table 1. *It is not as though the children at Table 2 and 3 were ignorant of what was being taught in the class, but rather that the patterns of classroom interaction established by the teacher inhibited the low-status children from verbalizing what knowledge they had accumulated.* Thus, from the teacher's terms of reference, those who could not discuss must not know. Her expectations continued to be fulfilled, for though the low-status children had accumulated knowledge, they did not have the opportunity to verbalize it and, consequently, the teacher could not know what they had learned. Children at Table 2 and 3 had learned material presented in the kindergarten class, but would continue to be defined by the teacher as children who could not or would not learn.

A second response of the higher status students to the differential behavior of the teacher towards them was to seek solidarity and closeness with the teacher and urge Tables 2 and 3 children to comply with her wishes.

The teacher is out of the room. Pamela says to the class, "We all should clean up before the teacher comes." Shortly thereafter the teacher has still not returned and Pamela begins to supervise other children in the class. She says to one girl from Table 3, "Girl, leave that piano alone." The child plays only a short time longer and then leaves.

The teacher has instructed the students to go and take off their coats since they have come in from the playground. Milt says, "Ok y'al, let's go take off our clothes."

At this time Jim says to the teacher, "Mrs. Caplow, they pretty flowers on your desk." Mrs. Caplow responded, "Yes, Jim, those flowers are roses, but we will not have roses much longer. The roses will die and rest until spring because it is getting so cold outside."

When the teacher tells the students to come from their desks and form a semi-circle around her, Gregory scoots up very close to Mrs. Caplow and is practically sitting in her lap.

Gregory has come into the room late. He takes off his coat and goes to the coat room to hang it up. He comes back and sits down in the very front of the group and is now closest to the teacher.

The higher-status students in the class perceived the lower status and esteem the teacher ascribed to those children at Tables 2 and 3. Not only would the Table 1 students attempt to control and ridicule the Table 2 and 3 students, but they also perceived and verbalized that they, the Table 1 students, were better students and were receiving differential treatment from the teacher.

The children are rehearsing a play, Little Red Riding Hood. Pamela tells the observer, "The teacher gave me the best part." The teacher overheard this comment, smiled, and made no verbal response.

The children are preparing to go on a field trip to a local dairy. The teacher has designated Gregory as the "sheriff" for the trip. Mrs. Caplaw stated that for the field trip today Gregory would be the sheriff. Mrs. Caplow simply watched as Gregory would walk up to a student and push him back into line saying, "Boy, stand where you suppose to." Several times he went up to students from Table 3 and showed them the badge that the teacher had given to him and said, "Teacher made me sheriff."

The children seated at the first table were internalizing the attitudes and behavior of the teacher towards those at the remaining two tables. That is, as the teacher responded from her reference group orientation as to which type of children were most likely to succeed and which type most likely to fail, she behaved towards the two groups of children in a significantly different manner. The children from Table 1 were also learning through emulating the teacher how to behave towards other black children who came from low-income and poorly educated homes. The teacher, who came from a well-educated and middle-income family, and the children from Table 1 who came from a background similar to the teacher's, came to respond to the children from poor and uneducated homes in a strikingly similar manner.

The lower-status students in the classroom from Tables 2 and 3 responded in significantly different ways to the stimuli of the teacher. The two major responses of the Table 2 and 3 students were withdrawal and verbal and physical in-group hostility.

The withdrawal of some of the lower-status students as a response to the ridicule of their peers and the isolation from the teacher occasionally took the form of physical withdrawal, but most often it was psychological.

Betty, a very poorly dressed child, had gone outside and hidden behind the door. . . . Mrs. Caplow sees Betty leave and goes outside to bring her back, says in an authoritative and irritated voice, "Betty, come here right now." When the child returns, Mrs. Caplow seizes her by the right arm, brings her over to the group, and pushes her down to the floor. Betty begins to cry. . . . The teacher now shows the group a large posterboard with a picture of a white child going to school.

The teacher is demonstrating how to mount leaves between two pieces of wax paper. Betty leaves the group and goes back to her seat and begins to color.

The teacher is instructing the children in how they can make a "spooky thing" for Hallowe'en. James turns away from the teacher and puts his head on his desk. Mrs. Caplow looks at James and says, "James, sit up and look here."

The children are supposed to make United Nations flags. They have been told that they do not have to make exact replicas of the teacher's flag. They have before them the materials to make the flags. Lilly and James are the only children who have not yet started to work on their flags. Presently, James has his head under his desk and Lilly simply sits and watches the other children. Now they are both staring into space. . . . (5 minutes later) Lilly and James have not yet started, while several other children have already finished. . . . A minute later, with the teacher telling the children to begin to clean up their scraps, Lilly is still staring into space.

The teacher has the children seated on the floor in front of her asking them questions about a story that she had read to them. The teacher says, "June, your back is turned. I want to see your face." (The child had turned completely around and was facing away from the group.)

The teacher told the students to come from their seats and form a semi-circle on the floor in front of her. The girls all sit very close to the piano where the teacher is seated. The boys sit a good distance back away from the girls and away from the teacher. Lilly finishes her work at her desk and comes and sits at the rear of the group of girls, but she is actually in the middle of the open space separating the boys and the girls. She speaks to no one and simply sits staring off.

The verbal and physical hostility that the children at Tables 2 and 3 began to act out among themselves in many ways mirrored what the Table 1 students and the teacher were also saying about them. There are numerous instances in the observations of the children at Tables 2 and 3 calling one another "stupid," "dummy," or "dumb dumb." Racial overtones were noted on two occasions when one boy called another a "nigger," and on another occasion when a girl called a boy an "almond head." Threats of beatings, "whoppins," and even spitting on a child were also recorded among those at Tables 2 and 3. Also at Table 2, two instances were observed in which a single child hoarded all the supplies for the whole table. Similar manifestations of hostility were not observed among those children at the first table. The single incident of strong anger or hostility by one child at Table 1 against another child at the same table occurred when one accused the other of copying from his paper. The second denied it and an argument ensued.

In the organization of hostility within the classroom, there may be at least the tentative basis for the rejection of a popular "folk myth" of American society, which is that children are inherently cruel to one another and that this tendency towards cruelty must be socialized into socially acceptable channels. The evidence from this classroom would indicate that much of the cruelty displayed was a result of the social organization of the class. Those children at Tables 2 and 3 who displayed cruelty appeared to have learned from the teacher that it was acceptable to act in an aggressive manner towards those from low-income and poorly educated backgrounds. Their cruelty was not diffuse, but rather focused on a specific group—the other poor children. Likewise, the incidence of such behavior increased over time. The children at Tables 2 and 3 did not begin the school year ridiculing and belittling each other. This social process began to emerge with the outline of the social organization the teacher imposed upon the class. The children from the first table were also apparently socialized into a pattern of behavior in which they perceived that they could direct hostility and aggression towards those at Table 2 and 3, but not towards one another. The children in the class learned who was vulnerable to hostility and who was not through the actions of the teacher. She established the patterns of differential behavior which the class adopted.

* * * *

The Caste System Falters

A major objective of this study has been to document the manner in which there emerges within the early grades a stratification system, based both on teacher expectations related to behavioral and attitudinal characteristics of the child and also on a variety of socio-economic status factors related to the background of the child. As noted, when the child begins to move through the grades, the variable of past performance becomes a crucial index of the position of the child within the different classes. The formulation of the system of stratification of the children into various reading groups appears to gain a caste-like character over time in that there was no observed movement into the highest reading group once it had been initially established at the beginning of the kindergarten school year. Likewise, there was no movement out of the highest reading group. There was movement between the second and third reading groups, in that those at the lowest reading table one year are combined with the middle group for a following year, due to the presence of a group of students repeating the grade.

Poor Kids and Public Schools

It has been a major goal of this paper to demonstrate the impact of teacher expectations, based upon a series of subjectively interpreted social criteria, on both the anticipated academic potential and subsequent differential treatment accorded to those students perceived as having dissimilar social status. For the kindergarten teacher, expectations as to what type of child may be anticipated as a "fast learner"

361

appear to be grounded in her reference group of a mixed white-black educated middle class. That is, students within her classroom who displayed those attributes which a number of studies have indicated are highly desired in children by middle-class educated adults as being necessary for future success were selected by her as possessing the potential to be a "fast learner." On the other hand, those children who did not possess the desired qualities were defined by the teacher as "slow learners." None of the criteria upon which the teacher appeared to base her evaluation of the children were directly related to measurable aspects of academic potential. Given that the I. Q. test was administered to the children in the last week of their kindergarten year, the results could not have been of any benefit to the teacher as she established patterns of organization within the class.[5] The I.Q. scores may have been significant factors for the first- and second-grade teachers, but I assume that consideration of past performance was the major determinant for the seating arrangements which they established.[6]

It was evident throughout the length of the study that the teachers made clear the distinctions they perceived between the children who were defined as fast learners and those defined as slow learners. It would not appear incorrect to state that within the classroom there was established by the various teachers a clear system of segregation between the two established groups of children. In the one group were all the children who appeared clean and interested, sought interactions with adults, displayed leadership within the class, and came from homes which displayed various status criteria valued in the middle class. In the other were children who were dirty, smelled of urine, did not actively participate in class, spoke a linguistic dialect other than that spoken by the teacher and students at Table 1, did not display leadership behavior, and came from poor homes often supported by public welfare. I would contend that within the system of segregation established by the teachers, the group perceived as slow learners were ascribed a caste position that sought to keep them apart from the other students.

[5] The results of the I.Q. Test for the kindergarten class indicated that, though there were no statistically significant differences among the children at the three tables, the scores were skewed slightly higher for the children at Table 1. There were, however, children at Tables 2 and 3 who did score higher than several students at Table 1. The highest score came from a student at Table 1 (124) while the lowest came from a student at Table 3 (78). There appear to be at least three alternative explanations for the slightly higher scores by students at Table 1. First, the scores may represent the result of differential treatment in the classroom by Mrs. Caplow, thus contributing to the validation of the self-fulfilling prophecy. That is, the teacher by the predominance of teaching time spent with the Table 1 students, better prepared the students to do well on the examination than was the case for those students who received less teaching time. Secondly, the tests themselves may have reflected strong biases towards the knowledge and experience of middle-class children. Thus, students from higher-status families at Table 1 could be expected to perform better than did the low-status students from Table 3. The test resulted not in a "value free" measure of cognitive capacity, but in an index of family background. Third, of course, would be the fact that the children at the first table did possess a higher degree of academic potential than those at the other tables, and the teacher was intuitively able to discern these differences. This third alternative, however, is least susceptible to empirical verification.

[6] When the second-grade teacher was questioned as to what significance she placed in the results of I.Q. tests, she replied that "They merely confirm what I already know about the student."

The placement of the children within the various classrooms into different reading groups was ostensibly done on the promise of future performance in the kindergarten and on differentials of past performance in later grades. However, the placement may rather have been done from purely irrational reasons that had nothing to do with academic performance. The utilization of academic criteria may have served as the rationalization for a more fundamental process occurring with the class whereby the teacher served as the agent of the larger society to ensure that proper "social distance" was maintained between the various strata of the society as represented by the children.

Within the context of this analysis there appear to be at least two interactional processes that may be identified as having occurred simultaneously within the kindergarten classroom. The first was the relation of the teacher to the students placed at Table 1. The process appeared to occur in at least four stages. The initial stage involved the kindergarten teacher's developing expectations regarding certain students as possessing a series of characteristics that she considered essential for future academic "success." Second, the teacher reinforced through her mechanisms of "positive" differential behavior those characteristics of the children that she considered important and desirable.

Third, the children responded with more of the behavior that initially gained them the attention and support of the teacher. Perceiving that verbalization, for example, was a quality that the teacher appeared to admire, the Table 1 children increased their level of verbalization throughout the school year. Fourth, the cycle was complete as the teacher focused even more specifically on the children at Table 1 who continued to manifest the behavior she desired. A positive interactional scheme arose whereby initial behavioral patterns of the student were reinforced into apparent permanent behavioral patterns, once he had received support and differential treatment from the teacher.

Within this framework, the actual academic potential of the students was not objectively measured prior to the kindergarten teacher's evaluation of expected performance. The students may be assumed to have had mixed potential. However, the common positive treatment accorded to all within the group by the teacher may have served as the necessary catalyst for the self-fulfilling prophecy whereby those expected to do well did so.

A concurrent behavioral process appeared to occur between the teacher and those students placed at Tables 2 and 3. The student came into the class possessing a series of behavioral and attitudinal characteristics that within the frame of reference of the teacher were perceived as indicative of "failure." Second, through mechanisms of reinforcement of her initial expectations as to the future performance of the student, it was made evident that he was not perceived as similar or equal to those at the table of fast learners. In the third stage, the student responded to both the definition and actual treatment given to him by the teacher which emphasized his characteristics of being an educational "failure." Given the high degree of control-oriented behavior directed toward the "slower" learner, the lack of verbal interaction and encouragement, the disproportionally small amount of teaching time given to him, and the ridicule and hostility, the child withdrew from class participation. The fourth stage was the cyclical repetition of behavioral and attitudinal characteristics that led to the initial labeling as an educational failure.

As with those perceived as having high probability of future success, the academic potential of the failure group was not objectively determined prior to evaluation by the kindergarten teacher. This group also may be assumed to have come into the class with mixed potential. Some within the group may have had the capacity to perform academic tasks quite well, while others perhaps did not. Yet the reinforcement by the teacher of the characteristics in the children that she had perceived as leading to academic failure may, in fact, have created the very conditions of student failure. With the "negative" treatment accorded to the perceived failure group, the teacher's definition of the situation may have ensured its emergence. What the teacher perceived in the children may have served as the catalyst for a series of interactions, with the result that the child came to act out within the class the very expectations defined for him by the teacher.

As an alternative explanation, however, the teacher may have developed the system of caste segregation within the classroom, not because the groups of children were so dissimilar they had to be handled in an entirely different manner, but because they were, in fact, so very close to one another. The teacher may have believed quite strongly that the ghetto community inhibited the development of middle-class success models. Thus, it was her duty to "save" at least one group of children from the "streets." Those children had to be kept separate who could have had a "bad" influence on the children who appeared to have a chance to "make it" in the middle class of the larger society. Within this framework, the teacher's actions may be understood not only as an attempt to keep the slow learners away from those fast learners, but to ensure that the fast learners would not be so influenced that they themselves become enticed with the "streets" and lose their apparent opportunity for, future middle-class status.

In addition to the formal separation of the groups within the classroom, there was also the persistence of mechanisms utilized by the teacher to socialize the children in the high reading group with feelings of aversion, revulsion, and rejection towards those of the lower reading groups. Through ridicule, belittlement, physical punishment, and merely ignoring them, the teacher was continually giving clues to those in the high reading group as to how one with high status and a high probability of future success treats those of low status and low probability of future success. To maintain within the larger society the caste aspects of the position of the poor *vis à vis* the remainder of the society, there has to occur the transmission from one generation to another the attitudes and values necessary to legitimate and continue such a form of social organization.

Given the extreme intercomplexity of the organizational structure of this society, the institutions that both create and sustain social organization can neither be held singularly responsible for perpetuating the inequalities nor for eradicating them (cf. Leacock, 1969). The public school system, I believe, is justifiably responsible for contributing to the present structure of the society, but the responsibility is not its alone. The picture that emerges from this study is that the school strongly shares in the complicity of maintaining the organizational perpetuation of poverty and unequal opportunity. This, of course, is in contrast to the formal doctrine of education in this country to ameliorate rather than aggravate the conditions of the poor.

The teachers' reliance on a mixed black-white educated middle class for their normative reference group appeared to contain assumptions of superiority over those of lower-class and status positions. For they and those members of their reference group, comfortable affluence, education, community participation, and possession of professional status may have afforded a rather stable view of the social order. The treatment of those from lower socio-economic backgrounds within the classrooms by the teachers may have indicated that the values highly esteemed by them were not open to members of the lower groups. Thus the lower groups were in numerous ways informed of their lower status and were socialized for a role of lower self-expectations and also for respect and deference towards those of higher status. The social distance between the groups within the classrooms was manifested in its extreme form by the maintenance of patterns of caste segregation whereby those of lower positions were not allowed to become a part of the peer group at the highest level. The value system of the teachers appeared to necessitate that a certain group be ostracized due to "unworthiness" or inherent inferiority. The very beliefs which legitimated exclusion were maintained among those of the higher social group which then contributed to the continuation of the pattern of social organization itself.

It has not been a contention of this study that the teachers observed could not or would not teach their students. They did, I believe, teach quite well. But the high-quality teaching was not made equally accessible to all students in the class. For the students of high socio-economic background who were perceived by the teachers as possessing desirable behavioral and attitudinal characteristics, the classroom experience was one where the teachers displayed interest in them, spent a large proportion of teaching time with them, directed little control-oriented behavior towards them, held them as models for the remainder of the class and continually reinforced statements that they were "special" students. Hypothetically, if the classrooms observed had contained only those students perceived by the teachers as having a desirable social status and a high probability of future success outside the confines of the ghetto community, the teachers could be assumed to have continued to teach well and, under these circumstances, to the entire class.

Though the analysis has focused on the early years of schooling for a single group of black children attending a ghetto school, the implications are far-reaching for those situations where there are children from different status backgrounds within the same classroom. When a teacher bases her expectations of performance on the social status of the student and assumes that the higher the social status, the higher the potential of the child, those children of low social status suffer a stigmatization outside of their own choice or will. Yet there is a greater tragedy than being labeled as a slow learner, and that is being treated as one. The differential amounts of control-oriented behavior, the lack of interaction with the teacher, the ridicule from one's peers, and the caste aspects of being placed in lower reading groups all have implications for the future life style and value of education for the child.

Though it may be argued from the above that the solution to the existence of differential treatment for students is the establishment of schools catering to only a single segment of the population, I regard this as being antithetical to the goals of education—if one views the ultimate value of an education as providing insights and experience with thoughts and persons different from oneself. The thrust of the educational experience should be towards diversity, not homogeneity. It may be utopian to suggest that education should seek to encompass as wide a variety of individuals as possible within the same setting, but it is no mean goal to pursue.

The success of an educational institution and any individual teacher should not be measured by the treatment of the high-achieving students, but rather by the treatment of those not achieving. As is the case with a chain, ultimate value is based on the weakest member. So long as the lower-status students are treated differently in both quality and quantity of education, there will exist an imperative for change.

It should be apparent, of course, that if one desires this society to retain its present social class configuration and the disproportional access to wealth, power, social and economic mobility, medical care, and choice of life styles, one should not disturb the methods of education as presented in this study. This contention is made because what develops a "caste" within the classrooms appears to emerge in the larger society as "class." The low-income children segregated as a caste of "unclean and intellectually inferior" persons may very well be those who in their adult years become the car washers, dishwashers, welfare recipients, and participants in numerous other un- or underemployed roles within this society. The question may quite honestly be asked, "Given the treatment of low-income children from the beginning of their kindergarten experience, for what class strata are they being prepared other than that of the lower class?" It appears that the public school system not only mirrors the configurations of the larger society, but also significantly contributes to maintaining them. Thus the system of public education in reality perpetuates what it is ideologically committed to eradicate—class barriers which result in inequality in the social and economic life of the citizenry.

References*

Adams, R. G. "The Behavior of Pupils in Democratic and Autocratic Social Climates." Abstracts of Dissertations, Stanford University, 1945.

* Although this article has been abridged, the references are in their original form—ED.

Anderson, H. *Studies in Teachers' Classroom Personalities.* Stanford: Stanford University Press, 1946.

Anderson, H.; Brewer, J.; and Reed, M. "Studies of Teachers' Classroom Personalities, III. Follow-up Studies of the Effects of Dominative and Integrative Contacts on Children's Behavior." *Applied Psychology Monograph.* Stanford: Stanford University Press, 1946.

Asbell, B. "Not Like Other Children." *Redbook,* 65 (October, 1963), pp. 114-118.

Austin, Mary C. and Morrison, Coleman. *The First R: The Harvard Report on Reading in Elementary Schools.* New York: Macmillan, 1963.

Becker, H. S. "Social Class Variation in Teacher-Pupil Relationship." *Journal of Educational Sociology,* 1952, *25,* 451-465.

Borg, W. "Ability Grouping in the Public Schools." Cooperative Research Project 557. Salt Lake City: Utah State University, 1964.

Clark, K. B. "Educational Stimulation of Racially Disadvantaged Children." *Education in Depressed Areas.* Edited by A. H. Passow. New York: Columbia University Press, 1963.

Coleman, J. S., *et al. Equality of Educational Opportunity.* Washington, D. C.: United States Government Printing Office, 1966.

Deutsch, M. "Minority Groups and Class Status as Related to Social and Personality Factors in Scholastic Achievement." *The Disadvantaged Child.* Edited by M. Deutsch, *et al.* New York: Basic Books, 1967.

Eddy, E. *Walk the White Line.* Garden City, N. Y.: Doubleday, 1967.

Frazier, E. F. *Black Bourgeoisie.* New York: The Free Press, 1957.

Freeman, R.; Whelpton, P.; and Campbell, A. *Family Planning, Sterility and Population Growth.* New York: McGraw-Hill, 1959.

Fuchs, E. *Teachers Talk.* Garden City, N. Y.: Doubleday, 1967.

Gebhard, P.; Pomeroy, W.; Martin, C.; and Christenson, C. *Pregnancy, Birth and Abortion.* New York: Harper & Row, 1958.

Gibson, G.: "Aptitude Tests." *Science,* 1965, *149,* 583.

Goldberg, M.; Passow, A.; and Justman, J. *The Effects of Ability Grouping.* New York: Teachers College Press, Columbia University, 1966.

Harlem Youth Opportunities Unlimited. *Youth in the Ghetto.* New York: HARYOU, 1964.

Henry, J. "Docility, or Giving the Teacher What She Wants." *Journal of Social Issues,* 1955, *11,* 2.

———. "The Problem of Spontaneity, Initiative and Creativity in Suburban Classrooms." *American Journal of Orthopsychiatry,* 1959, *29,* 1.

———. "Golden Rule Days: American Schoolrooms." *Culture Against Man.* New York: Random House, 1963.

Hollingshead, A. *Elmtown's Youth.* New York: John Wiley & Sons, 1949.

Jackson, P. *Life in Classrooms.* New York: Holt, Rinehart & Winston, 1968.

Kahl, J. A. *The American Class Structure.* New York: Holt, Rinehart & Winston, 1957.

Katz, I. "Review of Evidence Relating to Effects of Desegregation on Intellectual Performance of Negroes." *American Psychologist,* 1964, *19,* 381-399.

Kelly, H. and Thibaut, J. "Experimental Studies of Group Problem Solving and Process." *Handbook of Social Psychology,* Vol. 2. Edited by G. Lindzey. Reading, Mass.: Addison-Wesley, 1954.

Kohl, H. *36 Children.* New York: New American Library, 1967.

Kozol, J. *Death at an Early Age.* Boston: Houghton Mifflin, 1967.

Kvaraceus, W. C. "Disadvantaged Children and Youth: Programs of Promise or Pretense?" Burlingame: California Teachers Association, 1965. (Mimeographed.)

Lawrence, S. "Ability Grouping." Unpublished manuscript prepared for Center for Educational Policy Research, Harvard Graduate School of Education, Cambridge, Mass., 1969.

Leacock, E. *Teaching and Learning in City Schools.* New York: Basic Books, 1969.

Lewin, K.; Lippitt, R.; and White R. "Patterns of Aggressive Behavior in Experimentally Created Social Climates." *Journal of Social Psychology,* 1939, *10,* 271-299.

Lynd, H. and Lynd, R. *Middletown in Transition.* New York: Harcourt, Brace & World, 1937.

MacKinnon, D. W. "The Nature and Nurture of Creative Talent." *American Psychologist,* 1962, *17,* 484-495.

Merton, R. K. *Social Theory and Social Structure.* Revised and Enlarged. New York: The Free Press, 1957.

Moore, A. *Realities of the Urban Classroom.* Garden City, N. Y.: Doubleday, 1967.

Notestein, F. "Class Differences in Fertility." *Class, Status and Power.* Edited by R. Bendix and S. Lipset. New York: The Free Press, 1953.

Preston, M. and Heintz, R. "Effects of Participatory Versus Supervisory Leadership on Group Judgment." *Journal of Abnormal Social Psychology,* 1949, *44,* 345-355.

Reissman, L. *Class in American Society.* New York: The Free Press, 1959.

Riessman, F. *The Culturally Deprived Child.* New York: Harper and Row, 1962.

———. "Teachers of the Poor: A Five Point Program." Burlingame: California Teachers Association, 1965. (Mimeographed.)

Robbins, F. "The Impact of Social Climate upon a College Class." *School Review,* 1952, *60,* 275-284.

Rose, A. *The Negro in America.* Boston: Beacon Press, 1956.

Rosenthal, R. and Jacobson, Lenore. *Pygmalion in the Classroom.* New York: Holt, Rinehart & Winston, 1968.

Sigel, I. "The Piagetian System and the World of Education." *Studies in Cognitive Development.* Edited by D. Elkind and J. Flavell. New York: Oxford University Press, 1969.

Simpson, G. and Yinger, J. M. *Racial and Cultural Minorities.* New York: Harper & Row, 1958.

Smith, L. and Geoffrey, W. *The Complexities of an Urban Classroom.* New York: Holt, Rinehart & Winston, 1968.

Smith, M. "Equality of Educational Opportunity: The Basic Findings Reconsidered." *On Equality of Educational Opportunity.* Edited by F. Mosteller and D. P. Moynihan. New York: Random House, 1971.

Warner, W. L.; Havighurst, R.; and Loeb, M. *Who Shall Be Educated?* New York: Harper & Row, 1944.

Wilson, A. B. "Social Stratification and Academic Achievement." *Education in Depressed Areas.* Edited by A. H. Passow. New York: Teachers College Press, Columbia University, 1963.

Community Colleges
and Social Stratification

JEROME KARABEL

The expansion of the community colleges in recent years repeats an American pattern that couples class-based tracking with "educational inflation." Shaped by a changing economy and by the American ideology of equal opportunity, community colleges are moving toward vocational rather than transfer curricula and are channeling first generation college students into these programs. The author examines the social forces behind the community college movement and the social processes within the community colleges that have produced a submerged class conflict in higher education.

In recent years a remarkable transformation has occurred in American higher education, a change as far-ranging in its consequences as the earlier transformation of the American high school from an elite to a mass institution. At the forefront of this development has been the burgeoning two-year community college movement. Enrolling 153,970 students in 1948, two-year public colleges increased their enrollment by one million over the next twenty years to 1,169,635 in 1968 (Department of Health, Education, and Welfare, 1970, p. 75). This growth in enrollment has been accompanied by an increase in the number of institutions; during the 1960's, the number of community colleges increased from 656 to 1,100. Nationally, one-third of all students who enter higher education today start in a community college. In California, the state with the most intricate network of community colleges, students who begin in a community college represent 80 per cent of all entering students (Medsker & Tillery, 1971, 16-17). In the future, the role of community colleges in the system of higher education promises to become even larger.

A complex set of forces underlies this extraordinary change in the structure of American higher education. One critical factor in the expansion and differ-

I would like to thank Christopher Jencks, David Riesman, Russell Thackrey, and Michael Useem for their comments on an earlier draft of this paper. The author takes full responsibility for the views expressed in this article.

Harvard Educational Review   Vol. 42   No. 4   November 1972, 521-562

entiation of the system of colleges and universities has been a change in the structure of the economy. Between 1950 and 1970, the proportion of technical and professional workers in the labor force rose from 7.1 per cent to 14.5 per cent (Bureau of the Census, 1971a, p. 225). Some of this increase took place among traditional professions, such as law and medicine, but much of it occurred among growth fields such as data processing and the health semi-professions which frequently require more than a high school education but less than a bachelor's degree. Community colleges have been important in providing the manpower for this growing middle-level stratum and, if current projections of occupational trends are correct, they are likely to become indispensable in filling labor force needs during the next few years. Openings for library technicians and dental hygienists, for example, jobs for which community colleges provide much of the training, will number 9,000 and 2,400 respectively per year for the next decade. Overall, the largest growth area until 1980 will be the technical and professional category with a projected increase of 50 per cent (Bushnell and Zagaris, 1972, p. 135). Without these major changes in the American economy, it is extremely unlikely that the community college movement would have attained its present dimensions.

Although a change in the nature of the labor force laid the groundwork for a system of two-year public colleges, the magnitude and shape of the community college movement owe much to American ideology about equal opportunity through education. Observers, both foreign and domestic, have long noted that Americans take pride in their country's openness—in its apparent capacity to let each person advance as far as his abilities can take him, regardless of social origins. This perceived freedom from caste and class is often contrasted to the aristocratic character of many European societies.[1] America, according to the ideology, is the land of opportunity, and the capstone of its open opportunity structure is its system of public education.

Americans have not only believed in the possibility of upward mobility through education, but have also become convinced that, in a society which places considerable emphasis on credentials, the lack of the proper degrees may well be fatal to the realization of their aspirations. In recent years higher education has obtained a virtual monopoly on entrance to middle and upper level positions in the class structure. Table 1 shows that the probability of holding a high status job, in this case defined as a professional or managerial position, increases sharply with the possession of a bachelor's degree. This stress on diplomas has led to a clamor for access to higher education, regardless of social background or past achieve-

---

[1] Contrary to popular perceptions, American and European rates of social mobility, at least as measured by mobility from manual to non-manual occupations, are very similar. For data on this point see Lipset and Bendix (1959).

TABLE 1

Percentage of U. S. Younger Employed Males in Professional and Managerial Occupations, by Level of Educational Attainment, Latter 1960's

Level of Educational Attainment	Percentage, Professional and Managerial
High school graduation only	7
One or two terms of college	13
Three or four terms of college	28
Five to seven terms of college	32
Eight or more terms of college	82

Source: Unpublished tabulations of the October 1967, 1968, and 1969 Current Population Surveys of the Bureau of the Census, in which the occupations of younger persons, and the imputed earnings for the various occupations were related to levels of educational attainment. (Jaffe and Adams, 1972, p. 249)

ments. The American educational system keeps the mobility "contest"[2] open for as long as possible and has been willing and able to accommodate the demands of the populace for universal access to college.

Response to the pressure for entrance led to greater hierarchical differentiation within higher education.[3] Existing four-year colleges did not, for the most part, open up to the masses of students demanding higher education (indeed, selectivity at many of these institutions has increased in recent years); instead, separate two-year institutions stressing their open and democratic character were created for these new students. Herein lies the genius of the community college movement: it seemingly fulfills the traditional American quest for *equality of opportunity* without sacrificing the principle of *achievement*. On the one hand, the openness of the community college[4] gives testimony to the American commitment to equality of opportunity through education; an empirical study by Medsker and Trent (1965) shows that, among students of high ability and low social status, the rate of college attendance varies from 22 per cent in a community with no colleges to 53 per cent in a community with a junior college. On the other hand, the community colleges leave the principle of achievement intact by enabling the state colleges and univer-

[2] See Ralph Turner's "Modes of Social Ascent through Education" (1966) for a discussion of how differing norms in the United States and England lead to patterns of "contest" and "sponsored" mobility.

[3] For an empirical study of hierarchical differentiation within higher education, see Karabel and Austin (1975).

[4] The term "community college" is used in this study to refer to all *public two-year colleges.* Excluded from this definition are private two-year colleges and all four-year colleges and universities. In the text, the terms "junior college" and "two-year college" are used interchangeably with community college though they are not, strictly speaking, synonyms. The name community college has become the more frequently used because of the increasing emphasis of two-year public institutions on fulfilling local needs. Further, as the community college struggled to obtain a distinct identity and as greater stress was placed on two-year programs, the junior college label, which seemingly describes a lesser version of the four-year college geared almost exclusively to transfer, became increasingly inappropriate.

sities to deny access to those citizens who do not meet their qualifications. The latent ideology of the community college movement thus suggests that everyone should have an opportunity to attain elite status, but that once they have had a chance to prove themselves, an unequal distribution of rewards is acceptable. By their ideology, by their position in the implicit tracking system of higher education —indeed, by their very relationship to the larger class structure—the community colleges lend affirmation to the merit principle which, while facilitating individual upward mobility, diverts attention from underlying questions of distributive justice.

The community college movement is part of a larger historical process of educational expansion. In the early twentieth century, the key point of expansion was at the secondary level as the high school underwent a transition from an elite to a mass institution. Then, as now, access to education was markedly influenced by socioeconomic status.[5]

As the high school became a mass institution, it underwent an internal transformation (Trow, 1966). Formerly providing uniform training to a small group of relatively homogeneous students in order to enable them to fill new white-collar jobs, the high school responded to the massive influx of students by developing a differentiated curriculum. The main thrust of this new curriculum was to provide terminal rather than college preparatory education.

Martin Trow places this "first transformation of American secondary education" between 1910 and 1940. During this period, the proportion of the 14 to 17 age group attending rose from about 15 per cent to over 70 per cent. Since World War II, a similar transformation has been taking place in American higher education: in 1945, 16.3 per cent of the 18 to 21 age group was enrolled in college; by 1968, the proportion had grown to 40.8 per cent (Department of Health, Education and Welfare, 1970, p. 67). This growth has been accompanied by increasing differentiation in higher education, with the community colleges playing a pivotal role in this new division of labor. In short, educational expansion seems to lead to some form of tracking which, in turn, distributes people in a manner which is roughly commensurate with both their class origins and their occupational destination.

The process by which the educational system expands without narrowing relative differences between groups or changing the underlying opportunity structure may be referred to as "educational inflation" (cf. Milner, 1972). Like economic inflation, educational inflation means that what used to be quite valuable (e.g., a high

[5] Two of the most comprehensive recent studies of the influence of social class and ability on access to higher education are Sewell and Shah (1967) and Folger et al. (1970). George Counts (1922:149), in a classical empirical study of the American high school of a half century ago, concluded that "in very large measure participation in the privilege of a secondary education is contingent on social and economic status." Similarly, Michael Katz (1968), in a study of public education reform in nineteenth century Massachusetts, found that the early high school was overwhelmingly a middle class institution.

school diploma) is worth less than it once was. As lower socioeconomic groups attain access to a specific level of education, educational escalation is pushed one step higher. When the high school was democratized, sorting continued to take place through the mechanism of tracking, with higher status children taking college preparatory programs and lower status children enrolling in terminal vocational courses; similarly as access to college was universalized, the allocative function continued to occur through the provision of separate schools, two-year community colleges, which would provide an education for most students that would not only be different from a bachelor's degree program, but also shorter. The net effect of educational inflation is thus to vitiate the social impact of extending educational opportunity to a higher level.

If the theory of educational inflation is correct, we would expect that the tremendous expansion of the educational system in the twentieth century has been accompanied by minimal changes in the system of social stratification. Indeed, various studies indicate that the rate of social mobility has remained fairly constant in the last half-century (Lipset and Bendix, 1959; Blau and Duncan, 1967) as has the distribution of wealth and income (Kolko, 1962; Miller, 1971; Jencks, 1972). Apparently, the extension of educational opportunity, however much it may have contributed to other spheres such as economic productivity and the general cultural level of the society, has resulted in little or no change in the overall extent of social mobility and economic inequality.

To observe that educational expansion has not resulted in fundamental changes in the American class structure is in no way to deny that it *has* been critical in providing upward mobility for many individuals. Nor is the assertion that patterns of mobility and inequality have been fairly stable over time meant to reflect upon the intentions of those who were instrumental in changing the shape of the educational system; at work have been underlying social processes, particularly economic and ideological ones, which have helped give shape to the community college.

The thesis of this paper is that the community college, generally viewed as the leading edge of an open and egalitarian system of higher education, is in reality a prime contemporary expression of the dual historical patterns of class-based tracking and of educational inflation. The paper will examine data on the social composition of the community college student body, the flow of community college students through the system of higher education, and the distributive effects of public higher education. Throughout, the emphasis will be on social class and tracking. An analysis of existing evidence will show that the community college is itself the bottom track of the system of higher education both in class origins and occupational destinations of its students. Further, tracking takes place *within* the community college in the form of vocational education. The existence of submerged class conflicts, inherent in a class-based tracking system, will receive considerable attention, with special emphasis on the processes which contribute to these conflicts remaining latent. The paper will conclude with a discussion of the implications of its findings on class and the community college.

The Composition of the Community College Student Body

If community colleges occupy the bottom of a tracking system within higher education that is closely linked to the external class structure, the social composition of the two-year public college should be proportionately lower in status than that of more prestigious four-year institutions. Christopher Jencks and David Riesman, in *The Academic Revolution* (1968, p. 485), however, citing 1966 American Council on Education data, suggest that the "parents of students who enroll at community colleges are slightly *richer* than the parents of students at four-year institutions." This conclusion is derived from the small income superiority students at two-year public colleges had over students at four-year public colleges in 1966; it ignores public universities and all private institutions. Several other studies, most of them more recent, show that community college students *do* come from lower class backgrounds, as measured by income, occupation, and education, than do their counterparts at four-year colleges and universities (Medsker and Trent, 1965; Schoenfeldt, 1968; American Council on Education, 1971; Medsker and Tillery, 1971; Bureau of the Census, 1972).

Table 2 presents data showing the distribution of fathers' occupations at various types of colleges. Community colleges are lowest in terms of social class; they have the fewest children of professionals and managers (16 per cent) and the most of blue-collar workers (55 per cent). Private universities, the most prestigious of the categories and the one linked most closely to graduate and professional schools, have the highest social composition: 49 per cent professional and managerial and only 20 per cent blue-collar. Interestingly, the proportion of middle-level occupations shows little variation among the various types of colleges.

Having demonstrated the lower-middle and working-class character of commu-

TABLE 2

Father's Occupational Classification by Type of College Entered (percentages)

Type of College	Father's Occupational Classification			
	Skilled, Semi-skilled Unskilled	*Semi-professional, Small Business, Sales and Clerical*	*Professional and Managerial*	*Total*
Public two-year	55	29	16	100
Public four-year	49	32	19	100
Private four-year	38	30	32	100
Public university	32	33	35	100
Private university	20	31	49	100

Source: Medsker and Trent (1965)

TABLE 3
Family Income by Type of College Entered (percentages)

| Type of College | Family Income | | | | |
	Under $8,000	$8,000– 12,499	$12,500– 20,000	Over $20,000	Total
Public two-year	27.2	34.8	26.4	11.5	100
Public four-year	25.4	31.7	28.3	14.7	100
Public university	15.1	29.7	32.8	22.3	100
Private university	10.6	20.4	27.3	41.8	100

Source: American Council on Education (1971, p. 39)

nity colleges, it would seem to follow that college type is also related to family income. Table 3, based on nationally representative American Council on Education data for 1971, reveals systematic income differences among the student bodies at various types of colleges. Over one-quarter of all community college students are from relatively low income families (under $8000) compared with about 11 per cent at private universities. Affluent students (over $20,000) comprise 12 per cent of the student body at community colleges but over 40 per cent at private institutions. The four-year public colleges show income distributions between community colleges and private universities.

Prestige differences among colleges also correspond to differences in fathers' educational attainment. In Table 4, American Council on Education data for 1966 show that the proportion of students whose fathers graduated from college ranges from 15 per cent at community colleges to 72.6 per cent at elite institutions (colleges with average Scholastic Aptitude Tests over 650). Over one third of public two-year college students have fathers who did not graduate from high school compared with less than 5 per cent at elite colleges.

The data on occupation, income, and education all run in the same direction and testify to an increase in social class position as one ascends the prestige hier-

TABLE 4
Father's Education by Type of College Entered (percentages)

| Type of College | Father's Education | | | | | | |
	Grammar School or Less	Some High School	High School Graduate	Some College	College Graduate	Post-graduate Degree	Total
Public two-year	12.7	21.3	31.7	19.1	11.5	3.8	100
Public four-year	12.1	19.4	34.7	17.9	11.1	4.8	100
Public university	8.0	13.9	29.0	20.3	19.0	9.8	100
Private university	4.6	9.6	21.9	18.9	24.4	20.5	100
Elite[a]	1.2	3.5	10.6	13.1	31.3	40.5	100

Source: American Council on Education (1967, p. 22)
[a]Elite colleges are defined as institutions having average freshman SAT's over 650. For more data on elite colleges see Karabel and Astin (forthcoming).

archy of colleges and universities. Community colleges, at the bottom of the tracking system in higher education, are also lowest in student body class composition. That college prestige is a rough indicator of factors leading to adult occupational attainment and of adult socioeconomic status itself is borne out by a number of studies (Havemann and West, 1952; Reed and Miller, 1970; Wolfle, 1971; Pierson, 1969; Collins, 1971; Spaeth, 1968; Sharp, 1970; Folger et al., 1970). Thus, the current tracking system in higher education may help transmit inequality intergenerationally. Lower class students disproportionately attend community colleges which, in turn, channel them into relatively low status jobs.

However related attendance at a community college may be to social origins, students are not explicitly sorted into the hierarchically differentiated system of higher education on the basis of social class. More important than class background in predicting where one goes to college is measured academic ability (Folger et al., 1970, pp. 166–167; Karabel and Astin, 1975). Schoenfeldt (1968), using Project TALENT data, reports that junior college students are more like non-college students in terms of academic ability and more like four-year college students in terms of socioeconomic status. A review of research on the ability of junior college students by Cross (1968) concludes that they show substantially less measured academic ability than their four-year counterparts although there is a great diversity in academic ability *among* junior college students. In a sample of 1966 high school graduates in four states who entered community colleges, 19 per cent were in the highest quartile of academic ability (Medsker & Tillery, 1971, p. 38). As is common with aggregate data, generalizations obscure important variations among individuals. In California, where admission to the state colleges and university are limited to the top 33 1/3 and 12 1/2 per cent in ability respectively, approximately 26 and 6 per cent of students who choose a junior college would have been eligible for a state college or university (Coordinating Council, 1969, p. 79).

There is evidence that many high ability students who attend community colleges are of modest social origins. In California, for example, the proportion of eligible students who choose to attend the state colleges or university varies from 22.5 per cent among students from families with incomes of under $4,000 to over 50 per cent in the $20,000-25,000 category (Hansen and Weisbrod, 1969, p. 74). It is assumed that many of these low-income students attend a nearby two-year college. Table 5 estimates the probability of a male student entering a junior college (public and private). The likeliest entrant at a two-year college is the person of high academic ability and low social status followed by the high status student of less than average ability. These data, however, cannot be construed as providing the relative proportion of intelligent, poor students as opposed to mediocre, rich students in the community college; instead, they merely show the probability of attending a two-year college *if* someone falls into a particular category. Table 5 also illustrates that there is a diversity of both social class and academic ability in the

TABLE 5
Probability of a Male Entering a Two-Year College

Socioeconomic Quarter		Ability Quarter			
		Low 1	2	3	High 4
Low	1	.04	.07	.06	.16
	2	.03	.07	.10	.08
	3	.07	.11	.10	.08
High	4	.11	.12	.11	.05

Source: Schoenfeldt (1968, p. 357)

community college. Internal diversity notwithstanding, the community college does indeed stand at the bottom of the tracking system in higher education not only from the perspective of social class, but also from that of academic ability.

Cooling Out: Process and Functions

The preceding section on patterns of attendance among community college students showed large discrepancies between aspirations and their realization. Unrealized educational aspirations, almost always linked to a desire for upward mobility, reach genuinely massive proportions among community college students. Clearly, the social process which enables those who entered the junior college with high hopes never to be realized to adjust to their situation bears close investigation.

The key to this process is what Burton Clark (1960), in a classic case study of San José City College (a two-year institution), referred to as "cooling out." The community college, according to Clark, has three types of students; pure terminal (usually occupational), pure transfer, and latent terminal. The latent terminal student, the one who would like to transfer but who is not likely to meet the qualifications, poses a serious problem for the junior college. The crux of the dilemma is how to gently convince the latent terminal student that a transfer program is inappropriate for him without seeming to deny him the equal educational opportunity that Americans value so highly. Clark does not specify the class origins of these students, but since the modal community college student is of relatively low social status (Cross, 1971) and since SES is itself related to both academic ability and to the probability of dropping out of college, it seems fair to assume that many of them are working class or lower middle class. A great deal is thus at stake here: failure to give these students a "fair shake" would undermine American confidence in the democratic character of the educational system and, very possibly, of the larger society.

"Cooling out," the process described by Clark (pp. 71-76) of handling latent terminal students, begins even before the student arrives as a freshman. A battery of pre-entrance tests are given, and low scores lead to remedial classes which not only cast doubt on the student's promise, but which also slow his movement toward courses for credit. The second step is a meeting with a counselor to arrange the student's class schedule. In view of test scores, high school record, and the student's objectives, the counselor tries to assist the student in choosing a realistic program.[6]

The next step of the process Clark describes in his case study of San José is a specially devised course called "Psychology 5, Orientation to College." A one-unit mandatory course, it is designed to assist the student in selecting a program and places special emphasis on the problem of "unrealistic aspirations." Counselors report that the course provides an ideal opportunity "to talk tough" in an impersonal way to latent terminal students.

The cooling out process has, until this point, been gentle, and the latent-terminal student can refuse to heed the subtle and not-so-subtle hints he has been given. The fourth step of the process, however—dissemination of "need for improvement notices," given to students in courses where they are getting low grades—is impossible to ignore. If the student does not seek guidance, the counselor, with the authority of the disciplinary apparatus behind him, requests to see the student. All of this goes into the student's permanent record.

The fifth and possibly most decisive step of the process is the placing of a student on probation. This is to pressure him into a realistic program. "The real meaning of probation," says Clark, "lies in its killing off the hope of some of the latent terminal students" (p. 75).

The purpose of the drawn-out counseling procedure is not to bludgeon the student into dropping out, but rather to have the student himself decide to switch out of the transfer program. If the student can be persuaded to take himself out of the competition without being forced out of it (through being flunked out), he is much more likely to retain a benign view of the sorting process.

The opaqueness of the cooling out function is indispensable to its successful performance. In a revealing passage, Clark describes the nature of the problem:

A dilemma of this role, however, is that it needs to remain reasonably latent, not clearly perceived and understood by prospective clientele. Should the function become obvious, the ability of the junior college to perform it would be impaired. The realization that the junior college is a place where students reach undesired destinations would turn the pressure for college admission back on the "protected" colleges. The widespread identifica-

---

[6] In discussing the role of guidance in the junior college, it is interesting to observe the connection between the growth of the school counseling profession and educational tracking. As long as the curriculum at a particular level of schooling remains unified, there is relatively little need for guidance. However, when a number of curricula leading to occupations of varying prestige come into being, counseling becomes a virtual necessity. It is worth noting in this connection the long-standing enthusiasm of the business community for guidance programs. George S. Counts, in a study entitled *School and Society in Chicago* (1928), noted the fervor with which the Chicago Association of Commerce, the city's dominant business association, supported the establishment of a program of vocational guidance in the public schools in the early twentieth century.

tion of the junior college as principally a transfer station, aided by the ambiguity of the "community college" label. helps keep this role reasonably opaque to public scrutiny. (p. 165)

The implication of this passage, of course, is that the community college would be unable to perform its task of allowing high aspirations to gently subside if its social function were understood by those most directly affected by it. Clark considers "the student who filters out of education while in the junior college . . . to be very much what such a college is about" (p. 84), and refers to the "transforming of transfer students into terminal students" as the community college's "operational specialty" (p. 146).

One problem with Clark's analysis of the community college is that he perceives the "situation of structured failure" to emerge out of a conflict between the rigourous academic standards of higher education and the non-selective open door. What Clark has failed to do here is to take his analysis a step further to analyze the social function of standards. Rothbart (1970) notes that "objective" academic standards also serve to exclude the poor and minorities from the university. The even-handed application of these standards to all groups gives each individual the feeling that he "had his chance." Academic standards, far from being the quintessential expression of an objective ivory tower concept, justify the university as a means of distributing privilege and of legitimating inequality. This is not to deny that academic standards have important intellectual substance, but it is to say that standards do have a class function. Indeed, what appears to Clark to be a conflict between professors committed to standards and students who do not "measure up" is, in a wider sense, a conflict between low-status students demanding upward mobility and a system unable to fully respond to their aspirations because it is too narrow at the top. Academic standards are located in the midst of this conflict and serve as a "covert mechanism" which, according to Rothbart, enables the university to "do the dirty work for the rest of the society" (p. 174). The cooling out process, the opaqueness of which Clark himself stresses, is thus the expression not only of an academic conflict, but also of a submerged class conflict.

Community colleges, which are located at the very point in the structure of educational and social stratification where cultural aspirations clash head on with the realities of the class system, developed cooling out as a means not only of allocating people to slots in the occupational structure, but also of legitimating the process by which people are sorted. One of its main features is that it causes people to blame themselves rather than the system for their "failure." This process was an organic rather than a conscious one; cooling out was not designed by anyone but rather grew out of the conflict between cultural aspirations and economic reality. Commitment to standards, sincerely held by many academics, may have played a small part in this process, but professorial devotion to academic rigor could disappear and the underlying cultural and structural conflict would remain. Cooling out, or something very much like it, was and is inevitable given this conflict.

The cooling out process not only allows the junior college to perform its sorting and legitimation functions; given the class composition of the community college and the data on attrition, it also enables the two-year college to contribute to the intergenerational transmission of privilege (Bowles, 1971a and 1971b). At the bottom of an increasingly formalized tracking system in higher education, community colleges channel working-class students away from four-year colleges and into middle-level technical occupations. Having gained access to higher education, the low status student is often cooled out and made to internalize his structurally induced failure. The tremendous disjunction between aspirations and their realization, a potentially troublesome political problem, is thus mitigated and the ideology of equal opportunity is sustained. That community colleges have a *negative* impact on persistence, that they do *not* increase the number of bachelor's degrees, that they seem to provide the greatest opportunity for transfer (and hence mobility) to *middle* class students—these are all facts which are unknown to their clientele. The community college movement, seemingly a promising extension of equal educational opportunity, in reality marks the extension of a class-based tracking system into higher education and the continuation of a long historical process of educational escalation without real change.

Tracking Within the Community College—Vocational Education

The subordinate position of the community college within the tracking system of higher education has often been noted. What has been less frequently noted is that tracking also takes place *within* the community college. Two-year public colleges are almost always open door institutions, but admission to programs within them is often on a selective basis. What this generally means in practice is that students who are not "transfer material" are either tracked into vocational programs or cooled out altogether.

Class-based tracking, whether between schools, within schools, or both, is not new in American education. This pattern extends back into the early twentieth century, the period during which the American high school became a mass institution.[7] If the theory of class-based hierarchical differentiation in education is applied to the question of tracking within the community college, it would lead us to expect a relatively low class composition among students in vocational programs.

[7] When George L. Counts examined class differences in secondary schools in the early twenties, he wrote:

These differences in the extent of educational opportunity are further accentuated through the choice of curricula. As a rule, those groups which are poorly represented in the high school patronize the more narrow and practical curricula, the curricula which stand as terminal points in the educational system and which prepare for wage-earning. And the poorer their representation in high school, the greater is the probability that they will enter these curricula. The one- and two-year vocational courses, wherever offered, draw their registration particularly from the ranks of labor (Counts, 1922, p. 143). See also Trow, 1966; Cohen and Lazerson, 1972; Greer, 1972.

TABLE 6

Selected Characteristics of Students Enrolled in Three Curriculums in 63 Comprehensive Community Colleges (percentages)

Characteristics	College Parallel	Technical	Vocational
Father's occupation			
Unskilled or semiskilled	18	26	35
White collar	46	35	25
Parental income			
Less than $6,000	14	14	24
More than $10,000	36	28	21
Father's formal education			
Less than high school graduation	27	34	50
Some college or more	31	20	14
Race			
Caucasian	91	79	70
Negro	5	7	14
Oriental	1	7	7
Other	1	4	6

Source: Comparative Guidance and Placement Program, 1969. (Cross, 1970, p. 191)

Data presented in Table 6 show a pronounced class bias in the composition of community college students enrolled in vocational programs. Compared with students in transfer programs, vocational students are markedly lower in family income, father's education, and father's occupation. While almost half of community college students in the transfer curriculum are from white-collar families, only one-fourth of the students in vocational programs are from such backgrounds. Students enrolled in technical programs fall in between vocational and transfer students along various measures of socioeconomic status. Black students show themselves to be considerably more likely than white students to enroll in community college vocational programs.[8]

The relatively low social origins of vocational and technical students are likely to be reflected in their adult occupations. Community college occupational programs are broadly designed to prepare people for entrance into the growing technical and semi-professional stratum. Estimates as to the size of this expanding class suggest that it may comprise one-third of the labor force by 1975 (Harris, 1971, p. 254). This stratum occupies the lower-middle levels of the system of social stratification, but it creates a sensation of upward mobility among its members because it is representative of the change from a blue-collar (or secondary) to a white-

[8] Minority students are also disproportionately enrolled in two of the lower rungs of the higher education tracking system—community colleges and unselective black colleges. Patterns of enrollment, of course, vary from region to region with community colleges dominant in the West and black institutions more prominent in the South. For data showing that the proportion of minority students decreases as one progresses up the three-track California system see Coordinating Council (1969: 23) and Jaffe and Adams (1972: 232).

TABLE 7

Yearly Income of U. S. Younger Employed Males, by Level of Educational Attainment, Late 1960s (Base: High school graudation income = 100)

Level of Educational Attainment	Income	Percentage of All College Dropouts
High school graduation	100	—
One or two terms of college	110	40
Three or four terms of college	119	37
Five to seven terms of college	121	23
Eight or more terms of college	150	—

Source: Unpublished tabulations of the October 1967, 1968, and 1969 Current Population Surveys of the Bureau of the Census, in which the occupations of younger persons, and the imputed earnings for the various occupations were related to levels of educational attainment. (Jaffe and Adams, 1972, p. 249)

collar (or tertiary) economy. Since many members of this "new working class" originate from blue-collar backgrounds, their movement into this stratum does in fact represent mobility. Yet it may be conjectured that this perception of mobility is only temporary; as more and more people move into these jobs, the prestige of a white-collar position may undergo a corresponding decline in status.[9]

Evidence on the economic returns of these vocational programs is, at best, indirect, and empirical studies on this topic would be extremely useful. Yet it is apparent that, in general, having two years of college is not half as good as having four years (Bowles, 1971b, Jaffe & Adams, 1972). Table 7, based on recent Census Bureau data, indicates that the recipient of five to seven terms of college is closer in income to a high school graduate than to a college graduate. Possibly, there is some sort of "sheepskin effect" associated with the attainment of a bachelor's degree. But whatever the reasons, having part of a college education seems to be of limited economic value. Whether this is also true for community college students in programs specially designed to prepare them for an occupation remains to be seen.[10]

[9] At the same time, however, it is easy to forget that *absolute* changes in occupation, income, and educational attainment can have important consequences in everyday life and may raise general levels of satisfaction. Having more people attend college, while not narrowing the educational gap in relative terms, may lead to a more enlightened populace. Keniston and Gerzon (1972) attack the narrowly economic view of higher education and argue that important non-pecuniary benefits accrue from college attendance. Similarly, a change from a blue-collar to a white-collar economy may eliminate many menial tasks and hence lead to greater job satisfaction. Finally, an absolute increase in the standard of living, while not necessarily abolishing poverty (which, as Jencks argues, is primarily a relative phenomenon), may result in a higher quality of life than was possible under conditions of greater scarcity.

[10] Grubb and Lazerson (1972) report that economic returns to vocational education are almost uniformly low, but their review does not include studies of programs at community colleges. Some skepticism as to the allegedly high incomes of graduates of occupational programs for blue-collar jobs may, however, be expressed. Contrary to popular mythology about the affluent worker, the proportion of male blue-collar workers earning more than $15,000 in 1970 was a miniscule 4 per-

The Sponsors of the Vocational Movement

Unlike the movement for open admissions to college, which received much of its impetus from mass pressure, there has been little popular clamor for community college vocational programs. Indeed, most junior college entrants see the two-year college as a way-station to a four-year college and shun occupational programs (see the next section). Despite this, there has been an enormous push to increase enrollment in community college occupational programs. This push from the top for more career education marks one of the major developments in the evolution of the community college movement.

The interest of the business community in encouraging occupational training at public expense is manifest. With a changing labor force which requires ever-increasing amounts of skill to perform its tasks and with manpower shortages in certain critical areas, private industry is anxious to use the community college as a training ground for its employees. An associate of the Space Division of the North American Rockwell Corporation makes the corporate viewpoint clear: "industry . . . must recognize that junior colleges are indispensable to the fulfillment of its needs for technical manpower" (Ryan, 1971, p. 71). In the Los Angeles area, Space Division personnel and junior college faculty work together to set up curricular requirements, frame course content, determine student competence, and formulate "on-the-job performance objectives."

The influence of the business community on the junior college is exerted in part through membership of local industrial notables on community college boards of trustees. Hartnett (1969, p. 28) reports that 33 per cent of public junior college trustees are business executives and that over half of all community college trustees agree that "running a college is basically like running a business." Overt business interference in the affairs of the community college is, however, probably rare; the ideological influence of the business community, with its emphasis on pragmatism and economic efficiency, is so pervasive in the two-year college that conflicts between the industrial and educational communities would not normally arise. One imagines that Arthur M. Cohen (1971b, p. 6), Director of the ERIC Clearinghouse for Junior Colleges, is hardly exaggerating when he says that when "corporate managers . . . announce a need for skilled workers, . . . college administrators trip over each other in their haste to organize a new technical curriculum."

---

cent (Bureau of the Census, 1971: 30). Only 3 out of 10 blue-collar workers earned more than $10,000 in 1970.

We do not know what economic rewards accrue to graduates of community college vocational programs, nor do we know much about the occupational and economic status of the community college drop-out. This is fertile ground for empirical inquiry. A longitudinal study of three groups of high school graduates—students who do not enter college, community college drop-outs, and community college entrants who obtain a degree (A.A. or B.A.)—matching students with similar personal characteristics, would do much to illuminate the effects of attending a community college.

Foundations have also shown an intense interest in junior college vocational programs, an interest which is somewhat more difficult to explain than that of business and industry. The Kellogg Foundation, which over a period of years, has made grants to the community college movement totaling several million dollars (Gleazer, 1968, p. 38), has a long-standing interest in career training. In 1959, the general director of the Kellogg Foundation noted approvingly that the "community college movement can do much to supply the sub-professionals, the technicians so necessary to the professions and industry in the years ahead" (Powell, 1965, p. 17). Kellogg followed up on this interest in career education with grants to Chicago City Junior College in 1963 and 1964 for associate degree programs in nursing and business which came to $312,440 and $112,493 respectively (Sunko, 1965, p. 42). In addition, in the late 1950's, Kellogg made a several hundred thousand dollar commitment to support the American Association of Junior Colleges, the national organization of the two-year college movement which has itself been a long-time advocate of vocational programs (Brick, 1964).

The Carnegie Commission on Higher Education, financially sponsored by, but independent of, the Carnegie Corporation of New York, has also been active in sponsoring career education. In its widely read pamphlet, *The Open-Door colleges,* the Carnegie Commission (1970), made explicit policy proposals for community colleges. Members of the Commission came out strongly for occupational programs, and stated that they "should be given the fullest support and status within community colleges" and should be "flexibly geared to the changing requirements of society" (1970, p. 1). Later in the report (pp. 15-16) the Commission recommended that community colleges remain two-year institutions lest they "place less emphasis on occupational programs." Community colleges, the Commission said, "should follow an open-enrollment policy, whereas access to four-year institutions should generally be more selective." The net impact of these recommendations is to leave the tracking system of higher education intact. Considering the class composition of the community college, to maintain the status quo in higher education tracking is, in essence, to perpetuate privilege (see Wolfe, 1971).

The influence of foundations in fostering vocational education in community colleges is difficult to measure precisely, but it is clear that they have been among its leading sponsors.[11] State master plans (see Hurlburt, 1969; Cross, 1970) have also done much to formalize the subordinate status of the community college within higher education and to encourage the growth of their vocational curricula. The federal government, too, has promoted vocational training in the two-year institutions. Federal involvement dates back at least to 1963. At that time, Congress authorized the spending of several hundred million dollars to encourage post-

[11] Karier (1972) has written a provocative essay on the role of foundations in sponsoring educational testing. The role of far-sighted foundations in fostering educational reform, possibly as a means of rationalizing the social order, is a topic worthy of careful investigation.

secondary technical education. More recently, the Higher Education Act of 1972 (pp. 77-78) authorized $850,000,000 over the next three years for post-secondary occupational education. In comparison, the entire sum authorized for the establishment of new community colleges and the expansion of old ones is less than one-third as much—$275,000,000.

The language of the Higher Education Act of 1972 makes clear just what is meant by vocational education:

The term 'postsecondary occupational education' means education, training, or retraining . . . conducted by an institution . . . which is designed to prepare individuals for gainful employment as semi-skilled or skilled workers or technicians or sub-professionals in recognized occupations (including new and emerging occupations) . . . but excluding any program to prepare individuals for employment in occupations . . . to be generally considered professional or which require a baccalaureate or advanced degree. (p. 87)

The import of this definition of occupational education is to exclude four-year programs leading to a B.A. from funding. The intent of this legislation, which provides enormous sums of money for community college career education, is obvious: it is designed to fill current manpower shortage in the middle and lower-middle levels of the occupational structure.

The idea of career education which the U.S. Office of Education is "working to spread throughout elementary, secondary and at least community college circles" (Marland, 1972, p. 217) is that the student, regardless of when he leaves the educational system, should have sufficient skills to enable him to be gainfully employed. The idea is a worthy one, but it implicitly accepts the existing system of social stratification. The philosophy of career education is that the proper function of the educational system is to respond to current manpower needs and to allocate people to positions characterized by large disparities in rewards. Commissioner of Education, Sidney Marland, observes that no more than 20 per cent of all jobs in the 1970's will require a bachelor's degree; apparently, this is supposed to provide a rough index as to how many people should attend college for four years. Further, it is worth noting that career education does not seem to extend above the community college level. An idea whose "time has come," it somehow does not seem applicable to the sons and daughters of the middle and upper classes who attend four-year colleges and universities.

Federal sponsorship of vocational programs in the community college may have contributed to the development of a rigid track system (Cohen, 1971a, p. 152). By prohibiting the allocation of funds to non-vocational programs, federal laws have deepened the division between transfer and occupational programs. This division fosters separate facilities, separate brochures, and separate administrations. The result is a magnification of the differences between transfer and vocational programs leading to a decline in the desirability of occupational training.

Also at the forefront of the movement to expand vocational programs in community colleges have been various national higher education organizations. The American Association of Junior Colleges (AAJC), almost since its founding in 1920, has exerted its influence to encourage the growth of vocational education. Faced with the initial problem of establishing an identity for two-year colleges, the AAJC set out to describe the unique functions of the junior college. Prominent among these was the provision of two-year occupational training at the post-secondary level. In 1940 and 1941 the AAJC sponsored a Commission on Junior College Terminal Education. According to Ralph Fields (1962), a long-time observer of the junior college, this commission was instrumental in lending legitimacy to vocational training in the community college.

In recent years, the AAJC has continued its active encouragement of occupational programs in the community college. Numerous pamphlets, training programs, and conferences on vocational training in the two-year college have been sponsored by AAJC. In that the AAJC, the leading national association of junior colleges, has probably done more than any other single organization to give definition to the community college movement, its enthusiasm for vocational training takes on particular importance.

The American Council on Education, the umbrella organization for the various associations of higher education, is considered by many to be the leading spokesman for American higher education. It, too, has given major support to post-secondary technical education. In 1963, the Council sponsored a study of the place of technical and vocational training in higher education. One of the conclusions of the report was that "two-year colleges, if they are to assume their proper and effective role in the educational system of the nation, should make vocational and technical education programs a major part of their mission and a fundamental institutional objective" (Venn, 1964, p. 165). Edmund Gleazer, Jr. (1968, p. 139), Executive Director of AAJC, points to this report as critical in gaining acceptance for vocational training within the higher education community.

Finally, many American universities have looked with favor on the development of the community college into a "comprehensive" institution with occupational programs in addition to its more traditional transfer programs. From the origins of the junior college in the late nineteenth and early twentieth centuries as an institution designed to extend secondary education for two years in order to keep the university pure, there has been a recognition among many university academics that it is in their interest to have a diversity of institutions in higher education (Thornton, 1960, pp. 46-50). A number of observers have noted that the community colleges serve as a safety valve, diverting students clamoring for access to college away from more selective institutions (Clark, 1960; Jencks and Riesman, 1968; Cohen, 1971b). Elite colleges neither want nor need these students; if separate institutions, or, for that matter, vocational programs within these institutions help keep the masses out of their colleges, then they are to be given full support.[12] Paradoxically, the elite sector of the academic community, much of it liberal to radical, finds itself in a peculiar alliance with industry, foundations, government, and established higher education associations to vocationalize the community college.[13]

The Response to Vocational Education: Submerged Class Conflict

Despite the massive effort by leading national educational policy-makers to encourage the development of occupational education in the community college, student response to vocational programs has been limited. Estimates vary as to how many community college students are enrolled in career education programs, but the figures seem to range from 25 to 33 per cent (Cross, 1970; Ogilvie, 1971; Medsker and Tillery, 1971). Over two-thirds of two-year college entrants aspire to a bachelor's degree, and a similar proportion enroll, at least initially, in college-parallel or transfer programs. Many of these students, of course, are subsequently cooled out, but few of them seem to prefer a vocational program to leaving the community college altogether.

Leaders of the occupational education movement have constantly bemoaned the lack of student enthusiasm for vocational education (Venn, 1964; Gleazer, 1968; Carnegie, 1970; Medsker and Tillery, 1971; Cross, 1971). The problem, they believe, is the low status of career training in a society that worships the bachelor's degree. Medsker and Tillery (p. 140), for example, argue that "negative attitudes toward vocational education . . . are by-products of the academic syndrome in American higher education." Marland (1972, p. 218) refers to the difficulty as "degree fixation." The problem, then, since it is one of an irrational preoccupation with obtaining a traditional four-year education, leads to an obvious solution: raising the status of vocational education. This proposed solution has been suggested by the Carnegie Commission on Higher Education, the Office of Education, the American Association of Junior Colleges, the American Council on Education, leaders of industry, and scholars in the field of community colleges.

Despite the apparent logic and simplicity of raising the status of vocational education, the task presents enormous difficulties. Minority students, though more likely to be enrolled in occupational programs than white students, seem especially sensitive to being channeled into vocational tracks. Overall, students are voting with their feet against community college vocational programs.

This is not an irrational obsession with four-year diplomas on the part of the

---

[12] Amitai Etzioni (1970), chairman of the Department of Sociology at Columbia University, expresses this point of view well: "If we can no longer keep the floodgates closed at the admissions office, it at least seems wise to channel the general flow away from four-year colleges and toward two-year extensions of high school in the junior and community colleges." Vice President Agnew (1970), in a speech attacking open admissions, approvingly cited this quotation.

[13] See Riessman's "The Vocationalization of Higher Education: Duping the Poor" for an analysis of the movement to turn the community college into a technical institution. For a brilliant article on the elitism of leftist academics toward working-class students see McDermott (1969).

students. It is not just snobbish prejudice; there are sound structural reasons for the low status of career education in the community college. At the base of an educational institution's prestige is its relationship to the occupational and class structure of the society in which it operates (Clark, 1962, pp. 80-83). The community college lies at the base of the stratification structure of higher education both in the class origins of its students and in their occupational destinations. Within the community college, the vocational curriculum is at the bottom of the prestige hierarchy—again, both in terms of social composition and likely adult status.

It is unrealistic, then, to expect that community college vocational programs, the bottom track of higher education's bottom track, will have much status. It is worth noting that the British, generally more hardheaded about matters of social class than Americans, faced the matter of educational status directly some years ago. In the 1950's in Great Britain, there was a great deal of talk about "parity of esteem" in English secondary education. The problem was to give equal status to grammar schools (college preparatory), technical schools (middle level managerial and technical), and secondary modern schools (terminal). After considerable debate, the British realized that "parity of esteem" was an impossible ideal given the encompassing class structure (Banks, 1955; Marshall, 1965).

The educational establishment's concern with the low status of occupational programs in the community colleges reveals much more about its own ideology than it does about the allegedly irrational behavior of students resistant to vocational education. A great deal of emphasis is placed on improving the public image of vocational education, but little attention is paid to the substantive matter of class differences in income, occupational prestige, power, and opportunities for autonomy and expression at the workplace. The Carnegie Commission, whose ideology is probably representative of the higher education establishment, blurs the distinction between *equality* and *equality of opportunity* (Karabel, 1972a, p. 42). Discussing its vision of the day when minority persons will be proportionately represented in higher occupational levels, the Commission hails this as an "important signal that society was meeting its commitment to equality." The conception of equality conveyed in this passage is really one of equality of opportunity; the Commission seems less interested in reducing gross differences in rewards than in giving everyone a chance to get ahead of everyone else. The Carnegie Commission, reflecting the values not only of the national educational leadership but also of the wider society, shows concern about opportunities for mobility, but little concern about a reduction in inequality.

The submerged class conflict that exists between the sponsors of vocational education in the junior college, who represent the interests and outlook of the more privileged sectors of society, and community college students, many of them working class, occasionally becomes overt. At Seattle Community College in 1968-1969, the Black Student Union vigorously opposed a recommendation to concentrate trade and technical programs in the central (Black) campus while the "higher" semiprofessional programs were allocated to the northern and southern (white) campuses (Cohen, 1971a: 142). Rutgers (Newark) was the scene in 1969 of extensive demonstrations to gain open admissions to a branch of the state university. The import of the case of Rutgers (Newark) was that the protests took place in a city where students already had access to an open-door community college (Essex) and a mildly selective state college (Newark State). What the students were resisting here was not being tracked within the community college, but rather being channeled into the community college itself.[14] The well-known struggle for open admissions at CUNY in the spring of 1969 was not primarily for access per se, but for access to the more prestigious four-year institutions: City, Brooklyn, Queens, and Hunter.

The pattern in these isolated cases of manifest resistance to tracking within or between colleges is one of minority student leadership. In the United States, where race is a much more visible social cleavage than class, it is not surprising that Black students have shown the most sensitivity to tracking in higher education. Channeling of Black students to community colleges and to vocational programs within them is, after all, fairly visible; in contrast, the *class* character of the tracking system is much less perceptible. Were it not for the militancy of some minority students, it is likely that the conflict over vocational education would have long continued to manifest itself in enrollment patterns without becoming overt.

The class nature of the conflict over tracking has, however, not always been invisible. In Illinois in 1913, there was a battle over a bill in the state legislature to establish a separate system of vocational schools above the sixth grade. Business strongly backed the bill, sponsored by Chicago School Superintendent Edwin G. Cooley. The Chicago Federation of Labor, lobbying against the bill, expressed fear that it reflected

an effort on the part of large employers to turn the public schools into an agency for supplying them with an adequate supply of docile, well-trained, and capable workers [which] . . . aimed to bring Illinois a caste system of education which would shunt the children of the laboring classes at an early age first into vocational courses and then into the factories (Counts, 1928, p. 167).

After a bitter fight, the bill was defeated in the legislature.

The tracking which takes place in the community college is, however, much more invisible than that proposed in the Cooley Bill. For one thing, the community college, by the very use of the word "college" in its title, locates itself squarely within the system of higher education and gives it at least the minimal status which comes from being a college rather than a technical school. For another, the

---

[14] I am indebted to Russell Thackrey for pointing out the implications of the interesting case of Rutgers (Newark).

apparent emphasis of the junior college on the transfer function leads to a perception of it as a way station on the road to a four-year college. This view of the community college as a place of transfer rather than a track is strengthened by the subtlety and smoothness of the cooling out process. The community college is a "comprehensive" institution; like the high school before it, it provides preparatory and terminal education in the same building and offers sufficient opportunities for movement between programs to obscure the larger pattern of tracking. Finally, the very age at which students enter the community college makes tracking a less serious issue; there *is* a difference between channeling an eleven-year-old child and channeling a young adult of eighteen.

Whatever the differences between high school and college tracking, there is a marked similarity in the rationales given in each case for curricular differentiation. The argument is that a common curriculum denies equality of opportunity by restricting educational achievement to a single mode which will inevitably lead to some form of hierarchy. In 1908, the Boston school superintendent argued:

Until very recently [the schools] have offered equal opportunity to receive *one kind* of education, but what will make them democratic is to provide opportunity for all to receive such an education as will fit them *equally well* for their particular life work. (Cohen and Lazerson, 1972: 69)

Similarly, K. Patricia Cross (1971: 162), a leading researcher on the junior college, argues more than 60 years later:

Surely quality education consists not in offering the same thing to all people in a token gesture toward equality but in maximizing the match between the talents of the individual and the teaching resources of the institution. Educational quality is not uni-dimensional. Colleges can be *different* and excellent too.

In principle, colleges can be different and excellent, too. But in a stratified society, what this diversity of educational experiences is likely to mean is that people will, at best, have an equal opportunity to obtain an education that will fit them into their appropriate position in the class structure. More often than not, those of lower class origins will, under the new definition of equality of educational opportunity, find themselves in schools or curricula which train them for positions roughly commensurate with their social origins.

The current movement to vocationalize the community college is a logical outgrowth of the dual historical patterns of class-based hierarchical differentiation in education and of educational inflation. The system of higher education, forced to respond to pressure for access arising from mobility aspirations endemic in an affluent society which stresses individual success and the democratic character of its opportunity structure, has let people in and has then proceeded to track them into community colleges and, more particularly, into occupational programs within these two-year colleges. This push toward vocational training in the community college has been sponsored by a national educational planning elite whose social composition, outlook, and policy proposals are reflective of the interests of the more privileged strata of our society. Notably absent among those pressuring for more occupational training in the junior college have been the students themselves.

Discussion

The recent Newman Report on Higher Education (1971; 57) noted that "the public, and especially the four-year colleges and universities, are shifting more and more responsibility onto the community colleges for undertaking the toughest tasks of higher education." One of the most difficult of these tasks has been to educate hundreds of thousands of students, many of them of modest social origins, in whom more selective colleges and universities showed no interest. Community colleges have given these students access to higher education and have provided some of them a chance to advance their class position.

Despite the idealism and vigor of the community college movement, there has been a sharp contradiction between official rhetoric and social reality. Hailed as the "democratizers of higher education," community colleges are, in reality, a vital component of the class-based tracking system. The modal junior college student, though aspiring to a four-year diploma upon entrance, receives neither an associate nor a bachelor's degree. The likelihood of his persisting in higher education is *negatively* influenced by attending a community college. Since a disproportionate number of two-year college students are of working-class origins, low status students are most likely to attend those institutions which increase the likelihood that they will drop out of college. Having increased access to higher education, community colleges are notably unsuccessful in retaining their students and in reducing class differentials in educational opportunity.

If current trends continue, the tracking system of higher education may well become more rigid. The community college, as the bottom track, is likely to absorb the vast majority of students who are the first generation in their families to enter higher education. Since most of these students are from relatively low status backgrounds, an increase in the already significant correlation between social class and position in the tracking system of higher education is likely to occur. As more and more people enter postsecondary education, the community college will probably become more distinct from the rest of higher education both in class composition and in curriculum. With the push of the policy-planning elite for more career education, vocational training may well become more pervasive, and the community college will become even more a terminal rather than a transfer institution. These trends, often referred to as expressions of higher education's "diversity" and of the community college's "special and unique role" are the very processes which place the community college at the bottom of the class-based tracking system. The system of higher education's much-touted "diversity" is, for the most part, hierarchy rather than genuine variety (see Karabel, 1972a and 1972b), a form of hierarchy which has more to do with social class than educational philosophy.

The high rate of attrition at community colleges may well be functional for the existing social system. The cooling out function of the junior college, as Clark puts it, is what "such a college is about." Community colleges exist in part to reconcile students' culturally induced hopes for mobility with their eventual destinations, transforming structurally induced failure into individual failure. This serves to legitimize the myth of an equal opportunity structure; it shifts attention to questions of individual mobility rather than distributive justice. Cooling out, then, can be seen as conflict between working class students and standards that legitimize the position of the privileged—a veiled class conflict. Similarly, there is class conflict implicit in the differences over vocational education between the aspirations of students and the objectives of policy-makers. This has occasionally become overt, but the community colleges seem to serve their legitimizing function best when the conflict remains submerged.

Can the inability of the community college movement to modify the American class structure be overcome? An assessment of some specific reforms that have been proposed may yield some insight. One obvious reform would be to reverse the pattern that Hansen and Weisbrod (1969) document—simply to invest more money in the community colleges than in the four-year public institutions. The idea of this reform would be both to provide the highest quality education to those who have socioeconomic and cognitive disadvantages to overcome and to put an end to the pattern of poor people subsidizing relatively affluent people through public systems of higher education. This proposal, which may be justified on grounds of equity, is unlikely to make much difference either in terms of education or social class. A repeated finding in social science research, confirmed by both the Coleman Report (1966) and the recent Jencks (1972) study, is that educational expenditures seem to be virtually unrelated to cognitive development at the elementary and secondary levels, and there is no reason to believe that money is any more effective in colleges. However desirable a shift in resources from four-year colleges to community colleges might be on other grounds, it is unlikely to seriously affect the larger pattern of class-based tracking in higher education.

Another possibility would be to transform the community college into a four-year institution—the very proposal that the Carnegie Commission on Higher Education strongly opposes. The purpose of this reform would be to upgrade the status of the community college and to diminish the rigidity of the tracking system. Yet it is highly questionable whether making the junior college into a senior college would have any such effect; there are marked status distinctions among four-year colleges and, in all likelihood, the new four-year institutions would be at the bottom of the prestige hierarchy. Further, the creation of more four-year colleges would probably accelerate the process of educational inflation.

The proposal to vocationalize the community college exemplifies the dilemma faced by those who would reform the public two-year college. Noting that many community college students neither transfer nor get an associate degree, proponents of vocational education argue that the students should stop engaging in a uni-dimensional academic competition which they cannot win and should instead obtain a marketable skill before leaving the educational system. If one accepts the existing system of social stratification, there is an almost irresistible logic to the vocational training argument; there are, after all, manpower shortages to be filled and it *is* true that not everyone can be a member of the elite.

In a sense, the community colleges are "damned if they do and damned if they don't." The vocational educational reform provides a striking example of their dilemma, for the question of whether community colleges should become predominantly vocational institutions may well be the most critical policy issue facing the two-year institutions in the years ahead. If they move toward more career education, they will tend to accentuate class-based tracking. If they continue as "comprehensive institutions" they will continue to be plagued by the enormous attrition in their transfer curricula. Either way, the primary role of the colleges derives from their relation to the class structure and feasible reforms will, at best, result in minor changes in their channeling function.

That the community colleges cannot do what many of their proponents claim they are supposed to do does not mean that they can do nothing at all. They do make a difference for many students—providing them opportunities for better lives than their parents had. They are able to introduce some students, particularly those who are residential rather than commuter students, to ideas, influences, and ways of life that broaden their view of the world. And surely it is not beyond reason to think that better staff, counseling, and facilities could somewhat reduce the rate of attrition in the transfer curricula. It is not beyond hope to think that reform of the vocational tracks could encourage students not to fit like cogs into rigid occupational roles but to have some faith in themselves, their right to decent working conditions, and to some control over their own work so that they could shape the roles they are supposed to fit into. It may be that students and teachers intent on changing society could raise the consciousness of community college students about where they fit in the social system and why they fit where they do. All this is possible, important, and underway in many community colleges.

But as for educational reform making this a more egalitarian society, we cannot be sanguine. Jencks (1972) has shown that the effects of schooling on ultimate income and occupation are relatively small. Even if the community colleges were to undergo a major transformation, little change in the system of social stratification would be likely to take place. If we are genuinely concerned about creating a more egalitarian society, it will be necessary to change our economic institutions. The problems of inequality and inequality of opportunity are, in short, best dealt with not through educational reform but rather by the wider changes in economic and political life that would help build a socialist society.

Writing in favor of secondary education for everybody many years ago, R. H.

Tawney, the British social historian, remarked that the "intrusion into educational organization of the vulgarities of the class system is an irrelevance as mischievous in effect as it is odious in conception." That matters of social class have intruded into the community college is beyond dispute; whether the influence of class can be diminished not only in the community college but also in the larger society remains to be seen.

References*

Agnew, S. Toward a middle way in college admissions. *Educational Record* 51 (Spring, 1970), pp. 106-111.

American Council on Education, Office of Research. National norms for entering college freshmen—Fall 1966. ACE Research Reports, Vol. 2, No. 1. Washington, D.C.: 1966.

American Council on Education, Office of Research. The American freshman: National norms for Fall 1971. ACE Research Reports, Vol. 6, No. 6. Washington, D.C.: 1971.

Astin, A. W. *Predicting academic performance in college.* New York: Free Press, 1971.

Astin, A. W. College dropouts: A national profile. ACE Research Reports, Vol. 7, No. 1. Washington, D. C.: American Council on Education, 1972.

Astin, A. W. & Panos, R. J. *The educational and vocational development of college students.* Washington, D.C.: American Council on Education, 1969.

Banks, O. *Parity and prestige in English secondary education.* London: Routledge and Kegan Paul, Ltd., 1955.

Blackburn, R. The unequal society. In H. P. Dreitzel (Ed.), *Recent sociology No. 1.* London: Macmillan Company, 1969.

Blau, P. M. & Duncan, O. D. *The American occupational structure.* New York: Wiley, 1967.

Bowles, S. Contradictions in U. S. higher education. James Weaver (Ed.) *Political economy: radical vs. orthodox approaches.* Boston: Allyn & Bacon, 1972.

Bowles, S. Unequal education and the reproduction of the social division of labor. *Review of radical political economics,* 3 (Fall), 1971.

Brick, M. *Forum and focus for the junior college movement.* New York: Bureau of Publications, Teachers College, Columbia University, 1964.

Bureau of the Census. *The American almanac.* New York: Grosset & Dunlap, 1971a.

Bureau of the Census. Educational attainment: March 1971. Series P20, No. 229. Washington, D.C.: U. S. Government Printing Office, 1971b.

Bureau of the Census. Undergraduate enrollment in two-year and four-year colleges: October 1971. Series P20, No. 236. Washington, D.C.: U. S. Government Printing Office, 1972.

Bushnell, D. S. & Zagaris, I. *Report from Project FOCUS: Strategies for change.* Washington, D. C.: American Association of Junior Colleges, 1972.

Carnegie Commission on Higher Education. *The open-door colleges.* New York: McGraw-Hill, 1970.

Clark, B. R. *The open door college.* New York: McGraw-Hill, 1960.

Clark, B. R. *Educating the expert society.* San Francisco: Chandler, 1962.

Cohen, A. M. *et al. A constant variable.* San Francisco: Jossey-Bass, 1971a.

Cohen, A. M. Stretching pre-college education. *Social Policy* (May/June, 1971b), pp. 5-9.

* Although this article has been abridged, the references are in their original form — ED.

Cohen, D. K. & Lazerson, M. Education and the corporate order. *Socialist Revolution,* 2 (March/April, 1972), pp. 47-72.

Coleman, J. S., *et al. Equality of educational opportunity.* Washington, D. C.: U. S. Government Printing Office, 1966.

Collins, R. Functional and conflict theories of stratification. *American Sociological Review* 36 (December, 1971), pp. 1002-19.

Coordinating Council for Higher Education. *The undergraduate student and his higher education: Policies of California colleges and universities in the next decade.* Sacramento, Cal. 1969.

Counts, G. S. *School and society in Chicago.* New York: Harcourt, Brace, 1928.

Counts, G. S. *The selective character of American secondary education.* Chicago: University of Chicago Press, 1922.

Cross, K. P. The junior college student: A research description. Princeton, N. J.: Educational Testing Service, 1968.

Cross, K. P. The role of the junior college in providing postsecondary education for all. In *Trends in postsecondary education.* Washington, D. C.: U. S. Government Printing Office, 1970.

Cross, K. P. *Beyond the open door.* San Francisco: Jossey-Bass, 1971.

Department of Health, Education, and Welfare. *Digest of educational statistics.* Washington, D. C.: U. S. Government Printing Office, 1970.

Eckland, B. K. Social class and college graduation: Some misconceptions corrected. *American Journal of Sociology,* 70 (July, 1964), pp. 36-50.

Etzioni, A. The high schoolization of college. *Wall Street Journal,* March 17, 1970.

Fields, R. R. *The community college movement.* New York: McGraw-Hill, 1962.

Folger, J. K., Astin, H. S., & Bayer, A. E. *Human resources and higher education.* New York: Russell Sage, 1970.

Gleazer, E. J., Jr. *This is the community college.* Boston: Houghton Mifflin, 1968.

Greer, C. *The great school legend.* New York: Basic Books, 1972.

Grubb, W. N., & Lazerson, M. *American education and vocationalism: A documentary History, 1870–1970.* New York: Teachers College Press, 1974.

Hansen, W. L. & Weisbrod, B. A. *Benefits, costs, and finance of public higher education.* Chicago: Markham, 1969.

Harris, N. C. The middle manpower job spectrum. In W. K. Ogilvie, and M. R. Raines (Eds.), *Perspectives on the Community-Junior College.* New York: Appleton-Century-Crofts, 1971.

Hartnett, R. T. College and university trustees: Their backgrounds, roles, and educational attitudes. Princeton, N. J.: Educational Testing Service, 1969.

Havemann, E. & West, P. *They went to college.* New York: Harcourt, Brace, 1952.

Higher Education Act of 1972. Public Law 92-318. 92nd Congress, 659, June 23, 1972.

Hurlburt, A. L. *State master plans for community colleges.* Washington, D. C.: American Association of Junior Colleges, 1969.

Jaffe, A. J. & Adams, W. Two models of open enrollment. In L. Wilson and O. Mills (Eds.), *Universal higher education.* Washington: American Council on Education, 1972.

Jencks, C. & Riesman, D. *The academic revolution.* Garden City, N. Y.: Doubleday, 1968.

Jencks, C. *et al. Inequality: a reassessment of the effect of family and schooling in America.* New York: Basic Books, 1972.

Karabel, J. Perspectives on open admissions. *Educational Record,* 53 (Winter, 1972a), pp. 30-44.

Karabel, J. Open admissions: Toward meritocracy or equality? *Change,* 4 (May, 1972b), pp. 38-43.

Karabel, J. & Astin, A. W. Social class, academic ability, and college quality. *Social Forces,* May 1975, 53, 381–398.

Karier, C. J. Testing for order and control in the corporate liberal state. *Educational Theory,* 22 (Spring, 1972), pp. 154-180.

Katz, M. B. *The irony of early school reform.* Boston: Beacon Press, 1968.

Keniston, K. & Gerzon, M. Human and social benefits. In L. Wilson and O. Mills, *Universal Higher Education.* Washington, D. C.: American Council on Education, 1972.

Knoell, D. M. & Medsker, L. L. Articulation between two-year and four-year colleges. Berkeley: Center for the Study of Higher Education, 1964.

Kolko, G. *Wealth and power in America.* New York: Praeger, 1962.

Lipset, S. M. & Bendix, R. *Social mobility in industrial society.* Berkeley: University of California Press, 1959.

Marland, S. P., Jr. A strengthening alliance. In L. Wilson and O. Mills (Eds.), *Universal higher education.* Washington, D. C.: American Council on Education, 1972.

Marshall, T. H. *Class, citizenship, and social development.* Garden City, N.Y.: Anchor, 1965.

McDermott, J. The laying on of culture. *The Nation,* March 10, 1969.

Medsker, L. L. & Trent, J. W. The influence of different types of public higher institutions on college attendance from varying socioeconomic and ability levels. Berkeley: Center for Research and Development in Higher Education, 1965.

Medsker, L. L. & Tillery, D. *Breaking the access barriers.* New York: McGraw-Hill, 1971.

Miller, H. *Rich, man, poor man.* New York: Thomas Y. Crowell, 1971.

Milner, M., Jr. *The illusion of equality.* San Francisco: Jossey-Bass, 1972.

Morsch, W. O. *Costs analysis of occupational training programs in community colleges and vocational training centers.* Washington, D. C.: Bureau of Social Science Research, 1971.

Newman, F., et al. *Report on higher education.* Reports to the U. S. Department of Health, Education, and Welfare. Washington, D. C.: U. S. Government Printing Office, 1971.

Ogilvie, W. K. Occupational education and the community college. In W. K. Ogilvie & M. R. Raines (Eds.), *Perspectives on the Community-Junior College.* New York: Appleton-Century-Crofts, 1971.

Pechman, J. A. The distributional effects of public higher education in California. *Journal of Human Resources,* 5 (Summer, 1970), pp. 361-37.

Pierson, G. W. *The education of American leaders.* New York: Praeger, 1969.

Powell, H. B. The foundation and the future of the junior college. In *The foundation and the junior colleges.* Washington, D. C.: American Association of Junior Colleges, 1965.

Reed, R. & Miller, H. Some determinants of the variation in earnings for college men. *Journal of Human Resources,* 5, Spring, 1970, pp. 177-190.

Riessman, F. The 'vocationalization' of higher education: Duping the poor. *Social Policy,* 2, (May/June, 1971), pp. 3-4.

Rothbart, G. S. The legitimation of inequality: objective scholarship vs. black militance. *Sociology of Education,* 43 (Spring, 1970), pp. 159-174.

Ryan, P. B. Why industry needs the junior college. In W. K. Ogilvie & M. R. Raines (Eds.), *Perspectives on the Community-Junior College.* New York: Appleton-Century-Crofts, 1971.

Schoenfeldt, L. F. Education after high school. *Sociology of Education,* 41 (Fall 1968), pp. 350-369.

Sewell, W. H. and Shah, V. P. Socioeconomic status, intelligence, and the attainment of higher education. *Sociology of Education*, 40 (Winter, 1967), pp. 1-23.

Sharp, L. M. *Education and employment*. Baltimore, Johns Hopkins, 1970.

Spaeth, J. L. The allocation of college graduates to graduate and professional schools. *Sociology of Education*, 41 (Fall, 1968), pp. 342-349.

Sunko, Theodore S. Making the case for junior college foundation support. In *The Foundation and the junior college*. Washington, D. C.: American Association of Junior Colleges, 1965.

Thornton, J. W., Jr. *The community junior college*. New York: John Wiley, 1960.

Titmuss, R. M. The limits of the welfare state. *New Left Review*, 23 (September/October, 1964), pp. 28-37.

Trent, J. W., & Medsker, L. L. *Beyond high school*. San Francisco: Jossey-Bass, 1968.

Trow, M. The second transformation of American secondary education. In R. Bendix and S. Lipset (Eds.), *Class, status and power*. New York: Free Press, 1966.

Turner, R. Modes of social ascent through education. In R. Bendix and S. Lipset (Eds.), *Class, status and power*. New York: Free Press, 1966.

Venn, G. *Man. education and work*. Washington, D. C.: American Council on Education, 1964.

Watson, N. Corporations and the community colleges: a growing liaison? *Technical Education News*, Vol. 29, No. 2 (April/May 1970), pp. 3-6.

Wegner, E. L. & Sewell, W. H. Selection and context as factors affecting the probability of graduation from college. *American Journal of Sociology*, 75 (January, 1970), pp. 665-679.

Willingham, W. *Free-access higher education*. New York: College Entrance Examination Board, 1970.

Windham, D. M. *Education, equality and income redistribution*. Lexington, Mass.: D. C. Heath, 1970.

Wolfe, A. Reform without reform: the Carnegie Commission on Higher Education. *Social Policy*, 2 (May/June, 1971), pp. 18-27.

Wolfe, D. *The uses of talent*. Princeton, N. J.: Princeton University Press, 1971.

Ways of Seeing: An Essay on the History of Compulsory Schooling

DAVID B. TYACK

In this essay the author describes the rise of compulsory schooling in the United States and then views this phenomenon through five different explanatory models. The first two are largely political, revealing compulsory schooling as a form of political construction and as an outgrowth of ethnocultural conflict. Noting the rise of educational bureaucracies, the author next offers an organizational inter- pretation as a third way of viewing compulsory schooling. The last two models are largely economic: one depicts the growth in schooling as an investment in human capital, and the other, using a Marxian approach, shows compulsory schooling to be a means of reproducing the class structure of American society. In conclusion, Professor Tyack observes that alternative ways of seeing not only draw on different kinds of evidence, but also depict different levels of social reality and so aid us in gaining a wider and more accurate perception of the past.

I should warn you that what you are about to read is not a bulletproof, airtight, unsinkable monograph. It is an *essay* in the root sense of the word: a trial of some ideas. Kenneth Burke wrote that "a way of seeing is always a way of not seeing."[1] In our specialized age people are taught and paid to have tunnel vision—and such specialization has many benefits. Socialization within the academic disciplines focuses inquiry: economists explain events in economic terms, sociologists in socio- logical ways, psychologists by their own theories. Splintering even occurs within fields; Freudians and behaviorists, for example, see the world through quite dif- ferent lenses.[2]

Historians tend to be eclectic more often than people in other disciplines, but they often make their reputations by developing a single line of argument. The frontier was the major shaping force in American history, Turner tells us. Status anxiety is the key to the progressive leaders, Hofstadter argues. Economic interests

---

[1] Kenneth Burke, *Permanence and Change* (New York: New Republic, 1935), p. 70.
[2] Everett C. Hughes, *Men and Their Work* (Glencoe, Ill.: Free Press, 1958).

Harvard Educational Review   Vol. 46   No. 3   August 1976, 355–389

are the figure in the historical carpet, Beard claims. Other historians make their reputations by attacking Turner, Hofstadter, or Beard.[3] And so it goes.

Historiography normally is retrospective, telling us in what diverse ways scholars have explained events like the American Civil War. What I propose to do here is a kind of prospective historiography. I am impressed with the value of explicitly stated theories of interpretation but also struck by the value of discovering anomalies which any one theory does not explain. Thus, it seems useful to entertain alternative modes of explanation as a way of avoiding the reductionism that selects evidence to fit a particular thesis. Using different lenses to view the same phenomenon may seem irresponsibly playful to a true believer in any one interpretation, but at least it offers the possibility of self-correction without undue damage to an author's self-esteem.[4]

The topic of compulsory schooling lends itself to sharply different valuations, as the cartoons in figures 1 and 2 suggest. Earlier students of compulsion, like Forest Ensign and Ellwood Cubberley, regarded universal attendance as necessary for social progress and portrayed the passage and implementation of compulsory laws as the product of noble leaders playing their role in a long evolution of democracy.[5] Standing firmly on "the structure of civilization," as in figure 1, leaders used the mechanism of schooling to raise "American Social and Economic Life." In recent years radical critics have offered a quite different view of compulsory schooling. Figure 2 visually represents some of the elements of this revised interpretation. The school offers different and unequal treatments based on the race, sex, and class of incoming students. Compartmentalized internally, it produces a segmented labor force incapable of perceiving common interest. Rather than liberating the individual, the school programs him or her so as to guarantee the profits of the invisible rulers of the system. The school is thus an imposition that dehumanizes the student and perpetuates social stratification.[6] Such differing valuations as these necessarily influence explanatory frameworks and policy discussion.

In this intentionally open-ended essay, I first sketch what I take to be the phenomena of compulsory schooling that the theories should explain. Then I examine two sets of interpretations, political and economic, which I find initially plausible. Some of the explanations are complementary, some contradictory; some explain certain events well but not others. Although each discussion is brief, I have tried to state the theories fairly, believing it not very useful to shoot down

[3] Herbert Bass, ed., *The State of American History* (Chicago: Quadrangle Books, 1970).

[4] Edward N. Saveth, ed., *American History and the Social Sciences* (New York: Free Press, 1964).

[5] Forest C. Ensign, *Compulsory School Attendance and Child Labor* (Iowa City, Iowa: Athens Press, 1921); Ellwood P. Cubberley, *Changing Conceptions of Education* (Boston: Houghton Mifflin, 1909).

[6] A sampling of radical views can be found in writings of Paul Goodman, Ivan Illich, Michael Katz, and Samuel Bowles and Herbert Gintis (the last two are discussed below in the "Marxian Analysis" section).

FIGURE 1

Source: Edgar Mendenhall, *The City School Board Member and His Task* (Pittsburgh, Kans.: College
          Inn Books, 1929), frontispiece.

interpretations like ducks in a shooting gallery, only to bring out the *right* one
(mine) at the end. But naturally I have interpretive preferences. Therefore, I
intend to indicate what I see as flaws in the theories and anomalies they may not
explain. In my conclusion, I do not attempt to reconcile the various interpretations

FIGURE 2

Source: Diane Lasch, *Leviathan*, 1, No. 3 (June 1969), 12.

in any definitive way, but instead suggest what we can learn from such comparative
explorations.

What Needs to Be Explained?

At this point in my reading, I see two major phases in the history of compulsory
school attendance in the United States. During the first, which lasted from mid-
nineteenth century to about 1890, Americans built a broad base of elementary
schooling which attracted ever-growing numbers of children. Most states passed
compulsory-attendance legislation during these years, but generally these laws
were unenforced and probably unenforceable. The notion of compulsion appears
to have aroused ideological dispute at this time, but few persons paid serious at-

tention to the organizational apparatus necessary to compel students into class-rooms. Therefore, this phase might be called the *symbolic* stage. The second phase, beginning shortly before the turn of the twentieth century, might be called the *bureaucratic* stage. During this era of American education, school systems grew in size and complexity, new techniques of bureaucratic control emerged, ideological conflict over compulsion diminished, strong laws were passed, and school officials developed sophisticated techniques to bring truants into schools. By the 1920s and 1930s increasing numbers of states were requiring youth to attend high school, and by the 1950s secondary-school attendance had become so customary that school-leavers were routinely seen as "dropouts."[7]

Even before the common-school crusade of the mid-nineteenth century and be-fore any compulsory laws, Americans were probably in the vanguard in literacy and mass schooling among the peoples of the world. Although methods of sup-port and control of schools were heterogeneous in most communities before 1830, enrollment rates and literacy were very high—at least among whites. Public-school advocates persuaded Americans to translate their generalized faith in education into support of a particular institution, the common school. Between 1850 and 1890 public expenditures for schools jumped from about $7 million to $147 mil-lion. Funds spent on public schools increased from 47 percent of total educational expenditures to 79 percent during those years.[8] Table 1 indicates both the high initial commitment to schooling and the gradual increase in attendance and de-cline in illiteracy.[9]

Educational statistics and data on literacy during the nineteenth century are notoriously unreliable, but table 1 at least suggests the magnitude of change. The aggregated national data, however, mask very important variations in attendance and literacy by region (the South lagged far behind the rest of the nation); by ethnicity (commonly forbidden to read under slavery, Blacks were about 90 per-cent illiterate in 1870; and foreign-born adult whites were considerably less liter-ate than native-born); and by other factors such as social class and urban or rural residence. Furthermore, the use of the broad age range of five to nineteen (com-mon for both census and Office of Education statistics) hides variations in at-tendance at different age levels in different kinds of communities. In the industrial states, for example, children tended to start school earlier and to leave earlier than in farm states. In a census sample of both kinds of states, however, eight or nine

[7] For a more detailed explication of this phasing, see my study *The One Best System: A History of American Urban Education* (Cambridge, Mass.: Harvard Univ. Press, 1974).

[8] Albert Fishlow, "Levels of Nineteenth-Century Investment in Education," *Journal of Eco-nomic History*, 26 (1966), 418–24; Albert Fishlow, "The American Common School Revival: Fact or Fancy?" in *Industrialism in Two Systems: Essays in Honor of Alexander Gerschenkron*, ed. Henry Rosovsky (New York: Wiley, 1966), pp. 40–67.

[9] John K. Folger and Charles B. Nam, *Education of the American Population* (Washington, D.C.: GPO, 1967), chs. 1, 4; W. Vance Grant and C. George Lind, *Digest of Educational Statistics*, 1974 ed. (Washington, D.C.: GPO, 1975).

TABLE 1

Selected Educational Statistics for the United States, 1840–1890

	1840	1850	1860	1870	1880	1890
Enrollment rates of persons aged 5–19, in percentage (a)	37	42	49	60	58	64
Percentage of enrolled pupils attending daily (b)	–	–	–	59	62	64
Average length of school term, in days (b)	–	–	–	132	130	134
Percentage of population 10 years and older illiterate (c)	25–30	23	20	20	17	13

Sources: a) John K. Folger and Charles B. Nam, *Education of the American Population* (Washington, D.C.: GPO, 1967), chs. 1,4.

b) W. Vance Grant and C. George Lind, *Digest of Educational Statistics,* 1974 ed. (Washington, D.C.: GPO, 1975), p. 34.

c) Folger and Nam, *Education*, pp. 113-114.

out of ten children attended school from ten to fourteen. Finally, the percentages obscured the magnitude of the sevenfold absolute growth in enrollment from 1840 to 1890; in the latter year, over fourteen million children were in school. By the close of the nineteenth century the typical child could expect to attend school for five years, according to United States Commissioner of Education William T. Harris; Harris and many others regarded this as a triumph, and indeed by then the United States led the world in its provision for mass education.[10]

These changes in attendance and literacy before roughly 1890 took place with minimal coercion by the states—despite the fact that by then twenty-seven legislatures had passed compulsory-attendance laws. A survey in 1889 revealed that in all but a handful of states and individual cities the laws were dead letters. Indeed, in several cases state superintendents of education said that responsible local officials did not even know that there was such legislation.[11] Educators were often ambivalent about enforcement of compulsory-attendance laws. Often they did not want the unwilling pupils whom coercion would bring into classrooms. In many communities, especially big cities, schools did not have enough seats even for children who wanted to go to school. And many citizens regarded compulsion as

[10] Folger and Nam, pp. 25, 3, 211–68; William T. Harris, "Elementary Education," in *Monographs on Education in the United States,* ed. Nicholas M. Butler (Albany, N.Y.: J. B. Lyon, 1900), pp. 79–139.

[11] United States Commissioner of Education, "Compulsory Attendance Laws in the United States," *Report for 1888–1889,* I (Washington, D.C.: GPO, 1889), ch. 18, pp. 470–531.

TABLE 2

Selected Educational Statistics for the United States, 1900–1950

	1900	1910	1920	1930	1940	1950
Enrollment rates of persons aged 5–19, in percentage (a)	72	74	78	82	84	83
Percentage of enrolled pupils attending daily (a)	69	72	75	83	87	89
Percentage of total enrollment in high schools (a)	3	5	10	17	26	23
High School graduates as percentage of population 17 years old (b)	6	9	17	29	51	59
Percentage of population 10 years and older illiterate (c)	11	8	6	4	3	3
Estimates of educational attainment, in years (d)	—	8.1	8.2	8.4	8.6	9.3

Sources: a) W. Vance Grant and C. George Lind, *Digest of Educational Statistics,* 1974 ed. (Washington, D.C.: GPO, 1975), p. 34.
b) United States Bureau of the Census, *Historical Statistics of the United States: Colonial Times to 1957* (Washington, D.C.: GPO, 1960), p. 207.
c) John K. Folger and Charles B. Nam, *Education of the American Population* (Washington, D.C.: GPO, 1967), p. 114.
d) Folger and Nam, *Education*, p. 132.

an un-American invasion of parental rights. Except in a few states like Connecticut and Massachusetts, provisions for enforcement were quite inadequate.[12]

Phase two of the history of compulsory schooling, the bureaucratic stage, built on the base of achievement laid down during the symbolic stage. The basically simple structure of the common school became much more elaborate, however, and mass education came to encompass the secondary school as well, as indicated by table 2.

Public attitudes toward compulsory schooling appeared to become more positive in the years after 1890. This was true even in the South, which had previously resisted such legislation. States passed new laws with provisions for effective enforcement, including requirements for censuses to determine how many children there were, attendance officers, elaborate "pupil accounting," and often state financing of schools in proportion to average daily attendance. Age limits were

[12] Mary J. Herrick, *The Chicago Schools: A Social and Political History* (Beverly Hills, Calif.: Sage, 1971), p. 58; John D. Philbrick, *City School Systems in the United States*, U.S. Bureau of Education, Circular of Information, No. 1 (Washington, D.C.: GPO, 1885), pp. 154–55.

gradually extended upwards, especially under the impact of the labor surplus in the Depression, until by the mid-1930s youths were typically required to attend school until age sixteen.

Early in the century the great majority of teenagers in school were lumped in the upper grades of the elementary school as a result of the frequent practice of forcing children to repeat grades. In the 1920s and 1930s, however, the practice of "social promotion"—that is, keeping age groups together—took hold, and the percentage of teenagers in high schools increased sharply. The increasing numbers of children compelled to attend schools, in turn, helped to transform the structure and curriculum of schooling. Of course, there were still many children who escaped the net of the truant officer, many who were denied equality of educational opportunity: an estimated two million children aged six to fifteen were not in any school in 1940. But during the twentieth century universal elementary and secondary schooling gradually was accepted as a common goal and approached a common reality.[13]

Over the long perspective of the last century and a half, both phases of compulsory school attendance may be seen as part of significant shifts in the functions of families and the status of children and youth. Households in American industrial cities became more like units of consumption than of production. Indeed, Frank Musgrove contends that the passage of compulsory-school legislation in England "finally signalized the triumph of public over private influences as formative in social life and individual development; in particular, it tardily recognized the obsolescence of the educative family, its inadequacy in modern society in child care and training."[14] Advocates of compulsory schooling often argued that families—or at least some families, like those of the poor or foreign-born—were failing to carry out their traditional functions of moral and vocational training. Immigrant children in crowded cities, reformers complained, were leading disorderly lives, schooled by the street and their peers more than by Christian nurture in the home. Much of the drive for compulsory schooling reflected an animus against parents considered incompetent to train their children. Often combining fear of social unrest with humanitarian zeal, reformers used the powers of the state to intervene in families and to create alternative institutions of socialization.

Laws compelling school attendance were only part of an elaborate and massive transformation in the legal and social rules governing children.[15] Children and

[13] United States Bureau of the Census, *Historical Statistics of the United States: Colonial Times to 1957* (Washington, D.C.: GPO, 1960), pp. 207, 215; John K. Norton and Eugene S. Lawler, *Unfinished Business in American Education: An Inventory of Public School Expenditures in the United States* (Washington, D.C.: American Council on Education, 1946); Newton Edwards, *Equal Educational Opportunity for Youth* (Washington, D.C.: American Council on Education, 1939), p. 152.

[14] Frank Musgrove, "The Decline of the Educative Family," *Universities Quarterly*, 14 (1960), p. 377.

[15] John W. Meyer and Joane P. Nagel, "The Changing Status of Childhood," paper presented at the Annual Meeting of the Society for the Study of Social Problems, San Francisco, Calif., 1975.

youth came to be seen as individuals with categorical needs: as patients requiring specialized medical care; as "delinquents" needing particular treatment in the courts; and as students deserving elaborately differentiated schooling. Specific adults came to be designated as responsible for aiding parents in the complex tasks of child care: teachers, truant officers, counselors, scout leaders, and pediatricians, for example—not to mention Captain Kangaroo. Formerly regarded as a central function of the family, education came finally to be regarded as synonymous with schooling. The common query "Why aren't you in school?" signified that attendance in school had become the normal career of the young.[16]

Political Dimensions of Compulsory Attendance

Only government can compel parents to send their children to school. In legally compelling school attendance, the democratic state not only coerces behavior but also legitimizes majority values, as Michael S. Katz has argued.[17] Thus, sooner or later, any historian investigating compulsory school attendance logically needs to attend to political processes.

In recent years, however, few historians of American education have paid close attention either to the politics of control of schools or to the nature of political socialization in schools. Echoing Horace Mann's concern for social cohesion as well as social justice, R. Freeman Butts has suggested that both radical historians (stressing imposition by economic elites) and "culturist" historians (broadening the definition of education to include all "habitats of knowledge") have somewhat neglected the political functions of public schooling in both national and international contexts—what he calls civism.[18] Such neglect did not characterize much of the earlier work in the history of education, which like writings in other branches of history, had a marked political and indeed nationalistic flavor. Among political sociologists, the emergence of new nations has also aroused interest in the political construction of education.

I begin, then, with an examination of a broad interpretive framework which stresses education as a means of incorporating people into a nation-state and legitimizing the status of "citizen" and "leader." After noting difficulties in relating these notions to the loosely organized political system of the United States, I proceed to a rather different form of analysis—namely, one which seeks to interpret the passage of compulsory-schooling laws as a species of ethnocultural conflict. This explanation appears to fit phase one far better than phase two. To interpret

[16] Robert H. Bremner, ed., *Children and Youth in America: A Documentary History*, I–II (Cambridge, Mass.: Harvard Univ. Press, 1970–71).

[17] Michael S. Katz, "The Concepts of Compulsory Education and Compulsory Schooling: A Philosophical Inquiry," Diss. Stanford Univ., Palo Alto, Calif., 1974.

[18] R. Freeman Butts, "Public Education and Political Community," *History of Education Quarterly*, 14 (1974), 165–83.

phase two I draw upon what one historian has called "the organizational synthesis," an approach that seeks to explain political and social changes during the progressive era in terms of the growing importance of large-scale bureaucratic organizations and the attempt to resolve political issues by administrative means.

The Political Construction of Education

It is natural in the Watergate era to agree with Dr. Johnson that "patriotism is the last refuge of the scoundrel" and to suspect that nationalistic rhetoric about schooling disguises real motives. Yet I am struck by the range of ideology and class among persons in the United States who justified compulsory public education on explicitly political grounds. If the patriots were scoundrels, there were many of them in assorted walks of life. Moreover, nationalism has been associated with compulsory attendance not in the United States alone but also in European nations during the nineteenth century and in scores of developing nations today. In 1951 UNESCO sponsored a series of monographs on compulsory education around the globe; the organization assumed that all United Nations members agreed on "the general principle of the necessity of instituting systems of compulsory, free and universal education in all countries."[19]

How can one construe the political construction of education? Why does schooling seem so important to the modern state? In their essay, "Education and Political Development," John W. Meyer and Richard Rubinson have argued that modern national educational systems in effect create and legitimate citizens. New nations are commonly composed of families and individuals who identify with regions, religions, ethnic groups, tribes, or interest groups. Such persons rarely think of themselves as either participants in or subjects of the state. Indeed, the whole notion of universal citizenship might seem to them fanciful and implausible. Meyer and Rubinson argue that the central political purpose of universal education is precisely to create citizens and legitimize the state. Families in potentially divisive subgroups turn over their children to state schools to learn a common language, a national history, and an ideology that incorporates them as citizens into the broader entity called the state. The point is not that this new compulsory political socialization is actually successful in accomplishing its cognitive or affective tasks, but simply that the institutional process is designed to create a new category of personnel—citizens. Similarly, advanced education may create and legitimate elites. People who formerly ruled by hereditary right or other kinds of ascriptive privilege may still wield power, but the rituals of higher state education turn them into legitimate "civil servants." As states expand their control over new sectors of society, state schooling gives an apparently rational and modern justification for new social rules that replace the older ones based on regional, ethnic, religious, or

[19] Australian National Commission for UNESCO, *Compulsory Education in Australia* (Paris: UNESCO, 1951), preface.

family loyalties. By these means, education helps to institutionalize the authority of the state.[20]

It is a complicated argument. Let me illustrate with historical examples from American, French, and Prussian experience. After the American Revolution, numerous theorists like Thomas Jefferson, Benjamin Rush, and Noah Webster argued that without a transformed educational system the old pre-Revolutionary attitudes and relationships would prevail in the new nation. Rush said that a new, uniform state system should turn children into "republican machines." Webster called for an "Association of American Patriots for the Formation of an American Character," strove to promote uniformity of language, and wrote a "Federal Catechism" to teach republican principles to school children. Jefferson wanted to create state primary schools to make loyal citizens of the young. In addition, many early theorists wanted a national university to prepare and legitimate elites for leadership.[21] Similarly, French writers on education after the 1789 Revolution advocated a universal state system that would teach all French citizens to read and would give them pride in their country's history and political institutions. In both cases education was regarded as an instrument deliberately used to create a new status, to turn people with diverse loyalties into citizens of a new entity—the republican state.

The use of schooling as a means of incorporating people into the nation-state was not limited to liberal regimes, however. Compulsory schooling also served militant nationalism in conservative Prussia during the nineteenth century by attaching people to the centralized and corporate state. Victor Cousin observed in his report on Prussian education that the parental duty to send children to school "is so national, so rooted in all the legal and moral habits of the country, that it is expressed by a single word, *Schulpflichtigkeit* [school duty, or school obligation]. It corresponds to another word, similarly formed and similarly sanctioned by public opinion, *Dienstpflichtigkeit* [service obligation, that is military service]."[22]

To some degree the political construction of education I have sketched here does fit the development of compulsory schooling in the United States. As mentioned above, post-revolutionary writers on education stressed the need to use schools to transform colonials into citizens. Repeating their arguments, Horace Mann contended that common schools would imbue the rising generation with traits of character and loyalties required for self-government. Waves of immigration intensified concern over the incorporation of new groups into the polity. For a time the federal government took an active interest in schooling ex-slaves so that they,

[20] John W. Meyer and Richard Rubinson, "Education and Political Development," in *Review of Research in Education*, III, ed. Fred Kerlinger (Itasca, Ill.: F. E. Peacock, 1975), 134–62.

[21] David Tyack, *Turning Points in American Educational History* (Waltham, Mass.: Blaisdell, 1967), pp. 83–119.

[22] Cousins, as quoted in Edward Reisner, *Nationalism and Education Since 1789: A Social and Political History of Modern Education* (New York: Macmillan, 1922), p. 134; ch. 2.

too, might become proper citizens like their foreign-born fellow compatriots.[23] The national government even used schooling as a way to shape people conquered in war into the predetermined mold of republican citizenship: witness the fate of Native American children torn from their parents and sent to boarding schools, the dispatch of American teachers to Puerto Rico and the Philippines after the Spanish-American war, and the attempts to democratize Germany and Japan after World War II.[24] Even the Japanese-Americans "relocated" during World War II were subjected to deliberate resocialization in the camps' public schools.[25]

Clearly, Americans had enormous faith in the power of schooling to transform all kinds of people—even "enemies"—into citizens. The process of entry into the status of citizenship was rather like baptism; like the sprinkling of water on the head of a child in an approved church, schooling was a ritual process that acquired political significance because people believed in it. Characteristically, Americans intensified their attempts at political socialization in schools whenever they perceived a weakening of loyalties (as in World War I), or an infusion of strangers (as in peak times of immigration), or a spreading of subversive ideas (whether by Jesuits or Wobblies or Communists). Interest in compulsory attendance seems to correlate well with such periods of concern.[26]

There are problems, however, with applying this conception of the political construction of education to the United States. The ideas of the revolutionary theorists were not put into practice in their lifetime, for example. One could argue that early Americans learned to be citizens by participating in public life rather than by schooling and indeed, that they had in effect been American "citizens" even before the Revolution. Before the common-school crusade, educational institutions tended to reflect differences of religion, ethnicity, and social class—precisely the sorts of competing loyalties presumably detrimental to national unification. Furthermore, in the federated network of local, state, and national governments, it was by no means clear what "the state" really was. Although many advocates of compulsion turned to Prussia for evidence on how the state could incorporate the young into schools for the public good, opposition to centralization of state power was strong throughout the nineteenth century. The ritualized patriotism of Fourth-of-July orations and school textbooks was popular, but actual attempts to coerce parents to send their children to school were often seen as un-American

23 William Edward Burghardt DuBois, *Black Reconstruction in America, an Essay toward a History of the Part which Black Folk Played in the Attempt to Reconstruct Democracy in America, 1860–1880* (Cleveland, Ohio: World Pub., 1964), pp. 637–69.

24 John Morgan Oates, *Schoolbooks and Krags: The United States Army in the Philippines, 1898–1902* (Westport, Conn.: Greenwood Press, 1973).

25 Charles Wollenberg, *All Deliberate Speed: Segregation and Exclusion in California Schools, 1855–1975* (Berkeley: Univ. of California Press, forthcoming), ch. 3.

26 Howard K. Beale, *A History of Freedom of Teaching in American Schools* (New York: Charles Scribner's Sons, 1941); John W. Meyer, "Theories of the Effects of Education on Civil Participation in Developing Societies," unpublished paper, Dept. of Sociology, Stanford Univ., Palo Alto, Calif., May 1972.

and no business of the state. Prussian concepts of duty to the state sharply contrasted with nineteenth-century American beliefs in individualism and laissez-faire government. Different groups in American society tended to express different points of view about using the state to reinforce certain values and to sanction others.[27] I will explore this point in the next section on ethnocultural politics.

During most of the nineteenth century, the apparatus of federal and state control of education was exceedingly weak. Although leaders from Horace Mann forward talked of the virtues of centralization and standardization in state systems, state departments of education were miniscule and had few powers. In 1890 the median size of state departments of education, including the superintendent, was two persons. At that time there was one state education official in the United States for every one hundred thousand pupils. One pedagogical czar with effective sanctions and rewards might have controlled such masses, but state departments of education prior to the turn of the twentieth century rarely had strong or even clear-cut powers.[28] Federal control was even weaker, although some reformers dreamed of massive federal aid and extended powers for the Office of Education. In effect, the United States Commissioner of Education was a glorified collector of statistics—and often ineffectual even in that role. An individual like Henry Barnard or William T. Harris might lend intellectual authority to the position, but the Office itself probably had trivial influence on American schools.[29] De facto, most control of schools lay with local school boards.

So the theory of the political construction of education is powerfully suggestive, but the American historical experience raises certain anomalies. Most Americans during the early national period apparently felt no need to legitimize citizenship through formal state schooling, although that idea began to take hold by mid-nineteenth century. Until the end of the century there was considerable opposition to centralized state power, both in theory and in practice. Thus it is difficult to envisage *the state* during either period as legitimizing individuals as citizens through education or effectively extending its jurisdiction into other parts of society like the family.

Much of this changed in the era beginning roughly in 1890, as the notion of the state as an agency of social and economic reform and control took hold and an "organizational revolution" began. Thus it seems useful to supplement the broad theory of the political construction of education with two other interpretations that give a more focused perspective on the two phases of compulsion.

27 Merle Curti, *The Roots of American Loyalty* (New York: Columbia Univ. Press, 1946).
28 Department of Superintendence, NEA, *Educational Leadership: Progress and Possibilities* (Washington, D.C.: NEA, 1933), p. 246, ch. 11.
29 Donald Warren, *To Enforce Education: A History of the Founding Years of the United States Office of Education* (Detroit: Wayne State Univ. Press, 1974).

Ethnocultural Politics in Compulsory-School Legislation during the Nineteenth Century

During the nineteenth century Americans differed significantly in their views of citizenship and the legitimate domain of state action, including compulsory-attendance legislation. A number of interpreters of the political contests of the period have argued that these cleavages followed ethnic and religious lines. In a perceptive essay on this ethnocultural school of interpretation, James Wright notes that these historians dissent from both the economic class-conflict model of Charles Beard and the consensus model that emerged after World War II. The ethnocultural historians, he says, do not argue

> . . . a simplistic model in which ward heelers appeal to ethnic, religious, or racial prejudices and loyalties in order to divert attention from "real" economic issues. Rather, the real issues of politics have been those most significant relative to life style and values: prohibition, public funding or control of sectarian schools, sabbatarian laws, woman suffrage, and efforts to hasten or retard ethnic assimilation.[30]

Richard Jensen points out that religious congregations, often divided along ethnic lines, were very important in shaping political attitudes and behavior in the Midwest. Such sectarian groups provided not only contrasting world views but also face-to-face communities that reinforced them. Like Paul Kleppner, Jensen has identified two primary religious persuasions that directly influenced political expression. One was represented by the *pietistic* sects—groups like the Baptists and Methodists that had experienced great growth as a result of the evangelical awakenings of the century—which tended to reject church hierarchy and ritual and insist that right belief should result in upright behavior. Seeing sin in the world, as represented by breaking the Sabbath or drinking alcohol, for example, the pietists sought to change society and thereby, as Kleppner explains, "to *conserve* their value system and to restore the norms it preserved." The *liturgicals,* by contrast, believed that salvation came from right belief and from the preservation of the particular orthodoxies represented in the creeds and sacraments of the church. Liturgicals like Roman Catholics and Lutherans of certain synods tended to see morality as the preserve not of the state but of the church, the family, and the parochial school. According to both Kleppner and Jensen, the Republican Party tended to attract the pietists, the Democratic Party the liturgicals. By and large, the Republicans supported a "crusading moralism" for a single standard of behavior, while the Democrats spoke for a "counter-crusading pluralism."[31]

These politically important religious distinctions cut across ethnic lines. Al-

---

30 James Wright, "The Ethnocultural Model of Voting: A Behavioral and Historical Critique," *American Behavioral Scientist,* 16 (1973), p. 655.

31 Richard Jensen, *The Winning of the Midwest: Social and Political Conflict, 1888–1896* (Chicago: Univ. of Chicago Press, 1971), pp. 63–66, xv; Paul Kleppner, *The Cross of Culture: A Social Analysis of Midwestern Politics, 1850–1900* (New York: Free Press, 1970), pp. 71–74.

though old-stock Americans tended to be pietistic and Republican, the Irish Catholics to be liturgical and Democratic, for example, other ethnic groups, like the Germans, split into different camps. *The* immigrant vote was a fiction based on nativistic fear; canny politicians knew better. Furthermore, this kind of status-group politics needs to be distinguished from the theory of the politics of status anxiety or status discrepancy that was advanced by political scientists and by Richard Hofstadter in the 1950s. Status groups asserting themselves through the political process during the nineteenth century rarely saw themselves on the skids socially. Rather than regarding ethnocultural politics as in some sense pathological, it is quite as accurate to describe it as the positive assertion of groups that believed in their own values and life styles and sought to extend their group boundaries and influence.[32]

The politics of "crusading moralism" and "counter-crusading pluralism" often focused on issues like temperance or Sabbath observance and frequently resulted in blue laws, which, like dead-letter compulsory-attendance legislation, were often more symbolic assertions than implementable decisions. Republican politicians often winked at breaches of the laws where it was politically astute to do so. It was one thing to enforce prohibition in a town where the only public drinker was the town Democrat, and quite another to do so in German wards of Milwaukee. Laws which stamped the pietistic foot and said "Be like me" might satisfy symbolically without alienating dissenters by active enforcement.[33]

Were nineteenth-century compulsory-school-attendance laws of that character largely passed by Republican pietists? I don't know, but the hypothesis seems worth testing by evidence; perhaps by the political composition of the state legislatures that passed such laws and by values expressed in textbooks. For now, the interpretation seems plausible. Evangelical ministers were at the forefront of the common-school crusade as the frontier moved westward, and ministers like Josiah Strong saw the school as a bulwark of the evangelical campaign to save the cities. Public schooling was widely publicized as the creation of "our Puritan, New England forefathers." Pietists saw themselves not as an interest group but as representatives of true American values. People who wanted compulsory-attendance laws were presumably already sending their children to school; by branding the nonconforming parent as illegal or deviant, they thereby strengthened the norms of their own group (the explanation follows what can be called the tongue-clucking theory of the function of crime).[34]

[32] John W. Meyer and James G. Roth, "A Reinterpretation of American Status Politics," *Pacific Sociological Review*, 13 (1970), 95–102; Joseph R. Gusfield, *Symbolic Crusade: Status Politics and the American Temperance Movement* (Urbana, Ill.: Univ. of Illinois Press, 1963), chs. 1, 6, 7.

[33] Jensen, p. 122.

[34] Timothy L. Smith, "Protestant Schooling and American Nationality," *Journal of American History*, 53 (1967), 679–95; David B. Tyack, "Onward Christian Soldiers: Religion in the American Common School," in *History and Education*, ed. Paul Nash (New York: Random House, 1970), pp. 212–55.

Much of the rhetoric of compulsory schooling lends itself to this ethnocultural interpretation and further refines the theory of the political construction of education. In 1891 superintendents in the National Education Association (NEA) passed a resolution favoring compulsory education. The resolution's preamble stated that "in our free Republic the State is merely the expression of the people's will, and not an external governmental force." The NEA statement sounds quite different than the notion of a strong central state creating citizens through schooling, as in the view explored above. Why then, did the state have to compel citizens to send their children to school? Because compulsion created liberty.[35]

The assumptions behind this Orwellian paradox become more clear when one reads accounts of the discussions of compulsion which took place that year in the National Council of Education, the prestigious think tank of the NEA. A committee had just reported to the Council that the idle and vicious were filling the jails of the nation, corrupt men were getting the ballot, and "foreign influence has begun a system of colonization with a purpose of preserving foreign languages and traditions and proportionately of destroying distinctive Americanism. It has made alliance with religion. . . ." The committee was really saying that there were two classes of citizens, us and them. Said an educator in the audience: "The report assumes that when the people established this government they had a certain standard of intelligence and morality; and that an intelligent and moral people will conform to the requirements of good citizenship." Things have changed, he observed: "People have come here who are not entitled to freedom in the same sense as those who established this government." The question was whether to raise these inferior newcomers to the standards of the Anglo-Saxon forefathers or to "lower this idea of intelligence and morality to the standard of that class" of new immigrants from southern and eastern Europe. Republican liberty depended on a homogeneity of virtue and knowledge that only compulsion could create in the new generation. Almost without exception native-born and Protestant, NEA leaders in the nineteenth century took naturally to the notion that real citizens were those who fit the pietist mold.[36]

In 1871, in a speech on the "New Departure of the Republican Party," Republican Senator Henry Wilson linked compulsory schooling to nativist and Protestant principles. Pointing out that the Fifteenth Amendment had expanded suffrage to include Blacks and that unrestricted immigration was flooding the nation with millions "from Europe with all the disqualifications of their early training," he argued for an educational system that would transform "the emigrant, the freedman, and the operative" into proper citizens in accord with the "desirable traits

35 J. K. Richards, *Compulsory Education in Ohio: Brief for Defendent in Error in the Supreme Court of Ohio, Patrick F. Quigley v. The State of Ohio* (Columbus, Ohio: Westbote, 1892), p. 23.
36 National Education Association, *Journal of Addresses and Proceedings, 1891* (Topeka: Kansas Pub. House, 1891), pp. 295, 298, 393–403.

of New England and the American character."[37] An editorial in the *Catholic World* promptly attacked Wilson for wanting compulsory schooling to mold all "into one homogeneous people, after what may be called the New England Evangelical type. Neither his politics nor his philanthropy can tolerate any diversity of ranks, conditions, race, belief, or worship."[38]

Evidence of ethnic and religious bias abounds in the arguments about compulsory schooling throughout the nineteenth century. In the 1920s bias surfaced again in Oregon when the Ku Klux Klan and its allies passed a law that sought to outlaw private schooling. Two compulsory-schooling laws in Illinois and in Wisconsin in 1889 aroused fierce opposition from liturgical groups, especially German Catholics and Lutherans, because of their provisions that private schools teach in the English language and that they be approved by boards of public education. In both states Democrats derided the laws as instances of Republican paternalism and hostility to pluralism; defeated Republicans learned to disavow spokesmen who believed that extremism in defense of virtue is no vice. After the disastrous votes in 1892, one Republican wrote to a friend that "defeat was inevitable. The school law did it—a silly, sentimental and damned useless abstraction, foisted upon us by a self-righteous demagogue."[39] Both Kleppner and Jensen see these contests over compulsory instruction in English as classic examples of ethnocultural politics.[40]

These Illinois and Wisconsin conflicts may, however, be exceptional cases; other states passed similar laws requiring English-language instruction and state accreditation without such contests erupting. It is possible that there was bipartisan support for the ineffectual state laws passed before 1890 and that widespread belief in public education made consensus politics the wisest course. The South, which lagged in compulsory legislation, had few immigrants and few Catholics; its population was native-born and evangelical with a vengeance. How well does an ethnocultural hypothesis fit the South? Is the educational politics of race substantially different from white ethnocultural politics? Only careful state-by-state analysis can test the theory that ethnocultural politics was a key factor in compulsory-attendance legislation during the nineteenth century. But where there is the smoke of ethnocultural rhetoric it is plausible to seek political fires.[41]

In any case, the high point of ethnocultural politics of compulsory education was probably the nineteenth century. The assumption persisted into the twentieth

[37] Henry Wilson, "New Departure of the Republican Party," *Atlantic Monthly*, 27 (1871), 11–14.

[38] Editorial, *Catholic World*, 13 (1871), 3–4; John Whitney Evans, "Catholics and the Blair Education Bill," *Catholic Historical Review*, 46 (1960), 273–98.

[39] Jensen, pp. 122, 129.

[40] Kleppner, pp. 169–70.

[41] Horace Mann Bond has given us a brilliant analysis of how the politics of race mixed with the politics of competing economic groups in his *Negro Education in Alabama: A Study in Cotton and Steel* (Washington, D.C.: Associated Pub., 1939).

century that there were *real* citizens—those with the right heredity and principles —who needed to shape others to their own image. But at the turn of the century attention shifted to efficient organizational means for compelling school attendance.

From Politics to Administration:
An Organizational Interpretation

Despite some notable exceptions, open ethnocultural strife in school politics appears to have subsided during phase two of compulsory attendance. Many of the decisions that once had been made in the give-and-take of pluralistic politics now shifted to administrators within the system. At the turn of the century a powerful and largely successful movement centralized control of city schools in small boards of education elected at large rather than by ward. Furthermore, state departments of education grew in size and influence and led in the consolidation of rural schools and the enforcement of uniform educational standards. Advocates of these new forms of governance argued that education should be taken out of politics and that most decisions were best made by experts. Government by administrative experts was, of course, a form of politics under another name: decisions about who got what in the public allocation of scarce resources were simply shifted to a new arena. The line between public and private organizations became blurred as proponents of centralization urged that school systems adopt the corporate model of governance. As decision-making power shifted to superintendents and their staffs, the number of specialists and administrators ballooned. School systems grew in size, added tiers of officials, and became segmented into functional divisions: elementary, junior high, and high schools; vocational programs of several kinds; classes for the handicapped; counseling services; research and testing bureaus; and many other departments.[42]

The new provisions for compulsory schooling reflected these bureaucratic technologies. In city schools, in particular, large attendance departments were divided into supervisors, field workers, and clerks. Attendance experts developed the school census, elaborate forms for reporting attendance, manuals on "child accounting," and civil-service requirements for employment. By 1911 attendance officers were numerous and self-conscious enough to start their own national professional organization. Schools developed not only new ways of finding children and getting them into school, but also new institutions or programs to cope with the unwilling students whom truant officers brought to their doors: parental schools, day-long truant schools, disciplinary classes, ungraded classes, and a host of specialized curricular tracks. Local officials gathered data by the file full to aid in planning a

42 Marvin Lazerson, *Origins of the Urban Public School: Public Education in Massachusetts, 1870–1915* (Cambridge, Mass.: Harvard Univ. Press, 1971), chs. 5–9; Joseph M. Cronin, *The Control of Urban Schools: Perspectives on the Power of Educational Reformers* (New York: Free Press, 1973).

rational expansion and functional specialization of the schools. Doctoral dissertations and other "scientific" studies analyzed existing patterns of attendance and promoted the new methods.[43]

Surely one can find examples of these new techniques and institutional adaptations prior to phase two, but what I find striking is the very rapid increase in the machinery of compulsion and the structural differentiation of the schools in the years after 1890. A new method of inquiry called "educational science" helped educators to gather and process information so that they could not only describe quantitatively what was going on in schools, but also forecast and plan. In national organizations these new functional specialists shared ideas and strategies of change. Older local perspectives gradually gave way to more cosmopolitan ways of thinking. The new hierarchical, differentiated bureaucracies seemed to many to be a superb instrument for continuous adaptation of the schools to diverse social conditions and needs. Theoretically at least, issues of religion or ethnicity were irrelevant to decision making in such bureaucracies, as were parochial tastes or local prejudices.[44]

Samuel Hays sees the rise of large-scale organizations and functional groups as characteristic of many sectors of American society during the twentieth century. He points out that the new technical systems defined what were problems and used particular means for solving them. "Reason, science, and technology are not inert processes by which men discover, communicate, and apply facts disinterestedly and without passion, but means through which, through systems, some men organize and control the lives of other men according to their particular conceptions as to what is preferable." He argues that the rapid growth of empirical inquiry—normally called "science"—has enabled people in organizations to plan future courses of action. This differentiates these new technical systems from earlier bureaucracies. Not only did these new methods change decision making within organizations, but functional specialists like educators, engineers, or doctors banded together in organizations to influence the larger environment collectively as interest groups.[45]

How does this vision of organizational change help explain the enactment and implementation of compulsory schooling? John Higham has observed that "the distinctive feature of the period from 1898 to 1918 is not the preeminence of democratic ideals or of bureaucratic techniques, but rather a fertile amalgamation of the two. An extraordinary quickening of ideology occurred in the very midst of a dazzling elaboration of technical systems."[46] Robert Wiebe, likewise, sees the

[43] Frank V. Bermejo, *The School Attendance Service in American Cities* (Menasha, Wis.: George Banta Pub., 1924).

[44] Tyack, *One Best System,* part 4.

[45] Samuel Hays, "The New Organizational Society," in *Building the Organizational Society: Essays on Associational Activity in Modern America,* ed. Jerry Israel (New York: Free Press, 1972), pp. 2–3, 6–8.

[46] John Higham, "Hanging Together: Divergent Unities in American History," *Journal of American History,* 61 (1974), p. 24.

essence of progressivism as "the ambition of the new middle class to fulfill its destiny through bureaucratic means."[47] Thus one might interpret the passage of child-labor legislation and effective compulsory-attendance laws as the work of functional groups and national reform associations that combined ideological commitment with bureaucratic sophistication. These groups knew how to create enforcement systems that would actually work, and they followed up on their results. Active in this way were such groups as educators (who increasingly came to the forefront in compulsory-schooling campaigns), labor unions, the National Child Labor Committee, and elite educational associations (like the Philadelphia Public Education Association) with cosmopolitan connections and outlooks.[48]

In his essay, "The Emerging Organizational Synthesis in Modern American History," Louis Galambos says that historians of this persuasion believe

> . . . that some of the most (if not the single most) important changes which have taken place in modern America have centered about a shift from small-scale, informal, locally or regionally oriented groups to large-scale, national, formal organizations . . . characterized by a bureaucratic structure of authority. This shift in organization cuts across the traditional boundaries of political, economic, and social history.[49]

This interpretation has called attention to the fact that large-scale organizations deeply influence the lives of most Americans, and to a degree it has explained how. There is somewhat less agreement among historians as to *why* this shift has taken place or how to assess the human consequences. Most historians would agree that the rise of complex organizations relates in some fashion to new technology, new forms of empirical inquiry, and institutional innovations designed to cope with size and scope of functions. Economic historians like Thomas Cochran, Alfred Chandler, and Fritz Redlich have described how business firms changed from small, local enterprises (often owned and run by a single family) to vast and diversified multi-tier bureaucracies in order to cope with problems of growth of markets, complexity of production, and widening spans of control.[50] Raymond Callahan and others have shown how educational administrators consciously emulated these new business corporations.[51]

Although the new organizational approach in history may provide a useful focus for the study of compulsory attendance, especially in the years after 1890,

---

47 Robert Wiebe, *The Search for Order, 1877–1920* (New York: Hill & Wang, 1967), p. 166.

48 Walter Trattner, *Crusade for the Children: A History of the National Child Labor Committee and Child Labor Reform in America* (Chicago: Quadrangle Books, 1970).

49 Louis Galambos, "The Emerging Organizational Synthesis in Modern American History," *Business History Review*, 44 (1970), p. 280.

50 Thomas C. Cochran, *Business in American Life: A History* (New York: McGraw-Hill, 1972), chs. 9, 16; Alfred D. Chandler, Jr., and Fritz Redlich, "Recent Developments in American Business Administration and Their Conceptualization," *Business History Review*, 35 (1961), 1–31.

51 Raymond E. Callahan, *Education and the Cult of Efficiency* (Chicago: Univ. of Chicago Press, 1962).

the interpretation is not without flaws. It may not be sound to generalize urban experience to the educational system as a whole; bureaucratization was probably neither rapid nor systemic throughout American schools, but gradual and spreading from certain centers like drops of gas on water. The conceptualization of an organizational revolution is also somewhat rudimentary at this point, leading to the same dangers of misplaced concreteness one finds in the use of concepts like "modernization" and "urbanization." It is very important not to portray this kind of organizational change as an inevitable process. Some people helped to plan the changes and benefited from them, others did not; some results were intended, others were not. Schools are rarely so politically neutral as they portray themselves. One virtue of the economic interpretations to which we now turn is that they provide models of behavior that help to explain the interests or motivations of people who acted collectively in organizations.[52]

Two Economic Interpretations of School Attendance

It is misleading, of course, to attempt to separate economic interpretations too sharply from political ones. In the three variants of political models sketched above, issues of economic class are present even where, as in ethnocultural conflict, they may not be salient. Both of the economic interpretations I examine also involve political action. Not surprisingly, however, economic historians tend to focus on economic variables, and it is useful to see how far this kind of analysis carries us in interpreting school attendance.

Two contrasting views seem most relevant: human-capital theory and a Marxian model. Both have precursors in nineteenth-century educational thought, but both have received closest scholarly attention during the last generation. Both are related to political interpretations in the broad sense in which Thomas Cochran says that the economic order shaped the political order: "On the fundamental level the goals and values of a business-oriented culture established the rules of the game: how men were expected to act, what they strove for, and what qualities or achievements were rewarded."[53] Naturally, economic interpretations may differ in what they take to be the basic driving forces in historical events, and such is the case in the two models I explore.

Human-Capital Theory and School Attendance

Mary Jean Bowman has described the notion of investment in human beings "as something of a revolution in economic thought." The notion of investigating the connection between resources spent on increasing the competence of workers and

[52] For some of these criticisms of the "organizational synthesis" I am indebted to Wayne Hobson's unpublished manuscript, "Social Change and the Organizational Society," Stanford Univ., Palo Alto, Calif., 1975.
[53] Cochran, p. 304.

increased productivity and earnings was not entirely new, of course, but experience after World War II showed that "physical capital worked its miracles only in lands where there were many qualified men who knew how to use it (the Marshall Plan countries and Japan)." Economists interested in economic growth then began to analyze the effects of "human capital" on development and discovered that education appeared to have considerable explanatory power.[54]

Work on investment in human beings moved from general studies of the contribution of schooling to economic growth in whole societies to analyses of the rates of return of formal education to individuals. Economists treated the micro-decision making of individuals or families about schooling as a form of rational cost-benefit analysis. They developed increasingly sophisticated ways to estimate rates of return on investment in education by including not only the direct costs of schooling but also the value of foregone earnings and the costs of maintaining students as dependents. Albert Fishlow, for example, has calculated that during the nineteenth century the "opportunity costs" paid by parents about equalled the sums paid by the public to support all levels of the educational system. Despite disagreements over specific rates of return, most economists agree that schooling does have significant impact on growth and earnings.[55]

Although economists have only recently honed the theory of human investment, similar notions have been current in educational circles for a long time. An idea circulating among educators for over a century has been that schooling created economic benefits for the society as a whole through greater productivity and for individuals through greater earnings. The first influential advocate of this view in the United States was Horace Mann, Secretary of the Board of Education of Massachusetts, who devoted his *Fifth Annual Report* in 1842 chiefly to this theme. In his report Mann presented an economic justification for greater investment in schooling, but his arguments were soon picked up as justification for compulsory school attendance. As Maris Vinovskis has observed, Mann actually preferred to advocate education by noneconomic arguments—the role of schools in moral or civic development, for example. But in his fifth year as Secretary, when his work was under political attack in the legislature and when a depression was forcing government to retrench, Mann decided that the time had come to show thrifty Yankees that education was a good investment. He argued that education not only produced good character and multiplied knowledge "but that it is also the most prolific parent of material riches." As proof he adduced the replies of businessmen to his questionnaire asking about the differences between educated and uneducated workers. What his study lacked in objectivity and scientific rigor it made up

[54] Mary Jean Bowman, "The Human Investment Revolution in Economic Thought," *Sociology of Education*, 39 (1966), 113, 117; Berry R. Chiswick, "Minimum Schooling Legislation and the Cross-Sectional Distribution of Income," *Economic Journal*, 315 (1969), 495–507.

[55] Bowman, 118-19; Fishlow, "Levels of Investment," p. 426; Marc Blaug, *An Introduction to the Economics of Education* (London: Penguin, 1972), chs. 1–3.

in evangelical enthusiasm; Mann concluded that money spent on primary schooling gave an aggregate rate of return to society of about 50 percent. He claimed that education enabled people to become rational decision makers by "comprehending the connections of a long train of events and seeing the end from the beginning." In addition to instilling this orientation toward the future—perhaps of most benefit to entrepreneurs—schooling made workers punctual, industrious, frugal, and too rational to cause trouble for their employers.[56]

Although Mann's evidence was largely impressionistic, his questionnaire highly biased, and his conclusions suspect for those reasons, his report was welcome ammunition to school reformers across the country. The New York legislature printed and distributed eighteen thousand copies; Boston businessmen applauded him for proving that the common school was not only "a nursery of souls, but a mine of riches"; and a leading educator said in 1863 that Mann's report probably did "more than all other publications written within the past twenty-five years to convince capitalists of the value of elementary instruction as a means of increasing the value of labor."[57] In 1870 the United States Commissioner of Education surveyed employers and workingmen and reported results similar to those of Mann.[58] A committee of the United States Senate which took testimony on "the relations between labor and capital" in the mid-1880s found that businessmen and employees across the nation tended to agree that schooling increases the productivity and predictability of workers.[59] So fixed had this view become by the twentieth century—reflecting dozens of rate-of-return studies at the turn of the century—that a high school debaters' manual on compulsory schooling listed these as standard arguments for the affirmative:

> Education is the only guarantee of the prosperity of every individual in the State. Education will pay in dollars and cents.
> The education of the State and the wealth of the State bear a constant ratio, one increasing with the other.[60]

As human-capital theory has developed in recent years, economists have applied models of decision theory to the development of compulsory schooling in the nineteenth century. Generally they have focused upon individuals or their families and assumed that they make rational calculations of their presumed future benefits. For example, in their essay "Compulsory Schooling Legislation: An Economic

[56] Maris Vinovskis, "Horace Mann on the Economic Productivity of Education," *New England Quarterly*, 43 (1970), 562, 550–71.

[57] Vinovskis, p. 570.

[58] United States Commissioner of Education, *Report for 1870* (Washington, D.C.: GPO, 1870), pp. 447–67.

[59] United States Senate, *Report of the Committee of the Senate upon the Relations between Labor and Capital and Testimony Taken by the Committee* (Washington, D.C.: GPO, 1885), II, 789–90, 795–96, and IV, 504–5, 729–30.

[60] John S. Patton, ed., "Selected Arguments, Bibliographies, Etc., for the Use of the Virginia High School and Athletic League," *University of Virginia Record, Extension Series*, I (1915), 103–104.

Analysis of Law and Social Change in the Nineteenth Century," William Landes and Lewis Solmon adopted as their "theory of the determinants of schooling levels" the model that an individual "would maximize his wealth by investing in schooling until the marginal rate of return equaled marginal cost (expressed as an interest rate)."[61] They found that in 1880 there was a higher investment in schooling in states that had compulsory-attendance laws than in those that did not. But by also examining levels of schooling in 1870, when only two states had laws, they discovered that the states which passed laws during the 1870s had already achieved high levels of investment in public education prior to enactment of compulsory legislation. They concluded that compulsory-education laws did not much influence the supply and demand curves and were

> . . . not the cause of the higher schooling levels observed in 1880 in states with laws. Instead, these laws appear merely to have formalized what was already an observed fact; namely, that the vast majority of school-age persons had already been obtaining a level of schooling equal to or greater than what was to be later specified by statute.[62]

In other words, the legislation merely applauded the decisions of families who had concluded that schooling paid off for their children. But this does not explain why parents had to be forced by law to send children to school. In another article, Solmon admits that variation in state support for schooling "might reflect politics rather than individual market decisions, but even these are worked out in the 'political market place' and presumably reflect the tastes of the 'typical' individual."[63]

Why, then, pass the laws? Landes and Solmon argue that on the demand side, educators wanted "legislation that compels persons to purchase their product" (the laws did appear to increase the number of days the schools were open); and law may have had external benefits "to members of the community since it is a way of giving formal recognition to the community's achievement in committing more resources to schooling."[64] With regard to supply, since schooling was already widely available and most parents were sending their children anyway, the cost of passing the laws was minimal in light of the presumed gains.

Albert Fishlow reaches similar conclusions in his study of investment in education during the nineteenth century. He notes a rapid rise of spending on human capital in the industrialized nations of the United States, England, France, and Germany. But in contrast with the key role of the central state in Europe, Fishlow

---

61 William Landes and Lewis Solmon, "Compulsory Schooling Legislation: An Economic Analysis of Law and Social Change in the Nineteenth Century," *Journal of Economic History,* 32 (1972), 58–59.

62 Landes and Solmon, 77–78.

63 Lewis Solmon, "Opportunity Costs and Models of Schooling in the Nineteenth Century," *Southern Economic Journal,* 37 (1970), 72.

64 Landes and Solmon, pp. 87–88.

says, American investment arose from a local consensus on the value of education: "Under such circumstances, the educational commitment was a matter of course from parents to children rather than from community to schools."[65] Most parents, he argues, made the calculation that education was worth the price, both in public outlays and in private opportunity costs. But there were some families that did not make this decision, and Fishlow argues that "the entire history of compulsory-schooling legislation and of child-labor legislation is usefully viewed as social intervention to prevent present opportunity costs from having weight in the educational decision."[66]

The actual opportunity costs differed sharply between rural and urban communities and between richer and poorer families. Schools in farm areas could adjust the academic calendar to match the need for child labor in agriculture, thus nearly eliminating the need to forego the earnings of children. In cities, by contrast, work opportunities were generally not seasonal, and compulsory attendance effectively barred children from adding substantially to family income. In addition, the poor did not have the same opportunity to invest in their children as did middle- and upper-income families, since they could not generally borrow capital against their children's presumed higher future income. Thus the very large private contribution to schooling through the opportunity costs was a source of major educational inequality—one recognized, incidentally, by truant officers, judges, and other officials who confronted the problems of compulsory attendance firsthand.[67]

How convincing is the human-investment paradigm in explaining the history of school attendance? On the surface it appears to require quite a stretch of the imagination to envisage families actually making the complex calculations of future benefit embodied in some of the models of economists. But, as Mary Jean Bowman writes, "the economist is not concerned, as is the psychologist, with explaining individual behavior per se. If people behave *as if* they were economically rational, that is quite enough, provided we are dealing with multiple decision units."[68] The decision-making model is of course a conscious simplification, omitting factors of public welfare or intrinsic pleasure that probably do affect choice. If one defines as voluntary that school attendance which is unconstrained by law (in the absence of law, or beyond legally required years, or in communities where laws were unpublicized or unenforced), it does appear that voluntary attendance was influenced in part by the prospect of future economic advantage, for families always had competing demands on their incomes. And the evidence is quite convincing that compulsory laws were passed in states where most citizens were already investing in schooling up to the point required by law. A powerful recurring

65 Fishlow, "Levels of Investment," pp. 435–36.
66 Fishlow, p. 427.
67 Fishlow, p. 426; Solmon, 68–72.
68 Bowman, p. 120.

argument for compulsion was that taxpayers could realize the full return on their large investment only if free schooling reached all the children; the presumption was that children who were out of school needed education the most and would become an economic burden to the community if left uneducated. Hence there was a social benefit in investing in all children as human capital. Thus far the human-capital theory seems fruitful.

The kind of decision making assumed by this theory requires, I believe, at least some awareness of the economic benefits of education. Did nineteenth-century Americans, in fact, link schooling with economic success? In this century we have become accustomed to thinking of schools as sorters, as institutions that help to determine the occupational destiny of students. Increasingly, not only the professions but many other jobs as well have come to require educational credentials or prescribed levels of schooling even for entry-level positions.[69] Not only is this screening function of schools embodied in specific institutional arrangements, like high-school counseling programs, but it has also become common knowledge in the population at large. In 1973, 76 percent of respondents in a Gallup poll said they thought education was "extremely important" to "one's future success."[70]

There is little evidence, however, that citizens in the nineteenth century thought this way about schooling. Rhetoric about the purposes of education emphasized socialization for civic responsibility and moral character far more than as an investment in personal economic advancement. Indeed, there is some counter-evidence that businessmen, for one group, were actually hostile to the notion of education beyond the confines of the common school.[71] The arguments of Horace Mann and his early successors stressed not so much *individual* earnings as *aggregate* productivity and the workmanlike traits such as reliability and punctuality. The most influential spokesmen for nineteenth-century educators—people like William T. Harris—did stress a general socialization for work, but they tended to see success as the result of later behavior in the marketplace. Harris estimated that as late as 1898, the average person attended school for only five years. Out of one hundred students in all levels of education, ninety-five were in elementary, four were in secondary, and only one was in higher education.[72] Furthermore, family incomes were much lower in the nineteenth century than in mid-twentieth, and the structure of the labor force was far different. The percentage of the population engaged in agriculture dropped from 37.5 in 1900 to 6.3 in 1960, while the

---

69 Ivar E. Berg, *Education and Jobs: The Great Training Robbery* (New York: Praeger, 1970).

70 Stanley Elam, ed., *The Gallup Polls of Attitudes towards Education, 1969–1973* (Bloomington, Ind.: Phi Delta Kappa, 1973), p. 169.

71 Irwin Wyllie, *The Self-made Man in America* (New Brunswick, N.J.: Rutgers Univ. Press, 1954), ch. 3; Cochran, pp. 174–76.

72 Harris, 3–4, 54; Selwyn Troen, *The Public and the Schools: Shaping the St. Louis System, 1838–1920* (Columbia: Univ. of Missouri Press, 1975), ch. 6.

percentage in white-collar occupations rose from 17.6 to 43.5 in those years.[73] It is likely, then, that motives other than future rate of return on educational investments in individuals were more significant during the nineteenth century than in the twentieth. The micro-decision-making paradigm of human capital better explains our more recent history, when disposable family income has substantially risen, when parents are better educated and more capable of calculating future benefits, and when schooling has become far more important in sorting people into occupational niches.[74]

A Marxian Analysis

"We are led to reject the individual choice model as the basis for a theory of the supply of educational services," Samuel Bowles and Herbert Gintis have written.

> The model is not wrong—individuals and families do make choices, and may even make educational choices roughly as described by the human capital theorists. We reject the individual choice framework because it is so superficial as to be virtually irrelevant to the task of understanding why we have the kinds of schools and the amount of schooling that we do.[75]

Why superficial? Because the individual choice model provides only a partial interpretation of production, treats the firm "as a black box," and offers no useful insight into the basic question of how the capitalist class structure has been reproduced. The perpetuation of great inequalities of wealth and income over the past century and the development of schools as social institutions have not resulted simply from an aggregation of individual choices, Bowles and Gintis argue; rather, schooling has served to perpetuate the hierarchical social relations of capitalist production. In their view, society is not a marketplace of individuals maximizing their advantages but a class structure in which power is unequally divided. It may appear that the American educational system has developed in accord with "the relatively uncoordinated 'investment' decisions of individuals and groups as mediated by local school boards," but in actuality these "pluralistic" accommodations have taken place in response to changes in production "governed by the pursuit of profit and privilege by those elements of the capitalist class which dominate the dynamic sectors of the economy." By setting boundaries of decision—establishing the rules of the game—the capitalist class determines the range of acceptable choice in a manner that strengthens and legitimizes its position.[76]

[73] United States Bureau of the Census, *Historical Statistics of the United States* (Washington, D.C.: GPO, 1960), pp. 67–78.

[74] In "Education and the Corporate Order," *Socialist Revolution*, 2 (1972), p. 51, David K. Cohen and Marvin Lazerson point out that the "tendency to use market criteria in evaluating education flowered around the turn of the century"; for a survey of such studies, see A. Caswell Ellis, "The Money Value of Education," U.S. Bureau of Education, *Bulletin No. 22* (Washington, D.C.: GPO, 1917).

[75] Samuel Bowles and Herbert Gintis, "The Problem with Human Capital Theory—A Marxist Critique," *American Economic Review*, 65 (1975), 78.

[76] Bowles and Gintis, p. 75.

424

Bowles and Gintis are primarily interested in the consequences of the system of schooling rather than in the conscious motives of elites or school leaders. The important question is whether the outcomes of formal education have supported capitalism—for example, through differential training of workers and employers in ways that maintain the social division of labor. From this point of view, if Mann were a saint and yet his system of education perpetuated injustice because it supported exploitative relations of production, then the case for radical change would be all the stronger.

In developing their model of economic and educational change, Gintis and Bowles do not treat compulsory attendance in detail, but one can easily extrapolate an interpretation of compulsion from their theory. Their explanation has two major components. First, they account for educational reform periods, which shaped ideology and structure, as accommodations to contradictions engendered by capital accumulation and the incorporation of new groups into the wage-labor force. Second, they seek to demonstrate how the educational system has served capitalist objectives of achieving technical efficiency, control, and legitimacy.

"The capitalist economy and bicycle riding have this in common," they argue: "forward motion is essential to stability." As capital accumulates and new workers are drawn into expanded enterprises, potential conflict arises. Bowles and Gintis say that the contradictions inherent in this process gave rise to the common-school movement during the mid-nineteenth century, a time of labor militancy as the wage-labor force expanded and inequality increased. Such contradictions, they believe, also gave rise to the progressive movement at the turn of the twentieth century—a period of conflict between big business and big labor. Social discord stemmed from the integration of immigrant and rural labor into the industrial system. During these times, they argue, workers demanded more education, and "progressive elements in the capitalist class" acceded to the demands only insofar as they could adapt the school to their own purposes. Bowles and Gintis see educational development, then, "as an outcome of class conflict, not class domination." Workers won schooling for their children, but by controlling decision making in education and "suppressing anti-capitalist alternatives," the ruling class maintained the social relations of production while ameliorating conditions and dampening conflict. In this view, schooling has been a crucial tool for perpetuating the capitalist system amid rapid economic change. Periodically, when the schools ceased to correspond with the structure of production, major shifts in the scope and structure of education took place, dominated in the final analysis by the class that set the agendas of decision.[77]

How did schools meet the capitalist objectives of technical efficiency, control, and legitimacy? Gintis and Bowles claim that the social relations of the school closely matched the needs of the hierarchical relations of production. The school

[77] Samuel Bowles and Herbert Gintis, "Capitalism and Education in the United States," *Socialist Revolution*, 5 (1975), 111, 116–18.

prepared individuals differentially—in skills, traits of personality, credentials, self-concepts, and behavior—for performance in different roles in the economic hierarchy. This differentiation was congruent with social definitions of race, sex, and class. Thus, for example, when structures of production were relatively simple, schools concentrated on such qualities as punctuality, obedience to authority, and willingness to work for extrinsic rewards—all of which were useful in shaping a disciplined labor force for industry or commerce. As economic organizations became larger and more complex and the labor force increasingly segmented in level and function, schooling in turn grew more differentiated. This segmentation, coupled with differential treatment based on race and sex, helped to splinter employees into separate groups and to blind them to their common interest as workers. Schooling increasingly selected those who would get the good jobs; the rhetoric of equality of opportunity through education rationalized unequal incomes and status and legitimized the system. "The predominant economic function of schools," Bowles and Gintis observe, was "not the production or identification of cognitive abilities but the accreditation of future workers as well as the selection and generation of noncognitive personality attributes rewarded by the economic system."[78] As the work of different classes differed, so did the pattern of socialization in schools.

Just as Mann prefigured some of the human-capital theory, earlier Marxian theorists anticipated some of the Bowles–Gintis model, but they tended to see the laboring class as a more continuously active agent in educational change and capitalists as more hostile to public education. In 1883, for example, Adolph Douai, as a representative of the Socialistic Labor Party of the United States, presented a Marxist perspective on schooling to the United States Senate committee on the relations between labor and capital.[79] Half a century later, in the midst of the Great Depression, Rex David wrote a Marxian pamphlet on *Schools and the Crisis*.[80] Both strongly urged the creation of free and compulsory education for all young people; both stressed the opposition of capitalists to expanded educational opportunity; both saw teachers and other intellectual workers mostly as servants of vested interests but believed that educators could become an important means of spreading the light for socialism. For them as for a number of progressive labor historians, the working class was normally the dominant part of the coalition pushing for equality, and the ruling class was frequently hostile.

The interpretation of these earlier Marxists differs in emphasis from but does

---

[78] Samuel Bowles and Herbert Gintis, "The Contradictions of Liberal Educational Reform," in *Work, Technology, and Education,* ed. Walter Feinberg and Henry Rosemont, Jr. (Urbana, Ill.: Univ. of Illinois Press, 1975), pp. 124, 133; I have cited these essays by Bowles and Gintis because the more complete version of their analysis was not available at the time of writing. Now, see *Schooling in Capitalist America: Educational Reform and the Contradictions of Economic Life* (New York: Basic Books, 1976), esp. chs. 2, 4, 5, 7, and 9.

[79] Douai's testimony is in United States Senate, *Report on Labor and Capital,* ii, 702–43.

[80] Rex David, *Schools and the Crisis* (New York: Labor Research Assoc., 1934).

not directly contradict the Bowles-Gintis theory of educational change. Bowles and Gintis develop a more explicit model of how an apparently liberal educational system played a crucial part in reproducing unequal distribution of wealth and hierarchical relations of production. They further argue that owners and employers were not part of an undifferentiated group of capitalists but that the schooling reforms were engineered by those who controlled the leading sectors of the economy—exemplified by the corporate leaders at the turn of the century who sought to stabilize and rationalize the economy and supporting social institutions.[81]

Bowles and Gintis offer a general model of capitalist education rather than a specific interpretation of compulsory attendance. Thus what follows is my own extrapolation from their writing. Since they say that the "impetus for educational reform and expansion was provided by the growing class consciousness and political militancy of working people," presumably worker groups were advocates of universal attendance, perhaps aided by "progressive elements in the capitalist class." According to the theory that entry of new groups into the wage-labor force prompted demands for education, one might predict that the compulsory-education laws would appear first where the wage-labor force was growing most rapidly. At the same time, the ineffectiveness of these laws during the nineteenth century might be interpreted in part as a sign of ambivalence toward universal education among capitalists themselves (some might have preferred cheap child labor to the labor of schooled youth or adults, for example). On the other hand, phase two, the period of effective laws and increasing bureaucratization, might reflect growing capitalist consensus on the value of differentiated schooling in producing a segmented labor force for increasingly complex social relations of production. Indeed, the correspondence of the structure and processes of the schools with those of the work place is precisely the point of the analysis; changes in the latter drive the former.[82]

The Marxian model sketched here is to a degree congruent with both the general theory of the political construction of education and the organizational synthesis. It suggests, however, that the capitalist class, as the ruling class, defines the production of citizens through education according to its own interests in the political economy. It adds to the organizational synthesis an explanation of why the large organization became dominant: capitalists had concentrated their ownership and power. It does not deny the choice model of human-capital theory, but it declares that the choices have been set within a capitalist zone of tolerance; further, it adds the notions of class conflict and reproduction of social structure.

The Bowles-Gintis analysis addresses important questions and poses a clear, explicit model. In my view, however, this kind of class analysis does not sufficiently explain the motive force of religious and ethnic differences in political and social

---

81 Bowles and Gintis, "Contradictions."
82 Bowles and Gintis, "Capitalism," pp. 118, 126–33.

life, especially within the working class. It tends to downplay important variations among employers' attitudes toward child labor and the different forms of educa- tion. The older Marxist view here has some substance; as Thomas Cochran and others have documented, many businessmen were opposed to extension of edu- cational opportunity. The wage-labor hypothesis does not help us to understand widespread provision of schooling and numerous compulsory-schooling laws in communities and states in which the family farm was the predominant mode of production. As class analysis becomes further refined, however, it promises to add much to our understanding of both the continuities in social structure and the dynamics of economic and educational change.[83]

Conclusion

So what does one learn from exploring alternative ways of seeing compulsory schooling? Should one simply add them all together, like the observations of the blind men feeling an elephant, and say that the reality is in fact accessible only through multiple modes of analysis, that each mode is helpful but partial? Do some explanations fit only a particular time or place? To what degree are the in- terpretations mutually exclusive, and to what degree do they overlap? How might one test the assumptions and assertions of each by empirical investigation? Would any kind of factual testing be likely to change the mind of a person committed to a particular way of seeing or to a particular purpose?

The different kinds of interpretations do call attention to different actors, mo- tives, and evidence, and in this sense one could say that the historian interested in all the phenomena of compulsory schooling might simply add together the various sets of observations. Those arguing for the political construction of education emphasize the role of the state and stress the importance of incorporating a hetero- geneous populace into a unified state citizenry. The ethnocultural interpretation posits religious-ethnic differences as a motive force in political actions. The organi- zational synthesis stresses the role of the new middle class in changing the nature of American life through the creation of large organizations that dominate politi- cal and economic activities. Human-capital theorists focus on the family as a de- cision unit in calculating the costs and benefits of schooling. Finally, the Marxists see class struggle as the source of the dialectic that produces historical change. Each interpretation, in turn, directs attention to certain kinds of evidence which can confirm or disprove its assertions of causation: growth of new state rules and ap-

---

[83] On ethnic and religious dimensions to school politics see Troen, chs. 2–4; Diane Ravitch, *The Great School Wars, New York City, 1805–1973: A History of the Public Schools as Battlefield of Social Change* (New York: Basic Books, 1974), chs. 3–7. As Solmon and Fishlow indicate (see references in footnote 67 above), enrollments in rural schools in many parts of the nation were higher than in industrialized areas; almost two-thirds of the states that passed compulsory-schooling leg- islation prior to 1890 were overwhelmingly rural in the distribution of population.

paratus, religious differences expressed in political conflict, the rise of large organizations and related ideologies, the individual and social rates of return on schooling, and changes in the social relations of production and of schooling.[84]

There are problems with simple additive eclecticism, however. Some interpretations do fit certain times and places better than others, as we have seen. More fundamentally, the models deal with social reality on quite different levels: the individual or the family, the ethnocultural group, the large organization, and the structure of political or economic power in the society as a whole. Scholars advancing such interpretations often have quite different conceptions of what drives social change and hence quite different notions of appropriate policy. Some may concentrate on changing the individual, others on improving the functioning of organizations, and still others on radically restructuring the society. Ultimately, one is likely to adopt a framework of interpretation that matches one's perception of reality and purpose in writing, and thus simple eclecticism may lead to blurring of vision and confusion of purpose.

To argue that one should not mix interpretations promiscuously does not mean that it is unwise to confront alternative conceptualizations or to attempt to integrate them into a more complex understanding of social reality. This, in turn, may make historians more conscious of the ways in which theories and empirical research interact with one another, so that an anomalous piece of evidence may call a theory into question and a new mode of explanation may be generated.[85] One of my purposes in this essay has been to extend the boundaries of discussion about the history of American education. I have become convinced that much of the recent work in the field—my own included—has used causal models too implicitly. It has also tended to constrict the range of value judgments. Was schooling "imposed" by elites on an unwilling working class, for example, or was John Dewey a servant of corporate capitalism? Entertaining explicit alternative models and probing their value assumptions may help historians to gain a more complex and accurate perception of the past and a greater awareness of the ambiguous relationship between outcome and intent—both of the actors in history and of the historians who attempt to recreate their lives.[86]

---

84 Charles M. Dollar and Richard J. Jensen, *Historian's Guide to Statistics* (New York: Holt, Rinehart and Winston, 1971), chs. 1–2.

85 Martin Rein, *Social Science and Public Policy* (London: Penguin, 1976); Henry Levin, "Education, Life Chances, and the Courts: The Role of Social Science Evidence," *Law and Contemporary Problems*, 39 (1975), 217–40.

86 Robert K. Merton, "The Bearing of Sociological Theory on Empirical Research," and "The Bearing of Empirical Research on Sociological Theory," in *Readings in the Philosophy of the Social Sciences*, ed. May Brodbeck (New York: Macmillan, 1968), pp. 465–85.

Loss as a Theme in Social Policy

DAVID K. COHEN

Historians and social researchers have viewed social policy in America as primarily concerned with issues of equality. In this article, David K. Cohen argues that an equally important theme—a sense of loss—has gone largely unnoticed. Examining the role of loss in the historical development of social policy for public education, he demonstrates that policies aimed at creating equality have been confounded—and to some extent undermined—by policies aimed at repairing loss. The author contends that in general the sense of loss has led to a vision of community which is based on order and compulsion. He argues, however, that community may be organized on principles of reciprocity, equality, and choice. The author reviews alternative explanations for why the sense of loss has been pervasive and persistent; he offers the view that loss persists and community eludes us because of a particular cultural bias, and he illustrates how this bias continues to affect social policy.

Loss has been found. Again. Death has risen from the perfumed sanctuaries of Evelyn Waugh's *The Loved One* and is now headline news in pop sociology. Divorce and family dissolution are all over the pages of the popular social-science magazines. America's "lost ethnicity" has been a source of fascination—not to mention research funds and federal legislation—for nearly a decade now. Whether it is loss of community, family, intimate relationships, or life itself, the subject stimulates unusual interest among serious social scientists as well as trendy journalists. Some of this work seems especially penetrating—Elisabeth Kübler-Ross's book on dying or Peter Marris's *Loss and Change*.[1] Many other efforts provide only a steady stream of chic remedies: honesty for the dying; therapy for those newly alone; ethnic identity for the nearly-homogenized; and communes, extended families, and collectives for deracinated cosmopolites.

While loss is something of a novelty in current social thought, it is as ancient and serious a concern as any in Western thought. In social policy, its history has been somewhat less consistent. Loss has recently been taken up by analysts and commentators in a spirit of important discovery, but in fact the idea has been redis-

---

[1] Elisabeth Kübler-Ross, *Death* (Englewood Cliffs, N.J.: Prentice-Hall, 1975); Peter Marris, *Loss and Change* (New York: Pantheon, 1974).

Harvard Educational Review Vol. 46 No. 4 November 1976, 553-571

covered regularly for at least the last century and a half. Loss has been a central, though rather episodic, preoccupation in United States social policy.

One reason for this fitful concern probably is the equally episodic character of social dislocation. Another is the fact that most social scientists and historians concerned with social policy—like most Americans whose profession is the public domain—have thought that equality was the most striking feature of public life and policy in the United States. For example, traditional historians writing in the first six decades of this century celebrated the schools' role in advancing equality.[2] They recited sonorous narrative incantations about the extension of schooling, the rise of attendance, the expansion of access, and the spread of democratic control. Boosterism is in bad odor lately, but recent revisionist historians are no less concerned with equality—even though their tale is one of democracy denied.[3] They bemoan the forced draft of youthful masses into public schools; they morbidly measure the inequalities therein; and they carefully chronicle elite control of the enterprise. Social researchers interested in policy for education, whatever their ideologies, have had a similar preoccupation. This has been particularly evident in the last few decades as inequality in education has become a central focus of research on social policy.

This picture is not wrong. Social policy in United States education has been marked by continuing battles over equality. But the picture is incomplete, and that is one theme in this essay. If social policy has been shaped by contention over the extent of social democracy, it also has been the product of a mad rush to repair the traumas of becoming modern. If conflict over the extent of equality has been one major theme in the evolution of social policy, another has been the recurrent desire to recapture a community which seemed about to disappear. Beginning in the second quarter of the nineteenth century, there developed an acute sense that society was coming unstrung, that common values and cohesive institutions were eroding. This sense of loss powerfully influenced social policy. It evoked the belief that families were failing and produced efforts to shore them up or to replace them with new institutions. It evoked the belief that criminality and other forms of deviance resulted from the weakening of family and community bonds, and it produced efforts to invent institutions which could replace failing communities. It evoked the belief that primary institutions—families, churches, and communities—had lost their ability to pass a common culture along, and this became a powerful inspiration for the development of public education.

For the most part, commentators have ignored all this. Loss has been an important theme in social policy, but it has not been much represented in social policy analysis. This essay explores the idea that the imagery of loss has been a central

[2] For a perceptive bibliographic overview of this line of work, see Bernard Bailyn, *Education in the Forming of American Society: Needs and Opportunities for Study* (Chapel Hill, N.C.: Univ. of North Carolina Press, 1960), pp. 8–13.

[3] The outstanding works in this tradition include Michael Katz, *The Irony of Early School Reform* (Cambridge, Mass.: Harvard Univ. Press, 1968); and Samuel Bowles and Herbert Gintis, *Schooling in Capitalist America: Educational Reform and the Contradictions of Economic Life* (New York: Basic Books, 1976).

force shaping both Americans' vision of what is wrong with society and their efforts to set things right. It is an effort to call attention to a neglected theme in social policy, but it is not a celebration of loss. Rather, I will argue that social policy in education has been the product of mixed and conflicting metaphors about modernity. One vision evokes a sense of community lost, of rootless masses, of social incoherence and personal alienation. The other looks forward hopefully to the dissolution of frozen social hierarchies in the warm sunlight of equality. Distinct as these metaphors seem in principle, in practice they tended to merge. They represent two very different views about the problems of becoming modern, but somehow the schools' mission came to be understood as both repairing loss and creating equality. Much of what is most unique and problematic about social policy for education in America arises from the fusion and confounding of these two streams of thought.

In addition to exploring loss as a theme in social policy, I am interested in how the sense of loss has shaped our understanding of policy. Expectations of decay in family, community, and solidarity have been persistent since the 1840s, and once again today they are big news for social commentators and reformers. Intellectuals and policymakers have mostly accepted the calamitous forecasts of social collapse as though they were self-evident and have rarely subjected them to much skeptical poking and prodding. They also have welcomed the rather conservative remedies which were implied or prescribed. As loss is rediscovered, it may profit from a bit of critical scrutiny.

Lost Community and the Origin of Public Schools

Though most history books don't say so, one powerful motive for the establishment of public schools was concern about the decay of social order and the breakdown of collective values.[4] Between the 1830s and 1850s middle- and upper-class reformers, many of them public officials or clergymen, worried about the decay of community. They decried the breakdown of the family, bemoaned the destruction of a common culture, and fretted about urban crime, delinquency, and disorder. They pictured these developments as consequences of economic and social modernization, and they often wondered whether the cities would survive.

The traumas seemed particularly acute among poor and immigrant children. They appeared to be completely adrift—without intact families, decent places to live, or useful things to do. "Idle hands" was a common complaint in this reform litany, accompanied by worries about youthful criminality. Henry Barnard, who was superintendent of common schools in Connecticut in the mid-nineteenth cen-

[4] The analysis that follows is focused on the origin of public schools, and so it depends heavily on events and persons in the more urbanized and industrialized portions of early nineteenth-century America. The references are thus drawn nearly exclusively from New England, New York, and Pennsylvania; by the 1850s and 1860s the ideas and arguments had spread and gained credibility among reformers and some professionals—as they did in other cases as well—in many states in the settled Midwest. But there is little in this essay that applies to the South. In addition, it seems likely that quite a different story can be told about the rise of schooling in many midwestern, small towns; see Patricia Graham, *Community and Class in Education* (New York: Wiley, 1974).

tury and a leading figure in the New England school-reform movement, deplored "the example and teaching of low-bred idleness . . . in the densely populated sections of large cities, and all manufacturing villages . . . the deficient household arrangements and deranged machinery of domestic life."[5] Another commentator, several decades earlier, invited his readers to

> behold the streets, and lanes, and alleys of the metropolis, and other large towns and villages, crowded with squalid children, left, in utter neglect, to wallow in filth, to contract disease, and to acquire habits of idleness, violence, and vice. . . . From such a course of education what can be expected but a proficiency in vicious propensities and criminal practices:—what, in short, but that mass of juvenile delinquency which, in the present day, we have been forced to witness and deplore?[6]

Immigration and the dislocations of city life were thought to be breeding masses who had no intimate connection to society. Many reformers feared that urban America was creating a new antisocial man. Charles Loring Brace, a reformist Protestant minister in New York concerned with the problems of youth, articulated those fears. He felt that the city environment was simply destroying the fabric of society: families disintegrated under the impact of poverty; unemployment, drunkenness, petty crime, and personal incapacity followed; the churches struck him as too few and too poorly prepared to help very much; and other charitable organizations seemed even less adequate.[7]

In important respects this was true. Cities were chaotic, and voluntary agencies in the 1830s and 1840s were simply overwhelmed. The reformers believed that little natural community fabric was left to sustain and assist those in need. Reformers thought that primary institutions had been profoundly weakened by the new forces—industry, commerce, competitiveness, impersonality, and segregation—which had led to the rise of an urban manufacturing civilization; as the older community was washed away, little seemed left to stay rising waves of pathology.[8]

These notions were common to the period, but they were not unique to the United States. They represented only a somewhat less systematic version of worries about modernity which conservative European theorists had honed to a fine edge during and after the French Revolution. DeMaistre, Bonald, and other postrevolutionary European Traditionalists had bemoaned the corrosive effects of industry and urbanization;[9] they had mourned at length the loss of primary institu-

---

5 Since most of the citations are from primary sources which have very restricted availability, I have tried to use selections available in the several paperback compilations concerning the history of schools. Henry Barnard, *Sixth Annual Report of the Superintendent of Common Schools to the General Assembly of Connecticut, 1851*, rpt. in Michael B. Katz, *School Reform: Past and Present* (Boston: Little, Brown, 1971), p. 10.

6 "Account of the System of Infant Schools," *American Journal of Education* (1826), rpt. in Katz, p. 34.

7 For some of Brace's ideas, and further references, see Carl Kaestle, *The Evolution of an Urban School System* (Cambridge, Mass.: Harvard Univ. Press, 1973), pp. 77, 126–29.

8 Most traditional reformers were explicit in their view that these social problems were disorders—and pathological—and none saw them simply as conflicts. Barnard's views quoted just above are a fair example of this.

9 For a discussion of this stream of thought, see Robert A. Nisbet, *The Quest for Community*

tions; they had, indeed, developed a detailed political theology of loss. They held out no real hope for Europe. But if Continental critics of cities and industry despaired of recovering what had been lost, the Americans were of a different mind. Bitter as they were about the loss of community, it never occurred to American reformers to think the damage was irreparable. What they focused on, characteristically, was how to repair it.

Schools were central in their vision. Traditional American reformers were darkly despondent about the loss of primary institutions, but they were positively sunny about schools. Their ideas were expressed with varying degrees of humanity—some were insightful and generous while others ranged off to narrowness and bigotry—but they agreed that formal public education could inculcate the social morality and common sentiments which private institutions once had provided. Barnard observed, for example, that "the primary object in securing the early school attendance of young children is not so much their intellectual culture as the regulation of the feelings and dispositions, the extirpation of vicious propensities."[10] Another observer, advocating a system of infant schools, expressed the same point: "The incidental acquisition of useful knowledge . . . is but of small account, in comparison with that moral culture, with those habits of self-government, and with those feelings of mutual kindness, which form the characteristic tendencies, and indeed the grand recommendation, of the whole system [of schools]."[11]

Ideas about just how schools would work were fairly uniform. Most traditionalists thought of them as a redeeming environment. Much like those boarding schools for the poor which James Coleman proposed in the wake of his 1966 *Equality of Educational Opportunity*,[12] reformers hoped that schools would separate the deviant and deficient young from their inadequate surroundings, filling them with better sentiments and creating a new system of common morals. Some, especially infatuated with the schools' potential, expected that schools would even reform deviant families and communities by resocializing children to become natural missionaries in their own urban jungles. But most simply saw schools as an antidote to the poisons of slum life. The reformers thus varied in emphasis, and they argued about whether schools should be subject to direct public control, supported by public subventions to private organizations, or managed by some combination of the two. All agreed, though, that the point of public schooling was to create those collective sentiments and values which they feared were eroding. Schools would do intentionally and consciously what lost communities had once done reflexively and instinctively.

Thus, while these reformers were nostalgic, elegiac, and mournful for what was lost, while they were often bitter and resentful about the new peoples and pathologies of the cities, they were also profoundly hopeful about the schools' curative

---

(New York: Oxford Univ. Press, 1953); Hans Barth, *The Idea of Order: Contributions to a Philosophy of Politics*, trans. Ernest W. Hankamer and William M. Newell (Boston: Reidel, 1960).

10 Barnard, rpt. in Katz, p. 10.

11 "Account," rpt. in Katz, p. 33.

12 James S. Coleman, "Equal Schools or Equal Students?" *Public Interest*, No. 4 (Fall 1966), pp. 74–75.

powers. They offered up a terrifically gloomy account of what was happening in the cities, based on worries about the failure of institutions, elitist ideas about the inadequacy of immigrants and the poor, and a reading of history which portrayed economic change and urbanization as potentially destructive forces. Yet this dark diagnosis was married to a remarkably hopeful set of ideas about the creative power of institutions. Schools, the reformers thought, would recreate social solidarity by remaking personal values, sentiments, and ideas. Bureaucracies would be devised to organize and regularize this good work, harnessing the energies of many individuals and schools to a common social purpose, much in the spirit of business enterprise. Teachers and administrators would be trained by the thousands to staff these factories of the spirit—themselves turned out in a suitably common mold by new institutions of educational craft and science.[13]

It seems a colossal paradox. Schools would serve a nostalgic vision of small-town America combatting the corrosive evils of modern life. Yet they would be organized not on principles which avoided the future but which embraced it. The evils of modernity would be eliminated by the healing powers of modern rational institutions. At this distance, and in the less hopeful atmosphere of these days, it seems curious. After all, European thinkers who shared this distress with modernity specifically pointed out that efforts to salvage older social functions with newer rational institutions would only compound the fractures; they hadn't a whisper of hope about patching things up.[14] One wonders, why the difference?

One important reason is that Europeans experienced modernity as a profound wrench of change and dislocation. Americans, after all, did not have an ancient feudal society to lose, however rickety their inherited European social structure had become. And if traditional critics of modernity on both sides of the Atlantic were members of elites, the term "elite" had quite different meanings in Europe and America. Most European Traditionalists were nobles, heirs to a society which in principle placed them at what would have been for Americans of the period an unimaginable distance from ordinary citizens. The American connoisseurs of loss, on the other hand, were only clergymen, well-to-do businessmen, or public officials. Most of them were heirs only to money, many were social *nouveaux* in comparison to the Europeans, and their public offices were primarily elective, not hereditary. While the European Traditionalists' complaints were rooted in a confused mixture of leftover feudal realities and persistent medieval dreams, their American cousins discovered loss in a society much less rigidly stratified, with many more common social connections, and much more deeply penetrated by democratic ideas, politics, and social practices.

Thus, there were good social, political, and historical reasons why nostalgic American reformers responded to the sense of lost community in a characteristically hopeful manner. As a result, in seeking to preserve traditional values, they

13 These ideas about rationality and bureaucracy have been treated most wisely in Stanley Schultz, *The Culture Factory* (New York: Oxford Univ. Press, 1973), esp. chs. 5 and 6.

14 David Cohen, "Lemontey, An Early Critic of Industrialism," *French Historical Studies*, 4(1966), 290–303; David Cohen, "The Vicomte de Bonald's Critique of Industrialism," *The Journal of Modern History*, 41(1969), 475–84.

turned naturally to the rational design of new institutions and to the conscious construction of a social morality. As good Americans, progeny of low-church evangelism and the Enlightenment, they assumed that they could remake society simply by creating new organizations, by teaching good ideas, and by exemplifying sound sentiments. While ideas about loss have been endemic to all Western societies as they have modernized, the response of traditional American reformers was profoundly conditioned both by the facts of life in a society already strikingly democratic and by widespread optimism about the redeeming power of human institutions.

This curious concatenation of ideas had important effects on the way the schools' mission was conceived. Reformers could talk in one paragraph of the "ignorant," "uninstructed" children of immigrants, burdened by "the inherited stupidity of centuries of ignorant ancestors," polluting the cities like so much human offal. Yet in the next they could advertise the "winning ways" of a "primary school [which] is but a substitute for a good home."[15] Enlightenment hopefulness about the redeeming power of institutions was mixed with profound pessimism about the dissolution of modern society; democratic notions about the redemptive power of ideas and rational instruction were blended with depressing visions of the destructive power of urban rootlessness; evangelical hopefulness about human goodness and the universal availability of salvation were stirred into gloomy Calvinist ideas about the social obligation to punish deviants. Thus Henry Barnard could deplore on one page the "deficient . . . and deranged machinery" of city life and on the next extol schools as a reclaimer of "penury, ignorance and vice" into "economy and industry." He could celebrate school attendance as a "precious privilege" creating "that general virtue and intelligence which is at once the wealth, security and glory of a state" and then argue that the "right of suffrage should be withheld from such as cannot give the lowest evidence of school attendance and proficiency."[16] A more potent brew of democratic hopes and dark fears could hardly be imagined.

One consequence of these ideas was to profoundly imbalance ideas about the public schools' mission: the mere institutional handiwork of men, the schools would, in a few short years, repair what reformers saw as centuries-old traumas which had nearly overcome the central institutions of society. A second consequence was to weave a strange ambivalence into social policy for education: the wounds of modernization made public schools necessary, yet schools would be modernizing agencies. In one sense, therefore, social policy for education was classically conservative. Looking backward to the social and cultural ideal of an earlier time, schools would repair the damage of becoming modern: they would reform deviants, improve the deficient, and train up new generations of Americans in a common morality. Yet, in another sense, the new policies seemed quite modern. The principles of organization which reformers used in creating public schools involved Enlightenment views about the reforming power of new, man-

15 Boston School Committee, *1858 Annual Report*, rpt. in Katz, pp. 171–72.
16 Barnard, *Sixth Annual Report*, rpt. in Katz, pp. 11–13.

made institutions and nineteenth-century notions about the industrial division of labor, central bureaucratic control, and uniform rational procedures. Public schools would look back to an earlier social ideal, but they would be ordered along rational and bureaucratic lines.

Equality and Community

The concern with community was not peculiar to traditional reformers. Democrats had a major influence on the shape of social policy for education, and their hopes for the reforming power of popular institutions are well known. But their support for public schools was closely tied to the notion that community was a central problem for democratic reform. In the 1820s and 1830s many democrats advocated public schools on the grounds that equal education would provide a sort of social cement, sealing cracks in the social order that were due to social and economic divisions. They feared that political equality could not be sustained in the face of vast differences in wealth and social position, for privilege purchased power and encouraged separate enclaves of association. Pamphleteers for the Workingmen's Associations, for example, held that having private schools without public counterparts helped pass these distinctions from one generation to the next: class differences in access to private education reinforced economic barriers, perpetuated humiliating social distinctions, and threatened social fragmentation.[17]

Given this concern, it is not hard to understand the appeal of public schools. Democrats objected to a class-based "monopoly of talent" because they thought it would reinforce a class-based monopoly of power; they thought schools should be public because democracy could not work without a broad diffusion of knowledge and skills. And they believed that existing class barriers were divisive. A Workingmen's pamphlet from Pennsylvania explained how equal public schools could create community:

> Those cardinal principles of republican liberty which were declared in '76 . . . can only be sustained by the adoption of an ample system of public instruction, calculated to promote equality as well as mental culture—the establishment of institutions where the children of poor and rich may meet at that period of life, when the pomp and circumstance of wealth have not engendered pride; when the only distinction known will be the celebrity each may acquire by their acts of good fellowship when the best opportunity is afforded for forming associations that will endure through life, and where the obloquy attending the present system will not attach.[18]

[17] The ideas about the community-building features of equality and the divisive aspects of privilege were fairly widespread, even though democratic reformers were a diverse group, both politically and in terms of origins. For a general treatment, see Rush Welter, *Popular Educational Democratic Thought in America* (New York: Columbia Univ. Press, 1963), pp. 45–73. While the Workingmen were a minor political tendency with little direct effect (Welter, p. 45), their arguments about privilege, divisiveness, and equality were soon absorbed into the mainstream of liberal ideas about education (Welter, pp. 60–73).

[18] The Workingmen of Pennsylvania, "An Equal and Republican System of Mental Instruction," n.d., rpt. in David Tyack, *Turning Points in American Educational History* (Waltham, Mass.: Blaisdell, 1967), p. 145.

The Workingmen thought political democracy could not endure without social community, and they saw equality in education as one way to achieve community.

The argument seems a little out of place. One expects concern about community from conservatives, not from radical democrats. Certainly most egalitarians in the United States and Britain have found inequality obnoxious chiefly because it has impaired social opportunity or economic efficiency, not because it has imperiled social cohesion. In the second quarter of the nineteenth century, however, the connection between equality and community made sense even to egalitarians: they feared that America might come apart at the seams.

Not surprisingly, the connection has begun to seem more sensible recently as social fragmentation has once more become a major concern. Richard Titmuss, for example, recently wrote in *The Gift Relationship* that social policy should "promote an individual's sense of identity, participation and community and . . . discourage a sense of individual alienation."[19] He went on to argue that the ways in which societies organize institutions and social policies can affect the extent of community and held that egalitarian social policy could discourage alienation and create solidarity. The National Health Service, Titmuss argued, was the "most unsordid act of British social policy in the twentieth century [and] has allowed and encouraged sentiments of altruism, reciprocity and social duty."[20] This greater solidarity resulted, in part, from the fact that "the Health Service is not socially divisive; its universal and free access has contributed much, we believe, to the . . . choice to give . . . to unseen strangers."[21]

Thus, egalitarian social policy has seemed desirable for some radical democrats because it has promised community. They have hoped that equality would create collective sentiments and affections more generous and cohesive than those divisive feelings stimulated by stratified institutions. In the chaotic environment of early nineteenth-century American cities, the enormous appeal of social solidarity helps to explain the attraction of free common schools at that time. As in more recent United States history, it was hoped that equality and social integration were related.

These ideas are in striking contrast to the notions about loss which played such a large role in traditional reformers' ambitions for public schools. Whereas traditionalists worried about the social divisiveness due to economic change and urban life, democrats noticed the threats posed by inherited economic and social distinctions. Traditional reformers saw solidarity as a product of order, whereas democrats thought solidarity should result from greater equality. Community was central in both traditions of thought, but the perspectives were remarkably different. Democrats distrusted inherited institutions, wished to weaken their force, and hoped that greater equality would provide more coherence by reducing the power of old distinctions. Elite reformers grew nostalgic about inherited institutions, wished their authority were greater, and hoped that schools would provide co-

19 Richard Titmuss, *The Gift Relationship* (New York: Random House, 1972), p. 224.
20 Titmuss, p. 225.
21 Titmuss, p. 225.

438

herence by creating a new order similar to the old. Two more different ways of thinking about community and the state's role in creating it are hard to imagine.

But equal education was dear to democratic hearts for other reasons as well. Not even the democrats could advocate free public schools without pointing to crime, delinquency, and idleness. Schools for all, the Workingmen's pamphlets argued, would turn city youth away from such distractions.[22] These arguments were indistinguishable from those of Henry Barnard or other elite reformers. Additionally, in the second quarter of the nineteenth century, the acute sense of social instability made equal education especially appealing for many democrats. For those in the middle and lower reaches of the social structure, educational status seemed an attractive protection against social and economic uncertainty or dislocation. It was certainly a time in which once-settled social status and position seemed to become more fluid. Cities grew rapidly; immigrant labor threatened competition; manufacturing undermined handcraft; city neighborhoods became more segregated and former neighbors more distant. For many skilled workers and tradesmen, the stability associated with work and community position began to dissolve—or, at least, such were the perceptions of many urban Americans in the 1830s and 1840s.

In many respects, of course, these changes were devoutly wished by democrats. After all, democratic political ideas announced that all men were equal, but against the background of seventeenth- and eighteenth-century America, this meant severing the complex connections between an ordered and hierarchical society and its governing instruments. If men were to be politically equal, a much more neutral state would be required. Jacksonian rhetoric and popular culture announced the need for more neutral relations in public, but in the fluid and disorderly urban atmosphere of the time such democratic ideas and practices seem to have enhanced uneasiness about the loss of settled social position.

Democratic demands for free public schooling seem to have had a special meaning in this situation. Schooling presented itself both as a stable mark of status and as a necessity for democracy.[23] On the one hand, it was a particularly solid mark of status, one whose authenticity was unquestionable because schooling had been a possession of the classes. But, on the other hand, schooling was utterly untainted by its association with privilege. After all, was not popular education the Enlightenment's chosen weapon for breaking the chains of tradition and tyranny? Had not Jefferson said it was the key to sound republican government? Education, then, could be desired both because it embodied that specially solid status identified with a preserve of the privileged and because it was the key to popular sovereignty. Schooling was a mark of social position whose *bona fides* were assured by estab-

---

22 Tyack, p. 144.

23 Robert Wiebe has written, of a somewhat later period, concerning the same process of social disorganization and its impact on aspirations: "As this society crumpled, the specialized needs of an urban industrial system came as a godsend to the middle stratum in the cities. Identifying themselves by way of their skills gave them the deference of their neighbors while opening natural avenues into the nation at large. As much as any other twist, an earnest desire to remake the world upon their private model testified to deep satisfactions accompanying this revolutionary identity." Robert Wiebe, *The Search for Order* (New York: Hill & Wang, 1967), p. 113.

lished privilege and tradition, but democratic dogma freed it from guilty associations with wealth or power. It was, simply enough, the best of both worlds. And the new century was not very old before schooling also came to be seen as an important way of learning trades. For all these reasons, public education had an uncanny appeal: schooling would be a step up socially; it would be a sound social currency in an unsound world; it promised useful trades; and yet it was democracy incarnate.

Free common schools therefore satisfied both those private wants engendered by social competition and unsettling social change and those public needs identified with popular government.[24] If the state would provide schooling on a public basis and in a neutral fashion, it would meet both a new democracy's anticipated need for political competency and many citizens' desires for more—and more secure—personal status. This felicitous arrangement soon became a way of life in the United States, as a succession of public needs—economic development, social integration, and scientific advance—became entangled with the private wants of middling and less advantaged Americans. Social policy for American education has been a story of expanding public entitlements based on the identification of private needs for status and social advancement with public wants for a more fair and productive society.

Democratic ideas about free public education were thus mixed from the start. Equal schools would uplift a newly sovereign political mass, but they would also create community in place of social cleavages and divisive distinctions. Equal schools would bind up the interests of those peering at each other from the extremes of the social pyramid and would secure more solid status for those looking up enviously from near the bottom. Equality in education welded the public, political interests of democracy with the private, personal interests of democrats.

Equality and Loss

While in many important respects traditional and democratic ideas about public education were strikingly different, in practice the two traditions tended to merge. One reason for this fusion was the common hopefulness about modern institutions, and another was the common sense that schools could help with pressing social problems. Horrified as many traditional reformers were at the disorder of mass life in the cities, they were more unsettled by the prospective impact of the unlettered masses on what was already a democracy. While mourning the loss of a simpler and more cohesive community, they supported schools to undo the damage and extend community. And many democrats, fearful for both their own social position and the emerging political democracy, saw the remedy in state-supported common schools. Ideas about democracy and loss and about solidarity and equality thus tended increasingly to fall in with each other as reformers of various stripes united in support of free public schools.

24 These terms—private wants and public needs—are taken from Daniel Bell, "The Public Household," *Public Interest*, No. 37 (Fall 1974), pp. 29–67. Bell treats the expansion of social policy alluded to here at much greater length.

Strange as these alliances and blurred arguments may seem in retrospect, they have been quite functional. Most important they have produced broad agreement among rather diverse elements in the movement for public education. And in certain important respects things have changed little since that time. Social policy in education still rests on the same mixed ideas about equality and social control; schools still aim to repress deviance and release individual potential. Compensatory education programs, the most recent instance of this phenomenon, are based on notions similar to those which underlay the birth of public education in the cities. The "target populations" are pictured as deprived, deviant, asocial creatures in need of better behavior, brighter ideas, and sounder sentiments; yet these programs also claim to liberate the potential of children who are admitted to have been badly treated by society. Compensatory education is presented both as the best hope for nipping crime and delinquency in the bud and as a major step toward equality in a society generally unfriendly to the poor and to racial minorities. The programs generously propose better than equal treatment for the poor, but the treatment is labeled for the "culturally deprived." It is no wonder the programs have such broad appeal and equally unsurprising that they generate such ambivalent reactions among their "targets."

But if one practical effect of these confusions has been to create continuing support for the extension of public schooling, another—as the example of compensatory education suggests—has been to provoke tensions within the school enterprise. Because the central metaphors of social policy for education have been packed with contradictory ideas, educational practice has been pulled by conflicting tendencies. This conflict has long been manifest in such diverse matters as pedagogy, discipline, and schools' relations with parents. But it was most pronounced and important in school-attendance policy.

One tends to forget that the first fruit of the movement for public schools was not compulsory attendance. Rather, some states and localities simply sought to provide open access to schools by legislating the authority of local governments to maintain schools and sometimes by offering modest financial support. The notion was that state agencies had an obligation to provide a social service on an equal basis, but decisions about using the service were reserved to families.

As concern with social disorganization intensified around mid-century, policy, however, began to shift. State governments which had adopted permissive statutes began to pass compulsory-education laws. They repeated the old arguments about deficient children but added new ideas about the need to protect society from its young. In the 1870s, one state report held that "the primary object of the state, in bestowing free public education upon its citizens, is not to benefit individuals as such, but to qualify them properly for their relations and duties to each other."[25] The shift was even more clear in the words of a state superintendent from the same period:

The state builds prisons and penitentiaries for the protection of society, and taxes

[25] Quoted in Pennsylvania Board of Public Charities, *Report of 1871 of the State of Pennsylvania*, rpt. in Katz, p. 68.

society for the same. . . . Now to prevent crime, to anticipate and shut it off by proper compulsory efforts in the schoolroom . . . the state not only has the right to inaugurate such methods as may be deemed best, but is under strict obligation to do so by all means in her power.[26]

In a certain sense, as David Tyack has observed, the swing toward state compulsion was implicit in earlier reform ideas.[27] A large part of the motive for providing free access to schools was to protect society from deviants. If the deviants refused the advantages thus proffered, it made sense to impose the advantages to protect the community. Still, that is only logic. In historical fact, the incarnation of these ideas in statutes which compelled school attendance was a pronounced policy shift. The result was that schooling loomed somewhat larger as an agency for repressing deviance than as a force for liberating citizens.

The consequences have been felt ever since. One result, for example, was to help weaken the influence of communities over their schools, both in struggles over consolidation in the countryside and in wars over school control in the cities. For in both cases compulsion strengthened state agencies and professionals and thus encouraged more distance between communities and their schools. Another result was to raise legal and political questions about the legitimacy of private education and to help constrain diversity on that front. And another was to reduce the scope of family choice and individual liberty in schooling, as state requirements for acceptable education grew on the foundations of compulsion.

In many important respects, of course, these conflicts are inevitable, there being no known arrangement which perfectly harmonizes the interests of the state and citizens. But the mixed metaphors underlying social policy for American education didn't help. Free and equal schools were to promote common affections and a generous sense of community, and they were to liberate the potential of individuals. At the same time, however, schools were to impose better morals and behavior on deviant masses. The fact that these two notions became so closely woven together helps explain both the enormous appeal of schooling as an instrument of social policy and the deep conflicts in educational policy and practice.

Loss Persistent?

One remarkable point is how recurrent and unresolved the sense of loss has been. Anxiety about the decay of family, community, and tradition is easy to understand in the urban chaos of the 1840s, but these fears seem no less lively today. A major presidential report on contemporary problems of adolescence, for example, recently exhibited the same concerns. It bemoaned the development of a "youth culture" which it represented as "spinning out of control,"[28] a danger to the order

[26] Maine state superintendent, quoted in Pennsylvania Board of Public Charities, *Report of 1871 of the State of Pennsylvania*, rpt. in Katz, p. 68.

[27] David Tyack, *The One Best System* (Cambridge, Mass.: Harvard Univ. Press, 1974), p. 68.

[28] President's Science Advisory Committee (PSAC), *Youth in Transition* (Washington, D.C.: GPO, 1973), p. 130.

and integration of society.[29] These problems were traced to "the weakness of the family unit,"[30] because "in America . . . kinship structure is weakening in each decade . . . the nuclear family provides little psychic strength for its teen-age members, [and] the needs must be met from outside."[31] These developments were traced, familiarly, to the rise of an urban manufacturing civilization and the decline of agrarian society.

This might have been written long ago. Certainly, one could quote many parallel mournful diatribes of the 1840s and 1850s about how modern city life created "disobedient," "rebellious," and "wayward" youth. The similarities are probably so obvious as to require no emphasis. The only real difference, ironically, is that the presidential report argued that schools are partly to blame because they encourage age segregation and feed intergenerational antagonisms. Thus, more than a century ago, curing the pathologies of modern youth meant inventing schools to make up for the inadequate socializing force of family, community, and work; but the current fashion in remedying the pathologies is to get youth back into the worlds of work and adult experience and away from the false socializing influence of schools.

However ironic the contrasts and similarities, one is struck by how persistent the sense of loss has been and by how much it has shaped ideas about the defects of modern society and their cures. One wonders, why? Is the experience of loss objectively so central to modern life? Are we doomed forever to seek roots in a dry soil? Or does the experience recur only because the remedies undertaken thus far have been inadequate? If that were so, at least there would be the hope that we can find the right solutions.

Such queries have not often been raised to the level of self-conscious discussion. One reason is that the sense of loss is a central fixture in modern culture. The chief tradition of thought, as I have already suggested, assumes that the rapid deterioration of primary social institutions is a fact, that many of the central problems of modern society are traceable to this loss, and that the task of social policy is to repair the damage. These ideas are so deeply rooted in the culture that they are rarely examined. There is an alternative intellectual tradition, though, in which loss figures rather prominently—psychoanalytic thought—and here it has been subjected to some scrutiny. In Freud's view early estrangement is an occurrence which shapes individual experience in profound ways.[32] In general, though, the psychoanalytic perspective is focused mostly on individual pathology, and so these ideas about loss have rarely found their way into analyses of social policy. But in *Loss and Change,* Peter Marris draws heavily on this tradition to explore the societal impact of loss and to explain its role in social policy. The book offers a provocative alternative to accepted ways of thinking about loss.

Marris begins with a discussion of responses to death. In a study of London

29 PSAC, p. 132.
30 PSAC, p. 133.
31 PSAC, p. 116.
32 See, for example, Sigmund Freud, *Civilization and its Discontents* (New York: Norton, 1962), pp. 14–15.

widows, he advances the view that only those who expressed the grief and anger of bereavement were able to build new lives out of the ruins of the old. Others remained frozen in postures of repression and repetition—or they frantically searched for distracting novelties. Marris believes that in the face of emotional trauma personal change occurs by expressing the pain, recognizing ambivalence, and working through inner conflict.

Marris thinks "working through" is constructive. He believes that the recognition of loss and the expression of grief are essential to fusing what is usable from the past with what is needed in the present. And he argues that there are institutions and traditions which can help. In one example, Marris focuses on the invention of voluntary tribal associations by newly citified Nigerians. These associations were a response to the dislocations of modernization. They offered occasions to recollect and re-enact a life that had been lost. They provided some concrete links to once-potent forces in social life, a framework for mourning the old life, and ritual occasions for celebrating what had passed. Finally, they offered some social and economic services—like credit unions—which were useful in urban life.

These associations seem important to Marris because he believes they constructively express the conflict inherent in grieving. He thinks that if institutions recognize the ambivalence of loss as legitimate, if the conflicts are given play, then healthy change can occur. In his view this means that society should not try to ignore the reality of loss in change; it should not try to repress grief nor encourage novelties to distract from the pain. Marris thinks social organizations, just like the widows in London's East End, need time and support to work through their ambivalence. Society needs to recognize that conflict about loss and change is reasonable, and it needs institutions which help separate what is still useful from what is not.

It is not hard to see how Marris's analysis might illuminate the history of social policy in education. One could view the establishment of public schools as an effort to build barriers against loss, to preserve a past which seemed to be slipping away. Marris would doubtless say that the absence of institutions to legitimize grieving could help explain why efforts to recoup loss have been repeated from the beginning of social policy down to our own time. There is much in the public schools' history which could evoke the sense that loss that is not worked through will dog us, recurring because it is not resolved.

By implication, then, Marris offers one explanation of why the sense of loss has been so persistent in social policy: as America modernized we did not arrange policies and institutions to work through the experience. But if this explanation throws a novel light on the discussion of loss in social policy, it is not without a few problems. For one thing, while psychoanalytic ideas are an immensely rich source of interpretive insight, the prescriptions require a degree of self-consciousness and persistence which is neither easily achieved nor effectively carried through—even in individuals. Surprisingly, however, Marris hopes that society can be aware and insightful enough to create institutions which will help work through collective loss. The hope seems a bit unlikely. One possible reason is that the sort of neurotic repetition Marris's discussion evokes is usually wonderfully self-sealing. Neurotic efforts to preserve or re-enact something that has been lost typically involve resistance to information which confirms the loss and suggests the need to move on. Ordinarily such persons will not recognize the problem or seek treatment. Even among those who do acknowledge a problem, many will imagine its source to be external. Moreover, among the modest number who do seek help, the treatment will often be ineffective. Sometimes this is because the issue is too painful to approach; sometimes the problem is too deeply rooted to resolve; and sometimes the treatment is caught up in the repetition and becomes enmeshed in the pathology. Thus, if one extends the metaphor from individuals to organizations—something which is as risky as it is intriguing—there is plenty of experience which requires cautious expectations about the sort of remedies Peter Marris suggests.

A more serious problem is Marris's assumption that loss bedevils social policy because it is not confronted, worked through, and then consigned to its appropriate place. He sees loss as a real and objective phenomenon and holds that if we understand it and deal with it sensitively, it will not have pathological effects.

Perhaps. But the sense of loss may persist not only because it is an objective feature of modern social experience but also because it is a subjective feature of the way moderns view experience. Loss may seem important as much because it is a central theme in modern culture as because it is a fact of social reality.

The idea of loss, after all, has been a terrifically important theme in modern culture. When Rousseau and Locke sought to explain the nature of political liberty and political obligation, for example, they could do so only by referring to an earlier, more perfect condition—the state of nature—which was lost because it became corrupted. In laying down laws of history, Marx and other nineteenth-century *savants* told the story in terms of man's fall from a simpler and happier time, an age corrupted by the emergence of more rational social and economic relations. And Freud, in explaining psychic development, thought in terms of sensate and satisfied infancy lost in early estrangement from parents. Indeed, moderns from Rousseau to Dewey have portrayed socialization and personality development in terms of the loss of a simpler, unspoiled condition. There have been many arguments about whether human nature or social arrangements were responsible for the unhappy effects of early loss, but the imagery has been so pervasive as to often make growing up seem like running down.

Like most great cultural themes, though, loss has not been just an arcane idea preserved in Viennese consulting rooms or the British Museum. The notion has been so widely diffused that it has gradually become common cultural property, a lens through which experience great and small is passed. The sources of educated perception—such as Burke, Ruskin, Arnold, Thoreau, and Emerson—have taught us that turmoil, conflict, and dislocation are the hallmarks of being modern, the consequences of slipping away from a simpler condition in which life was more natural and relations more harmonious. Through religion and our generally nostalgic literary culture, these themes have passed insensibly not only into the common culture but also into the action of everyday life. They are manifested in the idealized portraits of small-town America in children's schoolbooks and in the syrupy fantasies about American families now current on television. It is surely no accident that the most radical remnant of the 1960s tried finally to reconstruct a simpler community in the green communes of Vermont and California. That simple, solitary life, after all, is what we think we lost on the way to the Industrial Revolution.

These arguments do not suggest that the loss Peter Marris discusses does not exist nor that the process of modernization is not wrenching. But they do suggest that our culture encourages a particularly powerful nostalgic view of such experiences. This nostalgic view, in turn, creates an imbalance in what we make of the experience of loss and the process of modernization. And this nostalgia helps to explain why the sense of loss persists through so much change, why the feeling of loss remains vital despite the fact that institutions which were supposed to collapse long ago remain functional—if somewhat altered. The sense of loss is a major theme in social policy as much because it has been a central preoccupation of modern culture as because it has been a central reality in modern society.

If this is true, it raises questions about the preoccupation itself. Raymond Williams has argued, for example, that the sense of loss, estrangement, and social pessimism which pervades post-1800 literary culture is only a manifestation of one response to modernity—and a profoundly conservative response at that.[33] He points out that the major British literary figures—men like Ruskin, Carlyle, or the expatriated T. S. Eliot—were deeply concerned with the loss of community, skeptical about democratic government, condescending to the bourgeoisie, and openly contemptuous of the industrial working class. In Williams's view these men incorrectly idealized pre-modern society and expressed unwarranted pessimism about the potential of popular institutions. Their legacy in social policy, he thinks, has been systematic underestimation of the prospects for democracy and social justice.

Williams's view makes some sense. Certainly ideas about loss have often had a decidedly conservative flavor. Certainly the public-school advocates who were most concerned about loss—Henry Barnard is a good example—were also the most worried about whether democracy would survive mass participation. Equally certainly, these ideas have had a generally conservative effect in American social policy. Nor is all this bookish argument. For if the sense of loss results as much from a specific nostalgic bias in the culture as from a particular social problem, then its persistence may have more to do with the way we have learned to think and feel than with the objective decay of primary institutions. And this would make one a little skeptical about social remedies, whether nostalgic or therapeutic. The preoccupation with loss and estrangement, after all, has remained a permanent fixture in modern thought in spite of repeated efforts to remedy the problem. Most observers have assumed that this meant the remedies were ineffective and the

[33] Raymond Williams, *Culture and Society* (New York: Doubleday, 1966).

446

problems persistent. But to the extent that the sense of loss is rooted more in the culture than in social arrangements, just to that extent would the feeling persist through all changes in the social arrangements.

Conclusion

Despite these cautions, one can hardly deny that the sense of loss is a regular feature of social life or that it has been an authentic feature of modernization. The question is not whether loss exists but rather why we experience it as we do, and what we make of it for social policy.

In that connection, I have delineated several alternative views. One is that the sense of loss persists because objective social and economic changes have obliterated the old order. Conservatives argue that community has been shattered, meanings disrupted, traditions uprooted. These qualities can be regained, they hold, only if society creates more solidarity through institutions which teach a common culture, inculcate a common morality, and foster a sense of order and hierarchy. A second view holds that loss is an inevitable part of change and modernization. The task of society is not to reconstruct the past but to create therapeutic institutions which will help us work loss through and accept change. By contrast, egalitarians have been ambivalent: early in United States educational history, democrats advocated equality partly because of uneasiness about a loss of order; more recently, some egalitarians have held that the sense of loss is a persistent illusion, fostered either by literary and political advocates of an old elitist culture or by disillusioned and nostalgic liberals. But all egalitarians agree, community can only be the product of more equality, greater reciprocity in social arrangements, and more social and economic sharing.

These varied ways to view loss are associated with equally varied views of social policy. Traditionalists saw social policy in education as an effort to replace what had been lost by inventing new forms of education: schooling would do consciously and deliberately what primary institutions had once done unconsciously and reflexively. Egalitarians, by contrast, have seen social policy not as an effort to reconstruct or emulate the past but as the key to a new future; they hoped equal schools would create relationships based on sharing and reciprocity and would thereby strengthen community. And, for Peter Marris, social policy can deal with loss by encouraging fuller and more conscious experience; the task is to build institutions which help express grief and come to terms with loss.

In past experience, of course, these alternatives have not always been clearly marked off; another point in this essay has been to suggest the complicated role which loss has played in social policy. I have been at particular pains to argue that social policy for schools in the United States rests on a fusion of two very different stories about becoming modern. The tension between these stories and the policies they imply has been built into the school enterprise. Understanding this clarifies a good deal about American education.

A final aim of the essay has been to sort out ideas about loss and community in order to subject them to a modest bit of critical scrutiny. One purpose in this has been to suggest that the tangled ways in which we think about loss obscure alternatives. I have called particular attention to the fact that order and tradition are not necessarily the only paths to community. Some egalitarians have argued that solidarity may be created through social policies which encourage equality, reciprocity, and sharing rather than through policies which encourage order, the repression of deviance, and the subordination of minority cultures.

A second purpose in this critical effort has been to show that while the tangled ideas underlying social policy have played a powerful role in the expansion of public education, there have been costs. One result is that we tend to identify community with a nostalgic vision of bygone, small-town America. Another is that we tend to identify equality with compulsion rather than with choice. Still another has been to obscure the differences between community based on order, hierarchy, and the dominance of established culture, and community based on economic reciprocity, social sharing, and a democratic culture.

These confusions strike me as even more important now, as loss is being revived again. Contemporary liberal reformers have begun to worry that the expansion of social programs since the New Deal has been counterproductive. Some, like Daniel Patrick Moynihan, fear that the growth of central reform institutions has tended to undermine local community government.[34] Others, like Nathan Glazer, think that liberal judicial reform in race relations has weakened community and reduced local control.[35] Still others, like Aaron Wildavsky, think that liberal ideas and social criticism have had a generally negative effect, weakening social bonds and institutions which ought to be strengthened.[36] Many wonder—like European conservatives after the French Revolution—whether the new rational institutions designed to solve social problems have not just eroded the older primary institutions which needed shoring up. Since these worries occur in a culture whose dominant intellectual tradition sees modernization as the story of loss, it has not been hard to interpret liberal or radical social policy as just another step in the process of deracination. As a result, there has been a growing tendency to picture reform as a central problem. In education, for example, it is now becoming an article of faith that schools cause the loss of community because they segregate children from real life. The last five or ten years have seen a rather remarkable reshuffling of ideas about social policy, so that solidarity and community now stand high on political agendas all around, and equality seems a threat or a delusion.

This will make it harder to see the profoundly different meanings which community has had in American social thought. And it will make it hard to see that there are profoundly different ways to think about repairing loss: more social reciprocity may be as plausible a remedy as more order. These confusions are not of our making. Their origins lie deep in the past, and of course the past cannot be undone. But perhaps it need not be redone either.

[34] Daniel P. Moynihan, *Maximum Feasible Misunderstanding* (New York: Random House, 1969).

[35] Nathan Glazer, *Affirmative Discrimination* (New York: Basic Books, 1975).

[36] Aaron Wildavsky, "The Strategic Retreat on Objectives," *Policy Analysis*, 2 (1976), 499–526.

Notes on Contributors

URSULA BELLUGI is Director, Laboratory for Language and Cognitive Studies at the Salk Institute for Biological Studies, San Diego. Among her professional interests are the study of sign language, the biological foundations of language, and language acquisition. She has contributed extensively to the literature on sign language and children's speech, and is coauthor of *The Signs of Language* (1979).

ROGER BROWN is Professor of Psychology at Harvard University. His special interests are social psychology and psycholinguistics. He is the author of *Words and Things* (1958), *Social Psychology* (1965), *A First Language: The Early Stages* (1973), and coauthor, with Richard Hernstein, of *Psychology* (1975).

JEROME S. BRUNER, formerly Professor of Psychology at Harvard University and Watts Professor of Psychology at Oxford University, is presently Sloan Fellow at Harvard and Visiting Professor at MIT. His major professional interests have been in the fields of cognitive and linguistic development and in the nature of the educational process. Professor Bruner's best-known works include *On Knowing: Essays for the Left Hand* (1956), *The Process of Education* (1966), and *Beyond the Information Given* (1972). His most recent book is *Under Five in Britain* (1980), and a collection of essays by former students and colleagues *The Social Foundations of Language and Thought: Essays in Honor of Jerome S. Bruner* (edited by D. R. Olson) is currently in preparation.

DAVID K. COHEN, Professor of Education and Social Policy at Harvard University, is particularly interested in the relations between social sciences and social policy, the politics of education, and the evolution of social policy. A widely published scholar, he was a contributing author of *Inequality* (1972) and coauthor of *Usable Knowledge* (1979).

JAMES S. COLEMAN is Professor Sociology at the University of Chicago, with special interest in youth and secondary education. His books include *Community Conflict* (1957), *The Adolescent Society* (1961), *Equality of Educational Opportunity* (1966), *Power and the Structure of Society* (1973), and *Youth: Transition to Adulthood* (1973).

JAMES BRYANT CONANT (1893–1978) served as President of Harvard University, 1933–1953. During his tenure he broadened the geographic and social representation of the student body and opened all departments of the University to women students. Following his retirement from Harvard, Conant served four years in the Federal Republic of Germany, first as United States High Commissioner and later as United States Ambassador. From 1957–1963 he conducted studies for the Carnegie Corporation on the American high school and the education of American teachers. Conant's books on education include *The American High School Today* (1959), *Education in the Junior High School Years* (1960), *Slums and Suburbs* (1961), *The Education of American Teachers* (1963), and *Shaping Educational Policy* (1964).

JOHN DEWEY (1859–1952) was the dean of twentieth-century American educators. As a philosopher, psychologist, and practicing educator, he had a profound effect on education in the United States and throughout the world. At the University of Chicago, where he headed the department of philosophy and education, 1894–1904, he initiated the progressive movement in educational theory and practice. Dewey was Professor of Philosophy at Columbia University, 1904–1930, and also helped to found the New School of Social Research, and was a charter member of the first teacher's union in New York City. His books include *Applied Psychology* (1889), *School and Society* (1899), *The Child and the Curriculum* (1906), *Democracy and Education* (1916), *Human Nature and Conduct* (1922), and *Art as Experience* (1934).

PAULO FREIRE has served as Fellow of the Center for the Study of Development and Social Change, Visiting Professor at Harvard University, Center for Studies in Education and Development, and General Coordinator of the National Plan of Adult Literacy in Brazil. Formerly Special Adviser in Education to the World Council of Churches in Geneva, Switzerland, he returned to Brazil in June 1980 as Professor of Philosophy of Education at the Catholic University of São Paulo and the State University of Campinas. His work includes *Pedagogy of the Oppressed* (1970), *Education for Critical Consciousness* (1973), and *Pedagogy in Process: Letters to Guinea-Bissau (1978)*.

ANNA FREUD, psychoanalyst and author, has been Director of the Hampstead Child-Therapy Course and Clinic since 1938. Noted for her contributions to psychoanalytic theory and to ego psychology in particular, Dr. Freud is the author of *The Ego and the Mechanisms of Defense* (1936), *Psychoanalytical Treatment of Children* (1946), and *Normality and Pathology in Childhood* (1965). She has also, in collaboration with Dorothy Burlingham, written two books about her experiences and observations during World War II, *Young Children in War-time* (1942) and *Infants Without Families* (1943).

CAROL GILLIGAN is associate Professor at Harvard University. She is a developmental psychologist and a member of the Laboratory of Human Development. Her research and writing reflect her interest in the moral and ego development of women, the transition between adolescence and adulthood, and the relation of judgment and action in real situations of moral conflict and choice.

CHARLES V. HAMILTON is Wallace S. Sayre Professor of Government at Columbia University. His chief professional interests are the American national government, and race and ethnic politics in America. Among his published works are *The Black Experience in America* (1973), *The Bench and the Ballot* (1972), and *The Black Preacher in America* (1972).

JOSEPH A. KAHL, Professor of Sociology at Cornell University, was Fulbright Lecturer at El Colegio de México in 1979. He is concerned with the problems of social stratification and development in Latin America. Professor Kahl is the author of *The Measurement of Modernism: A Study of Values in Brazil and Mexico* (1968), *Modernization, Exploitation and Dependency* (1976), and is currently preparing a revised edition of *The American Class Structure* (first published in 1957).

JEROME KARABEL is Senior Research Associate at the Huron Institute, Cambridge, Massachusetts. His present areas of professional interest are sociology of education, social stratification, and political sociology. A senior editor of the journal, *Theory and Society*, and coeditor of *Power and Ideology in Education* (1977), Karabel is currently at work on a book on politics and inequality in American higher education.

LAWRENCE KOHLBERG, Professor of Education and Social Psychology at Harvard University, is best known for pioneering a cognitive-developmental approach to moral reasoning. He is the author of numerous articles on moral development and moral education and is now preparing a three-volume edition of his collected works.

ABRAHAM H. MASLOW (1908–1970) was Professor of Psychology at Brandeis University, 1951–1969. Maslow was a principal proponent of humanistic or third-force psychology, a departure from Freudian and behaviorist psychologies. His work stressed healthy rather than unhealthy personality development. He was especially interested in creative persons and their self-actualization. He was the author of *Motivation and Personality* (1954), *Toward a Psychology of Being* (1962), and *Farther Reaches of Human Nature* (published posthumously, 1971).

ROCHELLE MAYER is currently on leave from the Research Division of Bank Street College, New York, to work on a book on infant development. She has coauthored *BRACE: An Instrument for Systematic Observation of Verbal Communication and Behavior in Educational Settings* (1976).

O. HOBART MOWRER, Research Professor Emeritus, University of Illinois, is now engaged in research in the field of clinical ecology. A prolific contributor to the literature of learning theory and of psychology generally, he is the author of *Learning Theory and Personality Dynamics* (1950), *Learning Theory and the Symbolic Processes* (1960), *The Crisis in Psychiatry and Religion* (1961), *Morality and Mental Health* (1967), and *Psychology of Language and Learning* (1980).

TALCOTT PARSONS (1902–1979) was Professor of Sociology at Harvard University, 1944–1973. Professor Parsons's major interests were sociological theory and the comparative analysis of institutions. He received honorary degrees from—among others—Heidelberg, Cologne, the University of Chicago, Boston College, and Hebrew University in Jerusalem, and was President of the American Academy of Sciences, 1967–1971. Parsons was the author of numerous books and articles in the field of social theory, among them *The Social System* (1951), *Essays in Sociological Theory* (rev. ed., 1954), *Family, Socialization and Interaction Process* (with R. F. Bales, 1955), *Politics and Social Structure* (1969), *The American University* (1973), *The Evolution of Societies* (1977), and *Social Systems and the Evolution of Action Theory* (1977).

RAY C. RIST is Professor in the Department of Human Ecology at Cornell University. Among his diverse professional interests are qualitative evolution strategies, youth unemployment, and European social policy. Formerly a Fulbright Fellow at the Max Planck Institute in Berlin and Associate Director of the National Institute of Education, Professor Rist is the author or editor of numerous books, including *The Invisible Children* (1978), *Guest Workers in Germany: The Prospects for Pluralism* (1978), and *Desegregated Schools* (1979).

CARL R. ROGERS is currently Resident Fellow at the Center for Studies of the Person in La Jolla, California. An eminent psychologist and Past-President of the American Psychological Association and the American Academy of Psychotherapists, Professor Rogers originated the nondirective, or client-centered approach to psychotherapy. In 1962–63 he was a Fellow at the Center for

Advanced Study in the Behavioral Sciences and he has taught at several universities, including the University of Chicago, Ohio State University, and the University of Wisconsin. Among his numerous writings are *Clinical Treatment of the Problem Child* (1939), *Client-Centered Therapy* (1951), *On Becoming a Person* (1961), *Freedom to Learn* (1969), and, most recently, *A Way of Being* (1980).

ISRAEL SCHEFFLER is Victor S. Thomas Professor of Education and Philosophy, Harvard University. Among his professional interests are the philosophy of language and the philosophy of education. He is author of *Conditions of Knowledge: An Introduction to Epistemology and Education* (1965), *Science and Subjectivity* (1967), *Reason and Teaching* (1973) and *Beyond the Letter: A Philosophical Inquiry into Ambiguity, Vagueness, and Metaphor in Language* (1979).

MICHAEL SCHUDSON is Associate Professor in the Departments of Sociology and Communication at the University of California, San Diego. He has also taught at the University of Chicago. The author of *Discovering the News: A Social History of American Newspapers* (1978), he is currently writing on the social role of advertising and on a theory of popular culture.

B. F. SKINNER, Professor Emeritus of Psychology and Social Relations, Harvard University, is currently engaged in an experimental analysis of behavior. The recipient of numerous awards and honorary degrees for his distinguished contributions to educational research and development in the field of experimental psychology, Professor Skinner has been a frequent contributor to the literature of behavioral psychology. Among his best-known works are *Walden Two* (1948) and *Beyond Freedom and Dignity* (1971). The second volume of his autobiography, *The Shaping of a Behaviorist*, appeared in 1979, following the publication of *Particulars of my Life* (1976).

STEPHEN SPENDER, British poet, playwright, and critic, is Professor Emeritus of English Literature of University College, London, and Honorary Fellow of University College, Oxford. He was for many years (1953–1967) an editor of the British literary journal, *Encounter*. One of the outstanding poets of his generation, Spender published his earliest poems in 1928; his *Collected Poems, 1928–1953* were published in 1955. He is also the author of plays and several books of literary criticism, among them, *The New Realism: A Discussion* (1939), *The Creative Element* (1953), *Chaos and Control in Poetry* (1966), *W. H. Auden: A Tribute* (1975), and *The Thirties and After* (1975).

DAVID B. TYACK is Professor of Education and History at Stanford University. Author of numerous publications, including *The One Best System: A History of American Urban Education* (1974), his major area of interest is the social history of American education.

HEINZ WERNER (1890–1964) received his doctorate in psychology at the University of Vienna in 1914. Joining the Psychological Laboratory of Munich and, later, the Psychological Laboratory of Hamburg, he advanced the argument that principles of development psychology are relevant to educators and to all of the life sciences. Among Werner's works are his well-known *Comparative Psychology of Mental Development* (1926) and three monographs: *The Origins of the Metaphor* (1922), *Basic Problems in the Psychology of Intensity* (1922), and *The Origin of the Lyric* (1924). Two volumes of his collected articles, *Developmental Processes*, were published in 1978.

452

The Editors: 1930–1980

Barbara E. Abrams	1954–55	Maureen D. Carlson	1959
Walter I. Ackerman	1954–55	Aaron S. Carton	1958–59
John E. Alman	1948–49	James H. Case	1967–68
Gordon M. Ambach	1965–66	Ray Castro	1973–74
James M. Anderson	1945	Bernard S. Cayne	1954–55
Wilton Anderson	1969–70	Courtney B. Cazden	1963–65
Albert S. Anthony	1946–47	Rachel Chaffey	1956
Richard N. Apling	1977–79	Barbara Chartier	1951–52
Reginald D. Archambault	1956–57	John L. D. Clark	1965–66
David K. Archibald	1961–62	Jonathan J. Clark	1965–66
Victor Atkins	1969–70	Walter H. Clark, Jr.	1960–62
Barbara J. Ayres	1952–53	Miriam Clasby	1970–71
		Michelle A. Coakley	1972–74
Neal A. Baer	1979–80	Morris L. Cogan	1951–52
Richard H. Balmenos	1959–60	Cherry W. Collins	1969–70
Mary Jo Bane	1969–71	Evan R. Collins	1940–44
Rhoda Baruch	1964	Susan Contratto	1968–69
Ralph Beatley	1947	William W. Cooley	1957–58
Rochelle Beck	1973–76	Trevor A. Coombe	1962–63
Harold Berlak	1962–63	Paul D. Courtney	1947
Hilda Bernstein (see Silverman)		Judith E. Cowen (see Fuchel)	
Carla F. Berry	1955	Patricia Cox	1974–77
William B. Bickley III	1975–77	Barbara H. Craig	1979–80
Arthur F. Blackman	1966–68	*Roger B. Crane	1959–60
Ben Bohnhorst	1950–51	Donald Cunnigen	1978–79
Barrie D. Bortnick	1965–67		
John C. Borton, Jr.	1968	Deborah P. Dale	1947
Raold W. Bowers	1949–51	Millicent P. Daly	1978–80
Norman J. Boyan	1948–50	Dolores M. Da Lomba	1974–75
*John Marks Brewer	1942–44	Hope F. Danielson	1957–58
Lynne T. Brickley	1977–79	Richard G. Darman	1970
Frances A. Bridges	1976–78	Mack I. Davis	1970–73
W. Douglas Brooks	1953–54	Lisa D. Delpit	1980
Charles E. Brown	1953–54	Daniel R. De Nicola	1969–70
George I. Brown	1957–58	Stephen R. Diaz	1975–77
Stephen I. Brown	1962–65	Ann L. Diller	1965–67
Larry N. Browning	1971–72	Paul J. Di Maggio	1974–77
Anthony Bryk	1973–74	*Norman R. Dixon	1953
Charles I. Bunting	1970–71	Simeon J. Domas	1948–50
Aaron C. Butler, Jr.	1954	Maureen Donnelly (see Carlson)	
John A. Butler	1972–74	Peter E. Donnelly	1947
		Kevin Dougherty	1976–78
Peter F. Carbone	1964–66	Clara C. Dreiss	1960–61
Richard F. Carle	1961–63	Raymond J. Dry	1950–51

* Deceased members

Peggy Dulany	1972–74	John K. Harley	1958
Annette Dula	1979–80	Willard W. Hartup	1952–54
		Penny Hauser-Cram	1980
John A. Easley, Jr.	1954–55	Chester M. Hedgepeth, Jr.	1976–77
Keith T. Edmonds	1976–77	Marvin Herrick	1952–54
*Esther P. Edwards	1960–63	Robert Herriot	1959–60
Frederick E. Ellis	1946	John D. Herzog	1959–61
Janet A. Emig	1962–64	Masinori Higa	1960–61
Todd I. Endo	1968–69	Thomas L. Hilton	1954–55
Terrie Epstein	1979–80	Marsha Hirano	1973–75
Claryce L. Evans	1971–73	Wells Hively II	1958–60
Eric L. Eversley	1973–74	Harold L. Hodgkinson	1956–58
Melvin Ezer	1957	*Henry W. Holmes	1934–46
		N. Deming Hoyt	1949–50
Aaron Fink	1951	Donna Hulsizer	1977–79
Kenneth L. Fish	1953–54	Lydia A. Hurd (see Smith)	
Sara A. Fisher	1964		
James T. Fleming	1962–64	Robert S. Ireland	1952–53
Joseph W. Fordyce	1948–49		
Donald Foster-Gross	1972–74	Greg Jackson	1974–76
Carla L. Friedman	1954–55	Jerry Jacobs	1979–80
Judith C. Fuchel	1953–54	David C. Jehnsen	1977–79
Michael Fultz	1980	John B. Jemmott III	1980
		Clifford V. Johnson	1969–70
Eric F. Gardner	1946	Melanie Hanson Johnson	1979–80
Gloria Garfunkel	1979–80	Helen M. Jones	1945
Andrew Garrod	1980	Kenneth J. Jones, Jr.	1962–63
Rev. Edwin K. Gedney	1947		
Fred Geis, Jr.	1967–68	Carl F. Kaestle	1968–69
Richard A. Geist	1967–68	Tomas M. Kalmar	1971–72
Stuart A. Gerber	1959–60	Max Kargman	1947
Kathleen Gerritz (see Weeks)		John S. Katz	1966–67
Joseph B. Giacquinta	1967–68	Michael B. Katz	1964–65
Maurice Gibbons	1967–68	Andreas M. Kazamias	1955–57
Hendrick D. Gideonse	1959–62	Chris D. Kehas	1961–62
W. King Gillen	1963–65	*Shildrick A. Kendrick	1950–52
George W. Goethals	1951–52	Harriet Kern (see Spivak)	
Stanley Goldberg	1962–65	Jane H. Kessler	1953–54
Wendy L. Gollub	1969–70	Richard J. King	1948–49
David W. Gordon	1971–73	Leopold E. Klopfer	1961–62
George J. Greenawalt	1961–63	Dennis S. Klos	1970–71
William Greenbaum	1970–73	Niilo E. Koponen	1963–66
Rogier A. Gregoire	1969–70	Nancy V. Kozak	1976–77
Calvin E. Gross	1951	Judith C. Kredel	1956–57
Robert J. Gross	1968–69	Phyllis Kuffler	1972–74
Tito Guerrero	1974–75	Dean W. Kuykendall	1945
Andre Guerrero	1978–79		
Florence C. Guild	1954–55	Magdalene Lampert	1978–80
		Roger L. Landrum	1976–77
James A. Hagler	1953–54	Ellen Lane	1948–49
Joseph I. Hall	1945	James D. Laurits	1950–51
Eber Hampton	1979–80	Charles W. Leftwich	1970
Emily Hancock	1979–80	Gloria Leiderman	1951–53
Walt Haney	1974–77	Judith Lemon	1973–75

George W. LeSuer	1955–56	Dennis K. Norman	1980
Lowell S. Levin	1951–54	Paul Nyberg	1954–56
Malcolm A. Levin	1965–66		
Sara L. Lightfoot	1969–70	Lydia N. O'Donnell	1978–79
Mona H. Lipofsky (see Rabineau)		Henry Olds, Jr.	1964–65
Paul R. Lohnes	1957–58	John J. O'Neill	1952–53
Richard H. Longabaugh	1959–61	Rev. Michael O'Neill	1965–66
*E. Jeffrey Ludwig	1966–67	John C. Osgood	1954–56
Carol Lukas	1973–75		
		Donald G. Palmer	1958–59
Grady McGonagill	1980	John C. Palmer, Jr.	1950–51
R. Gordon McIntosh	1966–68	Rosemarie L. Park	1971–73
David S. McLean	1945–46	John L. Parker	1967–68
Mark K. McQuillan	1977–79	Thomas D. Parker	1970–71
Donald J. Malcolm	1950	William O. Penrose	1946
Ian D. Malcolm	1949–51	Henry J. Perkinson	1957–58
K. Gerald Marsden	1963–65	Lauri Perman	1977–79
Daniel W. Marshall	1949–50	W. Lee Pierson	1969–70
Margaret Marshall	1971–73	Davenport Plumer	1966–67
Jane R. Martin	1957–59	Helen M. Popp	1962–64
Randy Martinez	1977–79	Douglas Porter	1956–57
Thomas Marx	1971–73	Jerilyn A. Posnik	1975–76
Prema Mathai-Davis	1975–77	Barbara S. Powell	1967–69
Robert Mathews	1977–78	Gordon M. Pradl	1969–71
Edward J. Meade, Jr.	1959–60	David Purpel	1958–59
Joseph Meier	1962–64		
Samuel Meisels	1970	David F. Quattrone	1971–73
Dolores Mendelson (see Da Lomba)			
Jonathan Messerli	1958–61	Louis Rabineau	1952
John A. Mierzwa	1960–61	Mona H. Rabineau	1956–57
Donald Mitchell	1949–50	Eugene Radwin	1976–78
Jacquelyn Mitchell	1978–79	Robert R. Ramsey, Jr.	1954–55
Joanne A. Mitchell	1964–65	Barbara Randell	1958–59
*Jeffrey P. Moeller	1976–77	Charles W. Read	1956–57
Marilyn D. Monteiro	1976–77	Freda G. Rebelsky	1960–61
Maurice R. Montgomery	1968–70	Horace B. Reed, Jr.	1957–58
Donald R. Moore	1967–69	Jack Reitzes	1961–62
Ralph L. Mosher	1960–62	Lauren B. Resnick	1959–60
O. Hobart Mowrer	1945–47	S. Earl Richards	1952–54
Frederick V. Mulhauser	1967–69	Robert C. Riordan	1969–72
Ruth H. C. Munroe	1961–62	Juna E. Ripoll	1954–55
Muchemwa Murerwa	1973–75	Marguerite Robertson	1951
Geraldine J. Murphy	1954–55	Joanne Robinson (See Mitchell)	
John Michael Murphy	1977–79	L. David Robinson	1968–69
Mary E. Murphy	1977–79	Wade Robinson	1959–60
		Jane Roland (see Martin)	
David A. Napior	1968–69	Peter S. Rosenbaum	1964–65
Paul Nash	1956–57	Bella Rosenberg	1974–77
George F. Needham III	1946	Stuart Rosenfeld	1974–75
*Gordon R. Neisser	1963–65	Kristine M. Rosenthal	1965–67
Beatrice K. Nelson	1968–69	Lawrence Rothstein	1974–75
Fred M. Newman	1962–64	Judge K. Rowley	1950–51
Irene A. Nichols	1955–58	*Phillip J. Rulon	1935–41
Gil G. Noam	1977–79	Rosemary E. Russo	1976–77

F. James Rutherford	1960-61	John E. Tirrell	1953-54
		Gregory E. Thomson	1969-70
Harriet Sachs	1955-56	David V. Tiedeman	1947
Edward P. St. John	1975-77	Hope F. Tower	1957-58
Nancy H. St. John	1961-62	Henry F. Trainor	1954-55
Samuel Salia-Bao	1979-80	Anne E. Trask	1958-59
Phoebe Salten	1976-77	*Raymond M. Travis	1954-55
Janet J. Sanfilippo	1965-66	John W. Tucker	1955
Marjorie D. Sanger	1947	Brenda Turnbull	1975-77
Cyril G. Sargent	1947	Ruth W. Twombly	1954-55
Jane Sargent (see Kessler)		David B. Tyack	1954-55
Alvin R. Schmidt, Jr.	1948-50		
Robert A. Schofield	1952-54	Reed T. Ueda	1977-78
Michael Schudson	1971-74	*Robert Ulich	1937-47
Robert B. Schwartz	1967-68		
Robert F. Schweiker	1950-51	J. Edwin Wade	1949-51
Penelope Scott	1950	Suzanne Wade	1979-80
David S. Seeley	1961-62	James M. Wallace	1965-66
Dean W. Seibel	1953-54	Joseph Walsh	1968-69
Margaret R. Shannon	1948-50	William S. Warren, Jr.	1955-56
Samuel N. Sheinfeld	1951	John W. Washburn, Jr.	1969-71
Mark R. Shibles	1945	William M. Weber	1971-73
Peter B. Shoresman	1961-62	Kathleen Weeks	1970-71
Carol Sienkiewicz	1980	Joel S. Weinberg	1962-64
Hilda I. Silverman	1964-65	Eleanor S. Weiss	1945
Wong Kooi Sim	1966-67	Heather B. Weiss	1972-75
Edward J. Simpkins	1969-70	Larry A. Weiss	1965-66
Theodore R. Sizer	1959-61	Robert C. Weller, Jr.	1950-51
John Sly	1958-59	Elizabeth A. Wescott	1973-74
Wood Smethurst	1969-70	John W. Wideman	1957-59
Henrietta T. Smith	1952-53	John B. Wight	1946
Louise Smith	1972-73	Claudia Wilds	1957-58
Lydia A. Smith	1955-59	W. Richard Willard	1955-58
John R. Snarey	1979-80	Lawrence V. Willey	1954-55
Ellen W. Solomon	1970-71	John Williams	1974-76
Harriet K. Spivak	1967-68	John N. Williamson	1968-69
Ernest Stabler	1950-51	*Howard E. Wilson	1934-44
Julian C. Stanley, Jr.	1948	Michael J. Wilson	1964-65
John N. Stauffer	1945	Kenneth M. Wilson	1952-54
William A. Stuart	1953-54	Thomas A. Wilson	1969-70
Marilyn Sullivan	1973-74	Maryanne Wolf	1975-77
		Ruth Hie-King Wong	1960-61
Diane S. Tabor	1970-72	Wilbur H. Wright	1946
Loong-Hoe Tan	1975-76		
Bridget Tancock	1960-61	Saul M. Yanofsky	1966-68
Merle W. Tate	1945	Joseph J. Young, Jr.	1954-55
Maurice M. Tatsuoka	1952-54	Lauren Jones Young	1979-80
Carol G. Taylor	1978-80		
Robert G. Templeton	1951-52	Janet Zeller	1975-77
Norman L. Thoburn	1952-53	Gail Zivin	1967-69
*Charles Swain Thomas	1931-36	Philip Phaedon Zodhiates	1979-80
George B. Thomas	1964-66		

Index

Barnard, Henry, 410, 432–433, 434, 436, 439, 446
Beard, Charles, 399, 411
Becker, H. S., 345, 346
Becker, Wesley, 20
Bedales (English coeducational school), 250
Beebe-Center, J. G., 67n
Behavior: "categorical," 36, 37; modifiable and non-modifiable, 55–56; modification of, 162, 165, 182, 198; child's experiences as, 169; relative to norm, 171; and behavior technology (neutrality of), 173; negative, reinforcement of, 364. *See also* Personality; Reinforcement
Behaviorism, 11, 138, 147, 169, 171, 398; and antibehaviorism, x, xi, 21, 149, 151; and "contingencies of reinforcement," 77, 78–80. *See also* Reinforcement
Belenky, Mary, 202n, 210
Bellugi, Ursula, xi, 21, 449
Bendix, R., 373
Bennett, John W., 344n
Bennett, Lerone, Jr., 319, 320
Bereday, G. Z. F., 10
Bereiter, C., 163, 173–174, 177–178, 187, 191
Berkowitz, L., 172
Bettelheim, Bruno, 162n
Black Panther Defense Fund, 16
Black Power (Hamilton and Carmichael), 14
Blacks: and search for legitimacy, xiii, 311–324; and Jensen-IQ controversy, 15–19; and *HER* editorial board, 17–18; linguistic system of, 21, 321, 352, 362; education for, 299, 300, 402, 408; and racial integration issue, 303–305, 311, 312, 321–322; academic achievement of, 306–307, 308–309, 310; and Afro-American culture, 312, 317, 319–321; and busing issue, 314, 317–318, 321, 322; self-image of (children), 314–315; Comprehensive Plan for, 322–324; and studies of ghetto school, 348–366; and community colleges/vocational education, 381, 388–389; illiteracy of, 402; suffrage for, 413. *See also* Equality/inequality of education/educational opportunity
Black Student Union (Seattle Community College), 388
Blau, P. M., 373
Bloomfield, Leonard, 119
Blough, Donald S., 80
Bonald, L. G. A., 433
Borg, W., 347
Boston Globe, 16n
Bowles, Samuel, 14, 380, 382, 424–427
Bowman, Mary Jean, 418, 422
Boyan, Norman, 257n
Brace, Charles Loring, 433

Braine, M. D. S., 129
Brandt, R. B., 176
Brazil literacy campaign, 327n, 337
Brick, M., 384
Brooklyn College, 389
Broverman, D., 203
Broverman, I., 203; et al., 205, 217
Brown, John, 230
Brown, Judson S., 61
Brown, Roger, xi, 21, 449
Brownell, William A., 41, 43
Browning, Larry, 17–18
Brown v. *Board of Education,* xiii, 6
Bruner, Jerome S., xi, 11–12, 449
Brunswik, Egan, 33
Buck, Paul, 7
Burke, Edmund, 445
Burke, Kenneth, 398
Bushnell, D. S., 370
Business community, xi–xii, 3; and vocational education, 383–384, 387; influence of, 417, 418; and opposition to education, 423, 426, 428. *See also* Capitalism; Labor force
Busing issue, *see* Blacks
Butts, R. Freeman, 406

California colleges, 369, 376, 381n
Callahan, Raymond, 417
Cambridge University, 247, 248
Cannon, W. B., 52, 67
Capital, human, *see* Human capital
Capitalism: class structure of, 424–428. *See also* Business community; Labor force; Social class
Carlyle, Thomas, 446
Carmichael, Stokely, 14
Carnegie Commission on Higher Education, 384, 387, 388, 392
Carnegie Corporation, 14, 384
Carnegie Endowment for International Peace, 5
Catholic World (periodical), 414
Census Bureau, *see* U.S. Bureau of the Census
Central nervous system, *see* Nervous system, central and autonomic
Chandler, Alfred, 417
Charterhouse (English public school), 247
Chicago: Board of Education, 312, 314; Family Education Center, 322–323; Association of Commerce, 378n; Federation of Labor, 389
Chicago City Junior College, 384
Child labor laws, 300, 417, 422. *See also* Labor force; Legislation
Children: as subject of *HER* articles, 20; -teacher relationships, 72–76, 245, 279, 281, 284–286, 289, 345, 346, 356, 363; school-age, drives of, 74, 75–76; ego and super-ego of, 75,

tary school, 259, 285, 302, 303; social class, and choice of, 269-270, 380n; and extra-curricular activities, 292; exposure to, and opportunity, 301, 303, 307; change in secondary-school, 302-303, 372, 405; black concern with, 320-321

Dare the School Build a New Social Order? (Counts), 4
David, Rex, 426
David Copperfield (Dickens), 253
Delinquency, 188, 283, 290-291, 294, 406, 432, 433, 439, 441; and truancy, 291, 402, 405, 415. *See also* Crime
Demiashkevich, Michael, 4
Democracy, 244, 316, 431, 435-440 *passim,* 446, 447; as *HER* issue, 5; educational, 181, 182-183, 198, 377, 391. *See also* Equality
Democratic Party, 411-412, 414
Deprivation: emotional, 73-74; effect of, 167; cultural, 173-174, 320, 441
"Deschooling," 162, 177
"Desirable trait" strategy, *see* "Bag of virtues" strategy
Development: structural-developmental theory, xi; maturationist theory, xi, 160, 162n, 164-168, 197; cognitive-developmental/interactionist theory, xi, 164, 165-171, 184, 187, 189-199; measurement of, 31-32; psychosexual stages of, 76, 165; of speech, studied, 116-134; as aim of education, 159-199; environmental-contingency theory, 164, 165, 168; cognitive stages of, 166-168, 171, 190, 194-199 *passim;* cultural factors in, 166; concept of, 189, 191, 192, 197; defined, 189. *See also* Moral development/morality
"Developmental-philosophic" strategy, 160, 183, 184, 187, 189-191
Developmental psychology, 31-45. *See also* Psychology(ies)
Developmental theory: as applied to women, 202-204, 230-237
DeVries, R., 193, 194
Dewey, John, ix, xi, 4, 137, 159-166 *passim,* 170-181 *passim,* 190-199 *passim,* 429, 445, 450
Dickens, Charles, 253
Didion, Joan, 212
Discovery (in learning), 89-100
Dollard, Charles, 7
Doll's House, A (Ibsen), 209
Dostoievsky, Feodor, 180
Douai, Adolph, 426
Douglass, Frederick, 319
Drabble, Margaret, 219
Drew, Dr. Charles, 321

Drive(s): and drive reduction, 48, 49, 61, 68, 85; in learning process, 51; learned, 56; of school-age child, 74, 75-76. *See also* Emotion
"Dropouts," 188, 377, 402
Dunbar, H. F., 67
Duncan, O. D., 373
Durbin, Marshal, 344n

Eckhardt, Meister, 151
Eddy, E., 349
Edi Ferreira, Maria, 340
Education: universal/compulsory (U.S.), xiv, 241, 299-301, 344, 369, 371, 380, 398-429; as term, interpretation of (by *HER* Editorial Board), 5; compensatory, 15-16, 19, 21, 312, 321, 441; aversive control of, 81-82, 84-85, 86; reformulation of aims of, 83-84; development as aim of, 159-199; strategies for defining objectives of, 159-160, 183-191; public, rise of, 298-299, 372; utopian, 338-339, 343, 366; as social process, 345-346, 349; as economic/social "investment," 382, 418-424; political construction of, 406, 407-415. *See also* Achievement, academic; Curriculum; Elementary school(s); Equality/inequality of education/educational opportunity; Ideology(ies), educational; Learning; Secondary school(s); Teacher(s); Teaching; Vocational education
Education, higher, 241, 259; selection for, 242-245, 276-278, 280, 290, 291-292, 294, 374-377; English, 247; aspirations for, 259-260, 266, 269-271, 272, 277; inequality of opportunity for, 300; curriculum for, 302-303, 372, 405; elitism/differentiation in, 369, 371, 372, 386-387, 391, 393, 407; stress on/demand for, 370-371; nonpecuniary benefits of, 382n. *See also* Community college movement; *individual colleges and universities*
Education Act of 1870 (England), 299
Educational aspirations: "common man" (U.S.) and, xii, xiv, 257-273
Educational goals and purpose, 144, 189; humanist view of, x; behaviorist view of, 11, 84, 87, 88, 173; progressive view of, 160, 163, 198-199; and acceleration vs. *decalage,* 195, 197. *See also* Ideology(ies), educational; Values
"Educational inflation," 372-373, 390
"Educational science," 416
Educational Testing Service (ETS), 277n
Effect: law of, x, 47, 48, 51, 68, 78; association and, 48-52, 60
"Effect" learning, *see* Learning
Ego (of child), *see* Children
Elementary school(s), 401; English, 247, 250; social class and status in, 259, 287-291, 293,

355-361, 364; curriculum, 259, 285, 302, 303; socialization and selection in, 276, 277-278, 285, 286-291; achievement in, 276, 277, 280-282, 287-291 *passim*; structure of class in, 278-280; family and peer group in relation to, 278-289 *passim*, 293, 294

Eliot, George, 207, 209, 219

Eliot, T. S., 446

Elitism, 179, 408, 417, 425, 429; in higher education, 369, 372, 386-387, 391, 393, 407; and educational reform, 429, 438, 439; American vs. European, 435. *See also* Social class; Values

Elkind, David, 12

Emerson, Ralph Waldo, 153, 445

Emotion: as response, x, 53, 56-57, 59, 61, 66-67; psychology of, 28; and appreciation, 29; and emotional deprivation, 73-74; and emotional development, 165. *See also* Drive(s); Fear

Empathy, *see* Guidance counseling

Empiricism: episodic, 92, 93; and empirical research, 109-114, 159, 170, 171, 184, 186, 416, 429; and "empirical" philosophy, 191

Encounter groups, 155

"Endocentric" construction, *see* Noun phrase(s)

Engelmann, S., 163, 173-174, 187, 192

England: adolescent experience in, xii, 246-256, 302; class system in, xii, 246-256, 299-300, 388; dual educational system of, 246-250, 254-255, 299, 303, 388; 18th-century restrictions on mobility in, 298; state support of schools in, 299-300; compulsory-school legislation in, 405; National Health Service in, 438

Enlightenment, the, 436, 439

Ensign, Forest, 399

Environmental-contingency theory, *see* Development

Equality: "law of" (Gestalt psychology), 35; women and, 206, 223, 228; economic, under capitalistic system, 424-427. *See also* Democracy; Social class

Equality/inequality of education/educational opportunity, 287; legislation toward, xi-xii; and political debate, xiii, 14; curriculum and, xiii, 300, 301-304, 390; and social policy, xiv, 180, 187-188, 365, 371, 377, 380, 392-393, 426, 431-432; talent and, 243, 244; concept of, 297-310, 311, 348, 370, 388; inequality defined (USOE survey), 305-306; effective, 307; criteria for, 315; compulsory education and, 405, 422; and loss, 431, 440-442; and community, 437-440. *See also* Social class; Socioeconomic status

Equality of Educational Opportunity (Coleman), *see* Coleman Report (1966)

ERIC Clearinghouse for Junior Colleges, 383

Erikson, Erik, 167, 202, 230, 235, 236

Ervin, Susan, 129

Esalen-type centers, 157

Essay Concerning Human Understanding (Locke), 136

Essentialist Committee for the Advancement of American Education, 4-5

Essex County College, 389

Ethnocultural conflict, *see* Culture

Eton College, 247, 248

Euthanasia, 222

Exercise, law of, 48n, 51n. *See also* Repetition

Existentialism, 150, 168, 208

Expansion (in speech development), *see* Imitation

Expectations of achievement, 280, 287, 290-291; by teacher (social class and), xiii-xiv, 282, 305, 344-366; conditioning and, 68; parental, 269, 271

Experience(s): and peak-experiences, 151-152, 155-157; progressive view of, 169, 170, 171; "miseducative," 170; absence of, 305, 356

"Experiential emptiness," 150

Experimentation: "pathogenic" procedure in, 65

Fallacy, *see* "Psychologist's fallacy"

Family, the, 275, 295, 309, 406; elementary school child and, 277-289 *passim*; women and, 295; preindustrial European, 297-298; weakening of, 405, 430-433 *passim*, 442-443; and "human capital" theory, 422, 428; educational choice by, 441, 442. *See also* Children; Parents

Fear: and defense/fear reaction, 50, 59, 60-61, 64, 65-66; learning of, 50, 53, 56, 59. *See also* Emotion

Featherstone, Joseph, 22

Feedback, 84, 155, 165; "natural," 168; parental expectations and, 269, 271. *See also* Information processing; Reinforcement

Ferster, Charles B., 78, 79

Fields, Ralph, 386

"Field theory," 68

Fishlow, Albert, 419, 421-422

Flexner, Abraham, 3

Folger, J. K., et al., 376

Follow Through: evaluation of, 19, 20

Ford, C. S., 53

Forster, E. M., 2, 254

Foundations: and vocational education, 384, 387. *See also* Business community

Frazier, E. F., 352

Free association, 152

Freeman, R., et al., 353

Freire, Paulo, xiii, 14, 20, 21, 450

French Revolution, 408, 433, 448

Freud, Anna, x, 162n, 450

Freud, Sigmund, 53, 152, 156, 161, 204–205, 209, 211, 443, 445; and Freudian theory, 58, 149, 150, 165, 167, 288, 398

Fuchs, E., 349

Fulton, J. F., 57

"Functors" (omitted forms), *see* Grammatical structure

Galambos, Louis, 417

Gallagher, Kathleen, xiv, 12

Gallup poll (1973), 423

Games: English attitude toward, 251, 253, 255

Gandhi, Mohandas K., 235–236

Garet, Michael, 21

Garvey, Marcus, 319

Gebhard, P., et al., 353

Geertz, Clifford, 22n

Gelb, Adhemar, 37

Gendlin, E. T., 104

Genetic (developmental) psychology, *see* Psychology(ies)

Geoffrey, W., 348

German gymnasium, 302

Gesell, Arnold, 161, 167, 268

Gestalt psychology, 35, 47; and "Gestalt-blindness," 39, 42

Ghetto schools, 316–317, 322; studies of, 346–366; social status within, 355–361, 364, 365–366. *See also* Blacks

Gibson, G., 346

Gideonse, Hendrik, 12

Gift Relationship, The (Titmuss), 438

Gill, R. Christine, xv

Gilligan, Carol, xi, 22, 207, 210, 232, 450

Gintis, Herbert, 424–427

Glazer, Nathan, 448

Gleazer, Edmund J., Jr., 384, 386, 387

Goldberg, M., 347

Goldstein, K., 37

Gouldner, Helen P., 344n

Grammatical structure, 120, 125; omitted form ("functors") in, 121–123, 124, 126, 127; induction of (by child), 126–134. *See also* Language

Great Depression, 405, 426

Grof-type work, 157

Gross, Neal, 10

Grotberg, Edith, 184

Group tests: inadequacy of, 43

Grubb, Norton, 19

Guidance counseling: "cooling out" process in, xiv, 377–380, 387, 390, 392; interpersonal relationships in, 101–114, 155, 245; congruence in, 102–104, 108, 110, 111, 113, 155; empathy in, 104–105, 107, 108, 110, 111, 113; cause and effect in, 112; value-free consulting model in,

172–173; in secondary schools, 242–245

Guide for the Perplexed (Maimonides), 89

Guthrie, E. R., 47

Haan, N., 192, 210, 211

Habits: vs. conditioned responses, 48, 51; inhibitory, 64n

Hall, G. Stanley, 162, 177

Hamburg Psychological Laboratory, 36

Hamilton, Charles, xiii, 14, 450

Hansen, W. L., 376, 392

Hare, R. M., 198

Harlem Youth Opportunities Unlimited, 346

Harris, N.C., 381

Harris, Neil, 19

Harris, Thomas, 4

Harris, William T., 403, 410, 423

Harrow (English public school), 247

Hartnett, R. T., 383

Hartshorne, H., 185

Harvard Business Review, 8–9

Harvard Crimson, 16n

Harvard Educational Review: history of, ix, 1–23; psychological perspective of, x, xi; students on editorial board of, xiv, 5, 6, 7–8, 9, 12; begins as *Harvard Teachers Record*, 1–5; citations of, 1n, 97; policy statement of (1945), 5–6; social science orientation of, 6, 7, 10, 14–15, 22; special issues/symposiums of, 9; emphasis of, on humanities, 10–12; circulation of, 13; and Jensen controversy, 15–19; -IBW agreement, 18; language as central concern of, 20–21

Harvard Graduate School of Education, 1, 2, 5, 7, 12, 22; journal's defense of, 3; expansion of, 13–14; Strike Committee, 16, 17

Harvard Law Review, 8

Harvard Psychological Laboratories, 80

Harvard Teachers' Association, 2, 8

Harvard Teachers Record, see Harvard Educational Review

Harvard University Laboratory of Social Relations, 257

Harvard University Press, 14

Havemann, E., 376

Hays, Samuel, 416

Headstart objectives, 184, 185, 186

Health, Education and Welfare, U.S. Department of, 369, 372

Hedonism, 46, 176

Hegel, Georg W. F., 165

Henry, Jules, 344n, 345

Heredity: and IQ controversy, 15–19

Higham, John, 416

Higher education, *see* Education, higher

Higher Education Act (1972), 385

Riesman, David, 7n, 8, 13, 98, 369n, 374, 386
Riessman, F., 346
Riordan, Robert, 325n
Rist, Ray, xiii-xiv, 451
Robinson, James Harvey, 4
Robinson, William H., 322
Rogers, Carl, x, 152, 155, 451-452
Romanticism, *see* Ideology(ies), educational
Roosevelt, Franklin D., 106
Roosevelt, Theodore, 319
Rose, A., 346, 353
Rosenkrantz, P., 203
Rosenthal, R., 346
Rothbart, G. S., 379
Rousseau, Jean Jacques, 161, 445
Roxbury Latin School, 241, 243
Rubinson, Richard, 407
Rugg, Harold, 4
Rule model, *see* Teaching
Rulon, Phillip J., 2, 5, 6-7
Rush, Benjamin, 408
Ruskin, John, 445, 446
Russian psychology/theory, 97
Rutgers University, 389
Ryan, P. B., 383

Salas, Dario, 341
San José City College: case study of, 377-379
Sartre, Jean Paul, 150, 151, 327
Satyagraha, 235
Scheffler, Israel, ix, 11, 452
Schizophrenia, 103, 109, 110, 111, 113
Schmidt, Alvin, 9
Schoenfeldt, L. F., 374, 376
Scholastic Aptitude Tests, 375
School attendance, 399; legislation for, 401-406 *passim*, 411, 412, 414, 417, 421, 422, 427, 428, 441-442; variations in, 402-403; and "pupil accounting," 404, 415; compulsory, politics of, 406-415; economic interpretations of, 418-428; 19th-century view of, 434, 436
School class: as social system, 274-296; elementary, 278-291; stratification, teacher expectations and, 345, 361. *See also* Expectations of achievement
Schools and the Crisis (David), 426
Schudson, Michael, xiv, 452
Schweitzer, Albert, 206
Science: simplicity ("parsimony") of, 46-47, 48; as model for education, 156; vs. philosophy, 175-176; "educational," 416. *See also* Empiricism
Scott, J. P., 55
Seattle Community College, 388
Secondary school(s): selection and guidance in,

241-245; in England, 247, 250, 388; differentiation and selection in, 291-295, 301; and opportunity, 300, 301; curriculum in, 301-303, 372, 405; as mass institution in U.S., 372, 380, 402, 404
Selection: for higher education, 243-245, 276-278, 284, 291; for future social status, 279, 287-291, 293; dichotomization in, 284
Self, the: humanistic/romanticist view of (and self-actualization), 150-151, 155, 161-162, 168, 170, 171, 179; and search for/discovery of identity, 150-154, 288, 438; women's conception of, 202-237; and adolescent identity crisis, 207, 209; and self-image of black children, 314-315
Semantics, *see* Speech
Senate, U.S., 420, 426. *See also* Congress, U.S.
Sentence(s): child's early construction of, 117, 120, 121-122; ungrammatical, of adults, 119; word order in, 119-120, 123, 124, 131; understanding of (in learning process), 140-141. *See also* Grammatical structure; Language
Sex differences, xi; and peak-experiences, 151-152; and morality, 205, 209-210, 236
Sex education: in England, 250-251, 253
Sex role(s): stereotypes of, 203, 209, 217; and homosexuality, 251, 294; of elementary and secondary school child, 277, 278, 291, 292, 295; peer groups and, 283, 292, 295; of teachers, 285-286
Sex segregation: in English schools, 250; in peer groups, 283; vs. coeducation in U.S. elementary schools, 285
Shakespeare, William, 236
Sharp, L. M., 376
Sidgwick, Henry, 180n
Sigel, I., 346
Simpson, G., 353
Simpson, Alfred, 7
Sizer, Theodore, xiv, 12, 13, 23
Skinner, B. F., x, xi, 11, 20, 60, 97, 148, 165, 169, 172-183 *passim*, 452
Slover, Loretta, 325n
Smith, Anne H., xv, 12
Smith, L., 348
Smith, M., 347
Social class: and social equality/inequality in U.S., xi-xiii, xiv, 243, 299-301, 366, 388; in England, xii, 246-256, 299-300, 388; and social mobility, xii, xiv, 242, 257-273, 277n, 298, 303, 370-373 *passim*, 377-382 *passim*, 388, 390, 392; and "common man" aspirations in U.S., xii, xiv, 257-273; and academic achievement, xii, xiv, 14, 188, 258, 270, 275-276, 304, 307, 309, 348; and teacher ex-

black, 316, 317, 321, 323; and subjective information about child, 347, 350-351; in ghetto school (study of), 351-357
Teaching: defined (vs. training), 54; and discovery, 90-91, 96, 98, 99-100; expository vs. hypothetical mode of, 91; philosophical models of (impression, insight, rule), 135-147; peak-experiences and, 156; quality of, as effect on achievement, 307, 348, 365. *See also* Education; Learning; Training
Teaching machines, x, 11, 77, 85-88
Tead, Ordway, 10
Technologies: value consequences of adopting, 173
T-groups, 155, 157
Thackrey, Russell, 369n, 389n
Thayer, V. T., 4
Theory Y industry, 157
Theresa, St., 151
"Third Force," x, 149-150. *See also* Psychology(ies)
Third World, 338, 339
Thomas, Charles Swain, 2, 5
Thoreau, Henry David, 445
Thorndike, Edward L., x, 46-47, 48n, 49n, 51n, 63-65, 68, 165
Thornton, J. W., Jr., 386
Thought and language, *see* Language
Tiedeman, David, 8, 10
Tillery, D., 369, 374, 376, 387
Titmuss, Richard, 438
Tolman, E. C., 50, 68
"Tracking," *see* Community college movement
Trade unions, *see* Labor force
Training: defined (vs. teaching), 54; "sensitivity," 105; of guidance counselors, 113-114. *See also* Teaching
Transcendentalism, 153
Trent, J. W., 371, 374
Trow, Martin, 372
Truancy, *see* Delinquency
Tufts, James, 180n
Turiel, E., 182, 195, 196, 210
Turner, Frederick Jackson, 398-399
Tyack, David, xiv, 452

Ulich, Robert, xiv, 5, 6
Ullman, A. D., 62
Uncertain Profession, The (Powell), 3
United Nations and UNESCO, 407
United States: social equality/inequality in, xi-xiii, xiv, 243, 299-301, 366, 388; status-education relationship in, 275, 380, 392; school systems, 278, 286, 295, 402; "youth culture" in, 290, 292-295; "abdication" of male in, 295;

school attendance statistics, 344, 369, 372, 403-404; secondary schools in, 372, 380, 402, 404; and federal support of vocational education, 384-385, 387; literacy in, 402, 403; public school expenditures in, 402, 404; political construction of education in, 406, 407-415; school administration in, 415-418, 435; social policy, loss as theme of, 430-448. *See also* Congress, U.S.; Education; Equality/inequality of education/educational opportunity; Legislation; School attendance; Social class; Supreme Court, U. S.; Values
U. S. Bureau of the Census, 370, 374, 382
U.S. Commission on Civil Rights, 312, 317
U.S. News and World Report, 15-16
U.S. Office of Education, 14, 385, 387, 402, 410, 420; Survey of Equality of Educational Opportunity, 304-306, 307
University of Chicago, ix
University of Oregon, 20
Uruguay: reading text published in, 342
Useem, Michael, 369n
Utopianism, 338-339, 343, 366
Utterance(s), *see* Verbalization

Values, 149-150, 162-163, 193; of learner, 153, 185; and value-relativism, 160, 172-180 *passim,* 187; and "value-neutral" psychology, 160, 172-173; and educational ideologies, 172-183; and "value-free" approaches, 190; of English youth, 255-256; of "common man" (U.S.), 262, 263, 268, 272; societal, 275, 282, 287, 313, 315; "alienation" from, 289-290; of teachers in ghetto school, 354-355; 358, 363-365; traditional U.S., 412, 431-437, 447. *See also* Attitudes; Culture; Democracy; Elitism; Expectations of achievement; Loss; Moral development/morality; Religion
van den Daele, L., 196, 197
Venn, G., 386, 387
Verbalization: single-word utterance (holophrase), 116; average length of utterance, in child's speech development, 117, 120-121, 129; of child in ghetto school, 351, 352, 354, 356, 358-359, 363. *See also* Language; Speech
Vietnam War, 5
Vigotsky, L. S., 43, 96
Vinovskis, Maris, 419
Vocational education, 199, 242, 301, 302; community colleges and, 373, 380-391, 392-393; sponsors of, 383-387; defined (by Higher Education Act), 385; response to, 387-391
Vogel, S., 203
Vote, the, 413, 436
Voting behavior: school class analogy to, 289

DATE DUE

MR 14 05			

DEMCO 38-296